# GOOD
# NURSERY G

*For Caroline, Georgina, Abigail, Alexandre and Leah*

# GOOD NURSERY GUIDE

## SUE WOODFORD & ANNE DE ZOYSA

**V**

VERMILION
LONDON

The authors would like to state that the information contained in this book was checked as rigorously as possible before going to press. Neither the authors nor the publisher can take responsibility for any changes which may have occurred since, or for any other variance of fact from that recorded here in good faith.

First published 1993

1 3 5 7 9 10 8 6 4 2

Text © Sue Woodford & Anne de Zoysa 1993

Sue Woodford and Anne de Zoysa have asserted their right under the Copyright, Designs and Patents Act, 1988, to be identified as the authors of this work.

All rights reserved. No part of this publication may be reproduced, stored in a retrieval system, or transmitted in any form or by any means, electronic, mechanical, photocopying, recording or otherwise, without prior permission of the copyright owners.

First published in the United Kingdom in 1993
by Vermilion
an imprint of Ebury Press,
Random House, 20 Vauxhall Bridge Road,
London SW1V 2SA

Random House Australia (Pty) Limited
20 Alfred Street, Milsons Point, Sydney,
New South Wales 2061, Australia

Random House New Zealand Limited
18 Poland Road, Glenfield
Auckland 10, New Zealand

Random House South Africa (Pty) Limited
PO Box 337, Bergvlei, South Africa

Random House UK Limited Reg. No. 954009

A CIP catalogue record for this book is available from the British Library

ISBN 0 09 177378 4

Editor: Alison Wormleighton
Designer: Bob Vickers

Typeset in Century Old Style by
SX Composing Limited, Rayleigh, Essex
Printed and bound in Great Britain by
Clays Ltd, St Ives, PLC

Papers used by Ebury Press are natural recyclable products made from wood grown in sustainable forests.

Front cover photograph: The Telegraph Colour Library

# Contents

Acknowledgements 7
Introduction 8
What to Look Out For 10
Types of Care for Under-5s 16
Nursery Terms & Abbreviations 18

Avon 21
Bedfordshire 29
Berkshire 31
Buckinghamshire 46
Cambridgeshire 59
Cheshire 70
Cleveland 75
Cornwall 77
Cumbria 85
Derbyshire 92
Devon 97
Dorset 105
Durham 109
East Sussex 113
Essex 123
Gloucestershire 133
Guernsey 139
Hampshire 141
Hereford & Worcester 151
Hertfordshire 160
Humberside 169
Isle of Man 173
Isle of Wight 175
Isles of Scilly 177
Jersey 178
Kent 179
Lancashire 190
Leicestershire 198
Lincolnshire 205

**LONDON** 210
Barking & Dagenham 210
Barnet 211
Bexley 216
Brent 216
Bromley 218
Camden 220
Corporation of London 225
Croydon 226
Ealing 230
Enfield 233
Greenwich 235
Hackney 237
Hammersmith & Fulham 242
Haringey 250
Harrow 251
Havering 252
Hillingdon 252
Hounslow 255
Islington 256
Kensington & Chelsea 260
Kingston-upon-Thames 273
Lambeth 275
Lewisham 282
Merton 284
Newham 287
Redbridge 288
Richmond-upon-Thames 289
Southwark 296
Sutton 299
Tower Hamlets 302
Waltham Forest 303
Wandsworth 304
Westminster 322

**MANCHESTER** 326
Bolton 326
Bury 332
Manchester 333
Oldham 335
Rochdale 335
Salford 336
Stockport 337
Tameside 339
Trafford 340
Wigan 342

**MERSEYSIDE** 344
Knowsley 344
Liverpool 344
Sefton 350
St Helens 353
Wirral 354

Norfolk 355
Northamptonshire 357
Northumberland 361
North Yorkshire 364
Nottinghamshire 372
Oxfordshire 374
Shropshire 386
Somerset 389

**SOUTH YORKSHIRE** 394
Barnsley 394
Doncaster 396
Rotherham 396
Sheffield 398

Staffordshire 402
Suffolk 406
Surrey 410

**TYNE & WEAR** 413
Gateshead 413
Newcastle-upon-Tyne 413
North Tyneside 419
South Tyneside 422
Sunderland 424

Warwickshire 427

**WEST MIDLANDS** 431
Birmingham 431
Coventry 434
Dudley 436
Sandwell 438
Solihull 438
Walsall 441
Wolverhampton 442

West Sussex 442

**WEST YORKSHIRE** 451
Bradford 451
Calderdale 460
Kirklees 462
Leeds 464
Wakefield 467

Wiltshire 468

**NORTHERN IRELAND** 471

**SCOTLAND** 479
Borders 479
Central 479
Dumfries & Galloway 480
Fife 481
Grampian 481
Highland 487
Lothian 487

Orkney 493
Shetland 493
Strathclyde 495
Tayside 500
Western Isles 503

**WALES** 504
Clwyd 504
Dyfed 506
Gwent 507
Gwynedd 508
Mid Glamorgan 508
Powys 510
South Glamorgan 513
West Glamorgan 516

Useful Organisations and Publications 517

Index of Nurseries by Name 519

Index of Nurseries by Region 524

# Acknowledgements

*Main Contributors:*
Carolyne Cullum
Yvonne Hales
Alison Kean
Margaret Mooney

Jill Sarginson
Ann Seed
Joanne Wace

We are grateful to the many friends, colleagues, nursery workers, parents and children who have helped us to research this book. It would never have been completed without the special endeavours of Alison Kean, our editorial assistant. Our thanks also to Dr Carol Goldstone and her colleagues at MAI Research, Alison Wormleighton, our editor at Ebury Press and, above all, the hundreds of nursery owners and teachers who opened their doors and welcomed us into daycare centres and nursery schools in literally every part of the British Isles.

*Please help us!*

We would welcome your reaction to the first edition of the *Good Nursery Guide*. Please let us know what you think about the facilities listed in this guide, or about any other examples of high-quality nursery care and education. All information will be gratefully received and treated in the strictest confidence. Please send your comments to:

Sue Woodford and Anne de Zoysa
Bringing up Baby Ltd
101 Frithville Gardens
London W12 7JQ

# Introduction

Nursery care and education in Britain is a mess. We have one of the worst records in Europe, no national childcare policy and no unifying agency to deal with a tangled web of piecemeal provision. There is an acute shortage of full-time daycare at prices all parents can afford and some groups are almost totally excluded – notably children under 2 years of age, families in rural areas and ethnic minorities. Although state nursery education is generally of high quality, it is part-time, or even less than part-time in certain areas and available to only 25 per cent of 3- and 4-year-olds. Staff/child ratios can also be as poor as 1:15. Although local authorities have no statutory duty to provide services for under-5s, except for children in need, they are responsible for registering and monitoring the quality of facilities in their areas – a task they are frequently under-resourced to carry out effectively and efficiently. The private and voluntary sectors struggle to meet increasing demand, with dedicated, overworked and poorly paid staff and limited resources.

There is little argument about the enormous benefits of good nursery education. Mounting research evidence also shows that children in daycare, provided it is of high quality, do better at school, stay in education longer, are more sociable and assertive and achieve better in later life than those who have had no nursery experience.

The main losers in this muddle are, inevitably, young children and their parents. Most parents have little or no choice of services and therefore put up with whatever is available, without question or complaint. Parents have a vital role to play in raising standards and ensuring and maintaining quality in nursery care and education. We have written the *Good Nursery Guide* because we are committed to the expansion of high-quality nurseries and nursery schools. By providing essential information and advice about a wide range of day nurseries, workplace nurseries, schools and classes, we hope that parents will be better-equipped to ask the right questions, evaluate services and, when necessary, complain. Information is a powerful tool, and with more power, parents can add their voices more effectively to the current debate about childcare in Britain.

Defining and assessing quality is, of course, subjective and complex. It is also a continuing process. Every child has different needs, and each parent is looking for something different when they choose a day nursery or nursery school. Some require flexible hours to fit their work patterns, while others look for affordability, young friends and stimulating play activities for their children, or strong educational programmes. Childcare professionals, with similar training, also have different objectives and priorities. There are those who emphasise health, care and safety, and others who see education as the priority. Few would disagree that quality should mean putting the development, needs and happiness of children first. Quality services must integrate care and education, in its broadest sense, and provide a warm, safe and homely environment. Quality must also be assessed in the context of the rights and expectations of children, parents, childcare workers and nursery teachers.

We have not attempted to follow the fashionable path of drawing up a league table of nurseries. We have selected just over 400, which in our judgement represent a wide range of different *examples* of good-quality nursery care and education. All entries and listings have been visited personally by us or one of our carefully briefed researchers. Nurseries have been selected in a variety of ways, by a rigorous process.

We wrote originally to all Directors of Education and Social Services throughout the United Kingdom, asking for their co-operation in sending out an initial questionnaire to day nurseries, nursery schools and nursery classes attached to primary schools. With a handful of notable exceptions, their help was less than overwhelming. We therefore compiled our own list and sent out 2250 questionnaires. We are grateful for the assistance and recommendations from National Childbirth Trust members,

Working for Childcare, the Midland Bank, Nursery World magazine and Childcare Links in Brighton. Over 600 questionnaires were completed and returned to us. Those which on paper did not meet the minimum standards set out in the guidelines and regulations of the Children Act 1989 were rejected and we arranged to visit the rest – some 450.

Each nursery received a visit lasting at least an hour and a half, in many cases much longer. Nursery owners, managers and teachers were generally welcoming, open and honest, although some were understandably reticent about sharing financial details with us. Staff salaries and nursery profits, particularly in the private sector, remain largely a trade secret. Some services were suspiciously clean, tidy and well ordered, but we tried to stay long enough to see behind the headlines. Every effort was made to look for those intangible qualities that go towards making a high-quality nursery. Atmosphere, ethos, the relationship between children and staff, and the degree of respect for children, are all difficult to assess and need time to observe. Our bottom line was always to trust our own instincts and to ask ourselves, 'Would I be prepared to send my child to this nursery?' No provider has had any editorial control over their entry. The responsibility is entirely ours.

As providers ourselves, we must declare an interest. However, after much heated discussion in the office and pleas from our staff, who felt our nurseries deserved inclusion, we decided to compromise by listing our own nurseries.

The length of each entry is not significant. The time lag between writing and publication inevitably means that some of the information which follows may unavoidably be out of date. Many local authorities are in the midst of upheaval, following implementation of the Children Act and swingeing budget cuts to Social Services and Education. Even as we write, these services are constantly under review.

We hope that the first edition of this guide will inspire parents, children and childcare professionals to visit nurseries and engage in lively debate about provision, standards and, above all, quality. Everyone has a part to play in achieving the aim we share – more and better-quality nursery services for our young children, available to every family who wants them, and at an affordable price. We look forward to hearing your response.

**bringing up baby**

Sue Woodford and Anne de Zoysa
Bringing Up Baby Ltd
London, June 1993

# What To Look Out For

Be sure to visit a nursery or nursery school during the day, when children and staff are there. Take your child/children with you and set aside enough time to soak up the atmosphere and have a thorough, unhurried look around. Try to see a number of facilities, so that you can compare services and talk to different providers. Ask other parents about their nursery experiences. Prepare your questions well in advance and make a list of the features that are the most important for you and your child's needs.

First impressions are very important. Check that the nursery is accessible. Note whether staff are welcoming and friendly when you arrive and whether someone has been assigned to show you round. Does the building feel right and smell clean when you walk in? We rejected a number of nurseries for this book because they smelt dank and musty; one even smelt strongly of alcohol. Noise levels may also be significant. If it is very noisy, are they the sounds of busy, excited children, staff shouting, or babies crying for attention? The first rule is to trust your instincts. If you are unsure, go back again and have a second look. If you decide you may want a place, register early, as waiting lists can be long.

## Premises

Premises come in all shapes and sizes, but must be warm, safe, clean and well maintained. Rooms should be light, airy and well lit, with enough space for children to move around freely. Floors should be clean and suitable for a range of different activities. It is essential for children in full daycare to have access to a safe, clean, securely fenced outside play area, paved and grassed, with a variety of outdoor equipment, preferably set on safety surfaces. A covered outdoor area for wet days is an added bonus.

The social and intellectual development of young children is not dependent on the amount of square footage or quantity of toys and equipment, unless both are seriously lacking. Much more important is the actual organisation of the space. Children learn best in small groups of five or six, supervised by one or two adults. They should be in small rooms or different areas (if the room is open-plan), with good-quality educational toys, books and equipment at child height, so that children can help themselves and put things away. Rooms need to look attractive and cheerful, with plenty of children's artwork and achievements displayed on the walls.

Check out the standard of the toilet and nappy changing facilities and the kitchen. Good nurseries also provide a staff room, laundry facilities and adequate storage. A nursery which is responsive to parents will set aside a room for their use while they are settling in new children and provide a parents' noticeboard for information.

## Staff

The calibre of staff and their relationship with the children they care for is crucial to the quality of any service. Look for staff who enjoy their work, are warm, caring and professional and will create a happy, stimulating environment where children can flourish. The tone is set by the principal, headteacher or nursery manager. Here again, first impressions can be telling. Check the head's qualifications and experience thoroughly. As a minimum, they should include a recognised childcare or teaching qualification, at least five years' experience working with groups of children of the age ranges using the facility and proven managerial skills.

Ask how the business side of the operation is run, how much time the person in charge spends with staff, children and parents and where his/her priorities lie. Private facilities need to be run on a sound business footing to ensure their survival, but if profit is a high priority, it is unlikely that enough money is being invested in staff, equipment and children. Remember to ask about staff qualifications and training opportunities. Quality care and education will rarely be found in nurseries where more than half the staff are unqualified, or if the nursery is full of young trainees and students.

There should be a good overall balance of staff, reflecting the social and ethnic mix of the children and the local community. If your child has special educational needs or disabilities, find out how much experience and support the nursery can provide in this area.

On your visits, spend time observing the way in which staff relate to children. The quality and content of conversations between adults and children in nurseries and classes play a vital role in children's social and intellectual development. Staff should be responsive to their needs, answering children's questions and requests and providing them with information. They should give reasons, explanations and frequent praise, even if a child gets it wrong. Children learn most through making their own choices and decisions and by doing things for themselves. Simply hugging and holding is not enough. Directing, controlling or interfering by staff will significantly weaken development. Many good nurseries operate a keyworker system, allocating one member of staff to each child, which enables children to develop a strong attachment to one particular carer or teacher and allows parents to communicate with a member of staff who knows their child well.

Stability and continuity are vitally important. American research indicates that day nurseries with high staff turnover produce children with poorer language skills and social development. Ask about staff turnover on your visits. Staff are more likely to stay in a job if they receive good pay and conditions, continuing training and some career opportunities. All good nurseries will have a strong training policy and budget, regular staff assessments and a written handbook for staff, detailing policies and procedures. Early-years workers generally have low pay and low status. Our survey of salaries shows some carers earning as little as £2.50 per hour. Highly qualified, experienced principals rarely receive more than £15,000 a year. This is particularly the case in the private and voluntary sectors. Local authority day nursery and education rates are higher, and we feel that pay amounting to less than two-thirds of the recognised local authority equivalent rate is unlikely to result in loyal, long-serving employees.

Finally, enquire about the catering and cleaning arrangements. Nurseries need a clean environment and wholesome food, but nursery nurses and teachers should not be involved in regular domestic chores. Their place is with the children.

## Staff/Child Ratios

The minimum acceptable levels of staffing in full daycare, recommended by the Children Act, are 1:3 for children from birth to 2 years old, 1:4 for 2- to 3-year-olds and 1:8 for 3- to 5-year-olds. Children with special needs often require higher ratios and, in our experience, babies should have a ratio of 1:2. Staffing levels for sessional care are less stringent. Local authority nursery schools and classes frequently have ratios as low as 1:13 or 1:15. Reception classes, which take children from 4 years old, can provide ratios as poor as 1:30.

It is essential to make sure that the nursery you choose is adequately staffed at all times. In nurseries with more than 20 children, the nursery principal should be supernumerary. Ask about ratios, count heads if necessary and find out what the arrangements are to cover staff holidays and sickness. Students, YTS trainees and work-experience pupils should not be counted in the ratios and should be supervised by staff throughout their stay. Staff numbers should be appropriately higher for outings, especially for swimming.

## Children

Observe and talk to the children when you visit a facility. Do they appear happy, confident, talkative and absorbed in their activities? How do they respond to strangers? In the best nurseries children have some control over what they do, are allowed to make suggestions and plan activities and, above all, are listened to. Happiness is difficult to define, but you will be able to sense the atmosphere. Worry if you see children wandering aimlessly around. Does the nursery have a good social and ethnic mix and are children with special needs welcome and well integrated? Watch the children talking and playing together and assess whether they treat each other and the staff with respect. Are they beginning to cope with sharing or helping each other? Social skills and independence are not acquired by osmosis, and a professional nursery will set aside time to teach good social behaviour.

## Parental Involvement

Parents should be active, valued partners in the care and education of their children. A nursery which does not encourage parental involvement is a bad nursery. Whichever service you choose, it is vital to feel welcome and comfortable about your child's life outside the home. Enquire closely about the attitude to parental involvement. A good nursery wants you to contribute as much as you can to nursery life. Parents need to feel they can telephone or visit whenever possible. There should be regular parents' meetings (at least three a year), opportunities to discuss a child's progress and achievements, and access to records. There may be a management committee with parent representatives, the chance to assist in the classroom or on outings, or fund-raising and social activities to organise. A regular newsletter can keep busy working parents in touch with the nursery. A well-run, professional organisation will provide parents with a clear and detailed brochure setting out the nursery's philosophy, aims, objectives and equal opportunities policy. Regular, good-quality communication between parents and staff is essential for your child's development and well-being. Parents should be allowed to contribute information about their child and play a role in discussions about curriculum and programmes, on a continuing basis.

## Phasing-In

Every nursery should have a settling or phasing-in policy for new children, which involves parents. Be prepared to set aside as much time as necessary to help your child settle happily into his/her new environment. Be guided by the carers/teachers or keyworker responsible for your child and be responsive to your child's particular needs. A successful phasing-in programme will result in your child's future happiness at nursery.

## Health and Safety

A healthy, hygienic environment and good, freshly cooked food are essential for the emotional and physical development of young children. There must always be at least one qualified first-aider on the premises at all times and a Health and Safety officer appointed. First-aid boxes should be checked regularly and should be out of the children's reach. Ask the nurseries and schools you visit for copies of their policies and procedures on the following, and if they do not have any be suspicious:

*Fire Procedure*

Check that the nursery has an up-to-date fire certificate, adequate fire extinguishers, smoke alarms and regular fire drills, particularly if children are above ground-floor level. All heaters and power points should be protected. The evacuation of babies is of particular concern – how is it done?

*Administration of Medicines*

No nursery should administer medicines unless a doctor has prescribed them and parents have given their written consent. Doses should be recorded in a drugs book and signed by two members of staff. To avoid cross-infection, staff should use disposable gloves for nappy changing and toileting, and wash their hands thoroughly before and after, with disinfectant soap. The changing table should be disinfected after use. Nappies should be put in sealed bags or closed chemical containers out of the reach of children. Each child should have an individual potty, washed and disinfected after use. Hand-washing for staff and children should be a regular, organised activity. Nurseries should be aware of the dangers of HIV and Hepatitis B, and should handle body fluids following procedures set out in local authority guidelines.

*Sleep*

Children should never share bedding. Each child needs his/her own set of bed linen, clearly marked and regularly laundered. Where possible, babies should have their own cot.

*Accidents and Emergencies*

Each nursery is required to keep an accident book for recording incidents, however minor. Ask to see it. There should also be clearly written procedures for dealing with emergencies – ask for a copy.

## Food and Mealtimes

Packed lunches are a poor substitute for young children. Nurseries and schools offering all-day care should have a regular, qualified cook and provide nutritious, balanced meals. Ask to see copies of menus. Mealtimes should be a learning experience and social occasion. Children can play a full part in laying tables, preparing and serving food and clearing up. Conversation round the table can develop language skills and teach children important social skills including table manners, politeness and sharing. Children enjoy food when they eat with their peers and carers. Parents who struggle to persuade their child to eat half a yoghurt and a few baked beans at home are often amazed by how much they eat at nursery. A good nursery takes account of special dietary needs and different cultural and religious backgrounds. In many of the best nurseries we visited, children were actively involved in preparing their own snacks and teas, often visiting local shops to buy the ingredients. Cooking is an activity which should be on the timetable of every nursery.

## Curriculum and Activities

Choose a facility which suits your needs and those of your child. Babies need a different and more flexible curriculum. Warmth, cleanliness, stimulation, good food, fresh air, a considerable amount of care and someone to give them immediate love and attention when they are distressed, are their priorities. They need a soft space in which to crawl without being trampled by older children, and they need stimulating, interesting toys.

We believe careful planning and preparation are the key to a good curriculum. Under-5s develop at different speeds and in different areas, and it is important that activities are designed for their individual needs. Care and education are inseparable at this age, but the overall aim of the curriculum should be the same for under-5s as it is for all children. This is set out clearly in the 1988 Education Act, which says that the curriculum should be a broad and balanced one which 'promotes the spiritual, moral, cultural, mental and physical development of pupils and of society', preparing children for the 'opportunities, responsibilities and experiences of adult life'.

Every nursery should have a wide range of good-quality, well-maintained, non-toxic educational equipment and materials suitable for the ages of the children using them. They should be bright, stimulating and accessible, designed to encourage overall development. Play is the most important learning tool for young children. No good nursery is without messy play – sand, water, paint, dough, clay and modelling activities. A wide range of picture and story books, including multicultural books and daily storytelling, is essential. Stories, pictures and activities which illustrate the cultural diversity of life in Britain and show images of men and women in non-stereotypical roles should be encouraged. Activities should be varied, child-centred and offer genuine learning experiences. Home corner, dressing up, role play activities, drama and mime all develop imagination and independence. Opportunities for children of all ages to develop oral and linguistic skills and practise other languages can be promoted through books, rhymes, storytelling, songs and conversations on a one-to-one basis or in small groups.

Pre-reading, pre-writing and basic mathematical concepts, computer skills and technology can be taught through projects, themes and structured activities. The daily programme should allow time for music, quiet activities and rest; periods of supervised, structured play and free play; and opportunity for self-expression. There should be periods of physical play inside and out – climbing, running, kicking, catching, dancing and simply letting off steam. Time should be set aside for one-to-one learning experiences, small-group activities and large-group activities. Fine motor and gross motor skills should be developed.

The balance between care and education can vary enormously from nursery to nursery, and it is important to choose a nursery with a balance that suits your philosophy and your child's needs. If you want your child to be a free spirit, do not send him/her to a highly structured educational establishment. If you are keen for him/her to be taught to read and write as early as possible, find a nursery which believes in teaching the 3Rs. No child should be pushed. Parents can sometimes have unrealistic educational goals for their children – be guided by the professionals and try to ensure that your child is in a nursery school where there are qualified teachers, experienced in the education of under-5s. The continuity between home, nursery and the wider community is important. Life at nursery should not exist in isolation. Regular outings, walks to the local shops, and contact with other nurseries and local primary schools should be part of the curriculum. Visits to the nursery by members of the community, such as doctors, nurses, firemen and police officers, help to make children feel they belong to society.

In a well-organised nursery, where children are loved and respected and are learning, there should be little need for discipline. However, ask the head what the discipline policy is and how they deal with discipline problems. There is no place whatsoever for physical punishment, shaking or shouting in any organisation catering for under-5s.

### Records and Reviews

Children's individual progress and development, their particular skills and talents as well as their problems, should be monitored and assessed on a regular basis. Make sure that you find out if children are regularly observed, who assesses them (usually the keyworker in conjunction with the head) and what records are kept. Parents have a valuable role to play in this process – after all, they know their child better than anyone. Their contribution should be encouraged and respected. All records and reviews should be available to parents and confidentiality assured. Find out how the information is used.

A good nursery or school will be able to call on the services of specialist teachers or advisers; for example, speech therapists, educational psychologists or language teachers. Staff and management should also have mechanisms for monitoring their own performance and that of the nursery as a whole. Ask about management meetings, staff meetings and self-appraisal. Who makes sure that the highest standards are achieved and maintained and how often does this take place?

### Cost

High-quality provision costs money. Unless a facility receives heavy subsidies or is run by the local authority, expect costs to be high and worry if they are not. If staff are paid reasonable salaries, and equipment and materials are good quality and regularly replenished, the cost of a full-time place in a day nursery can be comparable to a place at any top public school. Research has shown that facilities which are subsidised are likely to spend more on each child and their staff than those that receive no subsidy. Beware the childcare provider who gives the impression of being 'in the childcare business for the money', or who talks about children as 'units'. Luckily they are few, but they do exist and they are unlikely to be investing enough per annum in your child's care and education.

Make sure you know exactly what you are paying for and how you are expected to pay. Hidden extras can be a shock, and paying a term's fees up front is more painful than paying monthly in arrears. Our own particular prejudice is against nurseries that charge extra for everything – meals, outings, swimming, music, ballet, French, Tumbletots, etc.

If you can't afford the fees at the nursery of your choice, it is always worth asking if there are any subsidised places, hardship funds or bursaries. Try persuading your employer to contribute towards your childcare costs – the company may value your services enough to help.

### Insurance

Every nursery and nursery school must have up-to-date Employers' Liability Insurance and display the certificate prominently on the premises. Ask to see evidence of Public Liability Insurance as well. It is important that the nursery has insurance to cover children's outings, both during and outside nursery hours. If parents' or staff cars are used for trips, however short, appropriate additional cover needs to be arranged. It is a statutory requirement that all children travelling in cars or mini-buses must have individual seatbelts or baby seats. Enquire under what circumstances fees would be refunded if the nursery were forced to close down through fire, malicious damage or infectious disease.

### Some Questions You Should Ask

1. What are your staff/child ratios? (Do a head-count as you go round and don't include students or trainees.)
2. What qualifications or experience do staff have?
3. What is staff turnover like at this nursery? How many workers have left in the last year and why?
4. What happens when my child's keyworker or other staff are sick or on holiday?
5. What is the procedure if a child needs emergency medical attention?
6. How do you discipline children?
7. Do children play outside every day?
8. What do you do if I am late to collect my child?
9. How often do you increase your fees (if relevant)?

## WHAT TO LOOK OUT FOR

10. For private and voluntary services in particular – do you own or rent the building? How long before the lease runs out?
11. Do you accept children before they are potty-trained?

**Problem-solving**

If your child is attending a nursery and expresses unhappiness about the nursery, take the concerns seriously. If you yourself are worried, try to identify exactly what it is that concerns you and raise the matter with the nursery as soon as possible. Do not allow your worries to fester – act promptly. Talk to your child's keyworker (if applicable) and raise your concerns with the person in charge. Find out more about how the nursery is run; arrive early or unexpectedly, ask to sit in on a session, and talk to other parents to see if they share your worries.

If this fails to produce results and if the nursery is run by the council, an organisation, or a company, approach them. Serious problems that cannot be resolved directly with the nursery should be referred to your local Social Services or Education Department. Be prepared to take your child away and find alternative arrangements if your concerns continue.

# Types of Care for Under-5s

Provision for under-5s* takes many forms. Quality and quantity vary enormously across the United Kingdom. Depending on where you live, the main forms of childcare and nursery education provided by the public, private and voluntary sectors are likely to fall into the following categories:

## Playgroups

Often less than part-time childcare, and requiring some parental involvement. Open two or three hours a day, sometimes longer, for a few sessions each week, usually during school terms. Frequently run on a shoestring, with some qualified but many unqualified staff. Local authorities provide funding in some areas. Highly organised by the Pre-school Playgroups Association (PPA). Approximately 50 per cent of playgroup leaders have completed the PPA Foundation Course. Fees are minimal, and no meals provided unless an extended day is offered. No formal education; children learn entirely through play. Average annual expenditure per child £110.

## Local Authority Nursery Schools & Classes

Generally part-time, offering either morning or afternoon sessions five days a week. Occasionally, there are full-time places or extended-day provision until 6pm. Open term-time only – approximately 36 weeks a year. Staff are qualified, trained teachers, (Cert Ed or B Ed) assisted by NNEB nursery nurses. These are educational establishments, many increasingly favouring the High Scope approach. Staff/child ratios vary from 1:10 to 1:15. Students and parent helpers are often present. Ages range from 3 to 5 years old, and children tend to come from the immediate catchment area of the school. Priority to children with special educational needs and siblings. No fees, and voluntary contributions for snacks, outings and cookery classes. Non-statutory provision funded by local education authorities (LEAs).

Demand far exceeds current supply. Average annual expenditure per child £1100. Very uneven spread of provision and dependent on policies of individual local authorities. Often only available for one or two terms before school.

## Private Nursery Schools & Classes

Less than full-time care, similar hours to local authority nursery classes and open during term-time only. Many favour the Montessori philosophy of education and use Montessori teaching aids. Some are attached to pre-prep or prep schools. Staff are usually trained teachers and nursery nurses (qualified and unqualified). Fees variable, up to £900 per term. Registered by Social Services or the Department for Education.

## Day Nurseries

*Local Authority*

Run by Social Services departments for children from birth to 5 years old offering full or part-time places. Generally available only to children referred by Social Services, because of social, economic, emotional, physical or intellectual problems. Highly trained staff, NNEB qualified, others with social work, teaching or special needs training. They cater for less than one per cent of the pre-school population. Budget cuts have resulted in the closure of many local authority day nurseries and some areas have none at all. Fees very low, often depending on parental circumstances. Average annual expenditure per child £5500 per year.

*Private & Voluntary*

The fastest-growing sector in recent years, currently providing over 77,000 places across the country. Full-time daycare, often from 8am–6pm throughout the year, excluding bank holidays. They cater mainly for 2- to 5-year-olds, but increasing numbers are registering to take babies from 8 or 12 weeks old, to meet a

---

* Figures from the National Consumer Council.

huge demand. Registered by Social Services, who inspect to ensure quality. Standard and frequency of monitoring varies. Should have at least 50 per cent qualified staff, NNEB or equivalent. Primarily providers of care. Educational programmes and resources vary enormously, from excellent to very poor. Few employ qualified, trained early years teachers. Demand outweighs supply in many areas, particularly for baby places. Fees are low in some voluntary sector nurseries and extremely high in others. Some private nurseries in London are charging as much as £160 per week.

*Community Nurseries*

Set up and managed by parents, following local authority guidelines. Not many take children under 2 or 3 years. Often run on low budgets, because of their funding difficulties. Non profit-making, therefore endeavour to keep fees reasonable. Staff usually qualified nursery nurses.

*Workplace Nurseries*

Full-time daycare for working parents, sponsored by a range of public and private organisations for their employees. Health authorities, education and government departments lead the field. Some large private companies have followed their example, particularly during the boom years of the '80s, in order to retain their trained, female workforce. Places frequently restricted to employees only, although some workplace nurseries are available to the general community. Open 52 weeks a year. Fees similar to the private sector, with companies subsidising places for their employees on a sliding scale. Staff are usually NNEB qualified or equivalent.

## Registered Childminders

Women or, more rarely, men who look after children from birth to 5 years old in their own home, full-time, all year round. Required by law to register with Social Services, although an estimated 20 per cent do not. Many cater for babies. The majority are unqualified, although the local authority may help with training and equipment and pay for places. Numbers have increased dramatically since 1985, but many childminders have failed to re-register recently due to the stricter regulations brought in by the 1989 Children Act. Fees by negotiation.

## Nannies (Mothers' Helps & Au Pairs)

Full or part-time care for children of all ages, on a one-to-one or 'nanny-share' basis between families. Care usually in the home. Nannies live in or visit daily. Unregulated by any authority. Estimates suggest that approximately 40 per cent of nursery nurses who qualify each year become nannies. Many are also unqualified. Salaries, negotiated direct with employers, range from very little to £300 per week plus car and perks.

## Crèches

The term 'crèche' covers a range of provision. It is often an ad hoc childcare arrangement provided for an event, meeting or conference. It can also describe a day nursery specifically for babies, or an informal, private, home-based set-up, where children are left with parents or a crèche worker.

## Holiday Playschemes & After-school Care

Play activities for children of working parents. Operated by some local authorities, voluntary bodies or private providers. Open after school hours and during school holidays, particularly in the summer. Costs vary, but are usually reasonable. Quality of staff and equipment can be variable.

# Nursery Terms & Abbreviations

Over 40 separate qualifications are currently available to early years workers. Each provides a different training, lasts a different length of time and reaches vastly differing standards. There are almost as many theories and philosophies of childcare and nursery education as there are qualifications. To find your way around what one writer has described as 'the continuing under-5s muddle!', a whole new 'pre-school vocabulary' is required. We hope the following list of terms and abbreviations, all of which appear in the book, will help to clarify the information contained in our entries and listings.

**B Ed: Bachelor of Education**
A four-year course leading to an Honours Bachelor of Education degree and including a study of the art of teaching.

**BTEC: The Business and Technician Education Council National Diploma (National Diploma in Caring Services)**
A two-year nursery nurse training course, equivalent to two A-level GCSE passes. Tougher academic entry requirements than NNEB.

**Cert Ed: Certificate of Education**
Three-year non-degree teacher training course. Cert Ed, Teacher's Cert and Dip Ed are no longer awarded. Current teaching qualifications are **B Ed** and **PGCE**.

**(The) Children Act 1989**
Children under 8 years of age in any type of daycare facility, except those with private nannies, are the responsibility of local authorities, which must regulate, register, inspect and maintain standards in their area. They have a statutory duty to review all daycare provision and education services. These reviews are to be made publicly available by January 1994. The Children Act of 1989 allows the local authorities greater control and legislative powers, resulting in the well-publicised closure of some day nurseries and a drop in the number of childminders.

**City & Guilds: City and Guilds of the London Institute**
Offers a number of two-year courses in baby and childcare in colleges of further education throughout the country.

**CPQS (now known as DPQS): Certificate in Post-Qualifying Studies**
Further qualifying training for NNEBs, including managerial skills. Six modular units amounting to at least 720 hours of study.

**Dip Ed: Diploma in Education**
See Cert Ed.

**DFE: Department for Education**
Formerly DES (Department of Education & Science).

**DPQS: Diploma in Post-Qualifying Studies**
See **CPQS**.

**Family Grouping**
Also known as Vertical Grouping. Children of different ages are grouped together, as opposed to Horizontal or **Peer Grouping**.

**INSET**
In-Service Education for Teachers.

**Keyworker**
Many nurseries allocate a specific member of staff, known as a keyworker, to each child. Keyworkers build up a special relationship with the children and their parents.

**LEA**
Local Education Authority.

## Mont Dip: Montessori Diploma
A two-year teacher training course based on the philosophy of Dr Maria Montessori. The diploma can be done by correspondence or on a part-time basis. Not recognised as a teaching qualification in state nursery or primary schools.

## NAMCW: National Association for Maternal and Child Welfare
The Association runs a variety of certificate and diploma courses on family life and child development in schools and colleges.

## (The) National Curriculum
All children from the age of 5 are now required to follow the National Curriculum. It spells out the subjects children must cover and be assessed on at school. The first tests – Key Stage 1 – take place at 7. Many classes and nursery schools bear in mind the first attainment targets of the National Curriculum when they develop their own curricula.

## NNEB: National Nursery Examination Board
The best-known and longest-established childcare qualification. A two-year college training course; entrants must be 16 or over, usually with two or three GCSEs, grades A to C. No equivalent academic qualification.

## NVQ: National Vocational Qualifications
Still being developed by the National Council for Vocational Qualifications. Aims to allow candidates to be assessed and to gain a nationally recognised award while at their place of work. If successful will rationalise childcare training and improve the status of early years workers.

## OU/OU Childcare: Open University
Offers a wide selection of courses and is used by professionals keen to develop and update their skills.

## PPA: Pre-school Playgroups Association
Funds its own courses in conjunction with Social Services. The Foundation Course for group leaders has been replaced by a Diploma in Playgroup Practice – a 200-hour course in the development and needs of under-8s. Certification by attendance rather than assessment.

## Peer Grouping
Also known as Horizontal Grouping. Children of similar ages are grouped together, as opposed to Vertical or **Family Grouping**.

## PGCE: Post-Graduate Certificate of Education
A one-year post-graduate teacher training course. Candidates must already have a degree (in any subject).

## Pre-school Philosophies
The pre-school philosophies most likely to be encountered in early years education are:

### *Froebel*
Friedrich Froebel (1782–1852) was the German founder of 'the kindergarten' and the first educationalist to understand the value of exploratory and interactive play. Froebel's theories derive from the belief that there are certain 'invariant patterns' in a child's development which transcend gender, culture and race. These patterns of behaviour are observable and repeatable and can be channelled and used to teach acceptable social and educational skills.

### *High Scope*
The High Scope curriculum, developed in 1962 in Michigan by Dr David Weikart, sets out an educational programme for each child based on 'plan, do and review'. The onus is on the child to make his/her own decisions, approach tasks independently, and learn through initiative. The curriculum maintains that children learn best from activities which they have planned and carried out themselves. They are encouraged to be 'active learners'. Precise and dated observations and record sheets are kept to note particular achievements in each area of work.

### *Montessori*
Based on the philosophy and works of the Italian doctor Maria Montessori (1870–1952), who believed that it is in early childhood that personality and the mind are developed. It is a child-centred method of education, starting from the belief that all children want to learn and, given enough freedom, will become 'active learners'. The first six years of life are of paramount importance as children have 'absorbent minds' at this stage. Their learning environment is carefully structured and all equipment

and activities are conceived to encourage 'in-dependence and self-correction'. The Montessori teacher 'directs', but does not impose, learning.

### PPA
The Pre-school Playgroups Association (PPA) has a philosophy of learning through play. It recognises the importance of parental involvement, and parents are encouraged to make decisions in all areas, from curriculum-planning to the choice of equipment.

### Steiner
Based on the teachings of Rudolf Steiner (1861–1925), an Austrian philosopher whose method of education was centred on the spiritual needs of the child. Steiner taught that the very young child has an inborn affinity with the world and an innate appreciation of beauty and goodness. Education should foster the development of the spiritually sensitive 'whole person'.

### Reading Schemes
There are numerous reading schemes. Some have a pre-reading or introductory scheme suitable for pre-school children. All are graded, based on a combination of phonics (letter sounds) and sight reading (recognition of the whole word). Most first schools use more than one scheme, depending on the needs of the children. New Way (formerly Gay Way) and Ginn are two of the best known. Letterland, a pictogram system for teaching letter sounds, is very popular in many nursery schools.

### RGN, SRN, SEN
Professional nursing qualifications. A qualified nurse is now a Registered General Nurse (RGN).

### RSCN
A Registered Sick Children's Nurse.

### Special Needs
LEAs have a statutory obligation to identify children with learning, medical, psychological and physical difficulties, assess their needs and provide appropriate care and education. Government policy dictates that children with special needs should be integrated into ordinary nursery schools and day nurseries wherever possible.

### SS
Local authority Social Services department.

# Avon

The only county in England and Wales to offer more full- than part-time places in its nursery schools. About 20 per cent of all 3- and 4-year-olds attend either one of 16 local authority nursery schools or 55 nursery classes. The county's 97 private day nurseries charge an average £85 per week. Some have waiting lists of up to 60 names and children need to be registered as early as possible. Although the 14 local authority day nurseries are specifically for children in need, the council gives large grants to the voluntary sector to run affordable community nurseries, particularly for single working parents. This year's spending cuts seriously threaten this provision. Most of the pre-school care is based in Bristol, although there are nearly 2000 registered childminders who support the needs of the rural areas. Provision for under-2s is limited throughout the county.

**Further information**

For details on day nurseries, childminders and playgroups:

Department of Social Services
PO Box 30
Avon House North
St James Barton
Bristol BS99 7NB
Tel: (0272) 290777

For details on nursery schools, units and classes:
Education Department
PO Box 57
(address and telephone as above)

For more information on childcare, for both parents and carers, including after-school activities, health visitors and toy libraries:
Avon Parents' Network
28 Bright Street
Barton Hill
Bristol BS5 9PR
Tel: (0272) 413999

---

## CATERPILLARS DAY NURSERY

Royal United Hospital
Combe Park
Bath BA1 3NG
**Tel:** (0225) 824462 x4462

**Owner/Principal:** Jean Dinham, RGN, RSCN
**Type:** Day nursery offering full and part-time places and half-day sessions to NHS employees and local community
**Children:** 3mths–5yrs. 24 places. 80 on register
**Hours:** 8.30am–5.30pm
Early opening from 7.15am available on demand
Morning session 8.30am–1pm
Afternoon session 1.30pm–5.30pm
Open 52 weeks a year (excl bank holidays)
**Status:** Private, fee-paying
**Number of years open:** 2
**Meals:** Lunch, tea and snacks

**1992 fees:** £80 per week full-time – under 18 mths
£66 per week full-time – over 18mths
£17 per day – under 18mths
£14.75 per day – over 18mths
£9.50 per morning session – under 18mths
£8.50 per morning session – over 18mths
£8.50 per afternoon session – under 18mths
£7.15 per afternoon session – over 18mths
£2.50 per hour plus meals – under 18mths
£2 per hour plus meals – over 18mths
**Waiting list:** Very long – 60 names. Priority to NHS employees
**Registered by:** Avon County Council SS

**Premises** On the west side of Bath, near the main road to Bristol. A pre-fabricated, single-storey building in the hospital grounds on the quieter north side. Good car-parking facilities. The nursery occupies five main rooms and has its own loos, nappy changing area and kitchen. Children up to 2½ years use the Caterpillar Room which has a home corner and child-size kitchen, plentiful supplies of early learning equipment and toys, puzzles and a dolls' house. The Butterfly Room for older children has its own book corner, shelves filled with construction toys and bricks, musical instruments, television and nursery pets – a hamster and goldfish. An activity room offers sand and water play, a plasticine and cutting-out table, play dough, sticking, blackboard and a mirror. There is also a sleep room and an office. All are pleasantly decorated in pale blue or yellow and most rooms are carpeted. The outside area is securely fenced in. Fixed play equipment is installed on the grass to minimise accidents and other toys are used on the patio. Adjacent tennis courts are available for outdoor play in the winter when the grass is waterlogged. We especially liked a UVA filter sun verandah, where children can sleep outdoors in the summer.

**Owner/Principal & staff** Jean Dinham, RGN, RSCN, describes herself as an extrovert. She has 16 years' nursing experience and set up the nursery because she felt she needed a change. Now she very much enjoys being able to work with children who are fit and well. Of the six full-time staff, three are NNEB qualified and all have first aid training. Louisa is the senior nursery nurse who shares day-to-day responsibility with Jean. Another nursery nurse is particularly talented at art and craft work. Unqualified staff all have previous childcare experience. Staff meetings are held weekly and everyone is encouraged to share suggestions and criticisms. Staff divide the chores and all do their fair share of messy jobs. YTS and NNEB students attend the nursery for on-the-job experience and are closely supervised by staff, though not regarded as members of staff.

**Children & parents** Priority is given to NHS employees when allocating places, and parents represent most walks of hospital life: doctors, nurses, occupational therapists, lab staff. Most children are English, but there have been some other European nationalities in the past. Many children come from outside Bath, and consequently they go on to a wide variety of schools, mostly state primaries, but some private – in particular the Royal and the Park in Bath. Each child is allocated a keyworker for ease of assessment and to provide parents with a direct line of contact. The nursery operates an open door policy and children can be phased-in gently over a week or two, although not all parents take advantage of this.

**Curriculum & activities** Themes are planned in advance and last for a month or so, covering specific colours, seasons, etc. Activity sessions are linked to the theme of the month, as are stories, songs and artwork. Each day children are encouraged to make something for display or to take home. Little pre-school work is done and although books are in plentiful supply, no reading schemes are used. Children are encouraged to learn their names and recognise their photographs by changing round named place-mats at lunch and photos over coat pegs every day. Strong emphasis on motor skills, improving concentration, decision-making, sharing toys and tidying up. There is frequent opportunity for messy play, painting, sticking, cutting and drawing. Children all come together daily for music and movement sessions and to watch *Playdays*. During the summer, afternoon swimming sessions are held at the hospital's outdoor heated pool. A qualified lifeguard is always on duty. Small groups are taken on outings to local shops and the library and there are occasional trips into Bath by bus. Various emergency services have visited to allow children to clamber over vehicles and inspect uniforms.

**Remarks** Not a structured or academic environment, but a happy and well-organised nursery supplying a vital service. Jean Dinham hopes it will eventually become a workplace nursery for hospital staff only, but as long as supply does not meet hospital demand, places are still available to anyone prepared to join the long waiting list.

# CLYDE HOUSE DAY NURSERY

1 Nevil Road
Bishopston
Bristol BS7 9EG
**Tel:** (0272) 247488

**Owner/Principal:** Margaret Rudge, NAMH Dip
**Type:** Day nursery offering full- and part-time places
**Children:** 2–5yrs. 25 places. 60 on register
**Hours:** 8.15am–5.45pm
Flexible hours
Open 52 weeks a year
**Status:** Private, fee-paying
**Number of years open:** 5
**Meals:** Breakfast, lunch, tea
**1992 fees:** £70 per week full-time
£15 per day
£2 per hour
**Waiting list:** Reasonable
**Registered by:** Avon County Council SS
**Under same ownership:** Ashgrove Park Day Nursery, Ashley Down

**Premises** Turn-of-the-century house, occupying a corner plot, in the lively residential and business area of Bishopston, a local community of shops, churches, businesses and private houses. It is on the main bus route, 15 minutes from the centre of town. The owner lives on the first floor, and the ground floor houses the nursery. There are four main areas: children's room, playroom, kitchen and toilet/washbasin area. It is light, sparkling and spacious. Decoratively it is immaculate, but it avoids being clinical. Colourful adult-led art and craft is on the walls, but the children's own work is also at child height. The general feeling is one of warmth and homeliness. Efficient and well-labelled storage for the wealth of equipment and materials is not all easily accessible or at child level, but has been designed to maximise the floor space and activity areas for the children. Outside there is a grassed area in front of the house, stocked with hedges and trees, a bird table and feeder and seats for summer use. Adjacent to the garden, through iron railings and a gate, there is a tarmac playground, with bikes, trikes and a Wendy house.

**Owner/Principal & staff** Margaret Rudge, NAMH Dip, owns two nurseries and divides her time equally between them. She is a former childminder, nanny and teacher of mentally handicapped children. The nursery has a team of six workers, four full-time and two part-time. Four are qualified NNEBs, one a qualified special needs teacher. The only unqualified worker is a former YTS trainee, currently studying for a City & Guilds childcare qualification. A male student on work experience is a welcome and successful extra pair of hands. Staff are friendly and hard-working, and close to the children. We saw many hugs, willingly given on demand. Ancillary staff include a cook and cleaner. There is no training policy or budget for training but the nursery pays for staff to do first aid and food and hygiene courses. Staff/child ratios are 1:4 for 2- to 3-year-olds and 1:8 for 3-5-year-olds. Staff meetings are held monthly. Nursery nurses are encouraged to use their initiative and get on with the job. 'I do not spend my day telling staff what to to. They know what to do and do it,' says Margaret Rudge.

**Children & parents** A real mix of social and cultural backgrounds. The nursery operates family groupings and a flexible, informal keyworker system. The children bond naturally with certain nursery staff, but are not allocated. Close relationships with parents are considered crucial. Appointments are readily arranged and staff are always willing to talk to parents, even outside nursery hours. Phasing-in is done gently, according to the needs of each child and at no extra cost. The nursery welcomes children with special educational needs and children to whom English is a second language.

**Curriculum & activities** Margaret Rudge's personal philosophy is to provide flexible, quality care and pre-school preparation for as wide a range of children as possible. She takes no personal salary and ploughs any profits back into the nursery – for more equipment, better facilities and increased staff salaries. Long term, the business will buy the house, in lieu of a principal's salary. There is no structured learning as such, nor are there written programmes. Margaret Rudge prefers to call it a 'structured day'. All furniture is child-sized and in excellent condition. Equipment, for which the annual budget is £2000, is bright, clean and stimulating. There is a wide range of construction toys, musical instruments, craft materials and sand and water troughs. Paints are available at all times and the children are encouraged to express themselves freely. There is a pre-school group for the older children – they play games designed to develop number skills, take part in pencil-control activities, learn to follow instructions, and acquire listening skills. A good selection of real books is available, so that through sharing books and watching others use books, children learn important pre-reading skills and attitudes. There are name labels and signs everywhere. Children learn that print has meaning and to recognise their own names. There are no reading schemes. Every morning and afternoon the children get together for singing, storytime and playtime. There is music twice a day, and dance and movement daily. The nursery believes strongly in the value of outdoor play, and children spend a good part of the day outside, weather permitting. The children are active, interested and busy, with plenty of social action between individuals and groups. Piles of cushions in the book/quiet area provide a cosy place to read or sleep after lunch. Staff and children eat together. The nursery is a 'sugar-free zone', with wholefood, fresh fruit and milk only for snacks. All special diets are catered for.

**Remarks** Good, all-round care, education and facilities. Bursting with equipment. May not suit parents looking for stronger emphasis on formal school work, but pre-school education programmes are thorough. Children learn through play, in a flexible environment. Margaret Rudge points out that they are a day nursery, not a nursery school. There is a sister nursery half a mile away at Ashley Down.

## MEWS NURSERY

Carfax Garden
Henrietta Mews
Bath BA2 6LR
**Tel:** (0225) 443257/462089

**Owner:** Salvation Army Trustee Company
**Joint co-ordinators:** Sally Fenna, NNEB, Sue Yarlett, NNEB
**Type:** Day nursery offering full- and part-time places and half-day sessions
**Children:** 2–5yrs. 16 places. 42 on register
**Hours:** 8.30am–5.30pm
Morning session 8.30am–12.30pm
Afternoon session 1.30pm–5.30pm
Open 52 weeks a year
**Status:** Registered charity
**Number of years open:** 3
**Meals:** Lunch, tea, snacks
**1992 fees:** £17.50 per day
£10 per morning session
£9.50 per afternoon session
**Waiting list:** Moderate. Early registration advisable
**Registered by:** Avon County Council SS

**Premises** The architect-designed and renovated basement of the Carfax Hotel, built of Bath stone and centrally situated in Bath's famous Great Pulteney Street. Reached via Henrietta Mews, which runs behind, the nursery is approached through the hotel garden. There is on-street parking along Henrietta Mews. Short stops, for picking up and dropping off, can be made in the nearby hotel car park. Although the nursery is part of the basement of the hotel, the rear of the building is at ground level and there is plenty of natural light. The nursery consists of two adjoining, good-sized rooms. Tastefully decorated, it is in harmony with the quality of the building and the honey tones of its surroundings. One room is carpeted, while the other has a vinyl floor for messier activities. It is all light, bright and clean.

**Co-ordinators & staff** Sally Fenna and Sue Yarlett are joint co-ordinators. Both are NNEB qualified, with experience of nannying and work in nursery schools and day nurseries. Young, energetic and conscientious, they work well together, supporting each other in the day-to-day running of the nursery. There are three full-time nursery nurses and two part-timers – a minimum of three NNEBs in the nursery at any one time. Unqualified staff include a mature worker with grown-up children and classroom experience, and a school leaver. There is no training budget or staff training policy. The co-ordinators report to a management committee, which includes representatives from the Salvation Army, the hotel, interested members of the community and parents. The nursery offers two free places, which are allocated with the help of Social Services and local community groups. Staff from the hotel, especially the manager, take a great interest in the nursery, often popping in to see the children. Children react to visitors in a friendly and relaxed way. The nursery welcomes BTEC students on work experience and trainee nursery nurses. The staff/child ratio averages 1:4.

**Children & parents** The children come from a wide area, many parents commute into Bath, some from as far afield as Frome and Devizes. There is a good social and ethnic mix, including Spanish, Afro-Caribbean and Chinese children. The nursery has a small number of children with special educational needs and integration is considered beneficial for all the children. Priority places go to the Salvation Army and hotel staff. Parents are supportive and actively promote fund-raising activities. Parents' evenings, barbecues and coffee mornings are held regularly, both to raise funds and to enable parents to get to know each other and staff. Sally Fenna and Sue Yarlett believe that the key to a good relationship with parents is to be natural, honest and always ready to talk. There is an open door policy at all times. Settling in is done over three visits: on the first, parents stay with their child, on the second they stay in the building, and on the third they leave their child and return after an hour. When the children leave the nursery, they move to a variety of private and state schools.

**Curriculum & activities** There is no formal educational input. The nursery believes firmly in learning through play and the importance of free expression. There is a huge variety of stimulating, child-centred equipment, including multicultural equipment. Children learn to love books by being able to browse, listening to stories and sharing books with their peers and adults. Planned group activities take place using sand, water, paint and constructive and imaginative play materials. Time is set aside each day for children to relate to staff on a one to one basis. Emphasis is on social, physical and emotional development in a friendly, happy environment. Children's progress is monitored by the qualified staff on a termly basis. Limited pre-reading, writing and number work. Music and dance and movement weekly. Children have direct access to the pretty, secure hotel garden. Outdoor equipment includes a play house, climbing frame, bikes, sandpit, water play and a rocking boat. In summer, children plant flower baskets to decorate the wooden fence. Monthly library visits. Regular outings to nearby Henrietta Park and other beauty spots. Meals, prepared by the hotel cook, are social events, with children and staff eating and talking together.

**Remarks** Small, caring and homely nursery, with a friendly atmosphere. Formal educational input is minimal; the emphasis is on play and free expression. High-quality premises and standards of care. Links with Salvation Army and Carfax Hotel. Some subsidised places.

# RED HOUSE NURSERY

1 Cossins Road
Westbury Park
Bristol BS6 7LY
**Tel:** (0272) 428293

**Owners:** The Reverend Neville Kirby, Cert Ed, Dip Ed
Maggie Kirby, B Ed (Hons), M Ed
**Principal:** Maggie Kirby, B Ed (Hons), M Ed
**Type:** Day nursery offering full- and part-time places and half-day sessions (min 2 sessions a week)
**Children:** 2–5yrs. 35 places. 86 on register
**Hours:** 8am–5.30pm
Morning session 8am–12.45pm
Afternoon session 1pm–5.30pm
Open 51 weeks a year
**Status:** Private, fee-paying
**Number of years open:** 5½
**Meals:** Lunch, tea, snacks
**1992 fees:** £108 per week full-time
£12 per session
£50 non-returnable deposit
**Waiting list:** Long. Preference to children already attending part-time and to children with special needs
**Registered by:** Avon County Council SS

**Premises** A detached red brick 1920s house, in the bustling mixed community of Westbury Park. The house was bought six years ago, with the intention of creating a nursery school on the ground floor. The owners live above the shop. Alterations have been carefully considered, walls knocked down and areas opened up, with the needs of small children very much in mind. The nursery is open plan, but with three distinct areas – the Red Room has books, audio tapes, a vast selection of musical instruments, piles of constructional toys and imaginative play materials; the Clock

Room, with its resident grandfather clock, offers equipment for threading, drawing, chalking, sorting, science, domestic play and project work. In the newly built Garden Room are wet and dry sand, clay, paint, water for wet play. Office and staff room on the first floor. The house is warm, homely, very busy and there are fresh flowers in every room. The garden is small, but thoughtfully designed, part beautiful flower and water garden for nature studies, part play area. Directly opposite the house is Redland Green, a large, open, green-field expanse which the children use regularly.

**Owners/Principal & staff** The owners, Neville and Maggie Kirby, are both qualified teachers with a long history of lecturing, teaching and education-related experience. Neville is former Director of Studies and principal lecturer in the Department of Education at Bristol Polytechnic, and now honorary priest at St Albans Church, Bristol. Maggie has been headteacher of two Bristol schools and worked at Bristol Polytechnic as an Associate Director in the Education Department. She is also an international expert on dance and movement. There are 15 members of staff, including ancillary workers, all with relevant qualifications. The ten nursery workers have a range of nursery nursing and teaching qualifications – NNEB, B Ed or Cert Ed – and include two Honours graduates. Two teachers have special needs qualifications. There are five regular male members of staff: three full-time and two supply teachers. The staff/child ratio is an excellent 1:3 at all times. 'High ratios are important for the way we work,' Maggie says. 'We always have cover for holidays or when team members are on training courses. It also means staff can work individually with children or take them out, just like they would at home.' Staff training is a high priority with an annual training budget of £2000. Staff salaries are comparable to local authority scales, unusual in private nurseries. The Kirbys themselves do not take a salary, and feel strongly that nursery workers are underpaid for the work they do. Students are welcome on placement. The nursery also offers work experience for children from Bristol schools and sheltered employment for people with special needs who live nearby.

**Children & parents** The parents include a high proportion of professionals, with some cultural mix – African, Asian, French, Dutch, German and Polish. A mutual respect for *all* children is an essential element of the curriculum. Close relationships with parents are considered a crucial factor in good-quality care. 'The child is always seen in the context of the family. There must be respect and friendship between parents and staff,' Maggie Kirby insists. Parents are welcome to visit the nursery at any time (preferably not mealtimes) or telephone. There are regular parents' evenings, and parents help with outings and often join in the day's activities. Strong links with the local community are actively pursued. 'Lots of people call, bring flowers, play musical instruments or just talk to the children,' Maggie explains. Phasing-in is planned to meet the needs of each individual family and child. There is regular contact with local schools, with opportunities for nursery parents to meet primary school staff. Children with special educational needs are welcome and well integrated.

**Curriculum & activities** Everything is child-centred and child-oriented. The nursery is organised on a resource principle, with each environment having a different emphasis – books, tapes, music and imaginative play in one area, messy play in another and science, project work, threading, drawing, sorting etc in the third. There are elements of High Scope in the structure. Children take an active part in organising and choosing activities, carry them out, reflect on them and then put them away. They are free to move from area to area extending their play work with encouragement and guidance from staff. Equipment is high quality, well maintained and in abundance (annual equipment budget £3886), at child height and in a specific, marked place, so that children can easily find whatever they want. Topics are used, but not exclusively. Twice a day, children are grouped by age, each group led by a member of staff. Group time ends with lunch or tea, a social occasion, eaten with the same member of staff. The nursery is multicultural. Children are taught understanding and acceptance of other cultures and religious beliefs. Different festivals are celebrated as they relate to the children and their families. The nursery has a rich selection of quality reading materials, and there is some formal teaching of reading and writing, on an individual basis. Each child has a folder for letter formation work, writing patterns, photographs and examples of their achievements. The folder moves with them to their next school. Children's progress is monitored daily and full written records kept on each child. Other activities include daily music, with a huge selection of musical instruments, weekly dance and movement and library visits once a month.

**Remarks** An exceptional nursery, offering the very highest standards of care and education. Winner of the 'Under Fives Care and Education Award 1992', sponsored by *Nursery World* magazine and the Co-operative Bank. It would be difficult to improve on the ethos and professionalism we found at this nursery.

## REDROOFS NURSERY

24 Poplar Road
North Common
Warmley
Bristol BS15 5JU
**Tel:** (0272) 492700

**Owners:** Roger & Lesley Bates
**Principal:** Lesley Bates, NNEB, PPA
**Type:** Day nursery offering full- and part-time places and half-day sessions
**Children:** 0–5yrs. 32 places. 100 on register
**Hours:** 8am–5.30pm
Morning session 8.30am–1pm
Afternoon session 1.30pm–4.30pm
Open 52 weeks a year
**Status:** Private, fee-paying
**Number of years open:** 13
**Meals:** Lunch, tea, snacks
**1992 fees:** £89.25 per week full-time
£18.65 per day
£8.15 per morning session
£6.30 per afternoon session
**Waiting list:** 50 names. Early registration advisable
**Registered by:** Avon County Council SS
**Under same ownership:** Redroofs Nursery, St George, Bristol

**Premises** Purpose-built late '70s, pebble dash bungalow, next door to the principal's own house, prettily screened by trees and shrubs. On the very fringes of Bristol and North Common, Warmley is more a rural village than a suburb of a major city, but is accessible by public transport. The general layout of the nursery is open plan. There are two playrooms with a folding door between, an attractive conservatory/sleep room, a kitchen, a staff room and toilets. Decorations are in excellent condition, light and bright. The floor coverings – carpet, vinyl and stone – are suitable for every use. There is a reasonable outside play area with sandpit, climbing frame, bikes, trikes and Wendy house, and in the summer children use the swimming pool in the owner's garden. Nursery staff have been trained in life-saving skills.

**Owners/Principal & staff** Lesley Bates, NNEB, PPA, is Redroofs' owner and principal. A friendly, welcoming woman, she has run her own playgroup and set up two efficient and successful nurseries. She co-owns the nursery with her husband, who acts as administrator and looks after the financial side of the business. All seven nursery nurses are NNEB qualified. There are no qualified nursery or infant teachers on the staff. Recruitment policy includes choosing staff of both sexes, with a range of ages and social and cultural backgrounds, although there were no male carers when we visited and no apparent cultural mix. Students are accepted on placement, supervised by a full-time member of staff. There is no training budget. All staff have first aid certificates and occasionally attend other courses. Outside support workers include a visiting speech therapist, educational psychologist and hearing impairment teacher. The nursery operates a keyworker system and children keep the same keyworker throughout their stay. Staff turnover is not a problem, only one person having left in the two years prior to our visit.

**Children & parents** Reasonable social mix, little ethnic mix. The nursery successfully integrates children with disabilities and special educational needs including a blind child and children with Down's syndrome, hearing impairment, or speech difficulties. Good relationship with parents – open days, concerts and parents' evenings. Once a year there is a special meeting to explain the nursery's aims and objectives to parents and demonstrate exactly how children are taught through different play equipment. Staff are encouraged to talk to parents about their children at the beginning and end of each day. Prospective parents visit by appointment. When a vacancy arises parents bring their children in for a full session a week before they start. The day they begin, children arrive late and leave early.

**Curriculum & activities** The nursery

offers learning through play in an interesting, stimulating and secure environment. Furniture is child-size and equipment colourful and varied (annual equipment budget approx £2000). Everything is at child height, accessible and easy to see, including the fish tank and friendly cockatiel. There are plenty of books and opportunities to share them with adults and peers. Children learn letter names and sounds as part of developing their listening skills. They are taught to understand the importance of print through signs on walls and name labels on pictures and drawers. Activities are undertaken in small, age-related groups. There is a strong emphasis on communication and verbal development. Conversation is important. Children talk to each other, and staff constantly talk to children about what they are doing and why. Outdoor activities have high priority – swimming in summer, picnics, seaside outings, zoo and library visits. Music, dance and movement weekly. The nursery has its own mini-bus, so visits are frequent. Keyworkers monitor and assess all aspects of their children's development. Written records are available to parents.

**Remarks** High energy, imagination and good resources. Formal education is limited, with no qualified teachers on the staff, but the nursery offers quality care and pre-school learning in a homely, purpose-built environment. Lesley Bates owns a second nursery in the St George's area of Bristol, run by her daughter, Joanne.

## ROCKING HORSE DAY NURSERY SCHOOL

34 Northumberland Road
Redland
Bristol BS6 7BD
**Tel:** (0272) 240431

**Owner/Principal:** Julia Davies, SRN, RSCN
**Type:** Day nursery offering full- and part-time places
**Children:** 18mths–5yrs. 24 places. 62 on register
**Hours:** 8.30am–5.30pm
Open 50 weeks a year
**Status:** Private, fee-paying
**Number of years open:** 6
**Meals:** Lunch, tea, snacks

**1992 fees:** £85 per week full-time
10% sibling discount
**Waiting list:** Minimal
**Registered by:** Avon County Council SS
**Under same ownership:** Rocking Horse Day Nursery, Grange School, Warmley

**Premises** Large, late-Victorian detached house in a quiet, leafy suburb of Bristol. Parking for staff cars in front, on-street parking for parents. The nursery is on the ground floor, and the owner lives above. Two main activity rooms lead off a large hall. The rooms are spacious, homely and warm, generously decorated with children's artwork. Separate areas include a book corner, home corner, messy-play area and tables and chairs for tabletop activities. The toilets are bright and clean. There is an office/staff room upstairs. A small, enclosed garden, mainly grassed, includes sandpit, climbing frame, balancing beams, bikes and trains. A park, with a children's playground, is a short walk away, with no roads to cross. Children are taken to it by staff on a 1:2 ratio. The nursery also has regular use of a rumpus room in the local church.

**Owner/Principal & staff** Calm and quietly welcoming, Julia Davies, SRN, RSCN, owns and runs the Rocking Horse. An experienced children's nurse and lecturer in child development, she also runs a childcare consultancy, helping local employers create childcare facilities for their staff. A difficult task in a recession. The staff team consists of seven nursery nurses, all qualified NNEB nursery nurses. No staff member has a nursery teaching qualification. Julia's three teenage sons also enjoy helping in the nursery during the holidays. There is a system of open management. Julia makes the decisions about financial matters; all other decisions are reached jointly with the whole team. Staff are happy and committed and turnover is minimal. Staff meetings are held monthly, but group leaders and assistants discuss their children and current projects every two weeks. Training is considered important. All staff receive an in-house induction course and computer training. They also attend regular courses at the nursery nurses' college in Bristol, including first aid, equal opportunities and the DPQS. Students are accepted on placement. Ancillary staff include a cook and cleaner.

**Children & parents** The children come predominantly from middle class, professional families, and most have two working parents. There is some cultural and ethnic mix. Parental involvement is encouraged. Parents are invited to phone each day, attend parents' evenings and plays, and comment or complain about the running of the nursery. Children are divided into small family groups of three or four, each with their own group leader and assistant. A special area of the activity room is their home base. Parents are invited to become part of these small family groupings and to talk to staff in their child's group room. Nursery workers sometimes visit children and parents at home.

**Curriculum & activities** Children are given the space and freedom to learn through play. Equipment is educationally sound, of good quality and plentiful (annual budget £1000). Each group leader is responsible for providing a structured programme, at the same time allowing children the space to plan and create their own activities. Time is set aside for messy play – painting, craft, sand, water, play dough and gluing. There are quiet times for reading stories, conversation and language development. Music, movement, cookery, woodwork and studying creepy crawlies in the garden all form a regular part of the timetable. Pre-school children have a more structured learning programme. They are taught to recognise numbers from one to five and understand what they represent. They also learn basic matching and sorting, mathematical language (taller than/shorter than), experience of shape, colour and size as well as pencil control. Reading is not taught, but books are plentiful and readily available at child height. Good behaviour is encouraged and praised. An awareness of various cultures and religions is promoted and many different festivals celebrated. There are library visits every few weeks, as well as trips to the local shops and parks. The pet shop and post office are popular destinations. The nursery has a 'no junk food' policy and caters for any diet, including vegan.

**Remarks** A homely, well-organised nursery offering high-quality care from qualified and experienced staff. Low-key educational input; no qualified nursery or reception class teachers when we visited. Julia Davies owns another day nursery in Warmley, run along similar lines.

# Bedfordshire

One of the top counties in the country for nursery education, with 32 per cent of 3- and 4-year-olds in nursery schools or classes. A number of primary schools also incorporate a 'Four Plus Unit', enabling the majority of 4-year-olds to attend school full-time. Social Services run four day nurseries and six family centres for children in need. All have waiting lists. The council also sponsors places in the private and voluntary sectors. Most urban areas have a reasonable choice of services, but rural areas are frequently poorly served, relying on the county's 101 playgroups to help balance the uneven distribution. In the private sector, 44 day nurseries and 1330 childminders offer good provision for those who can afford their fees. To satisfy demand, Bedfordshire needs more nursery classes and more affordable full-time daycare. Neither the Director of Social Services nor the Director of Education responded to our letter requesting help with this guide. National Childbirth Trust mothers recommended a number of nurseries to us, and we sent out questionnaires to a range of facilities. Only four were returned.

**Further information**

For details on day nurseries, childminders and playgroups:
Department of Social Services
Under Eights Co-ordinator
Kingsway
Bedford MK42 9AP
Tel: (0234) 345331

For details on nursery schools, units and classes:
Education Department
County Hall
Cauldwell Street
Bedford MK42 9AP
Tel: (0234) 228179

## LAVENDERS DAY NURSERY

19 Bushmead Avenue
Bedford
Beds MK40 3QJ
**Tel:** (0234) 342818

**Owner:** Childbase Ltd
**Nursery Manager:** Ann Johnson, NNEB
**Type:** Day nursery offering full- and part-time places and half-day sessions
**Children:** 6wks–5yrs. 47 places. 70 on register
**Hours:** 8am–6pm
Morning session 8am–1pm (inc lunch)
Afternoon session 1pm–6pm
Open 51 weeks a year
**Status:** Private, fee-paying
**Number of years open:** 3
**Meals:** Lunch, tea, snacks
**1992 fees:** £100 per week full-time – under 2
£95 per week full-time – over 2
£11 per session – under 2
£10.50 per session – over 2
**Waiting list:** Long. Early registration advisable for baby places
**Registered by:** Beds County Council SS
**Under same ownership/management:** Woodlands Day Nursery, Milton Keynes, Bucks; Cedars Day Nursery, Leighton Buzzard, Beds; Meadow View Nursery, Newport Pagnell, Bucks; Lime Grove Day Nursery, Hemel Hempstead, Herts; Guy's Hospital Day Nursery, London, SE1; Sandfield Day Nursery, John Radcliffe Hospital, Oxford

## LITTLE SCHOOL FOR LITTLE SCHOLARS

49 Reginald Street
Luton
Beds LU2 7QZ
**Tel:** (0582) 453702

**Owner/Headteacher:** Maggie Christie, Mont Dip
**Type:** Montessori school offering half-day sessions only
**Children:** 2½–5yrs. 18 places. 36 on register
**Hours:** Morning session 9am–12 noon
Afternoon session 1pm–4pm
Open 36 weeks a year
**Status** Private, fee-paying

**Number of years open:** 7
**Meals:** Parents provide snacks
**1992 fees:** £273 per term for 5 sessions a week
**Waiting list:** Long. Early registration advisable
**Registered by:** Beds County Council SS

## SUNNYSIDE NURSERY

Summer Street
Leighton Buzzard
Beds LU7 8HT
**Tel:** (0525) 370243

**Joint Owners/Managers:** Brigitte Newberry, BTEC
Inge Newberry, BTEC
Heidi Newberry, BTEC
**Type:** Day nursery and nursery school offering full- and part-time places
**Children:** 0–5yrs. 68 places. 140 on register
**Hours:** 8am–6pm
Flexible hours
Open 51 weeks a year
**Status:** Private, fee-paying
**Number of years open:** 23
**Meals:** Lunch, tea. Parents provide snacks
**1992 fees:** £1.90 per hour – under 2
£1.70 per hour – over 2
80p per day for lunch for part-timers
**Waiting list:** Fairly long. Early registration advisable
**Registered by:** Beds County Council SS

## UNILEVER WORKPLACE NURSERY

Colworth House
Sharnbrook
Beds MK44 1LQ
**Tel:** (0234) 222589

**Owner:** Unilever Research
**Manager:** Debra Patchett, NNEB
**Type:** Workplace nursery offering full- and part-time places and half-day sessions to Unilever employees and local community
**Children:** 2mths–5yrs. 70 places. 80 on register
**Hours:** 8.15am–5.15pm
Morning session 8.15am–1pm
Afternoon session 1pm–5.15pm
Open 50 weeks a year
**Status:** Private, fee-paying

**Number of years open:** 3
**Meals:** Lunch, snacks
**1992 fees:** £353 per month full-time
£83.06 per week full-time
£9 per session
Subsidised rates available to Unilever employees
**Waiting list:** Early registration advisable
**Registered by:** Beds County Council SS

# Berkshire

No local authority day nurseries, but the council provides a 'small pot of money' to subsidise places in the private sector. Families with financial or social problems are encouraged to apply through their health visitor or the Social Services Department. The number of private nurseries has expanded to 57 over the last three years. They offer a wide choice and most have vacancies. Social Services have restructured their daycare system to take into account the widely varying needs of rural areas in the West and towns in the East such as Reading and Slough. The 1400 childminders cover all areas. The county is committed to nursery education and, despite financial restrictions, is slowly increasing provision. Currently 28 per cent of 3- and 4-year-olds receive a place, putting Berkshire in the top ten counties nationwide.

### Further information

For details on day nurseries, childminders, playgroups, crèches and playparks, contact your local Daycare Advisory Team:
Bracknell (0344) 426011
Maidenhead (0628) 32444
Newbury (0635) 46545
Reading (0734) 586111
Slough (0753) 531201
Wokingham (0734) 770407

For details on nursery schools, units and classes:
Education Department
Admissions & Transport Section
Shire Hall
Shinfield Park
Reading RG2 9XE
Tel: (0734) 233472

## ABACUS NURSERY SCHOOL

'Westside'
Oxford Road
Newbury
Berks RG13 1XB
**Tel:** (0635) 550134

**Owner/Headteacher:** Shelagh Lancaster, B Ed
**Type:** Nursery school offering full and part-time places and half-day sessions (min 3 sessions a week)
**Children:** 3–5yrs. 24 places. 56 on register
**Hours:** 8.30–5.30pm
Morning session 8.30am–12 noon or 1pm
Afternoon session 1.30pm–5.30pm
Open 47 weeks a year
**Status:** Private, fee-paying
**Number of years open:** 3½
**Meals:** Packed lunch, snacks
**1992 fees:** £75 per week full-time
£45 for 5 morning sessions till 1pm
£40 for 5 morning sessions till 12 noon
£40 for 5 afternoon sessions
£8.10 per session
£28 registration fee
**Waiting list:** Long for morning places, but all can usually be accommodated if prepared to be flexible
**Registered by:** Berks County Council SS
**Under same ownership:** Abacus Nursery Class, Newbury

**Premises** The ground floor of a large family house, set back from a fairly busy main road. Set in its own grounds, it has a securely fenced garden and spacious drive offering safe parking. The owner and her family live above the nursery. The front door opens on to a peg-lined hall, leading into three main nursery rooms. Totally refurbished three years ago, the rooms are brightly equipped and decorated in primary colours with plentiful displays of children's creativity. The red room is for messy play. The carpeted yellow room has generous space for floor activities – construction toys, large bricks and music and movement. The quiet room is blue, with child-size tables and chairs for table-top games, reading, pre-school work and a much-used computer. Light streams in. French windows in the blue and yellow rooms open on to a large, wide patio, surrounded by a higher level grassed area with a climbing frame and slide.

**Owner/Headteacher & staff** After 20 years' teaching and deputy headship in state primary schools, Shelagh Lancaster, B Ed, decided to go it alone. She opened Abacus in 1990, followed two years later by a nursery class in a local infants school. She is warm and friendly, with very definite views about the care, security, stimulation and learning environment young children require to develop their potential. The four full-time staff and one part-timer are all qualified and experienced – a mixture of teachers (Cert Ed, B Ed) and nursery nurses (NNEB, City & Guilds). They work as a close team. Each is responsible for a small group of children. Shelagh Lancaster's role is largely supervisory, but she is particularly involved in developing pre-reading and writing skills. Students from local schools and colleges come regularly for work experience. Monthly staff meetings are held. A training budget enables staff to update their skills and acquire additional qualifications.

**Children & parents** A good social mix, despite the fees. The limited ethnic diversity reflects the local population, with the children coming from all parts of Newbury and surrounding rural areas. Roughly two-thirds transfer to state primaries, a third to the private sector. Well-established links with local schools are partly a reflection of Shelagh Lancaster's contacts as a local deputy head. The school has particular expertise in dealing with speech and language difficulties and liaises closely with speech therapists. Parental involvement is a priority. Parents are invited to open mornings and afternoons, parents' evenings, a Christmas party and school outings. Children's progress is monitored regularly and detailed written reports discussed individually with parents. Shelagh's office is next to the front door and parents often call in to chat.

**Curriculum & activities** A happy, relaxed, but involved and busy atmosphere. The aim is for each child to develop at his or her own pace, but there are high expectations. 'We do not follow any particular school of thought, except that we should never underestimate what children can achieve,' says Shelagh Lancaster. The school is very much an educational establishment, where children come to learn. The curriculum for the 3Rs is carefully structured, incorporating the best of more traditional methods with new ideas and developments. There is an impressive range of exciting books, and home and school reading is encouraged, as soon as children seem ready. Letterland is used throughout and a number of different reading schemes, depending on a child's preference. Strong emphasis is placed on spoken language – staff are encouraged to listen to children and draw out the shy ones on a one to one basis. A comprehensive maths scheme introduces children to mathematical concepts and can take them all the way through to addition and subtraction when they are ready. Shelagh Lancaster stresses that the strongly educational programmes are balanced by a full and varied diet of other activities, to ensure healthy, all-round development. Children are grouped by age, and rotate between the three nursery rooms. There is plenty of opportunity for daily art and craft, music and fun on the computer. Dance and drama, outdoor play, impromptu walks and visits to the post office and shops are included in the timetable. There are monthly library visits and organised outings two or three times a year. Visits to the park by bus extend many children's experiences of transport. Equipment is plentiful, educational and carefully looked after (annual budget £1000).

**Remarks** A flying start. All the best aspects of nursery care and education have been carefully considered and put into action. Caring, very professional staff, and supportive parents. Strong, detailed educational programmes, but no pressure on children to do anything other than reach their full potential at their own pace. An excellent nursery school, with a headteacher who knows exactly what she is trying to achieve and how to achieve it. Places available if you are prepared to wait or accept afternoon sessions to begin with.

# AGNES HAYWARD NURSERY SCHOOL

29 Lincoln Road
Maidenhead
Berks SL6 5HW
**Tel:** (0628) 30259

**Owner/Principal:** Agnes Hayward
**Type:** Nursery school offering 5 morning sessions a week and 2 afternoon sessions (Tues & Thurs). Part-time places available
**Children:** 3–5yrs. 72 places. 180 on register
**Hours:** Morning session 8.45am–12 noon
Afternoon session (Tues & Thurs) 12.45pm–4pm
Open 40 weeks a year
**Status:** Private, fee-paying
**Number of years open:** 30
**Meals:** Milk or juice. Parents provide snacks
**1992 fees:** £3.70 per session
£2 registration fee
**Waiting list:** Over 100 on waiting list. Places can usually be found although not always full-time
**Registered by:** Berks County Council SS

**Premises** Don't be deceived by the look of the place – a pre-fabricated, very delapidated building in a tarmac yard. Although it looks like a temporary classroom in dire need of repair, the building has been standing for as long as the nursery. It is in a quiet street, close to local schools, with easy parking and a bus stop round the corner. Inside is a crowded but organised hive of activity. There are three classrooms, each warm, simply furnished and colourfully decorated, although one is smaller and darker than the rest. The playground is basic, with a small grassy area and a roundabout, climbing frame and other outdoor equipment. Outside play is confined to this area. The local park is never visited.

**Owner/Principal & staff** Agnes Hayward has been running her nursery school for nearly 30 years without any formal qualifications, having started as a childminder almost 40 years ago. She is the doyenne: planning and overseeing activities, writing letters, leading the team and keeping them up to standard. Her staff of 18 part-timers are unqualified, but sensible, mature and mostly very experienced. She refuses to use formal qualifications as a yardstick for judging staff. Her assistant, Mrs Boulter, has worked with her since 1959 and Agnes Hayward is planning for her own daughter to take over from her eventually. She trains her staff herself and has a detailed written policy and outline of staff duties – referred to as the 'bible' – which leaves little to chance. The nursery would not consider employing a man. 'We've got all the same interests and a man wouldn't fit in. It would spoil the atmosphere,' she says. Provided new staff live up to Mrs Hayward's requirements after a six-week trial, they become part of a strong, very long-serving and loving team. All of the current staff have been at the nursery for between five and 25 years. Ages range from late 30s to 60s. Staff meetings are not seen as necessary as they all work so closely together and have been operating in the same way for many years. Staff/child ratio is 1:6, very good for sessional care.

**Children & parents** The school is now on to second generation children. 'It's lovely to have the children of children,' Agnes Hayward says. There is a complete mixture of backgrounds and abilities. Over the years she has had children with 'almost every disability or special educational need you could mention'. There is also a cultural mix, including Asian and Taiwanese children. Some parents are unemployed or can only afford one or two mornings a week. Others – about 15 per cent – will be sending their children to private schools. Two places are subsidised by the council. Due to pressure for places, children who will be leaving early to go to other private nursery schools are not accepted. Phasing-in is done gradually. Agnes Hayward believes in 'school without tears', and parents are encouraged to join in with their children for as many weeks as necessary to settle them in. Even after a child is settled into the nursery, parents are encouraged to come right inside the classroom each day.

**Curriculum & activities** The school's philosophy is based on 'love and common sense' and requires good manners and presence of mind from everyone. All children spend each session in their classes with the same three members of staff. The 3- to 4-year-olds are divided into two classes and the 4- to 5-year-olds stay in one group. To ease the transition from one class to the next, rising-4s join the 'Big Class' for storytime for half a term before they move to familiarise themselves with staff and children. Afternoon sessions follow the same programme and were introduced simply to ease pressure on the waiting list. Some children move over to morning sessions when a place becomes available. Each session is disciplined and well structured, but it is made clear that staff are there to 'suggest rather than direct or impose'. Sand and water troughs, painting equipment, modelling clay, a Wendy house, a rocking horse, percussion instruments, books and a host of other educational toys and games have been amassed over the years. There is a calm, constructive atmosphere, with everybody interested and busy. Each day starts with free play, painting and puzzles, during which small groups are encouraged to come together for supervised pre-writing, reading and number work. Flashcards, a magnetic newsboard and computer word games are used and alphabet songs sung every day. Most children are 'reading ready' by the time they leave. Storytime is central to each session and includes discussion, finger games and songs. Reasonable behaviour is expected to ensure enjoyment for everyone, and anyone who is rude or persistently fidgeting is removed to sit on the 'silly chair' for a few minutes. The nursery has few rules, but any correction is administered with love, firmness and consistency. There are no written progress reports or records, but staff monitor development together, about once a month.

**Remarks** Agnes Hayward has been running her nursery school in the same way, with virtually the same staff, for nearly 30 years. Her old-fashioned methods and mature, motherly teachers are as popular today as they were a generation ago – and the school has never advertised. The structured curriculum provides solid pre-school preparation. A rare example of a nursery school where the total absence of formal staff qualifications appears irrelevant.

# CEDAR PARK SCHOOL – NURSERY CLASS

Bridge Farm Road
Twyford
Berks RG10 9PP
**Tel:** (0734) 340118

**Owners:** Partnership between Mr & Mrs Bradley and Mr & Mrs Christie
**Principal:** Sue Bradley, B Sc (Hons)
**Headteacher:** Diane Christie, B Sc, PGCE
**Type:** Nursery class in co-ed prep school offering half-day sessions and extended day care.
**Children:** 2–4yrs. 24 places. 44 on register
**Hours:** Morning session 9am–12 noon
Afternoon session 12.30pm–3.30pm
Extended day provision 8am–6pm
Flexible hours
Open 46 weeks a year
**Status:** Private, fee-paying
**Number of years open:** 3
**Meals:** Breakfast, lunch, tea, snacks
**1992 fees:** £470 per term for 5 sessions a week
£100 per term for 1 session a week
£1390 per term for full-time extended day
**Waiting list:** Long. Priority to siblings
**Registered by:** Berks County Council SS

**Premises** At a muddy turning off the main road just outside Twyford, the gates of Cedar Park School disappear into the hedgerow. A driveway leads to a large, whitewashed, recently extended house, set in two acres of mature gardens and woodland. In a former life this was a horticultural nursery. Throughout the house, newly converted rooms open on to patio or grass through French windows or stable doors. A vegetable garden, climbing frame area and pond are under development. Inside is a hive of activity, with three nursery rooms and a large hall with a screen dividing it into two classrooms. Walls are white throughout with either carpeted or tiled floors, and it lacks some warmth and homeliness. Kitchen, loos and nappy-changing areas are new, fresh and spotlessly clean.

**Owners/Principal, Headteacher & staff** Energy and enthusiasm from Sue Bradley, B Sc, the principal, complemented by her gentler partner, headteacher Diane Christie, B Sc, PGCE. Their teamwork started some years ago when both were deputy heads in a local independent school. They lead a fully qualified group of young, lively staff, nursery nurse and teacher trained, and encourage a co-operative approach through weekly staff meetings. The nursery is supervised by a full-time NNEB, who co-ordinates five nursery nurses. Additional formal teaching expertise is available when individual children are ready. Diane Christie teaches the 4-year-olds and Sue Bradley takes daily singing. A staff training and development budget is available for relevant courses. The school offers living accommodation for three full-time nursery staff.

**Children & parents** Local village parents and commuters using the nearby station are attracted to the full day care and education, a scarce combination in the area. Close links are maintained with independent schools, especially the partners' previous school. Children transfer to both the independent and state sectors. A varied combination of teaching sessions and extended daycare is offered. In the holidays and non-teaching hours, children all mix together, with some grouped by age according to activities and specific projects. Nursery staff are always available to talk to parents and there are two formal parents' evenings a year. The school is supported by an active Parents' Association which organises fund-raising activities and finances events.

**Curriculum & activities** Life is varied and never dull, with themes reflecting the seasons, current festivals and life in different cultures. Groups are organised so that a member of staff acts as informal keyworker to certain children, overseeing their progress and planning their activities. Each session starts in a group with the keyworker, for story, discussion, language development and an explanation of the activities on offer. Children then choose what they wish to do, supervised and encouraged by staff to ensure a balance of experiences. Early educational skills include pre-number and reading activities, with increasing emphasis on these for children over 4 years old. All tasks are geared to individual needs and readiness. An eclectic approach to early reading, incorporating phonics, look and say and enjoyment of books. The three nursery rooms are adapted to offer a full range of activities – messy play involving sand, water, paint and glue and quiet corners providing a wealth of books and interesting, attractive games, puzzles, toys, construction equipment and dressing-up clothes. Music is a major feature in nursery life, with daily sessions for each age group and regular productions for everyone, masterminded and written by Sue Bradley. After milk and music, time is set aside for outdoor play in the huge, imaginative garden. More music and movement precede a final story and discussion period, before the session closes. Many children stay for lunch or tea. Termly outings include trips to Kew Gardens, Bird World and Henley (by train). A written record of each child's progress is kept and all staff contribute comments. Much of the creative work is made into books, while other work is sent home. The younger group collate scrapbooks of work, which are taken home and worked on during holidays.

**Remarks** A strong educational establishment, offering extended day care, holiday cover and flexible hours for working parents. Partners have a clear vision, good resources and a traditional curriculum. As ever, the waiting list is long. Register early.

## CHILTERN NURSERY SCHOOL

Chiltern Nursery Training College
16 Peppard Road
Caversham
Reading
Berks RG4 8QS
**Tel:** (0734) 471847

**Owner:** Chiltern Nursery Training College
**Principal:** Ann Hicks, B Sc (Hons)
**Type:** Nursery school offering full- and part-time places and half-day sessions
**Children:** 3–5yrs. 40 places. 92 on register
**Hours:** 9am–3.30pm
Morning session 9am–12 noon
Afternoon session 1pm–3.30pm
Open 40 weeks a year
**Status:** Fee-paying, registered charity
**Number of years open:** 7 (in present building)
**Meals:** Lunch, snacks
**1992 fees:** £701 per term full-time
£529 per term for 5 morning sessions a week inc. lunch
£488.75 per term for 5 morning sessions a week excl. lunch

£294 per term for 5 afternoon sessions a week
**Waiting list:** Over-3s: moderate. Under-3s: long
**Registered by:** Berks County Council SS

**Premises** Once the college principal's private living quarters, the nursery has been extended and totally refurbished to a high standard. A mile from the centre of Reading, it is hidden away at the back of the glorious college grounds. There is one enormous ground-floor, south-facing room, carefully organised into smaller activity areas – the 'west wing' for table-top activities; the 'east wing' for messy and wet play; a science studio, a small office, a home corner and a library area. Light streams in from French windows along one entire side of the room, overlooking the gardens. Every square inch of wall space is covered with children's art and craft displays, parents' notices, curriculum plans, photographs and children's writing. There are impressive quantities of books and equipment throughout and a happy, lively, industrious atmosphere. Outside, a safely fenced play area contains sandpit, climbing frame, outdoor toys and a covered verandah.

**Headteacher & staff** The nursery is one of three on the campus, owned by the Chiltern Nursery Training College. The college, founded in 1931, offers a two-year training course in nursery nursing, leading to the NNEB qualification. The key to the success of this nursery is the universally admired headteacher, Ann Hicks, B Sc. Highly trained and with 27 years' teaching experience, Ann Hicks also lectures six hours a week at the College. Her deputy, Mrs Bell, is a qualified teacher of equal experience. Other full-time staff include three nursery nurses, all NNEB-qualified and Chiltern-trained, one with a DPQS. According to Ann Hicks, 'What makes this place are the six full-time nursery nurses in training we have at all times. They are full of enthusiasm and brimming with interesting and fresh ideas.' Chiltern students each spend a full term under supervision at the nursery during their second year. Their performance is assessed and forms part of their final examination result. There is an annual training budget and full-time staff attend in-house college courses and have access to Berkshire Social Services training.

**Children & parents** Parents are encouraged to be partners in educating their children and parental involvement is considered crucial. Although in approximately 50 per cent of the families both parents are working full-time, many still manage to take an active part in numerous activities. There are fun days, parents' evenings, coffee mornings and whole 'open weeks' for parents to come and spend time at the school. One parent takes small groups for French conversation, while others bring in food or read stories. Many work at the BBC Monitoring Station at the end of the road. Children are mainly middle class, but from a wide mix of cultures. Many children are bi-lingual. The majority transfer to local state schools.

**Curriculum & activities** The nursery is a 'teaching establishment', where children develop and learn in a secure, stimulating environment. The mornings are more structured than the afternoons, when younger children attend. The curriculum is planned well in advance and copies are displayed and discussed with parents. Teachers arrive early each morning to set out daily activities – painting, art and craft, science projects, pre-reading and early maths, home corner, imaginative play, play dough and free drawing. Children are encouraged to choose their own activity and to move freely from one to another. After milk and biscuits, they come together for 'big group' work – sharing news and stories, discussing current events. This is followed by work in small groups, with teachers offering individual help with pre-reading, pre-writing and maths. There are no worksheets and no reading schemes, as these are considered too limiting. Children are never pushed or made to compete with each other. The aim is to motivate each child to reach their full potential. The curriculum is multicultural, creative and varied. The emphasis is on fun and preparation for school. Termly topics, projects and interest tables are planned and discussed with students, children and parents. Everyone is involved. The Christmas display we observed was 'Christmas on Bondi Beach'. Detailed records are kept on each child's activities and progress. Television viewing of selected programmes occurs occasionally – recent favourites include *Sesame Street* and the Olympics. Other activities include daily outdoor play and use of the stunning college grounds, weekly music, dance and movement, frequent outings related to current topics and regular library visits. Equipment (annual budget £2750) and materials are plentiful and age related. Lunch is an important part of the day. Children and staff sit down together to eat and talk. Food looked and smelt delicious – freshly cooked in the college kitchens.

**Remarks** A wonderful nursery offering the best of care and education in just the right balance. A carefully planned and structured curriculum, which considers each child within the context of family and home. The nursery admits that the termly changeover of students is disruptive and can cause difficulties at the beginning of each term. However, full-time staff are well qualified, stable and very experienced. The students bring energy, enthusiasm and fresh ideas. Chiltern has one of the best relationships with parents we have come across. Parents are involved in every aspect of the nursery at all times. There is also a full-time day nursery and a workplace nursery on the same site.

# CHRIST THE KING (RC) PRIMARY SCHOOL – NURSERY CLASS

Northumberland Avenue
Reading
Berks RG2 8NR
**Tel:** (0734) 873819

**Owner:** Berks LEA
**Teacher-in-charge:** Irene Lindsay, B Ed
**Type:** Nursery class in Catholic primary school offering half-day sessions. No full-time places
**Children:** 3yrs 9mths–5yrs. 26 places. 52 on register
**Hours:** Morning session 9am–11.30am
Afternoon session 12.30pm–3pm
Open 38 weeks a year
**Status:** State nursery class
**Number of years open:** 3 (in current premises)
**Meals:** Milk
**1992 fees:** No fees
**Waiting list:** Long, but most children are offered a place eventually
**Registered by:** Berks County Council LEA

**Premises** An old classroom, converted three years ago so that the nursery school could relocate from its town site and join up with the primary school. It is a beautiful, bright, airy room, flooded with light from skylights and large windows, looking out on to a grassy outside area. Blue carpet, white walls, primary colours and a wealth of attractive, good-quality equipment, all create a lively and interesting environment. There is a raised area for the reading corner and doors opening on to the outside play area with a slide and climbing frame. A small shed houses trikes, bikes, barrows and outside toys. More resources for outdoor equipment would be welcome. A patch of garden allows children some experience of growing plants and flowers. The nursery benefits from being completely self-contained, but is also very much part of the school. The school hall is used regularly for PE and physical exercise during bad weather, and the nursery joins in school events and assemblies when appropriate.

**Teacher-in-charge & staff** Irene Lindsay, B Ed, organised and set up the newly located nursery. It was a challenge ideally suited to her extensive experience in early years education. She personifies her belief that the learning environment should be fun, but structured and consistent. Her NNEB nursery assistant, Marian, has been at the nursery for 22 years and shares her philosophy. Both women are firm but loving and they run an organised, disciplined nursery class. Parents often help and students undergoing teaching practice are frequently taken on. A staff development and training budget is available.

**Children & parents** Many of the children live within walking distance, on the housing estate surrounding the school. Others come from further away, specifically to attend a Catholic school. The nursery attracts a high percentage of Catholics, although non-Catholics are accepted. Most children spend three terms at the nursery before moving to primary school the term after their 5th birthday. Most transfer to local state primary schools, many to Christ the King. The nursery has experience with special needs children, but has only one such child at present. Parents regularly help in the classroom, especially to assist with outings. They attend parents' evenings, concerts, plays and social events. Discussion of children's progress is possible at any time, within reason. Parents are encouraged to accompany their children to the nursery once a week, over the half-term preceding their entry. Staff make some home visits.

**Curriculum & activities** The morning and afternoon sessions are run along the same lines, with the first hour involving free choice and movement between structured activities set up in each area of the nursery. One member of staff directs, observes and encourages in each area. Although children move freely, a check is kept to ensure each child has a balanced range of experiences. Group time with Irene Lindsay involves discussions, fun and games to develop language and concepts such as numbers, sounds, days of the week, the weather and colours. Outside play is then available or more choice inside, before storytime and tidying up. Milk is supplied on demand. Children are not divided into age groups until the term before starting school, when they begin to work through more structured tasks developing number, pencil-control and pre-reading and writing skills. All activities are tailored to each child's needs and interests. Weekly music sessions with a pianist are backed up by the use of tapes and singing at other times. Outings involve parents and vary from local trips to the library, church and leisure centre to whole-day visits further afield to a farm or the model village at Beaconscott. Spiritual development is a vital aspect of the curriculum and permeates all activities. Books, stories and different religious festivals are studied to explore aspects of Christianity.

**Remarks** A lively, caring and fun place to begin school life. Attractive surroundings and lots of the right things to do. Experienced, talented staff offer a strong curriculum within a structured, disciplined routine. Active, close relationship with the main school.

# LANGLEY MANOR NURSERY

Langley Manor School
St Mary's Road
Langley
Slough SL3 6BZ
**Tel:** (0753) 825368 or (0753) 577005

**Owners:** Chris & Sally Eaton
**Headmistress:** Sally Eaton, B Ed
**Nursery Headteacher:** Karen Cornell, BA, PGCE
**Type:** Nursery class in independent pre-prep school offering full-time places and half-day sessions, breakfast club and after-school club
**Children:** 2yrs 9mths–4½yrs. 24 places per session, 8 full-time. 40 on register.
**Hours:** 9.30am–3pm
Morning session 9.30am–11.45am
Afternoon session 12.45pm–3pm
Open 36 weeks a year
**Status:** Private, fee-paying
**Number of years open:** 3 in present building
**Meals:** Packed lunches, snacks
**1992 fees:** £844 per term full-time
£450 per term for 5 sessions a week
£1 per day for breakfast club
£4 per day for after-school club
**Waiting list:** 45 names. Preference to siblings
**Registered by:** Dept for Education
**Under same ownership/management:** Wheeler Manor School Nursery, Bucks; Cherry Trees Nursery, Berks; Iver Nursery School, Berks; Langley Nursery School, Berks

**Premises** Large, modern, brick-built, single-storey and set in its own grounds, with a swimming pool complex, Langley Manor School is impressive. The school takes 260 pupils including the nursery class. Facilities are excellent and available for use by the nursery – huge assembly hall, TV room, gym, library, art room, computer room, science lab, staff room, and extensive playgrounds. Everywhere is new, well planned and generously equipped. The nursery, known as the 'Lower Nursery', is on the ground floor, with a separate entrance and safely fenced outdoor play area. It is very much part of the school, sharing facilities and specialist teachers. The class is one large room with a home corner, book corner, prodigious amounts of equipment and toys – and two gerbils. The atmosphere is lively and industrious. Artwork throughout the school is stunning. Colourful displays of art, craft and writing cover the walls of the nursery.

**Owners, Headteacher & staff** The owners, Chris and Sally Eaton, B Ed, are young, approachable and successful. They own three nursery schools and manage a workplace nursery. Both are full-time and work long hours at Langley Manor School, Sally as headmistress, Chris as bursar. The headteacher of the nursery class is Karen Cornell, BA, PGCE, highly qualified and experienced. She has overall responsibility for the day-to-day running, but the curriculum is standardised across all the nursery schools owned by the Eatons. Karen is assisted by two part-time NNEB-qualified nursery nurses, one in the mornings, the other in the afternoons. There is also a full-time, unqualified nursery assistant. Morale is good and staff are keen to work at Langley Manor School. Visiting specialist teachers from the main school cover French, music, dance and art. No students. Staff training policy operates according to needs (annual training budget approx £2000). High calibre staff, who are long-serving.

**Children & parents** Parents are all local, from a range of cultural backgrounds. About half the children have two working parents, many self-employed. There is a strong Asian contingent, reflecting the area. Despite the recession, the numbers are high and the waiting list is long. A mini-bus service picks up children over 3 years old and brings them to school. The annual holiday summer school and Easter camp attract up to a hundred children. Parents are encouraged to become involved wherever possible. They are invited right inside the classroom to collect their children, stay for sessions and hear reading. They also help with swimming, fund-raising and a 'busy social diary throughout the year' – which includes plays, parties and barbecues. Most children stay on and move up through the school. Transfer to the two reception classes takes place at 4½ years, usually with ease, as the surroundings are so familiar. Communication and partnership with parents is at the heart of nursery beliefs.

**Curriculum & activities** Learning through play, with the emphasis on preparing children for entry into the reception class at 4½. It is based on Christian principles with the appropriate use of Bible references to encourage good moral conduct. A written Nursery Charter, compiled by the headmistress and her nursery leaders, outlines themes, topics, worksheets to be completed and developmental targets, reflecting a careful balance between care, play and education. Computers, with an abundance of software, are used. Science and mathematical teaching are in line with the Department for Education working paper for infant schools. Children are prepared so that they are familiar with the language and terms that will be tested at age 7. Praise is used freely. The nursery believes that if you expect the very best, children will reach their full potential. Weekly themes relating to children's everyday experiences are used to explore language, mathematics and science. Each session begins with a choice of free play, sand and water, art or cookery. During group play activities, small numbers of children are taken out to work individually on pre-reading, pre-writing and number work. Written work is done on worksheets, which either go home or are filed. Letterland is used throughout. There are no reading schemes until the reception class. Teachers keep checklists and detailed written developmental records on all children, which are available to parents. French twice a week, regular music, dance and movement, and outings. Swimming weekly in the school pool, with a resident coach. All children can swim by the time they are five.

**Remarks** Thriving, happy nursery school with all the advantages of being attached to a purpose-built, modern school, with excellent facilities and specialist teachers. Well resourced (equipment budget £3000 a year) and successful. Good relationship with supportive parents. This nursery is for parents who favour the private sector and can afford it. Unfortunately, Sally and Chris Eaton's longest running nursery, Langley Nursery School, falls short of the high standards set by their other nurseries.

# MARY SEACOLE DAY NURSERY

Terrapin Building
Coley Primary School
Wolseley Street
Reading
Berks RG1 6AZ
**Tel:** (0734) 391622

**Owner:** Mary Seacole Nursery and Educational Association
**Officer-in-charge:** Esther Fleary-Griffiths, NNEB
**Type:** Community day nursery offering full-time places
**Children:** 2–5yrs. 20 places. 20 on register
**Hours:** 8am–5.45pm
Open 50 weeks a year
**Status:** Fee-paying, registered charity. Run by management committee and subsidised by Social Services
**Number of years open:** 2½
**Meals:** Lunch, tea, snacks
**1992 fees:** £45 per week full-time
**Waiting list:** Extensive. Hopefully all will get a place, if only for a few months
**Registered by:** Berks County Council SS

**Premises** A lot is crammed into this terrapin building, but the two main rooms feel cosy, welcoming and secure with many interesting corners to explore. Bright, colourful displays reflect the multicultural philosophy that is fundamental to the Association. The Geldof Room is tiled, with a carpeted area and home corner, an impressive selection of woodwork tools and workbench, equipment for messy and creative activities as well as sand and water. Tables are pushed together at mealtimes to provide an eating area adjacent to the kitchen. Double doors open into the carpeted Biko Room, home to the nursery's pet fish and hamster and a book corner offering a broad range of reading material. Tables and chairs and units bulging with puzzles, games and equipment occupy all the remaining space. Windows on two sides of the building look on to the primary school playground and a grassy slope, shared with the school. The building is set in its own fenced area on the edge of the playground, providing a safe play area on an all-weather surface.

**Officer-in-charge & staff** The Mary Seacole Nursery was set up as a joint project between Social Services and parents and community leaders previously involved with the West Indian Women's Circle Nursery (which had to close) using funds frozen from the other nursery and additional council funding. Esther Fleary-Griffiths, NNEB, was employed to set up the new nursery in 1991 and has worked with great dedication to create a caring, stimulating and totally multicultural environment. Calm and committed, she presents a clear view of what she and her team are seeking to provide. Four of the team of five full-time staff are NNEB qualified, and all are experienced in child care. A male teaching student (an unusual asset in provision for under-5s) is enthusiastically welcomed back whenever he is available.

**Children & parents** Most children live in the immediate locality. Although the nursery was originally set up to fill the gap in provision for black children, at an affordable price, the intake of children is multiracial, from working and non-working families. Children move on to the neighbouring primary school or to other state and independent schools. The nursery has doubled its numbers since opening, and had a waiting list of 26 when we visited, reflecting the need for reasonably priced provision in the area. It is hoped that most children will eventually secure a place, even if only for a few months before transferring to primary school. The nursery operates an open door policy and believes that partnership with parents is the key to quality provision.

**Curriculum & activities** The aim is to enable each child, through a multicultural curriculum, to develop his or her skills and abilities in a warm, secure, caring, non-racist and non-sexist environment. The nursery strives 'to promote a positive image of all cultural backgrounds and to nurture personal development, awareness and self-esteem'. Children are organised into two groups of mixed age. Each member of staff acts as keyworker to five children and is responsible for recording their progress. The National Curriculum is kept firmly in mind and the day is carefully planned to include messy play, art and craft, stories, project work, educational activities and games, music and movement and at least an hour of outdoor play. Active sessions are followed by quieter discussion and stories. Equipment is varied and of good quality (annual budget £2000). During the younger children's rest period after lunch, early educational projects and pre-school activities, pre-reading and pre-writing work are covered by the older children. Topics are followed and changed regularly. An ongoing topic has been the alphabet, with a letter explored each week for six months. From 2.30pm onwards the day is less structured, with free play either side of tea. An outing is organised most weeks, to the library or parks, and regular visits further afield, to the market, a pantomime or Thorpe Park. Many outings involve the local community as well as the nursery. Food is prepared on the premises and looked appetising. Children are involved in helping to lay tables and serve food. Staff eat with children, making meals a time for socialising and conversation.

**Remarks** A shining example of what can be achieved by joint initiatives and partnership. Carefully considered multicultural philosophy is clearly followed and in great demand. Devoted, professional nursery staff and supportive parents. The nursery has ambitious expansion plans for the future which deserve to be funded and fulfilled. Extremely reasonable fees for full-time care.

# MEADOW NURSERY SCHOOL

Murray Road
Wokingham
Berks RG11 2TA
**Tel:** (0734) 733695

**Owner:** Meadow Nursery School Parents' Association
**Teacher-in-charge:** Dorn Share, B Ed
**Type:** Nursery school offering half-day sessions. No full-time places
**Children:** 3–5yrs. 30 places. 120 children on register
**Hours:** Morning session 9am–11.30am
Afternoon session 12.45pm–3.15pm
Open 36 weeks a year
**Status:** Fee-paying, registered charity, administered by parents' association committee
**Number of years open:** 15
**Meals:** Milk and biscuits
**1992 fees:** £3.50 per session
£2.50 registration fee
**Waiting list:** Long. Preference to siblings and children living within Walter County Infant School catchment area. Not all on list will be offered a place
**Registered by:** Berks County Council SS

**Premises** Two connected pre-fabricated terrapin buildings, set in the grounds of a local authority infant school. This nursery has mastered the art of maximum use of limited space. It is surrounded by a small, safely fenced, paved and grassed outside play area. Children also benefit from the use of the school playground and assembly hall. Parking is a headache. The school gate opens on to a busy, narrow through road to the station, with heavy commuter parking. Luckily, the majority of families live within walking distance. Inside, every inch of space in the two activity rooms is utilised, with a home corner, comfortable carpeted reading corner with big beanbags and an inviting display of books, a cluster of tables and a kitchen/cooking area in the first room. Past a very life-like telephone kiosk and a trolley full of musical instruments, you come to the second room, with water tray, art area, more tables and a further carpeted area, which at one point during the session housed a large climbing frame as well. Shelves packed with good-quality, well-cared-for materials separate the different activity areas within the two rooms. Light and airy, the neutral furnishings set off brightly coloured displays of children's masterpieces hanging from the ceiling and covering the walls.

**Teacher-in-charge & staff** In 1977, a group of parents concerned about the lack of pre-school provision in the area launched a project to set up their own nursery. In April 1978 Meadow opened – the first nursery school in Berkshire to be managed by a parents' committee. Members of the Parents' Association select an administrative committee annually and work exhaustively to raise funds for additional facilities and new equipment. Dorn Share, B Ed, the teacher-in-charge, joined the nursery in its early years as the assistant teacher, and took responsibility for running the nursery in 1984, just before the second room was added on and numbers increased. Her involvement and interest in the children are apparent, mixing a warm, gentle approach with firm expectations and structure. The three other female members of staff are all qualified, NNEB, B Ed, Cert Ed, and experienced. A close team, obviously enjoying the children's company. Two staff members and a parent volunteer work with Dorn at each session. The headteacher of the infant school liaises regularly to supervise the curriculum and advise on staff appointments. The staff training budget is limited, but five staff training days a year are taken – the most recent was a speech and language development course.

**Children & parents** Mainly middle class, comfortably-off families. Few ethnic minority children. The majority join the term after their 3rd birthday for two sessions a week, graduating to three sessions at 4 years old. They have the option of five sessions a week for the term before they enter school at 5. Virtually all move on to either Walter County Infant School, two steps away, or other state primaries. Very few opt for the independent sector. All of the families live within the infant school catchment area, many in the large private housing estate of Woosehill. Special needs children are welcome and the nursery successfully integrates children with learning difficulties, physical disabilities and Down's syndrome. The nursery has a strong relationship with parents, who are all members of the Parents' Association and through the committee run the nursery. Daily informal contact is continued with more formal open evenings to discuss each child's progress once a term. New parents are invited to an introductory evening. Parents are actively involved in many fund-raising activities.

**Curriculum & activities** The nursery aims to provide 'a safe and happy environment, where children can develop and mature and learn to co-operate and socialise'. During our visit, children were very obviously happy, enquiring and constructively busy. They were animated but polite, asking questions and chatting. Sessions begin with a variety of structured and open-ended activities, including creative art and modelling, pencil work, pre-school skills, board games, puzzles, construction toys, sand and water play and the home and book corners. Children are free to choose their activity, but encouraged and directed to join different groups to ensure they experience a balance of activities. Following outdoor play, there is milk and biscuits. Children choose a table to sit at and talk to the member of staff who joins their table. The whole class then comes together for discussion, and storytime, followed by more activities in small groups. The session ends with more conversation, games, songs and general fun for the whole group. Parents with particular skills or knowledge are quickly recruited to enliven sessions. Summer brings picnics in the playground and walks in the meadows. Topics change each term, with staff carefully planning the stages each child will be taken through. Detailed written programmes were being redesigned when we visited. Pre-school skills are based and planned with the National Curriculum Key Stage 1 in mind and often relate to activities which will continue on into infant school. Records on each child's progress are updated termly, with all staff contributing. A profile sheet is collated and discussed with parents, to be taken by children to their next school.

**Remarks** An excellent preparation for school, in a warm and happy atmosphere. Close liaison with the infant school. Premises are not perfect, and inside space is limited, but well organised. The outdoor play area is small. Meadow Nursery School owes its existence to an active group of parents who refused to accept that their children should miss out on the advantages of nursery education. The first nursery school in the country to be run by parents.

# NORLAND COLLEGE (NURSERY SCHOOL, DAYCARE UNITS & CHILDREN'S HOTEL)

Denford Park
Hungerford
Berks RG17 0PQ
**Tel:** (0488) 682252

**Owner:** Norland Nursery Training College
**Principal:** Louise E Davis, SRN, M Phil
**Type:** Nursery nurse training college, incorporating day nurseries, nursery school, workplace crèche and children's hotel, offering full- and part-time places and half-day sessions
**Children:** 6wks–5yrs (up to 8yrs in hotel). 134 places. 235 on register
**Hours:** 8am–6pm
Nursery school 9am–3pm
Morning session 9am–1pm
Afternoon session 1pm–3pm

Extended day care 8.15am–5.45pm
Hotel – 24hr care
Open 51 weeks a year
**Status:** Private, non profit-making
**Number of years open:** 101
**Meals:** Breakfast, lunch, tea, snacks
**1992 fees:** *Nursery School*
£600 per term full-time
£315 per term for 5 morning sessions a week
£285 per term for 5 afternoon sessions a week
*Day Nursery*
£95.20 per week full-time
£20.20 per day
£11.50 per morning session
£8.70 per afternoon session
*Children's Hotel*
£182 per week full-time
£28 per night
£40 Fri or Sat night
£40 single night rate
£55 registration fee
**Waiting list:** Long, but variable, depending on service required. Early registration advisable
**Registered by:** Berks County Council SS

**Premises** An elegant Georgian mansion set in over a hundred acres of rolling parkland in a position of splendid rural isolation. It has been a private house, convent and prep-school. The college, and its numerous childcare facilities used for training students, is approached via a long, winding drive from the A4. Public transport has failed to find this beautiful corner of Berkshire. Inside, the atmosphere is country house style, chintzy and very genteel. The principal's private apartments have been converted into the Primrose Nursery for babies under 12 months. It is a light, sunny, south-facing area with feeding room, kitchen and suite of bedrooms. Each baby has a cot and a big, old-fashioned, black pram. Children up to 3 years old are in the Daffodil and Bluebell Nurseries. All rooms are well equipped, cheerful and welcoming, with separate, safely secured outside play areas, generously filled with swings, climbing frames, sandpits and pram shelters. The nursery school for the over-3s, known as the Rose Garden, is a separate unit and consists of three classes. One is a day nursery for working parents, another a class for 3- to 4-year-olds, and the third is a pre-reception class for rising-5s. The children's hotel (known as 'Razzies' because the children reside there) offers 24-hour care for children up to 8 years old. Each child sleeps in a twin-bedded room with a Norland student. All the childcare facilities are well-decorated, with good-quality equipment (annual budget £25,000), but they are not lavish or glamorous. The 18th-century proportions of many children's rooms, the sheer size of the place and the equally unglamorous uniforms worn by the students and staff, make it difficult to create a homely, family atmosphere. Outdoor facilities are magnificent – numerous, beautifully equipped play areas (one recently cost £17,000), and the new Centenary Trail through the woods, completed to celebrate the college's 100th birthday last year.

**Principal & staff** The Principal, Louise Davis, SRN, M Phil, has been leading Norland College for 13 years and is approachable, down-to-earth and highly qualified. The day nursery is headed by Rosemary Best, NNEB, a Norland graduate. The recently appointed nursery school headteacher is Jamie Shaw, BA, PGCE, MA, Dip Child Development, and the matron of the children's hotel is Sally Hannam, NNEB (Norland). There are 30 qualified nursery nurses (20 NNEB, three B Ed/Cert Ed and seven SRN). All have first aid training, regularly updated. Staff receive competitive salaries and additional benefits. Staff meetings are monthly. There is an induction programme for new nursery workers and ongoing training and development. The college has a strong equal opportunities policy, although men are hard to find on the campus. To date, only one male student has applied, and was not accepted. Students all wear dull beige uniforms, including hat and gloves.

**Children & parents** Children of local Berkshire parents, many with working mothers. One or two places are subsidised by local companies. The children's hotel is used by Social Services for emergency and pre-fostering placements. Parents of children with special needs use it regularly for respite care. It is also popular with London parents going away for weekends and airline crews on short overseas trips. Children with special needs are welcome, provided they do not need specialist nursing care. There is an active PTA and parents are welcome to visit at any time and to take part in nursery activities. The main purpose of all childcare facilities at Norland is to provide a training ground for student nursery nurses.

**Curriculum & activities** The childcare philosophy is based on the teachings of Froebel and, to a lesser extent, a sympathy for Montessori methods, allowing each individual to develop independence and skills at his/her own pace. The real attraction at Norland is the high staffing ratios. The 15 babies are cared for by four trained staff and six students. In all the day nurseries there are ratios of 1:2 or 1:3. Each unit has a structured, but flexible, timetable, with a variety of activities and generous amounts of outdoor play and walks. Each child in the baby unit is checked every ten minutes while sleeping. Children in the nursery school are divided into three classes of 18 according to age. Each class has two Froebel-trained B Eds and two NNEB nursery assistants, plus students. The programme is planned, but informal. Strong art and craft work, daily music, stories, cooking, singing, environmental studies and computer work. Dance and movement twice a week with a qualified teacher. Nature and interest tables, book corner, play house, home corner and a telephone kiosk are also available. There is plenty of project work around themes and full use is made of the extensive outdoor facilities. Students organise outings and nature walks through the woods. Pre-reading, writing and number work increase as children become older. The pre-reception class is more structured with longer work periods. Children complete worksheets each day, which they take home, and when they are ready, the Ladybird, Ginn and Heinemann reading schemes are used. The extended day class follows a similar curriculum, but children are offered more rest and free play periods. Lunch and tea are provided. Children eat in a number of different dining rooms attended by large numbers of students.

**Remarks** Unparalleled surroundings, very high staff/child ratios and over a hundred years' experience in childcare. High-quality, trained staff and an unlimited supply of students from an élite and carefully selected group, many of whom will go on to become nannies to some of the richest and most famous families in the world. Well-resourced, child-centred and strong pre-school education. Fees commensurate with the quality of provision. The sheer size of the operation and 'those uniforms' may be too intimidating for some.

# ORCHARD DAY NURSERY

239 Henley Road
Caversham
Reading
Berks RG4 0LJ
**Tel:** (0734) 475797

**Owners/Principals:** Humphrey Boyd, BA, PGCE, CQSW
Jane Boyd, NNEB
**Type:** Day nursery offering full- and part-time places and half-day sessions
**Children:** 2–5yrs. 24 places. 45 on register
**Hours:** 8am–6pm
Morning session 8am–12 noon
Afternoon session 1pm–6pm
Open 50 weeks a year
**Status:** Private, fee-paying
**Number of years open:** 3
**Meals:** Lunch, tea, snacks
**1992 fees:** £83 per week full-time
£17.50 per day
£9.50 per session
£1.50 per day for lunch
£20 refundable registration fee
**Waiting list:** Variable but manageable
**Registered by:** Berks SS

**Premises** Big, detached family house with parking spaces in front on a busy main road leading into Reading. The entrance is down the side, into a small corridor with kitchen, loos and cloakroom. There are two main children's rooms – the Playroom which is carpeted, and the Messy Room which is not, and adapts to become a wet play area, dining room and cookery room. There is also a small, cosy, quiet room with soft beanbags, television and video. One of the most striking features of the nursery is the abundance of artwork and colourful craft displays (covering rather tired decoration) – a jungle display, alphabet display, caterpillar birthday chart and, best of all, a huge canvas painting which is worked on and added to continuously by children and staff. They have walked over it, daubed it, handprinted it and painted it with brushes – it is stunning, and still growing. The half-acre garden is an asset and well equipped for outdoor play. Animals are an important feature – the owners' two cats and dog roam freely throughout the nursery, being cuddled, smothered and pulled as they go. Three pygmy goats, rabbits, guinea pigs and chickens complete the menagerie. Future plans include building new cloakrooms and an extension to the rear, a pirate ship or spaceship for the garden and possible conversion of the garage into an after-school club.

**Owners/Principals & staff** Jane and Humphrey Boyd are the heart and soul of this nursery. Humphrey Boyd, BA, PGCE, CQSW, joined full-time last year – they needed his salary as a social worker up till then. The Boyds are brimming with enthusiasm and constantly looking for ways to improve the quality of their service. Extremely close contact with children and parents. Parents constantly drop in and one father comes for tea every day. There are four other nursery workers, all qualified NNEB and City & Guilds, plus two YTS students and a part-time cook. Staff are warm, friendly and positive towards the children – much praise, encouragement and cuddles.

**Children & parents** Happy, busy, confident children. Parents and children – mainly from the immediate neighbourhood, especially the local housing estates – feel very much at home in the nursery. About 50 per cent of children are full-time and will stay at Orchard until they go to school. Even then they keep coming back for tea and events. Parents are encouraged to spend as much time as possible in the nursery so they really understand how it works. They describe it as 'one big, happy family'. They are encouraged to visit other types of nursery provision in the area, so they can put Orchard in context. The nursery is particularly popular with separated and divorced families because of the love and stability it offers. Strenuous efforts are made to include both divorced/separated parents in nursery activities for the benefit of the child.

**Curriculum & activities** The Boyds are opposed to a didactic teaching approach for under-5s – their philosophy is that children will learn best if they are happy and secure and if activities available are stimulating and fun. They are anti-dogmatic, drawing from a range of theorists, but Piaget is favourite. Many different pursuits are available, including cooking, feeding and caring for animals plus visits, painting, working, reading, playing and selective television viewing. There is no pressure to work or complete assignments, but it is encouraged and results are impressive. The children love to learn. Each morning and afternoon there is a structured, disciplined time with tablework on letters, and topics incorporating science and counting. Work is done on worksheets by the younger group, in exercise books by the older children. The written work we were shown was of a high standard; good pencil control, careful colouring and excellent free-hand writing exercises. French was introduced by a volunteer teacher for a term, but has since lapsed. There are many social events for parents and children – coffee mornings with stalls and games, a summer fête with bouncy castle and more stalls and a pantomime trip at Christmas. Any new idea or experience is embraced, if it will be good for the children. The local agricultural college lends the nursery two newborn lambs for two weeks every spring so the children can hand-rear and look after them.

**Remarks** Jane and Humphrey Boyd and their two small children make this nursery special and very child-centred. Not for those seeking a structured, more traditional environment, or for anyone wary of mixing animals and young children, but a lovely, relaxed, family atmosphere. Your child could be very happy here.

# Buckinghamshire

Provision of pre-school education is poor, with only 15 per cent of 3- and 4-year-olds offered access to part-time classes. Parents complain of overcrowding and long waiting lists. One told us, 'The main state-funded provision is playgroups, which on the whole are over-subscribed and poorly equipped, many in claustrophobic church halls.' This year's budget cuts include £1.3 million from primary and nursery schools and £20,000 from special needs. In rural areas, childminders are often the only full-time carers available. There are no local authority day nurseries. The private sector provides 27 nurseries, offering over 800 places, but demand far outweighs supply. 'Most private nurseries have waiting lists so long you have to register as soon as your child is conceived,' according to the owner of a Montessori school.

### Further information

For details on private nurseries, childminders and playgroups, contact the Children's Daycare Advisor at the Social Services Department in your area:
Amersham, Beaconsfield
& High Wycombe (0494) 729000
Buckingham & Milton Keynes (0908) 835600
Aylesbury (0296) 383800

For details on nursery schools, units and classes:
Education Department – Central Services
County Hall
Aylesbury HP20 1UZ
Tel: (0296) 382641

---

## ACORN DAY NURSERY

17 South Street
Castlethorpe
Milton Keynes
MK19 7EL
**Tel:** (0908) 510309
**Owner:** Acorn Day Nursery Ltd
**Director/Manager:** Zoë Hedges, MA, PGCE
**Type:** Day nursery offering full- and part-time places and half-day sessions, plus after-school care for Castlethorpe School pupils only
**Children:** 3mths–5yrs. 36 places. 58 on register
**Hours:** 8am–6pm
Morning session 8am–1.30pm
Afternoon session 1.30pm–6pm
Short day 8am–3pm
Open 50 weeks a year
**Status:** Private, fee-paying
**Number of years open:** 4
**Meals:** Lunch, tea, snacks
**1992 fees:** £350 per month full-time
£84 per week full-time
£18 per day 8am–6pm
£14 per day 8am–4pm
£9.50 per morning session
£8.50 per afternoon session
10% sibling discount
£50 refundable deposit
**Waiting list:** Minimal
**Registered by:** Bucks County Council SS

**Premises** In an unspoilt Buckinghamshire village, not far from Milton Keynes. The building, once a Wesleyan chapel, was converted to a private house some years ago. The present owners now live upstairs and the ground floor has been equipped as a day nursery. There are two cheerful rooms for the six babies. Three more quaint, darker, but nevertheless cosy, rooms provide different activity areas for the three other age groups: a workroom, with books and tables; a large playroom with toys, Wendy house, climbing frame, dressing-up corner etc; and a messy-play/art-and-craft room. The walls are light pastel shades, relieved by old wood panelling and a colourful mural, painted by the village milkman. Very striking displays of children's combined work, but not many individual pieces. Cheerful old flowery carpet, and lino in the art room. There is a rather small garden off the art room, with a paved bike area, soft chips under the swing and a Wendy house. A good, well-equipped, council playground nearby is used regularly. The nursery also has weekly use of a local mini-bus, at low cost. Good street parking. No public transport, as Castlethorpe is off the beaten track.

**Owner/Manager & staff** Zoë Hedges, MA, PGCE, owns and manages Acorn. A young, energetic mother, and a former secondary school English teacher, she takes the older children for up to 25 hours a week and spends the rest of her time on administration. Her 13 female staff ('we probably wouldn't consider a man if one applied') comprise 11 NNEBs and two unqualified but experienced nursery workers. Nursery nurses are young, affectionate and committed. Jan Clarke, a registered nurse and NNEB, runs the baby room. The nursery operates a keyworker system. Each of the four groups of children has two members of staff allocated to them. Staff stay with the group for at least six months to allow for continuity. Three nursery workers, including the owner, have their own children at the nursery. Staff/child ratio is 1:3 for babies, 1:4 for older children. There is a lunchtime chef, teatime cook and NNEB and BTEC students as helpers. Staff meetings are held every six weeks, and time and money are set aside for staff to attend short training courses. The staff obviously work well, as a close-knit team, creating a warm, family environment. Visiting specialists take dancing, music and French.

**Children & parents** Mainly middle class with little cultural mix. A few live in the village, while others come from north Milton Keynes, Northampton and surrounding villages. The nursery is popular with staff from the nearby Foreign and Commonwealth Office. About 60 per cent of children have working mothers. Transfer is to Castlethorpe village school and a range of state and private schools elsewhere. The children seem very bright and cheerful, definitely enjoying their time at the nursery. There is an open door policy towards parents. Open days, parents' evenings, nursery plays and a termly newsletter keep parents informed. A huge display of photographs in the entrance hall allows them to see what their children have been up to on recent outings and activities. Children are required to attend for a minimum of two sessions a week; parents can stay with new children until they are settled.

**Curriculum & activities** Babies have their own separate suite, a playroom with a rather small cot room adjoining it for rests and changing area and cloakroom – there is a rocking chair and an electric swing to help settle them. When the babies are ready for more boisterous play they are gradually introduced to the activity rooms. The rest of the children are divided into three groups by age, Acorns, Squirrels and Oaks. Each morning and afternoon session consists of three 40-minute lessons with free play before and after. The three age groups spend 40 minutes in each of the three activity areas, twice a day. In the large room, they learn through play, with an excellent range of equipment – toys, games and books. The school has an exclusive deal with a supplier of educational toys and equipment to act as their showpiece nursery. They have an enormous amount of their equipment and constantly road-test new products for the company. In the workroom, worksheets are provided and all pre-school preparation skills are practised regularly. The whole nursery works on one theme or topic at a time, developing it in all areas and usually displaying the results in a group mural. Most of the National Curriculum up to Key Stage 1 is covered. Older children are taught more advanced reading and writing skills if they are ready. There are no written programmes. Keyworkers monitor each child's progress. Visiting teachers take groups for music, dancing and French. Children play outdoors in the small walled garden, babies are wheeled around the village in prams or buggies and older children are taken for walks to nearby farms or the local playground. Weekly swimming by mini-bus for Squirrels and Oaks and outings once a fortnight. The mini-bus is used regularly and means trips can sometimes be impromptu.

**Remarks** Homely setting and happy family atmosphere. The staff are lively and energetic. Well-balanced routine including excellent care and a variety of structured activities. Good preparation for school. Older children up to 8 years from Castlethorpe School come for after-school care and mix well with the younger ages, providing a stimulating link with the next stage. Fees restrict the cultural and social mix, while the out-of-the-way location and lack of public transport limits access.

## COPPICE NURSERY SCHOOL

Field Road
Bookerhill
High Wycombe
Bucks HP12 4LR
**Tel:** (0494) 521576

**Owner:** Bucks County Council
**Headteacher:** Pat Chuter, Dip Ed
**Type:** Nursery school offering half-day sessions, and limited full-time places for children with special educational needs
**Children:** 3yrs–4yrs 11 mths. 44 places. 88 on register
**Hours:** Morning session 9am–11.30am
Afternoon session 12.45pm–3.15pm
Open 36 weeks a year
**Status:** State nursery school
**Number of years open:** 29
**Meals:** Fruit and drinks
**1992 fees:** No fees. Voluntary contribution of £6 per term for materials
**Waiting list:** 80 already entered for next year. List is not closed as nursery always tries to take cases recommended by Social Services
**Registered by:** Bucks County Council LEA

**Premises** Purpose-built 1960s bungalow in the grounds of Bookerhill County Combined School. Two large L-shaped classrooms, a small staffroom/interview room, kitchen and cloakrooms. Recently redecorated throughout and extremely well equipped with educational games and toys – all available at child height. Several healthy-looking hamsters and guinea pigs live in odd corners. Wall space is limited, due to huge windows and bright curtains, but every available inch displays child-led art and craft, reflecting the current weekly topic. A third, much smaller, room acts as a home corner. When we visited, children were investigating a weather topic. Several girls were busy pulling hot and cold weather clothes out of two large suitcases and eagerly dressing up. There is a little library corner beside the head's office. Not many books on view, and children were busy turning it into a den. The large grassed outside playground includes an undercover paved area for wet weather play and a large sandpit, but little fixed outdoor equipment; most has been destroyed by vandals. Fencing seemed rather low for complete security.

**Headteacher & staff** Pat Chuter, Dip Ed, is a calm, quiet, mature teacher, unruffled by the boisterous activities going on around her. She was a secondary school PE teacher but retrained 18 years ago and worked in three state nurseries before coming to the Coppice. Her staff comprises two qualified teachers and four NNEBs, all mature women with many years' childcare experience. One has been at the nursery for 21 years, another for 17. A happy, well-established team. A welfare assistant is present for six hours a week to help with the children with special educational needs. Male NNEBs have been employed in the past, but proved unsuitable. NNEB, B Ed and YTS students are regularly on placement at the nursery. The staff/child ratio is officially 1:10, but in practice is often 1:5, an excellent ratio for sessional care in the state sector. Staff training is provided by the local education authority. The nursery operates a keyworker system, with each full-time member of staff responsible for a group of ten children. Veldees Brook, B Ed, teaches part time at the school and spends the remainder of her time on home liaison work, visiting special needs children in their own homes.

**Children & parents** A wide cross-section of children from High Wycombe, ranging from professional middle-class families to high-priority Social Services referrals. There are four places at each session reserved for children with special educational needs – cerebral palsy, autism, language and learning problems. The special needs children are completely integrated and difficult to identify. The nursery is noticeably multicultural, with a wide variety of races and religions represented. Education is seen as a joint venture with parents and the community. Warm and friendly relationships between parents and staff are encouraged through parents' representation on the Management Committee, home visits, parents' evenings and open days. Parents help with outings and fund raising. Children all transfer to local primary schools with close links to the nursery. Siblings of children already at the nursery can attend a Wednesday morning play session with mum to help familiarise themselves with nursery life, or come for a trial session with a parent.

**Curriculum & activities** The curriculum is implemented through play. It aims to encourage independence, curiosity, language and mathematical abilities and develop physical skills and co-ordination. The nursery operates a flexible version of the High Scope method. Each activity is broken down into planning time, activity/work time, recall/discussion time and tidy-up time. Children are free to choose whatever activity is available, including outside play, from an enormous selection of stimulating, child-orientated equipment and toys (annual equipment budget £6500). Art, craft, dressing up, home corner and music are also available. The children are lively and uninhibited, clearly enjoying their freedom, but in no way out of control. They work in groups of ten, under the guidance of two members of staff – two groups in each classroom. We observed one group working on the floor with a teacher, cutting out, colouring and sticking to make Christmas cards – each to his/her own ability and satisfaction; no one was using items pre-prepared by adults. Two other children nearby were totally absorbed in an educational computer game – the nursery has two computers. Programmes are planned half-termly in advance and broken into themes for each main room. Groups swap bases each half-term so that children can experience a different activity area. Pre-school preparation work takes place at the beginning and end of each session. Letter recognition, pencil control, colours, mathematical concepts, environmental studies and science are all part of the timetable and organised with the National Curriculum Level 1 in view. The staff room doubles as the 'Waldon Room' and is used for one-to-one sessions for children with special educational needs. Geoffrey Waldon was a British psychologist who devised a method of therapy for autistic children. His therapy has been extended to help children with cerebral palsy and physiological disorders. Using simple activity and construction toys recommended by Waldon, a teacher/carer sits behind a child, models the activity and then encourages the child to copy, helping and guiding if necessary, by use of hands only. There is no verbal communication. The Waldon method is most effective with children who have speech or communication problems as they cannot be discouraged by 'failing to understand an instruction'. Visits to the nearby woods take place once a term, and there are smaller group visits to local places related to a particular theme or topic – eg shops, post office, nearby Booker airport.

**Remarks** Lively, busy and crowded multi-cultural nursery, offering ideal preparation for the large classes of a typical primary school. Dedicated, experienced and long-serving staff team. A model of how children with special educational needs can be successfully integrated into normal nursery life. The lack of places unfortunately means that children can only be offered two terms of half-day sessions prior to starting at primary school. The nursery provides an excellent information booklet for prospective parents.

## EASTVIEW MONTESSORI NURSERY SCHOOL

Newport Road
Wavendon
Milton Keynes MK17 8AE
**Tel:** (0908) 583956

**Owners:** Maggie & Gunter Weber
Liz & Derick Wheelhouse
**Principals:** Maggie Weber, NNEB, Mont Dip
Liz Wheelhouse, Mont Dip
**Type:** Montessori nursery school offering full- and part-time places and half-day sessions
**Children:** 6wks–5yrs. 45 places. 42 on register
**Hours:** 8.15am–6pm
Morning session 9am–12pm
Afternoon session 1pm–4pm
Open 48 weeks a year
**Status:** Private, fee-paying
**Number of years open:** 6
**Meals:** Lunch, tea and snacks
**1992 fees:** £90 per week full-time – babies
£85 per week full-time – older children
£2.90 per hour for less than 15 hours per week
£2.70 per hour for more than 15 hours per week
£2 per hour afternoon places only
£20 registration fee
**Waiting list:** Minimal
**Registered by:** Bucks County Council SS

**Premises** Long, low, 1960s brick-built bungalow, formerly the home of one of the owners. The double garage has been recently converted to provide an additional room for ten babies. Situated midway between the villages of Woburn Sands and Wolverton on a main road into Milton Keynes, not far from the M1.

Babies and under-2s have their own nursery unit – the Lawns – with separate play and rest rooms and nappy-changing facilities. Nursery children have four large bright rooms, most overlooking the garden. The outside play area is well fenced, with a space set aside solely for babies and toddlers, a summerhouse equipped as a playhouse, outside climbing frames and swings and, beyond the grass, a pets' corner. Animals include ducks, goats, chickens, rabbits, guinea pigs and hamsters.

**Owners/Principals & staff** Maggie Weber, NNEB, Mont Dip, and Liz Wheelhouse, Mont Dip, met when they were both registered childminders and nursery nurses, living in the same village. Having opened the nursery six years ago, they became devoted to the Montessori method when they started a home-study Montessori course. In 1990, they converted Eastview to a Montessori-based nursery school. Maggie and Liz are mature, quiet, dedicated women, who have worked hard to build up the nursery. The third key member of the team is Maggie's husband, Gunter Weber, a big, serious man who is the nursery cook, maintenance man and, with the help of the children, also looks after the animals. Caring and teaching staff are all qualified NNEB, Mont Dip, or have an infant teaching qualification. The staff ratio is 1:3 for babies and 1:8 for older children in the nursery classes. Visiting specialist teachers come in weekly to teach music and movement and French. Maggie Weber is a qualified swimming instructor and takes children daily to swim in the pool at her own home, during the summer term. Parents pay extra for all specialist classes.

**Children & parents** Mainly white-collar workers and academics who work in Milton Keynes, including staff from the Cranfield College of Technology. Children move on to a mix of state and private schools. Children with disabilities are well integrated. Parents tend to be too busy working to take an active role in nursery life, but attend the termly parents' evenings and take advantage of the nursery's open door policy when they are experiencing problems. Children are confident and busy, with older children helping the younger ones. Parents have welcomed the change to a Montessori-based teaching programme, claiming that their children have become more independent and more caring over the past three years.

**Curriculum & activities** Classrooms contain a large collection of bright, new Montessori equipment which children choose and collect to work at on low tables. They use a variety of workbooks for practising number work and other pre-school skills. In addition to traditional Montessori letter recognition apparatus, all children use the phonic Letterland scheme. Ladybird books and readers from other schemes are readily available. The day is divided into 30-minute sessions, the children into family groups of eight to ten children. Every half an hour they move on to another area of free choice or a different group activity. In the craft room, children mix their own paints and produce work inspired by the current topic or project theme. Topics are planned six to eight weeks in advance and are often linked to outings or visitors to the nursery. Recent work has been built around visits from a dentist and a mounted policeman and a local train journey. Staff keep a low profile, allowing children to help each other, only intervening to demonstrate apparatus or offer guidance when really necessary. The nursery operates a keyworker system. Weekly progress reports are completed and available for parents to inspect and discuss. Detailed reports can be taken on to the primary or prep school. New parents are initiated into the Montessori philosophy and allowed to stay to phase in their children. Children and babies come together for group activities, including watching television programmes at certain times each day. Older children visit the baby unit regularly. There is also daily music, weekly French lessons and dancing and daily swimming in the summer. Maggie Weber and her husband are qualified swimming teachers and bronze medal lifesavers.

**Remarks** Caring, relaxed atmosphere, with mature, experienced staff, well qualified to care and educate. Not a 'smart' nursery and rather isolated from any local community, but children are happy and receive a solid pre-school education. The mini pets' corner is well organised for the benefit of the children. This is one of the few nurseries where there is a strong male role model at the centre of things. The nursery maintains links with Satsuki Kindergarten in Kyoto, Japan. Children regularly exchange artwork, educational materials and ideas with each other.

# LITTLE OAKS NURSERY SCHOOL

Sands Village Hall
Lane End Road
Sands
High Wycombe
Bucks HP12 4DA
**Tel:** (0494) 534377

**Owner/Headteacher:** Anna-Marie Sives, Mont Dip, PPA
**Type:** Montessori nursery school offering half-day sessions
**Children:** 2½–5yrs. 24 places. 48 on register
**Hours:** Morning session 9.30am–12 noon
Afternoon session (Mon & Tues only) 12.30pm–3pm
Open 37 weeks a year
**Status:** Private, fee-paying
**Number of years open:** 3
**Meals:** Mid-morning snacks, packed lunches
**1992 fees:** £5 per session
£4 for Wed afternoon gym session
£3 for morning riding
£10 registration fee
**Waiting list:** 60+. Most will be allocated places
**Registered by:** Bucks County Council SS

**Premises** Very large, fairly new, brick village hall, on the outskirts of High Wycombe. The nursery also has the use of cloakrooms, a kitchen and a smaller meeting room. The decorations are good but the rooms lack all the usual exciting children's artwork and craft displays, as staff are not allowed to hang anything on the walls. A temporary display board is brought out at each session. Wooden floors throughout, with plastic sheet put down for the art area. The nearest park and children's playground is 200 yards away, but visited in the summer only. Light and spacious, but definitely the atmosphere of a village hall rather than a nursery. Owner hopes to move to alternative premises of her own as soon as finances allow.

**Owner/Headteacher & staff** The owner and headteacher, Anna-Marie Sives, Mont Dip, PPA, is warm, dependable and committed. A former governess, she has previously worked in playgroups and reception classes. The nursery developed and expanded from a local scheme she pioneered to prepare playgroup children for main school. When we visited, her deputy, Cathy Pearcy, B Ed, was acting head, as Anna-Marie was recovering from a serious illness. There is a third qualified teacher, who is also responsible for setting the syllabus in reception classes throughout Oxfordshire, and two assistants PPA qualified. Visiting specialists include a weekly gym teacher (they considered a male applicant, but appointed a female) and a riding instructress. A group of PPA trainees are called on as supply teachers to cover for sickness and holidays, backed up by a team of parents, if necessary. Students on work experience and older women returning to work also use the nursery from time to time as a training ground. The caretaker of the building, a children's author, takes an active interest. Staff keep in the background, but offer support and guidance when it is needed. They have strong bonds with the children and each other. The staff/child ratio of 1:5 is very good for sessional teaching.

**Children & parents**ABwide social and cultural mix, from families on income support to others employing nannies. Many working mothers, mainly English, with a small Asian group. Most come from within a ten-mile radius. Children with special needs are welcome and are well integrated. Children transfer to the state and private sector. Parents are supportive and involved. The school has an open door policy, with a regular newsletter and an open evening each term. Children phasing-in spend one session with their parents and then stay on their own, provided they are ready. Parents help with outings and fund-raising and attend a summer sports day and Christmas nativity play. Children all wear uniform – dark blue sweatshirts, trousers or skirts with the school badge sewn on left breast, white socks.

**Curriculum & activities** The balance is about 75 per cent relaxed Montessori, 25 per cent reception class teaching and preparation for primary school. The day begins with a formal welcome and registration. Children help to set up the classroom, filling shelves with toys and equipment from the store. Small furniture, shelving, bookstands and a playhouse turn the hall into a series of self-contained activity areas. Toys are put on tables and are available on shelves at child height for children to choose and put back. There is a good range of Montessori apparatus, as well as free painting, sand and a dressing-up corner. Older children spend time every day working through worksheets, letter recognition, pencil control and other pre-school skills. The timetable is structured, but the emphasis is on good self-discipline. Children who failed to thrive in less structured playgroups settle well here. Staff allow children to organise their own activities, serve their own drinks and clear up. We observed plenty of cuddles and talk between children and staff. The general atmosphere is studious and quiet, relieved by a boisterous gym class on Wednesday afternoons. Children can also opt for a riding lesson in place of the Thursday morning session. A separate mother and toddler group has also been started in a side room, supervised by Anna-Marie Sives. There are special outings once a term, and visits to the local shops two or three times a week. Weekly music, dance and movement. Swimming twice a term.

**Remarks** Excellent nursery school in an area blessed with many playgroups but few nurseries, though the premises are not ideal. The mix of Montessori and reception class teaching offers a good balance. Staff are enthusiastic and well qualified; children happy and diligent. Many will have covered much of the work of a reception class when they transfer to full-time school.

# MEADOW VIEW NURSERY

Westbury Lane
Newport Pagnell
Bucks MK16 8PS
**Tel:** (0908) 216604

**Owner:** Childbase Ltd
**Manager:** Mandy Brown, NNEB
**Type:** Day nursery offering full- and part-time places and half-day sessions
**Children:** 6wks–5yrs. 46 places. 90 on register
**Hours:** 8am–6pm
Morning session 8am–1pm
Afternoon session 1.15pm–6pm
Open 52 weeks (excl bank holidays)
**Status:** Private, fee-paying
**Number of years open:** 4 in old premises.
New building opened Sept '92
**Meals:** Lunch, tea and snacks
**1992 fees:** £102.50 per week full-time – under 2
£92.50 per week – 2–5yrs
£11.50 per session – 1–2yrs
£10.50 per session – over 2

Sibling discounts
**Waiting list:** None
**Registered by:** Bucks County Council SS
**Under same ownership/management:** Woodlands Day Nursery, Milton Keynes, Bucks; Cedars Day Nursery, Leighton Buzzard, Beds; Lavenders Day Nursery, Bedford (see entry); Lime Grove Day Nursery, Hemel Hempstead, Herts; Guy's Hospital Day Nursery, London, SE1; Sandfield Day Nursery, John Radcliffe Hospital, Oxford

**Premises** The premises are immaculate: brand-new and purpose-built in 1992. The long, low, handsome building is owned by Childbase Ltd, an impressive operation providing private nursery care for over 500 children at several sites. The company has recently opened workplace nurseries at Guy's Hospital, London, and the John Radcliffe Infirmary, Oxford. Meadow View is their longest established nursery, but had been in its new premises for only four weeks at the time of our visit. Inside there are separate large rooms for each age group (babies 3 months–1 year, tweenies 1–2 years, toddlers 2–3 years and pre-school children 3–5 years), plus sleep rooms for babies and tweenies, a changing area and two cloakrooms, kitchen, staff room, utility room and office. There are several storerooms, including one in the hall where parents can leave buggies and car seats. Everything is beautifully designed. Excellent decorations – cream paint, varnished wood, friendly low 'saloon doors' between classrooms, colourful friezes, mobiles and displays of children's work. French windows open on to the garden from each room. Outside there is a narrow, landscaped garden running the length of the building, with a good paved patio and lawn, securely fenced and well equipped with swings, climbing frames, bikes and trikes. Safety flooring is due to be laid under the swings. Less than two hundred yards away there is a park and children's playground. Safe parking and easy access for parents.

**Principal & staff** Manager, Mandy Brown, is a vivacious, young NNEB, who has worked for private nurseries in Britain and the United States. Despite appearing too young to be in charge, she is very articulate and inspires confidence. Each room is run by a qualified NNEB, who acts as keyworker to the children in her room and is aided by an assistant. Teams change every two weeks and clear notices inform parents of the name of their child's current keyworker. Continuity of care does not seem to be a priority. The schedules are planned at monthly staff meetings. Staff, who are all young, are offered regular Saturday training sessions by the company as well as managerial training to provide a proper career structure. Children relate well to staff and call them by their Christian names. A qualified teacher visits for an hour each morning and afternoon to do more formal pre-school work with the oldest group. NNEB students from local colleges are welcome on placement, always as additional helpers. The best are sometimes offered a permanent job with the company when they graduate. A full-time cook prepares fresh meals and all special or religious diets are catered for. Staff ratios are 1:3 for babies, 1:6 for 2- to 3-year-olds and 1:8 for 3- to 5-year-olds, but 1:5 is preferred whenever possible.

**Children & parents** Mainly middle and upper-middle class and all white at present. Approximately half the children have both parents in full-time employment. Many live within a ten-mile radius, while others work locally and commute in. Children move on in equal numbers to state and private schools. Those we met were busy, articulate and polite to visitors. A large noticeboard in the entrance hall keeps parents informed about current activities, groups, keyworkers and menus. Parents are encouraged to be involved in everything – open days, plays and concerts, parents' evenings, activities and outings. They are always welcome at the nursery and their views and complaints listened to. Phasing-in of new children is done gradually, and parents stay with their children for about two hours for the first two or three visits.

**Curriculum & activities** Learning through play, with short periods of more formal teaching for pre-school children (3 years plus) by a qualified teacher. Each session (nearly five hours) follows a carefully structured timetable allowing for free play indoors and out, singing, supervised creative activities, storytime, 20 minutes' television viewing, a hot meal or snack break and one hour's teaching for the oldest group. Babies from 6 weeks old are cared for in a pleasant, spotlessly clean nursery each with his/her own cot, linen and equipment. Comfortable cane sofas give the room a homely feel. Breast-feeding mothers can visit at any time or leave expressed milk. Weaning and toilet training are undertaken in consultation with parents. The nursery offers only full-time care for babies. All the equipment throughout the nursery is first class – a credit to Mothercare, who supply most of it. Art, craft, dance and music and movement are regular features, but there is no permanent Wendy house or sand and water play. The nursery has a multicultural policy and, despite the lack of ethnic minority representation among staff and children, celebrates different cultural and religious festivals. Quality care is the priority. Teacher Bev Atkinson, Cert Ed, who was a secondary school French teacher, prepares worksheets for children to practise colours and letter and number work. She also spends two hours a week teaching French. There are 15 children in the group, but she tries to give as much individual attention as possible. There are no reading or maths schemes. Children's progress is monitored monthly. The whole nursery walks to the local park twice a term. There is an annual outing by coach to a farm or zoo and a library van visits occasionally. The previous premises had its own swimming pool and Mandy plans to reinstate swimming in the summer.

**Remarks** First-class facilities, provided by a very professional organisation. Ideal for the career mother looking for high-quality childcare, with some educational input. The regime is rather strictly timetabled, and there are quite large numbers of children in each group. Fees are higher than average for the area, but the facilities are superior and Childbase has an ambitious expansion and investment programme to fund. Some places are subsidised by Midland Bank for their employees. Mercedes-Benz has cancelled their company places as they were not taken up.

# NURSERYTYME

The Pavilion
Watermead
Aylesbury
Bucks HP19 3FX
**Tel:** (0296) 397407

**Owner:** Everglade Ltd
**Administrative Director:** Eileen Setchell
**Type:** Day nursery offering full- and part-time places and half-day sessions
**Children:** 3mths–5yrs. 68 places. 120 on register
**Hours:** 7.30am–7pm
Morning session 8am–1pm

Afternoon session 1pm–6pm
Open 51 weeks a year
**Status:** Private, fee-paying
**Number of years open:** 2½
**Meals:** Lunch, tea, snacks
**1992 fees:** £90.00 per week full-time
£21 per day
£11 per session
£2.95 per hour
**Waiting list:** None
**Registered by:** Bucks County Council SS

**Premises** An attractive new building originally designed as a cricket pavilion, on the edge of the Watermead residential and leisure complex – a desert which is still undergoing development. The private, enclosed gardens offer ideal hard and soft, wet and dry play areas, with good, new outdoor equipment, surrounded by open land and next to – but securely fenced-off from – a lake. The ducks come up for titbits through the fence at snacktime. Inside is a warren of small and medium-sized rooms, where children play in groups according to their age and interests. The largest room offers the oldest children, Toppers, a pleasant, sunny area with a kitchen/utility area adjacent for wet or messy activities. Other cosy, rather cramped rooms accommodate younger age groups, the Tweenies and Tiddlers, while upstairs, two fully-equipped nurseries provide cots, bouncers and playpens for the Babies and Toddlers. There are washrooms and loos on each floor, built to scale and including baby bath and shower. A dining room, used for art between meals, and the main kitchen are also upstairs. The whole building is well heated, carpeted, and magnificently equipped and decorated with mobiles and friezes and beautiful displays of the children's work. The only drawback is the lack of any large area indoors for group activities, although plans to build two large conservatories may resolve this.

**Administrative Director & staff** Nurserytyme is run as a business. The full-time administrative director, Eileen Setchell, is in overall charge and reports to the owners, Everglade Ltd. Down to earth and direct, she brings experienced business skills to the nursery, making the tightly-scheduled day run smoothly, while maintaining high standards of care. Although she is not involved in the day-to-day care and well-being of children, she knows them and their families well and offers a great deal of support to both parents and staff. Virtually all 18 staff have, or are training for, NNEB, PPA or BTEC qualifications. Carers work in pairs with groups of six or more children. Each two-person team is responsible for planning their own group activities. Students on NNEB courses and sixth-formers on work experience were much in evidence when we visited and appeared to be indistinguishable from members of staff. All wear uniforms – red sweatshirt and black trousers. Staff work shifts and rotate weekly between groups so that both children and staff get to know each other well and students gain experience with all age groups. Eileen admits staff turnover can be a problem, as can moving staff around to cover for sickness and holidays. At the time of writing, the nursery is without a full-time supervisor. Teamwork is run on democratic lines with everyone getting their fair share of 'dirty work'. All staff change nappies, feed, clean up. A note at the bottom of the Toddlers' timetable reads, 'NB cuddles are available throughout the day subject to lap space!'

**Children & parents** Children come from a wide catchment area, some parents travelling significant distances because the nursery is near their workplace rather than their home. The long, flexible opening hours are an attraction to parents who commute or work shifts. They are mainly white-collar workers, including several RAF families. The majority are English-speaking – some Asian, Italian, one Romanian child. The parents of one baby are both deaf, so staff are learning British Sign Language to help communication when the baby develops language skills. Children are happy, talkative, and fairly quiet. Good behaviour is encouraged. Open door policy towards parents with staff aiming to talk to them every day. Regular parents' evenings for more formal feedback.

**Curriculum & activities** The emphasis is on learning through play rather than acquiring skills in literacy and numeracy. All the popular PPA activities are encouraged, including plenty of painting and modelling. Enormous amount of new equipment, well designed and looking stunning. Good selection of books, well displayed at child height, supplemented by regular visits from the mobile library service. Children are grouped by developmental age and needs, with a timetable to suit their particular group.

Each child has his/her own care card which records all aspects of the child's development. No formal educational programme for the older children and no attempt to teach them to read, although twice-daily pre-school sessions include educational games, flashcards, number work, pencil control and telling the time. Art, craft, painting, play dough, water play, cookery and gardening are regular activities. Individual work and major group projects are encouraged. Each group plans themes a week in advance. There is no large indoor area for movement, dance, drama or gym, however, making it difficult for groups to come together indoors for mixed age/ability activities. Outdoor play twice a day, weather permitting – babies included, carefully screened by large sun umbrellas in the summer. No special outings. High standards of hygiene and safety are observed throughout. Meals are freshly cooked in a well-equipped kitchen by a full-time cook. Staff do not eat with children. Weaning and any special diets are catered for and recorded.

**Remarks** A commercial enterprise providing high-quality care for a large number of children in glamorous, if rather isolated, surroundings. Ideal for working parents requiring flexitime arrangement. Reasonably priced, no premium for babies and no waiting list. Visually stunning, with huge amount of equipment, but not for parents seeking more formal, strong, educational programmes to stimulate the spirit and mind.

## SIMPSON UNDER-5s RESOURCE CENTRE

211 Simpson Road,
Simpson
Milton Keynes
MK6 3AD
**Tel:** (0908) 670673

**Owner:** Bucks County Council SS
**Officer-in-charge:** Margaret Godfrey, NNEB
**Type:** Assessment centre and nursery offering full- and part-time places to children with special educational needs
**Children:** 3–5yrs. 20 places. 29 on register
**Hours:** 9am–4pm
Open 52 weeks a year

**Status:** Social Services nursery
**Number of years open:** 18 (It has been a resource centre for special needs children since 1987)
**Meals:** Lunch, snacks, vitamin drops
**1992 fees:** 30p per day
**Waiting list:** 14
**Registered by:** Bucks County Council SS

**Premises** 1960s brick bungalow converted for use as a nursery. Two classrooms, staff room, messy-play/storage room, toilets, office and kitchen. Flooring is mainly vinyl, with mats for children to sit on. A good-sized securely fenced garden, with trees and shrubs, runs around the building, and there is a variety of sturdy outdoor play equipment, with safety surface. A covered patio houses bikes and trikes. Children are brought in daily by bus, from a wide catchment area around Milton Keynes.

**Officer-in-charge and staff** Margaret Godfrey, NNEB, has been at Simpson for 17 years and has risen to the challenge of changing it from a nursery catering for the children of working parents to one dedicated to selected children with special educational needs. She has a staff of three full-time NNEB nursery nurses and a part-timer. They are mature, experienced women, well qualified for the very special work they do. Other staff include a voluntary helper for a visually impaired child and two cleaners. There are regular visits to individual children by speech therapists, educational psychologists and language teachers. Staff appear totally dedicated and conscientious. The staff/child ratio is 1:4. Carers cover for sickness and holidays as best they can – standby relief staff from Social Services rarely materialise. They work as a very close team. Weekly staff meetings plan the programmes and discuss individual children's development. There are a great many case conferences involving social workers and other professionals. The specialist work done at this nursery is recognised by increased pay scales. Generous training opportunities are also offered to staff.

**Children & parents** Mainly working-class families on income support, with some cultural mix. Some children come from foster homes. Children are referred by Social Services because they have serious emotional, behavioural or communication problems. Close relations with parents are often difficult, as children are bused in from a wide area. However, there are open days, and staff make home visits and keep in touch with parents by telephone. Each child has a small report book, which goes home weekly, explaining what activities they have done, highlighting their achievements and detailing behaviour. Parents are encouraged to comment and become involved – not all are co-operative. Phasing-in new children begins with a home visit, where staff explain the nursery philosophy and timetable. Once children start, parents can stay with them until they have settled in. The nursery aims to bring children to the stage where they can integrate successfully into their local primary school, at rising-5. For many, this is achieved. The nursery is the only assessment centre in Milton Keynes for children with special educational needs. When we visited, there were 14 children urgently waiting for places.

**Curriculum & activities** The centre aims to provide a range of services to meet the special needs of selected under-5s and their families and to offer information and support to voluntary organisations, professional workers and families. The emphasis is on care, and learning through play, but pre-school skills are introduced whenever possible, including letter recognition, pencil control and early maths. The daily timetable follows the same pattern as any nursery school – free play, group activities, imaginative and creative play, structured learning, music, singing and outdoor activities, including gardening. Staff and children find that a regular but stimulating routine promotes good behaviour. The programme is always flexible and adapts to individual children's needs. Children work in small groups, supervised by their keyworker. There are two full-time staff and a student in the large room and one nursery nurse with an assistant in the small room for older pre-school children. There is plenty of good, solid nursery equipment. The annual equipment budget is £2000. Constant hugs, cuddles and kisses from staff provide much-needed security and affection. Holding techniques are used to restrain, when necessary. Art and craft are a permanent feature and excellent therapy. Social-skills training is important, to help children develop the confidence and independence to enter mainstream primary school. There are monthly visits to the library bus, occasional small group outings by car and an annual outing by coach with parents.

**Remarks** A small, homely specialist unit for children with special educational needs – the only one of its kind in Milton Keynes – with exceptionally dedicated and qualified mature staff. This nursery offers children with special needs the opportunity to enjoy exactly the same pre-school nursery experiences as their peers, as well as any individual treatment or help they need. Without their time at Simpson, few would be able to transfer successfully to primary school. With the move to self-management, the future of the unit is uncertain. It is unlikely to be able to survive financially in its present form. Consideration is currently being given to a plan to offer five or more fee-paying places to the private sector. It is difficult to tell how the financial problems facing all Social Services departments will be solved in this case.

# WELLIES DAY NURSERY

1 Brook End
North Crawley
Newport Pagnell
Bucks MK16 9HH
**Tel:** (0234) 391600

**Owner/Principal:** Helen Hobbs, NNEB, RSH (Norland)
**Type:** Day nursery offering full- and part-time places and half-day sessions
**Children:** 0–5yrs. 45 places. 62 on register
**Hours:** 7.45am–6.15pm
Morning session 7.45am–1pm
Afternoon session 1pm–6.15pm
Open 48 weeks a year
**Status:** Private, fee-paying
**Number of years open:** 4
**Meals:** Lunch, high tea, snacks
**1992 fees:** £378 per month full-time
£20 per day
£12.50 per session
£30 registration fee
16% sibling discount
**Waiting list:** None kept. Babies are registered before birth
**Registered by:** Bucks County Council SS

**Premises** Wellies Day Nursery is difficult to find the first time – hidden away down a quiet country lane, near Newport Pagnell. The smartly converted farm cottages are an unlikely location for a large group of under-5s. The owner and her farmer husband live in a flat above. Inside, the building has been completely modernised to provide five spacious rooms with one age group in each room. There is a kitchen, utility room, office and cloakrooms. Decorations are plain, mainly white and grey, rather dull and slightly gloomy – only the pretty baby room seemed bright and cheery. There are friezes around the ceiling, a few pictures, some pinboards for children's work, basic shelves for storing toy boxes, but out of reach of children. Book racks are also well above child height; the windows are rather high. Not a homely environment. The large fenced play area outside at the back is surrounded by fields. There is a paved area for bikes, and a large lawn with outdoor play equipment. Absolutely no public transport. Gravel car park at the front for 15 cars.

**Owner/Principal & staff** Helen Hobbs, NNEB, RSH, owner and principal, was a Norland nanny to the children of the rich and famous (including TV personalities David Frost and Marsha Fitzalan's children), before she married a farmer and opened Wellies. She is young, attractive and obviously an astute, efficient business woman. Her own small child is at the nursery. Helen acts as administrator and floating replacement, covering for holidays and sickness. There are 12 full-time staff and two part-time, all white, middle class and female. They look very young, but in fact the age range is 19 to over 35. A lone male nursery nurse has recently left to set up his own nursery in Wales. More than half the staff have a formal childcare qualification. The five unqualified workers are experienced with young children. Some staff are long established, but in the baby nursery there has been a large turnover (12 in the last two years). Helen Hobbs is optimistic that this problem has now been solved. No staff training policy or budget, but Helen hopes to become an NVQ assessor in order to provide in-service training for unqualified staff. Staff work in pairs with their preferred age group. NNEB and BTEC students often assist them but are not left unsupervised. Staff ratios are 1:3 (0–2yrs), 1:4 (2–3yrs), 1:5 (3-5yrs). The nursery nurses we observed obviously relate well to the children. They were down on the floor at their level, playing with them and cuddling the little ones – more like mums than teachers.

**Children & parents** Inevitably with fees topping £100 a week, out of taxed income, the parents are almost exclusively middle class. There is a small Asian contingent. Two places are subsidised by Social Services. Most children transfer to primary schools around the region – Milton Keynes, Newport Pagnell, Olney, Northants villages. Children tend to start as babies and move up through the school. They leave the baby nursery as soon as they are mobile and spend a year in each room. Parents are welcome to visit or telephone at any time but tend not to become actively involved, except to help with outings. Parents' evenings are for the top group only. An open day was advertised for prospective parents, but very few people were able to find the building. Parents do not stay with their children for the phasing-in period. At our visit, children appeared happy, but fairly quiet and controlled.

**Curriculum & activities** Care and learning through play are the priorities for the first three years. More formal education is introduced for the older groups. The nursery is well equipped, but there did not seem to be many toys out. Children are offered small amounts in rotation, as part of a policy of not spoiling the children with too many toys. (The annual equipment budget is £1000.) Very little equipment is within their reach. There is no permanent Wendy house or home corner – these are provided from time to time. Art and craft materials are plentiful but, again, not freely available. Preparation for school is thorough. A qualified teacher visits each morning during term-time. The oldest children have lessons in reading, writing and number work. The day is carefully structured to provide play, work, art and craft, mealtimes and rest periods, with attention given to toilet routines, including tooth brushing times. All age groups meet together for outdoor play. Younger children spend as much time as possible in summer on the large sunny lawn and patio. Music and swimming take place weekly in term-time, as well as frequent country walks and visits to the farm adjacent.

**Remarks** Rather spartan and austere, which is part of the Wellies 'no fuss, no frills' image. High-quality care from young, enthusiastic staff – 'just like mum', but lacking the warmth and homeliness of more mature carers 'just like granny'. Good educational programmes from visiting teacher. Happy, but rather quiet and restrained children. Good manners, good care and no 'spoiling' of children.

## WESTON UNDERWOOD NURSERY CLASS

Weston Underwood Village Hall
Olney Road
Weston Underwood
Bucks
**Tel:** (0234) 711534 (school office)
**Owners:** Susan Marriott, B Ed
Jenni Birdseye
**Headteacher:** Elaine Burbeck, Cert Ed
**Type:** Nursery class offering half-day sessions. No full-time places
**Children:** 3–5yrs. 18 places. 50 on register
**Hours:** Morning session 9.30–12 noon
Afternoon session 1pm–3pm
Open 36 weeks a year
**Status:** Private, fee-paying
**Number of years open:** 5
**Meals:** None
**1992 fees:** £7.50 per morning session
£6.50 per afternoon session
£15 registration fee
**Waiting list:** Long. Early registration advisable
**Registered by:** Bucks County Council SS
**Under same ownership:** Filgrave School

**Premises** Old Victorian, stone village school, used primarily by the nursery but occasionally as a village hall. In the heart of the picturesque, tiny village of Weston Underwood, a few miles from Olney. The nursery comprises one very large, bright school room, with high ceilings and windows and fluorescent strip lighting, surprisingly warm and homely for its size. Children's artwork is on display throughout and much appreciated by the villagers who use the hall. The large schoolroom is rather sparse, lacking in nursery furniture. There is a kitchen, used for cookery classes and messy play, a furniture store and cloakrooms. The outside play area, a gravel playground, is rarely used. Likewise the nearest park, 200 yards away. Virtually no public transport reaches the village – parents can park on a gravel forecourt.

**Owners, Headteacher & staff** Susan Marriott, B Ed, and Elaine Burbeck, Cert Ed, were mums with young children when they set up the nursery class in 1988. Susan, glamorous and business-like, is a trained primary school teacher and Elaine, more motherly, a nursery teacher. It all began because they failed to find suitable nursery provision for their own children. They simply hired the hall, put a few advertisements around the area and opened their doors. Events snowballed. The nursery proved so popular and demand was so great that they now own Filgrave School, a private pre-prep school, which has a nursery class of its own attached. Susan Marriott visits the nursery daily, as proprietor and administrator, but the day-to-day running is delegated to Elaine. She is supported by a team of seven part-timers, a mixture of mature qualified teachers and experienced mothers, some of whom have worked in state schools. Staff are not as well paid as their counterparts in the state system, but are no less dedicated. The children treat them with respect, as teachers rather than companions. The child/staff ratio at 1:4½ is excellent for sessional care.

**Children & parents** Mainly middle class, but not exclusively. Predominantly English, but also a small group of part-Arab children. Parents travel from up to 15 miles away for a 2½-hour session. Some children transfer to Filgrave School, but many go on to local village schools, avoiding the large class sizes of primary schools in Newport Pagnell and Milton Keynes.

**Curriculum & activities** Learning is through carefully structured and planned play activities, supplemented by tuition in the basic skills that need to be acquired prior to school entry. A selection of activities is provided on a rotation basis – playing with jigsaws and construction toys, sand and water play, painting/craftwork, cookery. Hand-eye co-ordination is aided through threading, sorting, ordering and matching games. Tracing and writing patterns encourage pencil control. An awareness of letters, colours and number concepts is developed through supervised play and games such as Lotto, Snap and early dice games. Elementary reading skills are introduced when a child is ready. There is plenty of space for children to move freely between the rugs and tables, where all the activities are laid out – including a small bookstand, a cushioned cosy-corner, the worktable, where every child does at least one page of a home-made, individually tailored workbook, daily; and the headteacher's desk, where every child practises letter recognition or reading each day. This is principally a nursery where children come to learn. They learn to communicate, to do constructive art and craftwork and to socialise with other children. They cope well with the adult-sized furniture and toilets. The atmosphere is quiet, calm and friendly. The high ratio of staff to children allows each child much individual attention. Staff encourage good manners and respect. The emphasis is on preparation for school and a good command of language. A qualified music teacher visits three times a week, and there is music and movement once a week. An outing takes place only once a year.

**Remarks** This nursery class is an excellent preparation for school, offering carefully structured play, supplemented by more formal teaching, from qualified, experienced teachers. The rather sparse furnishings and lack of proper outdoor playground are compensated for by the extremely good staff/pupil ratio of 1:4½. In an area where Social Services only support playgroups, this class is a good alternative for parents anxious to give their children a more academic start.

# Cambridgeshire

There are nursery class places for only 12 per cent of 3- and 4-year-olds. Provision is unevenly spread throughout the county. A number of independent prep schools also have nursery classes. Hundreds of playgroups offer part-time, part-week sessions, but demand still exceeds supply. There is no shortage of private daycare, and some new nurseries have been forced to close because of lack of customers. Fees are too high for the majority of parents. Two thousand plus childminders are the most popular carers. The main issues facing parents in this county are the lack of affordable places (unemployment runs at 7.6 per cent) and local availability for families in rural areas. Most private nurseries only accept children over 2 years old. Nurseries that accept babies from 6 weeks old are always full and have waiting lists of up to one year.

**Further information**

For details on day nurseries, childminders and playgroups:
Department of Social Services
Services to Young Children and Families
Walden House
Market Hill
Huntingdon PE18 6NR
Tel: (0480) 425573

For details on nursery schools, units and classes:
Education Information Service
Castle Court
Shire Hall
Castle Hill
Cambridge CB3 0AP
Tel: (0223) 317391

## HARVEY ROAD DAY NURSERY

10 Harvey Road
Cambridge
CB1 2ET
**Tel:** (0223) 63860

**Owner:** Harvey Road Housing Association Ltd
**Manager:** Elizabeth Key, NNEB
**Type:** Day nursery offering full- and part-time places and half-day sessions
**Children:** 2mths–5yrs. 45 places. 50 on register
**Hours:** 8.15am–5.30pm
Morning session 8.15am–12 noon
Afternoon session 1.30pm–5.30pm
Open 51 weeks a year
**Status:** Fee-paying, registered charity
**Number of years open:** 26
**Meals:** Lunch, tea, snacks
**1992 fees:** £89 per week full-time – under 2
£79 per week full-time – 2–3yrs
£69 per week full-time – over 3
£59 per week for 5 morning sessions – under 2
£52 per week for 5 morning sessions – 2–3yrs
£46 per week for 5 morning sessions – over 3
£50 per week for 5 afternoon sessions – under 2
£44 per week for 5 afternoon sessions – 2–3yrs
£39 per week for 5 afternoon sessions – over 3
**Waiting list:** Variable – constant turnover
**Registered by:** Cambs County Council SS

**Premises** Two large, refurbished, Victorian terraced houses in the centre of Cambridge. Semi-detached, it divides naturally into two separate units – a baby section and a toddler and pre-school area for over-2s. Each has its own brightly coloured entrance, cloakroom and toilets. The floors above have been converted into flats for single-parent families. Staff room, laundry and storage are in the basement. Inside is airy and warm, with recently painted, slightly clinical white walls, relieved by bright displays of children's artwork. Babies have two adjoining rooms: a sleep room with cots, frilly curtains and soft, pastel colours; and a soft playroom with squidgy floor mats, indoor climbing frame, child-size furniture and toys. Older children have one large room, the length of the house, divided into different activity areas: tables and chairs for table-top activities, a book corner, a play area with floor mats and a huge playhouse full of domestic appliances. Between the separate sections, there is an impressive kitchen with commercial-scale, stainless-steel catering equipment. There is also a large office. A small open-air courtyard connects the two buildings. The huge garden is well supplied with swings, climbing frames, sand-pit and an imaginative play structure called 'the tower'. Parking is tricky, but it is generally accepted that cars are left outside with hazard warning lights left on at drop-off and pick-up times.

**Manager & staff** Elizabeth Key, NNEB, known as 'Matron', has been nursery manager for 15 years. A warm, confident, motherly woman, her aim is to maintain high standards of care in a homely atmosphere – an extension of family life. Matron leads a team of ten full-time nursery nurses; four are NNEB qualified, others are BTEC, City & Guilds. Most have many years' childcare experience, and some have been at the nursery as long as Matron. Ancillary staff include a cook, catering assistant, domestic/handyman/gardener and cleaner. Staff all have first-aid certificates and there is a small budget for further development. Welcoming and friendly, nursery workers work as a team, demonstrating close relationships with the children. Staff meetings are weekly. Keyworker system operates. Students from many different academic disciplines use the nursery as a training establishment.

**Children & parents** The Harvey Road Housing Association opened the nursery in 1967, with the specific aim of creating homes and nursery places for one-parent families. Mothers living in the flats above the nursery were able to return to work or further education, leaving their babies and toddlers safely downstairs. Fees from children from the outside community helped to pay nursery running costs and subsidised the tenants' places. As nursery costs have escalated, the system of cross-subsidy has become less viable. A bursary scheme has now been launched by the Association, sustained by donations from all sections of the community. Social Services referrals and children with special educational needs are welcome. Parents are enthusiastically accepted, represented on management and fund-raising committees and encouraged to call in during the day to feed their children. There is a 'mutual exchange' scheme, which allows parents and carers to swap information about their child, verbally or in writing. It is not intended to be a report on the child's progress. There are monthly parents' group meetings and regular events and outings for parents to socialise. Parents can celebrate their child's birthday at the nursery. Babies are phased-in over a period of a month, with a parent by their side. The nursery provides clothing, terry nappies, a cot and a pram for each child.

**Curriculum & activities** Learning through play in a calm, stimulating environment. Practical and social skills are taught at a speed to suit each individual child. Children choose from a large number of toys and activities (annual budget £2500) in family groups of four or five, with their keyworker. Music is important and there is an additional weekly session with a visiting music teacher. Songs, dancing, stories, art and craft and games are also on the daily timetable. Free play takes place in the play house, dressing-up corner, book corner and the garden. There are plenty of table-top and floor activities – construction toys, puzzles, cars, trains and games. A weekly project is studied and the subject displayed in the cloakroom, so that parents can bring appropriate materials to school or continue the learning process at home. Small groups of children are taken on outings to the shops, Botanical Gardens or other places of interest. There is no formal teaching of reading or writing. Numbers, words and letters are introduced through play activities, if appropriate. There are no qualified early years teachers on the staff. Children move from one activity to another at their own pace, guided by their keyworker, who makes sure they cover a mix of different learning experiences in a day. The day is relaxed and homely, with care and social training the priorities. Babies follow a similar routine, when they are awake. They play with developmental toys, roll together on a large, soft mat and are encouraged to feed themselves as soon as possible. Each child has his/her own potty, but no pressure is exerted to use it until the child is ready.

**Remarks** Professionally run day nursery offering love and high-quality care. Self-discovery and confidence are gained in a tranquil, homely atmosphere. No attempt to teach or achieve academically. Qualified, mature and loyal staff. Excellent social and cultural mix, helped by a bursary scheme for single parents.

## HISTON NURSERY SCHOOL

New School Road
Histon
Cambridge
Cambs CB4 4LL
**Tel:** (0223) 232351
**Owner:** Cambs County Council
**Headteacher:** Mandy Spencer, BA, Teachers' Cert
**Type:** Nursery school offering half-day sessions
**Children:** 3½–4½yrs. 80 places. 81 on register
**Hours:** Morning session 9am–11.30am
Afternoon session 1pm–3.15pm
Open 38 weeks a year
**Status:** State nursery school
**Number of years open:** 47, 32 on present site
**Meals:** Juice. Hot lunch for 11 children max. A child may attend for 1 or 2 lunches a week
**1992 fees:** No fees. 95p per day for lunch
**Waiting list:** 200 names. Priority to special needs and families living in Histon and Impington. Early registration advisable
**Registered by:** Cambs County Council LEA

## HUNTINGDON NURSERY SCHOOL

Ambury Road
Huntingdon
Cambs PE18 7AD
**Tel:** (0480) 453382
**Owner:** Cambs LEA
**Headteacher:** Barbara Talbott, Cert Ed
**Type:** Nursery school offering half-day sessions only
**Children:** 3½–4½yrs. 120 places. 120 on register
**Hours:** Morning session 9am–11.30am (12 noon inc lunch)
Afternoon session 12.45pm–3.15pm
Open 38 weeks a year
**Status:** State nursery school
**Number of years open:** 43
**Meals:** Milk or water. Lunch for 25 children attending morning session. Free meals for families on income support
**1992 fees:** No fees
**Waiting list:** Very long until 1995. Priority to special needs and families within catchment area. Apply after child's 2nd birthday
**Registered by:** Cambs County Council LEA

# JOINT COLLEGES NURSERY (JCN)

6B Chaucer Road
Cambridge CB2 2EB
**Tel:** (0223) 315084

**Owner:** Joint Colleges Nursery (Cambridge) Ltd
**Principal:** Thelma Rumball, NNEB, DPQS
**Type:** Day nursery offering full- and part-time places and half-day sessions
**Children:** 3mth–6yrs. 50 places (18 babies). 65 on register
**Hours:** 8.30am–5pm or 5.30pm (fines for late collection)
Morning session 8.30am–1pm
Afternoon session 1.30pm–5.30pm
Open 51 weeks a year
**Status:** Fee-paying registered charity, run by management committee of parents
**Number of years open:** 11 (7 years in current premises)
**Meals:** Lunch, tea
**1992 fees:** £97 per week full-time – under 2
£72 per week full-time – over 2
£61 per week for 5 morning sessions – under 2
£46 per week for 5 morning sessions – over 2
£45 per week for 5 afternoon sessions – under 2
£34 per week for 5 afternoon sessions – over 2
£20 registration fee. Deposit of 2 weeks' fees
**Waiting list:** Very long, especially for babies
**Registered by:** Cambs County Council SS

**Premises** Fantastic! A purpose-built chalet-style building (circa 1987) with big windows and sky-lights. Set back from a very pretty tree-lined street in a leafy, up-market neighbourhood close to Cambridge's Botanic Gardens. The beautiful, secure garden consists of grassy areas, wide patios with raised flowerbeds and plenty of sheds and outhouses for bikes, trikes, prams and outdoor equipment. The building is a non-traditional mixture of glass, wood and brick, surrounded by a verandah. Well used, but immaculate, with much use of plain varnished wood in the interior. The main entrance hall is a large open-plan area with folding doors which can divide into a messy play area and a quiet area. The two light, bright baby rooms (for children 3 months–2 years) each have their own nappy-changing room with loos, large sink and hand-wash basins. All is spotless, but homely rather than clinical. Staff ratio for babies is 1:3. Older children have a separate playroom with large bay window, carpeted area and playhouse. There is also an office, staff room, utility room and impressive kitchen with large-scale, catering-style stainless steel equipment.

**Principal & staff** Thelma Rumball, NNEB, DPQS, is a highly motivated, experienced and impressive woman. Her manner is gentle and smiling, but she seems able to address a dozen issues at once. Her wealth of experience includes special needs schools, residential homes, day nurseries, the deputy-headship of a Montessori school and work for the Spastics Society. She reports directly to the nursery's 12-member management committee (all current parents), consisting of accountants, lawyers, and academics, which meets every six weeks. There are 14 other members of staff, all qualified. One has been at JCN for ten years and another for nine years. Music, drama, etc, are done by parents, some of whom are professional musicians. Day release training for staff is encouraged.

**Children & parents** All from professional or academic backgrounds (approx 50/50). The nursery does not reserve places specifically for university children, but it does have close links with several colleges. JCN is built on land leased from the University, and much of the money raised to construct it was donated, or provided as an index-linked mortgage by Cambridge colleges. Children commute from a wide catchment area. The nursery was originally set up as a result of parental pressure and parents still have a great deal of control. Generally, relations are excellent. There is an open door policy and parents make a significant contribution to the nursery. Children's progress is entered on an index card system and parents have access to this at any time. Older children have work folders showing their personal levels of achievement, which go on to their next school with them. There are parent get-togethers before the AGM and a parent support group meets regularly.

**Curriculum & activities** There is a huge amount of equipment including a piano, and computer for the older children. Art and craft and ambitious project work in abundance. Our visit coincided with a summer-time project on flowers and leaves and a pond-life project with a large mural collage naming different pond animals and a baby bath complete with tadpoles, water boatmen and pond weed. Children are encouraged to be aware of other cultures and religions. There was a Passover project on the wall and a similar project on Buddhism had been done a month or so before. No formal reading or writing as such, but parents say almost all children are reading by the time they leave. A pre-schools activity co-ordinator provides the older children with gentle preparation for school. Local caterers provide food and supplies. Cooking is done on the premises and Thelma helps with the menus. Special diets are provided. Staff and children eat together – lunch is an important time for staff to relate to children. After lunch older children sleep on small stacking beds in the baby rooms and babies sleep in a platoon of large, old, Silver Cross prams in the garden, under the trees (weather permitting) or under cover of the pram shed.

**Remarks** A wonderful nursery and a great tribute to 'parent power'. A classic example of what can be done when a group of highly motivated, well-connected parents single-mindedly set out to achieve a clear objective. High-quality childcare at a reasonable price.

# KING STREET PLAYGROUP

Wesley Methodist Church
Christ Pieces
Cambridge
Cambs CB1 1LB
**Tel:** (0223) 316565

**Owner:** Wesley Methodist Church
**Principal:** Diana Newman, NNEB
**Type:** Playgroup offering morning sessions (min 2 a week)
**Children:** 3–5yrs. 24 places. 42 on register
**Hours:** 9.30am–12 noon
Open 36 weeks a year
**Status:** Fee-paying registered charity
**Number of years open:** 21
**Meals:** Snacks
**1992 fees:** £2.60 per sesssion
**Waiting list:** Always long. Early registration advisable
**Registered by:** Cambs County Council SS

# MILLINGTON ROAD NURSERY SCHOOL

4A Millington Road
Cambridge CB3 9HP
**Tel:** (0223) 356565

**Owner:** Millington Road Nursery School Trust
**Headteacher:** Helen Doodson, NNEB, Cert Ed
**Type:** Nursery school offering full- and part-time places and half-day sessions (afternoon sessions for younger children)
**Children:** 2½–5yrs. 80 places. 80 on register
**Hours:** Morning session 8.45am–12 noon
Afternoon session 1.30pm–3.30pm
Open 36 weeks a year
**Status:** Fee-paying registered charity
**Number of years open:** 30
**Meals:** Packed lunches, snacks, tea
**1992 fees:** £485 per term full-time
£227 per term for 5 morning sessions a week
£174 per term for 5 afternoon sessions a week
**Waiting list:** Moderate. First come first served
**Registered by:** Cambs County Council SS

**Premises** A picturesque wooden chalet on stilts with vast, fish-bowl windows, surrounded by trees, at the end of a quiet lane. It was purpose-built as a school during World War II, and the bunker is still visible at the back of the garden – well secured to avoid injury. The outside play area is huge, with excellent equipment – two play houses, climbing frames, a large sandpit, swings and trikes. Inside is spacious, sunny and cheerful: extremely well worn and in need of a coat of paint as well as more storage space, but child-oriented and friendly. An old building, it is hard to heat and difficult to keep clean. The head brings her two dogs to work each day and there are two tanks to house the nursery's stick insects. Children use three rooms: a big playroom, an art and messy-play room and a multipurpose room. There is also a staff room, cloakrooms and an office. A refurbishment programme progresses as funds become available. All the window frames are currently being replaced.

**Headteacher & staff** Helen Doodson, NNEB, Cert Ed, has been headteacher at Millington Road for seven years. An experienced primary and nursery school teacher who has worked in Britain and in the United States, she has a strong, but friendly and welcoming personality. Her main duties are the smooth running of the school, teaching the pre-school children and training students. There are four other nursery workers in her team, all qualified (NNEB, Cert Ed and City & Guilds), with a good mixture of teachers and nursery nurses. Most have a first-aid certificate. Students and sixth formers are accepted for training, including a number of men. No staff training policy or budget, although staff attend some specific courses occasionally. Staff/child ratio is 1:4 for afternoon sessions for 2-year-olds and 1:8 in the mornings. Staff have close relationships and socialise together outside nursery hours.

**Children & parents** The nursery was founded in 1963 to meet the needs of university students and staff, visiting academics and the local community. Run by a committee of trustees, which includes two parent-representatives, the nursery is a charity. All income is used for running costs or improvements. A co-operative scheme encourages parental involvement. Parents are asked to give three hours' help a term to the nursery, either in the playrooms or at home (eg preparing art activities, or washing the tea towels for a week). Those who do not participate pay £10 extra a term in fees. Parents are mainly local professional and university families. There is some cultural mix, with visiting students and academics from overseas – mainly the United States and Japan. A bursary fund is available to assist mature students living on grants, who would otherwise not be able to afford nursery fees. There is an open door policy; parents are welcome at any time and are invited to take part in every aspect of nursery life. Phasing-in of new children is done gently, with parents staying to settle their child. Regular coffee mornings are arranged for staff and parents to meet each other.

**Curriculum & activities** Learning is through play in a structured environment. Children are divided into three family groups, all of mixed ages and each following a different activity. They can move from group to group, with staff ensuring that every activity is experienced. Activities are changed during the day and nursery workers rotate from room to room. Children come together in two groups for newstime, stories, music and milk break. The nursery keeps the requirements of the National Curriculum in mind, but there is no emphasis on the 3Rs. Older children are taught basic number and letter recognition when they are ready and old enough to understand. Although this is not a Montessori school, many of the Montessori theories are in action. Older children help the younger ones; children choose their activities and express themselves freely. Individual fulfilment is encouraged. Strong emphasis is placed on vocabulary building and understanding words through stories, rhymes, discussion and imaginative play. Impressive art and craft work – clay, painting, printing, woodwork, cookery and other creative activities. Music daily – singing, movement, percussion and listening. Outdoor play at the end of each session in the large garden provides good scope for physical activity and large motor skill development. There is a weekly topic, which is developed at home and in the nursery. Children are self-confident and independent, learning to be members of a group and to share. The international flavour of the nursery helps them to understand different children and cultures around the world.

**Remarks** Relaxed, happy, caring and unpressured. The old building needs updating, but the happy atmosphere and qualified, dedicated staff reduce the shortcomings of the premises to a minor detail. Demand for places outstrips supply. Bursaries are available for the children of mature students.

## MONTESSORI SCHOOL, CAMBRIDGE

St Andrews Hall
Chapel Street
Cambridge
Cambs CB4 1DY
**Tel:** (0223) 350743

**Owner/Principal:** Julie Carroll-Watts, AMI Mont Dip (Association Montessori Internationale)
**Type:** Registered AMI nursery school offering morning sessions, and full-time places for older children
**Children:** 2½–7yrs. 28 places. 25 on register
**Hours:** Morning session 9.15am–12.15pm – under 4
Full day 9.15am–3.15pm except Wed – over 4
Open 36 weeks a year
**Status:** Private, fee-paying
**Number of years open:** 11

**Meals:** Snacks, tea, packed lunches
**1992 fees:** £675 per term full-time
£505 per term for 5 morning sessions a week
**Waiting list:** Long. Early registration advisable
**Registered by:** Cambs County Council SS

**Premises** A huge brick church hall in a quiet residential area, recently decorated and immaculately clean. High windows, but adequate natural light and pastel green walls. The nursery school shares use of the hall – everything must be set out at the beginning of each day and tidied away at the end. No permanent displays of children's artwork are allowed. Despite this limitation, once the room has been carefully prepared, everything below adult waist level seems perfect. Furniture is child-height, plentiful, high quality and made of natural materials. The collection of Montessori equipment and apparatus is the largest we have seen outside a Montessori college. The school has use of the hall, divided into two areas by curtains, toilets, kitchen, cloakroom, a storeroom and a large, modern ante-room with pink walls and lino floors for PE and music. The outside play area at the back of the church includes a garden plot for each child to plant and tend. The nearest park, a quarter of a mile away, is visited in all weathers to teach road safety and nature studies. Visitors are frequent and are treated very much as observers. Our researcher was asked to sit in a particular place, handed a pink laminated card, and asked to follow the visitors' code of conduct printed on it.

**Owner/Principal & staff** Julie Carroll-Watts, AMI Mont Dip, is a calm, unruffled, dedicated Montessori teacher, totally in control of her class. She was a traditional teacher in Australia and has worked in a variety of teaching posts around the world. Julie is assisted by two full-time members of staff, one a fine arts and music graduate, the other a qualified NNEB nursery nurse. A part-time Montessori trainee also works at the nursery and attends college on day release. Staff are quiet, calm and friendly – a multicultural team from Australia, India, Italy as well as Britain. After setting out the furniture and equipment each morning, they have coffee and biscuits and discuss the day's activities before children arrive.

**Children & parents** Predominantly white, middle class and Christian. Julie Carroll-Watts sponsors two places for children whose parents cannot afford the fees. Children come from as far away as Newmarket. There is an active parents' association, which meets monthly. Parent musicians play at school concerts and help with adult/child ratios on walks to the park and outings. Parents receive an annual report on their child's progress.

**Curriculum & activities** The nursery follows the Montessori philosophy of 'education for life'. Registration by the AMI ensures a high standard of equipment and staffing. Over £30,000 has been spent recently on a magnificent supply of expensive Montessori apparatus. The 'prepared environment' is an important aspect of the Montessori approach. Children have easy access to a range of experiences with appropriate educational aids. Practical life exercises such as washing dishes, polishing shoes or tying bows help children acquire basic skills and independence. Sensorial materials designed for touch, taste, smell and sound reinforce visual impressions and develop children's minds. Mathematics is a core subject. Numbers are introduced through the senses and basic concepts are taught, leading to simple addition and subtraction if a child is ready. Language is encouraged through stories, discussion groups and books. Reading and writing are approached via a wide range of activities and games, at each child's own pace. There is equipment for geography, botany, zoology, music, art and science. Each term, a project on a specific country is undertaken. All children have their own garden plot to plant. Other activities include dance and singing every day and playing musical instruments once a week. Children perform a concert every two weeks, and parents play instruments with them. Swimming and PE are undertaken once a fortnight. There is a weekly walk to the park for nature study, physical activity and road safety instruction. Each child is monitored daily and has his/her own curriculum for individual development. Their daily tasks are marked on a record card. Children are assigned one duty every day which they must fulfil – it may be pouring the juice or milk, or helping prepare snacks. Tasks are displayed on a duty board and announced at the morning registration. Birthdays are celebrated at a morning party and parents are asked to volunteer to give a ten-minute concert on party days.

**Remarks** An exemplary Montessori school, with high-quality equipment and an enriching environment. The calm, purposeful atmosphere fosters individual attention and growth. Each child's progress and development are carefully monitored and recorded. Despite the limitations of the building, the necessity to put everything away at the end of each day and the lack of parking, this is one of the best-equipped Montessori nurseries we have seen.

## OLD BUTTERY NURSERY SCHOOL

16 High Street
Willingham
Cambs CB4 5ES
**Tel:** (0223) 860263

**Owner/Principal:** Ro Asplin, City & Guilds
**Type:** Day nursery offering full- and part-time places
**Children:** 0–7yrs. 40 places. 79 on register
**Hours:** 8am–6pm
Open 52 weeks a year
**Status:** Private, fee-paying
**Number of years open:** 6
**Meals:** Breakfast, lunch, tea and snacks
**1992 fees:** £85 per week full-time – under 3
£80 per week full-time – over 3
£400 per term for 5 morning sessions a week – over 3
£1.85 per hour – under 3
£1.80 per hour – over 3
**Waiting list:** None
**Registered by:** Cambs County Council SS
**Under same ownership:** The Rosery, Cottenham; Stanton Farm Day Nursery, Landbeach

**Premises** An end-of-terrace, Victorian house and a separate single-storey, brick building, formerly a dairy. Willingham is a large village a few miles north of Cambridge. There are two classrooms in the old dairy and two in the house, each catering for different age groups. The walls are brightly decorated with characters from children's books and with children's artwork. The old dairy has its own cloakroom area. The house has toilets and an office upstairs. There is also a large kitchen. The garden is well equipped with outdoor toys and, beyond it, a separate nature area is used for environmental studies.
**Owner/Principal & staff** Ro Asplin, City & Guilds, owns two other day nurseries in the area, with over 200 children on their combined registers. She visits each nursery daily and aims to know all the children personally. Her staff team at the Old Buttery consists of 13 nursery workers. The majority are qualified NNEB or equivalent and there are two qualified nursery teachers. Unqualified helpers are generally in training through the PPA or regional college courses. All regularly attend external training workshops and seminars. Many staff and children come from surrounding army bases and move on every two years or so, which affects continuity. In the two years prior to our visit, six nursery workers had left.
**Children & parents** The children come from a wide catchment area, as the road network around Willingham is good. Parents are mostly middle-class professionals, reflecting the nature of the local businesses. Children are divided into groups according to age and ability, with members of staff assigned to each particular group. However, they eat, rest and do large-group activities together. They appear eager and interested in their work, and are obviously used to visitors. Ro Asplin works closely with parents. She holds open days and encourages parents to comment on their child's progress and well-being. Before a child comes to the nursery, he/she spends at least a morning there with a parent. They transfer to a variety of schools, including many of the private pre-prep schools in Cambridge. Children with special educational needs and disabilities are welcome and integrate easily into nursery life.
**Curriculum & activities** Learning is through educative play, with the emphasis on care. The nursery tries to follow a homely, flexible routine, within a daily structure. The school day begins with a story and topic work in small groups, and after milk and biscuits and outside play, ends with an activity – when all children come together – such as singing, music and movement, stories or discussion in a circle. After lunch, there is a rest and quiet time before afternoon art, craft and PE. The 'Little Ones', 1–3-year-olds, have a flexible routine. Part of their day is spent with the older children in homely, family groupings. The rest of the time, they enjoy free play with their peers – painting, listening to stories, doing puzzles, playing with toys suitable for their age or having frequent cuddles from staff. They are

encouraged to share, dress and feed themselves and learn to use a potty. Early manipulative skills are practised by sorting, sticking and craft work. Pre-prep children, aged 3–5, work with a teacher in small groups of four or five, depending on ability. Structured activities are designed to give children early practical experience of mathematical, scientific and linguistic concepts. Outdoor activities are undertaken in good weather – painting, football, throwing and catching, balancing and gardening. 'Much early science work can be done with a patient teacher, an interested child and a heap of soil,' Ro Asplin says. As their confidence grows, children are introduced to more formal reading, writing and number work.

**Remarks** Organised, well-planned day nursery. The emphasis is on care, in a stimulating, disciplined and homely environment. Intelligent pre-school programme and two qualified teachers provide a good grounding for primary school.

## ORCHARDS DAY NURSERY

Caxton Village Hall
Gransden Road
Caxton
Cambs CB3 7UR
**Tel:** (0954) 718098

**Owner/Principal:** Laura Gentry, Cert Ed
**Type:** Day nursery offering full- and part-time places
**Children:** 3mths–5yrs. 20 places. 30 on register
**Hours:** 8am–6pm
Flexible hours available
Open 50 weeks a year
**Status:** Private, fee-paying
**Number of years open:** 2
**Meals:** Breakfast, lunch, tea, snacks
**1992 fees:** £1.50 per hour full-time (min 30hrs per week)
£1.60 per hour (16–29hrs per week)
£1.75 per hour (less than 15hrs per week)
50p per day for lunch
Refundable deposit of 1 week's fees
**Waiting list:** Early registration advisable for baby places. Part-time places available
**Registered by:** Cambs County Council SS

## PARK ROAD NURSERY SCHOOL

241 Park Road
Peterborough
Cambs PE1 2UT
**Tel:** (0733) 343278

**Owners:** Mr and Mrs Boulton
**Principal:** Mrs Boulton, Cert Ed, Chartered Accountant
**Type:** Nursery school offering full- and part-time places and half-day sessions
**Children:** 2yrs 9mths–4yrs 11 mths. 40 places. 128 on register
**Hours:** 9am–4pm
Morning session 9am–12 noon
Afternoon session 1pm–4pm
Open 39 weeks a year
**Status:** Private, fee-paying
**Number of years open:** 7 (current ownership) (21 previous ownership)
**Meals:** Snacks, packed lunches
**1992 fees:** £2 per hour
**Waiting list:** Horrific. 200+ names
**Registered by:** Cambs County Council SS

**Premises** Five minutes' drive from Peterborough Cathedral and a few doors down from the well-known Kings School, the nursery is at the back of the owners' bungalow. It is in two parts: the Garden Room and the Pre-School Room, both in excellent condition. The Garden Room is a three-year-old purpose-built extension in the large garden. The younger children (2¾yrs) start here and use the two activity rooms and cloakrooms. The Pre-School Room occupies half the owners' bungalow – two rooms, in fact, which look out on to the garden – and occasionally spills over into the lounge for quiet work or interviewing parents. The most striking feature throughout the nursery is the huge amount of equipment – stacks of toys, books, puzzles, jigsaws and educational equipment, obviously bought at great expense. The large garden, a third of an acre in all, offers outdoor play space complete with summer house, trikes, bikes and climbing frame.

**Owners/Principal & staff** Run by an extremely experienced husband and wife team, both qualified teachers and known to everyone, rather formally, as Mr and Mrs Boulton. Mr Boulton still teaches part-time, but was away at the time of our visit. Mrs Boulton combines 13 years' teaching experience in a Peterborough infants school with a previous life as a chartered accountant – it seems to be a successful combination. She teaches seven hours a day, five days a week – a thoughtful, dedicated teacher who says, 'I am a firm believer that the more you expect from a child, the more you get.' Mrs Boulton's staff team is a mixture of mature, experienced women with years spent in primary schools and reasonably newly qualified NNEBs from nearby colleges who have done their practical training at the nursery. There are five full-timers (two NNEBs, one PPA, two unqualified) and three part-time staff. Many have been in post for over three years and all contribute positively to the running of the nursery.

**Children & parents** The catchment area encompasses the whole of Peterborough and villages beyond and the parents come from all social backgrounds and many different cultures. The nursery is well established and highly regarded in the area. Parents make considerable sacrifices to send their children. 'One mother walks six miles with her child to come here.' Languages include French, Italian, Portuguese, Polish, Japanese and Hindi. There is an open door policy towards parents, rather than formal parents' evenings, for which there is 'no need and no room' according to Mrs Boulton. Along with an excellent reputation, Park Road has earned itself one of the longest nursery waiting lists in existence. The places are allocated on a first-come, first-served basis, with preference to siblings. Children move on to either private or state education. Their future schools are all well known to Mrs Boulton, who is experienced in preparing each child individually for his or her chosen school.

**Curriculum & activities** No one particular philosophy or school of thought predominates here. The curriculum is based on sound educational principles and the timetable is structured with the emphasis on preparation for the reception class. Developing confidence and independence is also considered important. For each session, two activities are planned by different teachers on a rota basis, one 'work' and one 'craft'. Work time is a serious part of each day. Time is spent on pencil control exercises, pre-reading skills and scissor work – 'three very important skills required to prepare a child well for school,' says Mrs Boulton. Each day every child is expected to complete a worksheet, carefully graded and selected to suit their individual stage of development. The latter part of each session is known as 'table jobs' time, when tables are set up with a selection of jigsaws, educational toys, lotto and other games. Children are then taken from the group individually for one-to-one reading, writing and number work with a teacher. When a child is ready he/she takes home tins with words in them and reading books. Mrs Boulton has created her own reading scheme which is used throughout the nursery. Children love and take a pride in their work, and results are impressive. There is also time set aside for fun each day – outdoor playtime, free play, songs, music, dance and role playing in the home corner.

**Remarks** This nursery cannot be faulted. The level of care, stimulation and love is exceptional. It is not difficult to understand why parents are prepared to make substantial sacrifices to pay to send their pre-school children here. Park Road Nursery has built up a formidable, well-deserved reputation and, along with it, one of the longest waiting lists in the country. A totally professional school with a host of grateful parents, many of whom told us they did not believe it was possible to find a nursery school better than Park Road.

## ROSE COTTAGE DAY NURSERY

10 Meldreth Road
Shepreth
Near Royston
Cambs SG8 6PS
**Tel:** (0763) 262744

**Owner:** Susan Cook
**Headteacher:** Michaela Robinson, NNEB
**Type:** Day nursery offering full- and part-time places and half-day sessions
**Children:** 2–5yrs. 15 places. 48 on register Some after-school places for older children
**Hours:** 8.15am–5.45pm
Morning session 8.15am–1pm
Afternoon session 2pm–5.45pm
Open 52 weeks a year (excl bank holidays)
**Status:** Private, fee-paying

**Number of years open:** 3
**Meals:** Lunch, tea, snacks
**1992 fees:** £62 per week full-time
£13.50 per day
£8.50 per morning session (+£1 inc lunch)
£7.50 per afternoon session (+£1 inc lunch)
£1.50 per hour by negotiation
**Waiting list:** Minimal
**Registered by:** Cambs County Council SS

**Premises** Picturesque part thatched, listed, 19th-century cottage on two floors, attached to a small village store. The nursery, shop and surrounding buildings are all beautifully maintained. The front door of the nursery opens straight on to the pavement of a reasonably busy road, but is always kept locked, as is the side door. Parking is available at the side or on the road. The station is within easy walking distance and there is a bus stop a few yards away. Inside has been well converted and decorated. Lack of space is a problem and limits numbers to a maximum of 15 children at any one time, but creates a homely, family atmosphere. The tiled back room is ideal for art, craft and messy play and doubles as a dining room. Children's art covers the walls. Purpose-built cloakroom, loos and kitchen are spotless and newly equipped. The front classroom is carpeted throughout. The walls are pastel shades, adult-painted floor to ceiling with murals from stories – Snow White and the Seven Dwarfs on one, Beauty and the Beast planned for another. The front hall is used as a nappy-changing area and sleep room (not an ideal arrangement) with low beds stored under the stairs. The office, staff room and staff toilets are on the first floor. The garden is small and when we visited needed some upgrading – the grass has suffered badly from overuse. There is a Wendy house, swing and sandpit. At the bottom of the garden, a locked gate opens into Manor Gardens – an imaginative network of different gardens, each with its own character, linked by gates in walls and pathways between shrubs – reminiscent of the Secret Garden and a magical place for children to visit, but only under supervision.

**Owner, Headteacher & staff** Susan Cook, who owns Rose Cottage, launched the nursery and planned the conversion – the artistic murals are also her work. She is present at the nursery every day, but the headteacher is Michaela Robinson, NNEB, recently appointed. The limited number of children means a good staff/child ratio of 1:3 at most times. There are four full-time staff and two part-time. Their qualifications include PPA trained, with an Open University certificate in under-sevens and an SRN with ten years' playgroup experience. A dance and drama teacher visits weekly (£3 extra per session). Staff turnover has been a problem in 1992, with Susan Cook endeavouring to maintain continuity. No regular staff meetings, but staff are involved in decision-making and meet to discuss matters as they occur. Cambridgeshire Regional College and North Herts College use the nursery as a training establishment and for individual student assessments. In-service training of permanent staff is considered important, with a small (£500) training budget set aside.

**Children & parents** Children come from a wide catchment area – Royston and surrounding villages – travelling mainly by car, although some come by train and a very few walk. They are predominantly white and middle class, although there have been children from ethnic minorities in the past. The majority have working mothers, and some have nannies. Limited places are available for older children after school. Older brothers and sisters join in activities, stay for tea and are collected at 5.45pm. The children are quiet, but actively engaged in activities, and because the group is small (15 maximum) they know each other well. Staff do not raise their voices and during discussion children listen attentively and contribute eagerly. Parents are encouraged to spend as much time as possible at the nursery, observe the routines, see the daily menu and read the parents' noticeboard. Phasing-in new children is done over a period of time, with parents staying as long as they wish until their child is well settled. There are open days and a Christmas party for parents, but no regular parents' evenings. A clearly produced prospectus is available for parents.

**Curriculum & activities** No particular school of nursery thinking prevails here. The nursery describes its approach as broadly traditional, drawing on good practice from a variety of sources. It is responsive to the needs of children, their parents and the school to which they will transfer. The back room contains messy-play activities – sand tray, painting easel and two art tables, one for general art activities, the other for topic work. The carpeted front room is used for jigsaws, games and table-top or floor work. There is a book corner, Wendy house and benches for storytime, with boxes of toys underneath. Toys are laid out by staff at the beginning of the session, although children are asked to put them away when they have finished. Unfortunately many games are out of child reach and children have to ask an adult if they want to exchange a jigsaw, for example. There is a set structure to the day – a balance between choosing time, whole group and small group activities and outdoor play. Staff have a weekly timetable listing their responsibilities for each activity. There is a wide range of pre-school work suitable to each age group: art and craft to help develop painting, drawing, cutting and other motor skills, and constructional toys for imagination and motor skills. When children are ready they learn phonics and letter and word recognition, although no formal reading scheme is followed. Letter formation is learnt in stages from joining dots through copying patterns to forming letters. Worksheets are used. Games and activities develop sorting, sequencing and number skills and recognition of colours, shapes, sizes and numbers. Projects are also undertaken – 'Myself' and 'Spiders' were under way when we visited. The small number of children means plenty of individual attention and careful monitoring of each child's development. Children with special needs do well here, and the nursery works closely with health visitors and speech therapists. Outings are limited as children's hours at the nursery are so variable.

**Remarks** A flexible service tailored to the needs of individual parents. Well-planned and organised curriculum in a homely, family environment. The premises have character, but space is rather limited. A quiet, purposeful atmosphere.

# Cheshire

Cheshire aims to ensure that all young children have 'convenient, local access to services they require, when they need them, but with priority to children in need'. However, the council relies on the private, commercial and voluntary sectors for help in achieving their objectives. The county's eight nursery schools and 90 nursery classes cater for just over a fifth of 3- and 4-year-olds, on a part-time basis. Provision is irregular, especially in rural areas, although in some places it is offset by a rapid growth in playgroups and private nurseries. There are 335 playgroups. Working parents on above average salaries have a plentiful supply of private daycare to choose from – 82 day nurseries and over 2200 childminders. One parent we spoke to was delighted: 'Having moved to the south Manchester area from Kent, the provision and quality of private day nurseries is much higher and extremely good in comparison.'

**Further information**
For details on day nurseries, childminders and playgroups:
Department of Social Services
Inspection Unit
314 Chester Road
Hartford
Northwich CW8 2AB
Tel: (0606) 889773

For details on nursery schools, units and classes:
Education Services Group
County Hall
Chester CH1 1SQ
Tel: (0244) 602373

# BURNETT NURSERY

30 Lyon Street
Latchford
Warrington
Cheshire
WA4 1LN
**Tel:** (0925) 417985

**Owner:** Olive Higginson
**Type:** Private day nursery/nursery school offering full- and part-time places and half-day sessions
**Children:** 2–5yrs. 25 places. 50 on register
**Hours:** 8.30am–5.30pm
Morning session 8.30am–1pm
Afternoon session 1pm–5.30pm
Open 50 weeks a year
**Status:** Private, fee-paying
**Number of years open:** 5
**Meals:** Breakfast, lunch, tea, snacks
**1992 fees:** £57.55 per week full-time
£11.55 per day
£5.80 per session
**Waiting list:** Short. Places available at second nursery recently opened
**Registered by:** Cheshire SS
**Under same ownership:** Burnett Nursery II, Warrington

**Premises** A single-storey, brick-built, Victorian building rented from the adjoining Methodist church. Set in an old 'back to back' working-class area not far from the town centre, it is not the easiest of places to find. But initial impressions are deceptive. Inside, it is light, bright, spacious and airy with the neutral decor and furnishings brought to life by well-organised displays of children's work. There are two main nursery rooms, each with tables and chairs for work. One room has messy-play equipment and a piano, the other a play house, slide and an office area. The loos and changing facilities are down a corridor. The nursery also has the use of the adjoining church hall for Christmas concerts, plays, etc. There is an enclosed yard and grassy outside play area. A safe haven in an unlikely spot, with particular emphasis on security.

**Owner & staff** Olive Higginson opened the nursery when her own adopted sons started school. Her enthusiasm and commitment are obvious, so are her business and administrative skills, gained during many years as personal assistant to the MD of a large chemical company. She became involved with the PPA through her own children and, although she has no formal qualifications, she has her own very strong views on what children and their parents need from a nursery. Olive Higginson expects high standards from the children and her loyal staff, and has taken some time to build up the right team. She does not consider qualifications absolutely essential, although at the time of our visit, all carers were qualified NNEBs or City & Guilds. Olive Higginson spends only part of her time at the nursery, but she is very much in charge and always tries to be available to children, parents and staff, when needed. The day-to-day running of the nursery is in the hands of capable, caring, and well-managed staff. Staff/child ratio 1:6.

**Children & parents** Despite its working-class setting, virtually all children come from middle-class areas, to the south of Warrington. There is an impressive cultural mix, with French, Italian, German, Swedish, Muslim and Hindu children, occasionally with English as a second language. Approximately half have both parents working and attend full time. Parents are always welcome and new parents are encouraged to stay to settle their children in. Outings, concerts and open evenings are all well supported. The children are busy, polite and well behaved. The majority go on to state primary schools in the area, and roughly 25 per cent to the independent sector, most frequently Altrincham Prep or Tower College. The nursery has some experience of children with emotional difficulties and is willing to take children with special needs.

**Curriculum & activities** Children experience a structured day, with reading, writing and sometimes number work a priority for the older children. Free-play sessions with a wide choice of activities are interspersed with directed periods of craftwork, storytime, music, action songs, dance and movement. Educational TV programmes are used and children play outside during every session, weather permitting. Emphasis is on the emotional and social development of new children, who must attend a minimum of two sessions per week. Children are split into four groups according to age. Each group has its own nursery nurse who is responsible for their all-round care and development. Good manners are encouraged and expected, and discipline is firm but gentle at all times. The children enjoy an annual trip to nearby Chester Zoo, and occasional visits to other places of interest when relevant to the topic of the week. Olive Higginson's philosophy is one of 'child first', but within a disciplined, well-ordered programme. There is no pressure, but children go off to school confident and well advanced in pre-reading, pre-writing, number work and pencil control.

**Remarks** Now a well-established nursery, offering secure, structured and disciplined care in pleasant premises, at what are considered to be very reasonable fees. In an area with a substantial range of nursery provision, both private and local authority, demand for this particular type of care has been such that Olive Higginson has opened a second, almost identical, nursery on the other side of the town centre. Places are still available, but filling up fast.

## HAPPY DAYS NURSERY

Gadbrook Business Centre
Rudheath
Northwich
Cheshire CW9 7TN
**Tel:** (0606) 49424

**Owners:** Audrey Haffenden, Cert Ed,
Carol Potter
**Type:** Day nursery offering full-time places and half-day sessions
**Children:** 3mths–5yrs. 50 places. 100 on register
**Hours:** 8am–6pm
Morning session 8am–1pm (inc lunch)
Afternoon session 1pm–6pm (inc tea)
Open 51 weeks a year
**Status:** Private, fee-paying
**Number of years open:** 4
**Meals:** Lunch, tea, snacks
**1992 fees:** £84 per week full-time – under 1yr
£80 per week full-time – 1–2½yrs
£72 per week full-time – over 2½yrs
£16.80 per day – under 1yr
£16 per day – 1–2½yrs
£14.40 per day – over 2½yrs
£8.40 per session – under 1yr
£8 per session – 1–2½yrs
£7.20 per session – over 2½yrs
10% sibling discount
**Waiting list:** Full until September 1994.
Preference to siblings
**Registered by:** Cheshire County Council SS

**Premises** A pleasant single-storey, brick-built unit in the new Gadbrook Business Park, south of Northwich and only 15 miles from Chester. Set just off the main Manchester road, the nursery is easily accessible by car, and has good parking facilities. There is an enormous enclosed outside play area, with both grass and hard surfaces, and an attractive permanent outside playhouse sponsored by Barclays Bank. Inside is light, airy and very spacious with an enviable amount of room for storage, office, entrance hall, kitchen and utilities. It has been adapted very simply with the main open-plan area divided into two by cupboards, with a linking gate. The under-2½-year-olds are at one end, and the older children at the other. The babies have a separate sleep room with prams and cots and there is a quiet room for 'work' sessions with pre-school children. The emphasis is on flexibility, according to the ages of the children. The breeze-block walls are painted white and covered with attractive displays of the children's work. The entrance hall is welcoming and informative, with staff photographs, photo displays and scrapbooks showing some of the nursery activities.

**Owners & staff** The joint owners, Audrey Haffenden, Cert Ed, and Carol Potter, are caring, older mums whose skills and experience complement each other. This leads to very successful job sharing. Audrey is an experienced infant teacher who has lectured for the Open University. Carol has administrative and computer expertise and has completed a PPA playleaders' course. Audrey is responsible for the day-to-day care with the help of two NNEB supervisors who lead sessions, one in charge of babies, the other the older children. Carol deals with most of the administration, and major decisions are taken jointly. Either Audrey or Carol is always on site, although they are supernumerary, and have high staff/children ratios – 1:3 for children under 2½ and 1:5 for 2½–5-year-olds. All staff, even part-timers, work full days, for the sake of continuity. A keyworker system operates, with each worker having overall responsibility for a small group of children. The nursery is committed to training. They take NNEB and work-experience students and are hoping to start NVQ courses for all their own staff. In total there are ten full-time staff and 11 part-time. Fifty per cent are NNEB qualified, others are PPA playleaders or unqualified.

**Children & parents** Predominantly white and middle class, from a 25-mile radius of the nursery. Most children have two working parents, though not necessarily both work full-time. Roughly one-third of the children attend full-time for the whole day and many others attend for five mornings or five afternoons. The parents tend to lead busy, pressured lives and are not anxious to become involved in nursery activities. They need a reliable quality service to relieve them of one of their many pressures. Children appear busy and content and far too interested in what they are doing to take much notice of visitors. The nursery is happy to take children with special needs, provided that it is considered to be in the child's interest. They have experienced children with sight impairment, hearing difficulties and Down's syndrome. With the occasional exception, all the children go on to state primary schools. Audrey and Carol often take children to their new primary school to help settle them in.

**Curriculum & activities** The nursery follows the PPA philosophy of learning through play in a structured but flexible day. Each session begins with free play, offering a large variety of choices, including large climbing equipment, play house and quiet area with books. All children, regardless of age, are encouraged to take part in art, craft, messy play, music, songs and storytime every day. The older children, over 2½ years, experience two directed activity sessions during each session. These may include painting, gluing, jigsaws, sorting, matching, crayoning, cutting out, board games, etc. The pre-school group are taken out for pre-reading and pre-writing activities. Reading is not taught, although those starting to read at home are also encouraged to continue at the nursery. Each child's individual needs are carefully catered for by his/her key-worker. Audrey Haffenden says, 'We aim to get the child interested and keen to learn so that they will go on happily to school and flourish.' The owners continually appraise the standards and provision of care offered. There are written daily and weekly programmes for each age group, although flexibility is allowed to fit in with the moods and needs of each child. Written policies and procedures also cover every aspect of the running of the nursery, from discipline and the professional responsibilities of nursery nurses to fire drill, changing routines and staff disciplinary procedures. Maximum use is made of the large outside playspace. In summer most activities are moved into the open air and walks in the surrounding area are frequent. The daily cook prepares well-balanced meals in the spotless kitchen. Meals are an important occasion for socialising and talking.

**Remarks** High-quality childcare for working and non-working parents in spacious attractive surroundings. Good proportion of NNEB qualified staff. No academic pressure but good opportunities for free expression and individual development. With the exception of one of the owners, no staff with teaching qualifications or experience when we visited. Good childcare is in great demand in this area and anyone wishing to secure a place will need to plan well in advance. Good ratio of staff to children.

## LITTLE ACORNS DAY NURSERY

223 Wilmslow Road
Handforth
Cheshire SK9 3JZ
**Tel:** (061) 498 9251

**Owners:** Veronica Walker
Alan Walker
Jean Randles, NNEB
**Nursery Manager:** Jean Randles, NNEB
**Type:** Day nursery offering full-time places and half-day sessions
**Children:** 0–5yrs. 30 places. 42 on register
**Hours:** 8am–6pm
Morning session 8am–1pm (inc lunch)
Afternoon session 1pm–6pm
Open 50 weeks a year
**Status:** Private, fee-paying
**Number of years open:** 2
**Meals:** Lunch, tea, snacks
**1992 fees:** £100 per week full-time
£20 per day
£12.50 per session
£10 registration fee
**Waiting list:** Early registration for baby places advisable
**Registered by:** Cheshire County Council SS

## SMARTIES NURSERY

Gowy Bank Farm
Cotton Edmunds
Chester CH3 7PZ
**Tel:** (0829) 41608

**Owner/Principal:** Anne Williams, Cert Ed
**Type:** Day nursery offering full-time places and half-day sessions
**Children:** 1–5yrs. 36 places. 130 on register
**Hours:** 8.30am–5.30pm
Morning session 8.30am–12.30pm
Afternoon session 1.30pm–5.30pm
Open 48 weeks a year
**Status:** Private, fee-paying
**Number of years open:** 5
**Meals:** Lunch, tea, snacks
**1992 fees:** £19 per day – 1–2½yrs
£16 per day – 2½–5yrs
£10 per session – 1–2½yrs
£8.50 per half-day session – 2½–5yrs
£1.50 per day for lunch
**Waiting list:** Moderate
**Registered by:** Cheshire County Council SS

**Premises** Surrounded by farmland in rural Cheshire, just outside Chester, the nursery is the owner's former large modern home, now converted to a very high standard. The stables next door have been completely refurbished to provide an additional 12-place baby unit. Inside is tastefully designed, cheerful and welcoming. The original building is used by the older children and comprises a small 'teaching' room crammed with books and learning materials for pre-school skills; a messy room for art, craft, sand and water, with walls lined with children's artwork; a large carpeted playroom furnished with a home corner, dressing-up corner and piano for musical activities. This room has patio doors leading out into the outside play area. The relatively new baby unit for 1- to 2-year-olds is a large, bright room which can be partitioned off into cosier spaces when required. There is a scrupulously clean nappy-changing area and bathroom, with neat piles of disposable nappies on shelves. The unit also has its own kitchen for bottle and feed preparation and meals. Outside there are nearly three acres of play space including fields, a grassed playground with climbing frames and sandpit and a hard tennis court for bikes and trikes. The children have their own mini farm in the two fields – 12 sheep, Dusty the pony, two rabbits, a guinea pig and two rare breed hens. Prince and Scratch, the nursery dog and cat, wander about at will. The pièce de résistance is a wonderful indoor swimming pool, shared with the owner's brother, who lives next door.

**Owner/Principal & staff** Anne Williams, Cert Ed, owner and principal, is cheerful and fun. The children obviously love her warmth and laughter. A former secondary school teacher, she spends as much time as possible each day with the children and staff, employing someone else to do the bulk of the nursery administration. There are nine full-time staff; all except two are qualified and cover a wide range of skills. Three, including Anne Williams, are teachers, two are nurses and three NNEBs. The staff are friendly and relaxed. Children call them by their first names and relationships are clearly close and confident. Staff rotate around the different rooms. There is no keyworker system – children are free to bond with whoever they wish.

**Children & parents** The families come from a wide variety of social backgrounds, including the smart Cheshire set. Many are middle-class professionals, others farm workers. Parents drive from town and country so their children can attend Smarties. The children are phased in gradually when they start and parents encouraged to stay to settle them in. Communication between the nursery and parents is good – three newsletters a year give a written update and parents come in to talk to Anne or other members of staff whenever they feel it is necessary.

**Curriculum & activities** The nursery's philosophy of 'Learning Made Fun' is achieved through a rich, well-planned curriculum. Anne Williams believes in experiential learning with regular acting and 'doing' and many opportunities for language development. Creative play is important, with art activity twice a day incorporating paint, modelling, water and sand. Symbolic play using dressing-up clothes, home corner, shop corner and drama – children act out stories and put on puppet plays, which develop social skills and language. There is music and movement three times a week; swimming in the nursery indoor pool (staff are trained in life-saving) and cookery once a week. Horse riding is available at extra cost three mornings a week from a visiting instructress and is extremely popular. Pre-school academic work is carefully planned to prepare children for their various primary and prep schools. The three qualified teachers take children in small groups of four or five into the teaching room. Here children are introduced to science, and learn colour, shape and size by sorting and sequencing. Number work includes practical, written and conceptual use of numbers. Basic addition and subtraction will be introduced when a child is ready. The nursery has games and computer packages to practise these skills. Pre-reading and language skills are also developed. There is a letter of the week, as well as letter sorting and recognition. Practical pencil control is developed through colouring, dotting and joining.

The curriculum for babies is less structured and planned, but their room is filled with equipment designed to stimulate imagination and develop co-ordination and manipulative skills. Twice a day, whatever the weather, children help to feed and care for the farm animals.

**Remarks** A fabulous nursery, combining the best of care with strong educational programmes. Smarties is bursting with confidence and know-how and full of people – adults and children – who are having fun. The carefully planned, if rather overcrowded, curriculum guarantees an excellent start for any child. Staff qualifications cover a wide range of skills and subjects, including teaching.

# Cleveland

Cleveland is at the top of the league table for nursery education, with 58 per cent of all 3- and 4-year-olds in either a nursery school or class. Plans to open four or five new nursery classes each year until all primary schools offer nursery education have been shelved as a result of current spending cuts. Even those parents who opt for one of the 39 private day nurseries find no waiting lists and charges sometimes as low as £50 per week. The 656 childminders concentrate on offering babycare, before children move on to nursery education. Despite sending out 47 questionnaires to both the state and private sectors, only four private providers responded and no local authority nurseries or classes wished to be included in this guide.

**Further information**

For details on day nurseries, childminders and playgroups:
Department of Social Services
Registration and Inspection Unit
Gurney House
Gurney Street
Middlesbrough TS1 1JL
Tel: (0642) 264569

For details on nursery schools, units and classes:
Education Department
Woodlands Road
Middlesbrough TS1 3BN
Tel: (0642) 262953 or 262956

## GLENFIELD NURSERY SCHOOL

19 Albert Road
Eaglescliffe
Stockton-on-Tees TS16 0DA
**Tel:** (0642) 780552

**Owner/Principal:** Jean Brown, Cert Ed
**Type:** Day nursery offering full- and part-time places and half-day sessions

**Children:** 6wks–5yrs. 70 places. 63 on register
**Hours:** 7.30am–6pm
Morning session 7.30am–1pm
Afternoon session 1pm–6pm
Open 51 weeks a year
**Status:** Private, fee-paying
**Number of years open:** 2
**Meals:** Breakfast, lunch, tea
**1992 fees:** £60 per week full-time
£38 per week for 5 sessions
£14 per day
£8 per session

**Waiting list:** Early registration advisable for babies
**Registered by:** Cleveland County Council SS

# RAINBOW DAY NURSERY

1 Imperial Avenue
Norton
Stockton-on-Tees
Cleveland TS20 2EW
**Tel:** (0642) 555096

**Owner/Nursery Officer:** Linda Brooks, SRN, SCM, RMN
**Type:** Day nursery offering full- and part-time places and half-day sessions (min 2 sessions a week)
**Children:** 1mth–5yrs. 60 places. 80 on register
**Hours:** 7.30am–5.30pm
Morning session 7.30am–1pm
Afternoon session 1pm–5.30pm
Open 51 weeks a year
**Status:** Private, fee-paying
**Number of years open:** 14
**Meals:** Breakfast, lunch, tea, snacks
**1992 fees:** £55 per week full-time (inc meals and nappies)
£13 per day
£8 per morning session
£7 per afternoon session
10% sibling discount
**Waiting list:** Short. Places can always be found
**Registered by:** Cleveland County Council SS

**Premises** Large, detached, red-brick, Victorian house on the corner of a main road less than a mile from the city centre. The owner and her family live above the nursery. Children are divided by age and each of the six groups has its own 'base room'. The base rooms for over-2s are multi-purpose and also used as a quiet room and for art and craft. All rooms are supplied with a large amount of equipment and toys, stored in numerous stacking boxes and neatly labelled. Linda Brooks prefers not to invest in large play equipment as she feels this uses up too much valuable space. YTS trainees have painted several large and colourful murals around the nursery. There are two outside play areas, one behind the nursery and one to the side of the house. The smaller paved area is used more frequently in the winter. The larger side garden, with some grass, is popular in the summer. Nearby school playing fields are visited regularly.

**Owner/Nursery Officer & staff** Linda Brooks, SRN, SCM, RMN, has 25 years' nursing experience as a midwife and dental nurse and has worked all over the world. She has an Advanced Playgroups Certificate and set up the nursery 14 years ago. She employs 17 nursery nurses, 11 of whom are qualified, NNEB, BTEC and City & Guilds. Each room is led by an NNEB-qualified group leader. Ages range from 18 to 55, and nearly all have worked at the nursery for more than four years. Staff meetings are held once a month and staff are always involved in decison-making. Mr Brooks helps out regularly with repairs, finances, stores and liaison. Students and YTS trainees are welcomed and supervised by group leaders. There is no staff training policy or budget. The staff/child ratio across the nursery is 1:6. Staff wear badges displaying their Christian names and this is how children address them.

**Children & parents** The nursery has a wide catchment area – children travel in from up to 15 miles away. Most parents are white-collar workers and many work at the DSS and Barclaycard. There is little cultural or ethnic mix and very few single-parent families. Children go on to state primary schools all over the county and a small percentage to independent Red House. Group leaders are also keyworkers for the children in their group. Children change keyworker each time they change base room, every six or 12 months. Each keyworker is responsible for daily monitoring of the children in her group. Because of the size of the nursery, no more than two groups come together at a time for singing and meals. Children with special educational needs are welcome, but there is no wheelchair access or additional staff support. Parents are invited to open days twice a year and parents' evenings with guest speakers. They are welcome to spend time in the nursery, if they specifically ask to, but are discouraged from wandering about freely.

**Curriculum & activities** Each group has a planned pre-school education programme. The nursery sets out 'to teach all the children to recognise numbers, make use of colours, learn about letters, understand different words, distinguish different shapes, see size relationships, develop their reasoning ability, learn to sing with other children, enjoy stories and socialise with other children'. English is a core subject and includes pencil control, worksheets, reading using the Read Together scheme and matching pictures to words. Maths includes pencil work and worksheets, as well as counting aloud, singly and in groups. Science is a regular part of the timetable and is incorporated into projects, discussions, experiments, art and craft and outings. There are weekly library visits and swimming, baking, dance and movement, soft play and music. Horse riding features on the timetable and children are taken on outings to farms and the theatre. There is opportunity for free play at the beginning and end of each day.

**Remarks** Strong emphasis on the 3Rs, but no qualified nursery or early years teachers on the staff. Stimulating environment with good-quality, well-maintained equipment and resources. A huge selection of small table toys. Reasonable fees, considering the hours and quality of care.

# Cornwall

Although the local authority provides no day nurseries or playgroups, they do have two nursery schools and 30 nursery classes, offering part-time places only to 14 per cent of 3- and 4-year-olds. The decision not to provide day nurseries, they say, is due to the fact that many people in rural communities are without cars and would not be able to travel to them. There are about 17 private day nurseries for the working population, in towns such as Truro and Liskeard. The council claims there is no demand for nursery places in the country areas.

## Further information

For details on day nurseries, childminders and playgroups:
Under Fives Unit
13 Treyew Road
Truro TR1 2BY
Tel: (0872) 222312

For details on nursery schools, nursery units and classes:
Education Department
New County Hall
Treyew Road
Truro TR1 3AY
Tel: (0872) 74282

For a booklet providing information on family centres, health clinics, playgroups, toddler groups, toy libraries, GPs, etc:
Cornwall Under Fives Liaison Group
Cornwall Rural Community Council
9a River Street
Truro TR1 2SQ
Tel: (0872) 73952

For information concerning children with a physical or mental disability:
Children's Assessment Unit
City Hospital
Infirmary Hill
Truro TR1 2HS
Tel: (0872) 74242 ×2147 or ×6145

# GOOSEBERRY BUSH DAY NURSERY

Camborne School
Cranberry Road
Camborne
Cornwall TR14 7PJ
**Tel:** (0209) 713119
**Owner:** Cornwall LEA
**Supervisor:** Gill Smith, NNEB
**Type:** Day nursery offering full-time places and half-day sessions
**Children:** 3mths–5yrs. 24 full-time places. 30 on register
**Hours:** 8.30am–5.45pm (flexible)
Morning session 8.30am–12 noon
Afternoon session 1pm–5.45pm
Open 52 weeks a year (excl bank holidays)
**Status:** Fee-paying, non-profit-making community nursery
**Number of years open:** 2
**Meals:** Breakfast, lunch, tea
**1992 fees:** £10 per day
£6 per morning session
£5 per afternoon session
**Waiting list:** Small – for baby places
**Registered by:** Cornwall County Council SS

**Premises** A former classroom inside Camborne Community School – a typical, early-50s, state secondary school building. The room itself is large, airy and light. It is usually split into two by a set of low railings with a gate. There is also a toilet area, the use of a nearby kitchen and a dining lounge for parents and staff. The huge nursery windows look out on to a small garden – home to the pet rabbit. Regular visits are paid to the local park, a safe five-minute walk away.

**Supervisor & staff** Gill Smith, NNEB, is responsible for the day-to-day running of the nursery and employment of staff. Any financial decisions are made by the headmaster of Camborne school. Gill Smith trained as a nursery nurse in Manchester and began her career working with premature babies. In the past, she has set up a workplace nursery for NALGO and acted as a consultant for Berkshire County Council, advising on the setting up and running of their nurseries. Gill is a very caring woman, with strong views about nursery provision, which she believes should not be in the private sector. 'I feel through experience, that if someone is in business, their primary concern is money. When it comes to looking after children, good childcare should always be the priority.' Her warmth and genuine commitment to the children are obvious and shared by her permanent team of two full-time, qualified NNEB nursery nurses. There are also six or seven students and sixth-formers who work at the nursery as part of their practical training and who are expected to fulfil a regular, weekly commitment. At the time of our visit, there had been no staff turnover for at least two years, although staff cover for sickness and holidays has proved a problem because of the long hours and the financial burden.

**Children & parents** The children are happy and confident, experimenting with their activities and learning through play. They come from a wide variety of social and cultural backgrounds from Camborne and the surrounding area. Despite its idyllic setting, Camborne has severe economic problems, including high unemployment, and many of the children have to deal with severe social difficulties. Children in Need has recently funded a part-time place for a child with social problems. Parents are always welcome, although many work long hours. They can telephone at any time, and are encouraged to take an active part in the nursery. There is a parents' open evening for current and prospective parents to meet staff and regular coffee evenings for informal discussions between staff and parents. Parents come with their children for the first two or three visits to help settle in. Good communication occurs between staff and parents at the end of the day – unusually, staff are very willing to stay on in the evening to talk to parents on an individual basis.

**Curriculum & activities** There is no formal teaching of the 3Rs – learning is through play in a safe, clean, stimulating environment. Children are encouraged to develop social, physical and emotional skills through activities such as the home corner, books, sand and water, paint, puzzles and construction toys. The day begins with free play, followed by breakfast at 9.30am. Children are then split into groups according to age and ability to work on an activity related to the current theme. Older children complete their daily diary. The whole group meets together for stories and singing before lunch. Afternoon activities are art and craft orientated and very often take place outside, weather permitting. By the time children leave, they can usually recognise their own name, count well, know their colours and shapes and are independent enough to dress and feed themselves. Activities are well resourced and the furniture is bright and appropriate for the children. There is a home corner, many early-learning toys and a water area with measuring equipment. Library visits take place twice a term, and there are frequent walks to the park and occasional shopping or café expeditions. Staff are caring and demonstrative, and the nursery makes full use of the additional resources available in the big school, especially the drama and art departments. There is no pressure to achieve academically. The aim is to prepare children for an easy transition to school.

**Remarks** An excellent preparation for life in the reception class of a state primary school. Imaginative, homely and incredibly caring. Gill Smith inspires both staff and children. Very good value but clearly, with fees as low as this, there is not much money left over to invest in new equipment, staff training or extra staff cover.

# POLWHELE HOUSE

Truro
Cornwall TR4 9AE
**Tel:** (0872) 73011

**Owners/Principals:** Richard White, BA
Rosemary White, Cert Ed
**Nursery Supervisor:** Louise Keeler, SRN
**Type:** Nursery class attached to co-ed prep school offering full- and part-time places
**Children:** 3–4½yrs. 24 places. 20 on register
**Hours:** 8.30am–3.30pm
Open 36 weeks a year
**Status:** Private, fee-paying
**Number of years open:** 17
**Meals:** Lunch, snacks
**1992 fees:** £690 per term full-time
£1.17 per day for lunch
**Waiting list:** None. Children registered soon after birth
**Registered by:** Dept for Education

**Premises** The main school occupies a huge, stone manor house set in 34 acres, with sweeping lawns, mature shrubs and woodland. The pre-prep school, including the nursery class, is in the 900-year-old stable block, built around a sheltered courtyard and converted eight years ago. A car is essential to reach this rural enclave, two miles from the outskirts of Truro. The nursery classroom is welcoming and airy, full of imaginative art and craft work. It contains child-sized tables and chairs, a home corner, a small library and painting easels. Children have use of the computer room, gymnasium and dining room in the main school. Outside, there is access to hard and grass play areas, a courtyard and woodland walks, also swings, a climbing frame, wooden play houses and ponies to ride.

**Owners, Supervisor & staff** Rosemary White, Cert Ed, opened a small school for 3- to 7-year-olds in her own home nearly 20 years ago. Since then it has grown into a large co-ed boarding and day school, based on Christian principles. Her husband heads the prep school for 7- to 13-year-olds, while she is responsible for the pre-prep department. The day-to-day running of the nursery class is in the hands of Louise Keeler, a trained nurse, with no formal teaching qualifications, who says 'children are my calling'. She reports directly to Rosemary White, who visits the class daily and supervises afternoon playtime, so that she can get to know the children. There are two nursery assistants, one a trained teacher. Staff are young, middle class and outgoing. They relate confidently to the children. One member of staff is a music teacher and produces musical productions. A voluntary helper comes in daily to assist with reading and a student helper covers at lunchtime. The staff/child ratio averages 1:7 or better.

**Children & parents** The children of doctors, solicitors, accountants and businessmen. Several are bilingual with French and German parents. All wear a school uniform – grey with red trimming. The atmosphere is peaceful and relaxed. Children are visibly happy, talkative and well behaved. The rising-5s almost all move into the adjoining pre-prep school, but there is an informal assessment before they are offered a place. The school does not normally admit children with special needs, but currently offers refuge to a Romanian orphan and a Croatian. New children attend two days a week only and the older children are encouraged to help them settle happily. Parents are invited to open days, concerts, sports days and parents' evenings. They are welcome to visit whenever they wish, although few take up the offer.

**Curriculum & activities** Children experience a structured day, with as much individual attention as possible. There is an equal balance of discipline and fun and children are constantly praised. There is some religious content. Each morning the nursery joins the infant classes for assembly and there are prayers before and after meals and at the end of the day. Daily assembly is an important part of the programme. A typical day begins with tabletop activities, puzzles and drawing before assembly. This is followed by newstime, discussion about the weather, numbers, letters, singing and action songs in a large group. There is a strong music tradition in the school, beginning in the nursery class with daily singing and music making. Polwhele House is where the choristers from Truro Cathedral are educated. Children regularly listen to radio programmes, dance to tapes, do gymnastics and play outside each day. They are introduced to early science, and pre-literacy skills form an important part of the curriculum for older children. Reading is taught using the Ginn 360 reading scheme. A school mini-bus is available for visits to places of interest and there are walks to a nearby farm to study the animals. The school has an equestrian centre with an all-weather arena and ponies to ride. Achievement reports are compiled on each child – parents do not have access. Lunch is prepared in the school kitchens and nursery children eat in the main school dining room with staff.

**Remarks** A small, peaceful nursery class in a beautiful rural setting. Love, care and good resources, with an excellent balance between care and education. Mainly for parents wishing their children to stay at the school until their 7th birthday at least.

# ST MARTIN'S (C of E) PRIMARY SCHOOL – NURSERY UNIT

St Martin's Primary School
Lake Lane
Liskeard
Cornwall PL14 3DE
**Tel:** (0579) 344042

**Owner:** Cornwall County Council LEA
**Headteacher:** Anne Purdon, Cert Ed
**Type:** Nursery class in C of E primary school offering half-day sessions. No full-time places
**Children:** 3yrs 6mths–4yrs 9mths. 26 places. 52 on register
**Hours:** Morning session 9am–11.45am
Afternoon session 1pm–3.15pm
Open 38 weeks a year
**Status:** State nursery class
**Number of years open:** 14
**Meals:** None
**1992 fees:** No fees
**Waiting list:** Long. Not everyone can be guaranteed a place
Priority to regular churchgoers
**Registered by:** Cornwall County Council LEA

**Premises** Purpose-built, cheerfully decorated and well-maintained extension to main school building. Open-plan classroom with separate partitioned areas for cloakrooms, storage and reading. The book corner is enclosed behind a folding door and is generously stocked. The school is on a quiet side road with ample parking facilities and a local bus service. There is a large outside play area with grassy slopes and an area of hard surface for bikes and scooters. It is fenced in on three sides and open to the school playground on the fourth. With ample space on the doorstep, visits to the local park are unnecessary.

**Headteacher & staff** Anne Purdon, Cert Ed, has been headteacher of the nursery class since it opened 14 years ago. There is one other full-time member of staff, NNEB-qualified, mature and very experienced. Little formal management is required for such an intimate team and Anne and her assistant clearly have a friendly working relationship. The staff/child ratio of 1:13 is not ideal, but extra help is available from two young NNEB students and parents. Each week the headmaster of the primary school comes to read a story in the nursery class, and one of the male junior teachers frequently does the same. No staff training policy or budget. Staff meet once a term with local colleagues to share experiences and ideas. Nursery workers from all over Cornwall meet once a year for a similar exchange of views.

**Children & parents** Parents are socially mixed – some unemployed, others are oil rig workers, scrap metal dealers, farmers, teachers and doctors. Most children move into the main school, but some go to other local county infant schools and village primaries. Although the school has no special needs support, it has provided places for an epileptic child and another with cystic fibrosis. One child with cerebral palsy attends when well enough. The waiting list is long, and preference is given to siblings and children recommended by their local vicar. Those whose parents are regular church attenders have priority within that group. Children spend half an hour all together each day, so that they can identify with their class before dividing into smaller groups. Parents have been slow to take up invitations to parents' evenings, but have daily contact with nursery staff and are encouraged to come right inside the classroom to collect their children. New children are phased-in gradually. The headteacher lives locally, and makes a home visit to introduce herself to parents and new children before the beginning of term.

**Curriculum & activities** The nursery aims to provide an all-round education, based on Christian principles, in preparation for school. The playroom is full of stimulating activities, laid out and ready when children arrive. Each day is planned in advance and the timetable written down. Children have freedom to choose a wide range of play experiences – climbing frames, a Wendy house, sand and water play, painting, puzzles, dressing-up clothes, construction toys, clay, cutting and gluing. Books and stories are a key element of the curriculum and in constant use. Strong emphasis is placed on fostering an interest in and a love of books. Some structured learning is introduced in the last term, to prepare older children for their move to the reception class. Letterland is used for pre-reading skills and some practice in counting and numbers. Most leavers can recognise and write their names. There is daily singing, and four dance and movement sessions each week. A diary is kept for each day's activities. Religious content is not every day, but nursery children attend the main school assembly once a week and Christian teachings are included in books, stories and plays. Children appear busy, happy and talkative. They ask questions and relate well to staff and students.

**Remarks** A loving and secure environment, preparing children for their first school. Staff/child ratio of 1:13 does not allow for much individual attention. Happy, lively and well organised, although the headteacher feels they are not organised enough! The local community is expanding rapidly, but nursery provision in the area is not. The long waiting list means many disappointed parents and, more importantly, many children who are not given the opportunity to prepare properly for their first day at 'big school'.

# WHEELGATE HOUSE NURSERY SCHOOL

Trevowah Road
Crantock
Newquay
Cornwall TR8 5RU
**Tel:** (0637) 830680

**Owner/Head:** Gail Wilson, NNEB
**Type:** Private nursery school offering full- and part-time places and half-day sessions and baby crèche for under-2s 3 days a week.
**Children:** 2–7yrs. 24 places. 45 on register
**Hours:** 9am–3.30pm
Morning session 9am–12 noon
Afternoon session 12.30pm–3.30pm
Flexible hours
Open 40 weeks a year
**Status:** Private, fee-paying
**Number of years open:** 4½
**Meals:** Lunch, tea and snacks
**1992 fees:** £50 per week full-time
£30 per week for 3 days
£25 per week for 5 sessions
£15 per week for 3 sessions
£12 per day special rate 8.30am–5pm with meals
£1.50 each extra hour
£1 per day for lunch
£5 registration fee

**Waiting list:** Short. Places available
**Registered by:** Cornwall County Council SS/ changing to Dept for Education

**Premises** In a quiet valley, four miles from Newquay, between Cubert and Crantock. The wooden, purpose-built school is surrounded by an attractive and interesting garden in a pretty, rural setting. There is no public transport, but plenty of parking and turning space for several cars. The nursery occupies a large, airy, sunny room on the ground floor and is comfortably equipped. There is a small, carpeted baby room with cots for the thrice-weekly crèche and a special needs area – unused when we visited, as there were no children with special needs. The pre-prep school for 4½- to 7-year-olds is on the first floor. The garden provides many rich experiences, from a pigsty and chickens to a vegetable garden and pond with ducks and fish. The children use a fenced-in area for play and are supervised when they explore the rest of the 1½ acres. The school has a mini-bus for outings to the park in Newquay and the swimming pool.

**Owner/Head & staff** Gail Wilson, NNEB, is an enthusiastic, bubbly mother of five. She also fosters children and has taken an Open University course in educational psychology. She started the school in her own home, but when demand increased the current premises were built at a cost of £40,000. Parental demand has persuaded her to open a pre-prep section for children up to 7 years old. She employs a staff of three: one full-timer with a nursing qualification and two part-timers who are currently taking PPA and BTEC courses. Outside teachers spend an hour each week at the nursery for music and dance sessions. One of the part-time assistants is a talented artist. It is an intimate and friendly team which meets daily for planning and discussion. The nursery takes one student on placement. The staff/child ratio is 1:5.

**Children & parents** There is no cultural or ethnic mix in the area. Most children come from professional families. The local authority has placed one child from its 'at risk' register at the nursery. Seasonal workers from hotels and the holiday industry take temporary places during the summer months. Until now, children have moved on to local state schools in Cubert, Goonhavern and Newquay, but, according to Gail Wilson, many parents were unhappy with their children's progress at these schools and she hopes that more and more will be moving up into the recently opened Wheelgate House Pre-Prep School. Gail has had special needs experience and will accept children with all but the most severe disabilities. Social workers and health visitors are available to provide necessary back-up. In line with the nursery's strong belief that children function best in small groups of their own age, staff often work on a one-to-one basis with a child. Everyone comes together at least twice a day for stories and outdoor play. There are open days and a summer fête; parents are welcome to ask questions at any time. Children are accepted before they are potty-trained. Parents are not encouraged to stay too long on the first day, as staff feel this upsets the children. The children wear an optional uniform of school sweatshirt, yellow polo shirt and blue skirt or trousers. Small groups of children attend 'play therapy' afternoons, sponsored by the local Social Services.

**Curriculum & activities** Gail Wilson believes that childcare and learning go hand in hand. She and her staff start the learning process as early as possible. After settling into the school for a term, children are introduced to a series of graded worksheets and games. These are popular and, with supervision, help children to develop their confidence and independence. Each half-term a different project is studied (such as new life, weather or pets), which is drawn into various aspects of nursery life. Most of the 4-year-olds are learning to read using the New Way reading scheme. The decision to open the pre-prep section was prompted by the belief that children from Wheelgate were being held back in local schools, which they entered well ahead of their peers in numeracy and literacy. The usual nursery activities such as Lego, painting, junk construction and gluing are always on offer. The classroom walls are papered with colourful, imaginative drawings and paintings. Mobiles hang from the ceiling. Children are read stories for at least 20 minutes each day. Music, creative artwork, physical activities and environmental studies are important, including gardening, pond studies and farming activities. There are no written programmes or timetable, and no qualified early years teacher on the nursery staff. The children's progress is monitored termly and written reports produced for all children over 3½ years old. Parents have access. Physical contact is considered important. 'I want children to feel loved and to be in a homely atmosphere. We have an ancient armchair where children are cuddled when they need it,' the head told us. The school mini-bus is used for outings to farms, adventure playgrounds and the beach, as well as weekly library visits and the swimming club. Music and movement and swimming cost extra. Food is fresh and menus rather unusual. On the day of our visit, pigeon breasts were served for lunch. Fresh vegetables daily, mainly from the nursery's own garden.

**Remarks** Informal, family atmosphere, with a likeable head who enjoys laughing. Children make the most of an outdoor, rural life, visiting the lake (closely supervised), feeding animals and helping to pot plants. Educational programmes would benefit from the training and experience of a qualified nursery teacher – not on the staff at the time of our visit.

# TRELISKE PRE-PREPARATORY SCHOOL

Highertown
Truro
Cornwall TR1 3QN
**Tel:** (0872) 72616

**Owner:** Methodist Board of Management
**Headteacher:** Jane Grassby, Cert Ed
**Type:** Pre-prep section of Truro School offering full- and part-time places. 3yr-olds begin with 2 or 3 days a week
**Children:** 3–7yrs. 70 places. 50 on register
**Hours:** 8.40am–3.30pm
Open 36 weeks a year
**Status:** Private, fee-paying
**Number of years open:** 2
**Meals:** Lunch, tea, snacks
**1992 fees:** £795 per term full-time
Registration fee and deposit
**Waiting list:** Short. Places available
**Registered by:** Dept for Education

**Premises** An attractive, bungalow-style, purpose-built unit in the grounds of Treliske Preparatory School. Built in 1991 in what was the prep school's walled market garden. Willday House, as the pre-prep unit is known, has its own playground within these old walls. It is close to the main school building and surrounded by ten acres of beautiful grounds. The four classrooms, each with its own activity area, are set round a central hall with a specially designed glass roof to let in extra light. All are cheerful and well decorated with attractive curtains, fitted cord carpet and innumerable paintings and friezes covering the walls. There is a quiet/resource room with books and computer, a staff room and cloakrooms for each class. The main hall provides a piano, playhouse, books, interest tables and project displays. The playground, with grassy slopes and attractive old walls, provides a tarmac area for games and climbing frames. Children have daily access to main school facilities such as the indoor heated swimming pool, sports hall, dining room and playing fields.

**Headteacher & staff** Jane Grassby, Cert Ed (currently working on her M Ed), came to Treliske from a local county primary school to set up the new pre-prep section. She works closely with the Head of Treliske School, Russell Hollins, BA, B Ed, Cert Ed, and both report to the Methodist Board of Management in London, who own the school. There are three other qualified teachers and two auxiliaries, one unqualified. Teachers from the main school come over to Willday House each week to teach French, music and dance and cover for holidays and sickness when necessary. Staff meetings are held every Monday evening. They are a close-knit, friendly team, each with their own particular strengths and areas of expertise. NNEB, BTEC and YTS students are accepted. A staff training budget is provided by the secondary school. Teachers attend local county council and prep school courses.

**Children & parents** Nearly all pre-prep children transfer to Treliske main school when they are 7 and from there many will progress to Truro School. Both are co-educational and have day and boarding places. Pre-prep children all wear the navy blue and grey school uniform, and caps and hats are also worn. Parents are local farmers, doctors, dentists and other professionals. They are urged to become involved as much as they can in nursery life, and many become parent-helpers, assisting small groups with computing, cookery and painting. Children are grouped into classes by age, but these tend to break down into mixed-ability, friendship groups. The entire pre-prep school comes together at least once a day for assembly in the hall and sometimes to watch a particular television programme.

**Curriculum & activities** Treliske is a Christian Methodist School, although non-denominational. The daily, half-hour assembly includes Bible stories, and discussions about other religions and cultures. The Rotary motto 'service before self' is used to encourage regular charity work. The school's stated aims are: 'to ensure that numeracy, literacy and oracy are at the heart of the learning programme; to encourage a love of learning; to develop each child's imagination, creativity and sensitivity; and to help each child be self-aware and through this awareness to work amicably with others.' A structured programme of reading, writing and maths forms the core of each day's timetable and the half-termly projects. Shoes were the subject of a recent 'topic plan', which covered everything from designing a pair of mules to constructing the 'Old Woman's Shoe' from Duplo, measuring feet and choosing appropriate box and bag shapes. Another topic, on teddy bears, involved comparing teddies with real bears, discussing where wild bears live and planning a teddy bear's picnic. The school uses the Story Chest series and Ginn reading scheme. Other daily activities include painting and craft, sand and water, rhymes, songs, free play and outdoor play. Full-time children are taken swimming twice a week; the younger part-timers, once a week. Drama, games, PE and music take place once a week. When they leave at the age of 7, most children have a reading age well in advance of their actual age. The nursery is extremely well equipped, with a wide range of stimulating, child-oriented toys, games and computers. The annual equipment budget is generous – five per cent of revenue. Children's progress is carefully monitored on a regular basis and measured against the National Curriculum attainment levels. Parents are given written reports twice a year.

**Remarks** A new nursery providing a very high standard of care and education, with first-rate, purpose-built premises and rich resources. Carefully structured learning programme. Teaching of the 3Rs underpins all activities. Qualified, professional teaching staff and happy, busy and focused children. Treliske offers children a chance to stay in the same school from 3 to 13 years old. Places at Truro School are by competitive entry.

## WINDMILL NURSERY SCHOOL

Railway Terrace
Portreath
Camborne
Cornwall RR14 4LD
**Tel:** (0209) 842158

**Owners:** J & L Driver
M & B Jenkins
**Principal:** Janet Driver, B Phil Ed
**Type:** Day nursery offering full- and part-time places and half-day sessions
**Children:** 12mths–5yrs. 17 places. 50 on register
**Hours:** 8.30am–5.30pm
Morning session 8.30am–12.30pm
Afternoon session 1.30pm–5.30pm
Open 51 weeks a year
**Status:** Private, fee-paying
**Number of years open:** 4
**Meals:** Lunch, snacks
**1992 fees:**
£6.50 per morning session
£6.50 per 3½-hour afternoon session
£4.50 per 2½-hour afternoon session
£2.50 per lunchtime session
**Waiting list:** None
**Registered by:** Cornwall County Council SS

**Premises** A small, double-fronted former shop, on two floors with an adjoining dining room, set in a beautiful coastal village. Downstairs is one main workroom with areas set aside for different activities. Although small, every available space is utilised and the walls and ceiling are covered with colourful, well-designed displays. The tiny, paved front garden is decorated with window boxes and tubs overflowing with pretty coloured flowers. At the front, the huge picture windows of the playroom result in a certain lack of privacy for the children. Upstairs is an office and staff and children's toilets. Most parents bring their children by car – the bus route is seasonal and infrequent. There is easy access to the building with good short-term parking and some long term. Inside is well equipped, clean and recently decorated. At the back there is a newly built, well-fenced play area – concrete slabs with large outdoor toys, an area of wood-shavings underneath, a large slide and a small patch of grass.

**Owner/Principal & staff**  Janet Driver, B Phil Ed, co-owns the nursery and is responsible for the day-to-day running. She is a qualified teacher, with a specialist qualification in special educational needs. After 14 years in the state system working with children with special needs, she decided to adapt her knowledge and experience to under-5s. Her staff consists of two full-time carers and two part-time. Two are qualified NNEBs, two unqualified. The staff/child ratio rarely exceeds 1:4. Staff are consulted on all major issues and have a good relationship with each other and with the children. The nursery is a warm and welcoming place to visit.

**Children & parents**  Children come from a wide area, mainly middle class with a small number funded by Social Services. Parents talk to staff on a daily basis, but the nursery does not organise parents' evenings, open days, plays or concerts. There is a preparation pack for new parents and an informal talk. Parents can return as often as necessary with their child to settle in. Children with disabilities and special educational needs are well integrated and welcome. Janet Driver's expertise in this area is invaluable. Most children go on to state primary schools covering a wide area.

**Curriculum & activities**  The playroom is well equipped with small chairs and desks set together to make group tables. For relaxed activities such as story time or television viewing, there are more comfortable chairs and beanbags. A flexible home corner is regularly adapted to suit new topics. The session begins with constructive play – this can be dramatic, imaginative or domestic and includes pre-reading, writing and number skills, tracing, book work and worksheets. After break, children watch a short television programme and then enjoy outdoor play. Following this, craft activities begin, which can include painting, sticking, printing, making collage and cooking. The session ends with group singing, free play, stories and games. Children are encouraged to choose for themselves and motivated to try as many different activities as possible.

**Remarks**  Smooth-running, efficient small nursery with happy, well-cared-for children. Janet Driver is a formidable combination of good educationalist and good business woman. Committed, friendly staff. Limited by size of premises and actual space available to children.

# Cumbria

A quarter of all 3- and 4-year-olds attend nursery schools or classes part-time, before starting school at rising-5. Nearly 200 playgroups offer further part-time, part-week support. Full daycare is harder to find. Social Services provide four day nurseries for children in need and register a further 38 private nurseries. There are just 19 daycare places for every 1000 children. Most parents in this rural county rely on the extended family, friends or nearly 600 registered childminders.

**Further information**

For details on day nurseries, childminders and playgroups:

Department of Social Services
Lowther Arcade
Lowther Street
Carlisle CA3 8LX
Tel: (0228) 812814

For details on nursery schools, units and classes:

Education Department
5 Portland Square
Carlisle CA1 1PU
Tel: (0228) 23456

# BRAM LONGSTAFFE NURSERY SCHOOL

Island Road
Barrow-in-Furness
Cumbria LA14 2RN
**Tel:** (0229) 821359

**Owner:** Cumbria County Council
**Headteacher:** Ann Hardy, Cert Ed
**Type:** Nursery school offering half-day sessions. No full-time places
**Children:** 3–4½yrs. 208 places. 200 on register
**Hours:** Morning session 9am–11.30am
Afternoon session 1pm–3.25pm
Open 36 weeks a year
**Status:** State nursery school
**Number of years open:** 53
**Meals:** Milk and fruit
**1992 fees:** No fees
**Waiting list:** Minimal
**Registered by:** Cumbria County Council LEA

**Premises** This was the first nursery school in Cumbria, named after a local Labour councillor and former mayor of Barrow, the founder of nursery education in the town. He envisaged a nursery place for every child from the age of three. When the school opened in 1939, it took children from 2 to 4 years old; they attended from 8.30am till 4.30pm. Today there are no full-time places and children attend from the age of 3. A single-storey, C-shaped building, well maintained with a secure, large grass playground, it has four classrooms, with 26 children in each, leading off an internal corridor which runs around the building. Rooms are laid out in identical pairs, each with different resource bases including home and book corners. The library doubles as a television room. Children spill out of their classes into the corridor for messy and wet play. The nursery is close to Vickers dockyards, in a working class/industrial area. There are nearby beaches and nature reserves. Disc parking is available; a school bus delivers children who live more than two miles away.

**Headteacher & staff** Ann Hardy, Cert Ed, has been headteacher for over two years. She teaches full time and is also responsible for the internal organisation, management and control of the school. She is keen to involve the community in school life and would like to offer more flexible opening hours to fit parents' needs. Each class is led by a qualified teacher, with an NNEB nursery assistant. The team of seven female and one male teacher works closely together, offering a range of special skills in art, music and computing. Ancillary staff include a secretary, site manager and cleaner. Ann Hardy calls regular staff meetings to discuss the aims and objectives of the school and plan the curriculum. The nursery is a training establishment and there are always students, under supervision, on a variety of courses; post-graduate, B Ed, NNEB, student nurses and health visitors. Children address them by their Christian names. The school has an annual staff training and development budget of £1,500. The staff/child ratio is 1:13.

**Children & parents** A complete cross-section of the community. Apart from a small group of Americans with parents working in the area, all the children are English. As far as possible, children transferring to the same primary school are grouped together in class. The nursery feeds seven local primary schools. Special needs children have the support of a qualified, specialist teacher, a weekly speech therapist and a learning support teacher. Parents are always welcome in the school, to help with group activities, share books with children and assist staff with clearing up. As Ann Hardy is a teaching headmistress, appointments to see her must be made outside teaching hours. Phasing-in can be done gradually and new parents are invited to observe a session to see how the nursery works.

**Curriculum & activities** The flexible, broad curriculum encourages children to take part in a variety of activities and experiences. Equipment is of good quality and plentiful (annual budget £4000). Activities and themes are planned in advance and designed to develop children's thinking, knowledge, independence and self-confidence. Pre-reading, pre-writing, language and maths skills are practised each session. No reading schemes are followed, but children learn to form letters of the alphabet and recognise and write their own names. If a child is 'reading ready' parents are advised to consult their future primary school for the appropriate reading scheme. Science and a sense of history and geography are taught through projects. Technology and computer education develop confidence with computers. Creative work includes regular music and drama, painting, drawing, collage and modelling and role-playing in pretend situations. Full developmental records are kept and sent home termly and at the end of the year. Physical activity co-ordination and manipulative and motor skills are given free rein in the large, all-grass play area outside. The nursery promotes equal opportunities and recognises all religious and cultural backgrounds. Small groups of children go on local visits related to projects but the school is too big for major outings. Most children live within easy reach of the beach and lakes. There is no hall or space large enough for the school to meet together, but an outdoors 'teddy bears' picnic' is organised each summer for everyone. The school produces a well-illustrated and informative brochure for parents.

**Remarks** The first nursery school to be set up in Cumbria, it is large, well organised and run by a strong team of teachers and carers, dedicated to nursery education and ready to fight to secure its future. The headteacher has ambitions to turn the school into a nursery centre offering a range of care and education, with more flexible hours, catering for the changing needs of the community. Virtually all 3- to 4-year-olds in the area have a part-time nursery place. The nursery school also has a satellite class at South Newbarns Infant School.

# EARLY YEARS I

Castle Park County Primary School
Sedbergh Drive
Kendal
Cumbria LA9 6BE
**Tel:** (0539) 721812

**Owner:** Cumbria LEA
**Headteacher:** Joyce Hill, B Ed, M Sc
**Teacher-in-charge:** Veronica Broyd, Cert Ed
**Type:** Nursery class in state primary school offering half-day sessions. No full-time places
**Children:** 3–4yrs. 26 places. 52 on register
**Hours:** Morning session 9am–11.30am
Afternoon session 1.15pm–3.15pm
Open 40 weeks a year
**Status:** State nursery class
**Number of years open:** 15
**Meals:** None
**1992 fees:** No fees
**Waiting list:** Moderate
**Registered by:** Cumbria County Council LEA

**Premises** Purpose-built, early years unit, comprising a nursery and reception class, in the extensive grounds of Castle Park County Primary School. The school, on a mixed housing estate in a rural area, is within walking distance for most pupils, but a taxi is provided by the local authority for children from outlying areas. Well maintained and decorated, the open-plan nursery divides into three distinct areas. There is a carpeted area for physical and floor play with large, wooden climbing equipment and big wooden toys and cars. The quiet area for imaginative play is full of books, on racks at child-height, and this week the home corner is transformed into a doctor's surgery. The third area is for messy play, and subdivided into separate areas for water, sand, dough and paint. The pet gerbil lives here. A door leads out onto an outside tarmac playground for ride-on toys and a gentle grass slope. The nursery also has use of the school playing fields.

**Teacher-in-charge & staff** Veronica Broyd, Cert Ed, is a dedicated, experienced early years teacher, who has been at the nursery for five years. She believes nursery education is vital. 'It's an extremely important stage in a child's development. If the LEA fails to fund us in the future, we shall do everything we can to carry on. We would also like to come up with a financially viable way of increasing our numbers to meet the demand for places,' she says. Her nursery assistant is a qualified NNEB nursery nurse, hard-working and equally committed to early years education. They say they receive tremendous support from the primary school head and their parent governor. Weekly activities are planned at staff meetings. The staff turnover is low. The head told us, 'We have no difficulty attracting good staff as the school has such an excellent reputation. Staff, including nursery staff, are all considered equally important and are included in all aspects of planning.' NNEB students on work experience attend under supervision. A speech therapist visits the school for half a day each week, and nursery children are referred to her if necessary. Staff/child ratio is 1:13. A limited training budget enables staff to keep up to date with new ideas.

**Children & parents** The main catchment area is the local housing estate, both private and council. Children represent a broad social spectrum, from highly paid professional lies and those working in local industry, to the unemployed. Two places each session are reserved for children with special needs; the nursery has ramps for wheelchair access and disabled toilets. The majority of children move into the reception class next door – Early Years II – and on through the school. Parents are always made to feel welcome and are given time at the beginning and end of each session to talk to staff. Invitations abound to plays, concerts, parents' evenings, outings and events. New parents attend a talk, with slides, and are given an opportunity to look round in the summer before their child joins. There are home visits during a child's first term and parents attend in small groups to observe a session. Phasing-in is gradual, with parental involvement, although independence is encouraged as soon as possible. All children receive a written report in their first term and each summer. Children we observed were happy, noisy and busy. Despite the relatively low staff/child ratio of 1:13, they were focused and supervised.

**Curriculum & activities** The nursery aims to foster confidence, independence and decision-making. Some aspects of the High Scope approach are used and staff draw on research into early years education. They believe that real learning comes from experience. Children are offered many different opportunities for first-hand experiences and are closely observed. All activities are free choice, but staff gently guide children to others if they have been absorbed in one activity for too long. The curriculum is carefully planned around half-termly projects, for example, 'Me and Food', 'Me, People and the Community', 'Me and my Animals', 'Me, the Weather and Clothes'. Each topic is then explored from a range of different angles; creative, physical, moral, spiritual, technological, mathematical, multicultural, social, scientific and communicative. Care is taken to ensure that activities are appropriate to the age group and that they are also progressive and structured. Equipment is plentiful, of high quality, colourful, clearly labelled and easily accessible. Children are made aware of letter sounds and are able to associate words with them. The nursery believes strongly that reading is about understanding and fun, not just about getting the words right. There are no reading schemes. Children tidy up after their chosen activities and spend time together in a group singing, talking and listening to stories. Music and movement, PE and dance are undertaken once a week in the school hall, there are visits to the local post office, farms and transport depots – all linked to project themes. The annual picnic is on a double-decker bus.

**Remarks** Dedicated, enthusiastic staff, committed to the benefits of nursery education. The nursery is an integral part of the whole school. Children and staff are included in many school activities, and children progress naturally to the reception class. Well resourced with a wide variety of experiences and activities on offer. Demand far outstrips supply for nursery places in the town, and outlying areas in particular.

# NORTH WALNEY PRIMARY SCHOOL – NURSERY CLASS

Duddon Drive
Walney Island
Barrow-in-Furness
Cumbria LA14 3TN
**Tel:** (0229) 471781

**Owner:** Cumbria LEA
**Head** John Sharples, Cert Ed
**Teacher-in-charge:** Joyce Rushton, B Ed, Cert Ed, Dip Ed
**Type:** Nursery class in state primary school offering half-day sessions. No full-time places
**Children:** 3–4yrs. 26 places. 52 on register
**Hours:** Morning session 8.50am–11.15am
Afternoon session 12.50pm–3.15pm
Open 36 weeks a year (term-time only)
**Status:** State nursery class
**Number of years open:** 13
**Meals:** Snacks
**1992 fees:** No fees. 20p per week voluntary contribution for cookery and snacks
**Waiting list:** Minimal
**Registered by:** Cumbria County Council LEA

**Premises** Situated in the middle of a bleak council housing estate, next to a boarded-up school, at the end of the island with poor public transport. The nursery is in a purpose-built brick bungalow which is about 14 years old. A link room is being developed to connect the nursery to the main school reception area. Clean and well decorated, the nursery has one large room, divided into areas for different activities. The tiled wet area is used for painting, craft and water play. A large climbing frame dominates the room and is in frequent use. The room is divided into clearly labelled areas. The music area has a low stage, drums and a cassette player with microphone for karaoke sessions. There is a café/shop full of fruit and vegetables to buy; a home corner and ironing board; a quiet area for concentrating on puzzles, drawing and number work; and a well-stocked library. Outside there is a patio and a larger area of grass. Children are carefully supervised out here as the area is not secure. A grassy patch next to the old boarded-up junior school is used for running around. The local park is visited in the summer term, using the school mini-bus.

**Teacher-in-charge & staff** Joyce Rushton, B Ed, Cert Ed, Dip Ed, is enjoying her third year as teacher-in-charge at North Walney. A highly qualified educator, she has many years' experience with special needs children and has worked in a diagnostic unit for 2- to 6-year-olds, studying child development. She says, 'I am totally committed to nursery education. So many people belittle both nursery education and nursery teachers. It's important to emphasise that nursery education requires an intellectual as well as a practical approach to planning and structure. We are definitely not a playgroup.' Joyce works closely with Vicky, an NNEB nursery assistant, who is particularly artistic and has been at the nursery since its inception. NNEB students attend, under supervision. A health visitor, speech therapist and teacher for the hearing impaired visit regularly. The primary school training budget of £4000 is used for in-service courses and conferences for all teachers, including nursery staff.

**Children & parents** The school, which has a broad social mix and small ethnic mix, serves the whole island, covering three or four communities. It has excellent facilities for children with special needs; wheelchair access and disabled loos are available. It also has a very positive attitude towards parental involvement. Open days take place twice a term, and there are regular concerts, shows and parents' evenings. Parents are involved in all nursery activities, with job rotas for parent helpers, a regular newsletter, coffee mornings, and Tupperware parties; mums can also join in Friday afternoon swimming (£1 for mum, free for children). Parents can telephone at any time and children are also allowed to phone home. The partnership and communication between staff and families are close. Children are friendly and talkative, clearly having fun and enjoying themselves.

**Curriculum & activities** The nursery is based on a belief that children should have freedom to explore and grow in a carefully structured environment, without pressure. The nursery takes from the best of the teachings of Mildred Stevens (observe, teach, assess), High Scope (plan, do, review) and Portage (working closely with parents). The National Curriculum Key Stage 1 is kept firmly in mind. Reading and writing are taught, not formally, but through a self-registration process. Having seen their names written on everything they do, children grow to recognise them and by the end of the year they can write them. 'Our planning and provision is the first stage of pre-reading, pre-writing and pre-number skills. Care is taken to give security, reassurance, social and self-help skills,' Joyce Rushton says. A typical session begins with free play, including the opportunity for parents to take part, followed by a choice of structured activities and small-group work. After snacks and tidying up, the big climbing frame is available. Children then sit together to discuss topics and review the morning's achievements. Music and movement, singing and more boisterous activities follow. The session ends quietly in the library for stories and booktime. Two children at a time can ask their parents to join the end of each session. The timetable includes weekly swimming, outings to the local shops and music every day. Children attend main school assemblies, watch suitable videos, enjoy birthday parties, concerts, karaoke sessions and cookery classes and run a book club. The school is regularly visited by the fire brigade, police force, lifeboat service, dentist and school library van. Low-key religious content to the curriculum. 'We emphasise the foundations of spiritual life and introduce the concept of God.' Children's progress and development are monitored regularly, recorded monthly and reviewed each term. Parents participate in this process and have access to all files. A playgroup is run next door, supervised by Joyce Rushton, for 40 2- to 3-year-olds who are likely to attend the nursery class the following year.

**Remarks** A wonderful, happy atmosphere. Excellent relationship between the teacher and the nursery nurse. Good variety and high standard of child-centred equipment. The location is dreary and the outside area needs further attention, but these are minor details compared with the quality of pre-school education offered. More nursery schools like this one are needed on the island.

## ST AIDAN'S SCHOOL DAY NURSERY

St Aidan's School
Lismore Place
Carlisle CA1 1LY
**Tel:** (0228) 810959

**Owner:** St Aidan's Day Nursery Trust
**Manager:** Janice Hill, NNEB
**Type:** Day nursery offering full- and part-time places
**Children:** 6mths–5yrs. 23 places. 47 on register
**Hours:** 8am–6pm
Open 52 weeks a year
**Status:** Private, fee-paying, non profit-making
**Number of years open:** 3
**Meals:** Breakfast, lunch, tea, snacks
**1992 fees:** £90 per week full-time – under 2
£75 per week full-time – 2–3yrs
£63.50 per week full-time – over 3
Pro rata daily rate
**Waiting list:** Reasonable. About 15 names
**Registered by:** Cumbria County Council SS

**Premises** A joint venture between St Aidan's High School and the Midland Bank, the nursery provides an invaluable community service for working mothers. Five minutes' walk from the town centre, it is situated inside the school, in what used to be the cookery room, staffroom, kitchen and toilets and has a separate entrance and fenced-off play areas. The nursery comprises one large L-shaped room, dazzlingly bright, with two walls almost entirely windows. The room is divided into activity areas for craft, messy play, home corner, television, book corner, table toys and floor toys. There is also a bedroom, with rows of travel cots and beds, and a kitchen. Bright and welcoming, the nursery was completely refurbished two years ago and is in pristine condition. The walls are covered in colourful, creative artwork and displays. Children let off steam in a private, paved outdoor play area, used for bikes and trikes. There is also a 'park area' within the school grounds, used exclusively by nursery children. It contains a large sandpit, swings and a climbing frame, fixed above bark chips and protected by a beech hedge. The local park, a five-minute walk away, is visited twice a week.

**Manager & staff** Janice Hill, NNEB, has 20 years' experience caring for children. She has worked in Social Services day nurseries and a residential home for mentally handicapped children. She makes most of the day-to-day decisions, but overall responsibility for the nursery lies with a group of trustees. Seven staff, including two part-timers, are all qualified NNEBs. The team is happy and friendly, each contributing different skills, including artistic and musical (trombone and recorder). Special needs assistants and support workers attend for several hours a week and two NNEB students are present on placement. Monthly staff meetings are held in the evenings or at weekends. No staff development policy or budget, although both would be welcomed by workers. Very few courses are available in the area. The nursery belongs to the National Private Day Nurseries Association and hopes to start training initiatives with other association members.

**Children & parents** Professional working parents, from shopkeepers, nurses and clerical workers to bankers and building society managers. The Midland Bank uses eight places. Families travel in from up to ten miles away and parents work in Carlisle. Special needs children are well integrated; there are children with severe epilepsy, fragile X syndrome and visual impairment currently attending. A keyworker system is in operation. When a keyworker goes on leave, she leaves behind meticulous reports on her children. These are also available to parents. There are two parent representatives on the management board, alongside school staff, governors and Midland Bank representatives. There is at least one social event a term and the door is always open to parents.

**Curriculum & activities** The programme of activities reflects the wide range of ages and the children's differing needs. There is no formal teaching, although there are opportunities for the older children to do group work on numbers, colours, shapes, pre-reading and pre-writing skills. Learning is relaxed and nothing is forced on the children. Activities are geared to their interests and all play is considered educationally important. The programme allows each child to take part in creative and messy play, art and craft, constructional play, music and storytime. *Playbus* is watched in the mornings and dance, keep fit and aerobics are done at least three times a week. Afternoons are craft orientated and children sleep or rest after lunch. The importance of outdoor play is emphasised, and children play outside every day. Regular outings to local parks, town centre, Blackpool Zoo, roly poly clubs and library in the school mini-bus.

**Remarks** A professional and loving environment for children and parents. The nursery's position in a secondary school offers interesting opportunities for mixing with older children. The children are happy and outgoing, mixing naturally with special needs children. An invaluable service for working parents in a city where provision is totally inadequate, and a good example of how childcare partnerships can work.

# ST CUTHBERTS (RC) SCHOOL – NURSERY UNIT

East End
Wigton
Cumbria CA7 9HZ
**Tel:** (06973) 43119

**Owner:** Cumbria County Council
**Headteacher:** Sister Catherine, Cert Ed
**Teacher-in-charge:** Olivia Verwoerd, BA, PGCE
**Type:** Nursery unit attached to primary school offering half-day sessions (max 3 sessions a week)
**Children:** 3–4yrs. 26 places. 78 on register
**Hours:** Morning session 9am–11.30am
Afternoon session 12.45pm–3.15pm
Open 38 weeks a year
**Status:** State nursery class
**Number of years open:** 19
**Meals:** None
**1992 fees:** No fees. £1 a week voluntary contribution for snacks

**Waiting list:** Reasonable. Preference to Roman Catholics and siblings
**Registered by:** Cumbria County Council LEA

**Premises** Situated on the edge of town, overlooking fields and meadows from the back, the school serves three large housing estates, a mixture of council and private. It is on a busy main road, with strictly enforced traffic regulations and no public transport. The red brick unit is self-contained and set in a large grass and tarmac playground. The cheerful, airy, open-plan classroom is divided into separate work bases: one tiled for art, craft and baking; one carpeted for constructive play; and a home corner with pine furniture, piles of books and dressing-up clothes. Plenty of good-quality equipment (£5000 recently spent), but not overcrowded or cluttered.

**Teacher-in-charge & staff** Olivia Verwoerd, BA, PGCE, an experienced early years teacher, has recently taken over as teacher-in-charge. Her NNEB assistant is long-serving, with 20 years' experience and a close relationship with parents and the local community. BTEC students attend on placement most days, supervised by Olivia Verwoerd and their college tutors. Male role models are considered important and fathers are encouraged to help in the classroom as often as possible. Staff development programme and budget. Staff are all first-aiders and have High Scope training.

**Children & parents** The children come from a range of backgrounds and a large catchment area, as there are few nursery schools in the district. Many, but not all, are from Roman Catholic families. The majority transfer to local authority primary schools, while about 30 stay on at St Cuthberts. The serious disadvantage is that, because of demand for places, no child can attend for more than three sessions a week. Sessions are allocated according to whether children are from the immediate catchment area or come from further afield by car. Children with special needs are accepted only if they have a helper. Children wear a school uniform – red jumpers and grey skirts or trousers. Parents are encouraged to take part in assemblies and to visit, within reason, but not to stay for too long. They also help in the classroom when appropriate. There is an active parent/teacher group. New families receive an informal home visit and an introductory meeting at the nursery; children are phased-in, in groups of six, over the first few weeks of the autumn term. Relationships between staff, parents and children appear to be particularly good.

**Curriculum & activities** The nursery follows the High Scope method of plan, do and review. The timetable each week is carefully planned in advance to offer a rich variety of activities, which will prepare children for school. The day begins with free choice. Children plan their tasks – cooking, painting, sticking, threading, puzzles, peg boards, bricks, pull-along toys, home corner, etc. To avoid overcrowding, badges are supplied for each activity. Once all the badges have been allocated, no one else can join that activity. Staff guide and support, but try to keep a low profile and encourage independence. Children then come together to discuss what has been achieved and to tidy up. The main school hall is used for a session of music, movement, songs, PE or dance. Snack time is followed by work in small groups – matching, sorting, projects following themes and books. Books are plentiful, high quality and always available to look at and talk about. In the summer term children are taught to recognise letters, and are shown letter formation. No reading schemes are followed. Each session ends with religious instruction. Each half-term follows a religious theme, related to the current topic. Prayers and religious stories are an important daily ingredient. Children's progress is monitored carefully and recorded in writing. Parents are sent a report at the end of each year, together with some examples of their child's achievements.

**Remarks** An excellent nursery following the High Scope method. Plenty of opportunity for free expression and self-development in a structured, kindly and disciplined environment. Busy, fulfilled children and happy staff.

# Derbyshire

Half of all children under 5 in Derbyshire have some form of childcare provision open to them. The county is proud of giving mothers every possible support to return to work. The number of day nurseries has increased to 66 during the last few years, of which 16 are Family Support Centres run by the local authority. There are 17 local authority nursery schools and a further 9000 places in nursery classes and units attached to primary schools. Parents can also choose from 1600 registered childminders and over 300 playgroups. It sounds good, and has one of the best records. However, one parent told us, 'It depends entirely on where you live. Some parts of Derby, for example, have no provision, although in a few cases schools will take children early.'

**Further information**

For details on day nurseries, childminders and playgroups:
Department of Social Services
County Offices
Matlock DE4 3AG
Tel: (0629) 580000

For details on nursery schools, units and classes:
Education Department
(address and telephone as above)

# BUSY BEE DAY NURSERY

Newholme Hospital
Baslow Road
Bakewell
Derbyshire DE45 1AD
**Tel:** (0629) 814166

**Owner:** North Derbyshire Health Authority (Dales Locality)
**Manager:** Cathy Walker, NNEB
**Type:** Workplace nursery offering full- and part-time places to hospital staff and local community
**Children:** 3mths–5yrs. 30 places. 70 on register
**Hours:** 8am–5.30pm
Flexible hours
Open 48 weeks a year
**Status:** Private, non profit-making
**Number of years open:** 2
**Meals:** Lunch, tea, snacks
**1992 fees:** £14 per day full-time
£8 per morning session inc lunch
£11 per afternoon session inc lunch
£20 registration fee
**Waiting list:** Moderate
**Registered by:** Currently exempt as owned by Health Authority

**Premises** A delightful, grade II listed building, dating from 1841. Single-storey, built of Derbyshire stone, with mullioned windows, it was formerly a workhouse connected to the main hospital. The building provides a large activity room for babies and toddlers with a separate sleep area, and another even more spacious room for older children, plus kitchen, loos, storeroom and office. The baby room has a feeding area with non-slip floor and soft, carpeted play space, prettily decorated with murals and balloon-patterned curtains. There are cots for babies and mattresses for toddlers who need to sleep. The room is overflowing with brightly coloured toys, small slides, a trampoline and ride-on toys. The activity room for 2- to 5-year-olds is large and lofty, with two tiers of windows on both sides. Natural light pours in. The room is carpeted, except for a messy-play area, well furnished with child-sized tables and chairs and plenty of toys. The ceiling is very high and staff have stretched ropes across at normal ceiling height to provide hanging space for artwork. There is a good home corner and a quiet corner for naps and reading books. The outside play space, supplied with swings and climbing equipment, comprises a tarmac area for pedal toys and a small field for children to run in.

**Manager & staff** Cathy Walker, NNEB, a former nursery officer at Sheffield's Northern General Hospital and subsequently a playgroup supervisor, heads a team of eight, whom she describes as a 'lovely, bubbly bunch of girls'; all are NNEB qualified. There are also a few NNEB students on release courses from the local college and youngsters from the local comprehensive gaining work experience for childcare courses. The nursery operates as a training centre for childcare students, who are always supervised. Two nursery workers can sign for the deaf and some have first-aid training. Cathy reports to hospital manager, Brenda MacDonald, who was responsible for setting up the nursery. There is a very happy atmosphere at this nursery. Children and staff show genuine fondness for one another.

**Children & parents** Children come from a variety of backgrounds, mainly professional, or hospital and health service staff. They go on to local primaries, with some going to a private prep school in the area. In most cases, both parents work and this is something the nursery tries to take into account at all times. There are no inconvenient evening parents' meetings. Instead parents are made welcome in the nursery throughout the day and can speak to staff, or Cathy Walker, at any time without an appointment. Parents are encouraged to ring whenever they wish, if they are worried about their child. During our visit children appeared happy and busy, making good use of all the equipment and activities on offer.

**Curriculum & activities** A nursery policy of learning through play, though Cathy Walker would like to see a more structured approach for the older children. The Letterland reading scheme is used for letter recognition, and 5-year-olds are able to write and recognise their names. Themes are used to provide a focus to learning activities and there is plenty of creative and constructive play. Parents receive a termly record of their child's development and achievements. The nursery is strong on art and craft and there is some music every day. Children are taken on trips to the local park and library and go shopping for ingredients that are then used during baking sessions. A hot lunch, with two choices of main dish (one vegetarian)

and a pudding, is provided by the hospital. Snacks are prepared at the nursery. Special dietary needs can be catered for. Parents provide pre-prepared formula for babies.
**Remarks** Professional, caring service, with flexible hours to suit working parents. Places allocated on a first come first served basis. High-quality care at a reasonable price.

## GAMESLEY PRE-SCHOOL CENTRE

Winster Mews
Gamesley
Glossop
Derbyshire SK13 0LU
**Tel:** (0457) 865262
**Owner:** Derbyshire County Council
**Head of centre:** Lynn Kennington, B Ed
**Type:** Community nursery centre offering full- and part-time places and half-day sessions, plus parents' group and classes, toy library and parent and toddler group
**Children:** 0–5yrs. 80 places. 120 on register
**Hours:** 8am–5pm
Morning session 9am–11.30am
Afternoon session 1pm–3.30pm
Open 51 weeks a year
**Status:** State community centre
**Number of years open:** 20
**Meals:** Breakfast, lunch, tea, snacks
**1992 fees:** No fees. 65p per day for lunch for those not entitled to free meals
**Waiting list:** 70 under-3s, less demand for over-3s
**Registered by:** Derbyshire County Council SS

**Premises** Purpose-built, modern, open-plan nursery centre attached to a community hall, library and medical facilities, all serving the Gamesley Council Estate, an area designated as one of social priority. The nursery is bright, light and colourfully decorated with children's work. There is a large activity area, divided by movable units into a wet-play area, quiet area with books, two smaller group activity areas and a quiet room. Babies are in an adjoining room, with their own separate facilities. Each area is well equipped. One of the outside play areas has been recently resurfaced with astroturf, layers of sand and a synthetic fibre wall. There are three outdoor play houses, a slide and numerous ride-on toys. The under-3s have a rabbit and a guinea pig to look after.
**Head & staff** Lynn Kennington, B Ed (currently studying for a Masters degree), has been head of the centre for seven years. An experienced infant teacher, nursery teacher and community leader, with two children of her own, she is ably supported by a deputy, three supervisors, a community tutor and 13 nursery nurses. All the staff at the centre are well qualified and two of the NNEBs have additional CSS social work qualifications. There are three qualified teachers. Lynn reports to a board of governors, made up of representatives from health, Social Services, the LEA, centre staff, the community and parents. They meet three times a year. The majority of staff are mature women, and the nursery has an extremely happy atmosphere. Centre workers attend regular, relevant training courses and a team of peripatetic support staff, employed by the council, is available when required. There are four midday supervisors to cover during lunch each day. Students studying for NNEB, teaching or social work diplomas and trainee health visitors all come on placement for work experience. A highly professional, multi-disciplinary team.
**Children & parents** The school's intake is predominantly working class, all white, with limited cultural diversity. A high number of children come from single-parent families and parents who are unemployed. The centre aims to involve parents in the education and care of their children as much as possible, and offers help and support to the whole family. A member of staff visits new children at home prior to starting. Parents regularly meet together in groups, attend classes, go on outings with the children and help with fund-raising. There is a newsletter for information. The children are happy, talkative and very well supervised. Each has a keyworker to take care of their overall needs. Many children receive extra language help when they start at the centre. The nursery is waiting for a ramp for wheelchair access, but otherwise it can cater for children with disabilities and draw on the back-up services of the local authority. Children all move on to state primary schools, usually to Gamesley or to St Margaret's, Dinting.
**Curriculum & activities** The curriculum

is planned around play, language and experimental learning based on the philosophies of a number of early-learning gurus – Froebel, Steiner, Montessori and Vygotsky. Aspects of the High Scope method are used to encourage children to become decision-makers and to 'plan, do and review' their activities. It is an active learning process. The environment is carefully planned, with everything at child height, so that each child always has a wide range of choices available. The nursery is extremely well equipped, with every conceivable area of play, art, craft and creative activities covered. Annual equipment budget £3680. Parents are encouraged to participate. At the beginning of a session, they plan the choice of activities with their child, and at the end they discuss with them what has been achieved. There is daily storytime, dance and movement, music and outdoor play. Time is set aside especially for cuddles. Reading is not formally taught, though children are encouraged to develop their own early learning skills and are introduced to books from the Story Chest and the Oxford Reading Tree. There are occasional trips out with parents. All meals are prepared on the premises, in a spotless kitchen.

**Remarks**  A much-needed and well-used community facility, offering all-round family support. The centre encourages positive parenting, as well as providing high-quality childcare. Highly professional, multi-disciplinary team with a good support network. When resources allow, the centre hopes to acquire a computer for the children and a qualified teacher for the under-3s.

## LITTLE ACORNS DAY NURSERY

10 Thornhill Road
Derby DE3 3LX
**Tel:** (0332) 46088

**Owner/Principal:** Sarah Flinton, NNEB
**Type:** Day nursery offering full-time and part-time places and half-day sessions
**Children:** 3mths–5yrs. 35 places. 70 on register
**Hours:** 8am–6pm
Morning session 8am–12.15pm
Afternoon session 1.15pm–6pm
Open 51 weeks a year

**Status:** Private, fee-paying
**Number of years open:** 3½
**Meals:** Breakfast, lunch, tea, snacks
**1992 fees:** £75 per week full-time – under 2
£65 per week full-time – over 2
£16 per day
**Waiting list:** Small, but places cannot be guaranteed
**Registered by:** Derbyshire County Council SS

**Premises**  A pleasant, Victorian semi, with a large garden, converted into a nursery three years ago, it is set in a quiet side street in a leafy, residential part of Derby. The nursery offers three rooms for 2- to 5-year-olds, a baby room, toddlers' play room and dining room. All newly decorated to a high standard, it is light, bright and attractive. The baby room is divided into play and sleep areas, prettily decorated in pink and white and well furnished with cots, bouncing chairs, play mats and toys. Toddlers have a good-sized room, with play house and piles of toys, warmly carpeted and with lively murals on the walls. There is an extra room, with kitchenette, for meals and to use as additional play space. Older children use a cheerful room at the front of the house for free play, singing and dancing, storytime and television. They have their own play house and shelves full of games, books and toys. The 'Jungle', with jungle-pattern wallpaper and parrot decorations, is furnished with tables and chairs for writing, worksheets and constructive play. It doubles as a dining room at lunchtime. An art and craft room is used for messy play – sand, water, painting and craft. Outside, children can run about in a large, pleasant, grassy, walled garden, with a paved area for ride-on toys. There is also climbing equipment, swings, a play house and a sandpit.

**Owner/Principal & staff**  Sarah Flinton runs the nursery with the help of her husband, who handles the finances and maintenance work. She is NNEB qualified and has years of experience working in a nursery school and with special needs children. She employs a staff of nine – six NNEB qualified and three experienced childcare workers. YTS students help out from time to time. Staff are recruited through advertisements in local papers, and Mrs Flinton emphasises that qualifications are not always as important as experience. She looks for patience, an outgoing personality and a real liking for children. Most staff have been at the nursery since it opened and seem motivated to stay. There is no qualified teacher on the staff. All are young, jolly and smartly dressed in matching dark green sweatshirts bearing the nursery logo. They are kind and caring and have a good rapport with the children. Staff are encouraged to use their initiative and ideas.

**Children & parents** The children come from middle to high income families; a third of mothers work. Nearly all are white and British, and only a handful come from different ethnic backgrounds. The nursery would be happy to welcome children with special needs, and could cope with wheelchairs, but none attend at present. Children, who come from a wide catchment area, move on to state primaries or local private schools. After three years, the nursery has found it no longer needs to advertise widely, generally depending on word of mouth for new entrants. Parents are encouraged to talk to staff on a daily basis – there are no formal parents' evenings or meetings. A regular newsletter keeps parents up to date with nursery activities. Monthly diaries are kept on the progress and achievements of older children. Weekly records are kept for babies.

**Curriculum & activities** A learning through play approach. Mrs Flinton feels that formal education will start soon enough and wants children to enjoy themselves. Older children follow a pre-school learning programme, but there is no attempt to push them if they are not ready. By the time they leave at the age of 5, children can write and recognise their names, but there is no pressure to progress any further. There is a pre-school activities session every day in the 'Jungle' – usually first thing in the morning when children are fresh and alert. The timetable also includes a session of educational activities – colour, number and picture games, construction toys, drawing and writing skills. The rest of the day is taken up with art and craft, singing and dancing, stories, television, outdoor play and free play. During our visit, children were happily and busily occupied in small groups, supervised by a carer, and appeared to be thoroughly absorbed and having fun. A hot lunch is provided daily, cooked by Auntie Mavis. Special diets are catered for. Children stop for a mid-morning drink and snack and have a tea of sandwiches, biscuits and cake at 4pm. Under-2s are offered breakfast. Bottle feeds are made up at the nursery.

**Remarks** A delightful nursery with a truly homely atmosphere and stimulating activities.

## SUNSHINE DAY NURSERY

Walton Hospital
Whitecoats Lane
Walton
Chesterfield S40 3HN
**Tel:** (0246) 277271 × 5526
(0246) 208283

**Owner:** North Derbyshire Health Authority
**Manager:** Susan Hayley Buckley, NNEB, CPQS
**Type:** Workplace nursery offering full- and part-time places and half-day sessions to Walton hospital employees and local community
**Children:** 6mths–5yrs. 75 places. 180 on register
**Hours:** 7.30am–5.30pm
Morning session 7.30am–1pm (inc lunch)
Afternoon session 1pm–5.30pm
Open 52 weeks a year
**Status:** Fee-paying health authority nursery
**Number of years open:** 3
**Meals:** Breakfast, lunch, tea and snacks
**1992 fees:** £12.40 per day
£6.20 per session
£15 registration fee
**Waiting list:** Very long
**Registered by:** Derbyshire County Council SS

# Devon

No local authority day nurseries. The council subsidises places in private services for children in serious need. There are 52 private nurseries, concentrated mainly in Exeter and the coastal areas, with minimal waiting lists and fees of up to £80 per week. There is little choice for the average or low-paid worker. One council employee told us, 'If you were a mother of a two-year-old and you were offered a job, you would probably panic.' Pre-school education follows no clear pattern – some areas have no nursery units in their primary schools, while others have good provision, for no apparent reason. Only 12 per cent of 3- and 4-year-olds have access to one of the 60 nursery units attached to primary schools. Priority is given to children in need.

**Further information**

For details on day nurseries, childminders and playgroups, contact the Under Eights Development Officer through one of the 34 local Social Services offices. Details from:
Department of Social Services
County Hall
Topsham Road
Exeter EX2 4QR
Tel: (0392) 382563

For details on nursery schools, units and classes:
Education Department
(address as above)
Tel: (0392) 382000

## APPLEDORE NURSERY CLASS

Appledore Primary School
Richmond Road
Appledore
Bideford
North Devon EX39 1PF
**Tel:** (0237) 474365
**Owner:** Devon County Council
**Headteacher:** Malcolm Elliott, B Ed, Dip M Ed, CAPS (Certificate in Advanced Professional Studies)
**Nursery Teacher:** Wanda Moffat, Cert Ed
**Type:** Nursery class in state primary school offering morning sessions
**Children:** 3–4½yrs. 26 places. 26 on register
**Hours:** 9am–11.30am
Open 38 weeks a year
**Status:** State nursery class
**Number of years open:** 5
**Meals:** None
**1992 fees:** No fees. 25p voluntary contribution per week for cookery
**Waiting list:** Minimal. Most will secure a place. Register after 2nd birthday
**Registered by:** Devon County Council LEA

**Premises** Open-plan classroom in a modern primary school, part-shared with the reception class. The room is clean, colourful and inspiring, despite a shortage of space. Exciting, three-dimensional displays and children's work decorate the walls. The home corner is shared with the reception class, and messy play takes place outside in a covered area. Generous outdoor facilities offer playgrounds, fields, an open-air swimming pool and a wood for summer picnics. Wide, light corridors are used for computer work, cookery and interest displays.
**Nursery teacher & staff** Wanda Moffat, Cert Ed, has been at Appledore for just over two years, having previously worked in multi-racial, inner-city day nurseries in Liverpool and Leicestershire. She sees her role as innovative, 'to devise new and interesting ways of making learning fun'. Particularly concerned with equal opportunities, she has issued staff with 25 'intervention strategies' to encourage non-stereotypic attitudes towards boys and girls. These include useful advice such as, 'Never divide children into boys and girls for any activities. Introduce mixed sports, teach creative knitting to boys as well as girls, and invite male/female visitors in non-traditional occupations/roles.' The nursery's NNEB

assistant is Adele Behn, a calm young mother and experienced nursery nurse who works at another nursery in the afternoons. Both women confirm that much of the nursery's success is due to the support and commitment to good nursery provision of the headteacher, Malcolm Elliot. Staff meetings are held weekly and there is an annual staff INSET budget of £1100. The staff/child ratio is 1:13; parents are encouraged to assist in the nursery for appropriate activities.

**Children & parents** A wide social mix, reflecting the local area. Children stay at the school, moving on to the reception class at rising-5. Open door policy towards parents, who regularly volunteer to help out in the classroom. Fathers and grandparents are particularly welcome. Clear step-by-step instruction sheets allow families to learn how to use the computers, alongside their children. Home visits are arranged before new children begin. Nursery staff discuss the role of play in early learning and explain nursery procedures and phasing-in plans. They also advise parents on how to support their child's development at home and reinforce nursery learning. Children are encouraged to wear a uniform in the school colours of navy, red and sky blue. An active PTA raises funds for equipment and the maintenance of the swimming pool. A mother and toddler group, the Beehive Club, meets in the school hall on Tuesday afternoons to introduce future entrants to the school atmosphere in an informal way.

**Curriculum & activities** Learning through play, with the National Curriculum core subjects (English, Maths and Science) and foundation subjects (technology, art, history, geography, music and PE) very much in mind. Activities are ongoing throughout the morning, beginning with registration, news, discussion, storytime, songs and rhymes for the whole class. Strong emphasis on art and craft with a difference. Children were absorbed in making wonderful three-dimensional fluorescent string sculptures when we visited. Three times a week, there is food preparation – sandwich making, soups, pizza, birthday cakes and cheese snails (a favourite). Children are given clearly written recipes to take home. Pre-writing and pre-reading skills are practised regularly. The school hall is used daily by small groups of seven or eight children for PE, movement, dance or drama. There is music and songs daily, swimming in the school pool in the summer term and regular outings to the library, Westward Ho rock pools and anywhere relevant to the current themes or projects. Books can be borrowed each day and educational games, geared to developing particular skills, are taken home at weekends. Nursery staff are currently working together to devise a new, more workable system of record keeping to assess individual development and progress.

**Remarks** An impressive nursery class, with dedicated staff and helpful parents, totally supported by the headteacher. Children are clearly happy and challenged, valued for their thoughts, ideas and creations.

## HIGHWEEK NURSERY

Highweek County Primary School
Coronation Road
Newton Abbot
South Devon TQ12 1TX
**Tel:** (0626) 65550

**Owner:** Devon County Council LEA
**Nursery Teacher:** Jenny Buckle, Cert Ed (retired)
Diana Breund, Cert Ed
**Type:** Nursery class in state primary school offering morning sessions
**Children:** 3yrs 4mths–4yrs 10mths. 20 places. 20 on register
**Hours:** 9am–11.30am
Open 38 weeks a year
**Status:** State nursery class
**Number of years open:** 10
**Meals:** Mid-morning snack
**1992 fees:** No fees
**Waiting list:** 50 currently awaiting places. Termly allocation by selection panel
**Registered by:** Devon County Council LEA

**Premises** Across a tarmac playground, in the middle of a large council housing estate, and in a mobile classroom adjoining the primary school. There the greyness ends. Inside is clean, colourful, fresh and bright. Staff and parents work hard to create and maintain high standards for the premises. The small entrance lobby somehow manages to accommodate cloakroom, toilets, woodwork table and technology area. The classroom itself has windows on both sides, and a part carpeted, part washable floor for clean and messy play. The outdoor play space is small, an area between buildings, fenced at one end. There are two sheds, one for outdoor play equipment (no bikes though), the other for a toy library, open several times a week. The nursery also has use of the primary school facilities – a lush orchard, pond and conservation area – and shared use of playing fields across the road, attached to another school.

**Nursery teacher & assistant** When we visited Highweek, Jenny Buckle, Cert Ed, Froebel trained, was the nursery teacher in charge, assisted by nursery nurse Grace Job, NNEB. At the time of writing, Jenny is preparing to retire after 15 years as Devon's playgroup advisor and ten years as head of the nursery. She has also taken a leading role in setting up toy libraries across the county. Jenny Buckle will be greatly missed, but she leaves behind a nursery which is one of the best examples of good practice in the area. Her replacement is Diana Breund, Cert Ed. Jenny and Grace are a peripatetic team working mornings at Highweek and afternoons at a neighbouring nursery class. (Lack of funds prevents either nursery from providing full-time facilities despite prodigious waiting lists and overwhelming demand.) Staff attend Devon Education Authority in-service training days and an annual conference for all those working in under-5s education. Staff meetings are held weekly to plan themes, activities, outings and general procedures. Both teachers also attend staff meetings at the primary school and meetings of the school governors' nursery sub-group – the body responsible for major policy decisions at the nursery. The nursery accepts NNEB students for practical training.

**Children & parents** Highweek Nursery is used mainly by families on the large local council estate and a few in private housing. Children with special needs are a high priority for nursery education, so may come from further afield. There are many social problems. Until this class is made full-time, most of the 50 children on the waiting list will never get a place. Allocation is through a selection panel which meets termly. Developmental, behavioural and speech problems are common but children appear happy and relaxed. They progress readily to the infant school, having been well integrated already through using the gym every day and joining other main school activities throughout the year. Parents are actively involved and very welcome. They regularly help in the classroom, on a rota basis (dads are particularly supportive); attend family school assemblies, parents' evenings and open days, and provide extra pairs of hands on outings and swimming visits. Once or twice a term, parents come in to discuss their child's progress in maths, language, social skills, etc, on a more formal basis. Termly coffee mornings help to introduce new parents to each other, the staff and the system.

**Curriculum & activities** Learning through carefully structured play, aimed at teaching good habits, such as listening, concentrating, completing an activity and social skills. Scientific and mathematical concepts are acquired through sand and water play, woodwork, brick play, songs and rhymes. Parental involvement is considered vital. Plenty of opportunity for children to choose from many activities and experiences. Different stimulating environments have been carefully created: a cosy book corner, with children snuggled up on a settee, house plants, framed pictures on the wall and well-displayed, beautifully kept books; a home corner, with kitchen, table and boudoir; a music table, complete with stereo and record collection; and construction and table-top activities. Messy play is always available in some form – sand, water, painting, clay. Woodwork and technology – ie junk modelling, cutting and sticking – are always on offer and children can use the wall display areas themselves. Independence is encouraged in many ways. Children keep their own file of drawings and work. Adult-led group activities take place daily on the term's theme ('Homes' this term), ensuring all children have group work experience, learning to share and co-operate, express themselves and communicate with staff. Art is child-led – the huge wall display is clearly all their own work. The highlight of the morning is 'Cafe time', the mid-morning snack. The children organise a waiter/waitress rota and have a long menu, written and visual, to help with early reading skills. They all take part in preparing the food, for example spreading peanut butter or making biscuits. Music and movement follow in the school gym. There are weekly visits to the nearby swimming pool and other outings two or three times a term. Storytime is held in the local library once a fortnight.

**Remarks** An excellent nursery class in every way and one of the best examples of good practice in the county. The tragedy is that only 20 children benefit, for only 2½ hours a day. With scores of South Devon children waiting for nursery places it is absurd that this excellent resource is forced to close down in the afternoons. Primary head, Neil Graham, says, 'It would cost just an extra £10,000–£12,000 a year to open the nursery full-time and we could double our numbers.' The ball is now firmly in Devon Education Authority's court.

## LANHERNE SCHOOL NURSERY DEPARTMENT

Lanherne School
18 Longlands
Dawlish
Devon EX7 9NG
**Tel:** (0626) 863091

**Owner/Principal:** Pamela Robins, Mont Dip, Cert Ed
**Nursery Director:** Celia Hazeldene, Mont Dip, DPQS
**Type:** Nursery school attached to co-ed prep school offering full- and part-time places and morning sessions, plus out-of-school and holiday play schemes
**Children:** 2–5yrs. 30 places. 37 on register. Open 52 weeks a year (excl Christmas Day)
**Hours:** 9am–3pm
Morning session 9am–12 noon
Out of school care 8am–6pm
Holiday playscheme 9am–1pm
**Status:** Private, fee-paying
**Number of years open:** 13
**Meals:** Lunch, tea, snacks
**1992 fees:** £480 per term full-time
£375 per term for 5 morning sessions a week
25% sibling discount
**Waiting list:** None
**Registered by:** Dept for Education

**Premises** A handful of pre-school children in one room of a large Edwardian house has grown, over 13 years, into a small preparatory school. The nursery has taken over the whole of the ground floor of the house. Three wooden huts in the grounds accommodate the rest of the school. A large wooden classroom is used by all children for music, movement, dance, craft and technology and as a dining room. Four rooms are used by the nursery. A large classroom with lino floor for the rising-5s, with small tables and chairs, table-top toys and shelves of books. The 2- to 3-year-olds have an equally large, cosily carpeted room, with tables, home corner and space for floor toys. Across the hall there is a kitchen and a room for art and messy play. Although the premises are in need of some redecoration, the atmosphere is generally homely and stimulating. The nursery is clean and light, with big windows in most rooms. There is a good-sized garden.

**Nursery Director & staff** Celia Hazeldene, Mont Dip, runs the nursery school and is also the owner's daughter. The two other team members are a qualified teacher, Cert Ed, and a City & Guilds qualified nursery nurse. NNEB and BTEC students are regular attenders on placement from Torquay and Exeter colleges. There are no regular staff meetings, but children's needs and development are discussed daily. Specialist teachers visit the nursery for dance, music, Tumble Tots, swimming and French. Staff/child ratio 1:10.

**Children & parents** The children come from dual-income, working families and are driven in from Teignmouth or Dawlish. All attend for a minimum of five mornings a week and most move into the prep school at the age of 5. There is a strong Parents' Association, which organises two or three fund-raising events a term. Raising money for charity is an important part of the school's philosophy. It has an open-door policy towards parents, who can visit, telephone, attend parents' evenings and help with outings and activities. A regular newsletter keeps them in touch with nursery life. All children wear a grey school uniform.

**Curriculum & activities** There is an assembly every morning, followed by free play. The nursery loosely follows the Montessori approach to learning and play. Children are allowed to choose and initiate their own activities, including sand play, painting, cutting, imaginative play and licking and sticking. Montessori equipment is used, but not exclusively. There is no formal teaching. Teachers are available to guide, support and approve, not to direct or impose. Children are encouraged to discover for themselves and practise their skills in a safe, warm environment. This relaxed approach allows for a great deal of self-expression. Pre-reading and writing skills are encouraged. Phonics are taught and Montessori sandpaper letters demonstrate what a letter feels and sounds like. Furniture is labelled to help children link an object with the written symbol. The nursery uses different books, but no particular reading scheme. Children are encouraged to read anything they can. Weekly activities from visiting specialists include arm-band swimming, music, dance and movement, Tumble Tots, PE and ballet. Each session ends with all children coming together for storytime. No formal or written records are kept, and there is no written timetable or curriculum. Children's progress is monitored informally by the staff team on a daily basis.

**Remarks** Homely, easy-going school with caring, trained staff and happy children, clearly enjoying their play activities. Unstructured, informal atmosphere. The nursery appears under-resourced in certain areas and in need of more equipment and books.

# LEIGHAM INFANT SCHOOL – NURSERY UNIT

Leigham Infant School
Cockington Close
Leigham
Plymouth PL6 8RF
**Tel:** (0752) 778175

**Owner:** Devon County Council
**Teacher-in-charge:** Lorna Gough, Dip Ed
**Type:** Nursery class in state primary school offering half-day sessions. No full-time places.
**Children:** 3½–4½yrs. 26 places. 52 on register
**Hours:** Morning session 9am–11.30am
Afternoon session 12.45pm–3.15pm
Open 38 weeks a year
**Status:** State nursery class
**Number of years open:** 18
**Meals:** Snacks
**1992 fees:** No fees. £1 per week voluntary contribution towards cookery and outings
**Waiting list:** Long
**Registered by:** Devon County Council LEA

**Premises** A single-storey, square, concrete building with an interesting domed roof. Purpose-built in the mid-'70s. The cheerful entrance hall doubles as a cloakroom, storage space and small sitting area with low tables and chairs. The large, main, open-plan playroom has big windows and patio doors leading out on to a paved terrace. The floor is part carpet, part lino and there is soft, concealed strip lighting. Natural light also descends from the glass dome. Additional small rooms are an office-cum-library with a carpeted quiet-group area, a small staff loo, children's toilets and a kitchen for preparing snacks and for cookery lessons. Nursery children also use the main school hall for gym, PE and music and movement. Attractive displays of the children's work cheer up the building, which needs some redecoration. The school is at the end of a cul-de-sac in the middle of a large, mixed council and private housing estate. There is parking in the street, but most children walk to the nursery, up the short footpath running through the estate. The nearby park is rarely used.

**Teacher-in-charge & staff** Lorna Gough, Dip Ed, has taught in junior schools for the last 29 years, starting as a French teacher. Although very happy at the nursery, she is looking forward to early retirement. Her full-time assistant is Lyn Rose, NNEB, SRN. Two groups of NNEB students attend on alternate weeks and local sixth-formers help out on work experience. A rota of parents assist with activities such as cooking and craft work. Staff and students meet every Thursday after school to plan the next week's activities together. Lorna Gough reports to the headmistress of the school, but has never seen the governor allotted to the nursery. INSET training is available to teachers, but not the nursery nurse. Mrs Gough expresses reluctance at the idea of employing a male worker. 'Public opinion would be against it. It is an intimate job. Dressing up would be a difficult activity,' she says. There have been no staff changes in the last eight years. A well-established and long-serving team.

**Children & parents** The nursery is specifically for children who will be going on to Leigham Infant School. Many live on the surrounding housing estate, mainly from white, working class families. A number of parents work in the Plymouth dockyards. Entry to the nursery is by invitation only. A panel of selectors meets in the summer term to decide which children should have a place in the following September. Parents should put their child's name down at least a year in advance, but need a contingency plan as many will not be offered a place. Priority is given to single-parent families and the unemployed. Parents play an important role at the nursery and there is always a parent helper at every session. They are not encouraged to stay unless they are helping, as this delays the programme and routine. There is a limited number of children with special educational needs, but no special needs assistants. Staff/child ratio is 1:13, supplemented by ancillary helpers – parents, students and school pupils. Staff are available to talk to parents at the beginning and end of each session.

**Curriculum & activities** Daily activities are either set up ready for the children or strategically placed for free choice. Equipment is clearly labelled and available at child height. Each day usually begins with free play, followed by a group activity planned in advance. There is another period of free play before the end of the session. Drinks and snacks are available for children to help themselves. The main school hall is used for drama, or music and movement. The nursery keeps a record of each child's development for parents and the reception class teacher to see. Children take home dated examples of work and art on a regular basis. A copy of the Devon nursery curriculum is available for parents to study. The classroom is divided into different areas for a range of child-centred experiences. These include a home corner, water play area, sand and painting bases. Children have access to scissors, sellotape, junk boxes and glue at all times for creative work. Science and technology are encouraged as children explore their surrounding environment. On frequent walks they observe chimney smoke and houses, learn directions and the geography of the area and explore Plymbridge woods in all seasons. Simple resources are popular – for example, carrier bags are used for kites. A 'real' working telephone system operates across the nursery room, calculators are available and children have access to the infant school computer. There is a writing corner, with pencils, crayons, felt-tip pens, charcoals, chalks and different shapes of paper. Children are encouraged to write their own names from day one. Pre-writing and pattern skills are developed. A quiet room full of books, and easily accessible, is in constant use. Stories and rhymes are dramatised. Music and musical instruments are part of the daily timetable. Mathematical concepts are taught through construction toys, different sizes of bricks, Lego, Duplo and number and shape games. The correct terminology is always used for shapes, ie cylinders, oblongs etc. Children are busy, challenged and happy. Two or three short outings and one major outing are organised each term. Recent adventures include a trip to a fish market and train and ferry rides.

**Remarks** An excellent preparation for first school. The programme of activities and outings is exciting and stimulating. Caring, qualified staff, supporting enthusiastic and confident children. High level of co-operation between staff, parents and children. Vivid displays of children's projects, work and creativity successfully cover up the need to redecorate the building. Too many children are chasing too few places at this deservedly popular nursery.

## PIXIELAND I DAY NURSERY

Mount Gould Hospital
Mount Gould Road
Plymouth
Devon PL4 7PY
**Tel:** (0752) 272304

**Owner/Principal:** Caroline Francis
**Type:** Workplace nursery offering full-time places and half-day sessions to hospital staff and local community
**Children:** 3mths–5yrs. 24 places. 60 on register
**Hours:** 7am–6pm
Morning session 8am–1pm
Afternoon session 1pm–6pm
Open 52 weeks a year (excl bank holidays)
**Status:** Private, fee-paying
**Number of years open:** 9
**Meals:** Lunch, tea, snacks
**1992 fees:** £57.50 per week full-time
£5.75 per session
**Waiting list:** 10. Early registration advisable. Priority to hospital staff
**Registered by:** Devon SS
**Under same ownership:** Pixieland II, Plymouth

**Premises** Ideal! A purpose-built, chalet-style building with big windows, surrounded by a pleasant garden and play area. The nursery is set in the grounds of the hospital it serves, with easy road access and parking. The interior is freshly decorated, light and bright, and is divided into areas for different activities. Babies have their own fenced-off area where they can play safely, and yet be part of the larger nursery. They can watch the older children and as soon as they are able to walk, they spend time with the toddlers in the play room. The nursery is outstandingly well equipped with mountains of toys, games and equipment of every kind. It is immaculately clean and tidy, but colourful and cheerful too, with plentiful evidence of ambitious art work and projects.

**Owner/Principal & staff** Caroline Francis is an energetic young woman who started the nursery after working for some years as a nanny. She has no formal childcare qualifications. There was such demand for childcare amongst doctors and medical staff that she approached the hospital and suggested setting up a nursery on site. The Health Authority provided the perfect building. Caroline has been so successful as a manager that she has since opened Pixieland II which she manages for Devon County and Plymouth City employees. She divides her time between the two nurseries. Her seven staff, led by a nursery supervisor, are all qualified – three NNEB, three PPA Supervisor Certificates and one Mont Dip. Training is considered important and encouraged. The nursery pays 50 per cent of the costs of all training, which includes first aid, management training and PPA Supervisor Courses. Staff turnover has never been a problem – most stay for several years. Caroline encourages team spirit by frequent meetings and discussions with staff and parents. She is briskly efficient and business-like, but clearly popular with everyone. Staff also run a babysitting circle for parents outside nursery hours.

**Children & parents** Almost all are the children of hospital staff. Some come from outside if and when there is room. Many of the parents are nurses working unsocial hours. There is quite a social and occasionally cultural mix, with children going on to private and state schools. Parents play a very active part; some mothers slip out of the hospital during lunch breaks to feed babies or just to visit their children. The family atmosphere was much felt during our visit, when collecting parents stayed on to chat with staff. The nursery arranges various parties for children and parents during the year and has regular meetings to discuss children's progress.

**Curriculum & activities** The emphasis is firmly on learning through play, although Letterland is used for early reading to teach letters and sounds. The day begins with free play and messy play on a rota system – water play, play dough, painting, glueing, chalks. After milk and biscuits, there is storytime and songs followed by talks, games and project work. Projects are the key to learning here. A monthly topic is chosen, in consultation with parents and reflecting areas they want their children to explore, and woven into the various activities, along with a monthly colour, shape and letter of the alphabet. Other projects for the year cover spring, pets, food, safety, the sea and a summer outing to a farm in Cornwall. Each child builds up a folder of work during their time at Pixieland, which is handed on to their next school. Most children leave with a thorough knowledge of letters and are able to write their names. Construction play is on the timetable each day and there is plenty of scope for outdoor play – a soft area with playground equipment, a huge sandpit, bikes, scooters, etc and a big Swiss-cottage-style Wendy house. A ballet teacher visits once a week to give dance lessons, and a BBC computer is on its way. The nursery takes a fairly firm line over discipline. Staff will administer a sharp telling-off and, if misbehaviour persists, the child is separated briefly to allow a cooling-off period.

**Remarks** Masses and masses of equipment in a capably run nursery with excellent facilities. Very reasonably priced, but unfortunately only really available to hospital staff. A limited number of places for outsiders, although a place may be available at its sister nursery, Pixieland II.

## ST PETER'S (C of E) PRIMARY SCHOOL – NURSERY UNIT

Rendle Street
Stonehouse
Plymouth
Devon PL1 1VH
**Tel:** (0752) 667724

**Owner:** Devon County Council
**Principal:** Diane Bolton, Cert Ed
**Type:** Nursery class in state/C of E primary school offering morning sessions only
**Children:** 3yrs 3mths–5yrs. 26 places. 26 on register
**Hours:** 9am–11.30am
Open 38 weeks a year
**Status:** State nursery class
**Number of years open:** 6
**Meals:** Snacks
**1992 fees:** No fees
**Waiting list:** 30 names
**Registered by:** Devon County Council LEA

## TAVISTOCK NURSERY CENTRE

Bridge House
142 Plymouth Road
Tavistock
Devon PL19 9DS
**Tel:** (0822) 612362

**Owner/Head:** Lesley Griffiths, Cert Ed
**Type:** Day nursery offering full-time places and half-day sessions plus after-school/holiday playscheme
**Children:** 0–5yrs. 5–10yrs after-school club and holiday playscheme. 50 places. 90 on register
**Hours:** 8am–5.30pm
Nursery class 9.30am–12 noon
Open 51 weeks a year (excl bank holidays)
**Status:** Private, fee-paying
**Number of years open:** 3
**Meals:** Snacks and drinks. Packed lunches
**1992 fees:** £62.50–£72.50 per week full-time
£12.50–£14.50 per day
£6.25–£7.25 per session
Nursery class £4.20 per day
Sliding scale depending on age of child
**Waiting list:** None
**Registered by:** Devon County Council SS

**Premises** The owner admits that the Nursery Centre is not smart, so do not be put off! The premises are rented and were once a kitchen showroom on the outskirts of town. However, a great deal of imagination and care has gone into making the interior jolly and inviting – and there is plenty of space. The large interior of the showroom has been split up into six rooms accommodating the Caterpillar Nursery for under-3s and the Butterfly School and day nursery for 3- to 5-year-olds. Babies have a separate room. There are bright colours and children's paintings everywhere – the overall effect is lively and appealing. Outside, the same imaginative approach has turned a rather unprepossessing back yard into an attractive play area.

**Owner/Head & staff** The warmth and enthusiasm of Lesley Griffiths, Cert Ed, and her staff, are the strength and mainstay of this nursery. Lesley, a qualified teacher of 3- to 7-year-olds, was forced to give up work due to a period of ill-health. She was looking for a nursery where she could place her own children and, finding nothing suitable, set about starting one 'literally from my bed'. She followed a simple formula – 'I wanted to make it the kind of place I would like for my own children,' she says. And, in fact, her own toddler was to be found busily splashing paint on to paper during our visit. She is fiercely proud of the nursery and determined to make it as perfect as she can, following her own criteria. She is ably backed up by Alison Sleeman and Wendy Stephens, nursery officers in charge of the under-3s and the 3- to 5-year-olds respectively. There are nine members of staff, all with NNEB, PPA or City & Guilds qualifications, occasionally helped out by students.

**Children & parents** A wide social mix. The children come from differing backgrounds, ranging from single parents to professional, dual-income families. They go on to local state schools or private schools in the area. The transition from home to nursery school is eased by a home visit from a member of staff before a child starts at the school. They aim to make sure that each child will feel confident on arrival, having already met a member of staff at home.

**Curriculum & activities** No strong emphasis on formal teaching, but Lesley believes that every activity or game offers opportunities for learning and that the most important thing is to provide a learning environment with stimulation. Children take part in singing, dance and movement, drama, painting and craft. There are regular mini-gym sessions and outdoor play. Records are kept on each child's development, which parents can pass on to the next school. As the children approach school age, they follow a pattern of pre-school learning, and the term before they leave they are assigned to one teacher who will assess their progress. There is no pressure to read or write, but children who are ready to move on are encouraged. 'We don't push education. It must come from the child, but there is a stage when children are ready for reading, writing and arithmetic and we must cater for that,' says Lesley. Local schools are consulted about reading schemes, so that children can slot in easily when the time comes. There is plenty of free play, with great demand for the dressing-up box! There is no formal discipline. Disruptive behaviour is dealt with by giving the child extra attention, perhaps on a one-to-one basis for a while. 'We try to instil a live and let live philosophy.' A child with quite severe behavioural problems was successfully cared for at the nursery and staff are ready to take on children with disabilities. One of the nursery officers in charge has special training in this area.

**Remarks**  A thoroughly enjoyable nursery – the staff, demonstrably enthusiastic and cheerful, radiate team spirit. The children are busy and happy. Lesley Griffiths has succeeded admirably in her aim of providing somewhere for parents to leave their children in the certain knowledge that they will benefit from the experience. Not a high-status building, but adapted to the needs of children, staff and parents.

# Dorset

Childcare provision in the county is generally poor. There are no local authority nursery schools, and only one in 50 children is offered a part-time place in a nursery class. The extended family provides most of the county's childcare needs. If that fails, there are over 1000 childminders and 300 playgroups. 'If we had more money, we wouldn't spend it on nurseries. We would spend it on training people to provide more playgroups in rural areas,' says one under-5s support worker. The county's 42 private day nurseries are mainly concentrated in areas of dense population along the coast, to handle the demand from workers in the tourist industry.

**Further information**

For a Parent Information Pack listing private day nurseries, childminders, playgroups, health visitors, toy libraries and nursery units in primary schools:

Under Fives Support Workers (West Dorset)
County Hall
Dorchester DT1 1XJ
Tel: (0305) 224520

Under Fives Support Workers (East Dorset)
40 Lowther Road
Bournemouth BH8 8NR
Tel: (0202) 296071 × 226

# ANNETTE'S NURSERY

5 Harcourt Road
Bournemouth BH5 2JG
**Tel:** (0202) 428880

**Owners:** Annette and Rodney Drain
**Principal:** Annette Drain, nursery nurse trained in Denmark
**Type:** Day nursery offering full-time places and half-day sessions
**Children:** 2–5yrs. 20 places. 31 on register
**Hours:** 8.30am–5.30pm
Morning session 8.30am–1pm
Afternoon session 1pm–5.30pm
Open 50 weeks a year
**Status:** Private, fee-paying
**Number of years open:** 21
**Meals:** Snacks and drinks. Parents provide packed lunch
**1992 fees:** £13 per day
£8 per session
Refundable deposit of 1 week's fees
**Waiting list:** Short. Places available
**Registered by:** Dorset County Council SS

**Premises** Substantial, Victorian, brick-built house in a quiet, tree-lined street not far from the centre of Bournemouth. Close to several bus routes. Five rooms on the ground floor accommodate the nursery. 2-to-3-year-olds use the Honeybees' Room – light, bright and bursting with toys and equipment, including a goldfish. Older children use the larger Rainbow Room, equally generously equipped and home to three budgies. There is also a kitchen, kept out of bounds to children, and a cloakroom, where children hang their coats and change into indoor shoes. The secluded garden is used daily, weather permitting, and provides a climbing frame, slide and see-saw as well as a shed full of toys for pushing and pedalling. Nearby Kings Park and Shelley Park are visited every few weeks.

**Principal & staff** Annette Drain has many years' experience working with under-5s in Denmark – where nursery education is, she says, far ahead of ours. She met her husband while she was working in Britain as an au-pair. He has a mainly administrative role in the nursery, but has taken the PPA Foundation Course. Four of the six staff are qualified, NNEB, SRN, City & Guilds and PPA. Of the two unqualified workers, one is currently training and the other has been a registered childminder. Staff meetings are held each week, and although there is a wide difference in ages, all nursery nurses work together as a friendly team and sometimes meet socially. Students and trainees are present for part of the year and are supervised by members of staff. There are no peripatetic teachers, but Annette plays the guitar for daily music sessions.

**Children & parents** Parents are mainly professional, middle-class. There is only one non-English child at the nursery. Most transfer to local state schools, but a few will attend private schools such as Park School and St Thomas Garnett. Each child is allocated a key-worker to monitor progress, although children move from one member of staff to another during the course of a day depending on which activity they are doing. Phasing in is tailored to individual requirements, but once a child is settled parents are not encouraged to stay at the nursery as this can upset a child's routine. Since most parents are working, they are generally happy to hand over the responsibility to nursery staff.

**Curriculum & activities** Children pursue their different activities in small groups of not more than six, supervised by at least one adult. There are no formal lessons, but work includes some pre-school skills, as well as creative, imaginative, outdoor, social and musical activities. No particular teaching method is used and no reading schemes as it is felt these could confuse children when they move on to their different schools. Projects are topic-based and the rooms alive with exciting visual displays. A weekly timetable is posted on the noticeboard, but staff tend to improvise and tailor the curriculum according to the abilities of the children present. Extremely detailed achievement records are kept on each child, recording posture and large movement, vision and fine movement, hearing and speech, social behaviour and play. There are regular outings to the pet shop, library and a local shopping centre to see the fountains as well as the fire station and railway station.

**Remarks** Small, well-established nursery offering good-quality care. Kind, firm and sympathetic nursery nurses. Fees are kept to the lowest level possible, without compromising the quality of service.

## DORCHESTER COMMUNITY NURSERY SCHOOL

York Road
Dorchester
Dorset DT1 1QA
**Tel:** (0305) 265140

**Owner:** Dorchester Community Nursery School Association
**Principal:** Valerie Gould, Cert Ed
**Type:** Community nursery school offering half-day sessions only
**Children:** 3–5yrs. 128 places. 128 on register
**Hours:** Morning session 9am–12 noon
Afternoon session 1.30pm–3.30pm
Open 39 weeks a year
**Status:** Community nursery. Registered charity
**Number of years open:** 24
**Meals:** Milk and biscuits
**1992 fees:** £1.25 per hour
Flexible terms
**Waiting list:** Long. 50 names
**Registered by:** Dorset County Council SS

## PETER PAN DAY NURSERY

10 Charmouth Grove
Lower Parkstone
Poole BH14 0LP
**Tel:** (0202) 746909

**Owners:** Mrs M Cheer and Mrs I Hobby
**Principal:** Mrs M Cheer, NAMCW
**Type:** Day nursery offering full-time places and half-day sessions
**Children:** 18mths–5yrs. 26 places. 53 on register
**Hours:** 8.30am–5.30pm
Morning session 8.30am–12.30pm
Afternoon session 1.30pm–5.30pm
Open 52 weeks a year
**Status:** Private, fee-paying
**Number of years open:** 23
**Meals:** Snacks. Packed lunches
**1992 fees:** £45 per week full-time (no reduction for part week)
£9 per day
**Waiting list:** None
**Registered by:** Dorset County Council SS

**Premises** Ground floor of a brick, semi-detached house in a middle-class, residential area. The first floor is sub-let as a flat and has nothing to do with the nursery. Children occupy four rooms: a playroom for educational play and pre-school learning; a messy room for painting, sand and water play and pastry making; a dinner room for quiet activities and lunch; and the 'new room' or physical room which is set up for indoor play with slide, tunnel, stepping stones and other activities. The decorations are generally good, although the lighting seemed subdued. The back garden is used as often as possible for outdoor games, but visits to the nearby park have been stopped because of dogs fouling the play area. A large boat fills the front garden and actually blocks some light from the downstairs rooms.

**Owner/Principal & staff** Mrs Hobby is Mrs Cheer's mother, and mother and daughter have been running the nursery for over 20 years, in what was originally the family home. Mrs Hobby spends most of her time on administration and leaves the day-to-day running of the nursery to her daughter and their senior assistant, Susan Wright (PPA Foundation Course), who has worked at the nursery almost since it started. Amongst the six other members of staff there is one NNEB. The rest have some qualification, including City & Guilds and the PPA Foundation Course. Staff work well as a team and meet daily for a planning session. New members of staff are chosen for their ability to 'interact not interfere' and are required always to encourage rather than enforce. This is not a profit-making concern – the owners do not pay themselves salaries. They consider their work a vocational experience'. Staff are paid a small salary. The nursery tries to charge the lowest possible fees to make places affordable to as many people as possible.

**Children & parents** Parents are mostly teachers, nurses, office or bank workers and shopkeepers. There is little cultural or racial mix, reflecting the local community. Some children commute in from 30 miles away and consequently they go on to a wide range of state and private schools. Places are allocated on a first come first served basis, although there is preference to siblings. In some cases, priority may be given to single-parent families or other circumstances of hardship. Each child is allocated a keyworker and parents are encouraged to come and discuss their child's progress at any time. Children are phased-in gradually until they are settled and happy.

**Curriculum & activities** Children are divided into family groups of mixed ages, eight or nine to a group with two members of staff. They come together as one group each day for singing and nursery rhymes and for their mid-session snacks. Each group works its way through a weekly programme, planned in advance, and pre-school learning is actively encouraged. The owners keep in regular touch with local schools to ensure that their programme complements the primary curriculum. The reading schemes include Look & See and One to One, and most of the children are emergent readers by the time they move on. Children have access to painting, cutting, water and sand play, plasticine, home corner, dressing up box, improvised play with blankets and boxes, play dough and a well-stocked library corner. Children's work, mounted and named, is on display everywhere. Parents are keen on an organised and structured day, but the nursery tries hard to strike a good balance between structured activities and free play. A report book on each child, available to parents, is updated quarterly and includes information on the settling-in period and progress on colour recognition, letter and number work. There are no outside specialist teachers and no outings as it is felt children will benefit more from these on a one-to-one basis with parents.

**Remarks** Sound care and education at a very reasonable cost. Much cheaper than other nurseries in the area. Dedicated staff prepared to work for little or nothing so that fees can be kept down. Children are friendly and confident – totally absorbed in their activities. Long-running family concern.

# SEAWARD DAY NURSERY

61 Seaward Avenue
Southbourne
Bournemouth
Dorset BH6 3SJ
**Tel:** (0202) 424655

**Owners/Principals:** Jenny Mathews, SEN
Linda Moss, SEN
**Type:** Day nursery offering full- and part-time places
**Children:** 2–5yrs. 17 places. 42 on register
**Hours:** 8.30am–5.30pm
Open 50 weeks a year
**Status:** Private, fee-paying
**Number of years open:** 5
**Meals:** Lunch, tea
**1992 fees:** £14 per day
£8.50 per half-day
**Waiting list:** 6mths for part-time places
1yr for full-time places. 20 on list
**Registered by:** Dorset County Council SS

**Premises** Seaward is based on the ground-floor of Jenny Mathews' small detached house – set among holiday homes, B&B and small hotels, just off the Overcliff Road – an area where boats are more common than children in the back garden.

**Owners/Principals** This small, intimate, 'home from home' nursery is run by mature State Enrolled Nurses and long-time friends, Jenny Mathews and Linda Moss. Both have completed the PPA Foundation Course; Linda ran a playgroup in Poole for many years. They met 20 years ago, while working on NHS children's wards and now share the running of the nursery. They head a team of five young, part-time nursery nurses, three of whom are PPA trained, two are unqualified.

**Children & parents** The nursery aims 'to supply a trustworthy and crisis-free service for the professional career parent'. Children come from a wide catchment area; some move across from a nearby baby unit run by a former Seaward staff member. The majority tend to be the 'only child of professional parents' and leave to go on in equal numbers to state and private schools.

**Curriculum & activities** There is no pressure to achieve academically. The nursery encourages confidence, gained by learning through play, and concentrates on developing the desire to learn in each child. When we visited, children were absorbed in a number of different activities, including a huge table covered with junk. Facilities are cramped, but children were visibly happy and stimulated. There are no reading schemes and no written reports. Older children have a writing book and everyone takes some work home every day. Art and craft, music and dance, gym, piano and musical instruments feature daily. Dressing up is the most popular free-play activity. There are outings every day, weather permitting. The small garden and the play park, 200 yards away, are used in the mornings and expeditions to the beach take place in the afternoons. Children go down on foot and come up in the cliff lift. There are no parents' evenings – parents can come in and chat at any time, but are said to be too busy and wrapped up in their jobs for evening meetings. Food is an important part of nursery life, incorporating plenty of fresh fruit and vegetables, cooked by the owners themselves. Jenny and Linda are 'hot on table manners' and meals are a social occasion. Birthdays are very special days and always include a party.

**Remarks** A small, friendly unit with happy children and dedicated owners. It would benefit from more space and some updating of existing facilities.

# Durham

Durham County Council has made pre-school education a priority. After a three-year expansion plan, they now have 27 nursery schools and 84 nursery classes attached to primary schools. One of the top three counties in the country in terms of nursery provision, Durham offers nearly half its 3- and 4-year-olds a nursery place. However, the Council acknowledges that, while providing nursery education is beneficial to children, it does little to ease the childcare problems of working parents. There are six day nurseries run by the local authority targeted at children in need and 12 private nurseries, only a small number of which cater for babies and toddlers. With high unemployment in the area, a good supply of childminders and willing relatives, parents do not seem to be campaigning for more provision.

**Further information**

For details on day nurseries, childminders and playgroups:
Department of Social Services
County Hall
Durham DH1 5UG
Tel: (091) 386 4411

For details on nursery schools, units and classes:
Education Department
(address and telephone as above)

## APPLE TREE NURSERY

Sniperley Hall Cottage
Durham City DH1 5RA
**Tel:** (091) 384 4819
**Owner/Principal:** Marie-Thérèse Roberts
**Head Nursery Nurse:** Lynn Davison, NNEB, DPQS
**Type:** Day nursery offering full-time places only
**Children:** 2–5yrs. 25 places. 25 on register
**Hours:** 8am–6pm
Open 51 weeks a year

**Status:** Private, fee-paying
**Number of years open:** 4
**Meals:** Breakfast, lunch, tea, snacks
**1992 fees:** £80.52 per week full-time
**Waiting list:** Minimal
**Registered by:** Durham County Council SS

**Premises** Two miles from the centre of Durham, up a driveway off the busy A691. The bungalow is surrounded by open countryside and next to Sniperley Hall, a wing of which is the nursery owner's home. Outside play facilities are extensive, including an excellent, well-equipped adventure playground. All the rooms in the bungalow are used by the nursery. They include a dressing-up room, messy-play/dining room, quiet room and book area, kitchen, staff room, office and toilets. The rooms are well decorated and fully equipped and the walls clad with displays of children's artwork.

**Owner/Principal & staff** Marie-Thérèse Roberts bought the bungalow some years ago to avoid acquiring neighbours and converted it into a nursery when her third child was born. She still works two days a week for her husband's pipeline business, and is responsible for the administration and financial side of the nursery. She employs six young, full-time, qualified NNEB staff. There are no qualified nursery teachers on the staff. Lynn Davison is head nursery nurse. All wear old-fashioned navy or green uniform dresses and starched white aprons and are called 'Auntie' by the children. Marie-Thérèse Roberts explains, 'When I was a child, I used to stay with my grandmother in Germany and go to a nursery where the nursery nurses wore the same uniform. To me, starched white aprons are synonymous with security.' To the visitor, they appear to be in a time warp. Staff work as a close team, supported by visiting music and dance teachers, two sixth-formers doing community service (one hour a week) and, intermittently, students from the College of Further Education. Staff meetings are held monthly. There is no staff training budget, but there is a termly in-house training evening and always at least one person studying for the DPQS. The staff/child ratio is 1:5. An air of cool efficiency prevails.

**Children & parents** The children are from professional or business backgrounds, with both parents working full-time. A large proportion progress to private schools when they leave. They are divided into what the nursery calls 'Auntie' groups, and each keyworker or 'Auntie' monitors the children in her group. The nursery caters for children with special needs, provided that they do not need one-to-one attention. Children are polite, busy and quietly spoken. Parents are expected to take a keen interest in nursery activities and are invited to open days, sports days, the nativity play and parents' evenings. A termly newsletter is sent out. Criticism and suggestions are heeded.

**Curriculum & activities** Creative play and a stimulating, homely environment are the priorities, with the emphasis on a secure, happy atmosphere, where children can develop and learn new skills at their own pace. Equipment is abundant (annual budget £5000+), carefully looked after and easily accessible to children. The day begins with free play in all rooms, followed by registration and large-group time, with discussion and songs. Themes are followed and regularly changed and assessed. Children are divided into colour-coded ability groups for pre-school work. This includes number, literacy, pre-writing and easy science exercises. Children use worksheets and keep their work in files. When they are ready and interested, the Ginn reading scheme is used. Weekly music, puppet shows, dance and movement and computer time are available. Language development is considered important and children are encouraged to express themselves freely and politely. Their grammar is corrected. Children move from room to room at will, but all spend part of each day in their 'Auntie' groups following supervised activities. Outdoor play facilities are very good and the next-door farm is regularly visited. Outings are undertaken twice a year to a Christmas pantomime and a summer location. There are occasional visits from a clown or conjurer and a ballet display by dance students. Developmental records are kept on each child. A qualified cook provides freshly cooked meals and caters for all special diets.

**Remarks** A happy, efficient nursery offering good-quality day care. Beautiful rural surroundings and excellent outdoor play facilities. Although there are no qualified early years teachers, staff are professional and the atmosphere is calm and quiet. Starched white aprons and children calling staff 'Auntie' gives the nursery a slightly Victorian air. Parents love it – as their many letters of thanks testify.

## DURHAM UNIVERSITY NURSERY

The Vennel
Old Elvet
Durham DH1 3HN
**Tel:** (091) 386 2527

**Owner:** Durham University
**Officer-in-charge:** Jill Johnston, NNEB
**Type:** Day nursery offering full- and part-time places to university employees, students and local community
**Children:** 6mths–5yrs. 40 places. 46 on register
**Hours:** 8.30am–5.30pm
Open 48 weeks a year
**Status:** Private, fee-paying, non profit-making
**Number of years open:** 2
**Meals:** Lunch, tea, snacks
**1992 fees:** £86 per week full-time – under 2
£64 per week full-time – over 2
£18.20 per day – under 2
£13.80 per day – over 2
Reduced rates for university employees and students
**Waiting list:** Long. Early registration advisable
**Registered by:** Durham County Council SS

## KIRKLANDS DAY NURSERY

8 Bede Road
Barnard Castle
Co Durham DL12 8HD
**Tel:** (0833) 38961

**Owner/Principal:** Janice McGhie, NNEB
**Type:** Day nursery offering full- and part-time places and half-day sessions
**Children:** 2–5yrs. 20 places. 64 on register
**Hours:** 7.45am–5.30pm
Morning session 9am–11.45am
Afternoon session 1.15pm–4pm
Open 50 weeks a year
**Status:** Private, fee-paying
**Number of years open:** 9½
**Meals:** Breakfast, packed lunches, tea, snacks
**1992 fees:** £3.70 per session
£1.30 per extra hour
**Waiting list:** 16. First come first served
**Registered by:** Durham County Council SS

## NEWFIELDS CHILDCARE CO-OPERATIVE

St Oswald's Institute
Church Street
Durham DH1 3DQ
**Tel:** (091) 384 9072

**Owner:** Newfields Childcare Co-operative Ltd
**Nursery Officer:** Liz Porteus, NNEB, PCNN
**Type:** Day nursery offering full- and part-time places and half-day sessions
**Children:** 2–5yrs. 25 places. 60 on register
**Hours:** 8.30am–5.30pm
Morning session 8.30am–2pm
Afternoon session 2pm–5.30pm
Open 50 weeks a year
**Status:** Private, non profit-making co-operative
**Number of years open:** 9
**Meals:** Snacks, packed lunches
**1992 fees:** £50 per week full-time
£1.60 per hour morning session
£1.30 per hour afternoon session
**Waiting list:** Moderate. 24 names
**Registered by:** Durham County Council SS

**Premises** Close to the city centre, surrounded by Durham University buildings, the nursery is opposite St Oswald's Church and next door to St Oswald's Park. An old red-brick building, it consists of two rooms and cloakrooms attached to a church hall, which it also uses. There is no staff room, or children's rest room, but the premises have recently been completely refurbished to a good standard. The main play room is divided into activity areas and can be partitioned to create two separate play environments. Outside there is an enclosed yard – partly grass and partly concrete. Visits to the park next door are frequent. Parking is available on the main road or in side streets, and a regular bus service passes the front door.
**Nursery officer & staff** Liz Porteus, NNEB, also holds the Scottish Post-Certificate Nursery Nurse Diploma, and has been supervising the nursery for five years. Previously, she spent many years in Scotland in Lothian Region nurseries. At the time of our visit, she was anticipating a move to take charge of a new nursery in Durham city centre, leaving Newfields in the capable hands of its existing staff. It is expected that there will be some movement between the two nurseries, both of staff and of resources. The nursery is a co-oper-

ative; all the staff are joint owners and form a management committee with Liz Porteus in overall charge. There is a chairman and treasurer, both parents, and the Co-operative Development Association (CDA) send a representative to management meetings. They originally costed the nursery and helped with legal fees. All members of staff are either registered play leaders or qualified nursery nurses, three full-time and three part-time. There is no teacher on the team. Additional part-time help comes from YTS trainees, a sixth-form student, a university student, a community care worker and numerous students on one-day placement. Staff take full advantage of a wide range of training initiatives provided by the Co-operative Movement.

**Children & parents** A lively social and cultural mix, reflecting the cosmopolitan community of a busy university town. When they leave, nursery children go to church, state and private schools in the area. Some return overseas with parents who have been students at the university. Children with special needs are not accepted, because of the cost of extra staffing. The nursery also provides a crèche and baby-sitting services, a collection and delivery service to primary schools and cover before and after school hours for working parents. Children from other nurseries which close for school holidays are accepted, if there are places available. There is an open-door policy towards parents, who visit at any time and often cover for staff absences or share activities with their children. They are urged to become part of an extended family.

**Curriculum & activities** Learning through play, following PPA guidelines. A wide selection of reasonable-quality equipment is available (annual budget £1000 over three years). There are facilities for music and dance, modelling, sand and water play and imaginative play. Children move freely from one activity to the other, as they choose. There is no formal teaching of the 3Rs, but there are good supplies of books and stories to listen to. All children can recognise their name by the time they leave. Some basic mathematics and science are also taught through play. The stated nursery aims are to develop the children's capacity for learning, eye/hand co-ordination, creativity, balance, awareness and social skills. Projects and interest corners are developed, often as a result of something a child has brought in from home. There is no set timetable; the day simply evolves. Outings relate to topics and depend on staff availability. There is an annual trip to Preston Park and local visits to the Cathedral, library, railway station, botanic gardens and shops, in addition to nature walks along the river to look at the ducks and boats. A puppet company visits regularly as well as members of the police force and fire brigade. Children's progress is monitored once a term and parents have access to a written report.

**Remarks** A workers' co-operative, set up to provide high-quality childcare at an affordable price. Any surplus funds are reinvested in equipment or to subsidise places for low-income families. The nursery offers a vital service to working parents in an area where most playgroups are only open for a few hours a week and nursery schools close for the school holidays. Happy atmosphere and close relationships with parents.

# East Sussex

No local authority day nurseries and very few state nursery schools or classes. Special needs children are placed in the private sector at local authority cost. Of the 40,000 under-5s, only one in 30 will have the chance of part-time, state-run, pre-school education. Wealthy families use nannies or spend over £100 per week for a place at one of the 92 private nurseries in the county. Plenty of private provision for the 2- to 5-year-olds, but limited baby places. Some nurseries are closing down due to the recession. 'Working mothers simply cannot afford the high cost of quality care,' a nursery consultant in the area told us. Despite this year's financial constraints, East Sussex is hoping to achieve a net growth in nursery education.

**Further information**

For details on day nurseries, private nursery schools, childminders and playgroups:

Department of Social Services
County Hall
St Anne's Crescent
Lewes BN7 1SW
Tel: (0273) 481000

For details on nursery schools, units and classes:
Education Department (Admissions Section)
County Hall
St Anne's Crescent
Lewes BN7 1SW
Tel: (0273) 481000

For information and advice on all forms of childcare:
Childcare Links
1A Barracks Yard
Off North Road
Brighton BN1 1YA
Tel: (0273) 621277 (9.30am–3pm Tues, Wed and Fri)

---

## CLOCK TOWER NURSERY

Lewes Tertiary College
Mountfield Road
Lewes
East Sussex BN7 2XH
**Tel:** (0273) 483188 (× 299)

**Owner:** Lewes Tertiary College
**Supervisor:** Alison Fullick, NNEB
**Type:** Day nursery offering full- and part-time places, and half-day sessions, primarily for college staff and students; limited community places. Playschemes during Easter and summer holidays
**Children:** 6mths–5yrs. 20 places (only 2 places for babies under 18mths). 45 on register
**Hours:** 8.30am–5pm
Morning session 8.30am–12.45pm
Afternoon session 12.45pm–5pm
Holiday playschemes 9am–4pm
Open 36 weeks a year
**Status:** Private, fee-paying, non profit-making. Subsidised places for college staff and students
**Number of years open:** 2
**Meals:** Lunch, snacks
**1992 fees:** £6.50 per half-day session – staff and students
£8.50 per half-day session – community users
75p per day for lunch
**Waiting list:** Long, particularly for babies
**Registered by:** E Sussex County Council SS

**Premises** Only two years old, brick-built and specially designed to accommodate a college day nursery. Access is through the main college entrance with parking at the side of the building. Situated on the south side of Lewes, between the railway station and the leisure centre. Inside is light and airy but warm, with magnolia walls covered with pictures, bright blue windows and high ceilings. The large main playroom has masses of bright new furniture, toys and other equipment. There is a sectioned-off baby area and an area used for messy play. There are separate toilets and baby-changing facilities, an office and a very clean, well-equipped kitchen including washing machine and tumble dryer. Outside is a large, newly paved patio used for bikes and ride-on toys all year round, and in summer for sand and water play.

**Supervisor & staff** Alison Fullick, NNEB, who manages and supervises the nursery, reports directly to the college principal. She has experience in many aspects of childcare and plans to take her DPQS. She considers qualifications and a good age mix amongst staff to be important. All but one of the six staff are NNEBs and the unqualified member of staff has completed a PPA course. There is no qualified nursery or infant teacher on the staff. The nursery takes NNEB and BTEC students for work experience, and its own staff participate in relevant training courses whenever possible. They are a friendly group and very affectionate towards the children. Alison is available to parents whenever they feel the need to see her. Staff/child ratios range from 1:2 for babies up to 1:6 for the oldest group.

**Children & parents** Most parents are staff or students at the college. New parents are encouraged to bring their children along to holiday playschemes for a few days before the beginning of term. They then settle comfortably when parents start their courses. Parents receive regular newsletters, attend parents' evenings and help with fund-raising events to buy new equipment. Children are mainly British, with one or two Cypriot and Afro-Caribbean children, and all transfer to state primary schools. The nursery is willing to take children with disabilities and special educational needs, provided that they do not need one-to-one care.

**Curriculum & activities** Learning through play in a happy, stimulating and structured environment. There are many opportunities for free expression and creativity, including painting, clay modelling, play dough, dance and mime and a wealth of pristine, new equipment. There is no formal teaching, but older children can choose to participate in more directed learning sessions, and practise the pre-writing and pre-reading skills necessary for primary school. Even the older age group still has plenty of free play. Staff set aside time to talk to individual children, and records of each child's general development are kept. Children come together as one group during sessions for songs and storytime and play outside each session, weather permitting.

There is a summer outing and children attend suitable plays or concerts at the college.

**Remarks** A warm and friendly nursery which provides quality care to staff and students at the college. Limited formal education. Very good facilities and a high level of qualified, caring staff, but unfortunately very few places for community users.

# EARLY YEARS DAY NURSERY

41 Dyke Road Avenue
Hove
East Sussex BN3 6QA
**Tel:** (0273) 500151

**Owner:** Early Years Childcare PLC
**Manager:** Mary Powell, NNEB
**Type:** Day nursery offering full-time places and half-day sessions.
**Children:** 3mths–5yrs. 75 places. 103 on register
**Hours:** 8am–6pm
Morning session 8am–1pm
Afternoon session 1pm–6pm
Flexible hours
Open 52 weeks a year (excl bank holidays)
**Status:** Private, fee-paying
**Number of years open:** 3
**Meals:** Breakfast, lunch, tea
**1992 fees:** £97.50 per week full-time – under 18 months
£92.50 per week full-time – over 18 months
£11 per morning session
£10.50 per afternoon session
**Waiting list:** No waiting list kept. Vacancies for half-day sessions only
**Registered by:** E Sussex County Council SS
**Under same ownership/management:** Early Years Day Nursery, Brighton; Early Years Day Nursery, Worthing; Panda Tots Workplace Nursery, Crawley, E. Sussex; Butterflies Workplace Nursery, Runcorn, Cheshire

**Premises** Imposing, detached property in classy part of Hove. Upmarket features include sweeping, gravel driveway, immaculate gardens, wood panelling and an elegant, period staircase. The building is vast, catering for 64 babies and children. Surprisingly, the creation of a nursery this size has not destroyed the atmosphere of a real home. There are seven children's rooms, all with nursery names (Rainbow, Ladybird, Cherubs, Jolly Tots), providing four family rooms for 2- to 5-year-olds, two toddler rooms for 1- to 2-year-olds and a baby room for 3 months to 1-year-olds. The overall impression is one of quality, with money no object.

**Owners/Manager & staff** Early Years Childcare PLC was set up by two partners – a London accountant and a Sussex property developer. A third, working director, with NNEB qualification and years of childcare experience, then joined them. This is a profit-making business venture. The company has two other nurseries in Sussex, with a total of almost 200 full-time places for children aged 0 to 5 years. In addition, Early Years offer holiday playschemes and before- and after-school care. The Hove nursery is managed by Mary Powell, NNEB, a professional, mature, calm and decisive person. Formerly, she set up and ran a workplace nursery for the Next Group at their Crawley HQ. Mary has many years' experience of private and state-run nursery provision. She leads a team of 17 full-time staff, with qualifications varying from NNEB (nine) to BTEC (two), NAMCW (four) and Cert Ed (one). Only one member of staff is unqualified. Part-timers include a cook, housekeeper and administrative assistant. Staff are open and friendly and speak highly of Early Years as employers. There is no visible ethnic or cultural mix among staff, although the children are definitely very cosmopolitan. The nursery operates a keyworker system. The staff ratios are excellent – better than Children Act guidelines: 1:2 for babies, 1:3 for toddlers and 1:6 for children over 2.

**Children & parents** Of the 64 places, 55 are taken by two local companies – 50 places to American Express and five to HM Customs & Excise. Both subsidise places heavily according to their employees' salaries. The remaining nine places are open to the local community, and all are taken by affluent, professional, nanny-owning parents intending to follow the path of private education. The children come from Asian, European and British families in the main. Parents' evenings are held three times a year, with a chance to talk to each child's keyworker and visit the nursery at leisure.

**Curriculum & activities** Strong emphasis on high-quality care – meeting the child's needs through play and aiming for a happy, hygienic, secure environment. Consistent, professional nursery nurses with no pretence at formal education or teaching of the three Rs. There are no reading schemes, no exercise books. A broad curriculum is drawn up by Early Years and translated into age-related activities in each room. Topic and thematic learning runs through each area of the curriculum – art, language, maths, science, etc. Topics change every two weeks. Children's work is displayed on the walls, collated into an individual folder or taken home. There is a nursery class for those over 3½ years old. Small groups are taken out to a quiet room for more concentrated work on shapes, numbers, letters, pencil control and writing. Developmental checks are undertaken every two months and are accessible to parents. Outdoor play occurs daily in the vast garden. Wet-weather play is in a specially equipped indoor playroom. Other activities include woodwork, cookery, music and movement. Older children are offered regular outings to museums and the local swimming pool. Excellent home cooking prepared by male chef – the only male member of staff.

**Remarks** Impressive, high-quality, professional childcare on a large scale, but in a surprisingly homely and cosy atmosphere. Glossy, expensive and lavishly equipped, with corporate clients – mainly American Express employees – offered generous subsidies by their employers. The few places available to the community go mainly to professional parents or wealthy non-working mothers who believe in the benefits of nurseries. Early Years is an expanding company, with a thoughtful, winning formula. Other major employers would do well to follow the example of American Express and support nurseries of this standard for their staff.

# HAPPY DAYS DAY NURSERY

Annunciation Hall
Coleman Street
Brighton
East Sussex BN2
**Tel:** (0273) 694447

**Owners/Principals:** Hazel McLeod, BA, NAMCW
Caroline Marsland, BA, NAMCW
**Type:** Day nursery offering full-time places and half-day sessions
**Children:** 2–5 yrs. 24 places. 62 on register
**Hours:** 8.30am–5.15pm
Morning session 8.30am–12.15pm
Afternoon session 1.30pm–5.15pm
Open 50 weeks a year
**Status:** Private, fee-paying, non profit-making
**Number of years open:** 7
**Meals:** Snacks, packed lunches
**1992 fees:** £55 per week full-time
£6 per session
**Waiting list:** 60 names. Afternoon places available
**Registered by:** E Sussex SS

**Premises** Huge, airy, former school hall in a peaceful street, not far from Brighton town centre. Reception is warm and friendly. Two small areas of the hall are partitioned off to make a small office and a staff room. At the top end, a large kitchen leads out to an enclosed garden. The nursery has sole use of the hall – the church uses the kitchen twice a year. Happy Days has been put together with little money but much love. The owners, helped by their respective sets of parents, have decorated the hall themselves, laid carpets, built partitions, repaired the plumbing and turfed the garden. Instead of taking a salary, they have opted to equip the nursery. Fundraising has done the rest. All the equipment is high quality and expensive – wood not plastic, bright colours not dull. Half the space in the main hall is taken up by a vast selection of bright, soft, squidgy shapes, where children can climb, roll, bounce and let rip. Art is a strong influence throughout, with vivid displays everywhere.

**Owners/Principals & staff** Hazel McLeod and Caroline Marsland, both BA, NAMCW, job-share the running of the nursery. They went to college together, live together nearby with Hazel's husband and child and both come from the north (Liverpool and Manchester), but their personalities are very different. Hazel is direct and bubbly, Caroline more relaxed, but they are both dedicated to their work and closely involved with the local community. Staff queue up to work at this nursery. There are two full-time teachers and one who works 4½ days a week (half-day release attending a nursery supervisors' course) – all are NAMCW qualified. An unqualified part-timer works four days a week. Holiday and sickness cover is provided by a child psychologist and a male worker who is taking a special needs course. Staff are loyal and long-serving – the average length of stay is three years.

**Children & parents** To understand this nursery is to understand the crucial role parents play. They visit constantly – for coffee, lunch, tea, gossip, advice and DIY assistance. They are part of the very fabric of the nursery. Many are single parents, others have recently lost their jobs. Money is often a problem, which explains why Hazel McLeod and Caroline Marsland are determined to keep their fees low. Parents are attracted to the nursery because of its close parental co-operation. Many are teachers, social workers, nurses, doctors and students. Two are Social Services registration officers, responsible for maintaining high standards in nurseries in the county. The children, mainly English, are happy, curious and ebullient. Special needs children are welcome – one blind child attends and several with learning and behavioural difficulties. Although registered to take 30 children, numbers are deliberately kept to 24 'because it works better that way'. Despite the demand for baby places in the area, Hazel and Caroline refuse to take them, believing strongly that babies should be looked after in the home.

**Curriculum & activities** Sixty per cent of children go home at lunchtime, therefore mornings are the busy time. Groups are of mixed age as 'children learn so much from each other'. Themes are developed over a week or longer – safety at home and Vikings were the themes at the time of our visit – and each one covers history, geography, science and literature. Twice a day all children do a specific task together – pottery, play dough, tie dyeing, cookery. Art is central – 'we do everything you can possibly imagine with paint'. More structured, traditional work is done on an individual basis. There is one-to-one tuition on practical number work, number problems, letters, words, names and pre-writing and writing skills. Written work on paper or in workbooks is done every day. Activities are structured to avoid boredom, so that noisy times are followed by quieter activities and group work is followed by one-to-one teaching. There are also specific talking periods for sharing news and views. Detailed written records on each child are ongoing and open to parents.

**Remarks** Fun, happy atmosphere, with friendly staff and unusually close and successful parental involvement. Reasonable fees, good reputation locally and very democratically run.

# HILLBURY HOUSE NURSERY SCHOOL

1 Nizells Avenue
Hove
East Sussex BN3 1PL
**Tel:** (0273) 720517

**Owner/Principal:** Liz Travis, SRN, NNEB
**Type:** Day nursery offering full-time places and half-day sessions
**Children:** 2½–5yrs. 32 places. 96 on register
**Hours:** 8.45am–4.30pm
Open till 5.30pm on demand
Morning session 8.45am–12 noon
Afternoon session 1.30pm–4.30pm
Open 50 weeks a year
**Status:** Private, fee-paying
**Number of years open:** 7
**Meals:** Snacks, juice, milk
**1992 fees:** £5 per session
**Waiting list:** 30 – mainly for morning session
**Registered by:** E Sussex SS
**Under same ownership:** Hillbury House II, Hove

**Premises** The nursery occupies the ground floor of a 1930s-style detached house in a smart, residential street. The owner lives upstairs. Inside the nursery, everywhere is light, bright and newly decorated. The walls of the entrance hall are lined with children's paintings, carefully framed. Mobiles hang from the ceiling. Off the hall are the three main classrooms – a messy room for creative play, a free-play room bursting with equipment and a passive or quiet room for one-to-one tuition and concentrated schoolwork. Large patio doors lead on to a concrete play area with sandpit, a good selection of outdoor toys and equipment and the nursery pets, a rabbit and a guinea pig. A separate grassed area with climbing equipment is used mainly in summer, when the paddling pool comes out. The owner's own kitchen at the back of the house is used for preparing snacks and regular cookery classes.

**Owner/Principal & staff** A former playgroup supervisor, whose main ambition has been to own her own nursery, Liz Travis, SRN, NNEB, is young, determined and efficient. She plays an active role in the nursery 'from cleaning the loos to showing parents around or playing the piano for singing, music and dance'. A specialist dance teacher visits once a week. However, Liz Travis's primary concern is to see that both staff and children are happy. She has a small, very loyal staff of three full-time and two part-time nursery nurses. They all have the NNEB qualification and the majority have been at the nursery since it opened in 1986. Staff come through personal recommendation. There is even a waiting list of people who would like to work at Hillbury House.

**Children & parents** A genuinely mixed nursery, socially and culturally, including Greek, French and Spanish children whose parents attend the local language schools. About half move on to local state schools and the other half to private schools. Most of the mums do not work and the children generally attend for a couple of sessions a week – mornings are the most popular. Children with special needs are welcome and integrate happily. There is an open-door policy towards parents. Liz Travis considers daily parental contact very important – 'even if only to say good morning'. There is a parents' noticeboard in the hallway and annual open days when the immediate and extended family are invited. During the summer, a sports day, fancy dress day and a teddy bears' picnic all carry an open invitation to parents. Phasing-in is done over the first three sessions, but then parents are expected to leave. Generally, children are expected to be out of nappies when they start.

**Curriculum & activities** No particular theory or philosophy is subscribed to, but children are encouraged to develop basic learning abilities as well as social and physical skills. There is no rigid grouping, and sessions are worked around the three rooms, with children free to move from one room to another. Staff monitoring ensures that each child experiences all aspects of the curriculum. The atmosphere is busy, happy, achieving and slightly chaotic. Most of all, the children are having fun. At each session, children spend time in the messy room (overalls provided), experiencing woodwork, water play, sand play, painting, cutting, sticking and model making. Their imaginative skills are developed in the well-equipped free-play room. Here they have a Wendy house, dressing-up clothes, hospital, shop, wooden train and a wealth of table toys, including bricks, sticklebricks, puzzles and Lego. There is a piano, a carpeted book corner and a magnificent Winnie the Pooh mural. Impressive and imaginative artwork is everywhere. Schoolwork is done on a one-to-one basis in the quiet room. Children practise pencil control, basic mathematics, shapes, colours, matching, sizing and nature studies. Seasonal projects are popular for wall displays. During a session, each child is given two worksheets to complete with nursery staff. Children learn to write confidently and know the letters of the alphabet, the concept of numbers from one to ten and basic counting and addition by the time they leave. Work, paintings and models go home each day.

**Remarks** A small, caring nursery catering for the local community, where children can gain some pre-school skills. Relaxed, happy and homely. Register early for the morning sessions.

## MOTHERCRAFT NURSERY

193 Dyke Road,
Hove
East Sussex BN3 1TL
**Tel:** (0273) 736948

**Owner:** Brighton & Hove Mothercraft Training Society
**Principal:** Barbara Doust, SRN
**Type:** Day nursery offering full-time places and half-day sessions
**Children:** 18mths–5yrs. 39 places. 120 on register

**Hours:** 8.30am–5.30pm
Morning session 9am–12 noon
Afternoon session 2pm–5pm
Open 51 weeks a year
**Status:** Fee-paying – registered charity
**Number of years open:** 29
**Meals:** Snacks. Packed lunches. Microwave available
**1992 fees:** £13.50 per day 9am–5pm
£15 per day 8.30am–5.30pm
£6 per session
**Waiting list:** Very long. Children registered before birth
**Registered by:** E Sussex SS

**Premises** Red-brick, Victorian house on busy Dyke Road. Parking is limited, but many parents walk and leave pushchairs in the porch. The unremarkable exterior does not prepare the visitor for what is to come. The nursery is stunning. The two floors of the building have been totally refurbished – no expense spared, no attention to safety precautions overlooked. Out of the blue, the Mothercraft Training Society was recently left a substantial legacy – with it they have created a breathtaking, state of the art nursery. The ground floor accommodates the principal's office, a carpeted quiet room with soft chairs which convert into small beds, floor toys and a television and video; separate toilet and nappy-changing facilities, brightly tiled in bold, colourful designs; and a space-age kitchen with dining room next door. At the back, running the entire length of the building is the 'Big Room', which caters for the toddlers (18 months–2½ years) and leads out to a marvellously well-equipped outside play area with safety surface. Upstairs are three further rooms for the older children – messy room, quiet room and playroom – and more loos of the same high standard. There is a fully equipped staff room. On the top floor is the principal's flat. The whole interior is immaculate and superbly decorated; there are wonderful soft furnishings, enhanced by exciting displays of children's work. Art and craft whichever way you turn.

**Owner/Principal & staff** The Mothercraft Training Society is a voluntary organisation which has been providing quality care for mothers and their young children in Brighton since 1934. Long before the introduction of NHS clinics, they weighed babies, arranged test feeds, promoted breast feeding and arranged lectures and advice on pregnancy and parenthood. In 1958, the Society pioneered National Childbirth Trust relaxation classes for expectant mothers. From early days, Mothercraft-trained maternity nurses were sent out into the community to help new mothers. As demand for nursery places among working women increased, Mothercraft widened their remit to include childcare and opened their first playgroup in 1963. The current head of the organisation is Barbara Doust, SRN. Affectionately known as Sister, she is an impressive, mature woman with a gentle, smiling approach. She has been at Mothercraft for 17 years. It is clear that she is very much in charge, but enjoys a warm, close relationship with staff and children. Her recently appointed deputy, Irene Holbourn, NNEB, is an excellent support and responsible for the overall, day-to-day running of the nursery. She also covers for holidays and sickness and has particular responsibility for special needs children. All full-time nursery staff (eight in total) are qualified NNEB or NAMCW. The two part-timers are experienced, with children of their own, but unqualified. The staff/child ratio is at least 1:6. Staff are recruited through local advertisements and long-standing links with the NNEB course at Eastbourne College. Staff turnover has been a problem over the last year, because of the building works, but has now stabilised.

**Children & parents** Noisy, confident children, who are mainly, but not exclusively, from middle-class backgrounds. Mixed nationalities, including Arab, Indian, Chinese and Japanese as well as British. Children with special needs are welcome. After nursery the children move on to both state and private schools. Mums are a mixture of full-time and part-time working mothers and housewives. The nursery has a close relationship with parents, who are welcome to visit or telephone at any time. Sister Doust is always available to discuss problems or worries. There are regular open days, a parents' noticeboard with a copy of the day's timetable prominently displayed and a parents' suggestion box available for comments.

**Curriculum & activities** A wide range of expensive, high-quality play and learning equipment is available on both floors. Children are encouraged to develop through play in 'an environment free from prejudice' and at a pace appropriate to their needs. No child is pressured to do anything. The youngest, downstairs, have a planned but loosely structured day with a similar programme in the mornings and afternoons. Each session begins with free play – construction toys, book corner, Wendy house, painting, sand and water play, jigsaws – masses of wonderful equipment. This is followed by milk, conversation and storytime. Outside play includes gardening, sand and water play, climbing frame, push and pull toys and an outdoor Wendy house. Group play includes dressing up, story tapes, television, pre-school games, music and movement and cookery. Group activities culminate with all the children, upstairs and downstairs, coming together for singing and finger rhymes. Upstairs, the older children are divided into three groups – Lions, Tigers and Zebras. Each group moves from one room to another in turn. Pre-school skills are encouraged in the quiet room, with worksheets and activity books. Number and letter games, shapes, size, colour and the formation of letters and numbers are all practised. There is a weather board, nature table and book corner crammed with wonderful books in perfect condition. A very high standard of arts and crafts is displayed throughout the nursery. No peripatetic teachers – music and movement are included in the timetable.

**Remarks** This nursery shows just what can be done with a windfall. Mothercraft has spent lavishly but wisely. Relaxed, happy atmosphere with hardworking, qualified staff. Mothercraft children must be among the luckiest in Brighton. Perhaps more people could be persuaded to leave their money to improving nursery provision?

## ROYAL SPA NURSERY SCHOOL
Park Hill
Brighton
East Sussex BN2 2BT
**Tel:** (0273) 607480

**Owner:** E Sussex County Council
**Headteacher:** Liz Taylor, B Ed
**Type:** Nursery school offering half-day sessions. No full-time places
**Children:** 3yrs 1mth–4yrs 11mths. 40 places (10% for special needs). 80 on register

**Hours:** Morning session 9am–11.30am
Afternoon session 1pm–3.30pm
Open during term-time only
**Status:** State nursery school
**Number of years open:** 15
**Meals:** Juice and fruit
**1992 fees:** No fees. 50p per week for snacks and juice
**Waiting list:** Very long. Approx 250 for each term's intake. Many never get a place. Priority to siblings and children with special needs
**Registered by:** E Sussex County Council SS

**Premises** A semi open-plan, single-storey nursery school, purpose-built five years ago. Elaborate Greek columns outside, reminiscent of the Parthenon, modern functional concrete inside. The school is set in a third of an acre of outside play space, in beautiful Queen's Park, overlooking the duckpond. Parking is difficult. Inside there is a quiet room with small tables and chairs for pre-reading and number work, a story room with rocking horse, piano and television and another with small tables and chairs and easy chairs. All rooms have brightly coloured walls, covered with children's pictures and craft work. The large, main classroom incorporates a number of activity areas including a home corner, book corner and a messy-play area, complete with the nursery pet, a guinea pig. Outside, a safely fenced garden is equipped with sandpit, climbing frame and soft mat, all under cover, ample ride-on toys and a lovely wooden playhouse.

**Headteacher & staff** Liz Taylor, B Ed, has taught a variety of age groups, but prefers teaching nursery age children. She came to the school as deputy head and took over as headteacher three years ago. She leads a close-knit team of 2½ teachers, two NNEB nursery assistants and two ancillary workers – committed, creative and highly skilled women of different ages, ranging from 27 to 50 years old, all with a sense of humour. The experienced ancillary workers help with the disabled children. All staff participate in INSET training and development, although the annual training budget has recently been cut back. They have weekly staff meetings, more often if necessary. Teaching and NNEB students come to the school for work experience and parents are involved in helping during sessions, serving snacks, reading, sewing and assisting with outings or special events.

**Children & parents** Approximately half of the children live in the immediate vicinity of the school, others come from as far away as Hove. They usually attend for five morning or five afternoon sessions a week. Family backgrounds vary enormously. About 11 per cent are from ethnic minority groups and a further ten per cent have special educational needs, including a Down's syndrome child, asthmatics and children with developmental, language and behavioural problems. All are well integrated and benefit greatly from their time at the nursery. Most of the school's children transfer to local state primary schools, while some go on to independent schools such as Brighton and Hove High and St Mary's Hall. The children are talkative and busy, moving happily between their chosen activities. There is excellent communication between staff and parents, especially at the beginning and end of each term. Parents also actively fund-raise for the school.

**Curriculum & activities** The nursery philosophy gives priority to building children's confidence, respect, independence and self-esteem. Each day is carefully planned to provide children with a wide range of opportunities across the curriculum, helping make them socially aware, at ease and able to relate confidently to their peers. They learn mainly through structured play, both individually and in groups, with staff developing play experiences to extend thinking, pose problems or invite suggestions. There are a great variety of choices available, including art and craft materials, home corner, construction toys, puzzles, table-top games, number activities and physical and imaginative play. Equipment and resources are plentiful and well maintained. There is more focused teaching and group work through storytelling, drama, music and cookery. Although there is no formal reading or writing, activities are chosen to develop the necessary pre-reading and pre-writing skills, and many children can recognise and write their own name. Books are important. Children and adults make their own, there are well-chosen reference books on display and children can take books home. Much of the work is related to a topic or theme. Children have daily outdoor play whenever possible and are taken on outings throughout the year to farms, markets, beaches, castles and pantomimes. Record keeping is limited, but when a child leaves for full-time primary education a report of his/her development goes with them. Full use is made of the beautiful park surrounding the nursery.

**Remarks** It is worth waiting for a place at this very popular, happy and friendly LEA nursery school. Unfortunately, many children on the waiting list will be disappointed as demand far exceeds supply. Children reach a high standard of achievement. According to a 1991 Government Inspector's report, 'Royal Spa Nursery School is an effective school. The staff are committed and energetic. In some cases children are already working at or beyond Level 1 of the core subjects of the National Curriculum.' Resources are needed to provide more facilities like this in the county.

# TOM THUMB NURSERY SCHOOL & KINDERGARTEN

12 The Avenue
Eastbourne
East Sussex BN21 3YA
**Tel:** (0323) 647630

**Owner/Principal:** Anne Walker, SRN, SCM, Mont Dip, HV Cert, FWT Cert
**Type:** Day nursery offering full-time places and half-day sessions
**Children:** 18mths–5yrs. 63 places. 176 on register
**Hours:** 8.30am–5.30pm
Morning session 9am–12 noon
Afternoon session 1.30pm–4.30pm
Open 50 weeks a year
**Status:** Private, fee-paying
**Number of years open:** 8
**Meals:** Lunch, tea, snacks
**1992 fees:** £12.25 per day
£1.75 per hour + 85p per meal
£10 refundable deposit
**Waiting list:** Minimal. For babies only
**Registered by:** E Sussex County Council SS

**Premises** A huge, sprawling four-storey Victorian house in one of Eastbourne's main avenues. The entire house is given over to the nursery, with the kindergarten in the basement for toddlers 18 months to 2½ years old, two classrooms on the ground floor for 2½- to 3-year-olds and two classrooms on the first floor for the oldest group. The top floor is an adult area with staff room and office, and is rather gloomy and unwelcoming. The building is well used and rather battered in parts. At the back is a car-park for staff and parents and a small garden with four plastic rabbits.

**Owner/Principal & staff** Anne Walker, SRN, SCM, Mont Dip, HV Cert, FWT Cert, started a nursery eight years ago above a greengrocer's shop in Eastbourne, and moved to bigger premises when her reputation and the demand for places grew. She has many years midwifery and health visiting experience and is a constant source of advice and reassurance for parents and staff. Her husband owns a toy shop in town which supplies much of the nursery equipment. Staff are split between the three floors, each floor led by a qualified, experienced nursery nurse, assisted by two less experienced or unqualified helpers. Hardworking, enthusiastic and friendly, they span a range of different ages, personalities and skills.

**Children & parents** There is only one other nursery in Eastbourne which takes children under 2, and with only five baby places at Tom Thumb demand is inevitably high. Parents, about half of whom work full-time, are made to feel welcome and encouraged to participate. There is an annual parents' evening in June and a children's party at Christmas.

**Curriculum & activities** The curriculum varies according to the age group. In the basement kindergarten, there are liberal amounts of creative and free play, play dough and simple puzzles, although some colouring and pencil control exercises are done each day. The ground and first floors plan their curriculum yearly in advance, including project work. Each morning begins with group discussion, introducing a new letter, number, shape and colour. The children then split into groups for a number or letter exercise on worksheets, a practical task – puzzles, construction, table-top game – or an art or craft activity. The groups rotate so that each child completes three activities each day. Afternoons follow a similar timetable, with some outdoor play added. Reading schemes (Ladybird and Letterland) are used when a child is ready – usually after his/her third birthday. Written reports are prepared every ten weeks on all children over 2½. There are beach, park and library visits and regular outings to local places of interest.

**Remarks** 'A safe, secure and friendly environment for families who need affordable care' is principal Anne Walker's description of her nursery. No fancy frills or trimmings, but excellent value for money in an area with little or no childcare provision for low-income families and only a handful of baby places, no matter how much you can afford to pay.

# YOUNG SUSSEX

165 Portland Road
Hove
East Sussex BN3 5QJ
**Tel:** (0273) 777001

**Owner/Principal:** Ingrid Boyd, BA, Teachers' Cert
**Type:** Day nursery and nursery school offering full- and part-time places and half-day sessions
**Children:** 3mths–5yrs. 65 places. 150 on register
**Hours:** 8.30am–5.30pm
Morning session 8.30am–12.30pm
Afternoon session 1.30pm–5.30pm
Open 50 weeks a year
**Status:** Private, fee-paying
**Number of years open:** 3½
**Meals:** Lunch, tea, snacks
**1992 fees:** £9.50 per session – under 2
£7.50 per session – 2–5yrs
£1.30 per day for lunch
£1.50 per session for dance
**Waiting list:** Reasonable
**Registered by:** E Sussex County Council SS
**Under same ownership:** Young Sussex II, Hove; Young Sussex, Shoreham-by-Sea

**Premises** Victorian, brick-built school, with a 50-year-old concrete addition and large wooden office on one side. Situated in a busy area of town near all forms of public transport and with easy parking. The nursery occupies eight rooms, all on one level. It is a spacious, light and happy place, with huge supplies of colourful equipment and bright blue carpets, curtains and furniture. Babies and toddlers have their own carpeted day room, sleep room and spotless kitchen area. The over-2s have a messy-play room, quiet area, two general playrooms for puzzles, construction toys, home corner, dressing up, etc, and a physical playroom which doubles as a dining room with indoor climbing frame, slide and large play equipment. The premises are in very good condition inside and out. There is a moderate-sized outside tarmac play area with a climbing frame set on a wood-chip safety base.

**Owner/Principal & staff** Ingrid Boyd, BA, Teachers' Cert, has set up the type of nurseries she would have liked for her own children but was unable to find. Prior to opening Young Sussex in Hove and Shoreham, she taught child psychology to NNEB students. In the early days she had a 'hands on' role, though she has now become primarily a manager and administrator. However, she always visits each nursery at some time during the day and has a comprehensive understanding of the children and staff. Her supervisor and deputies are all NNEB trained and conscientious, gentle young women, concerned with maintaining high standards. All staff have some childcare qualification, usually NNEB, NAMCW, City & Guilds or PPA. They have good relationships with parents and have created a calm, well-organised and stimulating environment. NNEB students gain work experience here. The day we visited, there were 51 children and 13 nursery nurses. The keyworker system has been rejected here. Ingrid Boyd believes that it is important for children to know and trust all members of staff. Babies have two or three special carers.

**Children & parents** The children are predominantly middle class. Many professional parents – doctors, accountants and teachers – have children here. Others are footballers, nurses, hairdressers, owners of small businesses. Children are mainly white British or European, with a handful of Japanese, Kuwaitis and Romanians. They appear happy and chatty without being noisy, and seemed to be extremely polite to one another, staff and visitors. Some transfer to local state primary schools, while others move to independent schools such as the Fold and Kingscliffe. The nursery willingly integrates children with most special educational needs and disabilities, although sometimes, as in the case of twins with hydrocephalus, they need extra staff. Parents of new children are offered a minimum of two settling-in sessions, at no charge.

**Curriculum & activities** No particular philosophy. Ingrid says, 'We have taken the best of a variety of educational philosophies including Montessori and Steiner.' Children are provided with a mix of free play and structured learning activities. They are divided into groups according to age. The large numbers attending make it impractical to have periods all together. Each day is divided into two sessions and structured to include free indoor and outdoor play, interspersed with quiet periods of educational and creative activities, individually or in a small group. Each session includes music, storytime and a break for a drink and snack. Every day staff talk to, read to and play with individual children, both to help with their language development and to build up a strong relationship with them. Children often take special objects or toys to nursery to talk about at conversation time. Dancing, keep-fit, cookery and occasional visits to the park, library and places of interest are all part of the curriculum. Weekly gymnastics sessions are held at the local gym. Each child has a record book which staff fill in regularly. Once a year, a full progress report is done. Parents have access to all written records about their children. As children get older their periods of learning time increase and they are introduced to basic reading, writing and numeracy skills. When they are ready, they use the Ginn reading scheme. Most are ready for this, but those not willing are not pushed. There is a summer outing and Christmas party. 'The most important thing is that the child is happy. A happy child will learn, a well-cared-for child will learn,' says Ingrid. Lunches are provided by the school meals service.

**Remarks** A lovely nursery offering a very high standard of childcare. Kind, well-qualified staff, happy and interested children. Plenty of individual attention and the right balance between learning through free play and structured, guided activities. Excellent facilities for babies, with a very high standard of hygiene.

# Essex

One of the worst providers of nursery education in the country, despite a large population of young children. Only one in 40 children under 5 receives a part-time place before starting school. Many 3- and 4-year-olds compete for a few sessions a week in a playgroup. Full-time day nurseries are equally lacking. The private and voluntary sectors are unable to keep up with demand. There are already 77 private day nurseries, a backlog of applications still to be processed and more coming in. However, fees exclude all but high income earners. The number of childminders has dropped since the Children Act came into force, but appears to meet demand at present. The real need is for nursery education and affordable daycare.

**Further information**

For details on day nurseries, childminders and playgroups:
Department of Social Services
PO Box 297
Chelmsford CM1 1YS
Social Services Helpline Tel: (0245) 492211

For details on nursery schools, units and classes:
Education Department
Treadneedle House
Market Road
Chelmsford CM1 1LD
Tel: (0245) 492211

# ALEC HUNTER PLAYGROUP

Alec Hunter High School
Stubbs Lane
Braintree
Essex CM7 6NR
**Tel:** (0376) 321813

**Supervisor/Leader:** Wendy Rowlinson, PPA Foundation
**Type:** Playgroup offering 5 morning and 2 afternoon sessions a week, plus a parent and toddler group
**Children:** 3–5yrs. 26 places. 70 on register
**Hours:** Morning session 9am–12.10pm
Afternoon session 1.30pm–3.45pm
Open 38 weeks a year
**Status:** Fee-paying, non profit-making, voluntary playgroup
**Number of years open:** 21
**Meals:** None
**1992 fees:** £2.25 per morning session
£2 per afternoon session
**Waiting list:** Fairly long. Places usually found
**Registered by:** Essex County Council SS

**Premises** Full-size classroom in a concrete extension at the back of the Alec Hunter High School. Access via a side street, with parking spaces available. There is no nearby public transport. Interior decoration is simple and basic. Staff have painted the walls in their spare time. The classroom is large and light, with curtains screening the bottom half of the windows from the school playground. High school pupils are welcome to come into the nursery. The playgroup has the use of the school library and sometimes the ovens in the school kitchens for baking. There is a very limited outside area of concrete paving surrounded by a high fence. At present it contains a playhouse only, but more outdoor equipment is to be purchased once a safety surface has been laid. The playgroup also has access to the school playing fields.

**Supervisor/Leader & staff** Wendy Rowlinson took over from her neighbour as the playgroup leader three years ago, and completed the PPA Foundation Course. Eight of the ten staff also have the PPA Foundation course qualification, and most have first-aid training. All are former users of the playgroup who have gradually become more and more involved. Many have been close friends for years. Their ages range from mid-20s to late 40s. From time to time a father joins the team. Staff work on a rota basis, and put their names down for whichever sessions suit them best. Consequently there is always a member of the team available to cover for sickness and absence. Parents also help out regularly in the classroom, but the new Children Act means that parents with children below the minimum age limit of 3 can no longer bring them along. As a result, a number of helpers have been forced to drop out. Parents who help out get the session free for their child. Students and pupils from the school also attend for work experience. On the day we visited, the staff/child ratio was 1:6. The staff training policy encourages all workers to complete the PPA Foundation Course and first-aid training.

**Children & parents** The children are of mixed ability, the majority from one-parent and low-income families; many are unemployed. Nearly all go on to Becker Green and Chapel Green, the local primary schools. Due to demand for places, most children attend for only two sessions a week. Those wanting a third session must wait until the term before they commence school. Children are not divided by age and spend each session all together. The two afternoon sessions are kept mainly for younger children. Children with special educational needs are welcome. One child wears a body brace and there are others with speech, hearing and emotional difficulties. A parent and toddler group is held every Tuesday afternoon. This is used as a way of introducing new parents and children to the playgroup and its staff. Parents are welcome at any time and a complaints and compliments book is always available for comment or criticism. The playgroup has a float each year in the local carnival, as well as a teddy bears' picnic and a range of other fund-raising activities, all of which depend on parental support.

**Curriculum & activities** Learning through play, following PPA guidelines. Wendy Rowlinson emphasises that she and her staff are not teachers. They concentrate mainly on the emotional and social development of the children. There is a reasonable amount of equipment, including a climbing frame, water trough, sand tray which, when covered, doubles as a woodwork bench, dressing-up clothes and a book corner. A different theme is chosen for the interest table each month and there is plenty of creative play – drawing, painting, modelling and sticking. Children are not taught to read and write, but any child who shows interest is given encouragement. Formal education is minimal. Staff and helpers are instructed to use lower case letters and are provided with guidelines on letter formation. Each child visits the school library once a fortnight and the playgroup is gradually building up its own supply of books. There is a farm trip once a year and a Christmas party, attended by everyone. Children help to put together a personal folder in their last term describing their progress and achievements, which they take to their first school.

**Remarks** Dedicated staff who are paid very little and devote a great deal of unpaid spare time to the playgroup. Four places are subsidised by Braintree Comfort Fund and others, for children with learning difficulties, by the local authority. Staff recognise that the outside area is below standard, and are desperately trying to find the £10,000 required to lay a safety surface and buy equipment. Last year, for the first time, they were unable to break even and the High School stepped in to make up the shortfall.

## BO-PEEP DAY NURSERY

Rear of 74 Christchurch Road
Southend-on-Sea
Essex SS7 2EA
**Tel:** (0702) 467362

**Owner:** Steve Thomas
**Officer-in-charge:** Barbara Rayner, NNEB
**Type:** Day nursery offering full- and part-time places and half-day sessions
**Children:** 6wks–5yrs. 50 places. 85 on register
**Hours:** 7am–7pm
Morning session 8am–12 noon
Afternoon session 2pm–6pm
Open 50 weeks a year
**Status:** Private, fee-paying
**Number of years open:** 2½
**Meals:** Breakfast, lunch, tea, snacks
**1992 fees:** £80 per week full-time – under 2
£70 per week full-time – over 2
£17 per day
£35 per week for 5 sessions – over 2
£8.50 per session – under 2
£8 per session – over 2
25% sibling discount
**Waiting list:** None. Places available
**Registered by:** Essex County Council SS

**Premises** Purpose-built, modern two-storey premises on a quarter-acre site in a residential area of Southend. Plenty of parking outside. The main central playroom, with teaching/quiet room, messy-play room, dining room, kitchen, laundry, changing room and toilet block leading off, occupies the ground floor. Upstairs, babies have separate play and sleep rooms. There is also a staff room and office. Everywhere is light and well decorated, carpeted, well furnished and well equipped. A cheerful environment for young children. The dining room walls are papered with photographs of all the nursery activities since it opened. Outside, children have fenced-off grass and tarmac areas, a sandpit and Postman Pat climbing equipment, all used daily.

**Owner, Officer-in-charge & staff** Owner and administrator, Steve Thomas, is usually at the nursery full-time taking care of finance, administration and practical problems. He also does the shopping. Originally a wholesale greengrocer with a flagging business, he decided to redevelop the site, converting his warehouse into a nursery and doing much of the work himself. Barbara Rayner, NNEB, is the officer-in-charge of the day-to-day care of the children. She qualified as an NNEB 13 years ago and has previous experience as a nanny, working with handicapped children in a special school, and in an inner city local authority nursery. Seven of the staff are qualified, including four NNEBs and an SRN. Many of the part-timers are unqualified. There is no qualified teacher as yet. Staff vary in age and experience and appear to have good relationships with each other and the children. Students come for work experience. The day we visited, there were four babies with two carers, and 37 children over 2 years old with seven nursery workers. Steve Thomas and his team would welcome male nursery workers, but tell us that parents are very against the idea. 'They think it should be women's work,' he says.

**Children & parents** The children come from a wide range of backgrounds and cultures, including a handful from ethnic minority groups, mainly Chinese and Indian. Many of the children have working parents, some in highly paid jobs. Others are students whose children have subsidised places. Parents are encouraged to phone whenever they want, but not to visit too often, as this can unsettle the children. Staff are responsive to parents' and children's problems. Many of the children move to private schools in Westcliff and Southend – Eton House, Alun Court, Crowstone and Ridley School. Bournemouth Park is the most popular state school. The nursery is happy to take special needs children and the officer-in-charge has experience in this area.

**Curriculum & activities** Children learn through play, with lots of hugs and sitting on laps. Equipment is colourful and new (annual budget £1000) and there are opportunities for creative self-expression through painting, play dough, music and movement. The day starts with free play. At 9am children split into groups for structured activities. Stories and singing, with all the children, take place after lunch and break. Time is set aside each day for quiet storytime and looking at books. There is no formal teaching of the 3Rs, but older children are encouraged to develop pre-reading, pre-writing and pre-number skills before leaving for school. Cooking sessions take place twice weekly and music features daily, along with outdoor play. There are no outings, but visiting treats include a bouncy castle, a guitarist and lambs during the spring.

**Remarks** Excellent premises, converted to a high standard, with the owner doing much of the work himself. He and his staff have created a bright, welcoming environment for the children of working parents. Proposed plans to recruit a qualified nursery teacher and more qualified nursery nurses will enhance the quality of this service.

# BUBBLES DAY NURSERY AND NURSERY SCHOOL

Parsonage Street
Halstead
Essex CO9 2JT
**Tel:** (0787) 478434

**Owner/Principal:** Victoria Spencer, SRN, DN, HV
**Type:** Day nursery offering full- and part-time places. Nursery school offering 5 morning and 2 afternoon sessions a week
**Children:** Day nursery 3mths–4yrs 11mths. 24 places.
Nursery school 3yrs–4yrs 11mths. 14 places. 60 on register
**Hours:** 8am–6pm
Open 50 weeks a year
**Status:** Private, fee-paying
**Number of years open:** 4½
**Meals:** Breakfast, lunch, tea, snacks
**1992 fees:** *Day nursery*
£87 per week full-time – under 2
£85 per week full-time – over 2
£20 per day
£2.60 or £2.65 per hour depending on age
£1.50 per day for lunch
£1.50 for weekly swimming session
*Nursery school*
£32 per week (5 sessions)
£7 per session part-time
**Waiting list:** Moderate. Long for under-2s.
**Registered by:** Essex County Council SS

**Premises** A post-war HORSA unit, erected in the grounds of Richard de Clare County Primary School in Halstead. Just off the High Street, with easy access and ample parking. The large, solid, 40-year-old building has been well adapted to provide a very light and cheerful day nursery, with pretty curtains and pale blue floor coverings. The spacious, main playroom, with home corner and cosy quiet area, comfortable settee and television, is used by the over-2s. The baby room is partitioned off, with nappy changing facilities, playpen and pram. There is a separate sleep room with cots and an activity area for the under-2s. Other accommodation includes an office, hallway and cloakroom, kitchenette and staff room. It is a friendly, homely nursery, well equipped and full of toys. The more recently opened nursery school occupies two rooms in a nearby youth centre, on the same campus. The classroom is again bright and lively, with small tables and chairs, displays of work and a library table with books standing open to invite reading. Toilets are shared with the youth centre. Both the nursery and the nursery school have use of the large school grounds, incorporating a woodland and nature area, nature trail and separate, fenced-off play area with a pets' corner.

**Owner/Principal & staff** Victoria Spencer, SRN, DN, HV, has four children and trained as a health visitor. She ran a playgroup in New Zealand and the present nursery grew from a small crèche, which she started in an annexe of her own home. Her supervisors are all trained nursery nurses, and staff work closely together with a common consensus on good childcare. They all enjoy warm relations with the children. The owner is always present to co-ordinate activities and maintain personal contact with children and parents. Students come for work experience. The nursery school class is led by two trained infant teachers, who work with a nursery nurse assistant and an additional helper. The staff/child ratio is good; 1:3 overall in the day nursery, 1:5 in the nursery school. A male assistant in the nursery school has recently been replaced by a qualified worker in line with Children Act requirements for qualified staff. All nursery workers are offered first-aid training; the cost of other relevant training is shared between the nursery and staff.

**Children & parents** Children are from local families, many with two working parents. A small number of Chinese children attend. Others, whose families have special needs, are subsidised by Social Services. Parents of new children are encouraged to make frequent initial short visits, to settle them in successfully. Many progress to local state primary schools, a few to Gosfield and Sudbury in the private sector. Children attending the day nursery are offered the option of a place at the nursery school for part of the day after their 3rd birthday. Special needs children are welcomed and the nursery can call on Social Services for additional support if required. Parents are actively encouraged to phone during the day to enquire about their children.

**Curriculum & activities** The emphasis is on love, space, safety and early stimulation for under-2s. Babies from 9 months are encouraged to participate in outdoor and indoor activities, including painting and gluing. They also spend time with older children in a family setting as a natural way of learning. Over-2s learn through play. A wide range of activities and equipment are available all the time (generous annual equipment budget of £4000). They are encouraged to talk and listen and are introduced to shapes, colours and numbers. There are daily opportunities for imaginative play, art, craft, dance and movement. During outdoor play the children have access to the pets' corner for cuddling and feeding the rabbits and guinea pigs. A typical day in the nursery school includes pre-literacy skills, news, art and craft, outside play and physical games, stories, songs and rhymes. There is a strong emphasis on nature, centred on regular walks through the grounds to study animals, trees and plants. Children ready to read use the Oxford Reading Tree, Ladybird and Through the Rainbow schemes. Work is theme-based, using workbooks and 'Stagecoach Learning' worksheets. At the end of each session, achievements are discussed and displayed. Full written records are kept on children's activities and progress; parents have access to these. Music and swimming are undertaken once a week, and there are termly outings. Recently started 'Spotlight' sessions on Friday afternoons offer an introduction to music, dance and drama for older children. A good prospectus provides accurate and fair information for parents.

**Remarks** Small, warm and friendly. A nursery with a dedicated owner who has invested a good deal of time and money in the service. Quality care and very good value. Older children have the option of nursery education from qualified teachers to supplement their daycare.

# GRAYS HALL DAY NURSERY

Grays Hall
Rectory Road
Sible Hedingham
Essex CO9 3NU
**Tel:** (0787) 60746

**Owner/Administrator:** Jean Gooderham, Registered Childminder
**Senior Nursery Nurse:** Micki Asbey, NNEB, SEN
**Type:** Day nursery offering full- and part-time places and half-day sessions
**Children:** 0-5yrs. 30 places (6 for babies). 45 on register
**Hours:** 7.30am–6.30pm
Flexible hours
Open 52 weeks a year (excl bank holidays)
**Status:** Private, fee-paying
**Number of years open:** 2¾
**Meals:** Breakfast, lunch, tea, snacks
**1992 fees:** £84 per week full-time – under 2
£74 per week full-time – over 2
£17 per day – under 2
£15 per day – over 2
£13 per day (9.30am–3.30pm) – over 2
£9 per half-day (+ £1 inc lunch) – under 2
£8 per half-day (+ £1 inc lunch) – over 2
**Waiting list:** None. Places available
**Registered by:** Essex County Council SS

**Premises** A very attractive 17th-century listed building, next to the village church, and close to the A604 Colchester–Cambridge road. It is approached by a tree-lined driveway, leading to a private courtyard. The nursery uses five rooms on the two lower floors of the house. The upper floors are the owner's home. The babies have separate accommodation on the lower floor: a playroom, carpeted and well decorated, and a sleep room with cots and a single bed for toddlers. Upstairs there is an art and craft room leading off the kitchen, used for messy play, with room for four children at a time; a quiet room, also used as the dining room, with television, blackboard and library; and finally a room for imaginative play, with playhouse, home corner and beanbags for storytime. Other rooms include a kitchen, office/staff room and toilets. There is an acre of garden, which has two grassy areas set aside for the children's use, with a climbing frame, sandpit, bikes and tricycles, a picnic area and a flowerbed for planting seeds.

**Owner/Administrator & staff** Jean Gooderham has brought up five sons and is now a grandmother. Warm and motherly, she is known to the children as Auntie Jean and runs the nursery as one large, happy family. Her involvement is total, including all the cooking and administration. Senior Nursery Nurse, Micki Asbey, NNEB, SEN, worked on children's wards at Addenbrookes Hospital before moving to Grays Hall. All other members of the team have NNEB qualifications or childcare experience. There are four full-time nursery nurses and three part-timers, some of whom are registered childminders. All except two have completed the St John's first-aid course. The management structure is informal with staff gathering for discussions as necessary. There are brief meetings every day and serious matters wait until the evening. Most staff are happy to stay late if required. There is a good age range among staff, and they have warm relationships with the children. No staff turnover. No staff training budget, but some limited access to Social Services courses. Students on work experience attend regularly.

**Children & parents** The nursery is gradually building up a reputation in the area and aims to attract commuters, as well as local families. The social mix has widened considerably since it opened in January 1991; children come from a range of backgrounds, although there are no ethnic minorities in the area. Many parents are professionals or self-employed, while others are teachers or office workers. Virtually all work full-time. Children are divided into three age groups: babies (up to 18 months), toddlers (from 18 months to 3 years) and pre-school children (from 3 to 5 years). All children are brought together in the morning, at lunchtime and in the evening so that they can socialise with each other. Children with disabilities are welcome, but there is no wheelchair access. Parents are invited to look at their children's work every day.

**Curriculum & activities** The nursery's philosophy is 'Learning through play, leading to traditional learning methods as the child progresses'. Babies are provided with a large selection of toys, from cuddlies and dolls to shape sorters, Duplo and puzzles, to encourage hand/eye co-ordination, social skills and language development. Older children divide their time between the three upstairs rooms following a loosely structured timetable. Monthly topics are covered to help promote discovery and language development. Pre-school activities take place in the quiet room and older children learn pre-reading, pre-writing and pre-number work, although no child is pressurised into this. The Ladybird and Letterland reading schemes are available, and children have learnt to read a few words before they move to their next school. The quiet room is also used for daily music and movement sessions, accompanied by a piano, as well as many other instruments. There are twice-weekly nature walks. Visits take place to the library every fortnight and to primary schools for Harvest Festival and Christmas plays. The nursery maintains strong links with local primary schools and co-ordinates its pre-school learning with them. Progress and development are monitored and recorded once a term. Pre-school work is recorded weekly. Parents have access to all written reports.

**Remarks** A marvellous family atmosphere created by warm, mature staff led by Auntie Jean. Plenty of love, cuddles and security. No qualified teacher and an unstructured programme, but children are given a good grounding in pre-school skills by caring and loving staff. Among the lowest fees in the area.

# LITTLE SPARROWS NURSERY

High Street
Ingatestone
Essex CM4 9EY
**Tel:** (0277) 352123

**Owner:** Elim Pentecostal Church
**Supervisor:** Irene Turner, Mont Dip, PPA
**Type:** Christian day nursery offering full-time and part-time places. No sessions
**Children:** 2–5yrs. 15 places. 42 on register
**Hours:** 8.15am–5.45pm
Open 48 weeks a year
**Status:** Private, fee-paying, non profit-making
**Number of years open:** 5
**Meals:** Packed lunches, snacks
**1992 fees:** £14 per day
**Waiting list:** Long. 61 names
**Registered by:** Essex County Council SS

**Premises** A church hall, set back from the High Street in Ingatestone. Limited parking in front of the hall and a bus service along the High Street. The building is brick, single storey and consists of two rooms, a kitchen and office. The larger of the rooms feels warm and cosy in spite of its size; the smaller one, laid with carpet tiles which are due for replacement soon, is used as a playroom and quiet room. Both areas have part-panelled walls, with the upper half painted white. They are well lit, with large windows and strip-lighting. The property is well maintained and clean. Outside there is a concrete area for playing, a sand pit, bikes, a see-saw and a small garden with flower tubs. Next door is the local fire station, a source of great interest to children and staff, particularly when there is a call-out.

**Supervisor & staff** Irene Turner, Mont Dip, PPA, a former medical secretary, started the nursery four years ago, because she felt that private nurseries in the district were 'big business' and she wanted to run a non profit-making, family service at an affordable price. She also favours motherly staff to make the children feel secure. Social Services and the LEA subsidise some of the places, and support the nursery by providing a speech therapist, special needs teacher, physiotherapist and community physician when necessary. There is an impressive, dedicated team of nursery workers, two full-time and six part-time. All except two are qualified NNEB and PPA and they cover a range of ages and cultures. Male nursery nurses and students have proved a great success in the past. Irene Turner says, 'I would really like to have a permanent man on the staff. We have children who live alone with their mothers and it's nice for them to have male company.' Students always work under supervision from a qualified member of staff or a tutor. Staff are keen to take part in any additional training available, especially special needs courses. This is a particularly well-knit group of highly motivated nursery workers.

**Children & parents** The children come from a complete cross-section of the community, both culturally and socially. When they leave, they transfer to state and private schools in the district. Children work in groups for part of the time – for language work in the morning and number and science work in the afternoon. The rest of the day, they are free to choose their activities. They appear happy, busy and supervised in a sensible, understanding way. The nursery has set up a charity to help fund children with special needs. It is fully supported by parents, who firmly believe in the benefits of integration. There is an open-door policy, with parents encouraged to come in at any time. Particular problems can be discussed with Irene Turner by appointment.

**Curriculum & activities** The school is well resourced with stimulating toys and books (annual equipment budget £3600). Montessori equipment and methods are used, but not exclusively. There is a climbing frame, play house, sand pit and wheeled toys for riding. Art and craft work takes place every day and there is dancing. Reading is encouraged, and the 1-2-3 & Away scheme is used when a child is ready. No pressure is exerted and children develop at their own speed. Most can read basic words by the time they move on to the next stage. There are nursery pets – two hamsters and two rabbits – looked after by staff and children on a rota basis. Written records are kept, to which parents have access. Children are constantly monitored. This is a Christian nursery, and children are taught that God cares for them and has a special love for each one of them. They say grace at mealtimes and special prayers and are read stories with a moral or Christian message. There are occasional visits to farms, a steam railway or somewhere relevant to the current theme. The 4-year-olds are taken swimming in a hydrotherapy pool once a week.

**Remarks** A busy, friendly, relaxed atmosphere. The relationship between children and staff is natural and close. The Christian ethic is the mainstay of the teaching programme and is apparent in every aspect of the timetable. The nursery has a deservedly high reputation for its care of children with disabilities and special educational needs. Completely integrated, they are helped and loved by staff, children and parents and add a special dimension to the life of the nursery. Nursery provision in the area is very poor; Irene Turner has extended her facilities to provide a wider, family service. Fees are very reasonable for the quality of service.

# SCHOOLGATE NURSERY

Potter Street County Primary School
Carters Mead
Harlow
Essex CM17 9EQ
**Tel:** (0279) 416708 (owner's home)

**Owners/Organisers:** Wendy Smith, B Sc
Miranda Smith, NNEB
**Type:** Nursery school offering half-day sessions. No full-time places
**Children:** 3–5yrs. 24 places. 85 on register
**Hours:** Morning session 8.30am–12.30pm
Afternoon session 1pm–3pm
Open 40 weeks a year
**Status:** Private, fee-paying
**Number of years open:** 3
**Meals:** Juice and fruit
**1992 fees:** 75p per hour
**Waiting list:** 30 on list. Longer list for morning sessions
**Registered by:** Essex County Council SS

**Premises** A prefabricated, single-storey classroom, rented from the primary school. Completely refurbished by the Council two years ago, the large, light classroom is well equipped with trampoline, Wendy house, musical instruments, gym equipment and multi-purpose 'waffle' blocks which are used as seating and also for making planes, boats, trains and bridges. The entrance lobby houses a sand tray, puzzle table, nature table complete with worms and reading area. The nursery has use of a roped-off area in the school playground which can be extended when necessary. The swings in the recreation ground are visited once or twice a week, weather permitting, and children are led across to this holding on to a 'crocodile rope' – each child holds a loop in the rope and never lets go. They are accompanied by several members of staff and sing a song as they go. The owners' swimming pool is visited in similar fashion during the summer. Owner, Wendy Smith, is a former lifesaver.

**Owners/Organisers & staff** Wendy Smith, B Sc, has been running nursery schools for many years in different parts of the country, and in her own home for 14 years. Her daughter, Miranda Smith, NNEB, is her partner and together they are in charge of the team of one full-time and five part-time workers. Mrs Smith's sons also help out occasionally. The staff range in age from Flo, who is 76 and does the school bus run with her husband, to the youngest, in her early 20s. Beryl Coleman has taken the PPA Foundation Course and Kasloom Malik, the afternoon supervisor, is taking the City & Guilds course. They are a talented group; Miranda plays guitar and keyboard and Margaret Wright is a qualified dance teacher. Staff are addressed by their surnames except for Miranda who is known to everyone by her Christian name. Staff/child ratio is 1:6. They are a friendly, kind team who listen to the children and give cuddles when they are needed. The owners see the nursery as a labour of love and pay themselves only low salaries.

**Children & parents** In an area of high unemployment, many of the children come from distressing homes. Others, with single working parents, are collected by child minders at the end of their sessions. The local population consists mainly of manual and semi-skilled workers. A good cross-section of the local population attends the school, including the children of four of the school governors. There is some ethnic mix. The local authority pays for two places each week. About 60 per cent of children transfer to Potter Street school and the rest to other state schools in Harlow. In the past the nursery has successfully integrated a child with a heart condition and another with severe allergies. 'We are happy to take any special needs, and if necessary we would get appropriate staff and assistance from Harlow Council,' Wendy Smith says. If wheelchair ramps or other equipment were required, she would approach the Council for a grant and other support. Parents are welcome to discuss ideas or problems at any time and are involved as much as they want to be. Along with various computer companies in the area, they provide all the paper used in the nursery. Children appear happy, busy, polite and at times noisy. Special efforts have been made to encourage ethnic minority children, including language classes for parents in the lobby of the nursery and the appointment of an Asian supervisor.

**Curriculum & activities** The emphasis is on building confidence and self-esteem in preparation for life in large primary school classes. Children are given free choice within a loosely structured timetable and work their way around the abundant equipment (annual budget £1000) during the course of a session. The day starts with free play and breakfast from the 'snack bar' for any children who have not eaten at home. Mostly the children divide themselves into groups, choosing to be with their friends. The rising-5s are separated from the rest for pre-school work, though not forced if they prefer to do something else. Floor and table activities are followed by outdoor play, children's television, music, sand and water play, break and storytime. Workbooks are available for the older children and there is a generous supply of books. Most children leave reading-ready and some, with additional parental encouragement, are free-reading by the time they move up to their next school. Academic records are not kept as they have never been asked for. There is close involvement with the local community – Wendy Smith plays a leading role in the local Community Centre – and children have been sponsored to raise money for a local hospice. The accent is on communication, manners and consideration for others. Wendy Smith says, 'We like to think that we teach social skills, with a big emphasis on kindness. We try to say good things about each other and point out the goodness in each child. Even if the odd child is "naughty", we say he or she is "usually kind".' Music, dance and movement, drama and gymnastics take place often. Children also take part in Harlow's Tidy Up week each year. Outings to the local park for nature studies, library and fire station. There is an occasional puppet show, and also picnics, sports days and swimming (ratio 1:1) in the summer.

**Remarks** A school with a real sense of community. Caring, kindly staff prepare the 'whole child' for the harsh realities of life in a large primary school reception class. Exceptionally good value for money – Wendy Smith and her daughter are subsidising childcare in the area themselves.

# WATERSHIP DOWNS NURSERY SCHOOL

Downs Road
Maldon
Essex CM9 7HG
**Tel:** (0621) 858478

**Owner/Principal:** Barbara Payne, Cert Ed
**Type:** Nursery school offering half-day sessions, plus an all-day session on Friday for pre-school children
**Children:** 2yrs 10mths–4yrs 11mths. 26 places. 123 on register
**Hours:** Morning session 9.30am–12 noon
Afternoon session 1pm–3.30pm
Open 46 weeks a year
**Status:** Private, fee-paying
**Number of years open:** 13
**Meals:** Snacks only. Packed lunches on Fridays
**1992 fees:** £4.75 per session
**Waiting list:** Very long. 200 names (some registered at birth)
**Registered by:** Essex County Council SS

**Premises** Attractive, single-storey former chandlery, erected in the 1920s, overlooking the river Blackwater near the centre of Maldon. An interesting and exciting place for children from the moment they step into the front garden, with a pretty outdoor playhouse, dinghy, rabbits, guinea pigs and many outdoor toys waiting on the verandah. Inside is warm, stimulating and welcoming, full of high-quality, well-maintained equipment. There is a small cloakroom, a nature room, with excellent displays and materials, a large classroom, with quiet room adjoining, a small office and toilets. The main classroom has large windows and plenty of natural light. It includes a home corner, messy-play space, tables and chairs and a quiet room through an archway. The walls are covered with children's work. Next door to the nursery is a large grassy area, which is used for sports day and summer activities.

**Owner/Principal & staff** Barbara Payne, Cert Ed, opened this well-established nursery 13 years ago, after experience teaching reception class infants. She still takes overall responsibility and is always available to help children, staff and parents. Her team comprises a qualified nursery/infant teacher, an NNEB and four nursery workers – PPA and City & Guilds qualified. Three members of staff have been at the nursery since it opened. There are no staff turnover problems at all. Termly staff meetings are held, where staff 'bounce ideas off each other'. A first-aider is always on the premises. There is no formal training policy or budget. Barbara Payne attends courses and feeds back information to staff. NNEB students attend on placement and are provided with a 'student guide'. Barbara Payne says she would not employ male staff. 'I don't think a man would be interested, since there is no career structure for them. I also have the impression parents would be uneasy about a man working as part of the team.' The staff/child ratio is 1:6.

**Children & parents** The children come from mainly middle-class families. Many of the parents are self-employed or professionally qualified and commute to London. Some children are brought by nannies. There is a good cultural mix, with a small number of Chinese and French children for whom English is their second language. Each new child is informally assigned to a keyworker for the settling-in period. Most children go on to state primary schools in Maldon, and a few to independent Maldon Court Preparatory School and Elm Green. The nursery school is willing to take children with special needs, but is unsuitable for wheelchair use. At present they have a child with cerebral palsy. Parents are encouraged to chat to staff when they deliver or collect their child and are invited to special events such as the annual Nativity play and sports day.

**Curriculum & activities** The nursery philosophy is that the needs of the children are paramount. Using the best from many ideologies, including Montessori, Steiner, Froebel and High Scope, the aim is to provide a secure and happy environment, where children can learn new skills, gain independence and mix socially. The nursery school tries to strike a balance between free play and structured learning, sometimes dividing the children into groups. For the first hour and a half, children are free to choose from a variety of supervised activities. When they arrive, tables are already set out with creative activities such as finger painting, collage, model-making, puzzles, construction toys and project work. There is also the choice of outdoor play. After break, which is treated as a social occasion for staff and children to enjoy refreshments and a chat, they divide into two smaller groups for storytime. Sessions always end with everyone coming together for an activity, such as music, movement, singing or number games. Projects are important and are geared towards involving the children in the community around them. The emphasis is very much on well-presented displays to show children that their work is valued and appreciated. There are fresh flowers everywhere, a pleasant and unusual touch. Children learn pre-literacy skills and most go on to reading, when ready, using the 1-2-3 and Away scheme. Formal teaching takes place with qualified nursery teachers. Children are encouraged, but not forced, to take part. There are occasional trips to the library and an annual outing to the theatre or zoo. Formal written records of progress and development are not kept. Close liaison and regular conversations with parents are preferred.

**Remarks** A first-class nursery school – professional, disciplined and stimulating. Well-qualified, long-serving staff, high-quality equipment and a warm, welcoming atmosphere. Lovely outside play area. Hugely over-subscribed as there are no state nursery schools in the area. Registration at birth is recommended if possible. Very reasonable fees.

## WOODLAND LODGE KINDERGARTEN

Coach Road
Great Horkesley
Colchester
Essex CO6 4DX
**Tel:** (0206) 271448

**Joint Owners:** Anita Huckle
Mandy Jones
**Principal:** Jo Hopkins, NNEB, DPQS
**Type:** Day nursery and nursery school offering full-time places and half-day sessions
**Children:** 2–5yrs. 42 places. 140 on register
**Hours:** 8am–6pm
Morning session 8.30am–12.30pm
Lunch 12.30pm–1.30pm
Afternoon session 12.30pm–1.30pm
Open 51 weeks a year
**Status:** Private, fee-paying
**Number of years open:** 2
**Meals:** Lunch, tea, snacks
**1992 fees:** £18 per day inc all meals
£9 per session
£2.25 per hour by arrangement
£1.50 per day for lunch
£5 registration fee
**Waiting list:** Very long. First come first served. Preference to siblings
**Registered by:** Essex County Council SS

# Gloucestershire

Bottom of the league. There is no state nursery education whatsoever in Gloucestershire. Its 34,000 pre-school children have to wait until they enter primary school at 4. Working parents join long waiting lists for places in expensive private day nurseries and schools. The private sector offers 64 day nurseries, 250 playgroups and approximately 1000 childminders. The council blames lack of funding from central government for this failure, but points out that they have 14 family centres for children with special needs, mainly in areas of social deprivation. Two of these are in Cheltenham. They also provide seven opportunity groups attached to schools, which are run as playgroups, and integrate special needs children.

### Further information

For details on day nurseries, childminders and playgroups:
Department of Social Services
Under Fives Department
Cayley Hall
Shepherd Road
Gloucester GL2 6DW
Tel: (0452) 308337

For details on primary schools:
Education Department
Shire Hall
Westgate Street
Gloucester GL1 2TP
Tel: (0452) 425000

# BILSON FAMILY CENTRE

Bilson School
Station Street
Cinderford
Glos GL14 2JJ
**Tel:** (0594) 826605

**Owner:** Glos County Council
**Co-ordinator:** Helen Reed, Cert Ed
**Type:** Family Centre for under-5s and their families with part-time playgroup sessions, mother and toddler group and 'drop-in' sessions.
**Children:** Under 3 for mother & toddler group 3–5yrs for playgroup sessions. 25 places. 50 on register. 140 families use the centre
**Hours:** Family Centre open 9am–3pm
Playgroup session 9am–11am
Mother & toddler group 1pm–3pm
Open 39 weeks a year
**Status:** State family centre
**Number of years open:** 7
**Meals:** Mid-morning snack
**1992 fees:** 80p per playgroup session
30p for mother & toddler group
**Waiting list:** Minimal, for playgroup only
**Registered by:** Glos County Council SS

**Premises** A small, stone-built Victorian school converted to incorporate a large playroom, parents' room/kitchen, pram bay, office, baby changing facilities, toilets and a quiet room with comfy chairs, TV and upright piano. The Centre is very near the middle of Cinderford, previously a mining town, in the Forest of Dean. Most families live locally and many walk to the Centre. Although the building is in constant need of repair and redecoration, it is generally in good condition. There is a garden with adventure frame and swings at the back, fenced off from the adjoining Bilson School playground. The lobby area is covered with photographs of children and staff and large friezes of the children's work. Inside, the Centre is visually exciting, with walls covered with inventive collages, mobiles hanging from the ceiling and children happily glueing and painting. It is a friendly, welcoming and very busy place. The playroom is enormous, like a school hall and very well equipped with a large, specially built home corner, computer and book areas, climbing frame, slide, trampoline, aquarium and art and messy-play space with sink.

**Co-ordinator & staff** Helen Reed, Cert Ed, the co-ordinator, is a qualified teacher in her mid-30s, with four children of her own. She taught for two years at Bilson School and is a very able and artistic leader, who communicates well with staff, children and their parents. She reports to the headteacher of the school and is enthusiastically supported by a part-time teacher and a full-time qualified NNEB. They work well as a team, assisted during playgroup sessions by parents on a rota basis and volunteers from a local day centre. They also take NNEB students on work experience. There is close contact with Bilson School. Rising-5s who progress to the reception class there have the benefit of attending 'liaison sessions' before they start school full-time. Staff attend compulsory two days' training by the LEA annually and participate in other relevant training sessions wherever possible, such as music therapy or clumsiness in children. Staff have also attended High Scope training.

**Children & parents** Predominantly white, working-class, mostly low-income, unemployed or single parents living close by. Parents are actively involved and help at playgroup sessions. When a new child starts, parents are encouraged to stay as long as they wish, until the child is happy to be left. Most children move on to Bilson School, the state primary next door, and the rest to two other state primaries in the town. There are several special needs children attending playgroup, including a child with cerebral palsy and children with behavioural, speech and hearing problems. A parent or nursery nurse is often required to stay with each special needs child. No child is ever turned away because their parents are in financial difficulties. They are asked to give of their time and help out in some other way if they cannot afford to pay fees.

**Curriculum & activities** Staff provide a broad, balanced curriculum and follow the PPA philosophy of learning through play. They aim to ensure that each child develops as an individual and is secure, happy and confident. Children choose from a wide range of activities including art, craft and messy play, climbing frame, home corner, computer, looking at books and writing. Reading and writing are not formally taught, but children participate in pre-writing and pre-reading activities. There are lots of cuddles, and plenty of opportunities for self-expression. Children come together for the mid-morning snack, storytime, songs and rhymes and to watch TV. Each child's development is regularly monitored and their skills assessed. All children leave for school with an 'All About Me' report used by Gloucester education authority. Staff work closely with parents. Educational sessions for parents are held in the Centre in the afternoons, often with guest speakers, eg from Relate or the Open University. Parents get together to chat in the parents' room and are given a regular newsletter. There are children's outings and picnics several times a year and visiting entertainers.

**Remarks** High-quality pre-school care for children from low-income families, whose parents could not afford private nursery care. The Family Centre is a vital community resource, used regularly by over 180 families. As one parent put it, 'I would commit suicide if it wasn't here.' Staff would like additional resources to extend their hours and offer parents more opportunity to leave their children, while they pursue further education or re-training. Excellent relationships with Bilson School staff enable the playgroup to thoroughly familiarise children with the school before they start at five.

---

# THE COIGNE

Market Square
Minchinhampton
Stroud
Glos GL6 9JP
**Tel:** (0453) 882004

**Owner/Headteacher:** Angela Keen, Cert Ed (Froebel)
**Type:** Nursery school offering morning sessions
**Children:** 3–5yrs. 24 places. 49 on register
**Hours:** 9am–12 noon
Open 38 weeks a year
**Status:** Private, fee-paying, non profit-making
**Number of years open:** 12
**Meals:** Mid-morning snack
**1992 fees:** £3 per session
£20 refundable deposit
Sibling discounts
**Waiting list:** Long – 36 names
**Registered by:** Glos County Council SS

**Premises** Part of the ground floor of a large stone-built Victorian mansion, in the centre of the small Cotswold town of Minchinhampton. The school is hidden behind high dry-stone walls, in a quiet area with free parking nearby. It occupies three rooms plus toilets and cloakroom and has a large, lovingly kept, enclosed garden, designed with children in mind. There is a good variety of outdoor play equipment including a tree house, swings, see-saw, sandpit and chickens which the children help to look after. It obviously runs on a very tight budget and the interior, though light and homely, is in need of some refurbishment. The kitchen, not used for cooking, doubles as a quiet room with books, musical instruments, a table and chairs. The two large main playrooms are well equipped and very child-centred. One room has small tables and chairs, a large variety of games and puzzles, drawing and sticking materials and a sandpit. The other, slightly larger, has easels and paints, dry sand and water play, a home corner and many dressing-up clothes. Children are regularly taken next door to the owner's house for cookery sessions.

**Owner/Headteacher & staff** Angela Keen, Cert Ed, is a qualified nursery teacher who subsequently became involved in running playgroups. She started her own nursery 12 years ago after the birth of her third child. Only five years from retirement, she employs another infant/nursery teacher in her 30s as deputy and four additional helpers, all mothers themselves, and with the experience of working with young children. All except two have formal qualifications. Members of the team have complementary skills and interests. Two are very artistic and Linda Arnold, Angela's deputy, is an inspired storyteller, with an interest in special needs children. The staff are happy and confident and work well together. They take advantage of any training courses offered by PPA. The nursery also takes NNEB students on work experience placement.

**Children & parents** The children come from a very wide range of backgrounds, from the low-waged and unemployed, through local government workers, doctors and nurses, teachers and farmers to wealthy land-owners, but there are no ethnic minorities. A number come from lone parent families. New parents are encouraged to stay and settle their children in and all parents are welcome at any time. The children here are very busy and totally absorbed in their various activities. Many go on to local state schools, while others transfer to independent Wycliffe and Beau Desert School. Several children have speech problems, and the nursery liaises with a speech therapist. Some children have places subsidised by PPA and the local authority. The owner would like to be able to help more children from low income families.

**Curriculum & activities** Angela Keen is Froebel-trained and influenced by the Froebel teaching philosophy. Children have complete freedom of choice of activities, with as wide a variety of equipment and experiences, including outside play, available to them as possible throughout the session. There is no formal teaching, but any child who is obviously ready for more formal work is offered it. The nursery aims to expose children to a wealth of creative and imaginative experiences through play and to stretch them in all directions. There are lots of cuddles and sitting on laps, and stories and music when requested. Children are very well supervised inspite of the policy of freedom. Visitors, including policemen, nurses, firemen and teachers, are invited in to talk to the children as 'people who help us'. Children visit a local farm in spring to see the lambs and attend the Christmas play at the local school. Some of the furniture and equipment is a little tatty, but there is plenty of it, some home-made, but very child-centred, imaginative and well used. There is no structured learning as Angela does not feel that many children are ready for it nor are there written records.

**Remarks** A very popular mornings-only nursery, with a happy atmosphere and a warm sense of freedom. Children's imaginations are stretched and challenged and they have a great deal of fun. The headteacher puts affordability before profit and is running on a tight budget, so that she can cater for as many local parents as possible. The nursery is excellent value. It is also vital for the community. There are no state nursery schools in the area at all and the nearest playgroup is miles away. Angela is nearing retirement age and it may not be feasible for the nursery to continue independently, as the premises are part of her property. If the Coigne closes it will be a sad loss.

# POLLY'S DAY NURSERY

Brownshill Road
Brownshill
Stroud
Glos GL6 8AS
**Tel:** (0453) 731101

**Owners/Principal:** Ann & Anna Parrott, BTEC (Nat Dip Business & Finance)
**Type:** Day nursery offering full- and part-time places and half-day sessions
**Children:** 2–5yrs. 18 places. 50 on register
**Hours:** 8am–6pm
Morning session 9am–1pm
Afternoon session 1pm–5pm
Open 50 weeks a year
**Status:** Private, fee-paying
**Number of years open:** 3½
**Meals:** Lunch, snacks mid-morning and mid-afternoon
**1992 fees:** £13.50 per day
£6.60 per session
£1 per day for lunch for part-timers
**Waiting list:** Very short. Places always available
**Registered by:** Glos County Council SS

**Premises** A private bungalow in the sprawling village of Brownshill, just outside Stroud, with its own driveway in front and gardens to the side and rear. A quiet, peaceful Cotswold village, home to many professional families as well as retired people. There is parking space for four cars in front of the nursery and two openings on to the street to ease flow of traffic. The bus stop is 100 yards away, but public transport is not good, with only four buses a day to Stroud. There are four main nursery rooms; a 'wet room', for outdoor clothes and boots, messy play and meals and snacks; a playroom, with tables and chairs, drawing equipment, games, puzzles, building bricks; a quiet room with comfortable chairs and beanbags, television and video and piles of books; and a dressing-up room for imaginative play with a foldaway Wendy house, play kitchen, comfy sofa and of course dressing-up clothes. This room is where children have their afternoon sleep. There is also a kitchen with office area. Each room is light, well decorated and enhanced by large and colourful friezes and collages done by the children. The garden is secure and well looked after with space for running around and a small vegetable plot where children assist in growing strawberries and other healthy treats. There is an abundance of outdoor equipment: three swings, a slide, sand pit and several tricycles. Brownshill Playing Fields are a short walk away and are visited once a week for ball games.

**Principal & staff** Anna Parrott, BTEC, set up this nursery jointly with her mother, Ann, a qualified teacher. Young and ambitious, Anna has been working with children since she left school, although she is primarily responsible for the management and administration of the nursery. She employs four members of staff, two qualified and two unqualified, and delegates responsibility for the children to Lesley St John, NNEB (Norland), who has ten years' experience in a variety of different childcare posts and has worked with deaf and autistic children and other children with disabilities. Anna's mother, Ann Parrott, Cert Ed, is gradually increasing her involvement in the nursery. Bridget Lovell comes in part-time and covers staff holidays and sick leave. The team is happy and committed. All are given equal say in managing the nursery at monthly management meetings when staff rotas are worked out for each task, from cleaning the loos to supervising activities. A different member of staff cooks lunch each day. Vacancies are advertised locally, although only one nursery nurse has left so far. Anna says she would be happy to employ a man if he were right for the job. Local work-experience students help on a regular basis and are supervised by a full-time member of staff. Parents are notified in advance when a student will be attending. A qualified dance and music teacher comes in once a week.

**Children & parents** Children are all local, living within a six-mile radius of the nursery. Most come from successful, professional families – some have single parents. The majority will go on to state schools in Stroud and Minchinhampton, although a few go on to independent Wycliffe. Given Lesley St John's experience with special needs, the nursery is happy to accept children with disabilities and currently takes an epileptic child who requires a special diet. Children are divided into groups according to ability and the pre-planned staff rota means that they each receive attention from all members of staff during the course of a day. Anna believes this ensures they are not upset when a member of staff is absent. There is no longer an open-door policy for parents, as it was found to be too disruptive, upsetting the timetable and routine. Once a child has settled in, parents are expected to leave him/her with a member of staff at the door. A monthly newsletter is sent out which covers themes for play and work, the 'interest table', staff holidays and any reminders to parents. Parents are also given a daily report on their child. Children are accepted before they are potty-trained.

**Curriculum & activities** There is a structured timetable at this nursery which allows for free play as well as set activities and regular outside play. However, painting, water and sand play are available all the time, allowing the children some freedom of choice during their day. The day starts with free play and moves on to a set activity, which may be part of a monthly theme for wall display. It generally involves painting, cutting, sticking, stencilling and other motor skills. This is followed by break, story and songs and outside play. After lunch is rest time and the morning's timetable is then repeated in reverse, ending the day with an hour or two of free play. Within the structures imposed (timetables, groupings) there is still room for flexibility, and unless an activity is deemed unsuitable for a particular age group the children spend most of their time all together. On Thursday mornings the older children, aged 3 plus, have a 2½-hour pre-school session, in various groups determined by ability. During this time they concentrate on fine motor skills such as sequencing, threading, identification and pencil control. The LEA actively discourages nurseries from teaching children to read, so pre-reading and writing do not feature during these sessions. However, children are always encouraged to look at books and are read stories every day. One member of staff speaks French and children have a short French session daily. There is particular emphasis on social skills, and all the children we saw were extremely confident, well behaved and friendly. Each child is given a written report before he/she leaves, entitled 'All About Me', and the child is actively involved in putting this together. It is written in the first person and includes information such as 'I can use a knife and fork by myself', 'I know these colours well', and 'I can count up to . . .'

**Remarks** A well-balanced atmosphere of freedom and discipline. Excellent value for money and very popular, particularly with working parents. Young, energetic staff have warm, understanding relationships with the children, who are confident and happy. Although LEA restrictions prevent formal teaching, the children are thoroughly prepared to enter any of the local primary schools in this area.

## WESTFIELDS PRIVATE DAY NURSERY

121 Leckhampton Road
Cheltenham
Glos GL53 0DQ
**Tel:** (0242) 245307

**Owners:** David & Hilary Hatton
**Nursery Manager:** Hilary Hatton
**Principal:** Aileen Stewart, NNEB
**Type:** Day nursery offering full- and part-time places and half-day sessions
**Children:** 6mths–5yrs. 30 places. 75 on register
**Hours:** 8.30am–5.30pm
Morning session 8.30am–1pm
Afternoon session 1pm–5.30pm
Flexible hours
Open 51 weeks a year
**Status:** Private, fee-paying
**Number of years open:** 3¾
**Meals:** Lunch, tea, snacks
**1992 fees:** £85 per week full-time – under 18mths
£72 per week full-time – over 18mths
£2.05 per hour – under 18mths
£1.75 per hour – over 18mths
£1.25 per day for main meal
Childcare vouchers accepted
**Waiting list:** Moderate
**Registered by:** Glos County Council SS

**Premises** The elegant, ground-floor rooms of a large Victorian mansion close to the centre of Cheltenham. The owner lives upstairs. There is on-street parking and a nearby bus stop. The two big front rooms, with bay windows overlooking the road, are playrooms, one for the toddlers, aged 14 months to 2½ years, the other for older pre-school children. The toddler room provides a good range of toys. There is a tunnel and a see-saw for physical play and a television and music system. The pre-school playroom has similar furniture, television and a music centre, good educational toys, books and equipment. The messy room at the back of the house provides all kinds of art and craft, sand and water. Uninhibited sessions of self-expression were underway here when we visited. The 2½- to 3½-year-olds are based in this room, where they splash, paint and play every morning until it is their turn to go outdoors or swap rooms with the toddlers for more structured play or group singing. The baby unit is at the back of the house. It is equipped for four babies from 6 to 14 months and is divided between sleeping area and a soft, carpeted play space. There are beanbags, baby toys and yet another music centre. The nursery has a leafy garden with a paved area for bikes, a large lawn, a climbing frame and a shrubbery for hide and seek. All plants are child-safe. Garden toys are stored in the conservatory. Growbags are provided for the children to sow their own seeds. A low fence divides the play area from the owners' pretty garden.

**Owners/Manager, Principal & staff** Hilary Hatton and her husband set up the nursery when their own two children arrived. Neither has any childcare qualifications. Hilary realised that mothers with part-time jobs who cannot afford nannies need flexible, part-time childcare as do mothers 'who just want a few hours break'. Hilary manages the finances and staff, and is one of the few nursery owners to admit to us that her nursery makes a profit. The day-to-day running of the nursery is in the hands of Aileen Stewart, a lively, young NNEB. Half of the staff of ten are qualified NNEB or SRN, while the rest have childcare experience or a variety of childcare certificates. Half work part-time. There is no qualified nursery teacher. Training is limited, but the owner would do more if resources allowed. Staff meetings are held weekly.

**Children & parents** The parents, mostly professional, live or work locally. The majority of children attend part-time, for a minimum of two sessions a week. There are only three full-time children at present. The nursery integrates a small number of children with disabilities. Parents are welcome at any time, although they rarely take advantage of the open-door policy. Staff talk to them at the door and a diary is kept of each younger child's day. Phasing-in new children is done gradually, according to each child's needs. Parents are invited to all nursery activities. Children transfer to many different state and private schools, taking with them the local authority's 'All About Me' report, detailing their progress and development while at the nursery.

**Curriculum & activities** The nursery follows the PPA philosophy of learning through play. Children are divided into four groups according to age. Each group leader follows a daily written activity sheet, which lists the children in her group, what they are to do and the equipment to be used. Sessions are structured to include periods for free play and self-expression, discussion of 'our world', physical play, stories and quiet play. Children move from room to room according to their timetable. Music-making, songs, dance and listening are considered important and each room has a music centre. Messy play is available at all times – painting, dough, clay, sand and water, glueing and sticking – and children's work is tastefully displayed on the walls. Children are taught to recognise their own name, to dress and undress themselves, use a handkerchief, wash and dry their hands and tidy away after activities. There is no formal attempt to teach reading or writing. The nursery believes children should come fresh to this when they start school. They learn colours and numbers, and Letterland is used to teach letters. Older children do some pre-reading and writing skills, such as dot-to-dot patterns, letter formation, tracing, pencil control and following text from left to right. No swimming, library visits, visiting speakers or entertainers, and infrequent outings. Home-cooked lunches, which smelt delicious, and a very high standard of hygiene and safety throughout. Written timetables and procedures, but no written developmental records or assessments until children leave. The large, sheltered garden is used daily.

**Remarks** A well-equipped nursery with many stimulating activities and a warm, friendly atmosphere. Plenty of cuddles and staff actively involved with children. No qualified early years teacher on the team. Flexible hours to suit parents who work part-time. Reasonable fees for high-quality childcare. Elegant, tastefully decorated premises.

# Guernsey

No state nursery education on the island, although children start school as soon as possible after their 4th birthday. No plans to increase provision either. 'There is even less money available now than in the past,' says an Education Department spokeswoman. Parents and children are offered 'lead-in' classes, where they are allowed to visit the primary school of their choice one day a week in the term before the child starts full-time. There are four expensive independent schools, which take pupils at 4 years old. No local authority day nurseries and no budget to sponsor or subsidise places. Two playgroups take Social Services referrals only. The two private day nurseries are considered expensive for the area. There are 125 childminders charging approximately £2 per hour, and 26 playgroups, which together offer places to half the island's 3000 under-5s.

**Further information**

For details on all types of nursery education:
States of Guernsey
Children's Board
Edward T Wheadon House
La Trouchot
St Peter Port
Guernsey
Tel: (0481) 720500

## STEPPING STONES DAY NURSERY

Le Courtil Pignon
Les Grippios
Bordeaux, Vale
Guernsey
Channel Islands
**Tel:** (0481) 43456

**Owner/Principal:** Pam Davey, NNEB, SEN
**Type:** Day nursery offering full- and part-time places and half-day sessions
**Children:** 6wks–5yrs. 12 places. 24 on register
**Hours:** 8.30am–5.45pm
Morning session 8.30am–1pm
Afternoon session 1pm–5.45pm
Open 51 weeks a year
**Status:** Private, fee-paying
**Number of years open:** 2
**Meals:** Lunch, tea, snacks
Parents provide infant food
**1992 fees:** £80 per week full-time
£16 per day
£8.50 per morning session (inc lunch)
£7.50 per afternoon session
**Waiting list:** Long for full-time places. Part-time places available
**Registered by:** States of Guernsey Children Board

## TOWN MOUSE DAY NURSERY

9 Union Street
St Peter Port
Guernsey
Channel Islands
**Tel:** (0481) 724501

**Owner/Principal:** Kathryn Gamble, Teachers' Cert
**Type:** Day nursery offering full- and part-time places and half-day sessions
**Children:** 2–5yrs. 32 places. 32 on register
**Hours:** 8.30am–5.30pm
Morning session 8.30am–12 noon (1.30pm inc lunch)
Afternoon session 1.30pm–5.30pm (12 noon start inc lunch)
Open 51 weeks a year
**Status:** Private, fee-paying
**Number of years open:** 8
**Meals:** Lunch, snacks
**1992 fees:** £64 per week full-time
£18.50 per day
£11.50 per session (+ £2 inc lunch)
£10 refundable registration fee
**Waiting list:** Places available
**Registered by:** States of Guernsey Children Board

# Hampshire

Hampshire has the highest population of children under 5 in the country (103,500). There are no local authority day nurseries and no full-time places in any of the county's four state nursery schools and 30 nursery classes. An Education Department spokesperson admitted, 'Nursery education is not a priority for us at this time,' although they have recently introduced a policy of allowing children to start school during the year in which they are 5, rather than the term. Working mothers join the queues for private nursery places, provided they can afford fees of up to £100 per week. Most families rely on the region's 4000 registered childminders or 800 part-time playgroups.

**Further information**

For details on day nurseries, private nursery schools, childminders and playgroups:

Department of Social Services
Trafalgar House
The Castle
Winchester SO23 8UQ
Tel: (0962) 841841

For details on nursery schools, units and classes:
Education Department
The Castle
Winchester SO23 8UQ
Tel: (0962) 841841

For parents seeking pre-school advice and information:
Childcare Links
27 Guildhall Walk
Portsmouth PO1 2RP
Tel: (0705) 838880

---

## HOLLY TREE NURSERY SCHOOL

63 Portsmouth Road
Woolston
Southampton SO2 9BE
**Tel:** (0703) 445869

**Owner/Principal:** Heather Dawson, B Ed
**Type:** Nursery school offering full- and part-time places.
**Children:** 3–5yrs. 20 places. 55 on register
**Hours:** 9am–3.30pm
Open 48 weeks a year
**Status:** Private, fee-paying
**Number of years open:** 4½
**Meals:** Mid-morning snack only. Children bring packed lunches
**1992 fees:** £55 per week full-time
£2 per hour
£10 refundable deposit
**Waiting list:** Very long. Booking now for 1997/8. Early registration advisable
**Registered by:** Hants County Council SS

**Premises** A purpose-built addition to a big Victorian house with a large pleasant garden. The school occupies three rooms. The largest, which is light and cheerful and looks out over the garden, is used by the 3-year-old group and for joint activities. The 4-year-olds have their own room and a third room is used for messy play, paint, craft and cooking. The rooms are well decorated and equipped with plenty of toys and learning equipment. The attractive garden at the back of the house offers a paved play area with a cushioned section for outdoor apparatus, and a large lawn for games in dry weather. Access and parking are made easier by a large drive in front of the house which takes several cars. The only drawback is the location on a very busy road, but as the nursery is at the back of the house, traffic noise is reduced to a minimum.

**Owner/Principal & staff** Heather Dawson, B Ed, is an experienced teacher, who has worked in a reception class, secondary schools and adult education. A pleasant, calm woman, she goes out of her way to accommodate parents' wishes. 'I want to offer people what they really want' is her philosophy. She is completely flexible about how many sessions parents can take – or can afford. Although she is no longer involved in day-to-day teaching, Heather Dawson is very much a presence in the school. She greets parents at the door each day and is ready to discuss progress or problems with them. Her daughter, Simone, works at the nursery with her, as one of five members of staff – all qualified or currently training. Deputy Andrea Martin, NAMCW, is a kindly, mumsy figure, clearly very popular with the children.

**Children & parents** Most children live locally and come from varied backgrounds but what they all share is parents who place emphasis on early years education. Most parents choose the school because of the teaching philosophy and its reputation has spread by word of mouth. At 5 years most children go on to state primary schools. A small proportion go to local private schools. The children are confident, lively and chatty. Most wear an informal uniform of hollyleaf green sweatshirt or tee-shirt, though there is no pressure to conform. Staff wear a jolly hollyberry red sweatshirt.

**Curriculum & activities** Many children leave the school able to read and write fluently and all arrive at their new schools well ahead of the game. Heather Dawson believes that small children love to learn. 'They take enormous pleasure in their achievements. They're the ones who are keen to get on with their work. They go to their tables themselves and get their books out, often in preference to playing with toys.' For the first term children are encouraged to learn how to make friends and get on with each other. In the second term foundation work begins. Parents bring their children for a practice session before they start at the school and then stay for a short period. Heather Dawson has never had the experience of a child distressed by being left. 'I think children are happy here because it is small and cosy,' she says. 'We also ask parents to tell us if there is anything going on at home which could cause a child to be upset – marital problems or a new sibling, anything like that.' Each session is broken up into periods of group activity (formal learning); free play; music, painting and craft; outdoor or indoor games; storytelling or television. Most children come for at least three sessions a week.

**Remarks** A justly popular nursery school offering a good education without pressure, in a happy, relaxed atmosphere. Because of the limited numbers it is advisable to put children's names down before birth, if possible. Heather Dawson has put into practice her belief in creating a nursery where the child, not the profit margin, is of paramount concern.

## BOUNDARY OAK NURSERY GROUP

Boundary Oak School
Roche Court
Fareham
Hants PO17 5BL
**Tel:** (0329) 280955

**Owner:** Boundary Oak School Trust Ltd
**Headmaster:** Mr Bliss, Cert Ed
**Supervisor:** Pauline Odams, NNEB
**Type:** Nursery school in prep school offering half-day sessions. No full-time places
**Children:** 3–5yrs. 16 places. 32 on register
**Hours:** Morning session 9am–11.30am
Afternoon session 1pm–3.30pm
Open 36 weeks a year
**Status:** Private, fee-paying
**Number of years open:** 7
**Meals:** Milk and biscuits
**1992 fees:** £425 per term for 5 sessions a week £10 registration fee
**Waiting list:** Long. Priority to siblings
**Registered by:** Hants SS

**Premises** The nursery is part of a co-ed prep school set on a hill overlooking rolling countryside. It occupies one large room in a purpose-built annexe to the main school; the annexe also houses the school hall. The classroom is light and airy and well stocked with play and learning equipment. It is divided in two for messy play and more formal learning round small tables. The nursery room has a slightly formal feel to it, probably due to the fact that it is part of a school, but it is warm and comfortable with plenty of books and pictures. It has its own loos. The children are able to use the adjacent school hall for their extremely boisterous and noisy sessions of free play – the perfect racetrack for trikes and other vehicles. Soft mats are laid down for tumbling around on. Since the children only attend for 2½ hours a day, it is not considered necessary to provide an outside play area.

**Headteacher & staff** Pauline Odams, NNEB, has been headteacher at the nursery since it opened and is helped by a teaching assistant. Pauline is a calm, unflappable and understanding woman who does not believe in pressuring small children, although she does believe in a structured approach to learning. She offers encouragement through a merit system designed to give every child a chance to shine. Rare disruptive behaviour is dealt with by means of a 'naughty chair', where a child is put to sit for a brief period to allow him/her to cool off. Pauline Odams and her assistant have a warm and friendly attitude towards the children and believe in plenty of cuddles. In this relaxed, happy environment it is difficult to believe there are any discipline problems.

**Children & parents** Middle-class, but the school is at pains to deny that it is a 'snobby' prep school. Many of the parents make great sacrifices to meet the school fees. Most of the children move from the nursery school into the main school – it has only just become co-ed, so some girls still go on to the local girls' prep school. A few go into the state sector. The children are lively, articulate and confident and clearly enjoy their time in the nursery. Children with special needs are welcome and wheelchairs are no problem. There is an informal uniform – navy blue sweatshirts and tee-shirts with the school emblem and grey trousers or skirts.

**Curriculum & activities** The nursery aims to develop individual abilities through purposeful play and the structured teaching of language and numeracy skills. Each session is carefully planned to cover creative play, shapes, numbers, speech, vocabulary, written work and social skills. As the nursery is run very much as part of the school, it is possible to provide for individual needs. Where appropriate, very able children can move into the reception class early, or if a child needs to move at a slower pace, entry can be delayed by a term or two. Parental involvement is encouraged at all times, with parents invited to regular open days, concerts, parents' evenings and outings. This is a small class and relationships between staff, children and parents are close. Twice a year parents receive a detailed written report on every aspect of their child's progress and development. When children enter the class, they are assessed individually and divided into three groups, young (new children), middle (one term plus) and older (4 years and over). The young group begins a formal scheme of work aimed at socialising – making them aware of themselves and others, through developing language, movement and games. When they move into the middle group, more emphasis is put on the quality of work and developing their motor skills. They work towards correct formation of letters and numbers and colour recognition. At 4-plus, there is greater concentration on fine motor skills – working towards numeracy to ten, understanding quantity and recognising and writing numbers up to ten from memory. Writing and language continue so that by the time children leave, they can write their own names and recognise some sounds. Each child progresses at his/her own pace.

**Remarks** A real education and excellent grounding for under-5s in a gentle, structured and happy setting. Although there is a well-developed system of formal learning and discipline, the emphasis is on enjoyment. The children are exuberant and obviously having a great time. The children enjoy all the advantages of the nursery being attached to a well-equipped prep school, including swimming pool, tennis courts, computers, yet are shielded from the rough and tumble of school.

# KING RICHARD NURSERY

Allaway Avenue
Paulsgrove
Portsmouth
Hants PO6 4QP
**Tel:** (0705) 221196/370321

**Owner:** King Richard School
**Manager:** Carolyn Scott, NNEB
**Type:** Workplace nursery offering full-time places and half-day sessions to school staff, Midland Bank employees and local community
**Children:** 6mths–5yrs. 20 places (6 for babies). 22 on register
**Hours:** 8am–6pm
Morning session 8am–1pm
Afternoon session 1pm–6pm
Open 51 weeks a year

**Status:** Private, fee-paying
**Number of years open:** 3
**Meals:** Lunch, tea, snacks
**1992 fees:** £20 per day
£10 per session
**Waiting list:** Reasonable. Priority to staff at King Richard School
**Registered by:** Hants County Council SS

**Premises** A specially adapted area with its own entrance, occupying part of a large secondary school. Children spend their day in a large room, well lit and airy, with big windows opening on to an outside play area. The room is divided into different areas for different age groups and for various activities. Babies' feeds and snacks are prepared separately in a small kitchen. There are good toilet and changing facilities and a separate sleep room for babies. The nursery is well provided with toys and play equipment, but seems short of books. Although well decorated and bright, it is a little institutional due to the large size of the room and the unmistakable school atmosphere. There is a pleasant outside play area with sandpit, climbing frame and slide on a safety surface and a grassy area for games.

**Manager & staff** Carolyn Scott, NNEB, is young and enthusiastic. She is also a qualified childcare lecturer. Her deputy, Vanessa Windess, NNEB, is an easygoing, friendly young woman, and has a clear rapport with young children. Carolyn is answerable to a management committee, but is responsible for the day-to-day running of the nursery. She heads a team of four, all qualified NNEB or BTEC, plus one YTS student taking a course in childcare. Staff meetings are held regularly. Parents come in to chat about their children on a daily basis and parents' evenings are held each term. Staff turnover has been a problem due to husbands changing jobs and moving away.

**Children & parents** Mostly from professional backgrounds, many are the children of teachers at the school, who have priority for places. Six places are reserved by Midland Bank for its employees. Most children go on to state schools in the area, with only a few going to local private schools. Nearly all come from the immediate neighbourhood.

**Curriculum & activities** The emphasis is firmly on play. Carolyn believes in allowing children to develop at their own pace. There is little formal learning as such, but children coming up to school age are encouraged to master pre-school skills such as shape and colour, number recognition and pencil control. Worksheets are provided, if children really want to do them. There is no pressure to learn, but there is plenty of educational play and learning through activities. Through the day, groups of children take part in a number of activities, rotating from one member of staff to another. Each week, staff choose which activity they will be responsible for, changing frequently to maintain a fresh approach. The children are split according to age for parts of the day, but spend some time all together. A family atmosphere is encouraged, and older children play with the babies – under supervision of course. The nursery is informal and relaxed and children clearly look on members of staff as friends. There is plenty of art and craft, dancing and music and children are taken on trips to the local library to choose books. The nursery staff are working on fund-raising projects to buy more toys and equipment.

**Remarks** A small and efficient nursery offering high-quality care. Although it lacks cosiness, due to the large, open layout, staff have created a relaxed and happy atmosphere. The children are clearly very much at home.

# LITTLEWORLD NURSERY SCHOOL

47 Weyhill Road
Andover
Hants SP10 3AN
**Tel:** (0264) 351833

**Owner:** Littleworld Nursery Schools PLC
**Manager:** Jan Cubitt, NNEB
**Type:** Day nursery offering full- and part-time places and half-day sessions
**Children:** 6mths–5yrs. 60 places. 92 on register
**Hours:** 8am–6pm
Morning session 8am–12.30pm
Afternoon session 1.30pm–6pm
Open 52 weeks a year (excl bank holidays)
**Status:** Private, fee-paying
**Number of years open:** 2½
**Meals:** Lunch, tea, snacks

**1992 fees:** £75 per week full-time – under 3
£66 per week full-time – over 3
£19.45 per day – under 3
£17.30 per day – over 3
£9.75 per session – under 3
£8.65 per session – over 3
**Waiting list:** 6mths for over-2s. 9mths–1yr for under-2s
**Registered by:** Hants County Council SS

**Premises** The nursery occupies the whole of a large Victorian house on a pleasant residential road leading out from Andover town centre. All the rooms are large with high ceilings and big windows, letting in plenty of natural light. The house is divided into two, with babies and toddlers upstairs. Under-1s have a day room to themselves, carpeted and padded with playmats. The toddlers' play room is equipped with tables and chairs and has an uncarpeted area for painting and for sand and water play. Children nap in comfortable sleep rooms and use immaculate toilet and washing facilities. Downstairs, the 3- to 5-year-olds have three large rooms for different activities. A gloriously sloshy session of potato printing was going on in the messy room during our visit, while other groups of children were busy in the work room, furnished with tables and chairs, and the quiet room. The rooms do have a slightly spartan look. This is partly due to their size, but although the nursery is fairly well equipped, there is a need for more toys and books. Since our visit, some have been bought and there are plans to purchase more as money becomes available. Outside, there is a good-sized garden divided into a large, hard-surfaced area where older children play boisterous games and a small, grassed plot for the younger children. A hot lunch is cooked daily in a large, spotless kitchen.

**Manager & staff** Jan Cubitt, NNEB, in her early 30s, is a calm, capable woman who believes in a close liaison between staff and parents. There is a very strong sense of team spirit among the staff and Jan is plainly happy to muck in when necessary. We found her cooking lunch on the day of our visit, as a flu bug had struck down kitchen staff. Every morning and afternoon staff get together for coffee and biscuits in Jan's office to talk about the day's happenings or problems. Jan Cubitt does not work with the children on a daily basis, but handles all the administrative work. She is, however, a constant presence and often takes over storytime. She is backed up by two deputy managers – Jacky Taylor, NNEB, for the under-2s and Jean Atkinson, NNEB, for the over-2s. There are 17 other members of staff, all qualified, 50% NNEBs, and a cook.

**Children & parents** Children come from a variety of different backgrounds – professional, army and a smattering of single parents. Most stay all day, with over half attending full-time. Parental involvement is encouraged and invited. Parents drop in and chat with staff on a friendly, informal basis. Mothers of babies are told to come into the nursery whenever they like at any time of day, to see how their children are getting on. New entrants come to the school for visits before starting. Children plainly regard the nursery as a home from home, and treat it with a reassuring lack of reverence. During our visit we surprised two small truants enjoying an exciting, extra-curricular game of monsters in the cloakroom – until they were tracked down by a cheerful, but firm, member of staff and coaxed back to join the rest of their group. Most of the children transfer to state schools, with a few to local private schools.

**Curriculum & activities** Learning through play is the governing principle here. Toddlers listen to stories, sing rhymes, paint, model and play with construction games and educational toys. The over-2s build up pre-school skills in stages to suit their ages. Part of the day is spent at tables working on the usual pre-school activities – number recognition, colours, letters, pencil control, shapes and sounds – but the emphasis is strongly on play and fun. There is no pressure to learn, but all children leave well prepared for the reception class of their primary or pre-prep school. Part of every day is set aside for stories, rhymes, singing and music. Each group of children takes part in some creative activity – painting, modelling or craft. Plenty of time is allowed for free play – inside and out. There is generous room for boisterous indoor play in bad weather.

**Remarks** A well-run nursery with a motivated and efficient team in charge. High standard of care and excellent, immaculately clean premises. Plans are underway to improve on the equipment. The quality of staff and strong team spirit are impressive.

## MANOR HOUSE NURSERY

47 Gosport Road
Lee-on-Solent
Hants PO13 9EJ
**Tel:** (0705) 552018

**Owner/Principal:** Elizabeth Driver, PPA (Foundation)
**Type:** Nursery school offering half-day sessions. No full-time places
**Children:** 3–5yrs. 16 places. 40 on register
**Hours:** Morning session 9am–12 noon
Afternoon session 1.30pm–4pm
Open 36 weeks a year
**Status:** Private, fee-paying
**Number of years open:** 4½
**Meals:** Snacks
**1992 fees:** £4.75 per morning session
£4.25 per afternoon session
£10 registration fee
**Waiting list:** Minimal
**Registered by:** Hants County Council SS
**Under same ownership:** April Cottage Nursery, Gosport

**Premises** The downstairs rooms of a medium-sized Victorian house in a residential part of Gosport. The school is small and looks a little shabby, giving the impression of being well used, and abused, by children. It is more than adequately equipped (annual budget for equipment £1,300) and exudes a friendly, cosy atmosphere. There is a games room with a trampoline for indoor play and dancing, but only a very small outside play area. However, it is close to miles of beach, which the children visit frequently.

**Owner/Principal & staff** Elizabeth Driver is a qualified teacher of English as a foreign language, holds a PPA Foundation Course diploma and is the mother of two grown-up children. She started the nursery school when she found that there were none in the area. The school that began with one nursery teacher and three children now has thirty names on the waiting list, all of whom will be found places in time. Elizabeth Driver believes that young children are keen to learn and their enthusiasm should be encouraged. She decided to run a nursery school rather than a playgroup because 'so many playgroups I went to look at seemed to be a huge room with children running round and round and not doing anything constructive,' she says. 'I wanted to create somewhere with a happy atmosphere, where children could develop a wide range of interests.' The school is run by six members of staff, including Elizabeth Driver, all with some childcare qualification. Two are qualified nursery teachers. All staff attend regular training courses to update their skills and have first-aid certificates. Three peripatetic teachers visit to teach music, French and dancing.

**Children & parents** A fair mix, but largely middle class, with professional or naval backgrounds. All children attend for half-day sessions only. Children with special needs are welcome, but the school would not be able to cope with wheelchairs. Children with learning difficulties and behavioural problems have been integrated successfully. Staff have an informal and friendly relationship with parents, who are welcome to discuss problems at any time. A newsletter is sent out once or twice a term and there are plans to start a system of written reports, in line with Children Act requirements.

**Curriculum & activities** No written programmes or timetable, but this is very much a nursery school and formal learning plays a large part in each session. Children work in groups according to age and ability, gradually building on their achievements. By the time they leave many are reading and writing fluently and all have a good grasp of the basic skills. Each session also involves free play, painting and craft, computing and science. Music, French and dancing are taught at different times during the week – there is often keen competition for places during sessions when these extras take place. Children are taken to the beach in fine weather or play outside in the small garden, or the lane behind the house, where they ride bikes and trikes under supervision.

**Remarks** A popular and well-run nursery school in an area with very poor provision. The emphasis is on stimulation and encouragement. A cosy atmosphere with cheerful staff, who believe in plenty of cuddles. As it attracts many naval families, there is sometimes a high turnover of children.

# MAYFIELD JUNIOR SCHOOL KINDERGARTEN

Mayfield Road
Farnborough
Hants GU14 8LH
**Tel:** (0252) 523999

**Owner:** Farnborough College of Technology
**Officer-in-charge:** Nicola Blackman, NNEB
**Type:** Day nursery offering full-time places and half-day sessions
**Children:** 2–5yrs 11mths. 21 places. 50 on register
**Hours:** 8am–5.30pm
Morning session 8am–1pm (inc lunch)
Afternoon session 12pm–5.30pm (inc lunch)
Open 50 weeks a year
**Status:** Private, non profit-making
**Number of years open:** 5
**Meals:** Lunch, snacks
**1992 fees:** £67.50 per week full-time inc lunch
£6.75 per session
Discounts to College of Technology students
**Waiting list:** Short – places guaranteed
**Registered by:** Hants County Council SS

**Premises** Two large classrooms on the second floor of a modern, purpose-built junior school. Light and airy with quantities of artwork decorating walls, the nursery has a cheerful, busy atmosphere. Children have access to the large school grounds and their own play area. The classrooms are fairly well equipped, warm and carpeted. There is a separate staff room which is also used for story telling. Access is rather difficult for mothers trying to negotiate small babies and toddlers up the stairs and would be impossible for a physically handicapped child. The nursery, run by Farnborough College of Technology, was originally set up to cater for the children of students and staff, but is now open to the whole community.

**Officer-in-charge & staff** Nicola Blackman, NNEB, is young and energetic and has been running the Kindergarten for all five years of its existence. There are five other staff members, all qualified in child care (NNEB, PPA and City & Guilds) and holding current first-aid certificates. As they are employed by Hampshire County Council, the nursery is run to Council standards as far as health and safety are concerned. Nicola believes in making the transition between home and nursery as easy as possible and assigns new children to a key-worker. She is the one who greets the child in the morning and returns the child to its parent in the afternoon. There has been very little staff turnover and they are plainly an enthusiastic team. 'We've all worked in nurseries before,' Nicola says, 'and we think this one is the best.'

**Children & parents** Children are all local and tend to be from professional backgrounds or the children of students and lecturers at the college. The majority go on to state schools, some to the junior school housing the nursery. A few go to private schools. Lively, chatty and enthusiastic, the children throw themselves into all the activities. Children (and staff occasionally) wear striking, bright red sweatshirts, decorated with a vivid yellow Jemima Puddle-duck and ducklings. The nursery is situated on a former GLC overspill estate. Children from the community reflect the varied social and cultural composition of the housing estate.

**Curriculum & activities** Nicola Blackman believes very firmly that enjoyment comes before formal learning and that high-quality, imaginative staff come before glamorous, expensive equipment. Children are prepared for school and leave knowing their letters, but they themselves dictate the pace and there is no pressure on them to learn. The atmosphere is relaxed and children choose their own activities much of the time. There are no written programmes, nor a particular philosophy of childcare or education, nor any monitoring of developmental progress. The generous annual equipment budget of £2000, plus successful fund-raising – the Post Office's local information technology centre recently donated a further £2000 – makes for plenty of toys, games, puzzles and equipment. Two themes are chosen each week and art, craft, discussion periods and other activities are designed around the themes. Children divide into small groups for activities and come together at regular intervals for stories, music, dance and movement. Large chunks of the day are devoted to free play, with frequent outings to neighbouring parks and the local library. There are special outings twice a year at Christmas and in the summer. Lunch is an important part of the timetable, when staff and children eat and converse. All dietary needs are catered for.

**Remarks** A very happy nursery where children and adults plainly have a good time. Surrounded as it is by a busy junior school, the nursery feels part of a children's world – very informal and play-centred. Its non profit-making status keeps fees reasonable, with good discounts for students.

# PEAR TREE DAY NURSERY

14 Winchester Street
Farnborough
Hants GU14 6AW
**Tel:** (0252) 523029

**Owner/Principal:** Susan Lambert
**Supervisor:** Sarah Cole, NNEB
**Type:** Day nursery offering full-time places and half-day sessions
**Children:** 3–5yrs. 14 places. 19 on register
**Hours:** 8.30am–5.30pm
Morning session 8.30am–12.30pm
Afternoon session 1.30pm–5.30pm
Open 48 weeks a year
**Status:** Private, fee-paying
**Number of years open:** 5
**Meals:** Lunch, snacks
**1992 fees:** £65 per week full-time
£35 per week for 5 sessions (excl lunch)
£1 for lunch
**Waiting list:** 20 approx. No guarantee of places. Early registration advisable
**Registered by:** Hants County Council SS
**Under same ownership:** Connaught Castle Day Nursery, Aldershot

**Premises** 'Bijou' would be the estate agent's description of this nursery. It occupies the ground floor of the owner's small, Victorian, terraced house, set in a wide residential road in Aldershot. However, what it may lack in spaciousness is more than made up for in atmosphere. The nursery is in what used to be the sitting room and dining room and this gives it a homely, comfortable feel. The main room has been adapted to offer a sand and water play space and a carpeted area for other activities. There is a Wendy house and plenty of well-cared-for, interesting equipment. All available wall space is covered with children's artwork. The second room is used for quiet activities and eating, and is furnished with small tables and chairs. A spotless kitchen is used for preparing meals and for cookery sessions. The loos are upstairs, but children are always accompanied. The garden is surprisingly large and has been well adapted for a variety of different play activities. Children go out on all but the wettest days.

**Owner, Supervisor & staff** Susan Lambert, the owner and principal, worked full-time at Pear Tree until last year, when she opened her second nursery, Connaught Castle, in Aldershot. She has now handed over the day-to-day running of Pear Tree to Sarah Cole, NNEB. Sarah is a competent, qualified nursery nurse with 12 years of childcare experience. There are two other full-time staff members (NNEB and PPA qualified) and occasionally students on placement. Working together in such close proximity, the staff need to like each other's company and this comes across strongly. A cook comes in for two hours each morning, but in such a small nursery the budget does not stretch to other visiting specialist teachers.

**Children & parents** Quite a few of the children are from army families – based at Aldershot – and from professional families with working mums. All go on to state schools in the area. Parents are expected to take an active interest in the nursery and often contribute to topic work or help with outings. They receive regular newsletters about nursery life and are encouraged to come into the nursery whenever possible. Children's progress, achievements or difficulties are discussed whenever necessary or required. Informality is the key ingredient here.

**Curriculum & activities** The nursery's philosophy is based on providing maximum stimulation within a caring and loving environment. The curriculum is based on a 'theme' concept. A new theme is chosen each week and is introduced into as many activities as possible – art, craftwork, reading, discussions and sometimes even cookery. There is a sense of busy purpose in the nursery, and children rotate from one member of staff to another as the day progresses, to ensure plenty of variety. Deborah feels this is especially important for the children who stay all day, and she takes particular care to ensure that children do not repeat in the afternoon what they did in the morning. There are a couple of PE sessions each day as well as free play, and children also enjoy music and movement. Formal teaching of reading and writing is geared to the needs of individual children and is not top of the list of priorities, although particularly able children are catered for. All children have mastered basic skills by the time they leave for school. The nursery staff are prepared to take children with disabilities and special needs – although wheelchairs would be a problem.

**Remarks** The warm, caring atmosphere is immediately palpable. Children simply exchange one family home for another when they arrive each day. Minimal discipline, masses of cuddles. Space limits large-group activities and parents looking for formal, structured education or academic achievement could be disappointed. Places are available at the more recently opened Connaught Castle Nursery which is run along the same lines but housed in a leisure centre attached to a secondary school.

# STAUNTON PARK DAY NURSERY

Staunton Park Community School
Wakefords Way
Havant
Hants PO9 5JD
**Tel:** (0705) 498217

**Owner:** Staunton Park Day Nursery Management Committee
**Manager:** Gloria Whitney, NNEB
**Type:** Day nursery offering full- and part-time places and half-day sessions
**Children:** 6mths–5yrs. 30 places (10 for babies). 36 on register
**Hours:** 8am–6pm
Morning session 8am–1pm
Afternoon session 1pm–6pm
Open 51 weeks a year
**Status:** Private, non profit-making
**Number of years open:** 2½
**Meals:** Breakfast, lunch, tea, snacks
**1992 fees:** £77 per week full-time – under 2
£74.50 per week full-time – over 2
£18 per day – under 2
£17 per day – over 2
£9 per session – under 2
£8.50 per session – over 2
£50 refundable deposit

**Waiting list:** Variable. Early registration advisable for babies
**Registered by:** Hants County Council SS

**Premises** Part of the Staunton Park Community School complex, set in a semi-rural area north of Havant. The nursery is spacious, occupying two very large rooms opening off a central lobby. In addition, there are two sleep rooms for babies, a small kitchen and good toilet, washing and laundry facilities, all spotlessly clean. The rooms are reasonably well equipped with toys, games, art and craft materials and books, but the decoration and furniture look fairly shabby. 'We're working on it,' says manager Gloria Whitney. 'We started with very little. Everything has been begged, borrowed or stolen!' The nursery is bright and cheerful with plenty of light and colour provided by the children's lively artwork. There is a garden play area and children can use the school fields, tennis courts and sports hall.

**Manager & staff** Gloria Whitney, NNEB, is a charming woman, full of enthusiasm for the nursery and caring towards children and parents. She is anxious for each child to really enjoy their time spent at nursery and creates a relaxed, happy atmosphere. She is accountable to the management committee of the nursery, but is responsible for day-to-day administration and staff management. She heads a team of eight (two extra to be taken on if numbers reach their maximum), seven qualified and one trainee.

**Children & parents** Mainly middle class from professional backgrounds. The Midland Bank pay for four places, which are not always taken up by bank employees, and Hampshire Social Services will occasionally subsidise a case of special need. During our visit, the children seemed busy and happy. A row of jolly babies in highchairs were feeding themselves with varying degrees of success, supervised by obviously doting staff. Older children were clambering about on apparatus or working busily on a craft project. Discipline is maintained by generous praise and a star chart system. Difficult behaviour is deflected by diversionary tactics. Parents can talk over progress or problems informally on a daily basis.

**Curriculum & activities** Gloria Whitney believes in a flexible but planned routine. Mornings tend to be more structured, with nursery school activities and pre-school work.

Older children have worksheets and their own folders. There is no formal teaching as such; children are encouraged to learn through play. Older children follow a pre-school pattern of activities – letter recognition and simple letter sounds, tracing and following letter shapes. No reading schemes are used as Gloria Whitney feels it can have an adverse effect if they are different to those used at the child's primary school. Many of the activities are woven around themes, which change regularly. Afternoons are mostly taken up with art and craft and there is plenty of free play. Gloria Whitney admits that afternoons could be structured more effectively. Music and songs several times a week, regular outings and occasional dance and movement. The mobile library visits once a month. No written programmes or curriculum, and no written records of child development.

**Remarks** A well-managed and efficient nursery providing good childcare in a happy, friendly environment. The manager and staff are constantly on the look-out for ways to improve their facilities and equipment. Places for babies are keenly sought after.

## SUNRISE DAY NURSERY

Richard Aldworth Community School
Western Way
Basingstoke
Hants RG21 6HA
**Tel:** (0256) 56166

**Owner:** Hampshire County Council
**Manager:** Jill Lawless, BA (Hons), PGCE
**Type:** Day nursery offering full-time and part-time places and half-day sessions
**Children:** 6mths–5yrs. 30 places (9 for babies). 55 on register
**Hours:** 8am–6pm
Morning session 8am–1pm
Afternoon session 1pm–3.30pm or 1pm–6pm
Open 50 weeks a year
**Status:** Private, fee-paying, non profit-making. Jointly sponsored by Hants County Council and others inc Borough Council and Midland Bank
**Number of years open:** 2½
**Meals:** Lunch, tea, snacks
**1992 fees:** £85–£95 per week full-time depending on age

**Waiting list:** 40, but a place can nearly always be found
**Registered by:** Hants County Council SS

**Premises** Excellent. The nursery occupies a separate building, modern and purpose-built, at the edge of a large comprehensive-school complex, looking out over playing fields. The main room is enormous, light and airy, and divided into specific areas for various activities, the adjacent baby unit has been well adapted. Babies sleep in a row of new cots, or nap outside in prams during fine weather. The unit is provided with a changing area and full laundry facilities. All the babies wear terry nappies which are laundered by the staff. The under-2s have an indoor play area and separate outdoor play area, safely fenced. Older children have a messy-play area for sand and water, small tables and chairs for sit-down activities and a book/story corner. The fenced-off outside play area will be improved when permanent outdoor play equipment is installed.

**Manager & staff** Jill Lawless, BA Hons, PGCE, is a qualified nursery teacher with several years' experience. Young and energetic, she has very clear ideas about what a nursery's aims should be. She is supported by six other members of staff, all NNEB qualified. There are no peripatetic teachers at the moment though it is hoped that it will be possible to employ some in the future. A cook, qualified in food hygiene, comes in daily to make lunch and is ready to cope with any sort of special diet. A nursery management committee comprising nursery staff, elected parents' representatives and representatives from organisations sponsoring the nursery, the school and Hampshire Social Services meets regularly to decide policy and to monitor the effective running of the nursery.

**Children & parents** Owing to Basingstoke's shifting population of professional people working in the various businesses and industries in the area, sometimes only for a short period, the turnover of children at the nursery tends to be higher than elsewhere. There is a mixture of nationalities – mainly European. The majority of the children come from professional backgrounds and most go on to state schools; just a few to the private sector. Although there is a waiting list, places often become available as parents move away to other jobs. Parents are actively encouraged to come into the nursery and see what is going on. Transitional visits are arranged to help new children settle in. The nursery offers priority places to Basingstoke & Deane Borough Council, the Benefits Agency, Hampshire County Council Education Department and Midland Bank plc. There are also places available for the community.

**Curriculum & activities** Much thought has gone into the daily routine, which is very structured and busy. The emphasis is on stimulating the imagination and helping children to learn by discovery. Children are encouraged to develop skills through play. There is no formal teaching of reading or number work. Jill Lawless says, 'My philosophy is that small children will learn if it is fun. They have got at least 11 years of formal education ahead of them. We want them to develop at their own pace without pressure, become aware of themselves as individuals and learn to make their own decisions.' The daily routine is often based around a topic which is used for discussion, activities and games. Each topic is used to encourage basic skills in maths, language, science, art and social and physical development as well as emphasising multicultural and environmental awareness. Children take part in drama, music and movement, PE, painting and modelling. There is generous time and equipment for free play – the Wendy house is, as always, particularly popular. Pre-school work is done with children individually or in pairs. There are regular outings to the park, the library or the shops and occasional special trips. At the time of our visit, the children were engrossed in a story and did not hesitate to add their comments and ask questions. Although lively, they were extremely well behaved. Jill Lawless does not believe in using any form of punishment to maintain discipline. Good behaviour is encouraged through praise and children are only restrained to prevent them from hurting themselves or others. Babies and toddlers join the main nursery for some joint activities, especially lunch. Staff eat with the children in small family groups.

**Remarks** Extremely well-run and organised day nursery for working parents. Qualified staff only, offering a busy and varied daily programme. This is not a cosy, homely place – the enormous size of the main room militates against that. However, there is a warm, friendly staff team, close to children and parents as well. Despite the seemingly long waiting list, the nursery is confident that everyone can be found a place. Management have produced a very useful and well-written handbook providing information for parents.

# Hereford & Worcester

Parents in outlying villages have always relied on childminders, but over a third of the county's 1600 childminders have dropped out since the Children Act imposed tighter regulations. There are five subsidised local authority day nurseries, charging £45 per week. However, waiting lists are so long that it is almost impossible to get a place. The local authority also sponsors places for children in need in the private and voluntary sectors. Private nurseries have mushroomed over the last few years. There are now 94, with fees at least twice the subsidised rate. There are 25 nursery classes attached to primary schools, but state provision is sparse. Only seven per cent of 3- and 4-year-olds will be lucky enough to secure a place in a nursery class prior to starting school.

**Further information**

For details on day nurseries, private nursery schools, childminders and playgroups:
Department of Social Services
County Hall
Spetchley Road
Worcester WR5 2NP
Tel: (0905) 763763

For details on nursery schools, units and classes:
Education Department
Castle Street
Worcester WR1 3AG
Tel: (0905) 763763

# COMMUNITY DAY CARE GROUP

Worcester College of Higher Education
Oldbury Road
St Johns
Worcester WR2 6AJ
**Tel:** (0905) 748227

**Owner:** Worcester College of Higher Education
**Supervisors:** Bronwyn Mitchell, Residential Care Cert, and Community Daycare Group Committee
**Type:** Day nursery offering full-time and part-time places to college staff and students and local community
**Children:** 3mths–7yrs. 18 places (inc 5 for community). 33 on register
**Hours:** 8am–6pm term time
8am–5.30pm college holidays
Open 51 weeks a year
**Status:** Workplace nursery
**Number of years open:** 8
**Meals:** Mid-morning snack, packed lunches – microwave available
**1992 fees:** £9.05 per day – students
£10.30 per day – college staff
£12 per day – community users
**Waiting list:** Approx 12 names. Priority to students
**Registered by:** Hereford and Worcester County Council SS

**Premises** A wartime, block-built, single-storey building adjoining the college sick bay. Much in need of renovation, it was once a flat for five residential students. The entrance doubles as an office and cloakroom. It leads into a passageway with a small messy-play area, off which are the babies' day room, sleep room and larger play room for the older children. The kitchen is used as a utility room, not for cooking. The toilet area is primitive, but adequate. Though not ideal, it is a cluttered, small and friendly place with the jolly, patient and loving staff making up for the physical inadequacies of the building. Safe, quiet location in a far corner of the college campus, with a very large, outdoor, grassy play area and a smaller, paved, all-weather enclosure.

**Supervisor & staff** Bronwyn Mitchell holds a Residential Care Certificate and has been supervisor since the nursery opened eight years ago. Motherly and lively, she is a hard-working organiser, experienced childminder and residential care worker. She heads a stable and conscientious staff team (three full-time, three part-time), the majority of whom are qualified. Bronwyn herself is also involved in day-to-day care. The new principal of the college is a working mother who is committed to providing good nursery care on campus. The Community Daycare Group Committee, the college staff who run the nursery, are optimistic that it will soon be able to move into larger (and better) premises and expand its places to meet strong demand.

**Children & parents** The children come from a wide variety of backgrounds, often with single parents. Some lack emotional stability, while others have suffered more than one family breakdown. Initially shy of visitors, the children soon included us in their play and were keen for help with their dressing-up activities. The nursery is available to male and female mature students at the college and outside parents. Demand exceeds the number of places available for most sessions. Places are allocated monthly on a first come first served basis. Roughly half the children attend full-time. Community users, limited to five places including some local teachers, must guarantee to purchase a minimum of ten sessions per week. Parents are encouraged to organise certain social events themselves. This helps them to get to know each other, the children and staff – not always an easy task when they are studying full-time or working long hours. Many students enrol at Worcester College primarily because it provides nursery facilities. The parents, because they are in education themselves, often have strongly held views on childcare, and nursery staff do their best to comply with individual requests, eg no television.

**Curriculum & activities** Stability, security, independence and communication skills are high priorities. As many children do not live in traditional family units and spend long hours at the nursery, strenuous efforts are made to create a warm, homely environment. Some pre-reading and writing activities are available, but the emphasis is on structured play with staff supervision and intervention when necessary. The day begins with table and floor activities set out. Art, craft and water play are always available in the messy-play area and staff take turns to organise these, often around a weekly theme. Talking is very important, and so are ordinary everyday family experiences such as trips to the shops, walks to the park and outdoor play. There is concern that children should not become institutionalised and that when they move on to school, they are independent and equipped with the basic skills to cope with school life. Nursery workers are patient, kind, firm but loving. Staff and children are clearly having fun.

**Remarks** A safe haven for children, many of whose parents are trying to cope with the enormous stresses of combining child-rearing and further education on limited incomes. Hopefully the combination of a college principal enthusiastic about childcare and a committed management committee, will enable the nursery to expand into more suitable premises and flourish on a firmer financial footing.

# FIELDHOUSE MONTESSORI KINDERGARTEN

Station Road
Credenhill
Hereford HR4 7DW
**Tel:** (0432) 761250

**Owner/Headmistress:** Anna Ecroyd, Mont Dip
**Type:** Nursery school offering half-day sessions
**Children:** 2½–5yrs. 30 places. 28 on register
**Hours:** Morning session 9.15am–12.30pm
Afternoon sessions depending on demand
Open 39 weeks a year
**Status:** Private, fee-paying
**Number of years open:** 2
**Meals:** Snack
**1992 fees:** £350 per term for 5 morning sessions a week
£300 per term for 3 morning sessions a week
£250 per term for 2 morning sessions a week
£20 registration fee
**Waiting list:** 17 names. Preference to siblings
**Registered by:** Hereford & Worcester County Council SS

# HAWTHORN COTTAGE DAY NURSERY & SCHOOL

92-94 Blakefield Road
St Johns
Worcester WR2 5DP
**Tel:** (0905) 426611

**Owner:** Margaret Tilsley, Cert Ed
**Type:** Day nursery and nursery school offering full-time places and half-day sessions
**Children:** 3mths–5yrs. 10 places for under-2s. 40 places for 2–5yrs. 70 on register
**Hours:** 8am–5.45pm
Morning session 9am–12.30pm
Afternoon session 1pm–5pm
Open 49 weeks a year
**Status:** Private, fee-paying
**Number of years open:** 7
**Meals:** Lunch, tea, and mid-morning snack
**1992 fees:** £71.25 per week full-time
£15 per day
£7.50 per session
15% sibling discount
Free to children with special needs
**Waiting list:** Short
**Registered by:** Hereford & Worcester County Council SS

**Premises** Babies are housed in a small, solid brick and timber house next door to the Victorian parish hall used by the older children. They occupy two rooms on the ground floor – one for play, with its own changing facilities, the other a sleeping room with cots and large old-fashioned prams. The 100-year-old parish hall adjacent is home to 40 children over 2 years old. They have the use of two floors and a large covered outdoor play space at the back. The ground floor (2- to 3-year-olds) has a large play/activity room, two smaller quiet rest rooms, toilet and utility areas. Upstairs – for children who have mastered the climbing of stairs – the oldest group have four adjoining play and activity areas and their own toilets. It is a light, airy building which feels comfortable and well used, as does most of the furniture and equipment. In contrast, some of the collage displays are superb and very new, especially the 'Safari Park' up the main staircase, made after a recent visit. The budget for new equipment is small, and not high on the list of priorities, although the nursery would like a 'growing' garden area to improve the outdoor play facilities.

**Owner & staff** Originally a secondary school French teacher, Margaret Tilsley, BA, Cert Ed, became involved with under-5s after the birth of her own child with special educational needs. She helped to start a play group at the college of higher education where her husband works. The need for nursery facilities in the area was all too apparent and seven years ago she opened Hawthorn Cottage. She is a friendly, thinking and reliable older mum, with a wealth of experience, who has easy and warm relationships with her staff, children and parents. She clearly cares about them all and keeping everyone happy is top of her list of priorities. Several of the qualified staff have been attracted by the free childcare which working at the nursery offers them and are enthusiastic, both as users and workers. They are mostly in their 20s and include a well-integrated physically handicapped nursery assistant. The staff/child ratio is 1:3 for babies and 1:5 for over-2s.

**Children & parents** Although Margaret Tilsley would very much like to help children from less privileged backgrounds, the private/fee-paying nature of the nursery means that most come from middle-class, professional families whose parents work in the city. About a third attend full-time and most start at around 2 years. They are happy, confident and very free within the nursery's unwritten rules of play. Mothers are encouraged to spend time settling their children in, especially when they are tiny babies. A number of children have single parents, and very occasionally, in a case that she considers a special need, the owner will offer a free place, rather than lose the child because of the parent's lack of money. The nursery is also willing to take babies and young children with special educational needs and disabilities. Margaret Tilsley also has a particular interest in gifted children. The majority of children go on to a variety of state primary schools in Worcester, Malvern and Broadheath. A few enter schools in the private sector such as Sunnyside.

**Curriculum & activities** Independence, civilised, polite behaviour, confidence and self-esteem come before formal education here. The emphasis is on learning through play, in a happy and secure environment. In the mornings the 4-year-olds take part in pre-reading and writing activities, stories and board games in their own separate area and are encouraged, each according to their differing abilities. In the afternoons they join the 3-year-olds for free play with art and craft activities alongside. The staff assist and supervise where necessary but there is plenty of opportunity for free expression and role playing and a fair amount of noise and mess, until clearing-up time. Then children are expected to transform the chaos into order, which they do with enthusiasm. Margaret Tilsley uses her French language abilities to teach the older children a little each day, on an informal basis. All children take part in singing games, outdoor play and storytimes at different points of the day according to their age group. There is an annual Christmas theatre trip, a summer outing and local farm and park visits during the year.

**Remarks** A committed, caring owner, Margaret Tilsley leads a friendly team of carers and teachers who clearly enjoy their work and have genuine affection for the children. Despite lack of money, the nursery offers stimulation and security in a less structured, more flexible environment than many. A small corner of fun and humour in an area which has an abysmal record for nursery provision for the under-5s.

## MRS TIGGY-WINKLE'S DAY NURSERY

Stretton Nursing Home
Burghill
Hereford HR4 7RR
**Tel:** (0432) 761323

**Owner:** Eleanor Mansell, NNEB
**Type:** Day nursery offering full- and part-time places
**Children:** 6mths–5yrs. 30 places. 45 on register
**Hours:** 7.15am–5.45pm
Flexible hours
Open 51 weeks a year
**Status:** Private, fee-paying
**Number of years open:** 3
**Meals:** Lunch, tea, snacks
**1992 fees:** £1.08 per hour full-time (40hr week) 51 weeks a year
£1.20 per hour full-time (40hr week) excl holidays
£1.30 per hour (30–40 hrs per week)
£1.50 per hour part-time (under 30 hrs week)

£1 per day for lunch
10% sibling discount
**Waiting list:** None. Places available
**Registered by:** Hereford & Worcester County Council SS

**Premises** Since our visit, the nursery has moved to new premises four miles from the centre of Hereford. It is now in a Victorian house in the grounds of Stretton Nursing Home, with its own fenced-off outside area, and the run of the nursing home's extensive grounds – a rural and peaceful setting. Children are divided between two floors, with the babies and toddlers upstairs in two groups, and the older children split into three groups downstairs, including a pre-school group.

**Owner & staff** Eleanor Mansell, a qualified NNEB, set up Mrs Tiggy-winkle's three years ago, not long before the birth of her twins, who are an established part of the nursery. She is a calm but energetic leader. The nursery is her life, and her husband and family also contribute a great deal of time and effort to help make it a success. Eleanor leads the pre-school group herself. Unfortunately the qualified teacher who assisted her has had to leave due to ill health, but Eleanor hopes to find a suitable replacement as soon as possible. The toddlers and babies each have their own group leaders. All unqualified staff are taking part in training sessions and there is usually an average staff/child ratio of at least 1:4. There is a good age mix and staff co-operate extremely well. They create a happy, loving and busy atmosphere, caring for each individual child's needs. Eleanor's husband is at the nursery for some time most afternoons and she would be keen to take on a male member of staff full-time to redress the all-female balance.

**Children & parents** Many of the parents run their own businesses or are office workers at large companies based in Hereford. About half the children have two working parents and a third attend full-time. Despite the easy journey from the city centre to Mrs Tiggy-winkle's, many parents are unwilling to travel out of town for nursery care, with the exception of army families based on the other side of the river. Several children have single parents or broken families and the nursery has, on occasions, subsidised places in cases of exceptional need. The children are very well mannered, eager to participate, talkative and unusually considerate of each other. They transfer to a wide variety of state schools in and around the city, some into nursery classes at the age of 3, others into reception classes during the term in which they turn 5.

**Curriculum & activities** Children are encouraged to participate in organised messy activities such as painting, gluing and sand and water play from a very young age, each at their own level. The babies' sleep pattern is usually dictated by their home routine and in the waking hours there is stimulation and learning through play with a good range of toys and equipment and much one-to-one attention. The older children start and finish the day with free-play sessions. Organised art, craft, music and movement, stories and rhymes and sand and water play occur in between. The group of pre-school children from 3 to 5 years is kept deliberately small. They are taken out for sessions aimed at developing their concentration and memory skills and introducing them to pre-writing activities. Reading is not taught here because the schools the children move on to all have different approaches and the nursery does not want to cause confusion. There is a strong emphasis on creativity and imagination and a flexible approach which is receptive to the moods of the children. The rural setting also gives the children opportunities to learn about nature first-hand and to grow plants for themselves. Weather permitting they make good use of the large garden and plentiful outdoor play equipment.

**Remarks** Extremely good care at a very reasonable price which, when we visited last year, had not increased for two years. Long, flexible hours for working parents and easily accessible from Hereford. Friendly, helpful staff, who love and stimulate the children. Current parents strongly recommend it.

## OAK HOUSE NURSERY SCHOOL

Brampton Abbotts
Ross-on-Wye
Herefordshire HR9 5JD
**Tel:** (0989) 62304

**Owner/Principal:** Sue Marshall, PPA, Mont Dip
**Type:** Nursery school offering full- and part-time places and half-day sessions, plus 12-week holiday playscheme
**Children:** 18mths–5yrs. 36 places. 108 on register
**Hours:** 8.30am–3.30pm
Morning session 9.15am–12.15pm
Afternoon session 12.30pm–3.30pm
Extended day available 8am–5.30pm
Open 40 weeks a year
**Status:** Private, fee-paying
**Number of years open:** 6
**Meals:** Packed lunches, snacks
**1992 fees:** £12 per day
£6.50 per morning session
£6 per afternoon session
Extra charge for extended day
10% sibling discount
**Waiting list:** Minimal. For morning sessions only
**Registered by:** Hereford & Worcester County Council SS

**Premises** Two sets of double gates open off a narrow country lane into a large tarmac playground with gardens at the side. Oak House, the owner's spacious 1920s-style home, is on the edge of the peaceful village of Brampton Abbotts, surrounded by farmland, but only a few minutes from the centre of Ross-on-Wye. The premises are clean, tidy and well maintained. The whole building was extended and refurbished two years ago. The nursery occupies five rooms, including three large, carefully designed playrooms with bright furniture and carpets and a vinyl floor area where painting and messy activities take place. The walls are covered with children's pictures. There is a toilet off one playroom and a separate nappy-changing area with laundry facilities. Each playroom has a low-level wash basin. Children watch educational television programmes each day in the family sitting room, and snacks are prepared in the owner's kitchen. The gardens surrounding the nursery provide a safe, stimulating play area, with a huge variety of fixed outdoor play equipment – picnic tables, a lovely wooden play den, a roundabout, swings and climbing frames, all set on grass or wood-chip safety surface. The rural position can cause problems with cars trying to pass each other on country lanes. Absolutely no public transport available.

**Owner/Principal & staff** Sue Marshall, PPA, Mont Dip, works full-time in the nursery, involving herself in everything that goes on. A mother of four school-age children and former playgroup leader, she opened Oak House five years ago. Her lively, enthusiastic team of local women were all known to Sue Marshall before she employed them and were chosen for their 'genuine love of children, patience, understanding, proper qualifications and good balance of ages', she says. There are three full-time and three part-time workers, including two NNEBs and a qualified primary school teacher with 17 years' experience. Together, they offer a range of skills – music, art, drama and a sound knowledge of pre-school education and care. Staff are friends and work closely together, meeting daily to discuss ideas, plans and problems. Children are offered generous attention and cuddles. There is no staff training policy or budget. The staff/child ratio is 1:6. On the possibility of hiring male nursery workers, Sue Marshall says, 'We would have to sell it very carefully to our parents. This is a rural area. We're not as liberal as inner-city parents. I think they might be suspicious of a young man with under-5s.' The staff seem genuinely caring. We watched several of the smaller children put up their hands for a cuddle and they were immediately picked up.

**Children & parents** Local children from farming and allied services or professional backgrounds. Most of the mothers are in part-time employment. A small number come from the nearby market town of Ross-on-Wye. Children with special educational needs are happily integrated. Virtually all move on to local primary schools. Children are accepted before they are potty-trained, with parents supplying nappies. Parents learn of the nursery by word of mouth or attend a free mother and toddler group at the nursery on Friday afternoons (1.30pm–3pm). 'I feel very strongly that parents should be able to walk through the door at any time.' Sue Marshall says, 'I welcome any visit, at any time, about any matter.' There are also regular parents' evenings, open days and socials. New children are settled-in according to their individual needs. 'Some settle quickly, others take half a term. We don't rush anything. Mum can stay as long as necessary.'

**Curriculum & activities**  No single philosophy prevails although, having studied the Montessori method, Sue Marshall believes the school provides a balance of this with other sound methods. There is an excellent range of educational and play equipment, much of it nearly new. Children are grouped mainly by age, but this is flexible. Each class has a structured day, including plenty of time for free play and fun. The school encourages, but never forces, a child to do anything. Activities include sand and water play, dance and movement, nature walks, visits to garden centres, the zoo and farms and termly swimming. Staff listen to older children read individually every day. They are taught letter formation and number work, simple science and technology as well as participating in a PE session in the village hall each week. Art, craft and music daily. When children are interested and ready, they are provided with graded worksheets and introduced to the phonic alphabet using the Letterland scheme. Number work includes recognition and formation of digits and the meaning of shape, quantity, size and volume. Children's progress and development is monitored by staff, but no written records are kept.

**Remarks**  Friendly, enthusiastic and relaxed. A nursery with an unusually homely feel, offering good care and sound educational programmes, supervised by an experienced infant teacher. Reasonably priced, considering the facilities. Impressive owner, eager to provide the best possible care for each individual child. Holiday playscheme available for children from 3 to 8 years old.

# PAINTER'S COTTAGE
2 Post Office Lane
Kempsey
Worcs WR5 3NS
**Tel:** (0905) 820236

**Owner/Principal:** Mary Williams, BA, Cert Ed
**Type:** Day nursery and nursery school offering full-time places and half-day sessions, plus school holiday club for under-10s
**Children:** 3mths–5yrs. 42 places per day, 24 in nursery school and 18 in day nursery. Some children attend both. 80 on register
**Hours:** *Day nursery*
8.15am–5.45pm
Open 52 weeks a year
*Nursery school*
Morning session 9am–12 noon
Afternoon session 12 noon–3pm
Open term-time only
**Status:** Private, fee-paying
**Number of years open:** Day nursery 3 years
Nursery school 15 years
**Meals:** Day nursery: lunch, tea, snacks
Nursery school: milk and biscuits
**1992 fees:** *Day nursery*
£90 per week full-time – under 2
£75 per week full-time – over 2
£12 per session – under 2
£10 per session – over 2
*Nursery school*
£45 per week full-time
£5.40 per session
**Waiting list:** None
**Registered by:** Hereford & Worcester County Council SS

**Premises**  Attractive, late 17th-century cottage, with several later additions, just off the main A38 in the centre of Kempsey. Originally, the owner's family home with a separate purpose-built extension used to accommodate the nursery school. When the family moved, the cottage itself was converted and refurbished to a high standard to provide a bright, homelike day nursery for babies and toddlers. Simple white walls, stripped pine and natural-coloured, fitted carpets throughout, are enhanced by colourful displays of children's work and pastel friezes in the babies' rooms. The adjoining nursery school is upstairs, with one main open-plan classroom – resembling a comfortable, well-equipped infant reception class – and two additional work and art/craft rooms. At the back, there is a reasonably large, enclosed garden with grass and paved areas, a climbing frame and swings. A yellow line outside the building makes parking difficult.

**Owner/Principal & staff** Mary Williams, BA, Cert Ed, formerly a primary school teacher, set up the nursery school 15 years ago, to cater for her own children's needs and provide a stimulating educational environment for their early years. Initially it grew slowly until the expansion into full-time nursery care for babies from 3 months old took over the family home three years ago. Mary Williams is a professional, experienced leader with high expectations of her well-qualified staff and the children too. Although no longer involved in day-to-day care or teaching, she is always available to talk to parents and staff. She organises, co-ordinates policy and manages the nursery school and a holiday playscheme. Of her ten staff, eight are qualified, NNEB, B Ed, BA and BTEC. The two unqualified assistants are parents of past pupils. The nursery school is in the hands of Carole Smith, a graduate teacher with further training in the education of pre-school children. Joy Hadley, NNEB, is the welcoming, calm and friendly manager of the day nursery, with wide experience of day nursery work at supervisor level. Staff turnover is particularly low at Painter's Cottage – one member has 11 years' service. The five nursery school staff have 33 years' service between them. Mary Williams says the secret is an open, friendly atmosphere throughout, making staff feel valued, as well as better salary scales than her competitors. Staff relationships are warm and communication between day nursery and school is surprisingly good. Staff/child ratios are 1:4 in the nursery and 1:8 in the nursery school.

**Children & parents** The children come from a wide area. Most are white, middle-class, often from professional families where both parents work. They want more than just high-quality childcare and are impressed by the educational programmes offered by the school. They are also prepared to pay what is considered locally to be an above-average price. Parents are encouraged to spend time in the nursery before leaving young babies for the first time. They and staff jointly keep a 'nursery to home' book, where they enter relevant comments for each other's information. There is a good relationship with parents and an open-door policy. Older day nursery children regularly attend some of the nursery school sessions. Children are happy, well behaved, disciplined and extremely confident for their ages. They are expected to work hard and give of their best – and are rewarded for doing so with stars, praise and an extra cuddle. About a third leave before 5 years old to go on to a variety of independent schools. The remainder settle very quickly into their respective state primary schools in the term of their 5th birthday. Staff are happy to take on more children with disabilities or special educational needs, provided the proper support and back-up system are available.

**Curriculum & activities** The day nursery is a friendly, calm place where each child is given generous individual attention and access to plentiful toys and suitable equipment. Directed art and craft activities are provided for older toddlers not yet attending the school. Learning is primarily through creative play in a flexible but structured day, often dictated by the moods of the children themselves. Picnics, walks and playtimes with the nursery school children happen regularly. Mealtimes are an opportunity for children and staff to talk together in a family atmosphere. When children in the day nursery are ready for more formal learning, they have the option of attending sessions at the adjoining nursery school. Academic standards reached are high, with the emphasis on learning and achievement. All morning sessions and two afternoons a week are devoted to intellectual pursuits. The curriculum covers a range of vital subjects. Besides language, stories, rhymes, games and conversation, there is reading using a number of different pre-reading and reading schemes; the majority of rising-5s leave able to read well. There is also writing, including fine motor control such as cutting, colouring and drawing, leading to formation of letters; mathematics in line with National Curriculum requirements for level 1, including addition, subtraction, shape, time and measurement. Creative activities, dance, music, and PE are also an important part of the timetable. Two afternoon sessions each week are led by an NNEB nursery nurse at a more relaxed pace.

**Remarks** Caring, professional and experienced staff providing high-quality day nursery care and education. An exclusive, tasteful and well-equipped setting. Above average prices for the area. Well-established nursery school for parents wanting a disciplined and structured approach, with high expectations of early academic achievement, confidence and social success.

# SWANPOOL CHILDREN'S NURSERY

2 Alexander Road
St Johns
Worcester WR2 4AJ
**Tel:** (0905) 748478

**Owner:** Leysfield House Ltd
**Manager:** Connie Pickering, NNEB, RSCN, Mont Dip
**Type:** Day nursery offering full-time places and half-day sessions
**Children:** 2–5 yrs. 24 places. 35 on register
**Hours:** 8.15am–5.30pm
Morning session 8.15am–12.45pm
Afternoon session 1pm–5.30pm
Open 50 weeks a year
**Status:** Private, fee-paying
**Number of years open:** 3
**Meals:** Lunch, tea, snacks
**1992 fees:** £65 per week full-time
£13 per day
£8 per morning session (inc lunch)
£7 per afternoon session
**Waiting list:** None
**Registered by:** Hereford & Worcester County Council SS

**Premises** A refurbished black and white 50-year-old, three-bedroomed bungalow, with a pretty garden, including a vegetable patch. It is located in a quiet residential cul-de-sac just off the busy Malvern road. This nursery is just like home. Through the front door, the smell of home cooking greets you from the kitchen opposite and friendly staff offer a warm welcome. The two main play/activity rooms are at either end with toilets, an office and the kitchen off the entrance hall in the centre. It is a light, safe and warm place, comfortably furnished on a limited budget, with second-hand school tables and chairs, and effective collages and displays of the children's work everywhere. Maximum use is made of available space and you know that nothing is wasted here. There is a neat compost heap at the end of the garden and vegetables are grown in season. The nursery is within easy walking distance of a large park with children's play area and the river Severn where the children often go, in small supervised groups, to feed the swans. Easy access by car and bus.

**Manager & staff** Connie Pickering is an enterprising, energetic grandmother, who qualified as an NNEB and RSCN before having children of her own. Her involvement in the PPA movement led to a job as under-5s advisor for the local Social Services department, and an awareness of the deficiencies in nursery care in the area. She is the driving force behind the Swanpool nursery and leads a team of caring, thoughtful staff, several of whom are older women like herself with a wealth of practical experience in childcare. With young college leavers, YTS students and younger mums there is a real family feeling here, and though much of Connie Pickering's time is taken up with admin she still likes to lead regular afternoon sessions with the older children. Her husband looks after the accounts and knows the children well, as he visits regularly.

**Children & parents** Most are middle-class, from the new estates on the outskirts of the city, with both parents working, though not necessarily full-time. Several children have single parents, but fees can be a problem for these families, who desperately need such a service in an area where state nursery provision is minimal – available to only four per cent of under-5s. Roughly a third of the children attend full-time. Virtually all are white, as reflects the area. They are happy, confident and sociable with each other, the staff and visitors. Parents, especially fathers, are encouraged to pop in for lunch from time to time and they 'pay' by telling a story afterwards. Children are normally introduced to the nursery over a two-month period of visits, with mum and dad both involved in settling their child in. The transition period is not always easy for staff, but they say that it is well worth the effort and avoids future problems. Although they have no special needs children at present, the nursery would be happy to consider this. Most children go on to state primary schools.

**Curriculum & activities** A child-centred nursery which operates within a disciplined but flexible framework. There is spontaneity, especially in the summer, when they take advantage of good weather for outdoor activities and outings. Children are split into two groups according to age, and the younger ones start the day with free play. The mid-morning break is followed by organised art and craft activities and/or sand and water play but any child who does not want to join in can choose an alternative task. Individual needs are well catered for. Walks feature regularly for both groups, as do song-times and stories. There is a theme, and colour to each week and relevant visitors are invited. During 'blue week' the local police-woman called with her walkie-talkie and radioed in for a panda car which arrived with its blue light flashing, to be greeted by 24 children in police helmets, which they had made themselves. Pre-reading and pre-writing skills are encouraged by using practical activities, but there is no pressure to achieve academically. Good communication is encouraged by sharing thoughts and needs with the group. Early years mathematics is taught through play during normal routine activities. It is essentially practical – matching, counting, looking at volume and length and simple addition and subtraction. The nursery's prime aim is to assist each child to become secure and well balanced and make a confident transition to primary school. There is a happy buzz throughout the nursery, with fun high on the agenda. Wonderful home cooking by a local cook, who also spends time in the nursery and clearly loves her job.

**Remarks** Quality care at a reasonable price. Happy, unpressured, homely environment which is welcoming to parents. In an area where only seven per cent of under-5s receive any form of state nursery education, Swanpool provides a much needed service.

# Hertfordshire

One of the top ten counties in the country for nursery education, with 35 per cent of all 3- and 4-year-olds receiving a nursery place. Admission is on a first come first served basis, with priority to children with special needs. The Social Services register 19 private day nurseries and over 200 playgroups. The nine family centres they run are threatened by this year's round of budget cuts. They are also one of the few departments to provide training for nursery staff and childminders. A respite scheme offers breaks for parents with special needs children. Fees for some priority children placed with childminders are also subsidised.

**Further information**

For details on day nurseries, childminders and playgroups:
Development Officer for Children
Department of Social Services
County Hall
Hertford SG13 8DF
Tel: (0992) 556378

For details on nursery schools, units and classes:
Education Planning Manager
County Hall
Hertford SG13 8DF
Tel: (0992) 555864

# MARLIN MONTESSORI

1 Parkview Road
Berkhamsted
Herts HP4 3EY
**Tel:** (0442) 866290

**Owner:** Marlin Schools & Childcare
**Directress:** Sheila O'Neill, AMI Dip, Cert Ed, Dip Beaux Arts
**Type:** Montessori prep school offering full and part-time places and half-day sessions
**Children:** 0–7yrs 55 places. 40 on register
**Hours:** 8am–6pm
Morning session 8am–1pm
Afternoon session 1.30pm–6pm
School hours 9am–3.15pm
Open 48 weeks a year
**Status:** Private, fee-paying
**Number of years open:** 27
**Meals:** Breakfast, lunch, tea, snacks
**1992 fees:** £1.25–£3 per hour
**Waiting list:** Long for babies. Places can be guaranteed for older children
**Registered by:** Dept for Education
**Under same ownership:** Marlin Schools Hertfordshire – Kings Langley, St Albans, Rickmansworth; Marlin Schools Middlesex – Bushey, Harrow-on-the-Hill, Pinner

**Premises** A converted 1930s bungalow with a purpose-built assembly hall attached, in a residential area of Berkhamsted. Seven rooms for different age groups, kitchen and offices. The premises are in good condition, light and bright, with lively artwork on the walls. The kitchen is in the process of being refurbished. The atmosphere is homely and space is adequate, not generous. Outside, the garden is divided into three areas – a soft bark-chip surface under play apparatus, a concrete race track for bikes and trikes and a grassy area for romping around. Plenty of outdoor equipment to suit different ages and tastes. Long-suffering traffic wardens tend to turn a blind eye to short-term illegal parking outside.

**Owner/Directress & staff** Sheila O'Neill, AMI Dip, Cert Ed, Dip Beaux Arts, has a varied and international background; an American, she was born in Canada and lived in Ireland, France and Holland before settling in England. Her four children are Montessori-trained and work for her in the nursery group; Marlin Childcare is very much a family business. Sheila O'Neill has been teaching for 30 years and used to play an active part as nursery head, but now has a more administrative role, overseeing her eight nurseries. She employs a minimum of 13 staff at Parkview Road; 12 are qualified NNEB, Mont Dip, Cert Ed, B Ed, PPA or City & Guilds, and one is unqualified with years of experience in childcare. Peripatetic teachers come in to give lessons in ballet, music, gym, swimming, science, history and geography. The staff are mostly under 30 and work closely together. There is an excellent relationship between staff and children, with nursery workers ready to help and encourage and to give cuddles when needed. A very happy atmosphere. No training or development programme.

**Children & parents** The children, many of whom travel from Aylesbury, Rickmansworth and Milton Keynes, come from culturally diverse, middle-class families. Many go on to private schools in the area, as well as to state primaries. Children are divided into family groups and a keyworker is appointed to each group. All the children have lunch together, except for the babies, and sometimes join together for outdoor play. A simple uniform is worn by children over 2½, and babies wear nursery sweatshirts. Children with special needs are catered for but the nursery will only take children they are sure can be adequately cared for. Parents are welcome to talk to staff informally about their children and more formally at open days and evenings. Progress records are kept and reports prepared for children's next schools. Parents can visit the baby section at any time.

**Curriculum & activities** Teaching follows the Montessori method, but not slavishly. Care is taken to create an atmosphere where children want to learn and to provide them with stimulating and challenging activities. The day follows a structured pattern. Older children take part in discussions, artwork and cultural activities, interspersed with extras like swimming, gym and dancing as well as generous periods of free play. The aim of the nursery school is to make sure that all the time spent there has a purpose. Even mealtimes are used for learning. Children are encouraged to be independent, choosing their activities and helping to prepare them and to tidy up afterwards. Everything is accessible, on open shelves and in open cupboards. If they show a particular interest in any specific activity, it is developed. Most children can read by the time they leave the school. The Ginn reading scheme is used when children are ready. Those who leave at 7 rather than 5 sometimes attain reading ages of 10½. There is a busy timetable – storytelling, music and musical instruments, singing, outdoor play, computers, woodwork, gardening and cookery. Geography, history and biology are introduced through puzzles, books and toys. French is taught once a week. The school is well equipped with Montessori teaching equipment and apparatus, toys and books. Children work individually in small groups. Creative and imaginative play is plentiful and there are outings to various places of interest such as art galleries, museums, farms and the nearby adventure playground. Entertainers occasionally come in, but children often make their own entertainment, putting on plays and concerts with the help of staff. Children are prepared for entrance examinations to a variety of pre-prep schools and can stay at Marlin until they are 7.

**Remarks** An intimate, friendly nursery that children really enjoy coming to, with qualified, dedicated staff. Long waiting list for babies, but the numbers of older children are down due to the recession.

# MONTESSORI NURSERY & PRE-PREPARATORY SCHOOL

High House Farm
Takeley Road
Mill End
Takeley
Nr Bishops Stortford
Herts CM22 6PL
**Tel:** (0279) 870898

**Owners:** Geraldine & David Gibson
**Headteacher:** Geraldine Gibson, Cert Ed
**Type:** Montessori nursery school attached to independent pre-prep school, offering full- and part-time places and half-day sessions
**Children:** 2½yrs–7yrs+. 48 places. 120 on register
**Hours:** 8.15am–6pm
Morning session 9.15am–12 noon
Afternoon session 1.30pm–3.30pm
Open 51 weeks a year
**Status:** Private, fee-paying
**Number of years open:** 7 (5 in current premises)
**Meals:** Snacks, lunch, packed teas
**1992 fees:** £5.10 per session
£1.40 per day for lunch
20% discount to siblings and full-time children
**Waiting list:** Long. Approx 30–40 per term. Cannot guarantee places
**Registered by:** Dept for Education

**Premises** Situated along a country lane next to Stansted Airport. The school occupies three separate buildings rented from Stansted Airport, which owns the site. The main nursery is a 1930s converted farmhouse. A smaller, parallel group is housed nearby in the Garden Barn, a mobile classroom. Downstairs, the brick-built farmhouse has a long room for 28 children. The big bay windows overlook five acres of farmland – all available for nursery use. The room is well organised and equipped with a Wendy house, walk-in telephone box, computer and piles of games and puzzles stored at child height. Walls are bursting with art and there is evidence of topic work everywhere. The art room doubles as a dining room and the large spotless kitchen is used for cookery classes, as well as preparing meals. Upstairs there is a comfortable library with sofas, chairs and cushions. The hub of this floor is the Montessori room, full of specialist Montessori apparatus and activities. The head's and secretary's offices are nearby. Children only use the stairs under supervision. The Garden Barn is equipped in a similar way to the farmhouse. The children here share an art room with the reception class. Overall, the buildings are bright, newly decorated and well furnished. Access by car only, no public transport and no houses within walking distance. Huge outside play area with wooden-framed climbing apparatus and outdoor equipment – used three times a day in summer, at least once a day in winter. Airplane noise is not a problem.

**Owner/Headteacher & staff** Geraldine Gibson, Cert Ed, is headteacher and owns the school jointly with her husband, a computer engineer. She has diplomas in child psychology and computing, but is above all an educationalist. Of the 15 full-time teaching staff, all but two are well qualified. The two deputies are Montessori qualified and the rest of the team include a range of qualifications – Cert Ed, NNEB, Mont Dip, NAMCW and City & Guilds. Training is highly regarded and staff attend regular seminars and training courses to acquire additional specialist skills and update their knowledge. The staff complement includes a cook, secretary and a sizeable number of students. Training students is considered an important role of the school. The staff also includes a music specialist, and French and German teachers. There are two 'floating' teachers not based in specific classes, but available to cover for sickness or holidays.

**Children & parents** Mainly white and middle class with a smattering of Europeans, particularly French and German. The catchment area is wide – many of the parents travel long distances to work at the airport. The children transfer to a variety of schools in the state and private sector. Some leave in the term in which they will be 5, some at 6, others not until they are 8. They usually start in one of the two parallel nursery classes at age 3, or earlier if they can cope without a daytime sleep and their health visitor approves in writing. Throughout the school, children are placed in classes according to suitability and readiness, not age. There is an orderly, polite atmosphere. Children are confident and independent. Phasing-in new children is done gradually and parents are always welcome. There are regular parents' evenings, with talks on different subjects, such as the Montessori method, the use of computers in the curriculum and reading policies. Parents are very supportive and active. It was parent pressure which resulted in the opening of the pre-prep department. Strong fundraising programme for charities.

**Curriculum & activities** Very much an educational establishment, strongly influenced by the Montessori method, but not to the exclusion of all else. Computers are widely used and each classroom has its own, with software designed for each age group. Younger children work with pre-reading, number and simple language programmes, while older children use word processors, databases and adventure programmes. Equipment is plentiful and stored at child height. The intermediate nursery class (for the oldest children) is more formally arranged, like a school classroom. Children wear uniforms and sit in groups around tables, with the teacher at her desk. The library and the Montessori room, each with a qualified teacher based in them, take three groups of four or five children per session. In the Montessori room, children progress through the apparatus in a structured, calm atmosphere. In the library they become familiar with Letterland characters and work on pre-reading and writing exercises in workbooks. A wide variety of reading schemes are used and each child follows the programme most suited to his/her needs. The Ginn scheme is used for maths. All children begin French and German. Topics change weekly. Swimming once a week. The environment is an important resource. Guinea pigs, fish and rabbits are kept and the surrounding farmland used for regular walks. Outings in the summer include Hatfield Forest, Paradise Park and Wimpole Hall. There is regular monitoring of children's progress, with written reports for the older group, and parents are invited in to talk about development goals.

**Remarks** Very popular Montessori-based nursery school and pre-prep, with flexible hours and services for working parents. Structured learning and well-qualified staff in a polite, orderly atmosphere. Children can move up the school at their own pace, according to ability, not age.

## MOUNT CARMEL KINDERGARTEN

60A Sandpit Lane
St Albans
Herts AL1 4BW
**Tel:** (0727) 838480

**Owners:** Franco and Lucia Federici
**Principal:** Lucia Federici, Maestra Giardiniera (Italian Nursery Teacher)
**Type:** Nursery school offering full-time places and half-day sessions
**Children:** 3–5yrs. 20 places. 50 on register
**Hours:** 8.45am–4pm
Morning session 8.45am–12.45pm
Afternoon session 1pm–4pm
Open 40 weeks a year
**Status:** Private, fee-paying
**Number of years open:** 7
**Meals:** Snacks, packed lunches

**1992 fees:** £70 per week full-time
£8 per 4hr morning session
£10 per 5hr morning session
£6 per afternoon session
**Waiting list:** Long. 42 names. Early registration advisable. First come first served, but priority to siblings.
**Registered by:** Herts County Council SS

**Premises** The ground floor of a detached, modern house in a leafy area of St Albans. The three rooms used by the children are light and cheerful with varied examples of artwork and projects adding colour. Formal learning takes place in the classroom, carpeted and furnished with small tables and chairs. The Art Room doubles as an indoor play area – half of it is provided with tables for glueing, painting and craft and the other half is equipped with a trampoline, slide, plastic tunnel and other large equipment. Quiet play, stories and rest periods take place in the Garden Room, which is stocked with books, sleep mats, small chairs and a television set. Outside there is a paved patio area and a pleasant garden – small, but just enough room to allow children to let off steam. It has a playhouse, and outdoor toys and apparatus. There is a menagerie of pets which the children play with and help to look after – two fish, three tortoises, two guinea pigs, two rabbits, a canary and a budgerigar.

**Owner/Principal & staff** Lucia Federici is English, has Italian nursery teaching qualifications and is the mother of seven children. She employs six part-time workers; three qualified NNEB and City & Guilds, two unqualified and one City & Guilds trainee. Lucia Federici teaches full-time at the nursery and is an enthusiastic, energetic principal, who believes in providing a kindly, but structured and disciplined environment, to give children a sense of security and confidence. The young staff interact well with each other and with the children. The atmosphere is orderly, friendly and happy. Any unacceptable behaviour is dealt with by a friendly talking-to or explanation. The staff/child ratio is 1:5. No staff development policy or budget.

**Children & parents** The children are from high-income families and various cultural backgrounds, all local. The school fills its numbers by word of mouth, and a long waiting list suggests its popularity. Lucia Federici makes herself available on a daily basis to discuss children's progress or problems with parents and encourages parents to participate in nursery school life – helping with outings and events, coming to see concerts and plays, taking part in parents' evenings. Parents of new children are allowed to drop in whenever they like or to telephone to find out how their child is settling in. Children wear a uniform of school sweatshirt, white blouse and self-coloured trousers or skirt.

**Curriculum & activities** A structured, disciplined timetable, with all the expected pre-school learning and activities and strong emphasis on imaginative play and art and craft. Lucia Federici is keen to encourage children to take part in community activities, particularly fund-raising, and has a sheaf of press cuttings to prove their success in raising large sums of money for charity. The daily routine includes an hour in the classroom, spent on a structured programme of early learning and skill development, followed by free play, structured play, dressing up, singing, caring for pets and plants, storytime and outdoor play. Most children can read to some extent by the time they leave. The standard varies from being able to manage a few basic words, to free reading. The nursery uses the '1-2-3 and Away' reading scheme. Records of reading ability are kept, but there are no records of progress or development and no written programmes, policies or procedures. Equipment is bright and interesting (annual budget £1500). Religion forms a part of the curriculum and Lucia Federici is very keen on kindness, good behaviour and Christian values in her pupils. Prayers are said at the start of the day and before meals, and religious stories are read or told from time to time. Children talk openly about Jesus, God, death and heaven. Music is held three times a week, dance and movement daily and cookery every fortnight. Guest speakers visit regularly.

**Remarks** A good foundation in education and social behaviour, very much reflecting the principal's Christian values and aims. One drawback is the size of the garden, which the owners hope to extend by purchasing some adjoining land. Small school with a growing waiting list.

# NORTON ST NICHOLAS (C of E) SCHOOL – NURSERY CLASS

Norton Road
Norton
Letchworth
Herts SG6 1AG
**Tel:** (0462) 684201

**Owner:** Herts County Council
**Headteacher:** Bob Hopcroft, MA (Ed)
**Nursery Teacher:** Gill Watterson, B Ed
**Type:** Nursery class in state primary school offering half-day sessions. No full-time places
**Children:** 3yrs 10mths–4yrs 11mths. 26 places. 52 on register
**Hours:** Morning session 9am–11.30am
Afternoon session 1pm–3.30pm
Open 36 weeks a year
**Status:** State nursery class
**Number of years open:** 14
**Meals:** Snacks
**1992 fees:** No fees. 25p per week for lunch
**Waiting list:** Varies. Currently turning away 50% of applicants. Priority to siblings
**Registered by:** Herts County Council LEA

**Premises** A single-storey, flat-roofed, brick building in the school grounds, surrounded by a fenced garden and play area, set in a rural village of thatched cottages, with open fields beyond. The entrance opens into a cloakroom, decorated with cheerful, carefully mounted, self-portraits of all the children. The main open-plan room has cream-coloured walls and brightly coloured furniture. Part carpeted, part tiled for messy play, it is divided into flexible activity areas. A quiet room off the main area is used for stories, cassette listening, group discussions, puzzles and reading. There is also a television, computer and facilities for cookery classes. Outdoor equipment is plentiful and new – climbing frames, plastic barrels and tubes to crawl through, a large sandpit and a covered area for bad-weather play. A road has been painted on the tarmac biking area, with traffic lights, zebra crossing and roundabout. A new shed is bursting with sit-on cars, scooters and bikes, hoops, balls, beanbags and bats. Limited off-street parking can be a problem. The Letchworth and Baldock bus service stops right outside the school. Bus times miraculously coincide with school hours.

**Headteacher, Nursery Teacher & staff** The headteacher, Bob Hopcroft, MA, takes an active interest in the nursery class and visits regularly, often taking a session. Gill Watterson, B Ed, has been the nursery teacher for two years. Enthusiastic and confident, she has four years' teaching experience. She spends many extra hours preparing the classroom with stimulating and interesting activities and displays. Amanda Stephens, NNEB, is the nursery nurse assistant. Both women are relaxed and dedicated. They constantly update their skills through in-service training and external courses. Staff from the main school come to read stories at the nursery and cover for holidays and sickness. The staff/child ratio at 1:13 is not generous, but is augmented by teachers from the school, specialist teachers for children with special educational needs, language teachers and occasional students. About ten pupils a year from the local secondary school come for work experience.

**Children & parents** A varied social and cultural mix, from a wide catchment area, including Letchworth and Baldock (poorly served for nursery places). There is a small Asian contingent, mainly Indian. Three-quarters of the children move into the main school, and the rest go on to local primary schools. Partnership with parents is treated as vital and each session begins with a parent helping his/her child. The last quarter of an hour of Friday sessions is for parents to come and share books with their children in the library corner. The nursery door is always open to parents. They do not assist in the classroom, but organise and help with outings and fund-raising events. The term before a child starts, parents are invited to an evening when the nursery philosophy is explained. A week before the start date, a nursery teacher visits the family at home. Parents can stay for as long as necessary for the first session. Entry of new children is staggered over the first two weeks of term.

**Curriculum & activities** The nursery follows the High Scope philosophy. There is a structure to each session and importance is placed on the child's ability to make informed choices and develop independence. Children and parents together choose the activities for the first part of the session. Once activities are completed, children divide into two groups to

# ST CHRISTOPHER SCHOOL

The Montessori Department
Barrington Road
Letchworth
Herts SG6 3JZ
**Tel:** (0462) 679301

**Owner:** St Christopher School Educational Trust
**Headmaster:** Colin Read, MA
**Head of Montessori Dept:** Christine Laubin, B Sc (Child Development), Mont Dip, AMI Dip (Association Montessori Internationale)
**Type:** Montessori nursery school in co-educational boarding/day school, offering full-time places and half-day sessions
**Children:** 2½–5yrs. 40 places. 40 on register
**Hours:** 8.40am–12 noon – under 4
8.40am–3.20pm – over 4
Open 40 weeks a year
**Status:** Independent school with charitable status
**Number of years open:** Since 1920s
**Meals:** Snacks, lunch (strict vegetarian – no meat or fish)
**1992 fees:** £897 per term full-time
£634 per term for 5 morning sessions a week
£54 per term for lunch
**Waiting list:** Moderate. Preference to siblings and children of former pupils
**Registered by:** Department for Education

**Premises** The Montessori department (known as 'Monte') is set in its own grounds in the centre of the school estate. It occupies the ground floor of Arunfield, the headmaster's Edwardian house – he lives upstairs. The approach is on foot – no cars are allowed near the school – along a tree-lined drive, past lawns and greenhouses. The nursery has attractive play areas, mostly grassed, with generous outdoor play equipment – wooden climbing frame, sand pit, swings, etc. Children enter through the cloakroom area, where each child has a locker for wellingtons, another for outdoor shoes and a peg. The two large classrooms are spacious and light with big windows and timber-beamed walls and ceiling. Equipment is well organised and displayed at child height. A separate library is cosy and very well stocked. Flooring is mainly polished wood and children carry small mats to do activities on the floor.

report back. Each session includes a small-group time, when work is more focused and teacher-directed. Much of the equipment in the nursery is new, bright and stimulating. As much as possible is easily accessible to children. The home corner has new pine furniture – table, benches, washing machine, cooker, bed and sink unit – plus piles of dressing-up clothes, especially a wonderful collection of hats. There is a sand and water tray and plenty of low surfaces for children to kneel at to play. A recently acquired puppet theatre, with a large stock of glove puppets, is very popular. Strong emphasis on art and craft, using many different techniques. Gill Watterson is responsible for art throughout the school. Children are involved in preparation, mixing paints and making the play dough. Cookery takes place weekly. Pre-reading, pre-writing and numeracy are encouraged through topics and activities. Books are enjoyed in the quiet room and taken home to share with the family. Older children from the primary school visit for a short period each session to read to individual children. Writing grows naturally out of other activities. Each child has a 'list book' for their activities, where they draw, write the occasional letter and gradually copy words. When a child is ready, he/she is guided towards correct letter formation. Parents are given a copy of the correct alphabet and how each letter should be written, for reinforcement at home. All children do PE in the main hall once a week. Pre-number and mathematical skills such as matching and sequencing are learnt through puzzles, construction equipment, computer games and board games. Computer software ranges from pre-number to language development programmes. Achievement records are kept on all aspects of a child's development and passed on to the next school. The mid-session snack of juice and crackers is a social but orderly time when children are expected to show good manners.

**Remarks** An exciting and fun environment in which to learn, with wonderful resources. Enthusiastic and dedicated staff. Pressure for places has increased dramatically over the last two years.

**Director & staff** Christine Laubin, B Sc, Mont Dip, AMI Dip, studied child development at Cornell University, New York, before coming to London to gain a Montessori qualification. She taught at the nursery before having her family and returned five years ago to become director of the department. Her enthusiasm and outstanding organisational skills are evident everywhere. There is one other full-time member of staff, plus two part-timers who leave after lunch. All except one have Montessori qualifications. Christine Laubin reports directly to the head of the junior school, who in turn is responsible to the headmaster of the whole school. Continuity within the department is impressive; one teacher has been there for 11 years and another two for over six years. Sixth-formers from St Christopher and local schools, as well as students studying child development, all come in to help. A peripatetic music teacher visits. Children use first names to address all staff – a long-standing tradition throughout the school which is felt to build a bond of friendship at an early stage. 'From this grows the mutual respect on which relationships at St Christopher's depend.' Caring, gentle staff and children who are generally very kind to each other.

**Children & parents** Children enter Monte at the beginning of the term in which they have their 3rd birthday. Virtually all will continue their education within the school, moving into the junior department at 5½. Before they move up, the top group attend a weekly morning talk in the junior hall and nursery staff liaise closely with staff in the junior school. The reception class teacher is also Montessori trained. Children are middle-class, fairly local and from a wide range of nationalities and religions, including Sikh and Hindu. Many parents are attracted by the informality, freedom and child-based approach. Philosophies include a strict wholefood, vegetarian diet throughout the school and no toy guns, war toys or Action Men to be brought in. St Christopher has a very active Parents' Circle (the Guinness Book of Records lists this as the oldest parents' organisation in the country); nursery parents form a sub-committee and nursery reps are on the main committee.

**Curriculum & activities** Classrooms are divided into six main areas – closely following the educational vision of Dame Maria Montessori – practical life, sensorial, language, maths, art and other miscellaneous activities. There is much use of Montessori equipment. Practical life sessions offer the children the chance to gain competence and confidence in their immediate environment. This includes exercises in pouring, cutting, carrying, washing, sweeping up, dressing, ironing and cooking. The sensorial area includes problem-solving activities related to size, shape, colour, sound, taste, smell, texture and weight. The language area offers pre-reading and pre-writing exercises and games. When children are ready, they work through various reading schemes and books are sent home. Maths work is almost entirely concrete, using Montessori equipment – there is little emphasis on written maths. Painting and a craft activity are always available, encouraging children's own work with as little adult input as possible. Each child chooses his/her own activity and works independently. Everywhere children are carrying small trays with their chosen activity from the shelves to tables or a mat on the floor – movement is quiet and purposeful. Each task is completed and all equipment put away carefully in its proper place before another is begun. Staff work with children individually, in pairs, and in groups, monitoring their progress on a daily basis. When children are 4 years old, they can stay full-time. Afternoons are for more advanced learning activities and Fridays for special programmes such as swimming, cookery, woodwork and gardening. All-day children are also taken on outings – museums, bird sanctuary, etc. Staff meet privately with all parents twice a year to discuss their individual child's progress in detail. No written reports. Food and diet are a very important part of school life. The school is strictly vegetarian, with no meat or fish but a plentiful supply of grains, pulses, fresh fruit and vegetables together with dairy produce, cheese and eggs. Children can help themselves to a drink or snack at any time during the day. Lunch comes from the main school kitchens. Vegetarian packed lunches allowed. Staff eat with children and mealtime conversation is important.

**Remarks** One of the most well-established Montessori nurseries in the country. Informal, happy and very relaxed.

# TENTERFIELD NURSERY SCHOOL

London Road
Welwyn
Herts AL6 9JF
**Tel:** (043 871) 4564

**Owner:** Herts County Council
**Headteacher:** Janet Broom, BA, PGCE
**Type:** High Scope nursery school offering half-day sessions. No full-time places. Youngest start in afternoons and move up to morning sessions
**Children:** 3yrs 6mths–5yrs. 80 places. 80 on register
**Hours:** Morning session 9am–11.30am
Afternoon session 1.15pm–3.30pm
Open 36 weeks a year
**Status:** State nursery school
**Number of years open:** 52
**Meals:** Milk. Older children stay for lunch in their last term
**1992 fees:** No fees
**Waiting list:** Endless. 300 names. Names can be put down at birth
**Registered by:** Herts County Council LEA

**Premises** Purpose-built in 1965 on the corner of London Road and Becket Gardens opposite the local primary school. There are two large, sunny classrooms each with a recess area behind a folding screen which can be used for quiet concentration. One classroom houses a huge play house which can take whole groups of children for imaginative play sessions. Last year a new music room was built where children can experiment with rhythm and dance. Funds were raised by parents and the local community. There is also a kitchen, head teacher's office, staff room, parents/reading room and cloakroom. The nursery school has its own garden stocked with apple trees and a wide range of other attractive trees and shrubs. There is a fantastic selection of outdoor play equipment including a play house, miniature gipsy caravan, fire engine, concrete engine, hollow blocks, several climbing frames and a large shed full of push and pedal toys. A covered area allows children to play outside in bad weather. There is a local adventure playground, but with such a wealth of outdoor equipment on site, there is almost no need to leave the premises, except for special outings.

**Headteacher & staff** Janet Broom, BA, PGCE, has been headteacher at Tenterfield for the last 14 years. She is answerable to the ten school governors. Her staff are mainly part-timers, all qualified NNEB or Cert Ed; one has an additional Montessori diploma. Sybil McCoy, NNEB, the only other full-timer, has been at the nursery for 30 years. She has seen the nursery change from a formal hierarchy headed by 'Matron', to the current friendly, well-managed team. Janet Broom sees great advantages in having part-time staff because they are able to cover for each other during holidays and sickness. Under normal circumstances the same staff always work together mornings or afternoons. Each staff group meets once a week and the whole team meets twice a term. NNEB students come on placement and although there are no peripatetic teachers, governors and parents come in from time to time to read stories and help with special activities. One parent visits regularly to play the flute. Staff also use their special talents such as music, guitar playing, art and design. Janet has written a book about using computers with small children.

**Children & parents** There is very little racial or cultural mix in the area, but the school has a good mix of social backgrounds. Some children travel from Welwyn Garden City and Stevenage, but most are local and move on to local primaries – St Mary's JMI and Oakland JMI. A few transfer to independent Sherrards Wood. There are a variety of professional and non-professional parents. Children are divided at random into groups of ten, and unless there is a violent clash of personalities they stay in these groups until they leave. Each group has a different teacher every term. The Parents' Association is very active. The head encourages as much parental involvement as possible in the nursery curriculum. 'We feel our work in the school is very much a partnership with the parents.' Introductory evenings are held for new parents to explain the High Scope approach. Children are phased-in gradually and parents are welcome at almost any time except mealtimes.

**Curriculum & activities** Children start the day in their groups and spend half an hour on a pre-planned activity with their teacher. After this they move on to High Scope, which involves choosing and planning an hour's activity with the help of a member of staff. Children go off and carry out their planned projects, which are then discussed in small groups with the teacher when completed and tidied away by the children. Staff keep a low profile, guiding only when absolutely necessary. Children are then free to play indoors or outside on equipment of their choice. Janet stresses that the school encourages 'active learning'. Every half-term each group puts on a show for the rest of the school. There are frequent music sessions. Reading and writing are not taught per se, but with so many books and stories around, most children absorb the basics. The core curriculum subjects are language, mathematics, general knowledge and science. Religious knowledge, social skills, physical skills and creativity also form part of the learning structure and all of these subjects are incorporated into appropriate activities. Creative work includes moulding materials, painting (with feet, hands, brushes, combs, sponges), water play, woodwork, blocks and bricks, gardening and cooking. Special-interest tables are set out to encourage sensory study of a particular topic. LEA 'Early Years Records of Achievement' are kept on each child, and teachers are responsible for observation records on the children in their group. The Keel assessment method is used to double check on the school's findings, if a problem is identified. All written records are available to parents, although few ask to see them. The nursery produces a very useful prospectus.

**Remarks** A purpose-built nursery with an exciting range of facilities. The new music room is an inspiration. Excellent staff team, which works well together. Confident, independent children, who didn't want to go home at the end of the session we observed. The school is an integral part of village life and well supported by the community.

# Humberside

Humberside is proud of its record of providing pre-school education for 37 per cent of 3- and 4-year-olds, as well as 500 places for 2-year-olds. However, their nursery provision outside term-time is less impressive. There are no Social Services day nurseries; the council buys places in the 60-plus private day nurseries for children with special needs. Five workplace nurseries exist, with limited places for the general public. During school holidays parents turn to relatives or the 1000 registered childminders in the region.

## Further information

For details on day nurseries, childminders and playgroups:
Social Services Inspection Unit
Ashwell Centre
Ashwell Avenue
Greatfield Estate
Hull HU9 5LL
Tel: (0482) 706615

For details on nursery units and classes:
Education Department Area Offices
East Riding (0482) 861251
Grimsby (0472) 344122
Hull (0482) 223151
Scunthorpe (0724) 856101

For information and advice on all under-5s provision:
C.R.I.S.P.S.
County Hall
Beverley HU17 9BA
Tel: (0482) 885236

## ANCHOLME HOUSE NURSERY

North Lindsey College
Doncaster Road
Scunthorpe
South Humberside DN15 7OE
**Tel:** (0724) 281090

**Owner:** North Lindsey College
**Manager:** Mavis Diaper, NNEB, CPQS, City & Guilds
**Type:** College nursery offering full- and part-time places for college students and local community, plus after-school and school-holiday sessions for 5–8yr-olds
**Children:** 6mths–5yrs. 52 places. 98 on register
**Hours:** 8am–6pm
Flexible hours
Open 51 weeks a year
**Status:** Private, fee-paying
**Number of years open:** 7
**Meals:** Lunch, packed tea, snacks
**1992 fees:** £11 per day – under 2
£10 per day – over 2
Reduced rates for students
**Waiting list:** Priority to students and siblings. Remaining places open to local community
**Registered by:** Humberside County Council SS

## BRITISH RED CROSS EDUCARE NURSERY

40 Norwood
Beverley
North Humberside HU17 9EW
**Tel:** (0482) 881598

**Owner:** British Red Cross
**Manager:** Jill Adkins, NNEB, CPQS
**Type:** Day nursery offering full- and part-time places and half-day sessions
**Children:** 2–5yrs. 24 places. 65 on register
**Hours:** 8am–6pm
Morning session 8am–1pm
Afternoon session 1pm–6pm
Open 52 weeks a year
**Status:** Private, fee-paying
**Number of years open:** 2
**Meals:** Lunch, tea, snacks
**1992 fees:** £227.50 per month full-time
£52.50 per week full-time
£11 per day
£6.50 per morning session
£5.50 per afternoon session
£1 per day for meals
**Waiting list:** Varies
**Registered by:** Humberside County Council SS

## HULL UNIVERSITY UNION DAY NURSERY

Hull University
Cottingham Road
Hull HU6 7RX
**Tel:** (0482) 466274

**Owner:** Hull University Students' Union
**Manager:** Nicola McEvinney, SRN
**Type:** College day nursery offering full- and part-time places and 3 sessions per day, to college staff, students and local community
**Children:** 3mths–5yrs. 49 places. 70 on register
**Hours:** 8.30am–5.45pm
Morning session 8.30am–12 noon
Lunch session 12 noon–2pm
Afternoon session 2pm–5.45pm
Open 48 weeks a year
**Status:** Private, fee-paying, non profit-making
**Number of years open:** 19
**Meals:** Lunch and snacks
**1992 fees:** £4.77 per session – under 2
£4.64 per session – 2–3yrs
£4.01 per session – over 3
£25 refundable registration fee
Reduced fees for students and staff
**Waiting list:** Places available
**Registered by:** Humberside County Council SS

## VICTORIA HOUSE QUALITY CHILDCARE

73-75 Hook Road
Goole
North Humberside DN14 5JN
**Tel:** (0405) 769770

**Owner:** Rosalyn Spencer, BA, Cert Ed
**Type:** Day nursery and nursery school offering full- and part-time places and half-day sessions plus after-school care for 4–11yr-olds and holiday playscheme

**Children:** 6wks–5yrs. 34 places in nursery school plus 12 places in nursery (Babes 'n' Tots) for under-3s. 80 on register
**Hours:** 8am–5.30pm
Morning session 9am–11.45am
Afternoon session 1.15pm–4pm
Flexible hours available
Open 51 weeks a year
**Status:** Private, fee-paying
**Number of years open:** 9
**Meals:** Snacks, packed lunches
**1992 fees:** £15–£18 per day
£6.50-7.50 per morning session
£5-7 per afternoon session
Discounts for full-time attendance, siblings and early payment
£2-2.20 per extra hour
**Waiting list:** None. Places available
**Registered by:** Humberside County Council SS

**Premises** A large, Victorian house in a mixed residential area, within five minutes' walk of the town centre. The 'Babes 'n' Tots' annexe opened two years ago in the house next door. The owner and her family live above the nursery, which occupies two floors of number 73. The nursery school rooms include a messy-play room; a front playroom with construction and table-top toys, home corner, book corner and musical instruments, including a piano; a corridor with painting easels and a blackboard; a washroom; toilets and an office. Upstairs there is a large Rumpus Room, with climbing frame, trampoline and brightly coloured soft climbing equipment; a library; a classroom overlooking the river, used for group school-work and equipped with computers and television; a small kitchen and toilet area. The Babes 'n' Tots annexe is decorated with stunning animal and nursery rhyme murals, painted by local artists. There is peace and quiet in the Geese Room; messy play in the Jungle Room and other play activities in the Nursery Rhyme room. The enclosed garden has grass and concrete areas, a flower garden tended by the children and a wide selection of outdoor play equipment.

**Owner & staff** Rosalyn Spencer, BA, Cert Ed, taught in Bradford before moving to Goole and setting up the nursery, nearly nine years ago. A keen educationalist, she is a devout supporter of Human Scale Education (HSE) – a pressure group committed to campaigning for alternative schooling, based on flexible mini-schools and individually tailored educational programmes for small groups of children. Other supporters include Sir Yehudi Menuhin and Lord Young of Dartington. She has plans, supported by some of her parents, to open an independent 'free' school based on HSE principles. Rosalyn Spencer employs 12 nursery workers, five full-time and seven part-time. The full-time workers have recognised childcare qualifications and the team includes a trained reception class teacher. The part-time nursery assistants generally have the PPA Basic Playworker qualification, or BTEC, as a minimum. They are quietly organised and relate positively to the children. Training is ongoing and staff are encouraged to participate in relevant training courses. The nursery pays 50 per cent of the fees. Childcare students come for work experience. A keyworker system operates.

**Children & parents** Children come from within a ten-mile radius. Their backgrounds are socially, but not culturally, mixed; some come from single-parent families. Parents are always welcome at the nursery and often come in to help. They are allowed some say in its running and are invited to open days, concerts and parents' evenings and to assist on outings. Phasing-in new children is done gently, over a period of time. The nursery is happy to take children with special needs, provided the premises and staff ratios are suitable. The children transfer to a variety of state schools and a few to the private Minster and Deeds schools.

**Curriculum & activities** A flexible, individual approach, carefully planned to challenge each child. Nursery school sessions are structured to incorporate learning through a free choice of play, creative activities, educational group work in the quiet room, and physical activity in the Rumpus Room. Children are given careful guidance from staff, when necessary. A qualified early years teacher is present at morning sessions and each child is offered help with basic pre-literacy and number skills in a small group. Those ready are taught to read using the Open Door, Ginn, Story Chest and Oxford Reading Tree schemes. Early science is taught and a High Scope project will shortly begin. Afternoon sessions are more relaxed and based on learning through structured play. Interest tables and wall displays are lively, interesting and changed regularly. There is always outdoor play, newstime, storytime, singing or music and there are Zia, the tabby cat, a rabbit called Bubbles and a tropical fish tank to look after. All children are given the option of weekly swimming sessions and older children enjoy creative movement and gymnastics on Wednesday mornings. The physical environment for 'tinies' is very different, and although they enjoy a structured learning programme, the emphasis is on fulfilling their general needs and providing constant warmth and affection. Currently, children bring packed lunches, but there are plans to upgrade the kitchen facilities and introduce cooked meals.

**Remarks** An interesting and well-equipped nursery and nursery school, where every child is special. The owner is idealistic (she does not take a salary) and committed to an alternative education system. In a relatively low income area, where state provision for over-3s is increasing, the nursery school is finding it hard to remain financially viable.

## VILLAGE DAY NURSERY

31A New Village Road
Cottingham
North Humberside HU16 4LX
**Tel:** (0482) 876477

**Owner:** For Under Fives (part of the Daral Group)
**Manager:** Nova Spaven, NNEB
**Type:** Day nursery offering full- and part-time places, after-school club and holiday playscheme for children under 8yrs
**Children:** 3mths–5yrs. 39 places. 75 on register
**Hours:** 8am–6pm
Flexible hours
Open 52 weeks a year
**Status:** Private, fee-paying
**Number of years open:** 2½
**Meals:** Breakfast, lunch, tea, snacks
**1992 fees:** £63 per week full-time – under 2
£58 per week full-time – over 2
£1.95 per hour – under 2
£1.70 per hour – over 2
£10 registration fee
**Waiting list:** Places available
**Registered by:** Humberside County Council SS
**Under same ownership/management:**
Havelock Day Nursery, Grimsby, Humberside; County Hospital Day Nursery, Lincoln; Springfield Lodge Montessori Day Nursery, Humberside

**Premises** Large, detached, Victorian house close to the centre of the village, and three miles from Hull city centre. The nursery has sole occupation of the house. The interior colour scheme of grey walls and primary colours for doors and window frames is used in all For Under Fives nurseries. Babies have a separate area upstairs with four cots, highchairs, play mats and lots of bright and cheerful decorations. Toddlers from 1 to 2 years old have a room with slide, playmat, art materials and tables and chairs for group activities. Over-2s move between the quiet room for classwork, reading and imaginative play and the messy room providing water play, sand, and a plentiful supply of art and craft materials. There are imaginative displays of children's work throughout. The grassy garden, full of mature trees, is used daily in summer, but less often in winter because the grass becomes too muddy. King George's Playing Fields are visited twice a week. There is plenty of parking space at the back of the house and nearby bus and train services.

**Manager & staff** Nova Spaven, NNEB, has been at the nursery since it opened. She was previously deputy at Hull University nursery and also has experience in the state school system. Her role as manager is primarily administrative. She would like to spend more time caring for the children, but organising complicated, flexible staff rotas to fit in with a large number of part-time children is time-consuming. There are 11 female nursery nurses, seven full-time, four part-time. All except one are qualified, NNEB, PPA, City & Guilds. The part-timers work flexible hours and can increase to full-time care if required. Staff meetings are held once a term or when necessary. Staff are enthusiastic for further training and attend courses on first aid, Makaton, HIV and child abuse. There is no specific training budget and staff often pay for courses out of their own pockets. Ancillary staff include a YTS trainee, a cook and a cleaner. BTEC and NNEB students come for work experience. Staff/child ratios are 1:3 for under-2s, 1:4 for 2- to 3-year-olds and 1:8 for over-3s.

**Children & parents** Many children, a large number of whom are part-timers, are dropped off by professional parents commuting into Hull. There is a wide catchment area, but little cultural or ethnic mix though there are some Asian children from local medical families. Three places are subsidised by Beverley College of Further Education. Three-quarters of the children transfer to state primary schools, the remainder to the private sector. Children with special educational needs are welcome, provided they do not require one-to-one care. Babies and children under 2 are each allocated a keyworker who monitors progress and reports to parents. Older children are divided into family groups. A 'room supervisor' is in charge of each age group. Older children spend time together during breaks and lunch, but babies remain in their separate unit upstairs. Parents are invited to regular meetings, evenings, open days, a summer fair and Christmas activities and to help on nursery outings. The door is open to parents at any time.

**Curriculum & activities** The nursery's stated aims are, 'to give children the opportunity to develop their basic skills by providing the equipment to stimulate all round development through physical, intellectual, creative, imaginative, explorative, manipulative and social skills'. Over-2s have free range of the many activities on offer and move from room to room during the course of their day. Children are invited to take part in activities, but are never forced into something they would prefer not to do. The timetable is flexible, and used as a guide only. Children regularly participate in dance and music, and weekly baking sessions are held. There are no peripatetic teachers, but several members of staff speak different languages and some are very musical. No formal teaching of the 3Rs and no qualified teacher on the staff. Children are not taught to read and write, but attain a basic literacy through play, storytelling and a good supply of books. Most recognise their names and some letters and numbers by the time they leave. Basic factual records are kept on each child as well as notes on developmental progress, but there are no written programmes or policies. Nova Spaven is hoping to introduce more of the Montessori philosophy to the nursery over the next year or two, but with a meagre £750 annual budget for equipment her selection of Montessori teaching aids will be limited. Children are taken on outings to visit horses belonging to a member of staff and to the local railway station. The fire brigade has visited the nursery. Children often help prepare tea. Special dietary requirements are catered for.

**Remarks** Particularly flexible hours. Well-qualified, caring staff, although no early years teacher. Children learn through play and have access to all activities in a rather unstructured environment. Pre-school educational programmes lack planning and structure. Very reasonable cost for full daycare.

# Isle of Man

The Isle of Man has recently appointed a pre-school co-ordinator to assess the needs of the 4000 under-5s on the island. There are no local authority day nurseries, but the ten private facilities are reasonably priced at around £40 per week for a full-time place, although they are mainly run on an ad hoc basis with unqualified staff. Waiting lists can be long. 37 playgroups offer part-time provision, and around 112 childminders cater for working mothers. 'On an island which has a village atmosphere, it is usually the family who rally round when childcare is needed,' says a Council worker. Pre-school education is virtually non-existent, with only one nursery class available. The Education Department is planning to open a second one this year.

**Further information**

For details on day nurseries, childminders and playgroups:
Public Health Department
4th Floor
Markwell House
Market Street
Douglas
Tel: (0624) 685156

For details on pre-school education:
Education Department
Murray House
Mount Havelock
Douglas
Tel: (0624) 626262

# BEEHIVE KINDERGARTEN

Cronkville
Hillberry Road
Onchan
Isle of Man
**Tel:** (0624) 674655

**Owners:** Vivienne and Richard Welch
**Principal:** Vivienne Welch, PPA
**Type:** Day nursery offering full- and part-time places and half-day sessions, plus holiday playscheme
**Children:** 2–5yrs. 72 places. 206 on register
**Hours:** 8.30am–5.45pm
Flexible hours
Open 50 weeks a year
**Status:** Private, fee-paying
**Number of years open:** 7½
**Meals:** Lunch, snacks
**1992 fees:** £1.20 per hour
**Waiting list:** Moderate and variable
**Registered by:** Isle of Man SS

**Premises** A large, detached, turn-of-the-century house with various additions, extensions and conversions. Children's accommodation is all on the ground floor – seven rooms in total, including a converted double garage, a five-year-old extension and part of the ground floor of the main house. It is well lit and furnished, though much of the equipment and books are out of the children's reach. The rooms could have been warmer on the day we visited. Parking is available in a large forecourt. At the back an impressive, securely fenced, large garden and orchard. It has a paved area for push and pull toys, a zebra crossing for road safety lessons and a big playhouse in one corner. Rabbits and ducks are kept in pens and children care for them regularly.

**Owners/Principal & staff** Vivienne Welch, the principal, completed her PPA training at the Isle of Man College of Further Education. Her husband and co-owner, Richard, is a master mariner and has responsibility for administration and maintenance and helps with the cooking. Richard's mother, Mrs Welch Snr, an SRN, ran a nursery in Africa, and is often involved at the Beehive, on call when needed. There are 12 nursery nurses, seven full-time, five part-time, with a variety of qualifications and experience, including NNEB, Mont Dip and PPA. They come from many different backgrounds and cultures. Staff nationalities include French, Caribbean, Irish and Australian. Some are long-serving, in particular Stella Clayton, the music teacher, who plays the piano and organ at the nursery. Ancillary staff include a cook and a part-time groundsman. Students from schools and colleges and trainee nurses are accepted on placement. No training budget or policy. Staff/child ratio is 1:8.

**Children & parents** A complete cross-section of Manx family life, but no cultural diversity. There are no children with special educational needs or disabilities on the register. Children are well motivated and those we spoke to were very polite. New children are phased in gradually. Parents are invited to parents' evenings, open days and concerts, but an open-door policy is not encouraged, unless there is a problem to be sorted out. Parents meet regularly to plan fund-raising efforts.

**Curriculum & activities** Learning through play, with emphasis on 'the old-fashioned values of self-discipline and good manners. Sharing, caring and consideration are important.' Some Montessori teaching methods are used. Children are divided by ages into Baby Bees (2-year-olds), Honey Bees (3-year-olds) and pre-school Bumble Bees. Activities include cookery, water play, wet and dry sand, painting, cutting out, glueing, sticking, dressing up, role play and physical exercise. Projects and themes are studied and changed regularly. Art and craftwork on display was of a high standard, but mainly adult-led. Pre-reading, pre-writing and number work are introduced for older children in preparation for school. Each child has a workbook, which can be taken home at the end of term. Language development is important and children are encouraged to talk and express themselves as much as possible. French songs, rhymes and conversation daily. Swimming weekly, for pre-school children only. Music, dance and movement, musical instruments and traditional old nursery rhymes are enjoyed for at least half an hour each session. Daily outdoor play in the large garden, and emphasis on nature and environmental studies. The children were making bird cakes when we visited. The nursery is an active member of Friends of the Earth and paper is recycled. Regular outings are taken in the new school mini-bus. Each classroom is

well equipped with educational toys, puzzles, books, games and construction toys. The average annual equipment budget is £3000. There are no written programmes, policies or timetable, nor are there written records on individual progress and development.
**Remarks** Large, busy nursery, with spacious facilities and reasonable fees. Good range of activities and equipment and a lively mix of staff.

**Hours:** 9am–4pm Mon, Wed, Fri
9am–1pm Tues & Thurs
Open 50 weeks a year
**Status:** Private, fee-paying
**Number of years open:** 2½
**Meals:** Packed lunches, snacks
**1992 fees:** £1 per hour
**Waiting list:** Places available
**Registered by:** Isle of Man SS

## PALM TREE NURSERY
Elim Pentecostal Church
Park Road
Douglas
Isle of Man
**Tel:** (0624) 663847

**Owner:** Elim Pentecostal Church
**Nursery Supervisor:** Jill Madsen-Mygdale
**Type:** Nursery school offering full- and part-time places
**Children:** 2–5yrs. 20 places. 33 on register

# Isle of Wight

There are just four private and five local authority day nurseries on the Isle of Wight. Unemployment on the island runs at 12 per cent and most of the work is tourist-based and seasonal. Many parents need flexible childcare arrangements and choose from 235 registered childminders. Some charge as little as £1 per hour during the summer. Island families are close-knit and granny is traditionally used where formal provision is lacking. There are no local authority nursery schools and only four full-time places in the five nursery units attached to primary schools. Only 180 of the island's 7000 under-5s receive any pre-school education.

**Further information**
For details on all provision for under-5s except playgroups and childminders:
Early Years Unit
Education Support Services
Node Hill Annexe
Orchard Street
Newport
Isle of Wight PO30 1JZ
Tel: (0983) 520021

For details on playgroups and childminders:
Social Services Department
17 Fairley Road
Newport
Isle of Wight PO30 1UD
Tel: (0983) 520600

## BEMBRIDGE SCHOOL PRE-PREP DEPARTMENT

Hillway
Bembridge
Isle of Wight PO35 5PH
**Tel:** (0983) 873328 or 872101

**Owner:** Bembridge School
**Nursery Principal:** Barbara Field, Cert Ed, Adv Dip Ed
**Type:** Pre-prep school offering full- and part-time places and half-day sessions
**Children:** 3½–7yrs. 24 places. 20 on register
**Hours:** 8.30am–3.30pm
Morning session 8.30am–12 noon
Afternoon session 1pm–3.30pm
Open 35 weeks a year
**Status:** Private, fee-paying
**Number of years open:** 2
**Meals:** Lunch, snacks
**1992 fees:** £450 per term full-time – under 6
£750 per term full-time – over 6
£10 per day
**Waiting list:** Early registration advisable
**Registered by:** Dept for Education

## FIVEWAYS

Ryde School
Queens Road
Ryde
Isle of Wight PO33 3BE
**Tel:** (0938) 562229

**Owner:** Ryde School
**Master of Junior School:** Robert Waddington, BA, PGCE
**Teacher-in-charge:** Sally Davies, B Ed
**Type:** Nursery school attached to prep school offering full- and part-time places and half-day sessions
**Children:** 2½–4½yrs. 20 places. 24 on register
**Hours:** 8.45am–3.30pm
Morning session 8.45am–11.45am
Afternoon session 12.30pm–3.30pm
Open 35 weeks a year
**Status:** Fee-paying registered charity
**Number of years open:** 1
**Meals:** Lunch, snacks
**1992 fees:** £532 per term full-time
£317 per term for 5 sessions a week
£97 per term (£1.50 per day for lunch)
£10 per day
£5 per session
**Waiting list:** Places available
**Registered by:** Dept for Education

## STUDIO DAY NURSERY

Westmont School
Carisbrooke Road
Newport
Isle of Wight PO30 1BY
**Tel:** (0983) 523051

**Owner/Headmistress:** Jan Maclean
**Nursery teacher-in-charge:** Linda Tyrell, NNEB
**Type:** Day nursery in co-ed prep school offering full-time places and half-day sessions
**Children:** 3–5yrs. 20 places.
40 on register
**Hours:** 8.30am–3.45pm
Morning session 9am–12 noon
Afternoon session 1.30pm–3.30pm
Open 38 weeks a year
**Status:** Private, fee-paying
**Number of years open:** 15
**Meals:** Lunch, snacks
**1992 fees:** £310 per term for 5 morning sessions
£200 per term for 5 afternoon sessions
**Waiting list:** Small, by choice
**Registered by:** Dept for Education

**Premises** Westmont School is a long-established, independent co-ed school for 3- to 13-year-olds. It is housed in two converted Victorian villas, with an attractive garden in front and a large enclosed playground at the back. The front garden provides some barrier to noise from the busy main road. The nursery is in a large, light room, with French windows leading out to an enclosed, south-facing garden. The first impression of the school is depressing – the building is drab, unwelcoming and shabby and it desperately needs a good coat of paint. Not so the nursery, however, which is bright, warm and full of colour and vibrant displays of children's artwork. Nursery children have separate toilets and cloakroom and share a gym and music room with the rest of the school. Parking is a headache, but parents somehow seem to manage.

**Owner/Headmistress, teacher-in-charge & staff** Jan Maclean, the headmistress, bought the school 15 years ago, when she moved to the island with her husband, a doctor whose practice is two houses away. Linda Tyrell, NNEB, is in charge of the nursery. She is a traditional teacher/carer of the old school, in her early 60s, with a wonderful, quiet, no-nonsense approach. The children clearly adore her. She has a team of one full-time teacher and three part-time NNEB assistants. Staff appear happy and settled. There are daily nursery discussions about children and fortnightly formal staff meetings with the whole school. Specialist teachers visit for music, drama and computing.

**Children & parents** The school attracts children from all over the island and from varied backgrounds. There are only a handful of independent prep schools on the Isle of Wight and Westmont is considered to be one of the best. Parents who want their children to attend use the nursery to gain access to the rest of the school. Children with special needs are welcome. At present one deaf child is happily integrated. Parents are welcome to visit the nursery at any time, are invited to all nursery activities and support the school through an active Parents' Association. The correct school uniform of maroon, yellow and grey is compulsory for all age groups.

**Curriculum & activities** The emphasis is on social skills and independence in an ordered, stimulating environment. There is some structured work to give children a basic understanding of numbers and letters. The Ginn reading scheme is used if children are ready. Impressive standard of artwork. The timetable includes periods of free play, art and craft, music and movement, gym, gardening, outdoor physical play and PE. Nursery children have use of the school's BBC computers twice a week. Books and stories are important, plentiful and enjoyed. Children work at tables in small groups of four, clearly directed by the staff. The nursery aims to make the transition from home to school as pleasurable as possible and creates an atmosphere where children learn to mix socially and to become independent. The nursery is run on Christian principles, but is non-denominational.

**Remarks** A happy, traditional nursery for parents seeking entry to the island's oldest prep school, set up 100 years ago. Mature, experienced staff and good-quality, plentiful resources. The depressing, unwelcoming building desperately needs the same devoted love and attention received by the children.

# Isles of Scilly

There are no nursery schools or classes attached to the four primary schools on the islands. The 120 under-5s have no opportunity for formal education until they start school. For the last two years families have benefited from an under-5s development officer, but the post has been axed in this year's budget cuts. Full daycare is limited to four childminders. The council provides storytelling sessions in the library and monitors the two playgroups and three extremely part-time/part-week parent and toddler groups.

**Further information**

For advice and information on under-5s facilities:
Department of Social Services
Town Hall
St Mary's
Isles of Scilly TR21 0LW
Tel: (0720) 22537

# Jersey

Waiting lists are long for the island's 12 private day nurseries. Fees range from £50 to £80 per week and half the services take babies under 1 year old full-time. There are 26 very good playgroups. Part-time workers in the hotel industry rely on 219 registered childminders, who offer seasonal care for an average £1.80 per hour. Pre-school education for 3- and 4-year-olds is limited to classes attached to seven primary schools.

## Further information

For details on all types of daycare and pre-school education:
Education Department
Children's Service
PO Box 142
Highlands
St Saviour
Jersey
Tel: (0534) 509500

## ROUGE BOUILLON NURSERY

Rouge Bouillon School
Brighton Road
St Helier
Jersey
**Tel:** (0534) 30800

**Owner:** Jersey Education Committee
**Headteacher:** Wendy Hurford, Teachers' Cert
**Nursery Teacher:** Julie Rotherham, Teachers' Cert
**Type:** Nursery class in state primary school, offering half-day sessions. No full-time places
**Children:** 3yrs 3mths–4yrs. 20 places. 40 on register
**Hours:** Morning session 9am–11.30am
Afternoon session 12.45pm–3.15pm
Open 38 weeks a year
**Status:** State nursery class
**Number of years open:** 7
**Meals:** Snacks
**1992 fees:** No fees
£1 per week for snacks/outings
**Waiting list:** Massive. Early registration advisable
**Registered by:** Jersey Education Authority

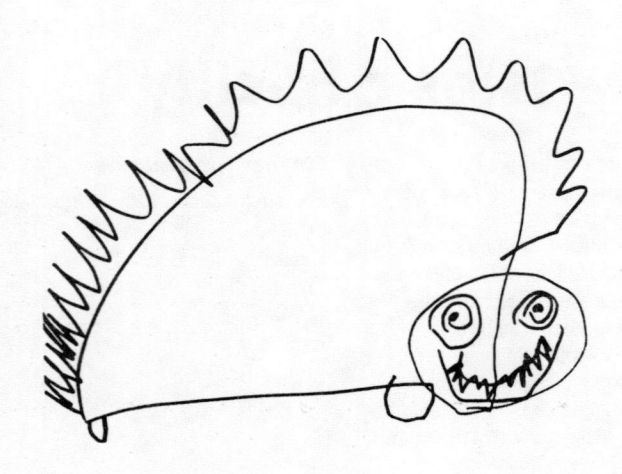

# Kent

Kent is one of the worst areas in the country for nursery provision, relying entirely on the private sector. It boasts 179 private day nurseries, the highest number in the country, but offers no local authority places, despite many known areas of social deprivation. However, there are five play centres run by the Thanet Under Fives Project which are totally funded by Social Services grants. Of the 4000 registered childminders, only 68 are supported by the council. Nursery education is also lacking, although efforts are being made to improve the situation. One nursery school and 29 nursery classes offer a part-time place to only 5 per cent of pre-school children. The council does have a 'rising-5s policy', which means that most 4-year-olds complete two terms at school before their 5th birthday. With over 100,000 children under 5 in the county, this does little to relieve the problems of working parents. Playgroups, many run on a shoestring and offering less than part-time care, are often the only solution. 'I run a playgroup in a village hall charging only £1.70 for a morning session.

Mothers in my area are desperate for childcare and couldn't possibly afford to go private,' says a local playgroup leader.

### Further information

For details on private provision:
Department of Social Services
Springfield
Maidstone ME14 2LW
Tel: (0622) 671411

For details on nursery schools, units and classes:
Department of Education
(Address and telephone as above)

For information, counselling, playgroups and parent groups in the Thanet area:
Thanet Under Fives Project
Newington Community Centre
Princess Margaret Avenue
Ramsgate CT12 6HX
Tel: (0843) 589481

---

## ABBEY SCHOOL DAY NURSERY

London Road
Faversham
Kent ME13 8RZ
**Tel:** (0795) 531408

**Owner:** The Abbey School (Kent County Council)
**Nursery Supervisor:** Fiona Kirby, B Ed
**Type:** Day nursery offering full- and part-time places to school staff and local community
**Children:** 0–5yrs. 18 places. 42 on register
**Hours:** 8am–5.30pm
Open 51 weeks a year
**Status:** Private, fee-paying
**Number of years open:** 2½
**Meals:** Breakfast, lunch, tea
**1992 fees:** £72 per week full-time
£8 per session
Sibling discounts
Subsidised fees for Abbey School teachers
**Waiting list:** Long, especially for baby places. Places cannot be guaranteed. Priority to teachers at Abbey School
**Registered by:** Kent County Council SS

**Premises** In the grounds of the Abbey School. The single-storey Rural Science building has been completely renovated and extended to create a modern, bright, purpose-built day nursery. It consists of two large main rooms – one for babies, the other for toddlers and pre-school children. Both rooms are warm, comfortable and equipped to a high standard, with carefully selected toys and apparatus to provide safety, stimulation and fun. Window decorations, colourful wall paintings and mobiles are much in evidence throughout. There is a porch for coats, toilets and a sparkling kitchen. Parking is easy and plentiful. The main road and public transport are a five-minute walk away. The nursery has a large, safely fenced playground and grassed area, maintained by the school gardener, with a good selection of ride-on toys, trucks and a sandpit. Children also have access to the school grounds and playing fields.

**Nursery Supervisor & staff** Fiona Kirby, B Ed, leads a lively team of four female workers, all full-time. Two are qualified – one NNEB, one BA. Of the unqualified staff, one is at present training (BTEC) and the other is a gym coach. Fiona Kirby reports to the head and deputy head of Abbey School and also has a parent-run management committee. Staff are young, friendly and relaxed. All have a keen sense of humour. Staff meetings are held once a month, when everyone voices their opinion. Training is encouraged and workers regularly attend short courses at the nursery's expense. The staff/child ratio varies between 1:4 and 1:5.

**Children & parents** Middle-class professionals, no ethnic mix. Priority to teachers at the school. At least half the children come from teaching families and most have two working parents. Two bilingual children – one Dutch, one German, attend the nursery. Virtually all the children transfer to local primary schools. Children with special needs and disabilities are well-integrated. The nursery currently has one child in a wheelchair. There is active parental involvement, including six parents on the management committee. The nursery has an open-door policy and holds open days and parents' evenings. Parents are welcome on outings and at activities. At the time of writing they are building a sandpit in the garden. Phasing-in is done gradually with parents and according to children's needs.

**Curriculum & activities** Discovery learning through play with a good balance of education and care. 'We aim to respect the uniqueness of each child and to offer a safe and secure environment, equipped to aid discovery and learning,' the prospectus asserts. Activities include ever-popular art, craft, music, drama and story-telling. Weekly gym. As the nursery is small, there is ample opportunity for one-to-one learning. Pre-reading, pre-writing, number work, science and technology are learnt, with support and gentle guidance from staff. No reading schemes. Children are free to explore the two rooms and the outside area. Emphasis is on inter-personal relationships, and teachers and carers have a warm, close contact with children. We observed many kisses and cuddles and saw children receive regular praise. 'No' and 'naughty' are words banned from the vocabulary of the nursery. Instead, children are offered a full explanation and shown a different, safer way to behave. Outings are a problem because of the size of the nursery and the need for extra staff to take children out. But there is regular outdoor play and walks in the school grounds. Equipment and furniture are still reasonably new and in good condition, suitable for each age group and properly used. Recent events include a puppet show, balloon making demonstration, music workshop and visit by a troop of clowns. A detailed written record of each child's progress is kept and given to parents when a child leaves.

**Remarks** Small, relaxed nursery, efficiently run by enthusiastic young staff. High-quality care, with some educational input. Emphasis on close relationships between carers and children. Might not be challenging enough for some over-3s because of limited numbers. This is the only nursery in the area offering places for children under 2 years old.

# ACORNS DAY NURSERY

Sevenoaks Primary School
Bradbourne Park Road
Sevenoaks
Kent TW13 3LB
**Tel:** (0732) 459162

**Owner:** Sevenoaks District Council
**Managers:** Company Child Care Ltd
**Principal:** Rachel Greener, NNEB, CPQS
**Type:** Workplace nursery offering full- and part-time places and half-day sessions to District Council and Midland Bank staff and local community
**Children:** 6mths–5yrs. 39 places. 30 on register
**Hours:** 8am–6pm
Morning session 8.30am–1pm
Afternoon session 1pm–5.30pm
Open 51 weeks a year
**Status:** Private, fee-paying
**Number of years open:** 3
**Meals:** Snacks, lunch, tea
**1992 fees:** £21.60 per day full-time
£11.36 per morning session

£10.24 per afternoon session
**Waiting list:** 10 names. Priority to District Council and Midland Bank employees
**Registered by:** Kent County Council SS

**Premises** In the grounds of Sevenoaks County School – a pre-fabricated building which used to be the school's assessment centre. The building is leased by the District Council, and management of the nursery is contracted out to Company Child Care Ltd, a small private company. The building is single-storey and sits alone, surrounded by the school playing fields. The nursery comprises one large room – the Badgers' Room – and two smaller rooms – Chipmunks and Squirrels. Well equipped, bright and cosy. A thoughtful choice of soft furnishings, curtain fabrics and colour schemes achieves a homely atmosphere. A staff room, kitchen, children's cloakrooms and office are somehow squeezed into the remaining space. The nursery has its own small fenced garden with large sandpit and safety surface and use of the pleasant, green school grounds. Parking inside the school campus is restricted to before 8.30am and after 4pm, because of the danger to school children. Easy parking in nearby streets.

**Managers, Principal & staff** Company Child Care Ltd, run by three women, two of whom are teachers, is a consultancy based in Hove, Sussex, specialising in advising councils, colleges and businesses on setting up workplace nurseries. This is the company's only nursery and the directors come in once a week in turn. They are responsible for ongoing staff training and general management of the nursery. Training is important and once a month the whole team receives a training session on various topics. Staff also attend day release courses. The day-to-day running of the nursery is the responsibility of supernumerary principal Rachel Greener, NNEB, CPQS, who is experienced in Social Services and private nursery care. Straightforward and straight-talking, she enjoys working at Acorns because, she says, 'I am really trusted and appreciated.' There are a further eight full-time female nursery staff, all qualified (NNEB or NAMCW). The nursery does not employ unqualified staff. They are assisted by two part-timers, a cook and an extra lunchtime helper, NNEB, who also covers for sickness and staff holidays. All the staff appear very young, but friendly and open. They work as a team, like each other and often socialise outside work.

**Children & parents** There are 12 subsidised places reserved for District Council employees (six baby places and six for over-2s) and six subsidised places for Midland Bank employees (three baby places and three for over-2s). All other places are available to outsiders, but there are no baby places left for the community. Ninety per cent of the children have two working parents and most live reasonably locally – Tunbridge Wells, Sevenoaks, Maidstone and Edenbridge. Mainly white, middle class. Some children travel long distances because their parents work nearby. It is nursery policy to restrict a child's stay at Acorns to a maximum of nine hours a day. Parents are as involved as working parents can be, but good lines of communication exist and there is an open-door policy. A parents' committee meets three times a year and parents are encouraged to talk to their child's key-worker at the beginning and end of each day. Parents and extended families take part in the Christmas party, Summer Fun day and festivals. There are regular parents' evenings. Parents are expected to take time off work to settle new children in slowly and smoothly.

**Curriculum & activities** Love, kindness and play dominate. The nursery provides a wide range of activities designed to develop the skills children need before transferring to school. The timetable is busy but flexible to the children's needs. Each nursery nurse is responsible for setting up different challenges for their own key children. Children are free to move from activity to activity, closely supervised by their carer. There is always a messy area, an art and craft project, sand and water and occasionally a cookery table. Older children do simple pre-reading and pre-writing exercises in small groups or individually. Everything is governed by choice and only attempted if a child is ready and interested. Worksheets are collated into workbooks. Older children also have news books for free drawing and writing. Activities are planned weekly in advance and displayed for parents to see and reinforce at home. Themes are decided termly in advance and great care is taken to include multicultural themes. The nursery encourages children to respect other cultures, ethnic backgrounds and people with different abilities. Equal opportunities are written into the curriculum. Girls spend time using construction toys, train sets and large equipment. Boys have opportunities to play in the home corner or care for dolls. Babies have daily records, which parents take home and add their own comments to – about sleeping patterns, eating habits or developmental milestones. Detailed written monitoring of all children. Impressive timetable and record keeping, always available to parents. Monthly library visits, daily music, dance and movement. Children go on visits once a week, sometimes to other nurseries and primary schools. Swimming in summertime only.

**Remarks** Very professional, loving care in a happy family nursery. The most striking feature was the number of smiling faces we observed – on children, staff and parents. For those who can afford it, this nursery provides one of the rare high-quality facilities in the county.

# ACORNS WORKPLACE NURSERY

Joydens Wood Infant School
Park Way
Bexley
Kent DA5 2HY
**Tel:** (0322) 550568

**Owner:** Kent County Council
**Nursery Managers:** Joy Hill, Teachers' Cert
Betty Field, Teachers' Cert
**Type:** Workplace nursery offering full-time places and half-day sessions to LEA employees, Midland Bank staff and local community
**Children:** 6mths–5yrs. 34 places. 60 on register
**Hours:** 8am–6pm
Morning session 8am–1pm
Afternoon session 1pm–6pm
Open 51 weeks a year
**Status:** Workplace nursery
**Number of years open:** 2
**Meals:** Breakfast, lunch, tea
**1992 fees:** £95 per week full-time – under 2
£85 per week full-time – over 2
£9 per session
£1 per day for lunch
**Waiting list:** Long. Most are found places eventually. Priority to Kent teachers and Midland Bank employees
**Registered by:** Kent County Council SS

**Premises** Two converted classrooms in the main infant school, approached by an unmade-up road in a rural, residential area. The brick-built, 1950s building with a pleasant outlook is five minutes from a bus service. Limited parking in school grounds, but plentiful on the nearby road. The nursery is light and well ventilated and has windows everywhere. There are five rooms. A colourful, carpeted room for the over-2s has tables, chairs and pictures all over the walls. A very comfortable and cosy room for the under-2s is filled with masses of colourful toys and soft seating as well as chairs. There is a carpeted and electrically heated sleeping area with cots for babies and mattresses for toddlers. The kitchen is fully equipped with microwave, fridge and freezer. The nappy changing room has a washing machine. It is all well cared-for, clean, tidy and spacious. Outside there is a fenced-in, grassy play area, used daily in good weather, and there are plans for an all-weather playground. Equipment includes tricycles, push-along toys, bats, balls and hoops. The only negative point is the steps down to this area. No toilets in the nursery – children use the school loos.

**Nursery Managers & staff** Betty Field and Joy Hill, both qualified, experienced teachers, job-share the position of nursery manager. Each works 20 hours a week. Their main duties are administrative and pastoral – looking after the needs of children and staff. Betty Field, promoted to manager two years ago, is a former infant school and music teacher. Joy Hill has a nursery teacher's qualification. A management committee, including parents' reps, oversees policy and general organisation. The staff team consists of six full-time and five part-time nursery workers. All are young and qualified. They cover a wide range of skills and talents – three teachers, Cert Ed and Mont Dip, four NNEB or NAMCW, three BTEC and one PPA. Some are musical, others artistic, and another is particularly good at bringing out shy children. No peripatetic staff are needed, but students attend on a regular basis. Staff relations are good. There is a formal staff meeting once a term, but each week an informal gathering takes place to discuss the week's activities. The staff/child ratio is 1:2 for under-2s, 1:5 at worst for over-2s. Regular in-house training and attendance at short courses is encouraged.

**Children & parents** A predominantly white, middle-class catchment area. Families are mainly professional, the majority with working mums. Midland Bank reserve five places and Kent County Council informs all teaching staff about the nursery. Other children come by word of mouth, although the nursery has advertised baby vacancies in the local papers. Most children transfer to state schools. There is a short phasing-in period for new children – usually two or three sessions. Parents are invited to plays, concerts and sports days. They are encouraged to help and generally become involved in the running of the nursery. The nursery has an open-door policy and staff are happy to see parents whenever necessary. Children with special needs are welcome at Acorns. At the time of our visit, they were looking forward to the arrival of an 18-month-old Down's syndrome boy. Children with special dietary needs and behavioural problems also attend. The children appear to be happy, confident and talkative, well supervised and busy.

**Curriculum & activities** No particular philosophy – direct experience through play in a calm, friendly, home-like atmosphere is considered the most important way of learning. There is no timetable as such; one activity flows into another. The nursery operates a keyworker system and thorough records are kept. Children are in groups of four or five, according to age, and come together for breakfast and sometimes tea. Equipment and furniture, including a climbing frame, dressing-up clothes, play dough and construction toys as well as table-top toys and puzzles, are plentiful and child-oriented. Basic number and reading skills are taught, but children are not expected to be able to read when they leave. Betty Field believes each child should be treated with care and gentleness and the right amount of firmness. If children are stimulated and happy, then learning will follow as a natural consequence. A topic is discussed and explored each week or fortnight. A typical day begins with breakfast all together at 9am followed by singing, an art and craft session in groups, and free play and storytime. After lunch, there is a television programme or sleep, free play, table-top games and tea at 3pm. Staff and children eat together and enjoy a happy and easy relationship. Physical contact is encouraged – cuddles, nappy-changing, bottle-feeding. Frequent outings are arranged to the police station, farms, other nurseries and a local aquarium.

**Remarks** Expensive for the area, but worth it if you can find the funds. Friendly and caring staff have created a homely and stimulating environment. Excellent staff/child ratios and plenty of well-maintained toys and equipment for each age group. Qualified teachers provide good educational input.

## CHEERFUL TOTS DAY NURSERY

68 Old Dover Road
Canterbury
Kent CT1 3DF
**Tel:** (0227) 464112

**Owner/Principal:** Elizabeth Mount, NNEB
**Type:** Day nursery offering full-time places and a range of different half-day sessions.
**Children:** 2–5yrs. 20 children max per session. 45 on register
**Hours:** 8am–6pm
Morning session 8am–12.30pm
or 9am–3pm
Afternoon session 1.30pm–6pm
Flexible hours
Open 51 weeks a year
**Status:** Private, fee-paying
**Number of years open:** 2½
**Meals:** Lunch, tea
**1992 fees:** £57 per week full-time
£32 per week 8am–12.30pm
£43 per week 9am–3pm
£25 per week 1.30pm–6pm
£12 per day full-time
£6.50 per day 8am–12.30pm
£9 per day 9am–3pm
£5 per day 1.30pm–6pm
£10 refundable registration fee
**Waiting list:** 20 on list but places always available
**Registered by:** Kent County Council SS

**Premises** A post-war, chalet-style, detached bungalow close to the centre of Canterbury with its own driveway. The building has been converted specifically as a nursery. Cars can drive right up to the front door for dropping off, as parking is not recommended on the main road. Bus and rail stations are close by. The nursery has one main activity room, a quiet room with home corner and reading area, a messy room for painting and experimenting and a classroom where older children take part in structured pre-school activities. All are colourful, warm and light with floor coverings appropriate to the purpose of the room. There is also a small extension used for sand and water play. The garden is available on a daily basis and has a patio and grassy area with climbing frames, a slide and swings.

**Owner/Principal & staff** Elizabeth Mount, NNEB, leads the team of four full-time, qualified staff (three NNEB and one BTEC). All are under 25 and for three of them this is their first job. The staff operate as a team, without a management committee, and as they live in the same area they often meet socially outside working hours. They have special needs and first-aid training. Some of the children attending the nursery have speech and social difficulties. Other than the principal and her deputy, staff have equal status, pay and holidays. Staff meetings are held once a month and Elizabeth tries to give them as much say in the running of the nursery as possible. Each member of staff is in charge of monitoring the progress of her particular group of children. Students attend the nursery every other week and are closely supervised by members of staff.

**Children & parents** The nursery covers a wide catchment area, from Margate to Sandwich. Most parents are dual-income professionals, although there is a high proportion of single-parent families in the area. There is some cultural mix, including Muslim children, some from mixed backgrounds, and one Danish boy who speaks no English. The majority move to state schools, some in outlying villages, and a few go on to Wincheap. Children are accepted before they are potty-trained. Non-working mothers are encouraged to help out at special events such as the summer fête. A real effort is made to get to know all the parents. New children are phased in gradually and the nursery operates an open-door policy, to build up a trusting relationship between parent and carer. Parents are given some say in the running of the nursery and are encouraged to comment or complain. There are special parents' evenings and open days throughout the year.

**Curriculum & activities** The nursery operates a structured routine of different play activities. Elizabeth explains that they aim to give each child some advantage when he/she moves on to primary school, since reception classes continue to get bigger and bigger. The younger children have a more flexible routine allowing them to learn colours, numbers, opposites, etc through play. The older group (3½ upwards) spend an hour and a quarter each day on pre-school skills. These include pencil control, learning to recognise and write their names, hand and eye co-ordination and letter and number work. Each child takes part in craft, construction, imaginative play, science and nature (taught by visiting students) and cookery. There is ample time for free play and outdoor play. Oxford workbooks 1 and 2 are used by the older children. Approximately a third are reading by the time they move on to their next school. Each child has a folder where records on number and letter recognition and physical development are kept. Parents have access to these if requested. Children spend most of their time all together, dividing into groups by age only for their more formal learning sessions. They also divide into different groups for meals each day so they get to know different members of staff. There is a spotless kitchen where cooked lunches are prepared. Special outings take place several times a year to a local farm, the theatre and to the shops.

**Remarks** Warm and caring atmosphere and responsive, talkative children. Staff are qualified, but young and relatively inexperienced. In the long term the nursery would benefit from further investment in toys and equipment and a more challenging programme for children over 3 years old.

## CLEVER CLOWNS NURSERY SCHOOL

Boxley Church Hall
The Street
Boxley
Nr Maidstone
Kent ME14 3DX
**Tel:** (0622) 761163

**Owners/Supervisors:** Susan Ford, PPA
Zenia Ring B Ed
**Type:** Nursery school offering morning sessions and longer sessions for 3½–5yr-olds
**Children:** 2–5yrs. 30 places. 35 on register
**Hours:** 9.30am–12.30pm
Extended session 9.30am–2.30pm Wed & Fri (3½–5yr-olds)
Open 39 weeks a year
**Status:** Private, fee-paying
**Number of years open:** 2
**Meals:** Packed lunches, snacks
**1992 fees:** £4 per session
£8 per extended session
**Waiting list:** Places available
**Registered by:** Kent County Council SS

## EAGER BEAVERS NURSERY

Beaver Green Infant School
Cuckoo Lane
Ashford
Kent TN23 2DA
**Tel:** (0233) 646662

**Owner:** Kent County Council
**Manager:** Jane Wakelen, NNEB
**Type:** Workplace nursery offering full-time places and half-day sessions to Council employees, Midland Bank staff and local community
**Children:** 6mths–5yrs. 30 places. 73 on register
**Hours:** 8am–6pm
Morning session 8am–1pm
Afternoon session 1pm–6pm
Open 50 weeks a year
**Status:** Self-funding workplace nursery
**Number of years open:** 3
**Meals:** Lunch, snacks
**1992 fees:** £66 per week full-time – under 2
£55 per week full-time – over 2
£6.60 per session – under 2
£5.50 per session – over 2
**Waiting list:** 25 names. Community places limited. Priority to Kent County Council employees and Midland Bank employees
**Registered by:** Kent County Council SS

**Premises** Well-maintained, flat-roofed, 60s brick building, in Beaver Green Infant School grounds. A main entrance hall, with kitchen area and toilets leading off. The main, oblong nursery room is laid out with child-size tables and chairs, table-top toys, crayoning table, number work table, Wendy house and log cabin. There is a quiet corner, with bench settee for singing and stories. Walls are bursting with artwork and displays of children's work. Long curtains can be drawn to divide the room into two cosier areas. A smaller baby room leads off. It is used for everything – playing, sleeping, changing (two sinks and a changing table) and eating. There is also a wet and dry room used for messy play and as a dining room – the floor is tiled and it is equipped with sand pit and painting and modelling materials. Tea is prepared in the staff room, which together with the supervisor's office next door is separated from the nursery rooms by a sturdy safety gate. The outside play area is securely fenced and very well equipped with outdoor toys. The nursery also has use of the infant school facilities including the playing fields in summer. There is a local park a few minutes' walk away. Good access by bus or car, with on-street parking.

**Manager & staff** Jane Wakelen, NNEB, worked as a nanny in the children's ward of a hospital and qualified eight years ago. She reports to a management committee made up of representatives from Kent Education and Social Services departments, Midland Bank and parents. The committee meets quarterly to discuss fees, staffing and all matters concerning the running of the nursery. Jane recruits outgoing, enthusiastic personalities and looks for friendly people who can work as part of a team. At present there are five full-time and two part-time nursery workers; four are qualified NNEB and NAMCW. They are encouraged to take part in decision making and contribute at regular staff meetings. They attend training courses enthusiastically and often socialise together after work. Two nursery nurses work exclusively in the baby room, to ensure continuity. Students visit on placement, but are always supervised by a member of staff and instructed not to answer parents' questions, as they may not be qualified to do so. The staff/child ratio in the baby room is 1:3, in the nursery 1:4. Staff appear close to the children and very approachable. The nursery would welcome some male workers, especially as there are a number of single-mother families, who would like more male role models in their children's lives.

**Children & parents** Broad social mix, some from the local council estate, others from professional and white collar management backgrounds. Some of the parents are unemployed or alone. There are no ethnic minorities. Most children transfer to the state system, especially the infant school next door, others to a local Catholic primary. There is a waiting list, with priority to Kent County Council and Midland Bank employees. The nursery welcomes children with special educational needs and can accommodate wheelchairs. There is an open-door policy towards parents, who can discuss anything with their child's key-worker at any time. Parents' evenings are held twice a year and also fund-raising events. Phasing in is done slowly with parents present for as long as they wish.

**Curriculum & activities** Eager Beavers learn through play. The day is not strictly regimented, rather one activity flows into another, but a general timetable is followed. The nursery provides high-quality care, encouraging all-round development – emotional, social, physical and intellectual. There is plenty of different equipment (annual budget £3000–£5000), in good condition, and children are well supervised at their many activities. No formal teaching is done, nor are there reading or maths schemes. The approach is very low-key with emphasis on art and craft, stories, songs and dancing and play with jigsaws, construction toys and in the home corner. Written development records and day books are kept on each child, available to parents on application. Children attend the infant school assembly once a week. The nursery has its own musical instruments and tapes and music is sometimes used as a calming background, especially at mealtimes. For most of the day, children work and play altogether, in family groupings, sometimes dividing into smaller age-related groups for particular activities or stories. Children are taught self-discipline, co-operation and independence. Those we observed were happy, busy and well adjusted to the nursery routines.

**Remarks** A happy, caring atmosphere, where children and staff work well together. One of the few full-time nurseries with baby places which is affordable to parents on average incomes. Unfortunately, places for the general public are limited.

## GRANGE HILL NURSERY SCHOOL

Goudhurst
Kent TN17 1JG
**Tel:** (0580) 211229

**Owner/Manager:** Sheila Klopper, BA (Oxon), MBE
**Teacher-in-charge:** Mary Watts, Makaton Course
**Type:** Nursery school offering 5 morning sessions a week and 2 afternoon sessions a week. All children go home for lunch
**Children:** 3–5yrs. 16 places per session. 40 on register
**Hours:** Morning session 9am–12 noon
Afternoon session 2pm–4pm Mon & Wed
Open 33 weeks a year
**Status:** Private, fee-paying
**Number of years open:** 28
**Meals:** Snacks
**1992 fees:** £32 per session
**Waiting list:** Places available
**Registered by:** Kent County Council SS

## LEAGUE OF FRIENDS DAY NURSERY

Kent & Canterbury Hospital
Ethelbert Road
Canterbury CT1 3NG
**Tel:** (0227) 451310

**Owners:** Kent and Canterbury Hospital & League of Friends
**Manager:** Julie Page, NNEB, DPQS
**Type:** Day nursery offering full-time places and half-day sessions to hospital staff, council employees and local community

**Children:** 2mths–5yrs. 55 places (25 for under 2s). 85 on register
**Hours:** 7.30am–6pm
Morning session 7.30am–12.30pm
Afternoon session 1pm–6pm
Open 52 weeks a year
**Status:** Fee-paying, registered charity
**Number of years open:** 3
**Meals:** Lunch, tea and snacks
**1992 fees:** £295 (£258 NHS staff) per month full-time – under 2
£276 (£239.40 NHS staff) per month full-time – 2–3yrs
£258 (£221 NHS staff) per month full-time – over 3
£184 (£163 NHS staff) per month for 5 sessions a week – under 2
£173 (£152 NHS staff) per month for 5 sessions a week – 2–3yrs
£163 (£140.80 NHS staff) per month for 5 sessions a week – over 3
80p per day for lunch
£25 registration fee
**Waiting list:** Priority to NHS employees and hospital staff. Some places for the community. Names taken during pregnancy. Cannot guarantee places for under-2s.
**Registered by:** Kent County Council SS

**Premises** Rather down-at-heel brick building in the hospital grounds, originally provided by the League of Friends as a recreation hall for nurses. The nursery is in a quiet area of the campus with generous parking space. Babies have their own purpose-built area providing a well-equipped day room and a sleeping room, which needs some redecoration. The main hall is divided into four age-related areas for the older children, with a good range of equipment for each group. There is also a kitchen, milk kitchen and loos. The toilets are quite a trek from the main playroom, with steps leading up to them. The garden, completely enclosed by a high wooden fence, has a large grassy area with playhouse. A nearby park is used regularly during the summer. The nursery is subsidised by the NHS insofar as the hospital provides the building, all services and maintenance free of charge.

**Manager & staff** Julie Page, NNEB, DPQS, is dedicated and determined. Her main ambition is to see childcare recognised as a profession. She is in charge of a staff of 12, most in their mid-20s. All except one are qualified childcare workers – including eight NNEB, a BTEC and one City & Guilds. Julie's role is administrative, but she ensures she has daily contact with all the children. Day-to-day supervision of the children is in the hands of her deputy, Vikki Bourne, NNEB. There are French, German and Turkish speakers on the staff. Staff meetings are held every six to eight weeks. Julie has a pool of 'flexi-staff', many of whom are qualified, who she can call on to fill in for holidays and sickness. Julie Page would like to see the status of nursery nurses raised and childcare seen as a profession. Until the salaries of nursery workers are dramatically improved (at this nursery, a senior nursery worker Grade B earns £8,300 per annum, and a qualified nursery worker Grade A £7,000) it is difficult to see how this will be achieved.

**Children & parents** Most places are taken by the children of hospital staff and four are held for council employees. Any remaining places are offered to the community. Children are 90 per cent British, but there is a German child and other cultural diversity. The catchment area is very wide, and few children transfer to the same school. The nursery operates an open-door policy and parents are welcome at any time, especially breast-feeding mothers. Many drop in at lunchtime. Parents are kept well informed, take a keen interest in the running of the nursery and are active fund-raisers through the parents' support group.

**Curriculum & activities** The day is loosely structured around periods of free play, art and craft, outdoor play and stories. Emphasis is on enjoying the various activities and having fun. There are no written programmes, no pre-school curriculum and no reading schemes. Staff see themselves as carers not teachers. Each group is provided with stimulation and encouragement. Children participate in music and songs daily, dance and movement weekly, library visits monthly. Developmental records and checklists are kept daily for babies, weekly for older children. Cooked meals are supplied by the hospital kitchens and any dietary requirement can be catered for.

**Remarks** Organised, relaxed and flexible day nursery geared as much as possible to NHS hospital working hours and patterns. Unfortunately, only limited places are available to the community. Nursery provision for under-2s in Canterbury is described as 'diabolical'.

## PARK PLACE NURSERY SCHOOL

24-25A Park Place
Margate
Kent CT9 1LE
**Tel:** (0843) 295151/298092

**Joint Owners:** Josephine Johnston, PPA
Ray Johnston
**Officer-in-charge:** Sharon Fountain, NNEB
**Type:** Day nursery offering full- and part-time places and half-day sessions
**Children:** 0–5yrs. 58 places. 135 on register
**Hours:** 8am–6pm
Morning session 8am–12.30pm
Afternoon session 1.30pm–6pm
Open 50 weeks a year
**Status:** Private, fee-paying
**Number of years open:** 3
**Meals:** Snacks. Children bring packed lunches
**1992 fees:** £70 per week full-time – under 2
£50 per week full-time – over 2
£11 per day
£5.50 per session
**Waiting list:** None
**Registered by:** Kent County Council SS

## ST HELEN'S MONTESSORI SCHOOL

Lower Road
East Farleigh
Maidstone
Kent ME15 0JT
**Tel:** (0622) 726219

**Owner/Directress:** Jeanette Dening-Smitherman, Mont Dip
**Type:** Montessori nursery school offering full-time places and half-day sessions
**Children:** 2½–5yrs. 32 per session. 60 on register
**Hours:** 9.30am–4pm
Morning session 9.30am–12.30pm
Afternoon session 1pm–4pm
Open 39 weeks a year
**Status:** Private, fee-paying
**Number of years open:** 4
**Meals:** Packed lunches, snacks
**1992 fees:** £290 per term for 5 sessions a week
£174 per term for 3 sessions a week
£58 per term for 1 session a week
**Waiting list:** Early registration advisable
**Registered by:** Kent County Council SS

## SEVENOAKS DAY NURSERY

Rear of Community Centre
Otford Road
Bat & Ball
Sevenoaks
Kent TN14 5DN
**Tel:** (0732) 460384

**Owner:** Sevenoaks Day Nursery Trust
**Nursery Leader:** Jean Sowten
**Type:** Day nursery offering full-time places and half-day sessions
**Children:** 2mths–5yrs. 37 places. 35 on register
**Hours:** 8am–6pm
Morning session 9am–12.45pm
Afternoon session 1.15pm–5pm
Open 52 weeks a year (excl bank holidays)
**Status:** Fee-paying registered charity
**Number of years open:** 4
**Meals:** Lunch, tea, snacks
**1992 fees:** £65 per week full-time
£13 per day
£5.50 per session
**Waiting list:** Approx 1 year. No one in need is turned away
**Registered by:** Kent County Council SS

**Premises** Three inter-linked, mobile Portakabins, providing a baby room, toddler room, classroom, toilets and kitchen. Situated behind Sevenoaks Community Centre, next door to a light industrial estate – not the smart end of town, but an area with a high proportion of under-5s and, until Sevenoaks Day Nursery opened its doors, no nursery provision whatsoever. After four years of solid fund-raising, the first two Portakabins opened for toddlers. In 1989 demand was so great and the waiting list grew so rapidly, that a further baby cabin was added – a gift from the insurance company Allied Dunbar, a local employer. Fees cover staff wages only, and fund-raising is vital to meet all other costs. Parents, local donors and Friends of the Sevenoaks Day Nursery regularly organise special events and appeals.

Their current target is £400,000 for a second 35-place nursery, to offer places to children on the long waiting list.

**Nursery Leader & staff** Jean Sowten leads the staff team. An experienced childminder and foster mother, she is currently studying for a formal qualification. Jean is a warm, mature, motherly figure, who has been totally converted to the advantages of nursery life over childminding, for babies and toddlers. There are nine full-time staff and five part-time. Just over half are qualified, NNEB, BTEC, NAMCW, many locally trained at West Kent College. The staff are not well paid (there was a wage freeze when we visited) but are extremely dedicated. Staff turnover is not a serious problem. Four nursery nurses are specially trained Portage workers, an early education programme for children with special educational needs. The nursery believes family groupings are important, with older children helping the younger ones.

**Children & parents** Sevenoaks Day Nursery is the brainchild of children's medical officer, Dr Olive Munro, who was concerned to offer the advantages of an integrated nursery experience to the many children with disabilities and special educational needs she encountered in her work. Approximately half the children have special needs, while the rest come from a mix of social backgrounds, including one-parent families and working mothers. Some children are subsidised by Social Services, others by the Education Department. Parents are actively involved in everything – they mow the lawn and tend the garden, decorate the nursery and buy equipment. One mother, a photographer, is responsible for the colourful photographic displays of nursery activities. A local publishing company donates books and the town librarian comes in to read stories and provide more books. Two hundred parents turned up to watch the annual Nativity play. There is a Parents' Association and parents are represented on the nursery Management Committee.

**Curriculum & activities** Learning is through play. Painting, water-play, model making and cookery are all regularly offered. Songs, music and percussion instruments daily. A specialist music teacher visits for an hour, every two weeks. The toddlers, often assisted by students from a local school, enjoy sticking, cutting, play dough and puzzles. Older children do some pre-school work, but in a very relaxed way. Reading is not taught, but children learn their colours, letters and name. Every year, the whole nursery does a project for display at Sevenoaks Town Library. There is also an art and craft extravaganza and a costumed play. Outdoor activities are in a safely fenced garden, surrounding the mobile classrooms. There is an annual summer outing for children and parents. Last year, British Rail donated two train carriages for a free day-trip to Hastings. For some of the mothers, a day out is a rare opportunity.

**Remarks** A warm and friendly nursery, established by Sevenoaks people and their friends for Sevenoaks children. Portakabins are not the most attractive or practical premises for nurseries, but this is a low-cost operation, meeting a desperate local need. Excellent integration of children with disabilities, special educational needs and social difficulties. Supported by experienced motherly staff and active parents. The nursery is dependent upon donations and fund-raising. This is an example of the community responding to Kent's lack of nursery provision by taking its own action.

# Lancashire

Lancashire has more local authority day nurseries and more nursery schools than any other county, but can only provide places for 18 per cent of 3- and 4-year-olds. It also has one of the highest populations of under-5s. 7000 pre-school children attend part-time nursery classes attached to primary schools. With a quarter of the 130 day nurseries run by the council, the private sector is forced to keep its fees reasonable, charging upwards of £7 for a half-day session. Many also cater for babies. There are over 1700 registered childminders.

**Further information**

For details on day nurseries, childminders and playgroups:

Department of Social Services
Inspection Unit
Beeches House
1 Garstang Road
Garstang PR3 1YD
Tel: (0995) 601008

For details on nursery schools, units and classes:
Education Department
White Cross Education Centre
Quarry Road
Lancaster LA1 3SQ
Tel: (0524) 67376

## COTTAM NURSERY SCHOOL

Sandy Lane
Cottam
Preston
Lancs PR4 0LE
**Tel:** (0772) 728035

**Owner/Principal:** Helen Bolton, B Ed
**Type:** Nursery school offering full- and part-time places and half-day sessions
**Children:** 2½–5yrs. 44 places. 110 on register
**Hours:** 9am–3.30pm
Morning session 9am–12 noon (or 1pm inc lunch)
Afternoon session 1pm–3pm
Open 37 weeks a year
**Status:** Private, fee-paying
**Number of years open:** 5
**Meals:** Snacks, hot lunches upon request
**1992 fees:** £8.80 per day
£1.50 per hour
**Waiting list:** Places available
**Registered by:** Lancs County Council SS

## CROSTON NURSERY SCHOOL

6 Station Road
Croston
Preston PR5 7RJ
**Tel:** (0772) 601074

**Owner/Principal:** Julie Dolan, NNEB
**Type:** Day nursery offering full- and part-time places and half-day sessions (2 a week min). After-school service
**Children:** 14mths–5yrs. 35 places. 49 on register
**Hours:** 8am–6pm
Morning session 8am–12.30pm
Afternoon session 1.30pm–6pm
Open 50 weeks a year
**Status:** Private, fee-paying
**Number of years open:** 5
**Meals:** Lunch, snacks
**1992 fees:** £68 per week full-time – under 2
£55 per week full-time – over 2
£38 per week for 5 sessions – under 2
£28.50 per week for 5 sessions – over 2
£15 per week for 2 sessions – under 2
£12 per week for 2 sessions – over 2
£14 per day – under 2
£11.50 per day – over 2
**Waiting list:** None. Places available
**Registered by:** Lancs County Council SS

**Premises** Housed in an old cinema, now converted into a Spar village shop on the ground floor. The nursery is upstairs, with a separate entrance from the street. The walls are covered with bright, colourful murals. The open-plan nursery is large and airy, but has the disadvantage of being on two levels. There are four steps from the classroom down into a play area. There are separate activity areas for under-2s and over-2s, a home corner, a carpeted area with bean bags, a messy-play area and plenty of space for riding around and physical play, as well as a cloakroom, toilets and a kitchen. A safe, well-fenced garden is reached down an outside staircase. It is partly paved, with wood chips under the slides and swings. The nursery pet, a rabbit, lives there too. Safety gates at the top of the stairs were in use and the door to the garden area locked. The front door is not locked, however. A bell rings in the nursery to tell staff that someone is on their way upstairs.

**Owner/Principal & staff** Julie Dolan, NNEB, is a qualified nursery nurse who has completed additional training for a teacher's certificate and has also worked with special needs children. She takes overall responsibility for the administration and day-to-day operation of the nursery. There are four full-time nursery nurses, one part-timer and a YTS student. Three are NNEB qualified, others City & Guilds. Staff ages range from 19 to 40. We saw hugs, cuddles and lots of physical contact between children and carers. Staff meetings are informal lunchtime gatherings, not formal meetings. Julie is supernumerary and covers for staff sickness or holidays. NNEB students are accepted for work experience. Staff training is limited. Social Services courses are less frequent due to local government cutbacks.

**Children & parents** The children are from diverse social backgrounds, with both parents working full-time. Most of them live within ten miles of the nursery and move on to village primary schools. They appear to be happy and very busy, so involved, in fact, that they take little notice of visitors. The nursery has an open-door policy (literally!), and parents can come and go as they please. If necessary, new children are phased-in slowly, but many start quite happily without. Children with special educational needs are welcome, but wheelchair access to the first floor is impractical. Nursery sweatshirts are available, but not compulsory.

**Curriculum & activities** Children begin the day with free play. A wide range of choices are available, including role play in the home corner and play house, table-top and floor games and messy play. Afterwards they help to clear up, before dividing into two groups for directed activity and conversation. There is a weekly theme and strong encouragement of self-expression. Children come together as one group to watch *Playbus* at storytimes (morning and afternoon) and to eat lunch. Older children participate in pre-reading and pre-number work, usually one to one with a member of staff. They are taught the Letterland alphabet and use Montessori sandpaper letters. As children progress to different schools, using a variety of reading schemes, the nursery does not follow any particular reading scheme. There is a computer in the classroom. Swimming, cookery sessions, dance and movement and music all take place on a weekly basis. There are regular nature walks in the village and trips to a local farm. The garden is used daily, weather permitting. Equipment, toys, games, books and materials are plentiful. There are no written programmes, policies or timetable. Weekly record cards are kept by staff on children's progress.

**Remarks** Friendly nursery with a good atmosphere and flexible hours. Fees are average for the area. Premises are a disadvantage, with stairs to negotiate down to the garden and a split-level play area, with more steps. We did not like the ease with which anyone could walk in off the street, through the unlocked front door.

## HEADSTART PRE-SCHOOL CENTRE

119a Oxford Street
Preston
Lancs PR1 3QN
**Tel:** (0772) 201004

**Partners:** Vivienne Hodgkinson, Geraldine Mahoney, Barbara Wilkinson and Anne Wynne-Jones (all NNEB)
**Managers:** Geraldine Mahoney, NNEB
Anne Wilkinson, NNEB
**Type:** Day nursery and workplace nursery offering full- and part-time places and half-day sessions to council employees and local community

**Children:** 3mths–5yrs. 34 places (8 for babies). 46 on register
**Hours:** 8.45am–5.45pm
Morning session 8.45am–12.45pm
Afternoon session 1.30pm–5.45pm
Open 51 weeks a year
**Status:** Private, fee-paying, women's co-operative
**Number of years open:** 4
**Meals:** Lunch and snacks
**1992 fees:** £75 per week full-time – under 2
£55 per week full-time – 2–3yrs
£50 per week full-time – over 3
£16.50 per day – under 2
£12.25 per day – 2–3yrs
£11 per day – over 3
£6.75–£9.75 per session
**Waiting list:** Baby places reserved by County Council. Places for over-2s available
**Registered by:** Lancs County Council SS
**Under same management:** Lancs County Council Workplace Crèche, Preston. Available to County Council employees only

**Premises** A beautifully decorated, light, two-storey 1970s house in the middle of a council house development, situated in a quiet area with little passing traffic. The baby unit is completely self-sufficient with its own bathroom, utility room and fire exit. The main playroom for over-2s is a large room with two smaller side rooms leading off it. One is a well-stocked library, the other an 'imagination play room', which can be made into literally anything. Upstairs, there is a schoolroom equipped with a fantastic selection of educational toys, a magnetic board for learning parts of the body, peg boards, language sets, lotto and a computer. There is not a spare inch of wall space anywhere in the nursery. Above the nursery is the Headstart Training Centre and a large drama room used by pre-school children. There are beautiful pale murals throughout. Children's paintings and collages, dozens of friezes, shelves full of colourful equipment and painted teddy bears complete the festival of decorations and colours. There is a garden surrounding the nursery, described by the managers as 'far too boring', which they plan to landscape with interesting, curving paths and trees. Currently it has a grassy area, where children can use bikes. A nearby park is used regularly for walks and nature rambles, weather permitting.

**Managers & staff** Geraldine Mahoney, NNEB, and Barbara Wilkinson, NNEB, both have extensive experience working in local authority nurseries. Geraldine is a specialist in baby care, while Barbara's special expertise is in drama, music and poetry. The six other female members of staff, and three paid trainees, form a close-knit, professional team. The majority are NNEB qualified, and some also have City & Guilds and CSS qualifications. All work full-time and wear bright pink uniforms. Training is considered an essential part of staff development and nursery workers are encouraged to take part in a wide range of outside courses as well as the nursery's own training programme. There are monthly workshops and weekly training sessions. Staff are valued and dedicated, in spite of lower than average remuneration. Peripatetic teachers come in for weekly dance and music sessions.

**Children & parents** Baby places at the nursery are all taken by County Council employees and babies eventually transfer to the Lancashire County Council Workplace Crèche close to County Hall, also managed by Headstart. Places for over-2s are open to the community and are frequently advertised. Parents are mainly white-collar workers, many dual-income, and there is some cultural mix. Every attempt is made to include parents in the running of the nursery, and monthly parents' meetings are held. There is a complaints box and when a point has been raised, a training session is built around the problem. The nursery welcomes all children and refuses to accept that children with special educational needs or disabilities are any different from all the rest. 'All children have special needs, and we do everything we can to meet their needs,' says one of the partners, Anne Wynne-Jones.

**Curriculum & activities** The nursery is bursting with equipment, games, toys and books. No particular philosophy is followed, but staff have devised their own, which incorporates the best from Montessori, Steiner and Froebel. Positive thinking is expected from staff at all times. Themes are used and last for as long as the children are interested, which may be days or weeks. The day starts with an hour of free play, followed by morning break. Children are then divided into three groups, Pixies, Elves and Gnomes, for an hour-long pre-planned session, with each group working on something different such as collages, a nature topic, messy play, acting out a story, number work or lotto. Children move around during the day between different groups. In the morning they are divided by age, and in the afternoon they play in mixed-age family groupings. After lunch, younger children have a sleep and older children rest, reading, listening to story tapes or watching a video. There is daily singing and stories, when all children come together, and weekly music and ballet sessions. Many of the pre-school children start to read, and the Story Chest and Ginn reading schemes are available for those who are ready. Detailed records are kept on each child, including their emotional needs, sleeping habits and health. 'Highlights books' are also kept, which include notes on children's progress and development. Meals are a social occasion and are seen as an opportunity for staff to interact with children.

**Remarks** Last year this nursery won the runners-up prize in the national Under-Fives Care and Education Awards. The nursery has a deservedly high reputation, and a strong management team. Staff are dedicated, highly motivated and skilled. Resources are plentiful and appropriate. A high-class nursery with a flexible, relaxed approach to play and learning. Excellent value for money and a wonderful start to any child's life.

## IRWELL VALE NURSERY SCHOOL

4 Milne Street
Irwell Vale
Ramsbottom
Rossendale
Lancs BL0 0QP
**Tel:** (0706) 825657

**Owner/Principal:** Janice Johnson, NNEB, PQC
**Type:** Day nursery offering full- and part-time and half-day sessions plus after-school care
**Children:** 3mths–5yrs. 21 places. 40 on register
**Hours:** 7am–7pm
Morning session 8am–12 noon
Afternoon session 1pm–6pm
Open 51 weeks a year
**Status:** Private, fee-paying

**Number of years open:** 3
**Meals:** Breakfast, lunch, snacks
**1992 fees:** £80 per week full-time – under 2
£65 per week full-time – over 2
£18 per day – under 2
£14 per day – over 2
£9 per session – under 2
£7 per session – over 2
**Waiting list:** None
**Registered by:** Lancs County Council SS

**Premises** Two of a terrace of three cottages, originally built to house local mill-workers. The mid-19th-century buildings are grade II listed and the owner lives in the adjoining cottage. There is a large, 'noisy' play room, brightly decorated with blue carpet, lively murals and children's artwork. It houses table toys, construction toys, toys for role play and imaginative play and music equipment. There is also a separate well-equipped messy-play room and a pastel-coloured quiet room for sleeping, storytime and other quiet activities, plus a utility/laundry room, bathroom and toilet facilities. The outside play area is clearly well used, but is tidy and provides swings, climbing frame and a baby swing on safety bark. There is Astroturf for ride-on toys. The surrounding fence is painted with cartoon characters. In summer children make frequent visits to the nearby park.

**Owner/Principal & staff** Janice Johnson, NNEB, PQC, worked for Manchester City Council before qualifying as an NNEB, and set up her own nursery when she needed nursery care for her second child. Now that both her children are at school, she has returned to college part-time and is studying to teach nursery nurses. She remains closely involved with the nursery and tries to see all parents each day. The day-to-day running is the responsibility of her deputy, also a qualified NNEB. The staff are a happy team. Of the seven nursery nurses, four are NNEB qualified, one PPA. Their special skills include art and music. They live locally and socialise together. There are lots of kisses and cuddles for the children, and staff actively take part in children's games and activities. Janice Johnson organises in-house staff training. The nursery is currently sponsoring a student completing an NVQ qualification in childcare. Janice Johnson says she would not employ a male nursery nurse. 'I don't think men have the right attitude when caring for young children. Perhaps that's too general, but that has been my experience.' Staff/child ratios are 1:3 for under-2s, 1:4 for 2- to 3-year-olds and 1:8 for over-3s. The day of our visit, there were six staff and 21 children. Staff meetings are held once a month. There is a strong sense of dedication among staff, who are not well paid. Janice Johnson says, 'We have odd weeks when we break even. I'm not in this for the money and I'll never make a fortune from it.'

**Children & parents** This is a typical village nursery with an exclusively white, middle-class catchment area. The majority of children have two working parents; many are doctors, teachers and bank managers. Parents are welcome at the nursery any time and their views are always carefully considered. Parents' evenings are thought unnecessary, as staff are always available to talk to parents. Each child has a designated keyworker, responsible for their overall care and development. Most children move to state primary schools in the area, a few to the private sector. The nursery is able to integrate children with special needs and currently has children with cerebral palsy and epilepsy, who spend most of their week at a local special needs nursery, but attend some sessions at Irwell Vale. The nursery's long hours are particularly favourable to working parents.

**Curriculum & activities** Learning through play, with plenty of choice. The aim is to teach children to be independent, confident and ready for school. Staff draw up a weekly timetable, with a new project or theme each week. The day starts with free play, anywhere in the nursery, until 9.30am, when children come together for a morning snack. They then split into small groups for a session organised by their keyworker. For most of the day children are free to choose between rooms and activities. Painting, play dough, water, puzzles, construction toys, home corner and books are always available. There is daily music, storytime and physical play sessions, inside and out. Baking and dance and movement are weekly events. Occasional group outings to Camelot Theme Park and other places of interest. Frequent walks around the village. Reading is not taught, but children are introduced to pre-reading, pre-writing and number work. Children can write their names and recognise shapes, numbers and letters by the time they leave.

There is no emphasis on academic achievement and no full-time qualified teacher on the staff. Attainment records are kept and taken on to primary school. A full-time cook offers nutritious, enjoyable food. Meals are prepared in the owner's immaculate kitchen.

**Remarks** A small, caring, village nursery, which offers good childcare to local working parents. Very long opening hours and a cost that fairly reflects the facilities provided. All staff have recognised childcare qualifications. Dedicated and loving atmosphere.

## LE MONDE PETIT

Bank Parade
Burnley
Lancs BB1 1UG
**Tel:** (0282) 427120

**Owner:** Le Monde Petit Ltd
**Principal:** Pamela Young, NNEB
**Type:** Day nursery offering full- and part-time places and half-day sessions.
**Children:** 6mths–5yrs. 80 places. 122 on register
**Hours:** 7am–6pm Mon–Fri
9am–5pm Sat
Morning session 9am–12 noon
Afternoon session 1pm–4pm
Flexible hours
Open 51 weeks a year
**Status:** Private, fee-paying
**Number of years open:** 3
**Meals:** Breakfast, lunch, tea and snacks
**1992 fees:** £75 per week full-time – under 2
£60 per week full-time – over 2
£17.25 per day – under 2
£15.25 per day – over 2
Hourly rates available on Sat
**Waiting list:** Waiting list for baby places. Places available for over-2s
**Registered by:** Lancs County Council SS

**Premises** In the centre of Burnley close to shops and offices. Originally a snooker hall, the building has been cleverly converted into a spacious, light and welcoming nursery. There is a vast main room (5500 sq ft) with a huge red and blue ball pool in the centre, decorated with large, adult-painted murals depicting familiar characters. A partitioned-off area is used for messy play and eating. The music room with a piano is also used for stories and other quiet activities. A self-contained baby area, with cots, prams and nappy changing facilities has places for 18 under-2s. There is also a pristine kitchen and loos. Security is taken seriously in such a central location, and the nursery is entered past a video monitor and an electrically locked door. Each parent is given a password and anyone unfamiliar collecting a child must know the password, or the child will not be released. Outside, a large walled lawn and tarmac area are used for riding trikes in the winter.

**Principal & staff** Pamela Young, NNEB, has many years' experience in private nurseries. Her role is mainly managerial, supervising the staff of 16 and liaising with parents. The all-female team is made up of ten NNEB nursery nurses, one qualified nurse and three nursery assistants, plus two cooks. A dance teacher comes in for regular music-and-movement sessions and the nursery is hoping to continue French lessons although it is currently without a teacher. One member of staff is a music specialist. Pamela Young has compiled a comprehensive staff manual covering every aspect of care for the over-2s and is currently working on a similar manual for the baby unit. Staff meetings are held every two or three months, but staff meet together every day during lunch and break times. NNEB and BTEC students are allocated to a member of staff for supervision. A close relationship between staff and children is evident.

**Children & parents** The catchment area covers a 20-mile radius. Many parents are professional, but there are also white-collar and blue-collar workers. Children progress to many different schools, and a significant number go on to private schools. They are a very happy, confident group, clearly enjoying themselves. Many apparently have to be dragged away at the end of a session. Children are divided into groups by age – Jelly Babies (6 months–2 years), Jelly Tots (2–3 years) and Jelly Beans (3–5 years). Staff change regularly from group to group. The nursery has wheelchair access and special toilet facilities and is happy to take children with disabilities, although currently there is only one part-time autistic child. Phasing-in is kept as flexible as possible to suit the needs of parents and children. Parents are invited to social evenings which sometimes take place outside the nursery. They recently organised a car treasure hunt.

**Curriculum & activities** A structured routine of free play, PE, messy activities, pre-school work and outside play. There is a fantastic supply of equipment, from the ball pool and play house to board games and puzzles – many Galt toys. Babies spend the day in their own unit, although older children are allowed to visit if accompanied by a member of staff. Jelly Tots and Jelly Beans both work their way through separate timetables each day, coming together after lunch and at the end of the day for free play and quiet time. Pre-school work includes number and colour work and some pre-reading. Flashcards are used, and most children are able to write their names before they move to their next school. Social skills are concentrated on initially, as these are considered vital before moving on to the more formal pre-school curriculum. There is much emphasis on PE, given the enormous amount of open space in the main room, and children have ample opportunity to practise all forms of agility. Individual activity sheets, covering the entire day and including any special instructions, are kept by staff for all under-2s. The nursery is planning to keep developmental charts for older children, but does not do so at present. There are occasional library visits and outings. Lunch is split into two sittings to accommodate numbers. There is a high standard of safety and hygiene throughout. Despite its size, the room is warm.

**Remarks** A very happy atmosphere. Children collected by their parents when we were there clearly did not want to leave. It is almost impossible to make a hall this size and height feel homely and cosy. Tiny children appear lost in the space. However, the nursery offers a structured play environment with qualified carers. Still feeling its way after only three years in business.

# MEADOW VIEW MONTESSORI NURSERY SCHOOL

25 Mitton Avenue
Rawtenstall
Lancs BB4 8UR
**Tel:** (0706) 831662

**Owner/Principal:** Susan Smith, Cert Ed, Cert Mont
**Type:** Day nursery and nursery school offering full- and part-time places and half-day sessions
**Children:** 2–5yrs. 15 places. 30 on register
**Hours:** 8.30am–5.30pm
Morning session 8.30am–1pm
Afternoon session 1pm–5.30pm
Open 51 weeks a year
**Status:** Private, fee-paying
**Number of years open:** 2½
**Meals:** Lunch, tea, snacks
**1992 fees:** £60 per week full-time
£13 per day
£7 per morning session
£6.50 per afternoon session
**Waiting list:** Moderate
**Registered by:** Lancs County Council SS

**Premises** A self-contained unit, formerly a large garage, adjoining the owner's modern, detached house, set in its own grounds on a small, secluded, private housing development surrounded by huge conifers. A bus service calls at the estate and there is easy access by car, with parking in front of the house. The nursery consists of one main, superbly decorated and equipped Montessori classroom, plus bathroom and toilet facilities. There are large, bright display boards, big picture windows at the front of the nursery and a splendid view overlooking the hills at the back. The immaculate and spacious garden includes a hard play area, lawns and brightly coloured outdoor Montessori equipment and toys.

**Owner/Principal & staff** Susan Smith, Cert Ed, Cert Mont, used to teach in further education and left to look after her young children. She completed a Montessori home study course and opened Meadow View just in time for her children to take advantage of it. At present she leads morning sessions and does all the administration. Her deputy is also involved in overall organisation. The three full-time and two part-time nursery nurses have been trained, by the owner, to use Montessori principles and apparatus. Staff are selected for their individual skills – one is particularly good at art. Two have Montessori teaching qualifications. There are no students or peripatetic teachers. Staff/child ratio is 1:4. Staff appear interested and involved with the children. They meet socially and hold formal staff meetings once every three months.

**Children & parents** A good mix of children, from varied social and cultural backgrounds, about half of them with two working parents. All live within a ten-mile radius of the nursery. Some parents are professionally qualified (barristers, teachers, social workers); others are local blue-collar workers. The nursery is small and staff know parents well. Parents help fund-raise for nursery outings and local charities. There is also a quarterly newsletter. New children usually start with an hour's session and build up slowly. Children are confident, busy and polite. Most transfer to state primary schools. There have been few requests for the nursery to take special needs children, but staff are able and keen to offer the support and care necessary.

**Curriculum & activities** A nursery based firmly on the teaching methods and principles of Dr Maria Montessori. The nursery environment is carefully prepared, with bright, stimulating Montessori equipment, easily accessible at child height. Children work in small family groups, choosing their own activities. Staff note exactly what each child has done. The whole group joins together for singing and music and movement, when the older children are encouraged to help the younger ones. Each morning after registration, children discuss the day, date and weather and sit down for at least half an hour of quiet, concentrated activity, followed by half an hour of active play, which could be a nature walk, art or craft. On the day of our visit, they were enthusiastically immersed in making a mixture to feed the birds, as part of a winter-time project. When they are ready, children are introduced to pre-reading, pre-writing and pre-number work through the current topic. Much work is done on a one-to-one basis, with equipment carefully presented to a child. There is plenty of practical life apparatus to encourage independence – dressing, undressing, tying laces, measuring, pouring and setting a table – as well as sensorial equipment. Children are treated as individuals and allowed to develop at their own pace, in a warm, secure environment. All aspects of children's progress are recorded daily and written up fully each month.

**Remarks** A lovely, small Montessori nursery school. Carefully designed and equipped to offer quality childcare and education. The commitment and warmth of teachers, combined with first-class facilities, makes this a very special place. Excellent relationship with parents.

## SUNFIELD DAY NURSERY

97–99 St Annes Road East
St Annes-on-Sea
Lancs FY8 3NF
**Tel:** (0253) 725898

**Owner/Matron:** Muriel Roberts, NNEB
**Type:** Day nursery offering full-time places and half-day sessions
**Children:** 9mths–5yrs. 32 places. 32 on register
**Hours:** 8.30am–5.30pm
Morning session 8.30am–1pm
Afternoon session 1pm–5.30pm
Open 52 weeks a year (excl bank holidays)
**Status:** Private, fee-paying
**Number of years open:** 31
**Meals:** Lunch, tea and snacks
**1992 fees:** £80 per week full-time – under 18mths
£55 per week – over 18mths
£45 per week for 5 sessions – under 18mths
£35 per week for 5 sessions – over 18mths
£55 deposit
**Waiting list:** 10 on list. Places can usually be found
**Registered by:** Lancs County Council SS

**Premises** The first floor of a large, detached, Edwardian house approached from the main road by a wide tarmac drive and double gates. Surrounded by a large garden with a tarmac playground, containing swings and climbing frames, set on areas of tree bark. There is a large Wendy house and sheds crammed with trikes and other outside play equipment. Each of the three age groups at the nursery has its own room and there is a special activities room for group project work. The main feature in the baby room is a large, purpose-built playpen which also acts as a sleeping area. The middle group is well supplied with sand tray, construction toys and plentiful early learning equipment. The pre-school room has a home corner, book corner, sand tray and other educational equipment. Walls throughout are decorated with teddies, murals and children's artwork. There is a park directly opposite, but it is never used by the nursery, because there are no dog-free areas.

**Owner/Matron & staff** Muriel Roberts, NNEB, qualified in 1949 in Yorkshire and set up Sunfield in 1962. She has maintained total involvement in the day-to-day running of the nursery since then. Her sister, who opened the nursery with her, has now retired, but comes in from time to time to help out with the finances. Her husband, also retired, is responsible for much of the administration. Muriel Roberts expresses great pride in her nine members of staff, all full-timers. Four are NNEB nursery nurses, including her daughter. No qualified nursery teachers on the staff. There are two YTS trainees. Other unqualified members of staff have been trained by Mrs Roberts herself, and have many years' experience. Staff are loyal and long-serving – two of them have been with her for 14 years. Another, who left last year, had worked at the nursery for 18 years. Ages range from the two YTS trainees in their late teens, to Muriel Roberts in her early 60s. Staff meetings are held when necessary, but generally about once a week. Outside teachers visit for weekly music and dance classes. No formal training policy or budget.

**Children & parents** St Annes is a genteel coastal resort, with large houses and wide avenues. Parents are prosperous, many dual-income, and tend to be doctors, hoteliers or running their own businesses. There is very little cultural mix either in the area or the nursery. Children go on to state schools and a significant percentage transfer each year to independent Arnold's School in Blackpool. The nursery is happy to take children with special needs and for the last year has been caring for premature twins. Children spend most of their day in their age groups, but all come together for free-play sessions at least once and usually twice a day. They are encouraged to build up relationships with all members of staff, not just those who are responsible for their particular group. Parents are made welcome at any time of day and a senior member of staff is always on duty to deal with any problems that may arise. Appointments, open days and parents' evenings are considered unnecessary as staff are always available.

**Curriculum & activities** There is no written curriculum or timetable, but all nursery activities are discussed with parents. The nursery aims to 'cater for all a child's needs in the best possible way, in a happy, loving and serene atmosphere'. Muriel Roberts feels that learning and caring go hand in hand, and that one cannot progress without the other. Children have access to a huge supply of educational equipment. Pre-school children are encouraged to read and write on a one-to-one basis 'as a mum would do it at home'. Some children are free-reading by the time they leave and all can write their names and recognise numbers. Written records are kept of pre-school work – parents have open access to these. Muriel Roberts keeps a keen eye on the emotional development of the children in her nursery, and care is taken to ensure that staff do not become too attached to any one child. There are regular outings for nature walks and to visit farms and a local agricultural college. The nursery operates an after-school pick-up service for children who go to the nearby school and have attended the nursery in the past.

**Remarks** Long-established and well-run nursery with caring, professional and very long-serving staff. We have received literally dozens of letters from parents recommending this nursery. Care and love in a happy, organised atmosphere.

# Leicestershire

Currently 22 per cent of all 3- and 4-year-olds can expect a nursery place, either full- or part-time. Some primary schools accept pupils at the beginning of the year in which they are 5. Social Services provide 15 day nurseries for children in need, 12 of them in Leicester itself. The private sector offers 60 nurseries, few catering for children under 2 years old. Nearly 600 childminders and 400 voluntary-run playgroups are also registered. Leicestershire has an acute shortage of affordable full-time care. In rural areas many working parents are forced to rely on the goodwill of relatives and friends.

## Further information

For details on day nurseries:
Department of Social Services – Children's Services
Inspection Unit
County Hall
Glenfield
Leicester LE3 8RL
Tel: (0533) 657433

For details on nursery schools, units and classes:
Education Department
(address as above)
Tel: (0533) 323232 or 656589

For details on childminders and playgroups:
Leicester West (0533) 777646
Leicester East (0533) 519027
South Leicestershire (0455) 636964
North Leicestershire
    Coalville (0530) 810521
    Loughborough (0509) 610311
    Lothley (0533) 302395
    Melton Mowbray (0664) 646989
    Oakham (Rutland) (0572) 722544

# ARK PLAYGROUP

Princess Avenue
Oakham
Rutland
Leics
**Tel:** (0572) 755776

**Owner:** The Ark Association
**Supervisor:** Mary-Jane Naylor, NNEB
**Type:** Community playgroup offering morning and afternoon sessions. No full-time places
**Children:** 2½–5yrs. 18 places. 120 on register
**Hours:** Morning session 9am–12 noon (3–5yr-olds)
Afternoon session 1pm–3pm (2½–3yr-olds)
Open 38 weeks a year
**Status:** Fee-paying registered charity
**Number of years open:** 10
**Meals:** None
**1992 fees:** £2.65 per morning session
£2.21 per afternoon session
**Waiting list:** None
**Registered by:** Leics County Council SS
**Under same ownership:** Ark Playgroup II, Oakham

**Premises** Ark Playgroup opened in 1983. Its success and growth are due to a group of dedicated local parents who decided to provide the pre-school facility they believed the community needed. The playgroup moved to its present site in Princess Avenue, on the western side of the town, in 1985. The wooden ex-scout hut has been totally refurbished, to provide a central carpeted area, a tiled kitchen/wet area, an additional quiet work room and a good-sized storeroom. At the rear of the single-storey building is a fully enclosed, impact-absorbent, safety surface with a variety of fixed climbing frames. Part of the area is grassed. Inside, pine panelling gives a welcoming warm atmosphere. The small size of the windows in the main area makes strip lighting necessary throughout the day. The building lies back from Princess Avenue down a short passageway. There is ample car parking space in the avenue. The premises are beautifully clean inside and well maintained outside. Management of the charity is vested in a Management Trust, to whom the Supervisor reports.

**Supervisor & staff** Mary-Jane Naylor, NNEB, is friendly, lively and full of ideas. She has been one of the driving forces behind the playgroup since its inception. A woman of considerable presence and tireless energy she is someone who makes things happen. Mary-Jane Naylor is assisted by four part-time staff, two of them qualified nursery nurses, and two fully qualified PPA. Since the opening of a second Ark playgroup in a large classroom at the Church of England Primary School, in School Road, Mary-Jane Naylor divides her time between the two establishments. The staff are friendly, enthusiastic and clearly love children. Students are accepted on a restricted basis and form an important part of the teaching resource. Staff take part in all local training initiatives, many organised by the Ark itself. There has been no staff turnover for years. The staff/child ratio is 1:8 morning, 1:6 afternoon.

**Children & parents** There is an unwritten contract that the playgroup is a joint venture between parents and management. The fees are kept reasonable and the playgroup is kept open only because of continual and successful fund-raising activities. Its growth over ten years is testimony to the commitment and enthusiasm of the Charity Management Trust, staff and local parents, who have supported the venture throughout. The playgroup receives no grants. The parents are an extremely dedicated and active group. Some were involved in the refurbishment of the premises, giving freely of their skills and time. The children are open, self-confident and eager to talk to adults, within the security of the playgroup. There is continuous coverage of playgroup activities in the local press, which helps to ensure its success and growth. There is an excellent social mix of parents and children. The playgroup has a complete open-door policy, which also encourages parents to act as additional volunteers. Parents are represented on the management committee. Children with special educational needs and physical disabilities are successfully integrated.

**Curriculum & activities** Learning through play in a safe, stimulating environment. Mary-Jane Naylor aims to make the playgroup a happy, thriving community, which prepares children as fully as possible for the start of their formal education. The emphasis is on fun. There is some religious content to all sessions. A substantial range of toys and books enables the children to pursue numerous activities (annual equipment budget £1000). No formal structure, no written timetable or programmes. Outings two or three times a term – the local Farm Centre is a regular attraction. No formal teaching of reading and writing, but the natural curiosity and desire to learn of the older children are supported and encouraged. There is close liaison with local reception classes, particularly since the second group has opened in a primary school classroom. Activities are laid out for children to choose – plenty of art and craft, messy play, construction toys, games and puzzles. Staff are heavily involved in helping and guiding children. Music, stories and singing are included in every session. The quiet room is used for more formal pre-school work. Areas include writing, maths, shape, colour and weight. Social skills are also taught. There is no pressure to achieve academically. Children are encouraged to be happy and enjoy themselves.

**Remarks** A thriving, extremely popular but rather unstructured playgroup, much loved by children and parents alike. Very reasonable costs mean a heavy reliance on fund-raising, by dedicated parents. Mary-Jane Naylor says, 'Nursery provision in Oakham is very poor – one local authority nursery school and no daycare places, private or Social Services. Our playgroups are essential.'

# DANESHILL NURSERY

1 Daneshill Road
Leicester LE3 6AN
**Tel:** (0533) 530856

**Owner:** Maralyn Timson
**Officer-in-charge:** Pat Perkins, NNEB
**Type:** Day nursery offering full-time places and half-day sessions
**Children:** 3mths–5yrs. 34 places. 36 on register
**Hours:** 8am–5.30pm
Morning session 8.30am–12.45pm
Afternoon session 1.15pm–5.30pm
Open 51 weeks a year
**Status:** Private, fee-paying
**Number of years open:** 7
**Meals:** Lunch, tea, snacks
**1992 fees:** £67.50 per week
£38 for 5 sessions a week
**Waiting list:** None kept – usually 3mths wait
**Registered by:** Leics County Council SS

**Premises** A substantial, three-storey, semi-detached, Victorian corner house in south-west Leicester. The property has been adapted to provide good accommodation, using the ground and first floors only. There are three separate rooms on the first floor for children over 3, toilet facilities, a large storeroom and an office for the officer-in-charge. The ground floor has separate rooms for babies and toddlers, a nappy changing room/washroom, a well-equipped kitchen, staff room and separate toilet facilities. The stairs are gated, top and bottom. Corridors are carpeted; rooms carpeted or tiled depending on use. The double-glazed windows let in adequate natural light. Outside play is in two securely fenced areas, alongside the house; one grass, the other tarmac. Parking is not available on the premises and the adjacent side street is heavily used.

**Officer-in-charge & staff** Pat Perkins, NNEB, a vivacious, experienced woman, has been responsible since the nursery opened seven years ago. Decisions affecting finance and long-term planning are taken jointly with the owner, Maralyn Timson. There are four full-time NNEB nursery nurses and a further four with the two-year City & Guilds qualification. Carers have a very wide range of experience, from 15 years to newly qualified. No one on the team has an early years teaching qualification. Pat Perkins believes that her staff benefit from a break at lunchtime, so they eat separately from the children, either in the staff room or off the premises. Lunch supervisors are employed to look after the children. The cook is a trained professional. Some of the nursery workers are also trained in first-aid, special needs and food hygiene. Staff meetings are held every month to review children's progress and discuss policy. Minimal staff turnover.

**Children & parents** Many parents come from outside the city travelling in to work. Good social and ethnic mix. There are professional middle-class families, further-education students and some low-income workers subsidised by their employers. Vacancies are filled by word of mouth almost before they occur. No formal waiting list is kept. An open-door policy towards parents means they can visit any time, except mealtimes. Regular parents' evenings and social events are held. Parents help with outings and their comments and suggestions are discussed and acted upon. There are limited formal links with local schools, since few children live in the immediate neighbourhood. Parents whose children previously attended the nursery recommend it highly and many stay in touch after their children have left.

**Curriculum & activities** Learning through play with some limited pre-reading, pre-writing and number work for older children. The emphasis is on art and creative activities. There is a good range of equipment and apparatus (small annual budget of £500), all appropriate to the ages of the children in the different rooms. Plenty of paint, crayons, puzzles and other table-top activities. Dance and music and movement sessions are held once a month, and songs, rhymes and action games on a daily basis. Children play outside every day, but there are no outings or local walks. There are no written educational programmes, timetable or reading schemes. Care is taken not to force formal work, but staff respond to interest and initiative with positive support and encouragement. Pencil control, cutting, glueing and sticking, joining dots and learning to recognise your name are all part of the programme. Detailed records are kept on each child's development. Children were all busily engaged in a wide variety of activities, well supervised by staff. Our one concern was that the front door was left unlocked during our visit, making it possible for anyone to walk into the nursery unannounced.

**Remarks** A happy, welcoming nursery organised by committed staff. Flexible approach – staff will always open earlier or stay later to fit in with the needs of working parents. The free, rather unstructured programme may not suit those looking for more formal learning. High parental satisfaction.

# LITTLE ACORNS NURSERY SCHOOL

382 London Road
Stoneygate
Leicester LE2 2PN
**Tel:** (0533) 705086

**Owner/Principal:** Sheelagh Shaen-Carter, BA, B Arch, PPA
**Officer-in-charge:** Judy Lewis, B Ed
**Type:** Nursery school offering full- and part-time places and half-day sessions
**Children:** 3mths–5yrs. 47 places. 95 on register
**Hours:** 8.15am–5.45pm
Flexible hours
Open 51 weeks a year
**Status:** Private, fee-paying
**Number of years open:** 3
**Meals:** Lunch, tea, snacks
**1992 fees:** £85 per week full-time
£19 per day
£13 per morning session
£10 per afternoon session
£5 registration fee
**Waiting list:** Long. Approx 50 names
**Registered by:** Leics County Council SS

**Premises** A large, detached, two-storey Edwardian house. The interior has been skilfully redesigned as a nursery by the architect owner and completely refurbished. Decorations are pristine, stair gates in position and used. There are a variety of classrooms and storerooms on each floor. The 3- to 5-year-olds use the first floor, which has an excellent fire escape. Toilets are available on both floors. There is a separate room for nappy changing. First-class washing facilities. The kitchen on the ground floor is well laid out and everywhere is scrupulously clean. All the latest facilities for health and safety are incorporated including toughened glass panels at ground level in the otherwise solid doors. The colour schemes are bright and there is ample natural light. Corridors and rooms are generally carpeted except for the toilets and messy play areas. Artwork decorating the walls is definitely child-led. A securely fenced area at the back provides a hard playground as well as grass. It is furnished with a good range of outdoor play apparatus. Car parking on the premises is limited, but there is ample space in the side road.

**Owner, Officer-in-charge & staff**

Sheelagh Shaen-Carter, BA, B Arch, PPA, is an architect with her own practice and a young daughter. As a working mother she became aware of the acute shortage of high-quality nursery provision in her area. 'It's particularly limited for babies from 3 to 18 months whose mothers want or need to go back to work. I want to make life as easy as possible for working parents,' she says. Little Acorns is her response to a desperate need. Day-to-day running of the nursery is the responsibility of officer-in-charge, Judy Lewis, B Ed, who is young, charismatic and thoroughly on the ball. Her team includes a deputy and four nursery nurses, all NNEB trained, plus a qualified teacher with over 20 years' experience, who has recently completed training in the assessment and recording of children's educational development. She teaches the oldest children. There are a further six assistants with a range of experience and basic training. Ancillaries are a cook and cleaner. In-house training is given to all staff, and first-aid certificates are encouraged. Staff turnover has been a problem in the past. However, Judy Lewis is confident they now have a strong, friendly and stable team, with good staff/child ratios.

**Children & parents** The children come from professional career families. Culturally mixed, they reflect the make-up of the city. The parents travel from a wide area, mostly outside the city, some to attend further-education courses. The children are lively, relaxed and courteous. They move on to a variety of schools in the state and private sector. The nursery does not have formal links with local schools. There is a limited open-door policy: parents can telephone, but visits are preferred before or after the school day. Phasing-in new children is done gently and parents are expected to visit at least twice with their child before starting. Open days, parents' evenings and nursery outings are well supported. Former parents are fulsome in their praise of the nursery.

**Curriculum & activities** No particular philosophy. The priority is that children should be happy and able to develop to the best of their abilities. There is a fully structured curriculum but enough flexibility to allow for the special talents of each individual child. Thoughtful written programmes and a detailed timetable for each age group. Peer groupings for the 2- to 5-year-olds, family groupings for babies. The day begins with free play offering a choice of floor and table-top activities – play dough, jigsaws, construction toys, drawing and colouring, cars, farm and zoo animals and reading for the over-3s. Drinks and biscuits offer a time for conversation, manners and special familiar nursery routines like smiling and waving to friends sitting opposite. Language development is a priority. There is a full range of directed activities to develop pre-reading and pre-writing skills – cutting, gluing, felt-tip pens, stories and books – plus plenty of art and craft and imaginative play. Equipment and educational toys are plentiful (annual budget £3000), of good quality and age-appropriate. Due to the layout of the building it is not possible for all children to come together as a group. Pre-school children, 3 to 5 years, follow a six-day rolling plan, so that children who only come one or two days a week do not miss out on important activities. The programme covers a different subject each day – language, maths and number work, phonics, art and craft, science topic and maths topic work. Activities are designed with the National Curriculum Key Stage 1 in mind. The approach to reading is multi-faceted with phonics, look-and-say and whole-book methods used, so that schemes can be tailored to meet individual needs. Letterland is the primary scheme. Music, dance, gym, cookery and gardening are regular weekly events. Throughout the day there are songs and rhymes. Outside play twice a day in good weather and regular walks. A major annual outing is organised for each age group. Tiny babies are fed, talked to, cuddled, played with and given regular sleeps. The children are offered physical warmth and much praise. Meals are a social occasion – an opportunity to discuss food and encourage table manners. Children lay the table, share out aprons and mats and, after the meal, clean their teeth and wash their hands and faces. Difficult or disruptive behaviour is dealt with by distraction if possible. If a child hurts another child, he or she is reprimanded, but more attention paid to comforting the wronged child. Children's progress is formally monitored approximately once a year.

**Remarks** A highly professional organisation with a rich, carefully planned diet of curriculum and activities. There now appears to be a strong stable team in place. Children are happy, challenged and having fun.

# MOUNTFIELDS LODGE NURSERY

Mountfields Lodge Primary School
Epinal Way
Loughborough
Leics LE11 0QE
**Tel:** (0509) 214119
**Owner:** Leics LEA
**Headteacher:** David Brown, B Ed, MA
**Teacher-in-charge:** Margaret Rogers, Cert Ed
**Type:** Nursery class in state primary school offering half-day sessions. No full-time places
**Children:** 4yrs 3mths–4yrs 9mths. 30 places. 60 on register
**Hours:** Morning session 8.50am–11.45am Afternoon session 1.15pm–3.15pm
Open 38 weeks a year
**Status:** State nursery class
**Number of years open:** 3
**Meals:** Snacks, drinks
**1992 fees:** No fees
**Waiting list:** Very long. 120 names. Not all are guaranteed places
**Registered by:** Leics County Council LEA

**Premises** There is a history of nursery provision on the present site dating back to 1952. The existing nursery classroom was purpose-built three years ago as an addition to the primary school. There is one large, central, open-plan classroom, part carpeted, part tiled. The ceiling is festooned with coloured cut-outs and the walls covered with colourful displays of children's named work. Areas off include a quiet room, washroom, cloakroom and en suite toilets. The large fenced-off outside area adjacent to the main school playground has a grass slope and tarmac play area. The school is next door to East Midlands Arts Centre and shares their generous parking facilities. This is a green-belt area on the south-western edge of town, surrounded by pleasant countryside and totally screened from the nearby main dual carriageway by thick trees. Poor public transport; access by car or on foot only.

**Teacher-in-charge & staff** Margaret Rogers, Cert Ed, has substantial experience as a qualified teacher. Efficient and organised, she has the knack of making everything appear simple and straightforward. At each session, she is assisted by a full-time NNEB qualified nursery nurse and a part-time ancillary, with years of nursery experience. Margaret liaises regularly with the head of the school and the Board of Governors who support and advise. Staff meetings are held daily, to plan activities and discuss children's progress. Staff training is important and paid for out of the main school budget. All staff have special needs training and experience. A variety of students – YTS, NNEB and trainee teachers – are welcome on regular placement during the year. There has been no staff turnover since the nursery opened. Nursery workers show respect for each other and work together as a happy close-knit team. The staff/child ratio is 1:10.

**Children & parents** The only state education nursery in Loughborough, it is available part-time to any child in the town on a first come first served basis. A complete social and ethnic mix with many different nationalities and backgrounds. Children come by car or many walk to the nursery. Five places are reserved specifically for children with special educational needs, some of whom start as young as 3. The majority are offered one or two terms of half-day sessions in the class before going on to full-time school. Many transfer to Mountfields Lodge, if they can secure a place. It is a very popular primary school and places are heavily oversubscribed. The nursery operates an open-door policy. 'We always welcome positive or negative opinions and will listen, discuss and act on them,' says Margaret Rogers. Parents are invited to become involved in every aspect of nursery life from settling in their own child to helping with cookery, computer classes and storytime. There is a strong partnership between nursery and parents to help ensure a smooth transition from home to school. Children are relaxed and self-confident, industriously working away at a range of tasks, oblivious to what is going on around them.

**Curriculum & activities** The main aim is to provide a safe, stimulating environment, where children feel happy, can be themselves and gain confidence in their abilities, and at all levels learn to work with and respect each other. Each session has a short religious content. Children are encouraged to become responsible, caring members of a multicultural society. The equipment and apparatus, sufficient but not generous, enable children to choose a range of planned activities and learning experiences. There are investigations of practical maths, science and technology. The finger dexterity of 4-year-olds on the two computers is amazing. Computer programmes support mathematical and phonic work and the computer is used every day. Strong emphasis on the love of books, stories, reading and writing, but no pressure to read or write. Children develop at their own pace. The priority is social development and self-motivation rather than academic achievement. Staff keep a low profile, but know when to intervene and when to leave children to their own experiences. There is no formal monitoring of children's progress, written programmes or records. Art and craft activities are many and varied. The children's achievements are valued and well displayed throughout the classroom. There is music, dance and drama every day; PE, with large and small apparatus, twice a week; weekly walks in the surrounding countryside and an annual coach outing. The nursery pets are two guinea pigs.

**Remarks** A stimulating environment, with experienced and well-qualified staff. Quiet, hardworking, interested children. The emphasis is on social skills and independence rather than teaching basics. The head would like to shorten the long waiting list and keep children for longer than one or two terms. As the LEA is currently proposing to allow children to start school in the year, instead of the term, in which they are 5, this may become possible. Despite clever organisation of space, the classroom remains small for a class of 30 4-year-olds.

## ST GABRIEL'S COMMUNITY CENTRE PLAYGROUP

Kerrysdale Avenue
Leicester LE4 7GH
**Tel:** (0533) 610711

**Playgroup leader:** Christine Campion, PPA (Foundation)
**Type:** Community playgroup offering 5 morning and 2 afternoon sessions a week, plus after-school care and 3wk holiday playscheme
**Children:** 2½–5yrs. 24 places. 38 on register
**Hours:** Morning session 9.15am–12 noon Afternoon session 1pm–3pm (Mon & Fri)
Open 38 weeks a year plus 3wk summer playscheme

**Status:** Private, fee-paying, non profit-making
**Number of years open:** 4
**Meals:** None
**1992 fees:** £1.50 per morning session
£1.20 per afternoon session
**Waiting list:** Variable. Places can usually be found
**Registered by:** Leics County Council SS

**Premises** A substantial, brick and cladding building, opened in 1989. Kate Bide, the centre manager, is a trained community worker responsible for the building and its use, reporting to a management committee. She has a strong personality and a thorough grasp of the many activities going on in the very busy community centre. The playgroup has shared used of the Green Hall, a large, high-ceilinged hall or gymnasium, which has direct access to the kitchen. All of the centre's facilities are available, including washroom and a baby changing area. There is a separate, recently constructed storeroom for equipment and toys. All apparatus has to be cleared away and set out daily. A more serious disadvantage of shared use is the difficulty in displaying children's art or in building up long-term interest tables. There is an outdoor, secure, enclosed ball court, used for outside play. The park is 200 yards from the centre. The building is well-lit, and designed for disabled access. All non-play areas are carpeted and well looked after. There is adequate car parking, and three major bus routes pass the door.

**Group Leader & staff** The driving force behind the playgroup is clearly Kate Bide, the centre manager. The day-to-day running of the group is in the hands of Christine Campion. She and the three full-time staff have completed the PPA Foundation Course. There is also a voluntary helper. The playgroup is considered an excellent resource for training local PPA students, who attend regularly on placement. Staff cover a good range of skills, talents, ages and cultures. There are two Gujarati speakers who provide essential communication links with local parents. All staff are trained first-aiders and are expected to complete the PPA Foundation Course. The staff/child ratio is 1:6. Staff meetings are held weekly.

**Children & parents** The children come from the local area, with a high Asian population. Seventy per cent of children are Gujarati- and Punjabi-speaking, the rest

English and Afro-Caribbean. Fees are kept deliberately low and can be varied according to parental means. There is a good social mix. The local primary school has a nursery unit, and many children leave the playgroup after their 4th birthday. Relations are good with the school, which actively encourages parents to send their younger children to the playgroup to prepare them for the reception class. Due to demand, two afternoon sessions have recently been introduced. The centre also runs a Free Time Club, offering after-school care and activities from 3pm–5.30pm to children up to 11 years old. Parents are encouraged to become involved, but it has proved difficult to motivate them. They are invited to meetings and to help with outings and activities.

**Curriculum & activities** Learning through play, following the PPA philosophy. There is a good range of furniture and equipment, and a small budget for replenishment. Activities include sand, water, books, cooking, bubble painting, balloon painting and Tumble Tots. There is a well-stocked dressing-up box for imaginative play as well as play dough, Duplo and bricks. When we visited, the children were indulging in energetic, boisterous play, which sounded noisier than it was in the large hall. The children are friendly, but a little shy of visitors. Staff work with small groups and spend time with each child. Children are encouraged to develop a love of books, and the library 'book bus' visits once a term. There is a good supply of multicultural books. Music and music making with percussion instruments and singing are an important part of the daily timetable. Children visit a nearby farm park regularly, particularly during festivals such as Diwali. There is no formal monitoring nor are developmental records kept.

**Remarks** The centre is a vital and sustaining part of the local Asian community. The playgroup provides a good-quality service, despite the limitations of shared premises and being a voluntary project without the resources of a private or statutory organisation. Structured play in a loving environment at a price everyone can afford.

# Lincolnshire

Only nine per cent of the county's young children receive nursery education before they start school at rising-5, putting Lincolnshire near the bottom of the national league table. There are only two state nursery schools and 20 nursery classes in the county. Demand is high and waiting lists long. Local authority daycare is limited to three family centres, catering for high priority cases only. The private sector offers 30 day nurseries, but many do not accept children under two years old. Nearly 1000 registered childminders and 300 part-time playgroups, many with waiting lists, provide the bulk of the area's pre-school services.

### Further information

For details on day nurseries, childminders and playgroups:
Department of Social Services
Inspection Unit
4 Lindum Road
Lincoln LN2 1NN
Tel: (0522) 569700

For details on nursery schools, units and classes:
Education Department
County Offices
Newland
Lincoln LN1 1YQ
Tel: (0522) 553271

# CARLTON ROAD NURSERY UNIT

Carlton Road Primary School
Carlton Road
Boston
Lincs PE21 8LN
**Tel:** (0205) 364674

**Owner:** Lincs LEA
**Teacher-in-charge:** Valerie Byers, Cert Ed (Froebel)
**Type:** Nursery unit attached to primary school offering half-day sessions. No full-time places
**Children:** 3–5yrs. 29 places. 78 on register
**Hours:** Morning session 9.15am–11.30am
Afternoon session 1pm–3.15pm
Open 39 weeks a year
**Status:** State nursery unit
**Number of years open:** 15
**Meals:** Snacks
**1992 fees:** No fees
**Waiting list:** Long. 85 names. Priority to oldest children in the catchment area
**Registered by:** Lincs County Council LEA

**Premises** Run as part of the primary school, in purpose-built, self-contained premises adjacent to the school. A single-storey, brick building. The unit primarily serves its immediate catchment area, a mixture of local authority and low cost private housing, but a limited number of children attend from further away. There are a number of different children's rooms: a large room for messy play and large apparatus; a lobby with interest tables; a large, light construction room, including the home corner; two quiet rooms for reading, storytelling and floor toys; and a wet-play room, clean, safe and well decorated, but not very warm. Good-quality and plentiful equipment (annual budget £1000). Windows everywhere, looking out on to a spacious, tarmac playground, with huge sandpits and other outdoor equipment. There is a grassy area for slides, climbing frame and a paddling pool.

**Teacher-in-charge & staff** Valerie Byers, Cert Ed (Froebel), is in her early 50s and has been teacher-in-charge of the nursery unit for 11 years. She has always worked with children, first as an infant teacher, then at the Froebel Institute in London, and intends to stay at Carlton Road until she retires. She spends approximately 25 hours a week teaching and the remainder on administration and organisation, setting high standards by example. Her assistants are four experienced NNEBs, two full-time and two part-time, with a range of different talents – two play the piano, one has special needs experience, another is an accomplished seamstress. There is very low staff turnover. Students, pupils from the local secondary school and various trainees come and go on work experience. Informal staff meetings are held daily, more formal ones weekly. Although staff work well together as a loyal, long-serving team, they rarely mix socially outside school hours. Staff/child ratio is 1:13. All staff would welcome a higher ratio. Nursery workers are allocated a proportion of the school's £3500 training and development budget to attend relevant courses.

**Children & parents** Almost without exception, the children move on to Carlton Road Primary. Children with special needs are welcome. The nursery has an open-door policy, with parents invited to all activities and welcome to assist in the classroom and accompany outings. Children are phased-in with their parents present only if a child appears seriously unhappy. Valerie Byers believes that nursery should be an extension of home life. 'In my opinion,' she says, 'without the nursery, there would be many more social problems in the area. The very low turnover of staff engenders a sense of continuity and trust in the parents and the wider community.'

**Curriculum & activities** The nursery bases its philosophy on the teachings of Froebel, believing that each child should be treated as an individual and taught according to his/her stage of development. The objective is to foster natural curiosity and a love of learning and to develop social and emotional skills. A stimulating, varied and safe environment is top priority. The nursery is always cheerful and welcoming, with every wall displaying children's work. Children are divided into groups of 13 for a structured, but flexible timetable of activities. The rooms are attractively and carefully prepared to offer a range of different experiences – art, construction, books, home corner, dry and wet sand, water, indoor and outdoor apparatus. Children come together for snacks, stories and discussion periods. Pre-reading, number and writing skills are practised in smaller groups each session. The Story Chest reading scheme is followed. Music with musical instruments and singing is a daily event. The library is visited once a term. There is no religious content to the day, but moral teaching, to promote kindness and consideration for others. Each session includes time set aside for well-structured, planned project work, culminating in imaginative and exciting wall displays. All projects cover every aspect of the curriculum – maths, language development and listening skills, writing, science, cookery, geography, art and music. Children are continuously monitored and a detailed record of progress and development goes with them to the reception class.

**Remarks** Dedicated and experienced teaching and support staff, who work exceptionally well as a team, serving an area with more than its fair share of social problems. Happy, caring and welcoming atmosphere. Outside the immediate area, nursery provision is poor.

# FIRST CLASS NURSERY SCHOOL

Old St Anne's School
Dudley Road
Grantham
Lincs NG31 9AA
**Tel:** (0476) 592655

**Owners/Principals:** Liz Morrison
Peter Morrison, Cert Ed
**Type:** Nursery school offering full- and part-time places and half-day sessions
**Children:** 2–5yrs. 30 places. 90 on register
**Hours:** 7.30am–6pm
Morning session 9am–12 noon
Afternoon session 1pm–4pm
Flexible hours
Open 51 weeks a year
**Status:** Private, fee-paying
**Number of years open:** 2½
**Meals:** Packed lunch, snacks
**1992 fees:** £5.40 per session
£1.10 per hour for any additional hours
10% discount for full-time places
**Waiting list:** None. Places available
**Registered by:** Lincs County Council SS

**Premises** An old, red-brick school building in a quiet side road with easy parking. There are three main rooms, all light, attractive and warm: a small, carpeted quiet room, also used as an office; the 'afternoon' room, used for music and woodwork, furnished with cabinets the children helped to make; and the open-plan main room with well-stocked reading corner and an organ and brightly decorated with children's pictures. There is also a kitchen, toilet area and staff loo. Outside, there is a large play area with a soft surface but no grass, used daily, weather permitting. There is a good supply of outdoor equipment, including play house, bikes, trikes, climbing frame and see-saw. A sandpit is planned. The local parks are not used, as there are no clean areas for children to play in.

**Owners/Principals & staff** Peter Morrison, Cert Ed, previously taught at Grantham College of Further Education. He and his wife are responsible for the day-to-day running of the nursery and head a team of three NNEB nursery nurses and an unqualified, but experienced, assistant. Ancillary staff include a YTS trainee and a music teacher who visits once a week for music and movement. Formal staff meetings are held every eight weeks or so, but staff discuss problems or developments as they occur. 'We believe in consulting and working with staff to make each day an enjoyable and profitable one for adults and children,' say the principals. They want everyone to have fun. The nursery has a list of back-up staff, mostly qualified, who can be called on to fill in for sickness or holidays. Parents also come in occasionally to help out. No staff training policy or budget.

**Children & parents** Very little ethnic or cultural mix, reflecting the local population. There is one bilingual child who speaks German at home. All children come from similar backgrounds, mostly professional. They are grouped according to their stage of development, which does not necessarily correspond with age. Parents' evenings are not considered necessary, as staff are always available to talk to parents. A newsletter is sent out and parents are openly invited to make suggestions and comments on the running of the nursery. Children all transfer to local state primary schools.

**Curriculum & activities** Learning through structured play. The main aim is for children to enjoy themselves, with some direction and encouragement from staff. Practical, social and pre-school skills are top of the agenda. Children spend most of their day in small groups within a clearly defined area and gradually work towards longer periods of concentration. Each day consists of sessions of free play, 45-minute work sessions, stories, rhymes and songs, as well as outdoor play and breaktime. No particular philosophy is followed, but the nursery puts children first, adapting to individual needs. The school is well supplied with art materials and equipment (annual equipment budget £2000), and walls are covered in exciting and colourful paintings and collages. The book corner is well displayed and provides a good selection of books for all ages, at child height. French is taught once a week to full-timers and there are weekly music and movement sessions for all.

**Remarks** A caring nursery school, with a well-balanced curriculum, allowing children to learn at their own pace. No liaison with local schools as yet. Geared more to sessional care than full-timers, but flexible hours mean that parents can choose the hours to suit their own timetables. Available places nearly always filled by word of mouth. Reasonable prices, with some discounts available. Poor state provision in the area. Private provision is plentiful, but of variable quality.

# HIGHGATE DAY CARE NURSERY

Old School House
Highgate
Leverton
Boston
Lincs PE22 0AW
**Tel:** (0205) 871038

**Owners:** Mr and Mrs D L Docking
**Supervisors:** Peta Docking
Joanne Reed, NNEB
**Type:** Day nursery offering full- and part-time places and half-day sessions
**Children:** 6wks–5yrs. 30 places. 48 on register
**Hours:** 8am–6pm
Morning session 8am–12.30pm
Afternoon session 1.30pm–6pm
Open 50 weeks a year
**Status:** Private, fee-paying
**Number of years open:** 2
**Meals:** Snacks, packed lunches

**1992 fees:** £62 per week full-time
£13 per full day
£1.60 per hour (min 3hrs)
**Waiting list:** None. Places available
**Registered by:** Lincs County Council SS

**Premises** Part of a former Victorian village primary school (closed because of falling numbers), dating from 1875. It stands in an acre of land, with a tarmac car park in front and a large, grass play area at the back. The nursery is in a quiet country road in a sleepy village, ten minutes' drive from Boston. The building is warm and light and in good repair. Children occupy the ground floor only. A late '60s back extension houses the main playroom. There is good natural light and low windows, allowing children to look out into the garden. Part carpet, part tiled, it has a messy-play and sand area and small tables and chairs for table-top activities. The hallway contains a comfortable sofa for reading and the nursery computer. The separate baby unit has light wood floors with rugs, lively pictures on the walls and cheerful curtains. It is furnished with a rocking chair, ample toys and child-sized tables and chairs. In addition, there is a sleep room, nappy-changing area and kitchen. There are plans to convert the school hall, currently used for storage, into a craft and soft-play room. The substantial outside area is securely fenced and locked, sheltered by beautiful, mature trees. Excellent variety of outdoor play equipment – climbing frame, tunnel, swings, slide, a wooden play house and picnic table. Nursery rabbits and guinea pigs live outside in summer.

**Supervisors & staff** Peta Docking is qualified in management and took a basic childcare course before opening the nursery. She shares the daily running of the nursery with Joanne Reed, an experienced NNEB, the senior nursery nurse. There is one other full-time NNEB nursery nurse and three part-timers. Three helpers are unqualified, but experienced; one is the mother of 12 children. There is no qualified early years teacher on the staff. 'Nursery nurses are few and far between in this part of Lincolnshire, as are nurseries. We attract each other by word of mouth,' Peta Docking says. The nursery is too new to have experienced staff turnover problems, but finding qualified workers in a rural area is not easy. Bubbly, enthusiastic, young staff. When we visited, there were just eight children and five nursery workers. The usual staff/child ratio is 1:5. A keyworker system operates when children first join. Staff meetings are held weekly.

**Children & parents** Almost exclusively the children of local farmers or farm workers, with others from medical and teaching backgrounds. The baby and toddler unit cares for children from 6 weeks to 2 years. The nursery takes children from when they are potty-trained until rising-5. Some leave at 3 to attend Conway pre-prep in Boston, while others stay and progress to local primary schools – Butterwich, Wrangle and Old Leake. The nursery is still establishing itself and numbers are low at some sessions. Children with special needs are welcome. Joanne Reed has speech therapy training, and there is wheelchair access to the building. The nursery currently has some children with delayed communication skills. Parents do not become involved in nursery activities or outings, but are invited to open days, talk to staff daily and receive a regular newsletter. Phasing-in is done to individual needs.

**Curriculum & activities** No particular philosophy. 'Our main concern is the happiness and welfare of the children in our care. We encourage children to develop at their own pace, to be independent, to play and to have fun,' says Peta Docking. Library visits take place once a fortnight, dance and movement weekly and music and basic French daily. Each child's keyworker and the senior nursery nurse monitor progress once a term. An achievement chart is kept for each child, including numbers and counting, colours, alphabet, shapes, left and right, directions, sizes and gross and fine motor control. There is a computer which children use for colour and shape matching. Lots of project work. Learning about the lifecycle of a butterfly, for example, involves hunting in the garden for caterpillars and watching the chrysalis produce a butterfly. Snails, ladybirds and other insects are studied. The rural location provides endless scope for nature work. Other recent projects have been 'Where we Live', 'Seeds' and 'Chicken and Egg'. Parents are kept informed of topics via the newsletter and are invited to bring relevant objects to the nursery. All equipment is clean and new, colour co-ordinated and stacked on shelves at child level. No reading schemes, but children can usually recognise about 30 words by the time they leave. No religious content and no out-

ings. The community policeman has visited the nursery. There is no qualified nursery teacher on the staff, but Peta Docking ensures that those who are ready are guided towards more formal learning activities.

**Remarks** A relatively new nursery that shows good promise. Excellent premises, equipment and spacious outside area. Young staff show warmth and affection for the children. Happy family atmosphere, based on sharing and discussion. Area desperately needs more provision for under-5s, of all types, but particularly low cost.

## TINY TOTS DAY NURSERY

68 Keddington Road
Louth
Lincs LN11 0BA
**Tel:** (0507) 601224

**Joint Owners/Managers:** Diane Dixon, NNEB Helen Towl, NNEB
**Type:** Day nursery offering full- and part-time places.
**Children:** 6wks–5yrs. 25 places. 41 on register
**Hours:** 7am–6pm
Flexible hours
Open 52 weeks a year
**Status:** Private, fee-paying
**Number of years open:** 3
**Meals:** Breakfast, lunch, tea, snacks
**1992 fees:** £2 per hour – under 2
£1.70 per hour – over 2
£3 per hour for two children
**Waiting list:** Early registration advisable, especially for babies under 18 mths
**Registered by:** Lincs County Council SS

# LONDON

# Barking & Dagenham

Strong commitment towards under-5s and the investment of resources. Since the 1980s, when primary school numbers started to fall, the Education Department has been adapting classrooms and opening nursery classes. Every school except one has a nursery class and there are 'definitely no plans to close any of them', the Education Department says, despite cuts in the education budget. Although there are waiting lists for popular schools, the majority of 3- and 4-year-olds receive a place if they want one. Most children in the borough start in the September after their 3rd birthday. Quality is high. Full day care is provided by registered childminders and six voluntary and private day nurseries. One subsidised community nursery charges £50 a week, the five private day nurseries between £70 and £80. Social Services subsidise 200 places, primarily for children in need, but there are a limited number of places for low-paid workers at £8 per day. Despite sending questionnaires to a range of nurseries and classes in the borough, none were returned to us.

## Further information

For details on day nurseries and playgroups:
Early Years Administrator
Tel: (081) 592 4500 × 2317
Childminding Advisors
Tel: (081) 592 4500 × 2394

For details on nursery schools, units and classes:
Education Department
Town Hall
Barking IG11 7LU
Tel: (081) 592 4500 × 3014

# Barnet

Nursery education has been a priority, with 30 per cent of 3- and 4-year-olds receiving a place. 'We are very, very child-centred and the quality of our nursery education is known to be high. We concentrate on emergent reading and writing and aim to make children independent thinkers,' an education officer told us. There is a carefully planned curriculum, tailored to the needs of each individual child, and close co-operation between nursery and primary school teachers. However, budget cuts worth £14 million put a serious question mark over the future of all non-statutory provision in the borough. Barnet has been the envy of many nursery teachers, particularly for its provision of advisory teachers and in-service training. These services may face the axe. The Early Years Inspector, who has recently left, will not be replaced and the many advisory teachers reduced to nil. 'Lack of resources is making a nonsense of the high standards we have fought to achieve,' says one officer. Full-time daycare is available for children in need in the borough's seven day nurseries (one has recently been closed). Local parents are campaigning vigorously to reverse the cuts. Most full-time childcare is provided by 900 registered childminders, charging £2–£2.50 per hour. The sole private day nursery in Barnet has fees of £100 per week.

## Further information

For details on day nurseries, childminders and playgroups:
West Area Under Eights Team
Barnard House
158 Burnt Oak Broadway
Edgware HA8 0UH
Tel: (081) 952 7722 × 3550
East Area Under Eights Team
42 Lytton Road
New Barnet EN5 5BY
Tel: (081) 449 5511

For details on nursery schools, units and classes:
Education Services
Friern Barnet Lane
London N11 3DL
Tel: (081) 368 1255 × 3047 or × 3006
Open Tues/Wed/Thurs mornings.

---

## HENDON COLLEGE NURSERY

Hendon College
Corner Mead
Grahame Park Way
Colindale
London NW9 5RA
**Tel:** (081) 200 8300 × 2029

**Owner:** Hendon College
**Nursery Manager:** Karen Neall, NNEB, DPQS
**Type:** Workplace nursery offering full-time places and half-day sessions to college students and staff and local community
**Children:** 2–5yrs. 20 places. 24 on register
**Hours:** 8.30am–5pm
Morning session 8.30am–11.55am
Afternoon session 1pm–5pm
Open 38 weeks a year (term-time only)
**Status:** Private, fee-paying, subsidised by college
**Number of years open:** 4
**Meals:** Snacks, lunch, tea
**1992 fees:** £78 (£26-£72 for college members) per week full-time
£9 (£3-£8 for college members) per session
Rates to college members dependent on salary
**Waiting list:** 60 names
**Registered by:** London Borough of Barnet SS

**Premises** On the fringes of Hendon College, surrounded by grass and trees. Easily accessible by public transport and car, with good on-site parking facilities. The nursery occupies the ground floor of a small brick building, which used to house old shower rooms, now completely gutted and refurbished. The college canteen is above. A ramp for disabled access leads up the main entrance into the cloakroom area. Everything is painted in bright primary colours – red pegs, blue lino, colour photographs of the children and a huge parents' noticeboard. The office on the left doubles as a staff room. Toilets are spotless and include a shower. There is a small kitchen. The children work and play in one big, L-shaped activity room, divided into sections for different activities. The book and quiet corner is cosy, carpeted and soft. It includes a good selection of books, a cardboard grandfather clock, television and computer. The main work area is set out with three tables and chairs, trays full of equipment and toys. A well-stocked home corner and separate wet/messy-play area, with sand and water play and painting easels, complete the different sections. Space is at a premium, but well organised, and the atmosphere is warm, happy and welcoming.

**Manager & staff** Hendon College nursery is the result of years of planning, scheming and hard work. Both the line manager in the student services department, Alan Scanlon, and the nursery manager, Karen Neall, NNEB, DPQS, have been involved in the project from the very beginning. Warm and approachable, Karen Neall has developed strong relationships with children, parents and staff. She loves her work and says she would never consider moving to any other nursery. The college has rewarded her loyalty with more and more responsibility – she is now in control of her own budget and makes most of the important decisions. All her staff – three full-timers and two part-timers – are qualified. The deputy, Diane, NNEB, DPQS, and one other full-timer have also been at the nursery since it opened. Staff turnover is rare. This is a close, solid and sociable team. Staff meetings often take place in their own homes and there is no need for rotas, as everyone works willingly at whatever needs to be done.

**Children & parents** There is a healthy social and cultural mix, with children coming from a wide catchment area. Thirteen subsidised places are reserved for college students and seven for staff and outsiders, who pay higher fees. Welcome at all times, parents are actively involved with the nursery and staff. Phasing-in takes as long as parents and children require. The majority of parents are students, including single parents, male and female. Currently, many are struggling to pay the fees. The college has set up a hardship fund and Barnet Social Services also fund some places. Karen Neall constantly wrestles with the dilemma of trying to make the nursery more affordable, without letting it go bankrupt. Parents discuss their child's progress with their keyworker once a term. The nursery also organises regular outings, Christmas parties and summer barbecues for children, parents and staff.

**Curriculum & activities** A weekly plan is drawn up by each member of staff in rotation and is clearly displayed for staff and parents to see. Work tends to be topic based and covers all aspects of the National Curriculum. The weekly plans have a strong multicultural element and cover creative work, maths, science, imaginative play and a special activity. Flexibility and choice are very important – no child is ever forced to do anything. There is no pressure on children and keyworkers ensure they develop at their own pace. The focus is on the importance of developing social skills, language ability through self-expression and pre-reading, pre-writing and pre-number work. On offer here is learning through play in a structured environment. The day begins with free play, followed by an activity for the whole group – songs, stories, sharing news. The latter part of each session is set aside for topic work – usually a choice of three different activities set out on tables; colouring, pre-writing, patterns, sticking, painting or cutting. Hand-written posters throughout the nursery spell out its philosophy and aims to parents. One explains the importance of play, another the value of books. Other activities include a weekly visit to the college gym, library visits, computer play, outdoor play twice a day and regular coach trips. The nursery's menus are restricted, as all meals come from the college canteen above the nursery. However, cookery is a popular activity with the children and parents are encouraged to bring in different cultural dishes to supplement the canteen diet.

**Remarks** Rapidly gaining a high reputation in the area with demand far outstripping the supply of available places. If the college could be persuaded to find funds, this nursery could increase the number of weeks it is open, expand its numbers and build a separate baby unit. There would be an immediate queue of customers clamouring for places.

# HENDON PRE-SCHOOL

20 Tenterden Grove
Hendon
London NW4 1TD
**Tel:** (081) 202 0263

**Owner:** Asquith Court Schools Ltd
**Headmistress:** Sarah Johnson, Mont Dip
**Type:** Nursery school offering full-time places and half-day sessions
**Children:** 3–5yrs 11mths. 90 places. 117 on register
**Hours:** 8am–6pm
Morning session 8am–1pm
Afternoon session 1pm–6pm
Open 50 weeks a year
**Status:** Private, fee-paying
**Number of years open:** 4
**Meals:** Snacks, lunch, tea
**1992 fees:** £115 per week full-time
£83 per week for 5 morning sessions
£57 per week for 5 afternoon sessions
£25 registration fee
**Waiting list:** None
**Registered by:** Dept for Education
**Under same ownership:** Breaside Pre-School, Bromley, Kent; Bush Hill Park Pre-School, Enfield, London; Meoncross Pre-School, Fareham, Hants; New Eltham Pre-School, New Eltham, London; Salcombe Pre-School, Enfield, London; Warsash Pre-School, Southampton, Hants; West Hampstead Pre-School, Hampstead, London; Westwood Park Pre-School, Southampton, Hants

**Premises** Desirable residential suburb, just off the North Circular Road. Imposing, detached prep-school with the pre-school purpose-built on to the side, complete with gravel driveway and well-planted, landscaped gardens. The building was bought as a school in 1989 and completely gutted and refurbished. The nursery comprises four classrooms in all, three on the ground floor and one in the basement of the main school. The playground is vast and completely fenced in. The pre-school nursery has its own outside area, with safety surfaces, playhouses, ramps, slides, ladders etc. No expense has been spared inside or out and every summer, when the school closes, more work is done. Classrooms are light, warm and very child-centred – two of the entrances are clearly for children only, as they are only just over a metre high. Carpentry work is of a very high standard – built-in play houses, colourful display boards and storage galore.

**Headmistress & staff** Sarah Johnson, Mont Dip, is described by her employers as 'dedicated and very dependable'. Her experience includes nannying, nursery nursing and teaching. She works an 11-hour day and has overall responsibility for everything except budgeting, which is kept firmly in the control of the owners, Asquith Court Schools Ltd. The group now has nine schools in total. Their director of operations, Jean Cross, B Ed, explained that they guarantee high quality by hiring very professional, experienced staff to teach and manage each school. Hendon Pre-School employs ten members of staff including Sarah. All are qualified, including four Mont Dips and three NNEBs. The emphasis is on education – each classroom is run by a Montessori teacher, who works from 8am to 4pm each day. Other staff act as assistants to the teacher. All children call teachers by their surnames, as part of their preparation for school.

**Children & parents** The nursery was set up specifically to feed the pre-prep section of the school and to meet the needs of working parents in the area. Of the most recent batch of 43 leavers, 33 moved over to the main school and the remaining ten to local state schools. A wide selection of nationalities, with a strong contingent of Japanese. One set of Japanese parents took their child away because they were worried he was not learning English quickly enough, surrounded by so many other Japanese children. Children are local and Sarah Johnson sees the school as a 'community nursery'. The atmosphere is noticeably quiet and well disciplined (until the children are let out into the playground). Parents are generally affluent and professional. Many use the pre-school because they want to secure a place at the prep-school. The majority are dedicated consumers of private education from an early stage.

**Curriculum & activities** Free play takes place until all the children have arrived at 9am, followed by group time, with strong emphasis on news and communication. This is followed by some form of writing exercise, a mid-morning snack and outdoor playtime. The 'real work' begins at 10.40am and continues for an hour, until lunch. Each afternoon begins with 1½ hours of school work, followed by tea. The day ends with all the children coming together in two classrooms for a range of different activities. Each child has a number book, news book, sound book and worksheets for colouring and writing exercises. Completed exercise books go home with teachers' markings and remarks intact. The Ginn reading scheme is used throughout the school and most of the 4-year-olds are readers. Some are very advanced and fluent. The approach is phonetic and the alphabet and simple words need to be mastered before a reading scheme is started. The preparation for school is intense but fun, and the results are impressive. The school gym and refectory are used regularly, particularly by the oldest group, so that the transition to 'big school' is smooth and gradual. Detailed reports are kept on each child. Younger group reports cover social/emotional development, concentration and language. Older group reports add maths, reading, writing and oral expression. The day is very structured and disciplined, but the children appear confident and independent.

**Remarks** Professional and efficient, with excellent facilities, amazing equipment and qualified staff. The owners have come up with a formula which they feel works and which they hope to duplicate throughout their other schools. High expectations are rewarded by impressive results. Too structured and rigid for some, but an excellent preparation for the rigours of private-school life in London.

## ST CATHERINE'S (RC) SCHOOL – NURSERY UNIT

Vale Drive
Barnet
Herts EN5 2ED
**Tel:** (081) 440 4946

**Owner:** London Borough of Barnet LEA
**Headteacher:** Julia Ross, Cert Ed
**Type:** Nursery class in state primary school
**Children:** 3–4yrs 11mths. 39 places for morning session, 26 places for afternoon session. 65 on register
**Hours:** Morning session 9am–11.30am
Afternoon session 1pm–3.30pm
Open 40 weeks a year
**Status:** State nursery class
**Number of years open:** 18
**Meals:** Snacks
**1992 fees:** No fees
**Waiting list:** Priority to Catholic children
**Registered by:** London Borough of Barnet LEA

## WESSEX GARDENS INFANT & NURSERY SCHOOLS

Wessex Gardens
Golders Green
London NW11
**Tel:** (081) 455 8798

**Owner:** London Borough of Barnet LEA
**Headteacher:** Moira Prunty, B Ed (Primary)
**Type:** Nursery class in primary school offering half-day sessions. No full-time places
**Children:** 3–5yrs. 52 places. 52 on register
**Hours:** Morning session 9am–11.30am
Afternoon session 1pm–3.30pm
Open 39 weeks a year
**Status:** State nursery class
**Number of years open:** 16
**Meals:** Children bring snacks
**1992 fees:** No fees
**Waiting list:** Moderate, getting longer. Priority to siblings and children going on to infant school
**Registered by:** London Borough of Barnet LEA

**Premises** An Aladdin's cave of treasures crammed into one large classroom on the ground floor of a large and busy primary school. It is impossible to stand up straight, there is so much children's art work hanging down from the ceiling. We visited only four weeks into a new school year, and there were vast displays of art and craft inside and out – including inspiring self-portraits of the children 'dancing on autumn leaves'. The whole class is overflowing with carefully researched and purposefully chosen equipment. A comfortable three-seater sofa by the door means parents and visitors will feel welcome at any time. The children move freely between different activity areas – art, messy play, writing, weighing and cookery. Outside, part of the infant school playground has been fenced off specially for the nursery and has its own sandpit, home corner and construction area. It is hard to believe the wealth of equipment available and impossible to describe it all. The school also has its own swimming pool.

**Headteacher & staff** Moira Prunty, B Ed, who comes from a family of teachers, is a very special woman with a genuine vocation. She trained in Scotland at the same college as her mother. Approachable, intelligent and mature, she gives everything to her job. Mary Parker, NNEB, NAMCW, the full-time nursery worker, is also committed and devoted. She and Moira spend many hours after work discussing the children and planning exciting programmes. NNEB students and many willing parents also help regularly. Teachers from the Infant School visit frequently, to seek Moira's advice.

**Children & parents** A tremendous mix of cultures and backgrounds, with over 28 different nationalities and almost as many languages – Hebrew is the most common, but a variety of Asian and African languages too. All families receive a home visit before children start school. The parents are active, involved and very supportive. The children are busy, absorbed, and visibly secure in their classroom environment. Special needs children are very welcome and expertly cared for – Moira is the special needs co-ordinator for the whole school.

**Curriculum & activities** Every morning and afternoon the nursery is carefully set up to provide a wide variety of activities – sand and water, cookery, writing, construction table and a home corner. Each teacher and helper is given a special responsibility, supervised by the head. Children are encouraged to learn through play, but the activities are all carefully planned so that children gain the maximum from them in every area of their development. For example, a cookery activity – making pizzas – teaches children about different ingredients and also about sharing, measuring, cutting and grating. Careful teacher-monitoring will ensure that through this activity, children learn about language, maths, motor skills, emotional and social development and science. There is also every opportunity to read and write. Paper and pencils are always available, writing is displayed everywhere and there is an incredible selection of books, which can be taken home. The door to the playground is always open. Each child is carefully observed at play to make sure they develop their full potential. Record keeping is considered vital – and all staff are involved. Ongoing records on each child and records on arrival and departure highlight progress in language, knowledge, understanding, literacy and imagination. Absolutely no discipline problems – children are far too busy and too well loved. Swimming once a week in the school pool.

**Remarks** After a three-hour visit we had to tear ourselves away. Moira Prunty agrees. 'When I first came, I knew this was the school for me. I had finally arrived.'

# Bexley

Near the bottom of the London borough league table for nursery education, but attempting to move up. Despite financial restraints and standstill budgets, four new nursery classes opened last year and the council's policy is to open two a year from now onwards. About 50 per cent of 3- and 4-year-olds may be offered a place in a nursery unit, and waiting lists are long. Expansion has not helped many parents. An Education Department spokesman honestly explains, 'We have reduced the waiting list, but now that there are twice as many places, those parents who don't get a place are even more dissatisfied. We are victims of our own success.' Full-time daycare is provided by the private sector. 700 childminders, paid a minimum of £1.40 per child per hour, provide most of the service. Four private nurseries are registered, charging £60 per week on average. 68 playgroups offer part-time sessions a few days per week. Questionnaires were sent out to a selection of nurseries in the borough, but none were returned.

### Further information

For details on day nurseries, childminders and playgroups:
Under Eights Section
Department of Social Services
Civic Offices
Broadway
Bexleyheath DA6 7LB
Tel: (081) 303 7777 × 2586

Nursery school admission is done directly through each school. Register your child on his/her 3rd birthday. For more details contact:
Nursery Admissions
Education Department
Hill View Drive
Welling DA16 3RY
Tel: (081) 303 7777 × 4465

# Brent

Brent Education Authority provides three nursery schools, one children's centre and 65 nursery classes offering mainly part-time places to 36 per cent of 3- and 4-year-olds. Full daycare is available to children in high-priority categories, in ten Social Services day nurseries. The majority of parents depend on the borough's 550 registered childminders. Those who can afford the fees have 44 private day nurseries to choose from. The Council acknowledges the importance of the voluntary sector and gives some grant aid, including funding to four of the 42 playgroups in the area. We sent many questionnaires to state and private sector services, but unfortunately received a minimal response.

### Further information

For details on day nurseries, childminders and playgroups:
Department of Social Services
Brent House
349 High Road
Wembley HA9 6BZ
Tel: (081) 904 1244 × 65864

For details on nursery schools and classes:
Education Department
Chesterfield House
9 Park Lane
Wembley HA9 7RW
Tel: (081) 900 5504

Brent Council publishes a useful booklet, 'Under Fives in Brent – A Guide to Facilities for Children Under Five in Brent'.

# NEWFIELD PRIMARY SCHOOL NURSERY UNIT

Longstone Avenue
London NW10 3UD
**Tel:** (081) 965 1376

**Owner:** London Borough of Brent LEA
**Headteacher Nursery Unit:** Sarah Cox, BA, PPE, PGCE, RSA, PPA
**Type:** Nursery class in state primary school offering full- and part-time places and half-day sessions
**Children:** 3yrs–4yrs 11mths. 30 places. 28 on register
**Hours:** Morning session 9am–12 noon
Extended day 8am–6pm
Open 49 weeks a year
**Status:** State nursery class
**Number of years open:** 6
**Meals:** Breakfast, snacks, hot lunch
**1992 fees:** No fees. Meals £1.30 per day
**Waiting list:** 30 names. Increasing each year
**Registered by:** London Borough of Brent LEA

**Premises** Purpose-built (1987) bungalow in the grounds of Newfield Primary School, surrounded by school playing fields and playground. The whole site is enclosed by tall, formidable iron railings. Newfield Nursery is one of nine state nurseries in Brent, offering extended hours and shorter summer holiday places. An urban development grant has been applied for to renovate and equip the outside play area. Inside there is a central, large play/classroom, with other areas and rooms leading off it. Newfield is the first nursery in the Borough to be built with its own parents' room (disgustingly smoke-filled on our visit). It is also used for neighbourhood English classes twice a week and as a drop-in centre for local childminders one morning a week. Other facilities include a kitchen, office-cum-staff room and quiet room for rest, stories, puzzles and other quiet toys. The children's space is divided into different workshop areas: carpeted parts for home and book corners, construction, dressing up; areas with washable, non-slip linoleum for messy play, painting and tablework like cutting and sticking, writing and drawing. Wall displays are creative and multicultural and follow the pre-planned themes for the term. These included 'Autumn', 'Babies', 'Getting to know each other and the nursery', and 'Diwali'. Overall impression, spacious and welcoming, but slightly dark and in need of some redecoration in parts.

**Headmaster, Nursery Unit Head & staff** The school's new headmaster, Mr Matthew, found time to welcome us warmly and to stress how important he feels nursery life is to the school. The headteacher of the nursery unit is Sarah Cox, mature, approachable and equally welcoming. Sarah Cox has more qualifications than a team of nursery workers, including an RSA qualification in teaching English as a second language in a multicultural school. She also has a working knowledge of Gujarati. Extremely open and honest, Sarah Cox wanted Newfield Nursery to be considered for this book so that more people would know that the state system *can* and, in some areas, *does* provide high-quality, comprehensive nursery education. The staff team is much larger than most state nurseries – four full-time teachers and one part-timer – with a minimum ratio of 1:7 (most nursery classes of 30+ would be allocated just one teacher and one assistant). Staff are lively and individualistic – one NNEB has seven children of her own, another, PPA qualified, has two degrees from Bombay. Between them they speak most of the languages in the classroom – Gujarati, Punjabi, Hindi, Urdu, Spanish, German and some French and Italian. They all have energy and inspiration, harnessed and led by the dynamic and sharp-witted Sarah Cox.

**Children & parents** Children start in September and October, if they are already 3 years old, and stay until they go to school at 4. Sarah believes this is too early, and that they are not ready to join a large reception class with only two teachers. Extended-day children vary in number. When we visited there were eight in all – children of working parents or students or referred by Social Services. Many of the children are bilingual from diverse cultural backgrounds. Some whose families are on income support, others with nannies – a reflection of the immediate locality. The ethnic mix has changed over the years from predominantly Afro-Caribbean and Irish to its present of mainly African (Ghanaian and Nigerian), European and Arab. So far, everyone on the waiting list has been found a place, but this is rapidly changing as word of the nursery's excellent reputation spreads. Parental involvement is considered vital, visits are welcome

at any time and individual parental talents seized on – to help with cookery, dance, music, languages, etc. Extended family is also included in the open-door policy.
**Curriculum & activities** Philosophy of learning through play activities, but also to 'reflect in the nursery environment, equipment and materials, the richness of cultures and wider multicultural differences'. Each term's projects and themes are planned well in advance and distributed to parents. Children are free to choose different activities under careful teacher supervision – writing and drawing in the office area, cutting, sticking, junk, cookery, home corner, dressing up, construction, etc. After juice and biscuits, there is storytime, music and songs in two groups. Children take a book home each day and parents write their comments on how their child has responded to it. Every child has a folder of their work during the year and a 'language development list' which records their progress – oral, written and story-telling. End-of-year written report, which goes on to the primary school. Parents have access to all written reports on their children.
**Remarks** Warm, caring and stimulating nursery, offering excellent range of pre-school activities and top-quality staff. In the face of severe local government cuts headteacher Sarah Cox faces a tough fight to defend Newfield Nursery's standards and extended hours.

# Bromley

Bromley's stated aims are excellent: 'To be sure that all nursery care shall provide a stimulating pre-school experience that will make the transition to infant school much easier for child and parent.' Unfortunately, Bromley provides little nursery care or education and only at full market rates. It is bottom of the London league table for nursery education, with only three nursery classes offering 161 places for 17,500 under-5s. Full daycare is almost exclusively private. Two Social Services day nurseries, managed by private contractors, provide 70 places for children in need. The private sector has recently expanded and provides 125 playgroups and 22 day nurseries, the latter charging from £65 to £100 per week. Response to our questionnaire was generally negative.

**Further information**
For details on day nurseries, childminders and playgroups:
Registration and Inspection Unit
Social Services Department
Civic Centre
Stockwell Close
Bromley BR1 3UH
Tel: (081) 313 4629

For details on the three nursery classes and a list of independent nursery schools and classes contact:
The Admissions Team, Pupil & Students Services
Education Department
Town Hall
Tweedy Road
Bromley BR1 1SB
Tel: (081) 313 4072 or 4058

# RAINBOW DAY NURSERY

13 Hayes Road
Bromley
Kent BR2 9AF
**Tel:** (081) 460 5335

**Owner:** Linda Williamson B Ed, RSA
**Matron:** Mandy Baines, NNEB
**Type:** Day nursery offering full- and part-time places and half-day sessions
**Children:** 2–5yrs. 25 places.
**Hours:** 8am–5.30pm
Morning session 8am–1pm
Afternoon session 1pm–5.30pm
Open 50 weeks a year
**Status:** Private, fee-paying
**Number of years open:** 6
**Meals:** Breakfast, lunch, tea
**1992 fees:** £17 per day
£10 per morning session
£8.50 per afternoon session
**Waiting list:** Reasonable
**Registered by:** London Borough of Bromley SS

**Premises** The nursery occupies the ground floor of a characterless three-storey semi, in a residential area, two minutes from Bromley town centre. Linda Williamson, B Ed, RSA, the owner, lives on the upper two floors with her family. The front forecourt is used as a staff car park – five cars can just about squeeze in. The long, turfed back garden is split into two by a fence. The nursery uses one half, offering sand and water play, trikes, balls, hoops, climbing equipment and a pet rabbit. Inside, there are now three main classrooms (a recent extension has provided the third), a kitchen, quiet room, cloakroom and tiny staff room. Space is at a premium. There are notices and noticeboards everywhere and some room left for children's artwork and displays. Parking outside is on yellow lines, but safe for rapid dropping off and picking up.

**Owner, Matron & staff** Dedicated and still unpaid after six years, Linda Williamson started the nursery for the benefit of her own child and because she wanted to do something for herself. She took a PPA course before opening, as her B Ed qualification is not recognised by Social Services. She still lectures at Orpington College on the BTEC Nursing Diploma course – 'It allows me to follow the latest theory in nursery nurse training and to stay completely up to date.' She describes herself as a 'straight person, who has an open relationship with staff and parents'. Nursery Matron, Mandy Baines, has been at Rainbow since it opened, joining as a nursery worker and progressing upwards. There are four other staff members, all young and qualified. French, ballet and music are taught by specialist visiting teachers at no extra cost to parents. Monthly staff meetings are social occasions around the dinner table. Training is considered important and time is set aside for staff to attend local courses. Linda Williamson and one other staff member are fluent in sign language (Makaton) and welcome children with hearing difficulties.

**Children & parents** The majority are from the local community, with a wide array of nationalities – British, Jamaican, Indian, French and Japanese. One of the nursery notices lists simple Japanese words and their pronunciation. Bromley is a popular town for Japanese bankers. Most parents work full-time, but somehow manage to collect their children by 5.30pm – a closing time stipulated by the local planning department. The nursery welcomes children with special needs. Bromley Social Services pay for two places at Rainbow and there is also one company-subsidised place. A very busy social diary entertains parents, children and staff and forges strong relationships. Annual events include Fun Days (for up to 100 people), barbecues, outings, Christmas parties, etc. However, there are no parents' evenings – in the past attendance has been low, with parents often too tired to attend after work. Showrounds are done individually at any time convenient for working parents.

**Curriculum & activities** No one particular philosophy or school of thought, but all activities are planned well in advance. Children are grouped by age in the three separate classrooms. The daily programme allows for free play from 8am to 10.30am and more structured activities from 10.30am to 11.30am and 1.30pm to 2.30pm. Children only start 'school time' when they are fully settled into the nursery routine. A small area off the kitchen is used for pre-school work. Each teacher takes a small group of children there in turn, and is responsible for setting work and laying out the relevant equipment and books. Careful records monitor the topics each child covers over the weeks, to make sure that every aspect of the

National Curriculum is covered. Subjects include language development, geography, maths, history, art, science and technology. Work is done on worksheets or in exercise books, which are accessible to parents, but kept at the nursery until a child leaves. There does not appear to be any pressure on children to work or achieve academic results. The programme incorporates plenty of choice and free play. Meals are an important social occasion, with staff and children sitting and talking together. A prize is given for the 'best table' each month, but every table wins something regardless. Each week 3½ hours are spent on specialist teaching which includes French, music, ballet and dance (modern and ballroom). The garden is used daily. Visits to the park and library are fortnightly. Swimming has just been added to the curriculum.

**Remarks** Premises may not be fantastic, but this is easily compensated for by the quality of care and the warmth of the staff. The owner, Linda Williamson, shows clearly how one person's dedication, hard work and love of children can benefit a whole community.

# Camden

With £1 million cut from the current Early Years Services budget, there is unlikely to be any growth in provision in the borough, despite a political commitment to expand nursery education and after-school care. Reorganisation, following the implementation of the Children Act, and the amalgamation of Social Services and Education departments under one management structure, should lead to a better use of resources. Several day nurseries have been merged to form two nursery centres, but this has only increased the number of places by ten. The local authority provides 11 children's centres and 19 playgroups. There is a strong voluntary sector, providing day nurseries and playgroups and 47 private day nurseries and nursery schools. 39 per cent of 3- to 4-year-olds can expect to secure a sessional place in one of Camden's nursery schools or classes. Priority is given to children with special needs. No charges for state provision, although extended daycare costs £25 per week. Fees in private nurseries vary enormously. 'Some are run with almost missionary zeal – one, owned by a 70-year-old who loves children, is only £25 per week, others rise to £130 per week,' say Social Services.

## Further information

All information on private, voluntary and local authority provision is available on the CINDEX system at all Camden's public libraries and civic centres. Printouts are free and updated every six months.

Education and Social Services Departments are at:
Crowndale Centre
218-220 Eversholt Street
London NW1 1BD
Tel: (071) 278 4444

## CAMDEN DAY NURSERY

123–127 St Pancras Way
London NW1 0SY
**Tel:** (071) 284 3600

**Owner:** Bringing Up Baby Ltd
**Principal:** Jackie Gardiner, NNEB
**Type:** Day nursery offering full-time places
**Children:** 6mths–3yrs. 16 places. 24 on register
**Hours:** 8.15am–6.15pm
Open 50 weeks a year
**Status:** Private, fee-paying
**Number of years open:** 1
**Meals:** Breakfast, lunch, tea, snacks
**1992 fees:** £130 per week full-time
£31 per day
£150–£200 refundable deposit
**Waiting list:** Reasonable. Early registration advisable
**Registered by:** London Borough of Camden SS
**Under same ownership:** Shepherd's Bush Day Nursery, & Annexe; The Park Nursery School, Wandsworth (see listings)

## FLEET STREET NURSERY

4th Floor
Wesley House
4, Wild Court
London WC2B 5AU
**Tel:** (071) 831 9179

**Owner:** Fleet Street Nursery Ltd
**Co-ordinator:** Jill Harrison, NNEB, City & Guilds Management
**Type:** Workplace nursery offering full-time places
**Children:** 3mths–5yrs. 25 places. 24 on register
**Hours:** 8am–6pm
Open 50 weeks a year
**Status:** Fee-paying registered charity
**Number of years open:** 6
**Meals:** Breakfast, lunch, tea
**1992 fees:** £135 per week full-time
**Waiting list:** Very long. 60 children on list
**Registered by:** London Borough of Camden SS

**Premises** In the heart of central London, the nursery is buried on the fourth floor of a six-storey former Methodist mission. Access is by lift, or stairs for the energetic. The outside play area is a roof garden, shared with Kingsway Nursery, another workplace nursery in the same building. Parking is impossible, but the nursery seems to have an understanding with the local traffic wardens. They and the police turn a blind eye to any vehicle parked outside for up to ten minutes, if it displays a special nursery ticket. Security is tight on the building and all visitors must report to reception. The nursery is spacious, colourful and expensively converted and equipped. The generous facilities include a separate parents' room, staff room, laundry room, three main children's rooms and 'the pit' – an imaginative indoor recreation area filled with coloured mats and climbing equipment. There are two serious weaknesses – the nursery has no immediate access to outside and is almost totally reliant upon artificial lighting.

**Co-ordinator & staff** Jill Harrison defeated strong competition to take over the job of co-ordinator 2½ years ago. Posts at Fleet Street Nursery are highly prized because of the nursery's reputation for top-quality care. There is no deputy, but staff are very supportive of each other and pull their weight if the co-ordinator is away. Staff meetings are held every Monday after work until 8.30pm. Jill Harrison also attends monthly meetings of the management committee – comprising past and present parents – to which she reports. Although she has the last word on the day-to-day running of the nursery, all major decisions are taken in conjunction with the committee. Despite hard work and long hours, this is a happy, well-led team. All staff are qualified NNEBs and there have been no staff changes for over two years. Staffing levels are 1:3 for babies up to 18 months, 1:4 for children from 18 months to 3 years old and 1:5 for children over 3.

**Children & parents** Fleet Street Nursery was originally set up for the use of media workers in central London by two of the main industry unions – the NUJ and SOGAT. It took six years of campaigning, fund-raising and searching for a suitable property to launch the project. The original funding, particularly from the GLC, has long since disappeared and the nursery is now required to be self-financing. Priority is given to media workers with employers who will subsidise their places. Companies with reserved places include London Weekend Television (five–six places) and Reuters (ten places). Camden Social Services also use two places for local residents. Donations towards running costs are regularly received from the Financial Times, the Guardian, LBC and the Press Association. Parents are very involved in the management of the nursery through the Committee and there are parents' reps for each of the children's rooms. All new parents are expected to take two weeks off work to phase in their children to the nursery routine and help them to bond with their keyworkers. Jill Harrison sees this period as crucial, as it is the only way working parents can really understand how the nursery operates and what their children are doing each day. During these two weeks, parents are asked to do anything from changing nappies to feeding babies. They report being exhausted and enlightened by the experience. Children are all full-time (part-timers must find someone to share the rest of their place) and siblings have priority. The nursery has an impressive mix of nationalities and languages. Children with special needs are welcome, but evacuation of the fourth floor in case of fire is not easy and excludes children with serious mobility problems. There are parents' meetings four times a year and an annual fund-raising barbecue.

**Curriculum & activities** The days and weeks are planned well in advance and the programmes for each week are prominently displayed for parents to see. Special attention is paid to National Curriculum subjects, and the timetable reflects this. However, the nursery believes strongly in learning through play and provides a wealth of educational toys and equipment to help each child develop at his or her own pace. Older children are encouraged to learn their letters, practise pencil control exercises and explore the world of maths and science. The reading approach is low-key, and there is no formal reading scheme. Children are allowed generous periods of supervised free play throughout the day. There are frequent walks to Coram Fields, Russell Square and the Embankment. A specialist music teacher visits on Thursday mornings and a computer is on its way, courtesy of the Financial Times. Fire drill is a regular part of the nursery routine because of its fourth floor location. Backpacks line the baby room to aid evacuation. Children eat in their own age groups with their carers. The baby room has the most bizarre eating routine: all the babies are stripped down to just their nappies to eat, so that they can try to feed themselves without adult interference. An extraordinary sight!

**Remarks** An early example of how well-organised and dogged pressure from unions and workers can persuade employers to invest in childcare. However, the actual number of companies involved is extremely small and the full cost of a place is high. The future of Fleet Street Nursery is in the balance – it should not be allowed to go under.

## STEPPING STONES NURSERY

North Bridge House School
33 Fitzjohns Avenue
London NW3 5JY
**Tel:** (071) 435 9641

**Owner:** Mr Wilcox
**Headmistress:** Mrs Allsopp, B Ed (Hons)
**Type:** Nursery school offering half-day sessions. Full-time places for over-4s
**Children:** 2½–5yrs. 50 places. 218 on register
**Hours:** 9am–3.20pm
Morning session 9am–12 noon
Afternoon session 1pm–3pm
Open 36 weeks a year
**Status:** Private, fee-paying
**Number of years open:** 31 (6 under present owner)
**Meals:** Snacks
**1992 fees:** £855 per term for 5 morning sessions a week
£1500 per term full-time – over 4
**Waiting list:** Long. Great demand for places
**Registered by:** Dept for Education

# ST LEONARD'S NURSERY SCHOOL

41 Brunswick Square
London WC1N 1AU
**Tel:** (071) 837 1039

**Owner:** London Borough of Camden LEA
**Headteacher:** Elizabeth Ferguson, Dip Ed, Nursery Nurse Dip
**Type:** State nursery school offering full- and part-time places and half-day sessions
**Children:** 3–5yrs. 60 places. 90 on register
**Hours:** 9.15am–3.30pm
Morning session 9.15am–11.45am
Morning session with lunch 9.15am–1pm
Afternoon session 1pm–3.30pm
Open 36 weeks a year
**Status:** State nursery school
**Number of years open:** 63
**Meals:** Lunch, snacks
**1992 fees:** No fees
**Waiting list:** 20 names. Can usually accommodate all the children on the list
**Registered by:** London Borough of Camden LEA

**Premises** St Leonard's has existed on this site since the 1930s, having started life as an orphanage for starving and homeless children living on the Thames embankment. It is situated in the heart of Coram Fields, in an almost rural setting, surrounded by green fields, a football pitch and a city farm. The building has seen better days, but the inside is well maintained, and children's artwork brightens up the otherwise dull premises. The nursery is spacious, light and well equipped. The two large, interconnecting classrooms lead directly on to a playground. The remaining rooms are made up of the headteacher's office, the secretary's office, staff room, parents' room, dining room/indoor playroom and children's cloakrooms – all on the ground floor. The playground is enormous, and due to serious fund-raising over the years, is very well equipped. There is a choice of play houses, assorted climbing frames, a large sandpit, tricycles and barrels.

**Headteacher & staff** Elizabeth Ferguson, Dip Ed, is a caring and experienced headteacher. She has Scottish teaching and nursery nursing diplomas and has taught or cared for children from 2 to 8 years old all her working life. With five children of her own, she also has first-hand experience of the stresses of motherhood. Elizabeth is keen to achieve greater recognition for her work and the nursery within Camden. Due to local authority cuts, by 1994 St Leonard's will be the only state nursery in the borough not attached to a school. Its future is uncertain although so far it has managed to survive from year to year. The team of two qualified teachers, three nursery nurses and a part-time assistant is very experienced. Ancillary staff include a cleaner, meal supervisors, a secretary and casuals. The longest-serving member has worked for the nursery for 18 years. Students are taken on placement from the local teaching and nursing colleges. Staff training consists of five INSET days a year, with a variable training budget up to a maximum of £950 per annum. Full staff meetings are held every two weeks, and room meetings daily.

**Children & parents** An amazing cross-section of cultures and professions. Priority is given to children who live locally. The short opening hours make it difficult for working parents to use the nursery, but some employ nannies or childminders as well. Parents include homeless refugees, cab drivers, market traders, nurses, brain surgeons, lawyers, doctors, students and lecturers. There are more than 30 different nationalities and some of the children are the third generation of their family to attend St Leonard's. Parents are encouraged to be involved with the curriculum and fund-raising. Elizabeth has developed very strong links with the community. Due to her outreach work, children from Great Ormond Street Hospital are allocated a number of places. Some have been hospitalised all their lives, others for shorter periods of time. They integrate well, are carefully monitored and benefit hugely.

**Curriculum & activities** The stated aim of the nursery is to 'foster children's overall development – social, emotional, intellectual, physical and spiritual – through the provision of appropriate play activities'. Children are encouraged to develop as individuals at their own pace. The two classrooms are set up with various activities before children arrive. There is always a wide choice of art and craft, junk modelling, sticking and cutting, creative role play in the home corners, large and small construction toys, musical instruments, books, computer, graphic work and puzzles. Children can also choose to play outside. All the work revolves around a central, half-termly theme, which is clearly displayed throughout the nursery and incorporates all the aspects of the curriculum including literacy, maths, science and technology. On our visit, the spring term theme was 'homes'. Goldilocks and the Three Bears were in the home corner and there were various wonderful art displays depicting the Big Bad Wolf and the Three Little Pigs at home. Records are kept on each child's development, monitoring their individual needs to ensure that they fulfil their potential. Children take most of their work home, although some samples are kept in individual files as examples of each child's progress throughout the year.

**Remarks** High-quality care and education for the local community. A wonderful mix of cultures and backgrounds, with caring and experienced staff. Large garden and green field site, particularly appreciated by inner city children. The nursery offers a lifeline to normality for a number of chronically sick children at Great Ormond Street Hospital. Both of Camden's other two nursery schools are to be closed, and it is by no means certain that this vital facility will continue to flourish.

## ST MARK'S SQUARE NURSERY SCHOOL

St Mark's Church
St Mark's Square
London NW1 8PG
**Tel:** (071) 586 8383

**Owner/Headteacher:** Sheema Parsons, B Ed, PGCE
**Type:** Nursery school offering full-time places and half-day sessions
**Children:** 2½–5yrs. 24 places per session. Some full-time places available for older children. 32 on register
**Hours:** 9.30am–3.30pm
Morning session 9am–12 noon
Afternoon session 1.30pm–3.30pm
Open 36 weeks a year
**Status:** Private, fee-paying
**Number of years open:** 10
**Meals:** Milk and biscuits, packed lunches
**1992 fees:** £595 per term for 5 morning sessions a week
£450 per term for 5 afternoon sessions a week
£50 registration fee
**Waiting list:** Variable. Some places available
**Registered by:** London Borough of Camden SS

**Premises** On the edge of Regent's Park, next to the Regent's Canal, St Mark's is a large and imposing church surrounded by its own enclosed gardens. The school is in a basement area at the back of the church, with separate entrance and garden. The large, centrally heated classroom is rather dark, with small windows, but well planned and equipped. The walls are alive with children's art and craft work. At the time of our visit, there was a Nativity scene, a maths graph measuring children's smiles, drawings and examples of free writing following a visit to the Tibetan exhibition at the Royal Academy. There are painting easels which are available at all times, a home corner full of interesting equipment and a well-stocked book corner. The room also offers a trampoline and shelves stacked high with toys and games. The outside area is small but safe and used regularly. There is also a small kitchen.

**Owner/Headteacher & staff** Sheema Parsons, B Ed, is direct and very involved. She also has extremely strong views about everything concerning the nursery – education, children, staff and parents. St Mark's is her 'vision'. The children, known as 'Markians', are taught 'her way' and staff are hand-picked to fit in with this vision. She says, 'I'm very choosy. I talk to prospective staff endlessly.' Sometimes new staff overlap the old for as long as six months. It is a small, loyal, qualified team consisting of deputy, Mont Dip; teacher, French and qualified for école maternelle; and an assistant. No students are allowed and visitors are limited as Sheema feels that both disrupt the children's routine. Sheema is a student of Jungian child analysis and has a post-graduate qualification in education. Time is spent each day talking to staff about their feelings and their relationship with the children. Twice a term staff meet for more formal discussions, sharing ideas and problems.

**Children & parents** Parents and children are carefully vetted and chosen only if they fit in with the philosophy of the nursery and respect what Sheema is trying to achieve. She says, 'I am very concerned about who I take on and look for parents with vision, who are more artistic – painters, writers, musicians.' Parents must demonstrate that they celebrate and value their children. Those who pass the test are rewarded with the head's total commitment. Sheema is always available to talk to parents and many become her personal friends. Children wear smocks and are encouraged to express themselves freely and show respect for each other and their teachers.

**Curriculum & activities** The nursery school aims to combine the best of the 'skills and discipline' approach of the private sector with the more 'child-centred, progressive and caring' emphasis of the state nursery schools. Based on a belief that under-5s have a far greater desire and ability to learn basic education skills than is generally acknowledged, the timetable is eclectic. Although planned, each day is flexible and responds to the moods of the children. Music, art, French, language, communication and educational outings (art galleries and ballet performances are particularly popular) all feature heavily in the curriculum. Younger children attend afternoon sessions, moving to the morning when they are considered more mature. A core of 12 children stay all day. Each session begins with free play, followed by a choice of art, maths or writing. Workbooks, worksheets or exercise books are used. Maths work is always project-based and graduates to addition, subtraction, tens and units. Creative writing begins with copying and moves on to free writing and using a wordbook/dictionary. Reading schemes are used, including Dragon books, New Way and anything else which captures a child's interest. Methods and equipment include Montessori, Fletcher, Nuffield and Breakthrough. French is integrated throughout the day, and the children speak it during break – two members of staff are fluent. The children are encouraged to share their dreams and news at this time. Often an interesting sentence from these conversations is written down and passed around. The weekly timetable allows for ballet, violin and T'ai chi lessons – martial arts are considered 'perfect for channelling anger'.

**Remarks** Deliberately small, stimulating, caring environment. An individual approach, heavily dependent on the ideals, passions and presence of the headteacher, Sheema Parsons. It is difficult to imagine that the nursery would continue without her. Friendly, professional teaching staff. Places available due to recession and head's policy of selection of parents and children. Markians usually do well at their chosen prep and primary schools.

# Corporation of London

A handful of services, designed to meet the needs of the 5000 residents only. At least 350,000 people pour into the City each weekday to work and there is virtually no provision for their children. There is a workplace nursery for staff and students of the London Guildhall University and one expensive day nursery primarily for Merrill Lynch employees which also offers places to the general public (for Broadgate Nursery, also in the City, see London Borough of Hackney). Local authority facilities include one nursery class and one children's centre, shared with Stepney. Enquiries from employers interested in setting up workplace nurseries have diminished sharply since the recession and there are no immediate plans to increase the number. Long waiting lists exist for every nursery place for under-2s.

**Further information**

No published lists. Information provided over the telephone:
Department of Social Services
Milton Court
Moor Lane
London EC2Y 9BL
Tel: (071) 332 1212

Education Department
Guildhall
London EC2P 2EJ
Tel: (071) 606 3030 × 1750

## CITY CHILD DAY NURSERY

1 Bridgewater Square
London EC2Y 8AH
**Tel:** (071) 374 0939

**Owner:** City Child Ltd
**Co-ordinator:** Linda Happy, NNEB
**Type:** Day nursery offering full- and part-time places to Merrill Lynch employees and those who live or work in the Corporation of London
**Children:** 3mths–5yrs. 30 places. 25 on register
**Hours:** 8.30am–6pm
Flexible hours
Open 52 weeks a year (excl bank holidays)
**Status:** Fee-paying, registered charity
**Number of years open:** 6
**Meals:** Breakfast, lunch, tea, snacks
**1992 fees:** £550 per month full-time
£26.10 per day
**Waiting list:** Long for babies. Places available from 18mths old
**Registered by:** Corporation of London SS

# Croydon

Close to the bottom of the London boroughs league table for nursery education, with only 13 per cent of 3- and 4-year-olds receiving nursery experience before school. However, the borough has made a public commitment to improve the situation and plans to increase the number of places at the rate of 260 per year. This year they have exceeded that total. Social Services provide four day nurseries and subsidise one private nursery for children in need. Nine private day nurseries offering full daycare charge £70–£80 per week. 800 registered childminders, some with fees as low as £45 per week, cater for all age groups, including babies. There is a Croydon Under Fives Forum (CUFF), sponsored by the Council and bankers, Hill Samuel, which collates all information about under-5s services and produces a useful booklet, 'CUFF Cares'. Some 90 playgroups offer half-day and occasional sessions.

### Further information

For details on day nurseries, childminders and playgroups:
Under Fives Team
Croydon Social Services
Tel: (081) 760 5439 or 5478

For details on nursery education:
Tel: (081) 760 5455

## BYRON INFANT SCHOOL – NURSERY CLASS

St David's (off Stoneyfield Road)
Coulsdon
Surrey CR5 2XE
**Tel:** (081) 668 0250

**Owner:** London Borough of Croydon LEA
**Headteacher:** Carolyn Childs, B Ed
**Nursery Teacher:** Maggie Anderson, Cert Ed, RSA Dip
**Type:** Nursery class in infant school offering half-day sessions. No full-time places
**Children:** 3–5yrs (children admitted in the year they become 4). 26 places. 52 on register
**Hours:** Morning session 9.15am–11.30am
Afternoon session 1pm–3.15pm
Open 38 weeks a year
**Status:** State nursery class
**Number of years open:** 2
**Meals:** None
**1992 fees:** No fees. £4.20 per term for milk and juice
**Waiting list:** Variable. Over 100 names for 1993 intake
**Registered by:** London Borough of Croydon LEA

**Premises** Attached to the infant school, in a quiet cul-de-sac, with a local bus service on the nearby main road. The accommodation is spacious and open-plan. The infant school building is single-storey and brick-built, with the internal walls part natural brick, part painted. The nursery class walls are covered with children's collages and paintings. New, exciting, child-centred equipment (£4500 setting-up budget) fills the classroom. The very large main room is divided into colour-coded sections (for example, red for maths, yellow for construction) with matching, colour-coded equipment and toys. There is a wooden, indoor climbing frame with thick rubber matting beneath it; a quiet corner for colouring and chalking on a blackboard; a messy area for painting, water and sand play; and a home corner for role play. A smaller, carpeted, quiet room, decorated with artwork, is used for story-telling, television and video, and contains an excellent selection of books at child-height. This is a mainly middle-class, urban area, ten minutes from the Downs. The playground is small but secure, with a paved surface, and is used under supervision only. The gates are kept locked until parents arrive to collect their children. There are plans to improve the outdoor facilities once funds are available.

**Nursery Teacher & staff** The nursery teacher, Maggie Anderson, Cert Ed, RSA Dip, who holds an additional special needs qualification, has been responsible for setting up the nursery at Byron. She works closely with her NNEB assistant. Welfare assistants from the infant school also spend time in the nursery, supporting individual children. Students are accepted on placement and parent helpers are welcome. A librarian visits twice a term, for book sharing and reading and to change the supply of books. There appears to be an excellent rapport between staff and children. The atmosphere is happy and friendly. Nursery staff meet daily and join a staff meeting of the whole school twice a week. There is a full training programme and budget for staff.

**Children & parents** Children of mixed nationalities, but predominantly white, many bilingual. All transfer to the infant school at age 5, well prepared for the transition. Children with special educational needs and disabilities thrive here and are extremely well supported. The parents come from a cross-section of the local community and are included as partners in the school from the very beginning. They can visit at any time to speak to staff and are invited to nursery events. There is an active PTA, which all parents belong to. Home visits are made before children begin and entry is staggered, two at a time, at weekly intervals, according to date of birth. Parents stay with children to settle them in. School uniform is optional – a brown or yellow tracksuit with yellow polo-neck jumpers.

**Curriculum & activities** Learning through structured play, language and first-hand experience. The rich curriculum covers language and literacy skills; maths, science and technology; human and social skills; moral and spiritual development; and creative, aesthetic and physical skills. Much work is based on half-termly topics. The equipment is of a high standard, and there are carefully planned activities, including painting, modelling, musical instruments, dance and movement and imaginative play, with dressing-up clothes or in the home corner, all encouraging free-expression. An impressive indoor climbing frame develops physical skills. Reading is fostered through stories and an extensive selection of story-books. Each child has a book bag, to carry a book to and from school each day, and a 'contact book' for teachers and parents to communicate information about the child's reading. Reading is not formally taught and few children can read when they move to the reception class. A love of books and a familiarity with them are considered more important at this stage. A profile folder is kept on each child to record progress and take to the reception class. There are occasional outings to the theatre and an annual summer trip to Chapel Farm in Woking. Visitors to the nursery are frequent, including theatre and puppet groups, musicians, parents with particular skills and representatives from the fire, police and health services.

**Remarks** New, exciting facility providing high-quality nursery education. Well-resourced, constantly reviewed and carefully planned curriculum. Experienced, enthusiastic staff. Parents are treated as equal partners in their children's education. Teachers are approachable and friendly.

## COULSDON NURSERY SCHOOL

Linden Avenue
Coulsdon
Surrey CR5 3BT
**Tel:** (0737) 553860

**Owner:** London Borough of Croydon LEA
**Headteacher:** Madeleine Branch, Cert Ed
**Type:** Nursery school offering half-day sessions. No full-time places
**Children:** 3–4yrs. 32 places. 64 on register
**Hours:** Morning session 9am–11.30am
Afternoon session 12.45pm–3pm
Open 40 weeks a year
**Status:** State nursery school
**Number of years open:** 57
**Meals:** None
**1992 fees:** No fees. 50p per week voluntary contribution to School Fund
**Waiting list:** Long. 140 names
**Registered by:** London Borough of Croydon LEA

**Premises** A 1930s, purpose-built, brick nursery all on one level. The roof and windows lack attention and the building requires modernisation. There are three children's playrooms, office, staff room, kitchen and cloakrooms. Inside is well maintained and clean, with a room for water play, one for messy play, painting or cookery and a third for concentrating and quiet studies, such as number or language work, table-top games and puzzles and construction toys. Everywhere is gaily decorated, proudly displaying children's artwork and achievements. The nursery is situated in a quiet cul-de-sac, not far from the railway station and local bus routes. Parking is no problem. There is ample space for outdoor play, with both grass and hard surface and a rubberised safety surface under the climbing frames. Children have access to a covered sandpit, numerous pedal and sit-and-ride toys, prams, wooden planks and blocks for construction play and a garden for growing bulbs.

**Headteacher & staff** Madeleine Branch, Cert Ed, came to Coulsdon Nursery in 1991 from Chipstead Valley Primary where she had been reception co-ordinator for seven years. She is assisted by two full-time teachers, both Cert Ed, two NNEB nursery nurses, one full-time and one part-time, and a welfare assistant. All are in their 40s. Madeleine Branch describes them as 'a great bunch, totally brilliant. As a new girl they have given me total support.' The school also draws on the expertise of special needs teachers, speech therapists and early years advisers, when necessary. Students on practical training are accepted and are supervised. A clerical assistant is the official first-aider to the school. Staff attend frequent courses to extend and update their skills. Mrs Branch would welcome a male nursery worker. 'It's nice for children without dads to have a male around and it gives a more natural environment,' she says.

**Children & parents** Children come from the immediate catchment area and are a complete social mix, with approximately 15 per cent from ethnic minorities. Special needs pupils are welcome and totally integrated. Most children continue in the state sector. Parents are supportive and included in all nursery activities. They have open access to staff at any time, to discuss problems or concerns, usually at the beginning or end of a session. All written records, except medical notes, are available to parents. New children and families receive a home visit from their teacher and nursery nurse, and an introductory meeting takes place at the nursery soon after a child has started. There is no PTA, but parents attend meetings, help with outings and fund-raising and enter their names on a 'Skills Directory', if they feel they have a particular area of knowledge to share with the class.

**Curriculum & activities** Learning through play, with the focus on educational activities, both individually and in groups. The nursery aims to provide a firm foundation for Key Stage One of the National Curriculum. There is no formal teaching of the 3Rs, but language development is important and most children recognise their names when they leave. Staff enable rather than direct. Each week's activities are carefully planned in advance around a theme. At the end of the week, staff evaluate, in writing, what has been achieved, how children responded to the activities and where improvements could be made. Children are carefully observed at every session, and in depth twice a term. A programme is then developed to meet their individual needs. In certain curriculum areas, the most able children are already working at levels well ahead of their age group. There are plentiful supplies of educational equipment (annual budget £2700) and a rich diet of play tasks; art, craft, design technology, graphics, writing and drawing, music and movement and gardening all feature regularly. The day we visited, it was the boys' turn to bake cakes for the mid-session snack. Outings are frequent – to farms, shops, building sites, churches – anywhere that will stimulate ideas and aid discovery and investigation. Doctors, nurses, new mothers, police and fire officers visit as often as possible to fit in with current themes. There is also a pets' visiting day. Multicultural projects and topics are used whenever possible. Consideration for others and social skills are encouraged.

**Remarks** High-quality education for those children lucky enough to secure a place. Carefully planned and carried out curriculum, which is constantly improved and evaluated by very committed staff. The headteacher is campaigning hard for a computer and for work to be done on the building, which does need some modernisation.

## PURLEY NURSERY SCHOOL

58 Pampisford Road
Purley
Surrey CR8 2NE
**Tel:** (081) 660 5639

**Owner:** London Borough of Croydon LEA
**Headteacher:** Marion Smith, Cert Ed
**Type:** Nursery school offering half-day sessions. No full-time places
**Children:** 3–5yrs. 60 places. 115 on register
**Hours:** Morning session 9am–11.30am
Afternoon session 12.45pm–3.15pm
Open 39 weeks a year
**Status:** State nursery school
**Number of years open:** 46 (15 in present building)
**Meals:** Lunch
**1992 fees:** No fees
**Waiting list:** Horrendous. 300 names. Priority to medical/social referrals, siblings and children within catchment area. Names taken after child's 2nd birthday
**Registered by:** London Borough of Croydon LEA

**Premises** A bright, spacious, purpose-built nursery within easy reach of Purley station. The building is only 15 years old and in pristine condition. One large, open-plan room is sectioned off into activity areas for painting, water play, small world, home corner, maths/investigation, games, graphics, construction, malleable materials, sand, puzzles and books. There are cheerful curtains and either carpet or vinyl on the floor. Wonderful displays of children's work and a wide selection of toys, equipment and books are everywhere. The atmosphere is busy, energetic and friendly. The playground is enormous, safe and child-centred. There is a huge sandpit, climbing frame with safety surface, wooden playhouse, rabbit hutch, telephone box and a wild-flower garden, plus a wide selection of trikes, buckets and spades. Children can spend as much time outside as they like, weather permitting, and many nursery activities frequently overspill into the garden.

**Headteacher & staff** Marion Smith, Cert Ed, originally qualified as a primary school teacher, but after a nursery teaching course in 1981 changed to the younger age group. She says she is now 'totally hooked on nursery teaching'. She is conspicuously warm and caring towards the children, and through careful planning provides them with a varied curriculum to meet individual needs. Marion Smith has hand-picked the team of two teachers (B Ed and Cert Ed) and four NNEB nursery nurses. Her deputy, Andrew, provides the male presence that many of the children lack at home. Lunch is organised by three dinner supervisors. A number of outside specialists offer additional support, from special needs assistance and speech therapy to bilingual and ESL teaching. Probationary teachers and NNEB or BTEC students on work experience also supplement numbers and bring in added skills. Training plays a key role and courses on first aid, speech therapy and behavioural difficulties are organised regularly. Staff are dedicated and hard-working – a happy, interactive group.

**Children & parents** A varied social and cultural mix, from doctors and solicitors to unemployed single parents. Asian, Greek, West Indian, African and Spanish children attend, although the majority are English. Children with various social, emotional, physical and linguistic needs are welcome and are expertly cared for. Home visits are arranged before children begin, and there is daily communication with parents. Children are phased-in over several weeks and parents can stay as long as they are required. There are three parents on the board of governors, which meets quarterly. Each child has a keyworker who changes every half-term. This means that each child is the joint responsibility of the nursery team.

**Curriculum & activities** The nursery philosophy is closest to the teachings of Froebel, who believed in 'beginning where the learner is', and taking each child forward at his/her own pace. Well-designed play opportunities and appropriate equipment are set up to foster the development of the whole child, with particular emphasis on intellectual development. The nursery is organised as a school workshop. Activities are laid out on tables by staff and cover all aspects of investigative, physical, manipulative, creative and cognitive play. The staff observe and support children, but do not direct, enabling them to become independent learners. The curriculum is topic-based, multicultural and varied. Photographic and written records are kept on each child's social, emotional and intellectual development. Parents have full access to these. There is regular swimming, dance and movement and outings to the library, theatre, Godstone Farm and local shops. There are two libraries run by the nursery: toys and puzzles can be borrowed on Wednesdays and books on Fridays.

**Remarks** A pleasure to visit. Stimulating, carefully planned nursery, organised by experienced and qualified staff. The high calibre of teachers, including a male teacher as deputy, and well-designed activities in a workshop environment offer children exciting pre-school learning.

# Ealing

A borough with a strong commitment to under-5s and the fourth highest provider of nursery education in London. Ealing offers a part-time place to nearly 50 per cent of 3- and 4-year-olds, in 44 nursery classes attached to primary schools and six nursery schools. Provision is expanding, with six new classes opening this year. Parents are free to apply to any school, irrespective of their catchment area. Past budget cuts have resulted in the closure of three Social Services nursery centres, leaving four. This year, across-the-board savings must be made. There are also seven local authority day nurseries for children in need. Provision for under-2s is generally poor, and facilities are unevenly distributed across the borough. The Southall area has more nurseries; Ealing has long waiting lists. There are 18 private nurseries, many in Ealing itself, charging £7–£15 per day, over 100 playgroups and a strong team of registered childminders costing up to £85 per week in central Ealing.

**Further information**

For details on all forms of childcare, nursery education and The Daycare Directory, contact:
Under Eights Section
Perceval House
Uxbridge Road
London W5 2HL
Tel: (081) 758 5969

For details on nursery schools and classes:
Schools Admissions
Education Department
Civic Centre
14–16 Uxbridge Road
London W5 2HL
Tel: (081) 758 5430

# BUTTONS NURSERY SCHOOL

99 Oaklands Road
Hanwell
London W7 2DT
**Tel:** (071) 840 3355
**Owner:** Loukes Leisure Ltd
**Principal:** Jane Loukes, SRN, RMN
**Type:** Nursery school offering full- and part-time places and half-day sessions
**Children:** 2½–5yrs. 25 places. 51 on register
**Hours:** 9.30am–3pm
Morning session 9.30am–12.30pm
Afternoon session 1pm–3pm
Before 9.30am and after 3pm by prior arrangement
Open 38 weeks a year
**Status:** Private, fee-paying
**Number of years open:** 3
**Meals:** Snacks and juice
**1992 fees:** £454 per term for 5 mornings a week
£339 per term for 5 afternoons a week
**Waiting list:** 1 year for morning places.
Afternoon places available
**Registered by:** London Borough of Ealing SS

**Premises** Refurbished builder's yard and warehouse near Ealing Broadway, comprising spacious dance studio/gym, large classroom with cloakrooms and small fenced garden, with a rabbit and guinea pig.
**Owners, Manager & staff** The owners, Anthony Loukes, B Sc Oxon, the former deputy head of a comprehensive, and Jane Loukes, SRN, RMN, ex-actress and ballet teacher, built up a thriving fitness and exercise centre for adults and children with a crèche attached. Demand for the crèche facilities developed into parental pressure for a more permanent, full-time day nursery. The manager, Gail Ross, NNEB, works mornings only and her staff were all unqualified when we visited.
**Children & parents** Children and parents usually join the nursery after attending the Loukes' fitness and exercise classes. The majority are local, middle-class professional families. Others drive to Hanwell from Chiswick, Acton and Shepherd's Bush. Children transfer to state and private schools in the area, many to Notting Hill and Ealing High School and the popular Latymer Upper School. It is a close-knit community (lots of siblings), with parents and children frequently socialising outside nursery hours. Parents are actively involved and committed to the nursery's programme of physical activities. Termly parents' evenings are well attended.
**Curriculum & activities** The emphasis is on learning through physical activity and energy. The weekly programme is packed with specialist classes in gymnastics, swimming, dance and movement, Tumbletots, ballet, music and drama. Activities coaches and teachers are well qualified and the swimming programme is excellent – your child will be able to swim five metres at 4 years old. A qualified lifeguard is on duty during all swimming lessons. However, the classroom is sometimes crowded, is not very welcoming and lacks artistic inspiration. It is set up with an art corner, writing corner and play/construction corner – children choose their own activity. Anthony Loukes, a mathematician, takes computing and maths classes. Worksheets go home each day and children also take a book home daily. Weekly French lessons. No written educational programmes.
**Remarks** Attractive nursery for the very energetic child, with the emphasis on physical activity. No real philosophy behind the non-physical side of the school.

# EALING MONTESSORI SCHOOL

St Martin's Church Hall
Hale Gardens
London W3 8NG
**Tel:** (081) 992 4513
**Owner/Principal:** Parin Jaffer, Mont Dip
**Type:** Montessori nursery school offering full-time places for over-3s and half-day sessions
**Children:** 2½–7yrs. 36 places. 36 on register
**Hours:** 9am–3pm (3–7yr-olds)
Morning session 9am–12 noon
Open 38 weeks a year
**Status:** Private, fee-paying
**Number of years open:** 20
**Meals:** Packed lunches

**1992 fees:** £800 per term full-time
£450 per term for 5 morning sessions a week
£150 refundable deposit
**Waiting list:** Long. Early registration advisable
**Registered by:** London Borough of Ealing SS

**Waiting list:** Long. Early registration advisable
**Registered by:** London Borough of Ealing SS
**Under same ownership:** Happy Child French Montessori School, Welsh Chapel, London W5; Happy Child Day Nursery, The Grove, London W5

## HAPPY CHILD DAY NURSERY

Green Man Passage
off Bayham Road
Ealing
London W13 0TG
**Tel:** (081) 566 5515

**Owner:** Ashoob Cook, BA
**Principal:** Majella Dunn, BA
**Type:** Day nursery offering full- and part-time places and half-day sessions
**Children:** 1–5yrs. 35 places. 50 on register
**Hours:** 8am–6pm
Morning session 8am–1pm (inc. lunch)
Afternoon session 1pm–6pm
Open 52 weeks a year
**Status:** Private, fee-paying
**Number of years open:** 3
**Meals:** Breakfast, lunch, tea, snacks
**1992 fees:** £105 per week full-time – under 2½
£80 per week full-time – over 2½
£24 per day. £45 for 5 mornings. £40 for 5 afternoons

## WEST ACTON FIRST SCHOOL

Noel Road
Acton
London W3 0JL
**Tel:** (081) 992 3144

**Owner:** London Borough of Ealing LEA
**Principal:** Wendy Dixon
**Type:** Nursery class in state primary school offering half-day sessions. No full-time places
**Children:** 3–4½yrs (children move up to main school in Sept of year in which they are 5). 54 places. 54 on register
**Hours:** Morning session 9am–11.30am
Afternoon session 1pm–3.30pm
Open 38 weeks a year
**Status:** State nursery class
**Number of years open:** 56
**Meals:** Milk. Children bring their own snacks
**1992 fees:** No fees
**Waiting list:** 100 names. Priority as identified by SS
**Registered by:** London Borough of Ealing SS

# Enfield

Nursery care and education are not a priority in Enfield. The borough supports the government's belief that parents should be left to make their own arrangements for pre-school children. One active campaigner in the field told us that the situation is desperate and getting worse. 'There's no probability of supply meeting demand. Nursery classes are not actually closing, but there is often no cover for teachers, so classes are temporarily closed if a teacher is ill or on holiday.' 20 per cent of the borough's 18,000 pre-school children receive a part-time nursery place, putting Enfield in the bottom quarter of London's borough league table. There are no local authority day nurseries – it is left to the private sector to provide 800 childminders, charging between £55 and £75 per week, and nine private day nurseries, which cost up to £110 per week. There are three college workplace nurseries. The borough's 86 playgroups offer part-time sessions at £2.50–£5 per session. There are waiting lists for virtually all private facilities. Parents are advised to register early. Response to our questionnaire in this borough was very disappointing.

### Further information

For details of childcare provision and a directory of services for under-8s, contact one of the six local centres:
West Enfield Tel: (081) 366 6565 X15025 or X15070
East Enfield Tel: (081) 366 6565 X5921
Ponders End Tel: (081) 805 2733 X8001
Edmonton Tel: (081) 807 3000 X2514
Palmers Green Tel: (081) 886 6555 X2676
Southgate Tel (081) 882 8061 X147

Primary Education Admissions are at:
Civic Centre
Silver Street
Enfield EN1 3XQ
Tel: (081) 366 6565 X13209 or 13211

## CAROL JANE MONTESSORI NURSERY SCHOOL

The Lodge
80 The Ridgeway
Enfield
Middlesex EN2 8JF
**Tel:** (081) 364 4440

**Owner/Principal:** Carol-Jane Medcalf, NNEB, Mont Dip
**Type:** Day nursery offering full-time places only
**Children:** 2–5yrs. 24 places. 60 on register
**Hours:** 8am–6pm
Open 51 weeks a year
**Status:** Private, fee-paying
**Number of years open:** 2½
**Meals:** Breakfast, lunch, tea, snacks
**1992 fees:** £90 per week full-time
£18 per day
No charge for bank holidays or Christmas week

**Waiting list:** Long. Full till '95. Early registration advisable
**Registered by:** London Borough of Enfield SS

**Premises** A charming old cottage, nestling between Lavender Hill Garage and a quiet tree-lined street of up-market, detached houses. There is a driveway, a small car park and two gardens. From the outside, the building looks like a large dolls' house. Inside consists of two reasonable-sized children's rooms, cloakrooms and a new extension, housing the staff room and a spotless, modern kitchen. The two small, secure gardens include a nature pond and outdoor climbing frames set on safety bark. Children also have access to the owner's nearby family home and four-acre garden. Here they can ride on the nursery's Shetland pony, Goldie, use the outdoor swimming pool or simply let off steam. Swimming takes place on a one-to-one basis, with a member of staff qualified in life-saving.

**Owner/Principal & staff** Carol-Jane Medcalf, NNEB, Mont Dip, is only 22 but worked in a local authority nursery and set up a private nursery in North London for a colleague, before opening her own facility. Her staff of four full-time and two part-time nursery workers have been carefully chosen to complement each other's skills. All are qualified NNEB or Mont Dip. The team appear very young and newly qualified. They relate well to each other and the children and socialise regularly after work. There is also a part-time cook.

**Children & parents** Parents travel great distances to bring their children to the nursery, some from Southend, a journey of an hour and a half. They are principally professional and affluent – doctors, nurses, accountants – although a few admit that they struggle to pay the fees. The cultural mix is rich and interesting, including a fair representation of Asian and Greek families. Staff and parents are friends and socialise together outside the nursery.

**Curriculum & activities** Children are taught in mixed age groups, so that they learn from each other, and older children care for the younger ones. The curriculum follows Montessori principles, but the nursery is not a strict Montessori establishment. A reasonable amount of Montessori equipment is provided. The top priority is to develop each child's independence and confidence and to use his/her inquisitiveness as a starting point for learning. The older ones do more, with worksheets, which are either taken home or filed in individual workbooks. The timetable allows for free play in the mornings and afternoons and for individual work, guided by a teacher, on pre-reading, pre-writing and number skills. Younger children concentrate on practical experiences. Pre-reading skills are developed through the use of Montessori letter and word boxes. No reading schemes are used, but books are plentiful and always easily accessible to children. Dance, French, cookery, riding and outdoor physical play are also on the timetable and taught by the energetic staff team. No specialist teachers visit.

**Remarks** Quality care and pre-school education, based on Montessori principles. Hardworking, energetic, and very young team of trained nursery nurses and Montessori teachers. Close and equal relationship between staff, parents and children. Within six months of opening, the nursery was full and now has a two-year waiting list. Enquiries average five a day.

# Greenwich

The borough has publicly stated its commitment to under-5s provision, 'but as far as demand meeting supply goes – it doesn't', they told us. 'Our ideal of expansion will have to wait until the future, when we can increase expenditure.' The most drastic early years cuts took place three years ago, hitting playgroups particularly badly. Further cuts are probably unlikely, for the time being at least, in case Greenwich finds itself in breach of the Children Act. Social Services day nurseries provide about 300 full-time places, with a further 400 names on the waiting list. Private nurseries charge an average £85 per week. The majority of working parents rely on relatives, or registered childminders whose fees are between £45 and £65 per week. 38 per cent of the borough's 3- to 4-year-olds can hope to experience some nursery education, in either a nursery class or early reception classes. 'Our commitment has to be to rationalise what we have got. All we can do is co-ordinate resources better, without incurring extra costs,' the Education Department says. Of 19 questionnaires sent to nurseries in the borough, only two were returned.

### Further information

For details on day nurseries, childminders and playgroups:
Early Years Day Care Section
Department of Social Services
147 Powis Street
London SE18 6PY
Tel: (081) 854 8888 × 2773 (duty service 9am–11.30am)

For details on nursery and early reception classes:
Education Department
Riverside House
Woolwich High Street
London SE18 6DF
Tel: (081) 854 8888 × 8043 (admissions)

---

## LINGFIELD DAY NURSERY

37 Kidbrooke Grove
Blackheath
London SE3 0LJ
**Tel:** (081) 858 1388

**Owner:** Dawn Smith
**Manager:** Tina Taylor, NNEB
**Type:** Day nursery offering full-time places and half-day sessions (min 3 sessions a week)
**Children:** 2–5yrs. 15 places. 31 on register
**Hours:** 8.30am–6pm
Morning session 8.30am–1pm
Afternoon session 1.30pm–6pm
Open 50 weeks a year
**Status:** Private, fee-paying
**Number of years open:** 3
**Meals:** Breakfast, lunch, tea
**1992 fees:** £100 per week full-time
£12 per session
£22 per day

**Waiting list:** 26 names. Rapidly building up
**Registered by:** London Borough of Greenwich SS

**Premises** The ground floor of a large, detached, Edwardian house, with gardens front and back, in a quiet, wide, no-through road. Parking is easy and most children arrive by car. The nearest bus stop is a long walk away. Children have two playrooms – the Busy Room is divided into two areas for free play, construction work, a home corner and art and messy play, while the Quiet Room is used for reading, puzzles, letter and number work, and for rest periods. A nature table and lively displays of children's paintings and artwork are set up in the hall. The building is spacious, light and very attractive. Children can move freely from one area to another, giving an open-plan feel to the nursery. There is a beautiful, large walled garden behind the house, ideal for outdoor play, with a well-kept lawn and paved area. Plenty of outdoor equipment and a children's bird-watching hut, with one-way glass. Swings, slide, climbing frame, water-play area and seed-planting patch are available. A teddy bears' picnic is held each year in Greenwich Park, a 25-minute walk from the nursery.

**Owner, Manager & staff** Dawn Smith started Lingfield three years ago and her daughter was one of the first pupils. She has no childcare qualifications. 'I'm very much the planner, scheduling, working out themes, dealing with administration and generally in control of decisions,' she says. Tina Taylor, NNEB, is the manager. Experienced in nursery school class work and special needs, she is a gentle woman who puts children first. Her team consists of three female nursery nurses (two NNEB, one PPA). Tina Taylor says, 'They all have one thing in common; a genuine love of children.' There is no qualified nursery teacher on the staff. The team discuss problems and plan activities at regular monthly meetings. Regular workshops are organised through the local college, to keep staff up to date with new ideas and developments.

**Children & parents** The children come from families with professional fathers and working mothers and are generally attending for the pre-school nursery education rather than the full-time care. Children travel a considerable distance to the nursery and progress to many different schools in the maintained and private sectors. Children with special needs are accepted, provided the nursery is sure that it can provide the attention they need. A speech therapist and educational psychologist visit. Children are happy, relaxed and totally absorbed in their activities. Parents are welcome to visit the school, but are asked to give advance notice, so that time can be set aside without disrupting the daily programme. Book and music weeks are organised and parents are invited to come in and read or play music to the children. New children are phased-in, with a parent, during an induction week. Newsletters are sent out informing parents of current themes.

**Curriculum & activities** Learning through play. The nursery is in the process of introducing the High Scope method. Children choose their particular activities, plan them, carry them out individually or in small groups, and then meet together with staff to discuss their achievements. Staff facilitate and guide, but do not direct or intervene. The programme revolves around changing themes, which are planned in advance. Equipment is plentiful, of good quality and easily accessible for free choice. Pre-reading and pre-writing exercises are practised regularly. No reading scheme is followed, and generally children cannot read when they leave, but firm foundations have been laid. There is music and movement, nature, science, number awareness, pencil control and language development through drama and discussion. Stories are read every day. Praise rather than criticism is given whenever possible. Discipline is firm but gentle, and unacceptable behaviour dealt with through explanation and discussion. Exclusion from a group activity is the ultimate sanction. The keyworker system operates. Keyworkers record children's progress and development and discuss their reports with parents. Outings often relate to themes – children visit the park, farms, and museums. Guests are frequently 'people who help us' – a nurse, police officer, fire officer, milkman with his float. All visits are followed up by role play and discussion. Meals are prepared by the cook.

**Remarks** Comfortable, homely atmosphere in a small, friendly nursery. Unpressured, with numerous opportunities for free play and self-expression. Cuddles freely offered and enjoyed. Not for the highly competitive.

# Hackney

Hackney aims to provide a nursery place for every 3- or 4-year-old who wants one. However, resources are sorely overstretched and the short-term objective is to reduce the nursery school waiting list from 1000 names to 500. Currently, approximately 36 per cent of 3- and 4-year-olds receive nursery education. The Council also aspires to increase its day nursery provision. There are 11 Social Services run nurseries and 17 community nurseries, subsidised by the local authority, but run by the voluntary sector. The maximum fees are about £45 per week. Additional provision comes from seven private nurseries (fees £70–£75 per week) and 41 playgroups. Hackney has 2 borough-funded nursery schools and 49 primary schools with nursery classes.

**Further information**
For details on all types of daycare and nursery education:
Hackney Town Hall
Information Department
Mare Street
London E8 1EA
Tel: (081) 986 3123

For lists, publications and details of Hackney's One Stop Shop:
Director of Education
Edith Craven Buildings
Enfield Road
London N1 5AZ
Tel: (081) 214 8400

## BROADGATE NURSERY
27-31 Earl Street
London EC2 2AL
**Tel:** (071) 247 3491
**Owner:** Susan Hay Associates Ltd
**Principal:** Jacky Roberts, NNEB
**Type:** Day nursery offering full- and part-time places to working parents
**Children:** 3mths–5yrs. 50 places. 18 on register
**Hours:** 8am–6pm
Open 50 weeks a year
**Status:** Private, fee-paying
**Number of years open:** 2
**Meals:** Breakfast, lunch, tea and snacks
**1992 fees:** £758 per month full-time – under 2
£693 per month full-time – over 2
£175 per week full-time – under 2
£160 per week full-time – over 2
**Waiting list:** Waiting list for babies, but places available for 2–5yr-olds
**Registered by:** London Borough of Hackney SS
**Under same ownership/Management:**
Floral Place Nursery, Islington (see entry); Sainsbury's Workplace Nurseries in Alperton and Dulwich

## DEFOE DAY CARE CENTRE
c/o Hackney College
Ayrsome Road
London N16 0RH
**Tel:** (071) 249 6947
**Owner:** Hackney LEA
**Co-ordinator:** Gloria Collins, SEN
**Type:** Community nursery offering full-time places
**Children:** 3mths–5yrs. 26 places. 26 on register
**Hours:** 8.30am–5pm (for children under 2)
8.30am–5.30pm (for children over 2)
Open 50 weeks a year
**Status:** Community nursery, 8 places full fee-paying and 18 assisted places. Non profit-making
**Number of years open:** 17
**Meals:** Mid-morning snack, hot lunch and tea
**1992 fees:** £45 per week full-time
Assisted places assessed by income
**Waiting list:** 150 for assisted places. None for full fee-paying places
**Registered by:** London Borough of Hackney SS

**Premises** Under threat of closure since 1980, but thankfully still surviving, this nursery staggers on in a small Portakabin in the grounds of Hackney College. Erected 17 years ago, with a ten-year life span, the building sadly shows its age and is in serious need of refurbishment, if not replacement. Inside it is divided into a baby room (for up to six babies), two toddler rooms, a tiny office, a kitchen and cloakrooms. The enclosed outside play area has a recently purchased slide, climbing frame and two colourful sit-on animals with springs. There is a constant struggle to balance the books and secure funding or grants for new equipment.

**Co-ordinator & staff** Despite the physical neglect and equipment shortages, there is an overwhelmingly warm, happy and loving atmosphere, provided by outstanding staff. Gloria Collins, SEN, is in charge. She has been at the nursery for '12 happy years' and intends to stay – 'They will have to put me outside with the furniture.' Her relaxed, infectious humour and complete dedication to the children are shared by the rest of her multicultural team – five full-timers and two who job-share (all qualified NNEB, City & Guilds and PPA). There is also an administrator, a City Training Student and an outpost worker. The outpost worker, who works closely with the nursery, parents and the community, has just been made redundant – her final brief is to secure 'just one more grant'.

**Children & parents** The nursery needs eight full fee-paying places to survive. At the time of visiting, they had only three. The remaining places go to students or are subsidised by Hackney Council who assess according to parental income. There are 150 names on the waiting list for assessed places. Children are all from the local community, predominantly black British, but including a range of other ethnic backgrounds. Many come from single-parent households. Parents are not always as supportive as staff would like but the children are bright, happy and busy.

**Curriculum & activities** Learning through play. The children choose a variety of different activities in a relaxed but focused way. Much of the work is practical and investigative, with a strong multicultural approach. The babies and toddlers get together on a daily basis to play with paint, water and construction toys. The older children use exercise books and worksheets every afternoon for pre-school work or numbers and letters. Reading books are taken home three times a week. Children's progress is discussed every three to six months and written records kept. Monthly outings are undertaken when funds allow and parents can be persuaded to help.

**Remarks** A lifeline for the local community. Outstanding, loving staff who will fight to the bitter end to keep this nursery open. Sadly, it becomes harder and harder each year.

# INDEPENDENT DAY NURSERY

Units 26/27 Independent Place
76 Shacklewell Lane
London E8 2HD
**Tel:** (071) 275 9499

**Owner:** Lilliput Ltd
**Company Directors:** Helen Jameson, MA (Cantab), ACA, Madeline Watson, M Ed, MIPM
**Manager:** Louise Hodgson, NNEB
**Type:** Day nursery offering full- and part-time places and half-day sessions. Some company places
**Children:** 6mths–5yrs. 30 places (inc 12 for under-2s). 18 on register
**Hours:** 8am–6.15pm
Morning session 8am–1pm
Afternoon session 1.30pm–6.15pm
Open approx 50 weeks a year
**Status:** Private, fee-paying
**Number of years open:** 2
**Meals:** Breakfast, lunch, tea, snacks
**1992 fees:** £148 per week full-time – under 2
£125 per week full-time – 2–3yrs
£95 per week full-time – over 3
**Waiting list:** Waiting list for under-2s. Places available for 2–5yr-olds
**Registered by:** London Borough of Hackney SS

# RAINBOW NURSERY I & II

Yorkshire Grove Estate
Nevill Road
Stoke Newington
London N16 8SP
**Tel:** (071) 254 7930

**Owner:** Rainbow Management Committee
**Head of staff:** Safirah Badat, NNEB, PQS
**Type:** Community nursery (Rainbow I)
Private day nursery (Rainbow II)
Both day nurseries offering full-time places and half-day sessions
**Children:** 2–5yrs. 35 places. 30 on register
**Hours:** 8am–5.30pm
Flexible half-day sessions available at Rainbow II
Open 50 weeks a year
**Status:** Private, fee-paying, non profit-making
**Number of years open:** 20 (Rainbow I)
2 (Rainbow II)
**Meals:** Lunch, tea, snacks
**1992 fees:** Rainbow I: £50 per week full-time (14 assisted places)
Rainbow II: £90 per week full-time
Refundable deposit
**Waiting list:** Rainbow I: long–1 year
Rainbow II: none yet
**Registered by:** London Borough of Hackney SS

**Premises** For a Portakabin nursery, this is surprisingly light, bright, warm and cosy, belying its age and contradicting all the normal prejudices against Portakabins. High railings protect the nursery and small play area at the back, in an attempt to keep out local vandals. There are two Rainbow nurseries. Rainbow I is a well-established, much needed community nursery. Spacious and well planned, it comprises one large children's area, three small classrooms, a kitchen, an office and cloakrooms. Rainbow II is a recent extension, into what used to be the car park. Built with help from local businesses, including the Midland Bank, it consists of one large children's room, a staff room and toilets. The two nurseries tend to operate as one and share facilities. The atmosphere is homely and stimulating – walls are plastered with creative artwork, language work, notices, programmes and information.
**Head of staff & staff** The head of staff, Safirah Badat, NNEB, PQS, inspires confidence. Warm and thoughtful, she has been in charge for the past five years. Although heavily pregnant when we met, she intends to return to work after maternity leave. 'I was very domesticated as a child and always wanted to work with under-5s,' she says. Her deputy, Rita Kirwin, SRN, has worked at Rainbow for ten years. The rest of the team, many of them long-established nursery workers, is made up of four qualified full-timers (two NNEBs and two currently being recruited) and three part-timers (one a qualified teacher, two unqualified but experienced). There is also a cheerful, highly organised administrative secretary who has been in the post since the very beginning. Staff reflect the community they come from and serve – their cultural backgrounds include Afro-Caribbean, Asian, Burmese, Greek and English.
**Children & parents** Rainbow I was founded in 1973 by the Afro-West Indian Women's Group, a group of black women who came together in the Stoke Newington area to organise and do something positive about the poor childcare provision in Hackney. With financial sponsorship from Save the Children Fund and Hackney Council, Rainbow Community Nursery was established. The nursery has strong roots in Hackney's Afro-Caribbean community, but is refreshingly cosmopolitan – a place where children from all backgrounds and cultures are welcomed to learn and play together. African, West Indian, Asian, Turkish and English children, all of whom live locally, make up this genuinely multicultural nursery. Parental support and interest are considered crucial and parents are expected to play a substantial part in running the nursery. The constitution requires at least five of the eight-person management committee to be parents of children currently attending the nursery. The entire committee, which meets monthly, comprises unpaid volunteers elected by parents and staff, past and present. Parents are also expected to help with fund-raising activities, as Hackney Council's grant only covers staff salaries and basic amenities. There are endless parties and events. Safirah Badat explains, 'We celebrate anything and everything and use food as our way of drawing people in.' Children all move on to the local state primary schools in the area.
**Curriculum & activities** Both nurseries combine free play with more structured, educational programmes. Each day begins and

ends with free play in the main playrooms. Different equipment is put out in rotation to avoid boredom. Group time follows and a chance to share stories, news, songs and music. For more structured work time, children divide into small groups according to age and move into their individual classrooms. Each nursery nurse organises her own group's work, according to a pre-planned theme, or the children's individual needs. All children have their own number and writing book and a folder for worksheets. Reading schemes are used, including Ladybird, and are taken home. Written developmental records are updated every six months. Parents have access to children's records and work. Time is also set aside for outdoor play, music and movement, keep fit, library visits, cookery and outings. The nursery has a wide variety of books, with stories from a range of cultures, some written in more than one language. Children are read a story every morning as part of their introduction to the new day. There are also strong artistic and craft programmes. Children with speech, hearing or other difficulties are catered for with the help of qualified staff and experts provided by Social Services. There is a firm policy for dealing with bullying or disruptive behaviour, but absolutely no corporal punishment.

**Remarks** A lifeline to the local community, as the very long waiting list testifies. A community-based nursery which caters for the social and educational needs of local children from all backgrounds and cultures. Long-serving, dedicated staff and supportive parents. Rainbow I and II are shining examples of high-quality nursery care and education at an affordable price. However, the future is uncertain, as Rainbow's grant from Hackney Council may well be threatened.

# WENTWORTH NURSERY SCHOOL

Cassland Road
Hackney
London E9 7BY
**Tel:** (081) 985 3491

**Owner:** London Borough of Hackney LEA
**Headteacher:** Carolyn Maples, BA, PGCE

**Type:** State nursery school offering full- and part-time places and half-day sessions
**Children:** 3–4yrs 11mths. 60 places. 90 on register
**Hours:** 9.15am–3.15pm
Morning session 9.15am–11.30am
Afternoon session 1pm–3.15pm
Open 38 weeks a year
**Status:** State nursery school
**Number of years open:** Approx 32
**Meals:** Lunch
**1992 fees:** No fees. £3.50 per week for lunch
**Waiting list:** Varies year to year
**Registered by:** London Borough of Hackney LEA

**Premises** Unusual, rather noisy setting for a state nursery school. Directly fronting a main road, on the ground floor of an ancient, four-storey, red-brick block of council flats. Once the old laundry rooms, ILEA converted it to a nursery over 30 years ago and doubled its size in the '60s. Light and cheerful, with windows everywhere, the nursery is huge. Bright blue paintwork and every square inch of wall covered with innovative children's work. There are two main nursery areas – the Yellow Room and the Red Room, with kitchen, staff room, staff kitchen, office and cloakrooms leading off them. The Yellow Room is home to a book and computer corner, home corner, graphics area and problem-solving section. The Red Room plays host to messy, arty, water, tactile and technical (junk building) activities. Access to the spacious outside area is directly from the Red Room. This is one of the best-equipped outdoor play areas we have visited, with six climbing frames, slide, enormous sandpit, trikes and push-and-pull toys.

**Headteacher & staff** Carolyn Maples, BA, PGCE, is experienced, motivated and well qualified. A local authority teacher, she retrained for nursery work – 'the best decision of my life. It's very satisfying work because you know the goals you are striving for.' She organises her 90 children and 13 staff with precision. Each member of staff is responsible for different activities at different times in the various rooms. All eight full-time staff are qualified – three are teachers (B Ed and Cert Ed) and five nursery nurses (NNEB). Part-time staff include an assistant, two special needs attendants (allocated two children), kitchen assistant and secretary. The quality, quantity and experience of staff are outstanding.

**Children & parents** Children join in the term of their 3rd birthday. There is a maximum of 60 children at any one time, divided into four groups, each with its own teacher and nursery worker. Each child also has his/her own key-worker. Children spend five terms at Wentworth, usually coming part-time for the first three or four terms, then full-time for one or two terms before moving on to an infant class. Most go on to local primary schools in Hackney, Tower Hamlets or Islington and a few go to church schools. The children are a wonderful mix of cultures and social backgrounds – Nigerian, Turkish, Vietnamese, Chinese, Ghanaian. The nursery accurately reflects the local community, which is mainly African, Asian and European. Parents put their child's name down for a place when the child is 2 years old. A decision is taken about two months before entry. Most children in Hackney will be offered a nursery place somewhere in the borough, but not necessarily at Wentworth, which is extremely popular. Most children live very close by and priority is given to those with identified special needs – eg language development. Home visits (keyworkers and one other member of staff) are done before a place is taken up. Parents are warmly welcomed at all times. There are regular coffee mornings and three parents' evenings a year. Future plans include a separate parents' room.

**Curriculum & activities** Everything is impressively organised and planned well in advance. Learning is through carefully monitored play. Staff take it in turns to be responsible for an area of the curriculum for a week at a time – this could involve preparing and laying out the graphic and number work areas, or the messy-play and art/craft areas or the library and book corner. One teacher will do nothing but read stories for a week. Each child spends time in both the Red and Yellow Rooms every day, where the child, not the teacher, chooses the activity. Activities are done everywhere throughout the building, inside and out, with constant encouragement and participation by staff. Half an hour before each session ends, children wind down with stories, songs and rhymes. Detailed monitoring of each child and written records of every type are kept. An Initial Observation Form, filled in with parents when a child starts, begins the process. There are ongoing Records of Achievement, covering all areas of language, social and physical development, technology, science and the humanities, done in the second, fourth and fifth terms. Staff also have notebooks in which they record exactly what their key children have done each session. The headteacher then transcribes these into each child's file. No child is allowed to concentrate on one activity only. Language development is central to nursery activities and a commitment to equal opportunities underpins all the work.

**Remarks** Busy, crowded and very stimulating. Some parents might prefer a quieter, less frenetic environment. The quality of staff is outstanding; premises, equipment and organisation faultless. State provision of this standard is hard to beat.

# Hammersmith & Fulham

It is Council policy that every 3- to 5-year-old in the borough will have a place in a nursery school or class by the year 2000. This means that over 2000 places must be created. New classes are opening every year, including five this year, funded from reserves. In order to avoid closing any of the eight Social Services day nurseries, but still meet tough financial targets, full- and part-time places are to be offered for sale on the open market. Initially there will be 30 'private' places, rising to 60 and distributed across the borough's eight nurseries. Costs will almost match the private sector at about £100–£120 per week for a full-time place. The workplace nursery for Council employees closed earlier this year, in order to save money. There are 300 registered childminders and a thriving private sector charging up to £150 per week.

**Further information**

For details on day nurseries, childminders and playgroups:
Under Eight Unit
Department of Social Services
164 King Street
London W6 9EJ
Tel: (081) 748 3020 × 5191/2/3 or 5155

For local authority nursery schools and classes:
Education Department
Banda House
Cambridge Grove
London W6 9JU
Tel: (081) 748 3020 (calls welcome from 2pm–4.30pm weekdays)

## BUSY BEE NURSERY SCHOOL

Addison Boys' Club
Redan Street
London W14 0AB
**Tel:** (071) 602 8905

**Owner/Principal:** Armine Pearson, Mont Dip, Primary Dip
**Type:** Nursery school offering morning sessions
**Children:** 2½–5yrs. 40 places. 37 on register
**Hours:** 9.15am–12.30pm
Open 36 weeks a year
**Status:** Private, fee-paying
**Number of years open:** 9 (5 under current ownership)
**Meals:** Biscuits and water
**1992 fees:** £425 per term for 5 mornings a week
£30 registration fee, plus £100 refundable deposit
**Waiting list:** Long. Automatic entry to siblings. Priority to children in area. Early registration advisable
**Registered by:** London Borough of Hammersmith & Fulham SS

**Premises** A converted church, currently owned and used by Addison Boys' Club. The nursery school has the use of two halls each weekday morning during term-time. The premises are warm but shabby and in need of re-painting and brightening up. The two halls are used for different age groups and provide ample space but lack natural light. Children's work is displayed on the walls, showing an impressive range of art and craft activities. There is an additional room for storytelling and quiet activities. Although rather tired and musty smelling, it is cosy and furnished with comfortable chairs. Situated in a quiet residential neighbourhood between Shepherds Bush and Hammersmith. No outside play area – children are occasionally taken to Brook Green, and an area of the larger hall is permanently cordoned off for boisterous playtime.

**Principal & staff** Armine Pearson, Mont Dip, Primary Dip, owns and teaches full-time at Busy Bee. An experienced primary school teacher, when she took over the nursery five years ago it was a Montessori school. She has gradually phased-out the Montessori teaching method as she felt it did not offer enough opportunity for play, although some Montessori equipment is still used. The nursery now follows Armine's own educational programmes. Her staff comprise five nursery teachers and two assistants. They have a variety of different qualifications including Mont Dip, NNEB and Occupational Therapy. Their different talents and strengths are reflected in the way the nursery is organised and in the balance between education and care. Staff interact well with children – all appeared warm, caring and cheerful. The staff/child ratio is 1:6. Students from Hammersmith College Day Care Diploma Course and some student teachers come on regular placement.

**Children & parents** Mainly local, from the middle-class residential streets in Brook Green, Hammersmith, Shepherds Bush, and around Olympia. The majority move on to local private schools. The large multicultural communities in these areas are not represented at the nursery. Children generally join the term in which they are 3. The small hall houses sixteen 3- to 3½-year-olds, and the larger hall takes twenty-four 3½–5-year-olds. Children are independent and extrovert and relate well to their teachers and each other. They call teachers by their first names, but are polite and respectful. Children with speech difficulties or dyslexia are especially welcome and are given particular individual attention. New parents and children are invited to a morning session prior to the child's first term. Once a child starts officially, parents can stay for the first two mornings only. Each member of staff is keyworker to six children. Parents can approach their keyworker whenever necessary to discuss any day-to-day problems. There is a parents' open morning to meet teachers once a year, and concerts twice a year. The principal is available to talk to parents by appointment.

**Curriculum & activities** Armine Pearson, a positive and lively woman, has developed her own educational programmes emphasising the importance of acquiring social skills first, gradually followed by reading, writing and arithmetic, but only when each child is ready and at their own pace. She uses many of her own worksheets and number and reading materials. The Letterland reading scheme is followed to introduce children to the phonic sounds of the alphabet. The Montessori sandpaper alphabet, One, Two, Three and Away, The New Way and Ginn 350 reading schemes are also favoured. Armine has created an interesting series of number mats to help children with their counting and number recognition. The floor mats are used rather like a game of hopscotch, with the children jumping from one to another and calling out the numbers as they land on a mat. By the time children leave at rising-5, they have a good basic knowledge of the 3Rs. Apart from worktime each session, there are art and craft lessons, with painting available at all times. Regular free-play activities include sand and water play, dressing up, a good range of play equipment and a large selection of books, including multicultural stories and pictures. Music is very important, with dance, movement and singing every day and drama once a week. Library visits take place three times a term. Sewing, gym, project work, storytelling sessions and occasional yoga are also fitted into the crowded timetable. There are no rewards and no punishments. Staff are loving but firm and discipline problems are non-existent. Three outings a year to places of interest like the zoo. Fees include a blue and white checked Busy Bee smock for all children. Staff monitor their six key children on a daily basis and meet twice a term to discuss each child's progress in detail. Written reports are kept on every child, for the use of teachers only.

**Remarks** A solid morning nursery, with impressive educational programmes, especially for the older children. Good balance between education and play, well supervised by patient, caring and qualified staff. Dull, disappointing premises, in need of decoration and lacking any outside play area. However, the overall atmosphere is friendly, warm and cheerful.

## L'ÉCOLE DES PETITS

2 Hazlebury Road
London SW6 2NB
**Tel:** (071) 371 8350

**Owner/Headmistress:** Mirella Otten, CAP (Certificat d'Aptitude Pédagogique – France)
**Type:** Pre-primary bilingual nursery school offering full- and part-time places, and half-day sessions for 2½–3½yr-olds
**Children:** 2½–6½yrs. 120 places. 120 on register
**Hours:** 9am–3.30pm Mon, Tues, Thurs, Fri
9am–12 noon Wed

Morning session 9am–12 noon (2½–3½yrs)
Open 35 weeks a year
**Status:** Private, fee-paying
**Number of years open:** 17 (2 at present address)
**Meals:** Lunch and snacks
**1992 fees:** £855 per term full-time – under 4yrs
£795 per term full-time – 4–6½yrs
£520 per five mornings – under 3½yrs
£20 registration fee, plus £500 refundable deposit
£28 for ballet
£100 for school bus
**Waiting list:** Long. Early registration advisable
**Registered by:** London Borough of Hammersmith & Fulham SS

# PUFFINS

60 Hugon Road
London SW6 3EN
**Tel:** (071) 736 7442

**Owner/Principal:** Fiona Talbot-Smith, Mont Dip
**Type:** Nursery school offering half-day sessions. No full-time places
**Children:** 3–5yrs. 20 places. 30 on register
**Hours:** Morning session 8.30am–12.30pm – older children
Afternoon session 1.30pm–4pm (3 days only) – younger children
Open 36 weeks a year
**Status:** Private, fee-paying
**Number of years open:** 9
**Meals:** None
**1992 fees:** £540 per term for 5 morning sessions a week
£325 per term for 3 afternoon sessions a week
£25 registration fee
**Waiting list:** Approx 18mths
**Registered by:** London Borough of Hammersmith & Fulham SS

**Premises** Puffins is discreetly hidden on the ground floor of a small Fulham house, in a quiet residential street. The owner, Fiona Talbot-Smith, lives in the corner house next door and has joined the two beautifully tended back gardens together, providing a large, peaceful, leafy area for the children. South Park is immediately adjacent. When the children step out of the nursery into the garden, they could almost be in the country. The nursery itself is homely, cosy, bright and spacious. Open shelving is crammed with exceptionally well-kept equipment and books. Parking is carefully monitored and parents and children are encouraged to walk – morning arrival times are staggered to avoid congestion in the street.

**Owner/Principal & staff** Fiona Talbot-Smith, who teaches full-time at the school, has a Montessori Diploma by correspondence and 19 years' teaching experience. She has a strong personality and very clear ideas about what she is trying to achieve – definitely someone who has the last word on everything. Her three staff (all qualified Montessori teachers) have been chosen for their 'common sense, warmth and love of children'. The New Zealander in the team also lives on the premises and doubles as nanny to one of Fiona's own children. Part-time staff include a tennis teacher who does ball skills with the children next door in South Park, a music and movement teacher and a ballet teacher. Only two staff have left since the nursery opened nine years ago. Staff get on extremely well together and often socialise outside school hours.

**Children & parents** The majority of children are local, mainly from the Peterborough Estate – a well-heeled, middle-class area. Most start at Puffins when they are 3 years old, although siblings may start slightly earlier. There is no real social or racial mix, but children with special needs are welcome. The aim of the nursery is to 'produce a happy, well-balanced child, ready in all respects to take the next step up the educational ladder'. All the children wear pinnies to protect their clothes and as a safety measure (easy to identify them when they are out). Parents come to the nursery by word of mouth and personal recommendation. All are professionals, with the mothers mainly housewives or part-time workers. The nursery has an open-door policy, and parents are encouraged to come in and talk about their children at any time. Prospective parents are shown round during ballet and music. There are no parents' evenings, as Fiona Talbot-Smith believes 'each child and family is different, and nothing can be achieved by talking to them as a group'. Children move on to private prep schools in the area.

**Curriculum & activities** Children are not accepted until they are 3 and then only for three afternoons a week to begin with. Afternoon children are moved up to the mornings when they can sit and concentrate for at least 20 minutes. The three afternoon sessions per week are more relaxed and flexible than the five mornings. Although all the teachers are Montessori trained, this is not a Montessori nursery in the true sense. There is definite teacher guidance in the choice of work and activities, and work is done mainly in groups at the table. At each session, 90 minutes is set aside for number, letter and topic work. Children are split into four groups by age, with a teacher. Each group rotates on a daily basis, so the children cover the same topics over a week. The Ginn reading scheme is used, and Scottish Primary Maths workbooks and sheets for maths. We observed the eldest group in the morning doing advanced news and writing work. The children were obviously enjoying their work and the atmosphere was calm and stress-free. A striking feature is the prime condition of all the books and equipment. The children obviously take pride in their school and tidying up is done with care and patience. Time is set aside to watch *Playbus* on television each morning, and all the children visit South Park daily. There is a Sports Day attended by parents each summer, and two plays a year (the Nativity play is written by their local homebeat police officer).

**Remarks** A small, cosy, family nursery school, catering very much for the immediate local community. Relaxed, happy, unpressured.

## QUEENSMILL NURSERY LTD

344 Fulham Palace Road
London SW6 6HT
**Tel:** (071) 381 2409

**Owner/Principal:** Hilary Allen, NNEB
**Type:** Day nursery offering full-time places only
**Children:** 3mths–5yrs. 26 places. 28 on register
**Hours:** 8am–6pm
Open 51 weeks a year
**Status:** Private, fee-paying
**Number of years open:** 7
**Meals:** Breakfast, lunch, tea
**1992 fees:** £30–£35 per day depending on number of days attended
**Waiting list:** Long. Early registration advisable
**Registered by:** London Borough of Hammersmith & Fulham SS

## ROSE MONTESSORI SCHOOL

St Albans Church Hall
Margravine Road
London W6
**Tel:** (071) 381 6002

**Owner/Headmistress:** Kate Gould, Mont Dip
**Type:** Montessori nursery school, offering half-day sessions. No full-time places
**Children:** 2½–5yrs. 24 places morning session, 14 places afternoon session. 38 on register

**Hours:** Morning session 9am–12.15pm
Afternoon session 1pm–3.30pm (except Fri)
Open 39 weeks a year
**Status:** Private, fee-paying
**Number of years open:** 9
**Meals:** Juice and biscuits
**1992 fees:** £450 per term for 5 morning sessions a week
£350 per term for 4 afternoon sessions a week
£15 registration fee
**Waiting list:** 3yrs for morning places. Afternoon places available
**Registered by:** London Borough of Hammersmith & Fulham SS

**Premises** On the first floor of St Alban's Church Hall, in the heart of Fulham, just off Fulham Palace Road, close to Charing Cross Hospital, the nursery is a vast, octagonal, high-ceilinged space. Incredibly light and well organised, yet warm and homely despite its size. Redecoration is needed, but the church is short of funds. Out of sheer desperation, headmistress Kate Gould has painted some of the windows herself and is now paving and turfing the small front area.

**Headmistress & staff** Kate Gould, Mont Dip, started as a teacher at Rose Montessori and within a year had bought the school and taken it over. In her mid-20s, she projects a mature, professional image and is committed to her work. Her two teachers, one full-time, one part-time, are both Montessori qualified. Kate Gould lectures at the London Montessori Centre once a week and has students from the Centre at the nursery on a regular basis. Staff appear confident, competent and mature. They relate well to the children and to each other, although they prefer not to socialise outside work. A specialist French teacher comes in twice a week and a male pianist also visits twice a week for music and movement.

**Children & parents** There are mixed age groups (from 2½-year-olds to 5-year-olds) in both morning and afternoon sessions. The children are almost one hundred per cent English, predominantly local and with large numbers of siblings. Children are close friends outside school. The parents are middle-class, nanny-employing professionals. Families in this area are larger than average (three or four children is common), filling up the large houses around Bishops Park. Most children go on to private education, although Bousfield and All Saints state primaries are also popular.

**Curriculum & activities** About 80 per cent Montessori, 20 per cent undirected, creative play, with a home corner, messy play, art and craft. Morning and afternoon sessions follow the same pattern, although French is done in the mornings only and the afternoon sessions are shorter. A session begins with 75 minutes of work. Children go to one of the three separate areas set out with Montessori equipment – practical life, numbers and letters – and choose an exercise to do, with teacher guidance. Each child is given a folder, with a number and a word book, and work is done in these each day. Standard Montessori equipment is used throughout – sandpaper letters, numerical rods, sound and word boxes, etc. The New Way reading scheme is followed and children are encouraged to be reading by the time they leave. Each teacher is keyworker to a group of children, whom she monitors regularly until they leave. Juice and biscuits follow work time, and the lights are dimmed to create a quiet atmosphere. Next, after a mass visit to the loos, they split into two groups for storytime. The remainder of the session is devoted to free creative play – painting, play dough, construction toys, art and craft. There is a Christmas play and summer concert. Written records or reports are frowned on and considered misleading. The ideal is to maintain constant supervision and observation of the children and continuous contact with parents.

**Remarks** A happy, well-equipped, smoothly run Montessori school, which deserves the strong reputation it enjoys in the area.

## SHEPHERD'S BUSH DAY NURSERY & ANNEXE

101 Frithville Gardens
London W12 7JQ
**Tel:** (081) 749 1256
(081) 749 1255

**Owner:** Bringing up Baby Ltd
**Principal:** Emma Harvey, NNEB, RSH (Norland), Mont Dip
**Head of Baby Unit:** Anne Wilkinson, NNEB
**Type:** Day nursery offering full- and part-time places
**Children:** 6mths–5yrs. 35 places. 45 on register
**Hours:** 8.15am–6.15pm
Open 50 weeks a year

**Status:** Private, fee-paying
**Number of years open:** 4
**Meals:** Breakfast, lunch, tea, snacks
**1992 fees:** £142 per week full-time – under 18mths
£135 per week full-time – over 18mths
£34 per day – under 18mths
£32 per day – over 18mths
£150–£200 refundable deposit
**Waiting list:** Reasonable. Early registration advisable
**Registered by:** London Borough of Hammersmith & Fulham SS
**Under same ownership:** Camden Day Nursery, Camden; The Park Nursery School, Battersea (see listing 5)

# SINCLAIR NURSERY SCHOOL

Garden Flat
142 Sinclair Road
London W14 0NL
**Tel:** (071) 602 3745

**Owner:** Sinclair Nursery School Trust
**Principal:** Cathy Burnaby-Atkins, Mont Dip
**Type:** Montessori nursery school offering half-day sessions. Full-time places available Wed and Thurs
**Children:** 2½–5yrs. 16 places morning session (for older children). 12 places afternoon session. 28 on register
**Hours:** 9.15am–4.15pm Wed, Thurs
Morning session 9.15am–12.15pm Mon–Fri
Afternoon session 2pm–4pm Mon–Thurs
Open 36 weeks a year
**Status:** Fee-paying registered charity
**Number of years open:** 10
**Meals:** Milk and biscuits. Packed lunches
**1992 fees:** £475 per term for 5 morning sessions a week
£315 per term for 4 afternoon sessions a week
£90 extra per term for full days
£175 refundable deposit
£20 registration fee
**Waiting list:** Variable, but healthy. Full for next 12 months
**Registered by:** London Borough of Hammersmith & Fulham SS

**Premises** Discreetly hidden below-stairs in the lower ground floor of a very ordinary suburban house, sub-divided into flats. From the outside, the only sign of child life is the artwork on the windows. Indoors, there are just two children's rooms with cloakrooms, loos and a small office sandwiched between them. Huge windows lighten this semi-basement area. The back room leads on to a small London-style patio garden, all concrete but safely enclosed.
**Owner/Principal & staff** The nursery is owned by the Sinclair Nursery School Trust, a charity administered by trustees, elected by the parents from among their number. The principal, Cathy Burnaby-Atkins, Mont Dip, joined Sinclair after a seven-year commitment to Dr Rolfe's, another established Montessori nursery in the area. Cathy is a strong admirer of Dr Maria Montessori and applies her teaching methods and philosophy to everything she does. 'I am a good old-fashioned Montessori teacher, with very high standards.' She describes herself as 'very stubborn and bolshy', yet strikes the visitor as caring and warm-hearted, with total dedication to her work. There is one other full-time qualified Montessori teacher, who works closely with Cathy. One Montessori student at a time is accepted from St Nicholas or the London Montessori Centre to train at the nursery.
**Children & parents** The children live locally, many within walking distance. Parental involvement is very important and treated as essential since any parent is a potential trustee. Many parents become personal friends and some are even related – Cathy's sister sends her child to the nursery. Nannies and au pairs are regular employees of the predominantly professional, middle-class parents. Mainly British, but some French, Swedish and Nigerian families. Children move on to a mix of state and private schools in the area. The parents are active in many aspects of the school – parents' evenings, concerts and plays and serious fund-raising to help with equipment and running costs.
**Curriculum & activities** The school is run on three basic principles. Each child is an individual and is encouraged to develop at his/her own pace. Discipline is friendly and understanding, promoting respect and kindness to one another. The routine is flexible, leaving room for spontaneity. Although a devotee of Montessori teaching, Cathy Burnaby-Atkins incorporates imaginative play and worksheets into the programme, in the belief that Maria Montessori would have understood the need to adapt to modern times. Each session, children are divided into two classes according to age.

Cathy takes the older group in the back room, and her co-teacher, Sally, is with the younger ones in the front room. Children begin a session with at least 1–1½ hours of worktime. They choose work from the shelves of Montessori equipment, or from the smattering of puzzles, construction games and worksheets. During this time, each child receives individual attention from their teacher. They go over letters, numbers, pre-reading and pre-writing work, all done on worksheets or in news and number books. Letters and words go home in Montessori boxes together with books for further work and consolidation. Art is a strong feature, with regular music, singing and movement. Afternoons are more relaxed, as there are fewer children and they are younger. The work is simpler, mainly using practical life exercises and concentrating on handwriting skills. Children learn to play together, share toys and develop artistic and manipulative skills. There are weekly projects for everyone, covering varied topics including numbers, colours, letters, shapes and current affairs. The garden is used whenever possible and includes a small growing area where children have their own plants. Outings take place once or twice a term to local places of interest. There is also a Christmas Nativity play and a summer concert.

**Remarks** Small traditional Montessori nursery with a secure family atmosphere. Very close relationships between children, teachers and parents. As trustees and active fundraisers, parents are a driving force. Not necessarily lively or busy enough for all tastes, but nevertheless a happy, stimulating nursery.

# STUDIO DAY NURSERY

93 Moore Park Road
Fulham
London SW6 2DA
**Tel:** (071) 736 9256

**Owner/Principal:** Jennifer Williams, NNEB (Norland)
**Type:** Montessori day nursery offering full- and part-time places and half-day sessions
**Children:** 2–5yrs. 30 places. 50 on register
**Hours:** 8am–7pm Mon–Thurs
8am–6.30pm Fri
Morning session 8am–12 noon
Afternoon session 12 noon–7pm, flexible
Open 50 weeks a year
**Status:** Private, fee-paying
**Number of years open:** 6
**Meals:** Breakfast, lunch and tea
**1992 fees:** £119.50 per week full-time
£24.90 per day
£12 per session
£4.50 per week or 90p per day for lunch
**Waiting list:** Deliberately short to avoid disappointment. Morning sessions always oversubscribed
**Registered by:** London Borough of Hammersmith & Fulham SS

**Premises** Initial disquiet at the unprepossessing and rather shabby exterior is immediately lifted when you get inside. A long, white, tiled entrance hall with colourful collages leads through a glass-roofed central area, now used as a messy-play and art room (it used to be a small garden), into the main ground-floor classroom. The building is a converted house and photographer's studio in the heart of Fulham. It is full of light, with white walls and primary colours, and children's work well displayed. A striking royal blue carpet is so eye-catching (and clean!) that it makes the other main classroom, in the basement, seem much lighter than it actually is. The first floor is the principal's own flat, but nursery meals are prepared in her kitchen daily and the children have cookery classes there. Unusually, the nursery has no outside play area, but the park is close. Every day, all the children are taken to Eel Brook Common, 200 yards away, across Harwood Road. An elaborate system of tying reins together and hand-holding negotiates children across this fairly busy road.

**Owner/Principal & staff** Jenny Williams, Norland trained, NNEB, RSH, has owned and run the Studio for five years. She describes herself as 'hard-working' and a 'self-taught business woman', but is clearly much more. She inspires strong loyalty from her six full-time staff – all qualified NNEB and Mont Dip, and leads with a thoughtful, calm and caring style. Staff turnover is not a problem. Teachers are well managed and independent. Jenny Williams no longer teaches, although she fills in for sickness and staff holidays, but will always make herself available to talk to parents, children and staff.

**Children & parents** The nursery is relentlessly middle class (Fulham, Richmond, Wimbledon, Clapham, etc), nanny-employing and culturally diverse (French, African, Eastern European), reflecting the catchment area. Fashionable London's children's entertainer 'Smarty Arty' regularly performs at the Christmas party and children's birthday parties held at the nursery. Many parents, but not all, are dual-income professionals; numbers have not dropped despite the recession. As expected, the children are happy, friendly, articulate and confident, responding positively to their artistic and stimulating environment. Children with special needs are welcome – the nursery has taken deaf children and a child with cerebral palsy (the nanny stayed with the child at the nursery). Jenny Williams is herself partially deaf, and has particular awareness of children with special needs. She is often the first to pick up hearing difficulties or learning problems, and is a firm believer in integrating children with disabilities into the nursery. Children are accepted before they are potty-trained (parents supply nappies) and are encouraged to come out of nappies only at their own speed. The nursery has a close and warm relationship with parents.

**Curriculum & activities** This is primarily a Montessori nursery, and the philosophy is evident throughout. There is a strong emphasis on learning and 'schoolwork', numbers, writing and reading. Academic achievement is important here. Every morning and afternoon, 45 minutes is set aside for small groups of five to go down to the 'work room' in the basement with a teacher. Children start the work programme when they are considered ready, usually at 2½–3yrs. Concentration downstairs is intense, but children seem to enjoy it. Work continues throughout the year without a summer break. Books are prominent, plentiful and at child height. At the time of visiting, the project was on space, as one child's godfather was an astronaut! All activities involve dividing the nursery into mixed age groups of five to eight children. Each group follows a different activity – cooking, project work, art, drama and elocution, nature study. This enables each child to do every activity on a regular basis, whether they attend morning or afternoon, full-time or part-time. Each child's progress is carefully monitored. All their work is kept in a 'work folder' which is discussed with parents twice a year. A daily record of academic progress (numbers, letters, pencil control, etc) is entered on each child's work card. When a child leaves, he/she takes a detailed report from each teacher. Food is a serious and enjoyable business at this nursery. The food is prepared and cooked by the staff (some of whom are ex-ski-chalet girls), with help from the children. Special dietary needs and preferences are catered for.

**Remarks** Excellent nursery offering good all-round care, combined with a strong educational programme. Very popular, but if parents are prepared to be flexible about days or times and don't mind waiting, then limited places are available.

# Haringey

For some years Haringey's policy has been to provide a nursery place for every 3-year-old who wants one. 'We're not quite there, but almost,' explains one of their education officers. 'The aim is for every child to receive a full year of nursery schooling in addition to three full years in infant education.' 43 per cent of the borough's 3- and 4-year-olds currently receive a nursery-class place, putting Haringey in the top ten of London boroughs. 'We are also at the forefront of multilingual teaching. At the last count, over 100 languages were spoken in our children's homes. We are geared to second language learners in our nursery provision.' Reorganisation following the Children Act has resulted in the Education Department taking on the daycare provision previously run by Social Services. The council hopes, by amalgamating resources, to provide parents with a fuller service, including extended-day facilities and holiday playschemes. The local authority runs four under-5s centres (two have recently closed) and two family centres, which take children under 2. These now sell 30 per cent of their places – rates are £85 per week for under-2s, £47 per week for over-2s. Despite the fees, there are long waiting lists. The private sector contributes a further 450 places, and nearly 450 registered childminders. 'Like everyone else we are struggling with ever-shrinking budgets, but demand for under-5s provision does not go away,' says one of Haringey's early years officers. 'Haringey spends above other boroughs on its nursery education, and offers good training provision and advisors, but our budget is dropping to 60 or 70 per cent of what it was.' None of our questionnaires were returned from Haringey.

## Further information

For details on daycare services:

North Daycare Team
Tel: (081) 889 0011

South Daycare Team
Tel: (081) 809 4466

For details on nursery education and a directory of borough services, contact:

Early Years Service
Education Department
48–62 Station Road
London N22 4TY
Tel: (081) 975 9700

# Harrow

Early years services are not a high priority and Harrow is near the bottom of the London league table. It has no local authority nursery schools and only 19 nursery classes in primary schools, offering 18 per cent of 3- and 4-year-olds a nursery education. The voluntary sector is strong, and includes 48 non profit-making day nurseries, many with waiting lists. Private nurseries and nursery schools, incorporating Montessori schools and various denominational groups, provide a further 27 facilities. Two local authority day nurseries cater for children with special needs. Most parents rely on the borough's 800-plus childminders. The Social Services department is divided into three areas, with a pre-school advisor in each to help and assist carers and parents. There are also special ethnic minority advisors.

**Further information**

Under Eights Helpline
Tel: (081) 863 5544 (9am–11am each weekday)

For details on day nurseries, childminders and playgroups:
Department of Social Services
429–433 Pinner Road
Harrow HA1 4HN
Tel: (081) 863 5544

For details on nursery schools, units and classes:
Education Department
Civic Centre
Station Road
Harrow HA1 2UW
Tel: (081) 863 5611 × 2307

## CRICKET MONTESSORI SCHOOL

Harrow Cricket Club
Payne's Folly
Wood End Road
Harrow
Middx HA1 3PP
**Tel:** (081) 422 0932
(081) 863 6653 or (081) 954 2124 home

**Owners/Principals:** Edwina Shackleford, Cert Ed, FIPS, MATS (LMC)
Marilyn Bruni, MATS (LMC)

**Type:** Montessori nursery school offering morning sessions
**Children:** 2yrs 9mths–5yrs. 20 places. 17 on register
**Hours:** 9.30am–12.30pm
Open 33 weeks a year
**Status:** Private, fee-paying
**Number of years open:** 1½
**Meals:** Snack
**1992 fees:** £400 per term
£2.50 for French lesson (optional)
£20 registration fee
**Waiting list:** 24 names. First come first served. Preference to siblings
**Registered by:** London Borough of Harrow SS

# Havering

Just four per cent of the borough's 6000 3- and 4-year-olds receive nursery education, putting Havering next to Bromley at the bottom of the London league table. Three Social Services day nurseries provide exclusively for children in need, although this is supplemented by a sponsorship scheme. Havering subsidises fees for low-income families attending the seven private nurseries or 91 playgroups. It is a borough of social extremes, with pockets of serious deprivation in the midst of stockbroker belts. Local authority provision concentrates on those in need or with disabilities and there are no plans to increase provision. Demand for day nurseries and childminders appears to be declining, but there is an overwhelming need for sessional playgroups. None of the initial questionnaires we sent to nurseries and schools in this borough were returned.

### Further information

For details on all under-5s provision:
Under Eights Section
Inspection and Monitoring Unit
Directorate of Social Services
Mercury House
Mercury Gardens
Romford RM1 3DS
Tel: (0708) 772933

# Hillingdon

Despite cuts in nursery funding, Hillingdon has the third-best record of all 33 London boroughs for nursery education provision. 48 per cent of 3- and 4-year-olds attend nursery classes part-time. Places have increased by 1200 since 1992. However, supply does not meet demand and parents are advised to register early at their local school. The borough's five day nurseries have long waiting lists and cater exclusively for children in need. Twenty private day nurseries, including five workplace facilities, offer full daycare to parents who can afford fees. Seventy playgroups offer sessional, part-time places. £14 million has been cut from this year's budget, a cut of 20 per cent. Non-statutory Social Services provision has been cut to the bone. Three under-5s resource centres are to close, and funding will be withdrawn from many playgroups. A desperate situation.

### Further information

For details on all types of childcare and nursery education:
Uxbridge Children and Families Team
Hillingdon Education and Community Services
Civic Centre
High Street
Uxbridge UB8 1UW
Tel: (0895) 250494

# BREAKSPEAR NURSERY UNIT

Breakspear Infant School
Bushey Road
Ickenham
Uxbridge UB10 8JA
**Tel:** (0895) 630411

**Owner:** London Borough of Hillingdon LEA
**Headteacher:** Melanie Proctor, B Ed
**Type:** Nursery class attached to infant school offering half-day sessions. No full-time places
**Children:** 4–5yrs 4mths. 40 places. 60 on register
**Hours:** Morning session 8.45am–11.25am
Afternoon session 12.45pm–3.25pm
Open 39 weeks a year
**Status:** State nursery unit
**Number of years open:** 11
**Meals:** Snacks
**1992 fees:** No fees
**Waiting list:** Long
**Registered by:** London Borough of Hillingdon LEA

**Premises** A purpose-built, self-contained block with a main, open-plan area for play, plus two bays, one for reading, the other for construction toys. Leading off the main area are a kitchen, children's loos, cloakroom, large store cupboard and the garden. Inside, the nursery is busy and bustling. It takes some time to tread a path across the room, around tables and chairs, past children absorbed in their activities and fascinating theme tables, snack tables and activity areas. Every available space is used to maximum effect. The nursery is extremely well equipped and the rather cramped room is intelligently laid out. Light streams into the room, although staff complain that there are too many windows. The garden is as well looked after as the schoolroom. There is a grassy area with large play equipment including a slide, a barrel and a trampoline. A covered area includes a selection of other activities including painting, an imaginative play area, a sand tray and a construction area.

**Headteacher & staff** Melanie Proctor, B Ed, is headteacher and Holly Winchcombe her NNEB assistant. Melanie qualified six years ago and then taught reception and junior infants in Leeds. She joined Breakspear in 1990. Her assistant joined at the same time, after experience in Social Services nurseries and as a childminder. They clearly have a strong relationship with the children and involve themselves thoroughly in all activities at child level. Their first priority is to produce children who are happy and secure in their environment, as they believe that no real learning can take place until this has been achieved. Staff meetings with the infant school teachers take place weekly. Nursery staff have two formal planning meetings a term and regular discussions whenever possible. The infant school has a government education support grant for training for staff, allowing nursery workers to update and improve their knowledge. The staff/child ratio is 1:15, a ratio which Melanie feels makes it difficult to meet the needs of every child.

**Children & parents** Relaxed and happy children. The classroom is very noisy and the children are obviously at home here. They are given freedom to choose their activities and wander the room at will, settling to different tasks as they go. There is so much to do that it would be unrealistic to assume a child could experience everything, but each individual concentration span is catered for. Strenuous efforts are made to give all children on the waiting list at least two terms in the nursery before they enter the reception class. Most are aged between 4 and 5 years. The intake is mainly from local, middle-class families, with approximately ten per cent Asian. The school is becoming increasingly popular with the local Asian community. Parents are encouraged to join a classroom 'helpers' rota', to assist on outings and to attend meetings and a termly assembly arranged especially for them. Appointments can be made at any time to discuss individual progress and a regular newsletter is sent out. Phasing-in is done slowly, over time. There is an annual Christmas play.

**Curriculum & activities** Learning through play and experience, on a self-service basis. Children do not lack variety or balance in their activities. Melanie Proctor plans the curriculum well in advance and knows exactly what she expects each child to experience during the course of a term. From the master plan she designs weekly and daily plans, detailing how the room will be laid out and which staff will supervise which activity. Nothing is left to chance. Play experiences available each day include sand, water, paint and a design and technology area providing heaps of junk in ordered boxes where children can glue, create and design whatever they wish. In the reading bay there is an area with headphones and story tapes with books, where children can listen two at a time. A computer provides an introduction to keyboard skills, and there are programmes for drawing and composing music. There is a cookery table, a home corner with dressing-up clothes, a comfortable reading area with fish tank and a 'small world' area on the floor where children play out events and make sense of the world around them using a dolls' house, zoo, farm animals and toy vehicles. Practical exercises involving maths, counting, ordering, patterns and shapes, measuring, learning to tell the time and weighing are undertaken. Pre-reading skills are developed and children work towards the Oxford Reading Scheme used by the main school. Children can take books home as soon as they are ready. A warm and close relationship exists with the primary school. Nursery children visit regularly and take part in assemblies and school plays.

**Remarks** An incredibly stimulating nursery class, providing opportunities for children to develop in all areas. Good equipment and resources, but above all committed and energetic staff, are its main strengths.

## GATEHOUSE NURSERY II

The Old Vicarage
High Street
Harmondsworth
Middx UB7 0AQ
**Tel:** (081) 759 0518

**Owner:** Linda Lloyd
**Principal:** Ella McLoughlin, NNEB
**Type:** Day nursery offering full-time places and half-day sessions by arrangement
**Children:** 3mths–5yrs. 60 places. 29 on register
**Hours:** 8am–6pm
Sessions available by arrangement
Open 51 weeks a year
**Status:** Private, fee-paying
**Number of years open:** 1
**Meals:** Breakfast, lunch, tea, snacks
**1992 fees:** £100 per week full-time
£10 per session

**Waiting list:** None
**Registered by:** London Borough of Hillingdon SS
**Under same ownership:** Gatehouse I, West Drayton, Middlesex; Gatehouse County Nursery, Longlevens, Glos

## WONDERLAND NURSERY LTD

Forte Crest Heathrow
Sipson Road
West Drayton
Middx UB7 0JU
**Tel:** (081) 759 2323 × 4335

**Owner/Headmistress:** Diane Lyddon, NNEB, Social Worker Cert
**Type:** Day nursery offering full-time places and half-day sessions
**Children:** 3mths–5yrs. 41 places. 46 on register
**Hours:** 8am–6pm
Morning session 8.30am–12.30pm
Afternoon session 1.30pm–5.30pm
Open 52 weeks a year
**Status:** Private, fee-paying
**Number of years open:** 4
**Meals:** Snacks, lunch
**1992 fees:** £88 per week full-time
£44 per week for 5 sessions
**Waiting list:** Long for babies, none for over-2s
**Registered by:** London Borough of Hillingdon SS

**Premises** The first floor of the Forte Crest Hotel, near Heathrow Airport. An unlikely setting for a nursery, but it works well for both parties – the hotel has the benefit of an in-house nursery, while the nursery makes full use of the hotel's catering, laundry, cleaning and leisure facilities. It is approached via a back entrance, more like a tradesman's entrance, but once inside, the space is well planned and light. The former accounts office has been transformed into a baby room, main children's room with adjoining cloakrooms and messy-play room, small office, kitchen, laundry and baby changing area. A fenced-off piece of secluded land is used for outdoor play.

**Headmistress & staff** Diane Lyddon, NNEB, ran the nursery for two years before the hotel sold it to her. She has many years' experience in nursery schools and Social Services day nurseries and sits on a number of childcare advisory committees. She is open and straightforward with staff, parents and children. All five members of staff are qualified NNEBs and appear competent and happy.

**Children & parents** Parents work locally for the major companies around Heathrow. Some travel in from Surrey, Herts and Bucks. Professions range from dentists, doctors and nurses to shop assistants and hotel workers. Ten places are subsidised by the hotel for their employees, and a further two places by the local authority.

**Curriculum & activities** Emphasis is on learning through play. 'We are not teachers, we are nursery nurses,' says Diane Lyddon. The staff rotate between rooms organising different activities. The messy-play room is used for manipulative play with sand and dough, painting, glueing and modelling. The main room is set up with a construction table, an easy table with simple activities for the youngest age group, a writing table – for simple tracing, colouring and free writing – and an imaginative table. Children are encouraged to move around the room and sample as many activities as they wish. At lunchtime the tables are cleared and different activities put out for the afternoon session. There is no formal teaching, but simple name recognition, number and pencil control exercises are undertaken. Work is filed or pinned up or goes home. There are also abundant books, a computer, home corner and musical instruments.

**Remarks** Experienced, well-motivated staff providing warm, loving childcare. Lack of formal educational programmes and first-floor hotel location may put some people off. However, the nursery offers a varied curriculum in a safe, happy environment and at a reasonable price, by London standards.

# Hounslow

Hounslow claims to lead the country in nursery education. Every one of their infant and primary schools has a nursery class and every 3½-year-old is offered a morning place, while 4-year-olds attend in the afternoons. Provision is high-quality and free. However, the borough has been forced to make £2.5 million pounds worth of cuts, and all non-statutory nursery classes face possible closure. A campaign to save them is gaining strength. 'We're running a positive campaign, celebrating what we have, which is outstanding. It is not the local authority's wish to make cuts. It's central government funding that has been cut,' a spokesperson told us. Social Services daycare provision has not been so badly hit, although there have been staff cuts, resulting in the loss of some places. The 19 extended-hours daycare schemes and five day nurseries for children in need remain open. Fifteen private day nurseries offer long hours for working parents. Our nursery questionnaire fell upon stony ground in Hounslow.

**Further information**

Constantly updated information on schools, classes and playgroups is available on the Hounslow View-Data Service at all libraries. The Education Department deals with nursery classes at:

Hounslow Civic Centre
Lampton Road
Hounslow TW3 4DN
Tel: (081) 862 5363 or 5367

For details on day nurseries and other early years provision:

The Under Eights Team
Department of Social Services
Brentford Area Office
26 Glenhurst Road
Brentford TW8 9BX
Tel: (081) 570 5372

## CORNER HOUSE DAY NURSERY

Heathfield Gardens
Chiswick
London W4 4JU
**Tel:** (081) 995 7585

**Joint Owners:** David Lilley
Heidi Clapp
**Principal:** Heidi Clapp, NNEB, RSH (Norland)
**Type:** Day nursery offering full-time places only

**Children:** 3mths–5yrs. 54 places. 44 on register
**Hours:** 8am–6pm
Open 52 weeks a year
**Status:** Private, fee-paying
**Number of years open:** 2
**Meals:** Breakfast, lunch, tea
**1992 fees:** £146 per week full-time – under 2½
£117 per week full-time – over 2½
**Waiting list:** Long for under-2s. Early registration advisable
**Registered by:** London Borough of Hounslow SS

# Islington

The Education Department is responsible for all early years provision, daycare and education, which leads to a well co-ordinated service. The borough is divided into four areas, with several neighbourhoods in each area, supervised by an Under Fives Development Officer. Full daycare is available in 29 community nurseries, eight local authority day nurseries and all-day playgroups. Twelve private day nurseries are registered. Fees vary, but can be as high as £700 per month. Nursery education is offered to 38 per cent of 3- and 4-year-olds, which puts Islington at number 12 in the league of 33 London boroughs. There are 3 nursery schools and 43 nursery classes attached to primary schools. Information is difficult to get, as budget cuts have led to redundancies among registration and inspectorate staff. It is essential to identify your neighbourhood and track down the local development officer in order to obtain information on provision in your area.

### Further information

For all enquiries and information, including a directory of services and details on your neighbourhood Under Fives Development Officer, contact:
Under Fives Development Officers
Education Department
Laycock Street
Islington
London N1 1TH
Tel: (071) 457 5635

## FLORAL PLACE NURSERY

2 Floral Place
Northampton Grove
Islington
London N1 2PL
**Tel:** (071) 354 9945

**Owner:** Susan Hay Associates Ltd
**Principal:** Tracy Burt, NNEB, DPQS
**Type:** Day nursery for working parents offering full- and part-time places (min 2 days a week)

**Children:** 3mths–5yrs. 50 places. 48 on register
**Hours:** 8am–6.30pm
Open 50 weeks a year
**Status:** Private, fee-paying
**Number of years open:** 3
**Meals:** Breakfast, lunch, tea and snacks
**1992 fees:** £715 per month full-time – under 2
£650 per month full-time – over 2
£165 per week full-time – under 2
£150 per week full-time – over 2
£50 registration fee plus £250 refundable deposit
**Waiting list:** Baby places full nine months ahead. Places available for 2–5yr-olds
**Registered by:** London Borough of Islington SS

**Under same ownership/management:** Broadgate Nursery, Hackney (see listing); Sainsbury's Workplace Nurseries, Alperton and Dulwich

**Premises** The ground floor of an attractive converted warehouse, which used to be a perfume factory. There are separate sections for babies and older children. Both consist of open-plan rooms imaginatively architect-designed to allow the child maximum control of his or her environment. For the older children there are bean bags, a junk corner neatly sorted into different categories, a large messy-play area, a sand trough, piles of books and generous equipment for painting, sticking, cutting and drawing, all neatly arranged – and still there is ample open space for running around and playing games. The floor is a warm red, non-slip lino and there are stable doors, half yellow, half blue. The rather daunting size of the room is made more friendly and manageable by the careful positioning of wooden furniture and storage units. One end of the toddler room (over 18mths) is entirely taken up by an expensive two-storey wooden play structure which can become anything a child wants it to be. A small area of this structure with table, chairs and cushions is known as the Cuddle Corner. The baby room is long and has a built-in sink and changing area; beyond is the sleeping area with a dormitory-like arrangement of neat white cots and on the other side, a play area. Each unit has its own kitchen, loos and nappy changing area. In the toddler room there is also an office, a sleeping room with more serried ranks of white cots, and a small quiet room for reading stories and other activities requiring concentration. The offices of Susan Hay Associates are above the baby unit. Outside there is a small play area where trikes can be ridden. Terraced with brick and concrete slabs, it has no grass or trees, but has been brought to life by the addition of low wooden partitions painted with flowers in brilliant colours. There are welcoming tubs of real flowers and herbs, tended by the children, also decorated with painted flowers and fruit.

**Principal & staff** Tracy Burt, NNEB, DPQS, leads the Floral Place team of ten full-time staff, all of whom are qualified, the majority NNEB. There is a lone male who has a social work qualification. Tracy is highly motivated and extremely organised; prior to Floral Place, she set up a successful workplace nursery in the City. She spends roughly two-thirds of her time at Floral Place; the rest is allocated managing other Susan Hay nurseries in London. The team also comprises a part-time (NNEB) nursery helper, a cook and two part-time housekeepers. Students from the local college attend frequently. Two dance teachers come in once a week for a music and movement class (which costs extra). There are fortnightly staff meetings and regular training sessions. The company employs a training officer.

**Children & parents** There is genuine regret that the type and cost of the nursery excludes all but middle-class, mainly white children. Most live locally, many with parents who run small businesses from home. The nursery has daily contact with most parents, but the majority are too short of time to become further involved. There are ten baby places and 30 places for children over 18 months. The nursery operates a keyworker system, and parents can request a 'keyworker session' whenever necessary. Detailed and impressive notes, including photographs, are kept on each child. No written reports are sent out and the onus is on parents to request information. Parents' evenings are held every two months, with invited guest speakers. A parents' noticeboard displays a planning chart for the week, and daily diaries for each child show what they ate, how long they slept and what they most enjoyed doing during the day. Full-time and part-time parents are expected to stay with their child for the first day or two, to settle in. There is an open-door policy, although parents rarely make use of it.

**Curriculum & activities** The philosophy here is that every activity should be available to all. There is totally integrated care and education throughout the age range. Projects and themes, which may last for weeks, are planned in advance at staff meetings. Children are then invited to join in activities, which they may or may not choose to do – they are not divided into set groups and are never forced into doing anything. Mealtimes are the only limitation on their freedom, and their options are deliberately limited prior to a meal to allow for clearing up and calming down. The nursery uses what it describes as 'the best from every teaching method' and this includes some Montessori teaching, as well as worksheets and a vast array of different matching games, puzzles and other educational toys. Some children are emergent readers by the time they leave, although many have not actually reached school age by the time they move on. Pre-school activities tend to be done in the early afternoon when younger children are asleep. Susan Hay Associates employs an Education Director, as a consultant, and she is involved in advance planning for the pre-school age group. A vast amount of toys and equipment is available at child height at all times. Staff organise special activities daily – painting, modelling, storytime, singing and dancing. Tracy Burt points out that the music and movement class 'is more structured than anything else we do' and involves disciplinary skills such as taking turns, listening, stopping, and studying rhythm. Because of numbers for music, the children are divided into two groups – the only time that this is ever done.

**Remarks** Considered to be a model of good practice locally and on a national level. Costs, among the highest in the country, illustrate just how expensive it is to provide high-quality childcare and education on a commercial basis. Company has actively tried to persuade major and local employers to subsidise places for their workers, but with only limited success. Six companies currently subsidise one or two places each. Extremely switched-on, intelligent and well-paid staff. Very carefully thought-out environment – perhaps too thought out. Nursery would perhaps benefit from being more cosy and homely.

# LITTLE PEOPLE

44 Whitehall Park
London N19 3TN
**Tel:** (071) 281 5951

**Owner/Headmistress:** Molly Molloy-Madigan, SRN
**Type:** Day nursery and nursery school offering full-time places and half-day sessions
**Children:** 2–5yrs. 27 places. 29 on register
**Hours:** 8am–5pm
Morning session 9am–1.30pm
Afternoon session 1.30pm–5pm
Open 47 weeks a year
**Status:** Private, fee-paying

**Number of years open:** 4
**Meals:** Lunch, tea, snacks
**1992 fees:** £125 per week full-time
£16 per session
£25 registration fee
**Waiting list:** None. Some afternoon vacancies
**Registered by:** London Borough of Islington SS

**Premises** Through the green, stained-glass door into the sweet-smelling world of Little People – London's first holistic nursery. Beautifully designed by the owner's architect husband, the nursery is in the lower half of the owner's substantial Victorian family home. Visitors and children are requested to take their shoes off at the door and pad gently along the green carpet and linoleum. It is not the artwork on the walls or the state of the decor that first strikes the visitor, but the scent of essential oils, which burn on mantelpieces in every room, and the sound of soft music or dolphin and whale sounds everywhere. The nursery comprises a messy-play room cum dining room, a conventional classroom, a rest and quiet room known as the Dolphin Room, small toilets without doors, an office, a kitchen and an organic garden. There is equipment in abundance, including a wide range of high-quality wooden toys, educational and art materials, books, cuddly toys and expensive furniture.

**Owner/Headmistress & staff** Molly Molloy-Madigan is in her own words 'Irish, a State Registered Nurse, aromatherapist and 30-something . . . Little People was born when I couldn't find anywhere I would be happy to leave my daughter when I needed to go back to work. I didn't go into the project with views on whether it would be a good business deal. I just wanted to give other children what I hoped to give my own child.' Molly's strong views are implemented by a hand-picked, carefully trained team of qualified nursery workers. There are two full-timers, Michelle, an NNEB from Jamaica, and Kris, from Michigan, with a Mont Dip and Early Childhood Degree and one of the few full-time male nursery teachers we met. Working alongside them are several part-timers, including an Australian teacher, a Brazilian art teacher and artist, and the all-important nursery cook. Specialist music, dance and French teachers all visit once a week. Staff are highly motivated, committed wholeheartedly to the philosophy of the nursery and unwavering in their healthy approach to life.

**Children & parents** All English and very local. Mainly professional families – graphic artists, designers, journalists, teachers, TV producers. Parents choose Little People because they share Molly Molloy-Madigan's strong beliefs about aromatherapy, organic vegetarianism, homeopathy etc. Phasing-in new children is done with care and much patience. Only one new recruit is taken on at a time, with one member of staff solely responsible for successfully settling in each child. Parents' evenings are held three times a year, one of which is organised by parents themselves. A close relationship exists between parents and staff, past and present. All the children so far have gone on to the more liberal private schools in the area – Charterhouse Square, St Christopher's, King Alfred's.

**Curriculum & activities** The nursery's philosophy is to develop the whole character of each child, enhance trust and self-esteem and instil confidence. There are written weekly and daily programmes, which are on display for parents and teachers. The timetable 'offers a structure but allows for spontaneous decisions'. Children are grouped for each activity – music, art, nature studies, French – according to how well they get on and how they work best together. Each morning at 9.30am, a teacher takes a group for 'a language or number experience, drawing or pre-writing exercise'. Each child will be carefully observed and individual needs and strengths noted and developed. Work is either displayed on the walls, taken home or put into the child's developmental file. Detailed developmental records are kept on each child (a page from each teacher weekly), which are passed to the next school. Language, written or oral, is considered crucial to all activities and is encouraged through stories, conversation and play. No reading schemes are followed, although some children leave ready to read. There is weekly French, music and ballet from specialist teachers at no extra cost, as they are seen as a vital part of the curriculum. Aromatherapy, massage and reflexology are built into the timetable, usually after rest time. Part-time children are massaged in groups of four, while full-timers receive a full individual body massage once a week. Children are also taught to massage each other as part of learning to care for each other; touch is believed to be vital to a child's bonding, communication, security and self-confidence. Very strong art and craft programme designed by the specialist art teacher. The first-aid box is full of homeopathic medicines – arnica for bumps, belladonna for fevers. Food plays a central role in the nursery and the kitchen overflows with beans, pulses, grains and spices. The meals, all vegetarian, are definitely not to every child's taste. Menus include red snapper with grapefruit, rice wrapped in seaweed and peanut stew.

**Remarks** Aromatherapy, massage and reflexology for under-5s, in London's first holistic nursery. This is not a run-of-the-mill nursery. However, if you leave your prejudices at the door with your shoes it is an extraordinarily loving and stimulating nursery, full of very happy children. Interesting and interested staff, better qualified than many nursery workers and highly motivated. The danger is that such a cosy, cuddly, gentle start could make it difficult to adapt to the real world of prep or primary school.

# Kensington & Chelsea

Kensington and Chelsea sent us their review of daycare services, which identifies the borough's problems, mainly arising from its wide social mix. The report highlights inadequate provision in the Earls Court area, not enough educational emphasis in daycare and an over-weighting of children in need in the six Social Services day nurseries. The private sector supplies most of the borough's services. 68 private day nurseries offer over 1700 full-time places, with fees rising to £150 per week. The number of registered childminders fluctuates. At present it is just over 100 charging from £56 to £75 per week. The council runs three excellent childminding groups, where minders and children can meet on certain days to exchange ideas and socialise. Nursery education is currently available to 28 per cent of 3- and 4-year-olds. The Education Department is examining the possibility of expanding nursery provision by restructuring entry into reception classes.

### Further information

For details on all childcare and education services, and a copy of 'A Guide to Daycare Facilities for Under Eights in Kensington and Chelsea', contact:

Under Eights Section
Room 140/B
Town Hall
Hornton Street
London W8 7NX
Tel: (071) 937 5464 × 2422/2340

---

## ACORN NURSERY SCHOOL

2 Lansdowne Crescent
London W11 2NH
**Tel:** (071) 727 2122

**Owner/Principal:** Jane Cameron, B Ed
**Type:** Nursery school offering full-time places and half-day sessions
**Children:** 2½–5yrs. 56 places. 90 on register
**Hours:** 9am–4pm
Morning session 9am–12 noon
Afternoon session 1pm–4pm
Open 36 weeks a year
**Status:** Private, fee-paying
**Number of years open:** 14yrs previous site
1yr present site
**Meals:** Snacks, packed lunches
**1992 fees:** £575 per term for 5 sessions a week
£100 per term for extra session a week
£10 registration fee plus £500 refundable deposit
**Waiting list:** Very long for morning places.
Long for afternoon places
**Registered by:** Royal Borough of Kensington & Chelsea SS

**Premises** A large, rambling, grey brick vicarage opposite St John's Church, in the elegant residential part of Notting Hill Gate. The nursery school occupies the basement and elevated ground floor, and entry is down the side of the building. There are amazing displays of children's artwork, collages, writing and photographs and a constant buzz of activity everywhere. Downstairs consists of a large children's room leading on to the sloping front garden. It includes a home corner, piano and child-size tables and chairs. A smaller, back room is used for quiet teaching in small groups. Overflowing with shelves of books, the walls groan with exhibits of topic work. Upstairs is a vast, wooden-floored classroom – welcoming, light and highly organised. Also on this floor is the treasured and well-used reading room, where reading is taught and practised daily. Outside, a small muddy patch of grass is best ignored in favour of the glorious communal gardens beyond it.

**Owner/Principal & staff** Jane Cameron, B Ed, is an intelligent, mature woman, who owns and runs an outstanding nursery school. She is involved in every aspect of Acorn, commanding the respect and loyalty of staff, children and parents, and constantly in demand. Children look to her for cuddles, hand holding, guidance and approval – all of which she gives in abundance. Eight full-time staff and three part-timers – all but two Montessori or NNEB qualified – make up the team. Teachers are carefully selected to provide a variety of personalities, talents and special interests. The longest-serving member is Bridget, the specialist reading teacher. She has been at Acorn for eight years, listening to children practise their reading, preparing letter and word boxes and encouraging hundreds of children to love books and enjoy learning to read. Lucy, the deputy head, who holds a B Sc and Mont Dip, has been a loyal, committed teacher for seven years. Staff morale and team spirit are high. The nursery is flooded with applicants wanting to work here, but new staff usually join through personal recommendation. Higher than average staff salaries, particularly for senior staff.

**Children & parents** Acorn has one of the best reputations in the area. Parents come by word of mouth and advertising has never been necessary. The children come from wealthy families in the surrounding Notting Hill, Bayswater, Holland Park and Kensington areas. Parents are very actively involved, supportive and influential. Jane Cameron says, 'Without the parents, I would not be here today.' They fought to secure her new, more spacious premises when the previous landlords, a local church, insisted that the school move out. Parents willingly pay a £500 deposit, knowing that it helps the school financially. Many waive its repayment when they leave. Parents organise their own evenings and frequently sit and observe sessions in the classroom. Many attend the daily 'Good morning' song. An open-door policy is encouraged at all times and parents take advantage of it. Children are happy, noisy, articulate and interested, with a strong sense of belonging. Many return to visit or help out long after they have left. Long-term family connections, with third and fourth siblings now attending.

**Curriculum & activities** A structured and busy timetable, which also allows space for fun and letting off steam. The programme is drawn up weekly, so each teacher knows in advance her specific responsibilities and which group of children she is responsible for that week. A session normally begins with the group welcome, songs and shared news. Children then split into separate mixed age groups for an hour of either work time, art or a geography, history or science topic. Older children help the younger ones. The newest children start by using Montessori apparatus and simple practical maths exercises. The older children work with more abstract concepts, do worksheets or write their numbers or news in exercise books. Phonetics are taught throughout and several reading schemes are used including New Way, Bangers & Mash and Ginn, which are taken home when the child is ready. Teachers keep written records of what each child has learnt or read during the session. All day children, mainly the rising-4s, are given more individual tuition in the teaching room downstairs. Music, art and craft, dance and outdoor physical play are important ingredients of every session. French and swimming are done weekly. The atmosphere is industrious, bustling and, above all, great fun. Results are impressive in academic areas – reading, writing and number work – but equally exciting in other, less formal parts of the curriculum. A Nativity play is performed every Christmas and concerts the other two terms. Evening concerts at which ex-Acorn children perform are also held. A sports day is held on the last day of the summer term.

**Remarks** One of the best private nursery schools we have visited. Committed, qualified teaching staff, and excellent premises. A balanced diet of creative and intellectual activities in a well-planned structured programme. Close, warm relationship between teachers and parents. Lively, interested children. School and parents' committee currently looking at ways to set up a fund for children whose parents cannot afford full fees.

## HOLLAND PARK DAY NURSERY & SCHOOL HOUSE

5 & 9 Holland Road
London W14 8HJ
**Tel:** (071) 602 9266 or 9066

**Owners:** Kitty and Christopher Mason
**Officers-in-Charge:** Steve Kennedy, NNEB
Sophie Bashall, NNEB, Mont Dip
**Type:** Day nursery and Montessori nursery school offering full- and part-time places and half-day sessions.
**Children:** Day Nursery 12wks–2½yrs
School House 2–5yrs
59 places (3 for under-1s). 45 on register
**Hours:** Day Nursery 7.30am–6.30pm
School House 8.30am–6.30pm (7.30am start available to children who move up from Day Nursery)
Day Nursery open 51 weeks a year
School House open 36 weeks a year
**Status:** Private, fee-paying
**Number of years open:** Day Nursery 3
School House 1
**Meals:** Breakfast, lunch, supper, snacks
**1992 fees:** *Day Nursery*
£160 per week – under 1yr
£150 per week – 1–2yrs
£145 per week – over 2yrs
£35 per day – 1–2yrs
£30 per day – over 2
£17.50 per session
£600 deposit or 1mth fees
*School House*
£1160 per term 9am–4pm
£585 per term for 5 sessions a week
£640 per month full-time – 2–3yrs
£550 per month full-time – over 3
£28 per day – 2–3yrs
£26 per day – over 3
£250 deposit
£25 registration fee
**Waiting list:** Very long for babies. Places available at School House
**Registered by:** Royal Borough of Kensington & Chelsea SS

**Premises** On a main road, close to one of West London's busiest intersections, in two almost-adjacent and immaculately converted flats. The Day Nursery is in a well-lit basement and consists of three rooms, as well as an office, staff room, bathroom and kitchen. Children spend most of their time in the main room, with a pretty bay window and window seat, overlooking a tiny office and staff room tucked away under the pavement. It is homely, well decorated and equipped with a large supply of toys. The dining room cum art room overlooks the garden at the back and is simply furnished, with tables and chairs. There is a baby room with three cots and a big toy cupboard, where the babies come for quiet periods. The patio garden provides just enough space for riding tricycles. A major programme of improvements is underway outside, and will eventually link it with the much larger School House garden next door. The recently opened School House has been refurbished to a very high standard. There are two large classrooms, one on each floor, both with adjacent, carpeted quiet rooms for imaginative play, stories and sleeping. The upstairs classroom, used by pre-school children, is full of Montessori and art and craft equipment. The downstairs classroom, next to the kitchen, doubles as a dining room. It has a piano and French windows leading into the garden, which is entirely safety-surfaced and contains a large sandpit, balancing bars and a climbing frame. Great attention to detail throughout; there are two handrails on the staircase, one at child height.

**Officers-in-charge & staff** The owner of the nursery, Kitty Mason, is no longer responsible for the daily running of the nursery. Her role is restricted to financial administration and management. Steve Kennedy, NNEB, has been in charge of the Day Nursery for the last two years. More comfortable with children than adults, he is experienced in special needs care and has worked in a number of Social Services day nurseries. Steve is responsible for a group of four full-time NNEB nursery nurses, another with a City & Guilds qualification and a cook. The officer-in-charge of School House, Sophie Bashall, NNEB, Mont Dip, leads a team of four full-timers, two NNEB, Mont Dip, one NNEB and a nursery nurse currently studying for her Montessori Diploma. In addition, there is a qualified, term-time-only teacher, a full-time cook and a part-time worker who comes to sit with children during their afternoon sleep. Staff meetings are held separately for each premises, every four to six weeks. An outside ballet teacher visits the School House on Fridays. One of the full-time nursery nurses teaches French. A keyworker system operates. Each keyworker is responsible for five children, and is expected to update the developmental records for each of those children. A staff training and development policy is followed.

**Children & parents** Nearly all dual-income, high-earning parents, many working in the City and at nearby Middle Eastern embassies. The majority live in the borough, many within walking distance. All children go on to private schools, mostly local. Children attending full-time are phased-in gradually and parents are asked to make themselves available over a two-week period. Children who do not speak English as their first language are given longer to settle in, and parents provide a list of key words in their own language to allow a basic degree of communication. There are no specialist EFL teachers.

**Curriculum & activities** Both nurseries work to a very structured routine. According to the nursery brochure, even free play is structured! Under-2s enjoy a day of table-top activities, outdoor play, singing, art, reading, construction activities and floor play. Circle time precedes every meal. Babies and toddlers spend most of their day together, but the babies have their own room for quiet periods and sleep. Steve emphasises that everybody joins in with main room activities, and babies have their fair share of the fun with finger paints, stripped down to their nappies. The local swimming pool is visited twice a week, in groups of four. Library visits are frequent. On Wednesdays there are outings relevant to the current theme. Children in School House are divided into their classes for most of the day. The under-3s have the most relaxed environment and concentrate on learning basic skills such as colour recognition and shapes. Pre-school children have access to a good selection of Montessori equipment used in conjunction with many other toys, puzzles and workbooks. Montessori reading cards are used, as well as the phonetic alphabet and there are pre-reading and pre-writing exercises every day. Children who are ready will be reading and writing by the time they leave. French is taught in the School House twice a day using songs, videos, rhymes and conversation. Children who are learning English do not attend these sessions. The school has its own mini-bus for swimming and outings.

**Remarks** Still the only nursery in the Royal Borough of Kensington & Chelsea taking children under 1. Excellent facilities in an upmarket, homely environment. Plenty of stimulating activities, and well-qualified staff. Great attention to detail and no expense spared on the conversion and equipping of the building. The most expensive nursery and nursery school in West London.

# IVERNA GARDENS MONTESSORI SCHOOL

Armenian Church Hall
Iverna Gardens
London W8 6TP
**Tel:** (071) 486 7208

**Owner/Principal:** Felicity Marrian, Mont Dip (St Nicholas)
**Type:** Montessori Nursery School offering half-day sessions during term time. No full-time places
**Children:** 2½–5½yrs. 36 places. 69 on register
**Hours:** Morning session 9am–12 noon
Afternoon session 1.30pm–4pm
Open 36 weeks a year
**Status:** Private, fee-paying
**Number of years open:** 5
**Meals:** Juice and biscuits
**1992 fees:** £590 per term for 5 sessions a week
£15 registration fee plus £500 refundable deposit
£28 per term for French
**Waiting list:** Huge. 60 names
**Registered by:** Royal Borough of Kensington & Chelsea SS

**Premises** Just off High Street Kensington, Iverna Gardens is a surprisingly quiet and peaceful crescent of smart mansion blocks. The nursery is approached through a safe, enclosed courtyard. The main front door opens into a small lobby and then into the main hall. The hall itself is only about 20 years old, incredibly light, spacious and in excellent condition. The hall is used at weekends and in the evenings for functions and children's parties. There is a solid wood floor and a stage which pulls out from the end wall. The nursery is meticulously set up well in advance of each session. The walls are covered with children's artwork, project work and charts of every description. An enormous aquarium catches the eye as soon as you walk in. Downstairs there is an open-plan area used as an office, a group room (for French), cloakrooms, a small kitchen and a further modest carpeted classroom for teaching and project work. There is no real outside play area (the courtyard is used) and no nearby park.

**Owner/Principal & staff** Felicity Marrian, Mont Dip, bought the nursery in January '92, but has been running it as principal since Sept '91. With two children of her own, she is a mature, calm and dedicated teacher who works hard to achieve high standards and expects the same from her staff. Her love of children and passion for her work are immediately apparent. She employs six teachers in the mornings and seven in the afternoons, when the children tend to be younger. Six are Montessori qualified (all St Nicholas), and the seventh has an NNEB. Her deputy, Kasia, is Polish and, according to Felicity, 'very gentle, and an inspiration to work with. She always sees things from the child's point of view.' Staff appear receptive, caring and mature. Recruitment is done by taking on Montessori students who come on a termly basis for practical experience. French is taught weekly by a visiting teacher from the Frère Jacques French Club.

**Children & parents** The parents tend to be heavy-weight middle-class professionals, dual-income earners with nannies, mainly local. A high proportion are bankers, from mainly American banks, and there are also consultants, musicians, actors, hoteliers – but few housewives. The range of nationalities is amazing: languages spoken by children include French, Italian, Spanish, Parsee, Serbo-Croat, Chinese, Swedish, Greek, Urdu. Children are not accepted until they are potty-trained or before 2½ years. All siblings are accepted for the morning session. Special needs children are welcome.

**Curriculum & activities** This is a nursery run on traditional Montessori lines. Felicity Marrian is a strong believer in the philosophy and teachings of Maria Montessori. Children are given great scope for individual choice and work, but every activity and every child is closely monitored and recorded in writing. Daily records are kept by each teacher on every child; some, but not all, are available to parents. Wall charts record the subjects each child has covered and what work still needs to be done. Morning and afternoon sessions are identical. Time is set aside for each child to work individually with a teacher in numbers, colours, shapes, reading and writing. Work is done with the aid of Montessori equipment (eg sandpaper letters and numbers) either on worksheets or in exercise books. Each child has a number book, writing book and scrapbook for his/her best worksheets and drawings. All books go home when finished. The majority of the work is phonetically based. Children learn letters, move on to three-letter words and then to free writing or reading schemes. A variety of reading schemes (New Way, Bangers & Mash) are used to avoid boredom and encourage choice. Reading books go home as 'homework' or 'funwork'. Homework is popular with the nursery's high-achieving parents, but can lead to competitiveness and too high expectations. Plenty of project work (wonderful wall display on the Seaside and Beach), beautifully written up with photographs, and 'there is always time for painting'. In the quieter downstairs room a teacher and five children sit at each of two tables. One group does project work, the other number work, reading or writing. French and music are once a week. Visits from people talking about their jobs occur regularly or fit in with project work (eg a project on the senses led to a visit from a blind person). There are three parents' evenings a year and school plays at Christmas and in the summer.

**Remarks** Impressive results achieved through detailed, well-thought-out preparation, hard work and thorough record-keeping. It would be difficult to find a more motivated group of teachers and children. Slightly higher fees, but worth it.

## KNIGHTSBRIDGE KINDERGARTENS

St Andrew's Church Hall
Park Walk
London SW10 0XX
**Tel:** (071) 351 0368

**Owner/Principal:** Judy Ewing-Hoy, Cert Ed (Oxon)
**Type:** Nursery school offering five morning sessions a week and optional extended day
**Children:** 2½-5yrs. 40 places. 17 on register

**Hours:** 9am–12 noon (Mon–Fri)
Extended day till 3pm (Mon–Thurs)
Open 38 weeks a year
**Status:** Private, fee-paying
**Number of years open:** 7 in Knightsbridge. 1 at present address
**Meals:** Packed lunches and snacks
**1992 fees:** £650 per term for 5 morning sessions a week
£15 per session for extended day
£30 registration fee plus refundable deposit of half a term's fees
**Waiting list:** Short
**Registered by:** Royal Borough of Kensington & Chelsea SS
**Under same ownership:** Knightsbridge Kindergartens, Knightsbridge

**Premises** Newly refurbished church hall adjoining St Andrew's Church in Park Walk, half-way between Fulham Road and the King's Road. The nursery has sole use. There are three classrooms, one of which is actually in the church, although enclosed behind mainly glass walls. They are light and colourful, with newly sanded floors, fresh white walls and pretty red and white gingham curtains at the leaded windows. There is a different room for each age group. The church garden is used by the school on an almost daily basis. It has a large grassy area, securely fenced, and attractive, carefully tended flowerbeds.

**Owner/Principal & staff** Judy Ewing-Hoy, Cert Ed, has been principal of the Knightsbridge Kindergarten since it opened in Knightsbridge seven years ago, and has quadrupled the number of places she can offer by opening this new nursery. She currently employs four full-time teachers, all Mont Dip or NAMCW, but will be taking on more as numbers increase. They are intelligent, young and mature. Suzanne Corlett, Cert Ed, is in charge of pre-school education at both schools. Stephanie Kramer, a native French speaker, comes in once a week to give a half-hour French lesson to each class. A ballet teacher and pianist from the Chelsea Ballet School visit each week for a music and movement session. Staff from both schools meet at the beginning of each term, and there are regular staff meetings at each school.

**Children & parents** The children are privileged and local, although a few live outside the borough. They are immediately recognisable in a uniform of vivid scarlet blazers and hats, as they walk through Kensington Gardens in a long crocodile. Each child wears a wide belt attached to a safety rope, to prevent them from wandering off. Almost all go on to smart private schools in Chelsea and Kensington. A variety of different nationalities attend, mainly European.

**Curriculum & activities** The Kindergarten places great emphasis on pre-school learning, although children are not under pressure to develop faster than is realistic. The youngest group are introduced to some of the Montessori practical life exercises, as well as pencil control, colouring in, shapes and colours. Older groups move on to exercise books and workbooks and do a great deal of pre-reading, pre-writing and pre-maths work. 'Nearly all the staff have taught older pre-prep children in the past and know how important correct letter formation is – they have been made aware of the problem at the other end,' explains Judy. Children who are ready to read are introduced to the New Way reading scheme. Generally, all children leave for their next schools able to read a simple book. Children also enjoy plenty of art and collage making. There are stunning examples decorating the walls, some adult-led and some clearly done by the children themselves. There is also exciting imaginary play using a dressing-up box, toy theatre and hand puppets, a shop and a home corner. Each child has a yearbook, which is filled during the course of the year with examples of his/her work and photographs demonstrating progress. Children all wear bright red coats and hats or blazers and caps as outdoor uniform.

**Remarks** A cheerful and cosy church hall, providing three excellent classrooms. Strong emphasis on pre-school work, but plenty of scope for creative and imaginative play. Dedicated, intelligent, qualified staff working with children in small groups. Staff/child ratio is 1:6 for the oldest children. Plenty of individual attention.

## LADBROKE SQUARE MONTESSORI SCHOOL

43 Ladbroke Square
London W11 3ND
**Tel:** (071) 229 0125

**Owner:** Peter Tausig
**Headmistresses:** Sophia Russell-Cobb, Mont Dip
Philippa Drinkwater, Mont Dip
**Type:** Montessori nursery school offering half-day sessions. Some full-time places for 4–5yr-olds
**Children:** 2½–5½yrs. 60 places. 107 on register
**Hours:** 9am–4pm
Morning session 9am–12 noon
Afternoon session 1.30pm–4pm
Open 32 weeks a year
**Status:** Private, fee-paying
**Number of years open:** 15
**Meals:** Mid-morning snack, packed lunches. Full-timers bring packed lunches.
**1992 fees:** £550 per term for 5 morning sessions a week
£490 per term for 5 afternoon sessions a week
£100 refundable deposit
**Waiting list:** Huge. 2 years minimum. Register names at birth.
**Registered by:** Royal Borough of Kensington & Chelsea SS
**Under same ownership:** Hill Top School, Hampstead

**Premises** A gracious, four-storey, Victorian townhouse overlooking Ladbroke Square in the heart of Notting Hill Gate, Kensington. The nursery is bursting out of its premises – every nook and cranny is used. There are six different sized classrooms, an assembly hall (a rare facility for a nursery), an office and cloakrooms, all newly decorated. As soon as you step inside you can feel the warmth and homeliness of this nursery. Everything is child-centred and child-oriented. The artwork on display is spectacular. Every child who attends the nursery has contributed to the Noah's Ark frieze which climbs the staircase, two by two, to the top of the house. Each classroom is vibrant with creative and colourful wall displays. Fresh flowers in vases, seeds growing in pots, nature corners, etc, add to an atmosphere brimming with energy and ideas. There is a well-kept patio-style garden at the back, but the nursery regularly uses the 6½ acres of Ladbroke Square Gardens (the largest private square in London), with its tennis court, children's playground, adventure playground and carefully tended lawns (dogs on leads only). There are staggered arrival times to cope with the number of cars. Neighbours complain about double-parking outside and parents ignore pleas from the nursery to park legally further down the road.

**Headmistresses & staff** For the past four years, Sophia Russell-Cobb, Mont Dip, and Philippa Drinkwater, Mont Dip, have shared the role of headmistress. They both have young children of their own and job-sharing has worked remarkably well (they overlap once a week). As they were both full-time teachers at the school for many years before becoming headmistresses, they know each other and the school extremely well and share the same caring approach and philosophy. The nine teaching staff are qualified Montessori teachers who have worked at the nursery for between two and eight years. They are all young (late 20s, early 30s) and very loyal. Teachers at Ladbroke Square rarely raise their voices to children. One of the most notable aspects of the nursery is the warmth and tenderness of the relationships between staff and children. The nursery also accepts Montessori students on practical placement and supervises their training. The actual owners of the nursery have changed three times over the last 12 years, each time leaving the headmistresses a free hand. The current owners, however, also run the Hill Top School in Hampstead and it is too early to say whether they may want to take a more active role.

**Children & parents** The children are confident, extrovert and comfortable with their teachers, each other and visitors. They are obviously used to strangers observing classes, and after an initial welcome, settle down to work immediately. Each of the two classes has mixed age groups (family groupings) ranging from 2½ to 5 years. The young ones have to be out of nappies, but can be in trainer pants. The 4–5-year-olds are the only children to stay all day. The parents are successful professionals in banking, law, business, television and the arts. The majority of mothers work, so there is a high proportion of nannies. Nationalities are varied, including American, French, Italian. Parents are welcome to visit during the day by prior appointment. A parents' social evening takes place at the end of the Christmas term, and there are two plays a year and a summer sports day and picnic. Once a year parents are invited to discuss their child's progress with teachers and sit in on a class. Favourite schools, when they move on, are Thomas's, St Paul's Girls' Prep, Wetherby, the American School, Norland Place and the French Lycée. A handful go on to the state schools, particularly Fox.

**Curriculum & activities**  The programme is varied and busy as there is a great deal to fit into 2½–3 hours. Morning and afternoon sessions are basically the same. Every day, at the beginning of each session, there is a 15-minute assembly. Each teacher takes a turn at conducting assembly, and themes are developed over the week. We witnessed the dissection of a fish in full view of the children, who were enthralled. Assembly is also a time for sharing news, songs and prayer. Teaching is Montessori-based and the majority of equipment is Montessori. French is taught to the children for 30 minutes by the Club Frère Jacques. Ballet and French are optional. Food is not provided, but full-timers bring a packed lunch.

**Remarks**  Despite the huge waiting list this is definitely a school worth waiting for. A delightful Montessori nursery, with dedicated and caring staff.

# MRS MYNORS' NURSERY SCHOOL

The Garden Flat
4 Chepstow Villas
London W11 2RB
**Tel:** (071) 272 7253

**Owner:** Mrs Robert Mynors
**Principal:** Jane Ritchie, Mont Dip
**Type:** Nursery school offering half-day sessions during term-time. No full-time places
**Children:** 2½–5yrs. Approx 30 places per session. 60 on register
**Hours:** Morning session 9am–12 noon
Afternoon session 1pm–4pm
Open 36 weeks a year
**Status:** Private, fee-paying
**Number of years open:** 18

**Meals:** Juice and biscuits
**1992 fees:** £594 per term for 5 sessions a week
**Waiting list:** Long – priority to siblings
**Registered by:** Royal Borough of Kensington & Chelsea SS

**Premises**  The nursery is in the basement of a large house in a genteel, tree-lined street; wealthy neighbours include pop stars, actors, aristocracy, society photographers and minor royalty. The school has been in this street for 13 years, first at No 11 and now at No 4. Over the years, neighbours have expressed strong objections to its presence, claiming a nursery school in their street devalues their properties and causes parking and noise problems. Planning consent has been consistently difficult and contentious. However, the school now has a permanent home and permanent planning permission, although neighbours still monitor the parking and noise very closely. The nursery itself is homely, bright and clean. The three smallish classrooms are cosy and decorated with stunning artwork by the children. The principal's sole regret is that there is no big room where all the children can get together for activities like music and dance. A conservatory is used for messy play and art, and a small kitchenette provides juice and snacks. There is a large, beautiful garden at the back, which the children use frequently.

**Principal & staff**  Although the school's founder, Mrs Mynors, has now retired to the country, her influence is still strong. She visits once a week to see the nursery and talk to the principal. She appointed Jane Ritchie, Mont Dip, three years ago, after head-hunting her from the reception class at Wetherby, a local boys' prep school. Calm, rather precise and dedicated, she is very much a 'hands on' principal and teaches the oldest class four days a week, preparing them for entry to preparatory and primary schools. Some schools in the area have entrance exams even at 5 years – Jane Ritchie knows exactly how to prepare pupils for these, with a minimum of stress. There are six teaching staff (five NNEB and/or Montessori qualified and one unqualified with extensive childcare experience) including the principal, and they all started at the same time as Jane Ritchie. This is a team which knows each other extremely well and is very involved with children and parents. Many of the teachers supplement their salaries by working as holiday nannies to the children during school holidays. There are regular visiting music teachers, but no students.

**Children & parents** Most of the children live locally and reflect the affluence of the area. Priority is given to families living in the street or within walking distance. The most famous children to come through the doors have been Prince William and Prince Harry, bringing with them an entourage of bodyguards, detectives and the world's press. Royal patronage has made this the 'in place', but it is a great credit to Jane Ritchie and her staff that the school continued to run calmly and smoothly while the princes were there. Needless to say, the children are a confident, privileged bunch, encouraged to have a go at anything and everything. The nursery aims to develop their confidence, prepare them for school and, above all, treat them as individuals. Praise is seen as a prime motivator, and physical contact (lots of hugs) is encouraged. The parents are professional and well-heeled. About a third of the mothers work. Only four families are without a nanny. Parents have high expectations and can be forceful. Parents' meetings, concerts and plays are all well attended. New parents can stay with their children to help settle them in.

**Curriculum & activities** No one particular philosophy or method is followed. 'We will adapt a philosophy to suit the individual child.' There is no great pressure to get the children reading and writing either. 'We feel it is important to allow them to express themselves and enjoy their time at the nursery, as the pressure is so great when they get to school.' Different activities are set out on tables or the floor and children move freely from one to another. There is a 'magic box' full of magical objects to stimulate discussion and focus young minds. Half an hour is set aside each session for structured learning of numbers and letters. Art and craft, songs and music take place daily, and French and music and movement once a week. Children's progress is assessed once a term by the staff team.

**Remarks** This is a lovely school, but, for the privileged few only. If you put your child's name down at birth and live nearby you might just be lucky and secure a place. Morning places are taken up entirely by siblings.

# POOH CORNER MONTESSORI SCHOOL
Christchurch Hall
Victoria Road
Kensington
London W8 5RQ
**Tel:** (071) 937 1364

**Owner/Principal:** Victoria Morris, NNEB (Norland), Mont Dip
**Type:** Nursery school offering 5 morning sessions a week for 3–5yr-olds, plus 4 afternoon sessions a week for 2–3 yr-olds
**Children:** 2–5yrs. 28 places. 28 on register
**Hours:** Morning session 9am–12.15pm (3–5yr-olds)
Afternoon session 1.30pm–3.30pm Mon–Thurs (2–3yr-olds)
Open 36 weeks a year
**Status:** Private, fee-paying
**Number of years open:** 20
**Meals:** Juice and biscuits
**1992 fees:** £580 per term for 5 morning sessions a week
£480 per term for 4 afternoon sessions a week
£15 registration fee. £200 deposit – refundable
**Waiting list:** Long. Approx 120 for next 2 years
**Registered by:** London Borough of Kensington & Chelsea SS

**Premises** In the heart of Kensington, close to Gloucester Road, a Victorian-gothic church hall, sandwiched between Christchurch and Cornwall Gardens. The hall feels more like a vestry, with narrow, leaded windows and stained, vaulted ceiling. It is small and dark, but very intimate. The walls are lined with cupboards bursting at the seams with equipment and toys. The hall is used occasionally for functions by the church. There is an enclosed garden at the side of the hall, where children are allowed to use their tricycles on the flagstones.

**Owner/Principal & staff** Vicky Morris, NNEB (Norland), Mont Dip, has been principal of this well-established nursery school for the last four years, and taught at Pooh Corner for some time before taking over. In the past 20 years the nursery has had four owners, but has always been in the church hall and always run in much the same way. Vicky's deputy, Mona Starkis, Mont Dip, and the two other members of staff, are all qualified (either Mont Dip or

NNEB). Vicky believes that however good the Montessori training is, it does not necessarily prepare staff for the semi-potty-trained child, and therefore she prefers to have at least one non-Montessori member of staff. 'Finding the right staff is always the most difficult part of running a nursery.' Every now and again, Norland NNEB students come and work at the nursery. Last year some Japanese NNEB students, who spoke little or no English, spent time training at the nursery. They were very popular with the European children, but the Japanese children refused to communicate with them. Staff turnover has been a problem in the past, but the team now appears relatively stable.

**Children & parents** The children live in one of the most expensive districts of London. All of them move on to private schools. There is a mix of nationalities – many French children, most of whom progress to the Lycée, as well as American, Dutch, Scandinavian and Arab – but the majority are British and extremely well-off. There are three intakes a year, but very few places are available by the start of the summer term. Children must be potty-trained before starting. Despite the starting age, many, particularly girls, manage to achieve this by the age of two.

**Curriculum & activities** This is a Montessori school, implementing the Montessori philosophy of learning. Afternoon sessions are for the youngest children (2- to 3-year-olds), mornings for the older ones (3- to 5-year-olds). The 3-year-olds are moved up to morning sessions either when they're ready, near their third birthday, or when there is space. The afternoon sessions concentrate on sensorial and practical life exercises: art, craft, sticking, play dough, puzzles as well as regular singing and number rhymes. Children are free to use whatever Montessori equipment they choose, provided they have been introduced to it first. There is usually an organised craft activity, as well as a run in the garden, milk and biscuits and stories. The morning session follows a similar pattern, but is more structured. There is always a special activity of the day – when we visited the children had been making calendars for Christmas. They are divided into three groups by age and ability and spend 1½ hours each session in their groups. In the middle group, children start learning their letters and numbers, using the Montessori sandpaper letters and numbers. The alphabet is taught phonetically. The older group move on to word boxes and the majority are capable of addition and subtraction up to ten by the time they leave – some have reached 20. The standard of handwriting and pencil control is impressive and exercise books are used to reinforce each new letter and number learnt. The timetable also includes art, nature study, simple geography, history, current events, practical life and acting – the dressing-up box is ever popular. Each term has its own theme; in the autumn term it is usually animal related, the Easter term concentrates on ponds, rivers and spring, and in the summer, when the average age of the children is higher, a country is studied. A music and movement class is held on Thursday morning. Detailed notes are kept on the development of each child including their letter and number comprehension, but no written reports are prepared unless requested by parents. The nursery policy is to discuss progress face to face.

**Remarks** Exclusive, long-established nursery school for the sons and daughters of affluent Kensington residents. Unlike many church halls, this one is warm and cosy, in quiet and pretty surroundings. Interesting staff from varied backgrounds. Montessori philosophy of learning underpins everything, but also a wide range of other ideas and equipment built up over 20 years. No obvious pressure, but nonetheless a determined concentration on the 3Rs and academic achievement. Aims to give a child the best possible chance to beat the hot competition for places in London's elite private schools.

---

# ST JOSEPH'S (RC) JMI SCHOOL – NURSERY UNIT

Cadogan Street
London SW3 2QT
**Tel:** (071) 589 2438

**Owner:** RC Archdiocese of Westminster/Royal Borough of Kensington and Chelsea
**Principal:** Jill Hunt, BA (art & design), Mont Dip
**Type:** Nursery unit in Catholic primary school offering full- and part-time places and half-day sessions

**Children:** 3yrs 8mths–5yrs 3mths. 12 full-timers per day and 8 part-timers per session. 28 on register
**Hours:** 9am–3.15pm
Morning session 9.30am–11.30am
Afternoon session 12.45pm–3.15pm
Open 40 weeks a year
**Status:** State nursery class
**Number of years open:** 15
**Meals:** Lunch and snacks
**1992 fees:** No fees. 75p per day for lunch. £1 per week for snacks
**Waiting list:** Very long. 200 names
**Registered by:** Royal Borough of Kensington & Chelsea

**Premises** A pre-fabricated, temporary classroom, more like a hut, which has seen better days. There are plans to build another similar room for the nursery on the other side of the main school, but it looks as if the current building will be home for some time to come. It is sandwiched between the school and the street, leaving a small but adequate playground – all tarmac – with fixed climbing frames and a slide. Accommodation is limited – the classroom is open-plan and full of child-size furniture, a home corner, equipment and toys, with loos and a storage area opening off it. Staff have to go to the main school staff room if they need a break. However, it is a bright, welcoming and totally child-centred environment. There is a central passageway dividing the room in two. On either side of it are bays set up for different activities: a writing and literacy corner with desk and miniature typewriter (with 'come and write a letter' written in four languages above the desk); a maths and science corner; a home corner which is transformed into all sorts of different uses relating to whichever projects are in progress; and a computer corner.

**Principal & staff** Jill Hunt, BA, Mont Dip, is the calm, gentle and unflappable head of the nursery class. She joined the upper infants class at St Joseph's six years ago and has been head of the nursery class for the last two. Her degree in art and design means that there is a strong emphasis on art and craft – fabric dyeing was in progress on the day of our visit. She is assisted by Caroline Wade, NNEB, who has been working in the nursery class almost since it started 15 years ago. Together they plan in advance all projects to be undertaken during the term. The weekly plan is posted on the parents' noticeboard. A student on placement is sometimes present.

**Children & parents** At the time of our visit, five out of 28 children on the register were British. The rest were mainly Portuguese or Philippino, but there were also some Spaniards, South Americans and Poles. Most families live locally, within walking distance. Many parents work in local shops or in service in the up-market Chelsea homes which surround the school. One child in the past has gone on to private school, but all the others move up to the reception class at St Joseph's. The school is used to children who speak little or no English and would be happy to accept children with disabilities. New children are phased-in, one or two a day, at the beginning of each term, and parents encouraged to stay with their child for as long as necessary – this could be a day or a week. In the last few years fewer and fewer parents have been available to join in school activities and outings as the need for second incomes has increased.

**Curriculum & activities** The curriculum is planned but not structured, although it is geared towards the National Curriculum. Jill explains that the learning process is 'almost subliminal'. One or two projects are undertaken each term and are drawn into every aspect of the child's day. Recent projects have been on India, when the home corner was transformed into an Indian grotto with drapes and colourful fabrics, and Babies, with the home corner transformed into a clinic. Mothers with newborn babies came to the school to demonstrate breastfeeding and bathing. When we were shown round, the current topic was Ourselves, chosen specifically because it would provide maths and science opportunities. Children had been learning about tallest, shortest, symmetry, counting and matching as well as the senses, functions of the body, mirrors and reflections, health and hygiene. Each week is planned around different elements of the project including design and technology, art and craft, maths, science, language and literacy, outside play, health and hygiene, social study, RE and music. Reading and writing are strongly encouraged once a child is ready, and books are taken home each day. The playground is available at all times. Children proudly showed us the potted daffodils they were growing. The main school's music

were growing. The main school's music specialist spends 20 minutes in the nursery class every Tuesday and Thursday, while Jill Hunt runs an art and craft session in the school. Mrs Glover, trained in special educational needs, takes a bookmaking session. Religious content to the day is 'more incidental than planned', but this is a Catholic school and a prayer is said before lunch and at the end of the day. Rules are kept to a minimum and mainly apply to the outside area for the children's own safety. Disruptive behaviour is nearly always cured by masses of hugs and distraction. Profiles – including photographs – are kept on each child and added to whenever there is anything of note. Jill feels that a photograph of the child with a particularly good piece of work or creative achievement is much more explicit than an adult's written notes.
**Remarks** Peace and happiness in the very heart of London. Children visibly responding to the warmth and affection shown by both members of staff, and each working at his/her own pace and routine. A confident and cosmopolitan group, showing a great deal of independent thinking. Excellent art and craft work. High-quality nursery provision, but as almost always, totally insufficient to meet the local demand.

## ST PETER'S NURSERY SCHOOL

St Peter's Church Hall
59a Portobello Road
London W11 3DB
**Tel:** (071) 243 2617

**Owner:** St Peter's Management Committee
**Headteacher:** Susan Weatherley, NNEB
**Type:** Christian community nursery offering half-day sessions, and some full-time places for older children. Afternoon session for youngest children
**Children:** 2½–5yrs. 48 places. 41 on register
**Hours:** 9.15am–3.15pm
Morning session 9.15am–12.15pm
Afternoon session 1.30pm–3.30pm
Open 46 weeks a year
**Status:** Community nursery school. Some subsidised places
**Number of years open:** 2
**Meals:** Snacks

**1992 fees:** £30 per week for 5 sessions (benchmark for non-subsidised fees)
£3–£8 additional contribution for full-day
**Waiting list:** Reasonable. ⅓ to be church attenders
**Registered by:** Royal Borough of Kensington & Chelsea SS

## TADPOLES NURSERY SCHOOL (formerly Ifield Road Nursery School)

Park Walk Play Centre
Park Walk Primary School
Park Walk
London SW10
**Tel:** (071) 373 1160

**Owner/Directress:** Claire Dimpfl, Mont Dip
**Type:** Montessori nursery school, offering full- and part-time places and half-day sessions
**Children:** 2½–5yrs. 26 places.
**Hours:** 9.30am–3pm (for children over 4yrs)
Morning session 9.30am–12.30pm
Afternoon session 1pm–3pm
Open 36 weeks a year
**Status:** Private, fee-paying
**Number of years open:** Opening Sept 93 in current premises. 11 years in previous premises
**Meals:** Packed lunches, snacks
**1992 fees:** £700 per term for 5 morning sessions and 3 afternoon sessions a week
£450 per term for 5 morning sessions
£250 per term for 3 afternoon sessions
£10 registration fee
**Waiting list:** Places available
**Registered by:** Royal Borough of Kensington & Chelsea SS

## WORLD'S END BEGINNERS' NURSERY SCHOOL

1 Shalcomb Street
London SW10 0HZ
**Tel:** (071) 352 2126

**Owner/Principal:** Belinda Howard, Mont Dip
**Type:** Nursery school offering full-time places and half-day sessions
**Children:** 2–5yrs. 30 places. 25 on register
**Hours:** 9.30am–3pm
Morning session 9.30am–12.30pm
Afternoon session 12.30pm–3pm
Open 36 weeks a year
**Status:** Private, fee-paying
**Number of years open:** 18
**Meals:** Snack, packed lunches
**1992 fees:** £1100 per term full-time
£600 per term for 5 morning sessions a week
£500 per term for 5 afternoon sessions a week
£20 registration fee
£28 per term for French lessons
**Waiting list:** Places available
**Registered by:** Royal Borough of Kensington & Chelsea SS

## ZEBEDEE NURSERY SCHOOL

St Paul's Church Hall
Onslow Square
London SW7 3NX
**Tel:** (071) 584 7660

**Principal:** Su Gahan, NNEB
**Type:** Christian nursery school offering half-day sessions. Full day twice a week for 4–5yr-olds
**Children:** 2½–5yrs. 52 places. 52 on register. 50% of places for Christian families
**Hours:** 9am–3.30pm Mon, Tues, Thurs (4–5yrs)
Morning session 9am–12.10pm (3–5yrs)
Afternoon session 1.30pm–3.30pm (2½–3yrs)
Open 38 weeks a year
**Status:** Church-run, fee-paying, with 5 assisted places
**Number of years open:** 10
**Meals:** Juice and biscuits only. Children attending for full day bring packed lunch
**1992 fees:** £475 per term for 5 morning sessions a week
£340 per term for 5 afternoon sessions a week
£25 registration fee plus £250 refundable deposit
**Waiting list:** Moderate
**Registered by:** Royal Borough of Kensington & Chelsea SS

**Premises** The nursery is in a church hall tucked away at the back of Onslow Square down a pretty side alley, well stocked with shrubs and flowers. Onslow Square is a private garden square in a classy residential part of South Kensington. The main hall is reasonably light and opens off a small entrance hall. The older children (4–5-year-olds) are taught separately in a small carpeted upstairs room, which has its own entrance and is rather isolated from the main nursery. Onslow Square gardens are used almost daily as a playground. However, the new Children Act has created problems. Staff ratios for going to the park under the Act must now increase from 1 teacher to 8 children to 1:3. This means recreation will become a difficult logistical exercise.

**Principal & staff** All staff are devout Christians and belong to different congregations (two from St Paul's). The former principal has left to travel and visit other Christian nurseries across the world, but when she returns she will set up a new nursery, Zebedee 2, at St Dionis' Church, Parsons Green. Her former deputy, Su Gahan, NNEB, has taken over the running of this nursery. Su was involved in setting up Zebedee ten years ago and taught here for five years before leaving to become a counsellor. She returned to Zebedee four years later to concentrate solely on the older children and develop their educational programme. She feels her strengths lie in teaching and treats her children with love and respect. There are three teachers (one Montessori qualified), including a qualified dance teacher with a Montessori correspondence qualification. A ballet teacher visits once a week.

**Children & parents** Parents travel to this nursery – school runs are organised from as far away as Camberwell and Clapham. Approx 50 per cent are local Christian families from St Paul's and Holy Trinity Brompton, and the rest come because it is convenient or because of the school's good reputation. Su is keen to attract more non-Christian families. Many children are siblings (they currently have the fifth child of one family). When children leave, parents are invited to contribute to a bursary fund which subsidises places for families struggling with fees. Subsidies can be as high as 75 per cent, and applications are made to the chairman of the trustees.

**Curriculum & activities** There are two groups within the school – a morning nursery school and an afternoon playgroup. Both are run on the basis of a strong Christian belief, which underlies all the work with the children. Three to four Christian themes each term are communicated to children through songs and Bible stories and by learning relevant verses from the Bible. Staff and children pray together in small groups, and once a week the whole school worships together. Zebedee is also a Montessori-inspired nursery, so children are given some choice in the activities they want to do during work time and carry them out individually. The children are divided, by age, into groups of six. All children do number, reading or writing work and a creative project every day. Younger ones do more practical work, simple pencil control exercises (tracing, colouring, etc), construction games and some written letter and number work. The 3- to 5-year-olds are given two pieces of written work each day, which must be completed before they go on to colouring or simpler tasks. Children who are 4 or 5 work in their own classroom upstairs – this has improved their concentration and output. All written work is done with workbooks or exercise books. Out of the group of eight, two are good readers and the rest are on New Way's early readers. Books and schemes used are the New Way reading scheme, Letterland and Heinemann Educational Infant Mathematics. There is an option for 4-year-olds to stay until 3.30pm on two days a week. They bring packed lunches and there are extra activities for them such as craft, cooking, projects, games in the gardens, music and musical instruments, stories and outings. The whole nursery comes together twice a week for topic work. Each term has its own particular big event. At Christmas it is a Nativity play, at Easter a dance display and in summer a sports day and a two-hour parents' evening.

**Remarks** A Christian nursery school with a good reputation in the area, only two minutes from South Kensington station. Strong community feeling and some subsidised places.

# Kingston-upon-Thames

Nursery education is reasonably extensive, with places for 34 per cent of all 3- and 4-year-olds. The Education Department claims more nursery class places than children to fill them – unique! The most helpful early years liaison officer we found in London worked here. She sent a long, hand-written letter with full details and a list of relevant publications. However, she only had two days left in the job – her post had been abolished as part of the borough's cuts. The Early Years Centre had lost its manager, and was in the throes of moving. The future looks uncertain. For day care, there are 420 registered childminders, charging approximately £2 per hour (list from the Early Years Centre); 47 playgroups (£1.70–£5 per session); 17 private day nurseries, charging between £55–£100 per child per week for over-2s. The two borough day nurseries have been almost exclusively for children in need. There is also concern that the cost of childcare is too high and that the excellent free nursery classes for 3–4 year-olds do not solve the problem for working parents. These nursery classes are attached to 17 primary schools with 1,258 places and only 1,243 children aged 3–4 in 1992.

## Further information

For details on day nurseries, childminders, playgroups and a clear, well-written summary of all services, contact:
Early Years Resource Centre
132 Kingston Road
New Malden KT3 3NX
Tel: (081) 547 6576

For details on nursery schools and classes:
Education Department
Guildhall
Kingston-upon-Thames KT1 1EU
Tel: (081) 547 5252

# LATCHMERE INFANT SCHOOL NURSERY

Latchmere Road
Kingston-upon-Thames
Surrey TW9 2DW
**Tel:** (081) 546 6507

**Owner:** London Borough of Kingston-upon-Thames LEA
**Headteacher of infant school:** Patricia Mellor, Cert Ed
**Deputy Head:** Susan Robb, Dip Primary Ed (Scotland)
**Nursery Manager:** Janie Manuel, Cert Ed
**Type:** Nursery class in state school offering half-day sessions. No full-time places.
**Children:** 3½–4½yrs. 26 places. 52 on register
**Hours:** Morning session 9am–11.30am Afternoon session 12.50pm–3.20pm Open 39 weeks a year
**Status:** State nursery class
**Number of years open:** 3½
**Meals:** Children bring fresh fruit or vegetable snack
**1992 fees:** No fees
**Waiting list:** Huge. 112 names. Priority to siblings and area health requests. Early registration advisable
**Registered by:** London Borough of Kingston-upon-Thames LEA

**Premises** New, creatively designed, purpose-built nursery on one floor, within the grounds of the popular Latchmere Infant School. The front of the building is modern, cheerful and welcoming, with colourful arched windows. A large, part-grassed, part-tarmac play area abuts the side and rear of the building, well equipped with fixed climbing frame, trikes and bikes and construction blocks. Inside is mainly open-plan, but welcoming and friendly. The classroom is organised into areas, each incorporating an aspect of the National Curriculum, but also giving the space a warm, more homely feel. The various work stations provide for construction work, creative and messy play, language studies, music and musical instruments, group activities and a quiet book corner. The walls are filled with artwork and projects, and the room is bursting with equipment, furniture, books and toys. The staff room, large cloakroom area and children's loos are brightly painted and cheerful.

**Nursery Manager & staff** Janie Manuel, Cert Ed, is responsible for the day-to-day running of the nursery. She is a cheerful extrovert with 18 years' teaching experience. When we visited, she was busy playing the guitar for an enthusiastic singing lesson. The children were totally absorbed. She is assisted by Lisa Drew, NNEB, also very experienced and calmer. Together they provide a knowledgeable team which liaises regularly with Susan Robb, the deputy head of the school, who is in overall control of the planning and supervision of the nursery and reception classes. This ensures continuity in education and care, when children move on. Nursery also relies on regular voluntary help from parents.

**Children & parents** All children are from the immediate local community, about five per cent from ethnic minorities. Latchmere Infants has a dynamic headmistress and a strong reputation. Children with disabilities and special educational needs are encouraged to apply and offered extra attention from the deputy head. Parents are actively involved and organise a rota of one or two parent volunteers to assist at each session. A parent is also elected annually to organise coffee mornings for new parents, help with fund-raising and act as a general representative on important issues. Parents and children are invited to an open morning the term before children are due to start. Entry is in September only, staggered over the first few days to allow children to be introduced gradually. Janie and Lisa conduct home visits and have drawn up an Early Years Profile – a detailed written profile of each child filled in by teachers, children and parents in their home environment. Good relationships with parents are considered vital. Open evenings are held once a term and the nursery has an open-door policy for day-to-day discussions.

**Curriculum & activities** Janie Manuel is impressed by High Scope and subtly incorporates it into the structure of the nursery, where possible. This method aims to make children more aware of their environment and responsible by allowing them to plan, execute and review their own activities, with gentle adult guidance. Sessions begin with group discussion about what is available for work and play. Children then choose their activity and finally talk about what they have achieved and learnt. Teachers monitor each activity closely and try to help children in small groups of four when possible. The emphasis is on language input, with frequent use of writing and language games. Art is an extremely strong subject in this nursery. Every wall is positively covered with genuinely child-directed work – among the most wonderful creative artwork we have seen. Still more artwork is taken home. Children usually spend a year in the nursery before moving up to one of the three reception classes, where they will be offered a full- or part-time place depending on age. Full-time school does not begin until they have turned 5 years. Dance, movement, music and singing take place daily and there is a weekly swimming session in the main school. Children are monitored constantly by staff, who also have weekly curriculum meetings. Monthly liaison meetings with teachers in the reception classes ensures continuity and guarantees that nursery children are well prepared for life in the main school. The term before they move up, each child spends a few hours a week in the reception class.

**Remarks** Cheerful, homely nursery offering high-quality stimulation and a thorough preparation for school, at an affordable price. Despite its short life, this nursery has established an excellent reputation and built up a hopelessly long waiting list. The successful headmistress of the main school has chosen an experienced, cheerful team to ensure the building of a well-organised, smooth-running nursery class. Open, friendly, creative – and very difficult to secure a place.

# Lambeth

The borough declares in its recent review of services for under-8s, 'Lambeth would like to see affordable services available for each child whose parents seek it, and in a form appropriate to the needs of each child.' However, due to central government funding cuts, nursery services in the borough face reductions, not the 70 per cent increase necessary to fulfil its aim. 'In practice, the emphasis is as much on defending current services as it is upon developing new ones,' an official told us. Lambeth spends £4 million on its 11 day nurseries and over £500,000 on grants to voluntary nurseries and playgroups. A further £400,000 is allocated to subsidising places with registered childminders. Strenuous efforts are made to charge affordable fees. A full-time Social Services nursery place costs £45 per week (real cost £145 per week), and grant-aided voluntary nurseries charge up to £30 per week. The 400 registered childminders charge £40–£65 per week. Grant-aided playgroups are approximately 55p per session. The borough has one of the highest birthrates in London, reflected in a 25 per cent increase in the number of under-5s between 1981 and 1989. The number of daycare places does not come anywhere near to meeting demand. Lambeth estimates that 50 per cent of its 3- and 4-year-olds have places in nursery units, nursery schools or classes. The 38 classes attached to primary schools (plus five at church schools) have long waiting lists. The borough believes demand is such that it could fill each class over again, if resources allowed.

## Further information

For details on day nurseries, childminders and playgroups:
Department of Social Services
Mary Seacole House
91 Clapham High Street
London SW4 7TY
Tel: (071) 926 4510

For details on nursery schools, units and classes:
Education Department
Frontline Services
50 Acre Lane
London SW2 5SS
Tel: (071) 926 2270 or 2266

# CALDECOT PRIMARY NURSERY CLASS

Caldecot Road
Camberwell
London SE5 9RN
**Tel:** (071) 274 1342

**Owner:** London Borough of Lambeth LEA
**Nursery Teacher-in-charge:** Bridgid Buckley, BA, PGCE
**Type:** Nursery class in primary school offering full-time places and half-day sessions
**Children:** 3yrs 4mths–5yrs. 25 places (15 full-time). 35 on register
**Hours:** 9.15am–3.30pm
Morning session 9.15am–11.45am
Afternoon session 1pm–3.30pm
Open 38 weeks a year
**Status:** State nursery class
**Number of years open:** 15
**Meals:** Juice, milk and biscuits, lunch
**1992 fees:** No fees. 50p per day for snack. 80p per day for lunch
**Waiting list:** 105. Demand far outstrips supply
**Registered by:** London Borough of Lambeth LEA

**Premises** Cheerful, south-facing rooms on the ground floor of a typical tall, red-brick, Victorian school building, adjacent to King's College Hospital on Denmark Hill. Surrounded by a sea of uncompromising tarmac and fairly intimidating from the outside, the school has nevertheless done everything it can inside to create a warm, colourful and welcoming environment. The nursery class is in two rooms knocked together and painted an attractive shade of pale pink. The atmosphere is homely, with vividly coloured decorations of all kinds on the walls, an inviting selection of cushions and beanbags in the carpeted reading/quiet area and plentiful supplies of equipment. French windows lead from the classroom directly on to a small outside play area (tarmac with some safety surfacing), fenced off from the main school playground. There is a limited amount of outdoor equipment, but Ruskin Park is just round the corner and is visited regularly for playtime and nature study. Children's loos and washbasins are in a specially partitioned-off area. All full-timers keep their own toothbrush for daily use after lunch.

**Teacher-in-charge & staff** Bridgid Buckley, BA, PGCE, a former infant teacher, took over the running of the class in 1992. She is assisted by an experienced and long-serving NNEB nursery assistant, Joy Andrews, and a lunchtime supervisor. Staff meetings, with the whole school, take place twice a week. There is a strong staff training and development programme. Each week's programme is carefully planned in advance and the schedule pinned on the class noticeboard for parents to read and discuss with staff.

**Children & parents** Although culturally diverse, the children are principally Afro-Caribbean from working-class backgrounds, some on the Social Services 'at-risk' register, others from socially deprived homes. Despite their many problems, the children are happy, interested and stimulated. The staff are experienced in dealing with learning and emotional difficulties. Parents are encouraged to support the school and become involved in class activities, although in practice this does not happen frequently. There are parent-teacher social evenings, evenings to discuss children's progress and regular newsletters. Children are phased-in, by attending for only an hour a day to begin with. Full-time children are usually in the older group, preparing for the reception class in the main school. Children at risk are sometimes accepted at a younger age. All children wear a uniform – grey trousers or skirts, with a white shirt and brilliant red V-neck jumper.

**Curriculum & activities** The nursery class is in control of its own budget and is well provided with equipment and generous supplies of art and painting materials (annual budget £1000). Each day starts with group time, when children sit in a circle on the carpeted area for the register and to sing songs. Then they move on to the day's activities, which have already been set up. There is more or less free choice, but 'free time' becomes subtly more structured as children approach the move to main school. Available activities include project work, art and craft, sensory/science, construction/maths, some reading exercises using flashcards, 'group experience' and music. The day we visited, children were sharing two large, mouthwatering platefuls of kiwi fruit, bananas and oranges which they had helped to chop up. Songs, stories, discussions, games and outdoor play take place each session. Children are encouraged to take books home from school at the end of the week, but there is no formal teaching of reading or writing. The school has a well-stocked library which is used regularly by the nursery class, but otherwise there is little contact with the rest of the school. Assembly is attended on rare and special occasions, for example, harvest festival. Lunches at Caldecot Primary are a special culinary experience and a major social occasion. The nursery class eats in the classroom, and tables are set with tablecloths and homemade table mats decorated with each child's name. Staff often eat with the children. Full-timers have a brief quiet period after lunch before the afternoon session commences. Afternoons tend to be less structured as the full-time children are often quite tired. Regular outings are taken in the school minibus.

**Remarks** A striking, colourful and happy place. A great asset to the neighbourhood and a caring, homely refuge for many of the children. Nursery provision is generally poor in the area and the waiting list is huge. Preference to siblings, those living closest and children with difficult home circumstances. Unhappily, after this excellent preparation for school, there is no guarantee of a place in the reception class.

# DAISY CHAIN MONTESSORI SCHOOL

Stockwell Methodist Church Hall
Jeffreys Road
London SW4
**Tel:** (071) 738 8606

**Owner/Headteacher:** Lucy Gordon-Lennox, Mont Dip
**Type:** Nursery school offering half-day sessions. Some full-time places for older children
**Children:** 2½–5yrs. 40 places. 45 on register.
**Hours:** Morning session 9.30am–12.30pm (older children)
Afternoon session 12.30pm–3.30pm
Open 32 weeks a year
**Status:** Private, fee-paying
**Number of years open:** 4½
**Meals:** Juice and biscuits

**1992 fees:** £500 per term for five morning sessions a week
£450 per term for 3 sessions a week (new children only)
**Waiting list:** No
**Registered by:** London Borough of Lambeth SS

**Premises** Leafy, but rather down-trodden area, between Clapham North and Stockwell tube stations. The church hall is a flat-roofed, brick building, extending out behind the church. An overgrown but very pretty garden with colourful flowerbeds, and splashes of jazzy primary colours on doors and walls, helps to minimise the building's institutional feel. The hall itself is large, bright and airy. A warren of hospital-style corridors leads to other tucked-away, but equally bright and sunny rooms, one of which is used for nothing but sand and water play. Only the main hall has to be cleared away (about once a week), so the nursery feels well established and at home and displays a stunning array of colourful wall charts, collages and children's art work. The stage at the far end of the hall is decorated with a splendid backdrop (three double sheets sewn together) which the children have spattered, smeared, wiped and painted with a striking riot of primary colours. The hall is set out with the usual small tables and chairs and has been broken up into more homely, manageable areas by the clever placing of bookcases, shelves and pretty flowery plastic floormats. One side of the stage is fenced off and forms a walkway into a large room behind, which is used by the 2½- to 3-year-olds. There is also a spacious hallway, a kitchen, a quiet room for serious concentration and a messy room.

**Owner/Headteacher & staff** The headteacher Lucy Gordon-Lennox, Mont Dip, is young, friendly and full of ideas. She aims to make her nursery school a lively, happy and enjoyable experience for children and staff. Since she qualified, she has worked in one other Montessori school in London and spent six months setting up nurseries in a South African township. Ms Gordon-Lennox only teaches three hours a week herself, but is an ever-present force in the mornings, explaining her role as 'helping to keep the spark going'. Her afternoons are taken up with administration. She expects her staff to be 'prepared to roll up their sleeves' and visits other nurseries whenever she can to help stay on her toes – 'you've got to keep working at it'. A student from the London Montessori Centre helps out two mornings a week – 'full of fresh ideas from the previous day's tutorials'. There are eight staff in total, seven full-time and one part-time. Five are qualified Mont Dip, one is NNEB. They are young, lively and enthusiastic.

**Children & parents** Despite its location in the heart of one of London's most culturally and socially diverse areas, there is no social or racial mix. The nursery children are, without exception, from white, middle-class, professional families. Lucy Gordon-Lennox has offered two free places to Lambeth Social Services for children from local estates, but the offer has never been taken up. The majority go on to private, pre-prep schools in the area. New arrivals are thrown in at the deep end – there is no phasing-in, although the youngest sometimes start with just three visits a week and can choose to spend the first term or two at the quieter afternoon sessions. The oldest children can stay all day, in preparation for school.

**Curriculum & activities** This is not a strict Montessori school, although most of the essential Montessori equipment is available. The day 'just seems to happen' around a core of roughly timetabled subjects; these include singing, nature, painting, news, co-ordination, projects and history of art – the latter being an ambitious and interesting programme built around the subject matter and styles of some of the great paintings. Children are taught to read and write and do simple number work. There is also plenty of scope for fun, with daily games in the church grounds or the park at the end of the road. Other activities include gardening by the front door (growing tomatoes and spring onions), making bread and cakes, dressing up, library visits, and work on topical and cultural subjects. We saw work in progress on a hibernation project and a harvest-festival box full of goodies. Despite a slightly chaotic atmosphere, children were bright, articulate and chirpy.

**Remarks** A church hall that actually works as a nursery. One of the lightest, most spacious and welcoming we have seen. Staff brimming with enthusiasm, clearly kept on their toes by a dynamic head teacher. A very jolly place to be.

# THE OVAL MONTESSORI NURSERY SCHOOL

88A Fentiman Road
London SW8 1LA
**Tel:** (071) 735 4816
**Owner/Principals:** Annabelle Mattingley, Mont Dip
Rebecca Grainzevelles, Mont Dip
**Type:** Montessori nursery school offering half-day sessions. No full-time places
**Children:** 2½–5yrs. 14 places per session. 28 on register
**Hours:** Morning session 9.15am–12.15pm
Afternoon session 2.15pm–5.15pm
Open 30 weeks a year
**Status:** Private, fee-paying
**Number of years open:** 3½
**Meals:** Juice and biscuits
**1992 fees:** £410 per term for 5 sessions a week
£12 per term for yoga
**Waiting list:** 40
**Registered by:** London Borough of Lambeth SS

**Premises** Attractive basement flat in well-kept early Victorian terrace of large town houses, between Vauxhall and the Oval. The entrance is via area steps below the main front door, past a pretty garden full of pink roses and herbaceous plants. A wooden hut at the bottom of the garden is used as an office. Children arrive for each session through the office and garden from a mews behind. This keeps them off Fentiman Road, which is used as a main thoroughfare between Clapham Road and South Lambeth Road. The nursery classroom is a light and attractive U-shaped room. In the centre of it a separate room has been built to accommodate child-size loos and hand basins. Handwashing seems to be a central and highly social activity at the nursery. There is a kitchen and cloakroom to the rear of the building leading into the garden. The classroom is neat, bright and tidy. Pale pink painted walls are sparsely decorated with hessian noticeboards displaying home-made maps of the world and framed black and white posters bearing Montessori quotations. With its small tables and chairs, cork-tiled floor and child-height shelves, full of wooden boxes and trays of Montessori equipment, it ressembles a very comfortable miniature office. The garden, a rather bare, sandy affair, is due for refurbishment and will include an area of wood chippings. There will be ramps to make access easier for disabled children.

**Principal & staff** Oval Montessori is owned and run by Rebecca Grainzevelles, Mont Dip, who owns the house and lives upstairs, and Annabelle Mattingley, Mont Dip. This is a pure Montessori nursery, every teacher is Montessori trained and qualified, and staff vacancies are only advertised at Montessori colleges. When we visited, Annabelle was teaching with Caroline, a Dutch Montessori teacher. Fourteen children were engaged in six different activities, wholly absorbed in what they were doing. The atmosphere is quiet and industrious. Instructions are almost whispered. One rather boisterous little boy was asked calmly and gently to use his 'inside voice', rather than disturb the rest of the class. Students from Montessori colleges come on placement for one or two weeks at a time and pupils from the local secondary school sometimes arrive for work experience.

**Children & parents** Fentiman Road covers the whole social scale, from the very affluent in large early-Victorian semis on one side, to the South Lambeth council estate on the other. Children at the nursery are surprisingly representative of this mix and there are one or two low-cost places sponsored by the owners, to help maintain it. Places have also been offered to Lambeth Social Services, but they have failed to respond. Children with special needs are welcome. A high percentage go on to the local state school, others to private schools like Hill House and Newton Prep. The nursery goes to great lengths to explain the Montessori method to parents. All new parents attend special 'parent education evenings', where they are shown the Montessori equipment used by the 3- and 4-year-olds. There is another, similar evening where the more advanced equipment for older children is demonstrated. Each term, parents are encouraged to sit in on a session and children take their parents round the equipment.

**Curriculum & activities** Learning in a Montessori classroom begins with practical-life materials. Equipment is used to teach skills such as pouring, tying bows and laces, folding and sewing. Children continue these exercises and also move on to work with sensorial apparatus using seminal Montessori equipment like the pink tower, cylinder blocks, the broad stair and touch boards. These lay the foundations for all further work in maths and language. Virtually all the equipment in the nursery is Montessori and is used to teach a wide range of subjects – geography, history, science, biology, geometry and algebra. Children move from one Montessori exercise to another at their own pace, choosing whatever piece of equipment attracts them. In each session about 1½ hours is devoted to Montessori-led work. Other activities include languages (French, German and Dutch), yoga, swimming and outings. Many activities are linked to special projects, for example visiting Chinese New Year celebrations was part of a project on SE Asia. The day we observed, children were studying primeval forests and fossils – they had painted a background for a prehistoric forest and were about to make fossil-shaped biscuits.

**Remarks** A well-managed nursery with a social conscience. The children are happy, calm and hardworking in a homely, organised environment. We hope that predicted management changes will not affect the future of this school. Devotees of Maria Montessori should join the waiting list now, as the school takes only 14 children each session.

## TOAD HALL NURSERY SCHOOL

37 St Mary's Gardens
Kennington
London SE11 4UF
**Tel:** (071) 735 5087

**Owner/Principal:** Vivien Rees, NNEB, Mont Dip
**Type:** Montessori nursery offering half-day sessions. No full-time places
**Children:** 2½–5yrs. 20 places. 40 on register
**Hours:** Morning session 8.30am–12 noon
Afternoon session 1pm–4.30pm
Open 40 weeks a year
**Status:** Private, fee-paying
**Number of years open:** 8
**Meals:** Juice and biscuits
**1992 fees:** £485 per term for 5 sessions a week
£37 per week for 5 sessions
£25 registration fee
**Waiting list:** Morning places full a year ahead. Afternoon places available
**Registered by:** London Borough of Lambeth SS

**Premises** A quiet location in the heart of Kennington, not far from the Imperial War Museum. Toad Hall has the tattiest exterior of all in a terrace of small Victorian houses. The interior also needs redecoration. Wallpaper is peeling off in places and there is an air of scruffiness throughout. The owner lives above the nursery on the upper floors of the house which look to be in a better state of decoration. The main room on the first floor is the most attractive and is set out with Montessori equipment and a reading corner. There is a grubby, comfy room with miniature armchairs, which houses a fantastic selection of children's books for all ages – a small library in fact. Downstairs is a messy-play room used for music sessions, with a piano, sand play and painting equipment. Next door is a classroom looking on to a patio at the back. The children are not allowed to use the patio because the Council is worried about noise. The nursery is currently negotiating with the Council to be able to take groups of five or six children outside at a time. For the same reasons, Toad Hall does not have access to the communal gardens in front of the house. Instead they use the parks in West Square and beside the Imperial War Museum.

**Owner/Principal & staff** Vivien Rees, NNEB, Mont Dip, is the dedicated, full-time principal and owner. Living above the nursery means total involvement, and in the past she used to launder and iron all 40 of the children's pinafores, although this is now the parents' responsibility. Her deputy, Carolyn Greenwood, Mont Dip, who has been at the nursery for five years, shares day-to-day responsibility for the school and its ever-changing and inventive curriculum. The staff are all Montessori-qualified, but interpret the philosophy liberally. One who speaks fluent French gives a French lesson once or twice a week. A ballet teacher comes in weekly.

**Children & parents** There is very active parental involvement and questionnaires are sent out to make sure everyone has some input and that parents are happy. Many parents come in to talk to the children about their jobs and others to play musical instruments for them. Most live locally. Some parents are local shopkeepers, which Vivien Rees feels gives the school a real sense of community. The children come from a wide assortment of backgrounds and cultures and progress to many different schools, mostly private. They wear smocks purchased from the school. This is a new development – Vivien Rees used to provide them free (made up by her mother in the country).

**Curriculum & activities** A liberal Montessori-based approach, with the emphasis on learning through play. Children are encouraged to progress at their own pace, but expected to be able to read and write well by the time they leave. Sessions begin with free play in the main room. Activities include drawing, cutting, painting, sand and water play, handicrafts and educational games. An hour of schoolwork, in small groups of five children supervised by a qualified Montessori teacher, follows. There is a good selection of Montessori and other equipment (annual budget £4000) for pre-reading, pre-writing and number work. After worktime, all the children sit together in a circle on cushions for group discussions, songs, stories and French conversation. Different projects are covered each term and full use is made of the nursery's huge supply of well-cared-for books. Music, ballet and regular outings take place regularly at no extra cost. Each child receives a comprehensive termly report, covering social skills and discipline as well as progress in maths, reading, writing, history, science, etc.

**Remarks** In spite of its unattractive premises and lack of outdoor facilities, this is an amazingly popular nursery school which has never needed to advertise and has a long waiting list, especially for morning sessions. Needs some care and attention to detail, *and* a major redecoration programme. Happy smiling children, clearly enjoying their first school experience.

# WILLOW NURSERY SCHOOL

Clapham Baptist Church
823–825 Wandsworth Road
London SW8 3JL
**Tel:** (071) 498 0319

**Owner/Principal:** Clarinda Weir, Mont Dip
**Type:** Montessori nursery school offering morning sessions
**Children:** 2½–5yrs. 40 places. 39 on register
**Hours:** 9am–12 noon
Open 36 weeks a year

**Status:** Private, fee-paying
**Number of years open:** 11
**Meals:** Juice and biscuits
**1992 fees:** £475 per term for 5 sessions a week
£410 per term for 3 sessions a week
£300 returnable deposit
**Waiting list:** Places often available in Sept. 3 intakes a year
**Registered by:** London Borough of Lambeth SS

**Premises** An ugly church hall, opening directly on to busy Wandsworth Road. A large entrance hall allows parents to collect and organise their offspring in safety before heading into the traffic, parking problems and busy bus lanes outside. The nursery uses two rooms, one a large, white and reasonably airy hall, with a rather grubby wooden floor and equally grubby rugs, and another smaller room used for prayers by the church. The prayer room is used by the younger children for the first part of each morning, before they join the rest of the school in the main hall. Tables and chairs must be cleared away after each session. No outside play area.

**Owner/Principal & staff** The driving forces behind the Willow for the past six years have been Susie Poë and Sarah Ward, both Mont Dip and both dynamic and committed. They have built up a loyal following and a long waiting list, but have now decided to retire. The nursery has been handed over to Clarinda Weir, Mont Dip, who has worked as a teacher at the school for the past two years.

**Children & parents** The clientele is professional, mainly European and prosperous. Some children move on to the popular state-run Honeywell and Macaulay primary schools, but the majority find places in private prep schools – Eaton House, Dulwich Prep, Finton House. New children are admitted at the beginning of each term and the youngest stay together during group time for the first term only. From then on, they move to a mixed ability, mixed age group of seven or eight children until they leave.

**Curriculum & activities** Classwork is Montessori based and all the teachers have a Montessori qualification, although the calm, concentrated atmosphere of many Montessori schools was missing on the day we observed a session. Most of the books in the book corner were borrowed from Wandsworth Library and were two weeks overdue. Nursery philosophy is that learning should be stimulating and fun. Above all, children are encouraged to enjoy themselves in a happy atmosphere. Sessions begin with children working individually, using the Montessori equipment set out on shelves around the room. Younger children practise fine motor skills with exercises such as glueing, sticking and folding, in small groups. Older children learn reading and letters phonetically, in the Montessori way. Teachers offer each child individual attention. Projects are followed and changed regularly – nocturnal animals were being studied when we visited. Lively paintings of owls, foxes and hedgehogs decorated the walls. Free play indoors offers dressing-up clothes, a limited home corner and a good selection of educational toys. Music, dance and movement take place weekly, accompanied on the piano or accordian by a visiting specialist teacher. There is an annual sports day and a nativity play or concert at Christmas. Record cards are produced half-termly for the use of teachers only. No written programmes or procedures are available. Parents receive a full report when their child leaves.

**Remarks** One of the best-established nursery schools in Clapham. Over the years it has built up a strong and loyal following. The new management will have to work hard to maintain the standards set by the previous charismatic owners. Disappointing premises.

# Lewisham

Early years provision remains a high priority in Lewisham. The Council says, 'Our aim is ultimately that our services will be available to all, but this is unlikely in the near future, because of lack of central government funding.' 37 per cent of 3- and 4-year-olds receive nursery education, but places are not guaranteed. 'It is important to put your child's name down at the school of your choice soon after their 2nd birthday,' the education department advises. There is an acute shortage of affordable full-time daycare, although the Council gives £836,000 to 19 voluntary groups. Budget cuts look set to affect the 11 Social Services children's day centres. 469 childminders provide the bulk of the area's daycare facilities, backed-up by part-time playgroups, some supported by the local authority. There are 20 private and 7 workplace nurseries, charging an average of £95 per week. Significant achievements have been made in the borough's co-ordination of services and their geographical distribution over the last two years. Lewisham is one of the few boroughs to support the training of nursery staff and childminders and to develop an early years curriculum.

## Further information

For information and details on all types of daycare and nursery education:

Under Eights Section
Laurence House
1 Catford Road
London SE6 4SW
Tel: (081) 695 6000

All publications relating to early years services can be obtained from the One Stop Shop at the above address.

## GOLDSMITHS' COLLEGE NURSERY

University of London
30 Lewisham Way
London SE14 6NW
**Tel:** (081) 692 7171 Ext. 2253

**Owner:** Goldsmiths' College
**Nursery Organiser:** Elaine Tait, NNEB
**Type:** College nursery, providing full- and part-time places for college employees and students only.
**Children:** 3mths–5yrs. 20 places. 20 on register
**Hours:** 8.30am–5.30pm term-time
9am–5pm during college vacation
Flexible hours
Open 50 weeks a year
**Status:** Private, fee-paying
**Number of years open:** 16
**Meals:** All meals prepared and brought each day by parents. Juice and milk provided
**1992 fees:** £66.71 per week full-time – staff
£39.52 per week full-time – students
£14.92 per day – staff
£10.25 per day – students
£8.27 per session – staff
£5.15 per session – students
**Waiting list:** Long and getting longer. 60 on list and can take up to 18 months to get a place
**Registered by:** London Borough of Lewisham SS

**Premises** The nursery is housed in an end-of-terrace basement adjacent to the main college building. Entry is via the college car park through a seriously rotting wooden porch. The smell of dampness lingers inside. The nursery is on two floors, with a large, light, L-shaped room on the first floor used by the toddlers, and downstairs a baby room which looks straight out on to the legs of passers-by and the wheels of buses and juggernauts on Lewisham Way. There is a small, newly acquired room for the pre-school-age group and a dining room, also used as office and staff room, with a small kitchen area. The nursery's strongest feature is its pretty, fenced garden. It is partly paved and partly grassed, and in the summer is used almost all day. Only three out of the twenty children attending the nursery have gardens at home, and consequently staff try to use it as much as possible.

**Nursery Organiser & staff**  Elaine Tait, NNEB, the nursery organiser, has a team of four NNEB-trained staff in all, one YTS trainee and two unqualified assistants, one of whom is about to start the PPA Diploma course on day release. Staff are gentle, confident and clearly used to working under pressure. The staff work three different shifts and term-time only. There is a nursery advisory group which meets once a term and includes the nursery organiser and various college personnel, including the vice-president of the Students' Union.

**Children & parents**  Parents are welcome in the nursery at any time of day and children are phased-in gradually. Significant fund-raising is done by already hard-pressed parents, which provides a sizeable amount of the nursery's equipment and toys.

**Curriculum & activities**  Since places at the nursery are highly sought after, any combination of days and hours is possible as there will always be someone else to fill in a gap. However, there are only eight places available during the holidays, allocated on a first come first served basis. There is a strong emphasis on craft work at the nursery, with some stunning examples in the walls. Music students from the college visit occasionally for musical sessions. Little emphasis is placed on pre-school work at present, mainly because the new room for 3- to 5-year-olds has only just opened. However, Elaine is planning to visit other nurseries to study their methods and will be introducing a more structured learning environment for this age group this year. Record-keeping is also fairly rudimentary – the only information kept is on the child's admission form – but this is also due to improve. The nursery has no cooking facilities and parents are required to provide lunchboxes and picnic snacks as the college canteen does not provide child-size portions. Children eat in relays with the others in their age group because of the space problem.

**Remarks**  A nursery which is providing a vital service under difficult circumstances. Goldsmiths' needs to appreciate how many people rely on it totally for their work and study. When a place becomes vacant, it is generally filled again within a couple of hours. The length of the waiting list bears testimony to the urgent need for nursery places and the degree to which Elaine Tait and her team are trusted.

## VILLAGE MONTESSORI SCHOOL

Kingswood Halls
Kingswood Place
London SE13 5BU
**Tel:** (081) 318 6720

**Owner/Principal:** Catherine Westlake, Mont Dip
**Type:** Montessori nursery school offering half-day sessions
**Children:** 3–5yrs. 20 places. 40 on register
**Hours:** Morning session 9.15am–12 noon
Afternoon session 1pm–3.45pm
Open 36 weeks a year
**Status:** Private, fee-paying
**Number of years open:** 30
**Meals:** Milk
**1992 fees:** £348 per 12-week term for 5 sessions a week
£319 per 11-week term for 5 sessions a week
£15 registration fee
**Waiting list:** Variable. First come first served
**Registered by:** London Borough of Lewisham SS

# Merton

A borough dedicated to nursery education, offering excellent provision for 56 per cent of 3- and 4-year-olds. All 28 county first schools and almost all of the nine church primaries have nursery units or classes – many purpose-built. 'Just lovely places to be,' is how one parent describes them. Merton is second only to Newham at the top of the London boroughs league table, and the second-best provider of nursery education in the country. Currently re-organising services following the Children Act, to form an Early Years Assessment Unit, the borough is concentrating on the development of the 'whole child' in its nursery schools. Observation notebooks have been designed to monitor each child's skills and abilities, compiled by parents and teachers. Merton provides two full-time day nurseries with 100 places for children in high-priority categories. There are four private day nurseries, 39 playgroups offering part-time sessions, and registered childminders.

### Further information

All daycare information is handled by:
The Under Eight's Dept
Merton Social Services
Worsford House
Church Road
Mitcham
Surrey CR4 3BE
Tel: (081) 640 1171

For details on nursery schools and classes:
Education Department
Civic Centre
London Road
Morden SM4 5DX
Tel: (081) 543 2222

## BUSHEY FIRST SCHOOL – NURSERY UNIT

West Barnes Lane
London SW20 0BZ
**Tel:** (081) 946 6439

**Owner:** London Borough of Merton LEA
**Headteacher:** Brenda Spencer, BA, MA
**Type:** Nursery class in state primary school
**Children:** 3–5yrs. 104 places. 104 on register
**Hours:** Morning session 9am–11.30am
Afternoon session 12.45pm–3.10pm
Open 38 weeks a year
**Status:** State nursery class
**Number of years open:** 8
**Meals:** Milk
**1992 fees:** No fees
**Waiting list:** Priority to siblings and those living nearest to the school
**Registered by:** London Borough of Merton LEA

## GROVE NURSERY SCHOOL

28 Wilton Grove
Wimbledon
London SW19 3QX
**Tel:** (081) 540 2388

**Owner/Principal:** Vivienne Kimber, Cert Ed
**Type:** Nursery school offering half-day sessions. No full-time places
**Children:** 2½–5yrs. 28 places. 56 on register
**Hours:** Morning session 9.30am–12.30pm (older children)
Afternoon session 1pm–3pm (younger children)
Open 36 weeks a year
**Status:** Private, fee-paying
**Number of years open:** 7
**Meals:** Milk and biscuits
**1992 fees:** £385 per term for 5 morning sessions a week
£280 per term for 5 afternoon sessions a week
**Waiting list:** Long. Early registration advisable
**Registered by:** London Borough of Merton SS

**Premises** The nursery rents the wooden pavilion belonging to Wilton Tennis Club and has shared use of the large, recently decorated clubhouse. Big picture windows look out over the busy tennis courts, and double doors lead out on to a generous grassy area used for outside play. Old-fashioned playground games such as hopscotch, hoops and ball games are favoured. The neighbourhood is suburban, residential and surrounded by trees. Parking is unrestricted. Strenuous efforts have been made to make this feel like a school, not a clubroom. Artwork is displayed on one side of movable wall dividers, equipment strategically placed and different areas turned into a home corner, book corner and project area. But at the end of the day, everything has to be put away and hidden and the artwork turned round to face the wall. Tennis Club members do not want any sign of the nursery when they take over in the evenings and at weekends.

**Owner/Principal & staff** The principal, Vivienne Kimber, is a qualified teacher with experience in state infant and primary schools. She has also taught in South America. When she failed to find a suitable nursery for her own two children, she started the Grove. From its early beginnings with just eight children, it has grown to a thriving concern with 28 children per session and a long waiting list. Not surprisingly, she is keen to acquire her own premises and continue to expand the school. Vivienne Kimber is very much an educator, with strong views on the role of nurseries, believing their prime focus should be educational. She teaches full-time at the Grove with a loyal staff of four (three qualified NNEB, PPA, Cert Ed and one unqualified, but a 'natural'). Experience and qualifications are important, but Vivienne also chooses staff from a 'gut feeling', after observing them at work in the nursery for a day. She looks for caring workers with initiative, then trains them and sets the teaching level herself. Although she admits that she is not very good at delegating, her staff have been with her for over two years and work together as a strong team.

**Children & parents** The school attracts a sizeable local element, with mainly Wimbledon parents, although some travel in from Surbiton, Kingston and New Malden. The parents are professionals – accountants, doctors, teachers, nurses, bankers. There has been a Japanese contingent, and now there is a Scandinavian group. The social mix is lessening due to recession, although Vivienne tries to keep the fees reasonable enough to encourage a wide range of children and parents. The afternoon sessions attract more of a cultural mix and also include two children with special needs. A few mothers work, but the majority are housewives – two were on the tennis courts when we visited. Vivienne's son, James, also attends. Leavers move on to an equal mixture of state and private schools in the area. The youngest children (2½-year-olds) begin with the two-hour afternoon sessions and when they are ready, usually after two terms, they move up to the longer morning sessions, where they can stay until they go to school. This can be as old as 5 if they are going on to some private schools like Wimbledon High.

**Curriculum & activities** There are written programmes which change every term, and a structure for each day. The day begins with registration, circle and news and then children 'show' something they have brought in to talk about. Pre-reading, pre-writing and pre-number work is done at tables with approximately six children to each teacher. No child is allowed to be aimless. Ms Kimber believes that state primary schools are failing badly in teaching reading and consequently finds herself doing more formal teaching to compensate. The 3-year-olds learn Letterland, which they love and which teaches them the names and sounds of letters. A variety of reading schemes are used depending on the child – 1-2-3 and Away, New Way, Ginn and the Crown Readers – popular with the boys. Of the 20 leavers in September 1992, all were starting to read well and six were free readers. Ms Kimber says it is never a question of forcing the children; they are so receptive and so eager to learn that she has difficulty keeping up with them. She firmly believes she can improve intelligence at this age. Motor skills are developed by regular sticking, spotting, circling and some colouring, although colouring is not considered to be an essential skill. Number skills are even more important. Children count everything – fingers, toes, noses, crayons. Parents are informed in advance of projects and themes and encouraged to reinforce the school work at home. All children have a work folder and their progress is carefully monitored by staff and overseen by the principal. The emphasis on educational basics still leaves time for art and craft ('painting is for pleasure, not for taking home'), percussion and music making, dance and movement. Ms Kimber is particularly keen on drama – every day children do some improvisation. The highlight of the year is the Christmas show where morning and afternoon children come together and ad lib a Christmas entertainment (past productions include The Snowman and the Nutcracker Suite).

**Remarks** A structured learning environment which also allows enough freedom and space for children to develop and choose their own activities. Happy, absorbed children. One of the most child-centred and positive nurseries we have visited. Dedicated staff who rarely say 'no', 'can't' or 'don't do that' and never seem to raise their voices. We hope Vivienne Kimber will achieve her ambition to find new premises and expand her school.

# WIMBLEDON PARK MONTESSORI SCHOOL

Wimbledon Park Hall
170 Arthur Road
Wimbledon
London SW19 8AQ
**Tel:** (081) 944 8584

**Owner/Headmistress:** Victoria Wilberforce-Ritchie, Mont Dip
**Type:** Montessori nursery school offering half-day sessions. No full-time places
**Children:** 2½–5yrs. 28 places. 48 on register
**Hours:** Morning session 9am–12.15pm
Afternoon session 1.15pm–4.30pm
Open 40 weeks a year
**Status:** Private, fee-paying
**Number of years open:** 2
**Meals:** Children bring fruit, nursery provides milk
**1992 fees:** £440 per term for 5 sessions a week
£370 per term for 4 sessions a week
£320 per term for 3 sessions a week
£15 per term for swimming
£25 registration fee plus refundable deposit
**Waiting list:** Minimal. A few afternoon sessions available
**Registered by:** London Borough of Merton SS
**Under same ownership:** Kingston Vale Montessori School, Kingston Vale, London, SW15

**Premises** Local authority council hall, on a small but busy high street in a primarily residential area, close to Wimbledon Park Station. Access is from a side street, where parking is easier. Bright, airy and spacious, the nursery is one huge room with large, leaded windows along both sides and a pitched roof. The wooden shelves and furniture storing Montessori equipment are moved around to provide smaller, cosier areas where children work in groups. A good-sized kitchenette in one corner is used for snacks and cookery classes. There is also a stage, used for the Christmas pantomime. Outside is a large concrete playground with a good selection of outdoor equipment and toys. There are occasional visits to Wimbledon Park, a five-minute walk away. The main disadvantage is the shared use of the hall – for weddings, scout meetings and keep-fit classes.

**Owner/Headmistress & staff** Victoria Wilberforce-Ritchie, Mont Dip, is a young, dynamic and gregarious headmistress, bubbling with energy and enjoyment. She set up Wimbledon Park two years ago and a year later took over another well-established Montessori nursery in Kingston Vale. She has 11 years' teaching experience, combined with four years as a recruitment consultant. An efficient manager, she divides her time equally between the two nurseries and tries to spend as much time as possible with the children. Wimbledon Park has a team of three young, qualified Montessori teachers, carefully chosen to provide a balance of personalities, from calm and quiet to the more extrovert and sociable. Teachers alternate weekly in selecting projects for the children. This allows them each a degree of independence and responsibility. They hold daily discussions on the progress of the children. Montessori students regularly assist the staff. A visiting music teacher attends weekly bringing with her a variety of musical instruments. Stable staff team, all in their post for over two years.

**Children & parents** Children live locally, and come from professional backgrounds. Most mothers do not work outside the home, but those who do tend to be bankers or solicitors. There is a large foreign contingent, especially from Japan, Sweden, Denmark and Poland. National identity is valued at the nursery, and parents are encouraged to visit to share their national costume, festivals and dishes with the children. Parents' evenings are held twice a year and an annual sports day with Kingston Vale. Introductory visits for new children take place the term before they start. The nursery has a close relationship with parents and an open-door policy. Victoria will even take children home if a parent is unable to collect. Children wear a colourful uniform (optional) – consisting of a bright yellow or blue sweatshirt, trousers and T-shirts for summer, endorsed with the school logo of two dancing teddy bears. The majority of children transfer to local private prep schools. The nursery is beginning to face increased competition, as state primary schools in the area are starting to take children at 3 years old and private preps and pre-preps are opening nursery classes.

**Curriculum & activities** Montessori-based teaching, using Montessori equipment and apparatus, but other methods, including Letterland, are also integrated. The emphasis is on fantasy, imagination and fun, with colouring competitions, paint and chalk work, movement and dance, cooking and swimming all part of the curriculum. There are also library visits and visits to the local bank and bakery. Victoria Wilberforce-Ritchie says, 'We like to include as many extra activities as we can, as cheaply as we can.' Morning and afternoon sessions are identical. Children are divided into three family groupings (mixed ages), each group provided with the same equipment. The first hour and a half is dedicated to letters, numbers and practical life. Equipment includes dressing frames, sound boxes and sandpaper letters. The groups then take turns to listen to a story, play outside and share the fruit they have brought to school. Circle time follows, when the whole class comes together to discuss a topical subject. Projects are also important. When we visited, everyone was preparing for a Hallowe'en party – children and teachers planned to dress up, and parents had agreed to bring the food. Children take home all their work at the end of each week. Detailed record cards are kept on each child for the benefit of students, as well as parents.

**Remarks** Young, new and enthusiastic Montessori-based nursery, with emphasis on imagination and fun. A welcome addition to the local community. Shared use of hall premises means that all work and equipment must be put away at the end of each day.

# Newham

Excellent nursery education, offering nearly 5000 part-time places for 3- and 4-year-olds, putting Newham at the top of the league table of London boroughs. Eight nursery schools and 46 classes in primary schools are currently available, and the Education Committee has agreed a continuing programme of expansion. Newham has the highest birthrate in the country and an interesting demographic profile. After a protracted decline until 1987, the population is now growing faster than any predictions, with births exceeding deaths by almost 1000 a year. Nearly half the borough's residents are under 34 years old, and a high proportion are from ethnic minority groups. Since 1981, the number of under-5s has increased by 20 per cent. A third of births are to single mothers, and one in three households relies on income support. There are heavy demands on nursery and childcare services. Social Services provide five children's centres for children in need, which may be affected by this year's budget cuts. Most full-time care is offered by 418 registered childminders. Eight voluntary and private day nurseries cost £65–£85 per week.

**Further information**

For details on daycare and nursery education in the area:
Early Years Unit
Department of Social Services
99 The Grove
Stratford
London E15 1HR
Tel: (081) 534 4545 × 25054

## OOPS-A-DAISY

The Halls
St Philip and St James Church
Whitwell Road
Plaistow
London E13 8BP
**Tel:** (071) 474 8737

**Owner:** Newham Community Employment Project
**Principal:** Sharon Mc Nicholas, NNEB

**Type:** Day nursery offering full- and part-time places
**Children:** 6mths–5yrs. 25 places. 24 on register
**Hours:** 8am–6pm
Open 51 weeks a year
**Status:** Private, fee-paying, non profit-making
**Number of years open:** 2
**Meals:** Breakfast, lunch, tea, snacks
**1992 fees:** £75 per week full-time
25% sibling reduction
**Waiting list:** None at present, but varies
**Registered by:** London Borough of Newham SS

# Redbridge

Nursery education provision is inadequate, offering a nursery place to only 16 per cent of 3- and 4-year-olds and putting Redbridge near the bottom of the London boroughs league table. The Education Department plans to increase places by opening two new nursery classes each year. Waiting lists are extremely long and priority is given to older 4-year-olds. There are three family centres run by Social Services in Ilford, Chadwell Heath and Woodford Green, but access is restricted to children with priority needs. The private sector offers 18 day nurseries, half of which take babies. Fees range from £75 to £85 per week. The borough's 480 registered childminders can charge even more, starting at £75 and rising to £100 per week, in more prosperous areas. Sessional care is provided by 72 playgroups and private nursery classes. Recession has hit the private sector badly. At the time of writing, there are vacancies everywhere and fees have dropped. Despite sending questionnaires to a range of services in Redbridge, none were returned to us.

### Further information

For details on day nurseries, childminders and playgroups:
Directorate of Social Services
Ley Street House
497 Ley Street
Ilford IG2 7QX
Tel: (081) 478 3020 × 5459

For details on pre-school education:
Education Department
Lynton House
255-259 High Road
Ilford IG1 1NN
Tel: (081) 478 3020 × 3147

# Richmond-upon-Thames

Near the bottom of the league table for nursery education, with only 18 per cent of 3- and 4-year-olds in nursery schools or classes, and waiting lists everywhere. The private and voluntary sector provides over 4000 places in 17 private day nurseries, 79 playgroups and with 430 registered childminders. Fees average £80 per week for a childminder and £90–£100 per week for a private day nursery. Baby places are very restricted, as only four nurseries are registered to take children under 2. Richmond Social Services runs three day nurseries for the assessment of children in need, and has a small budget to help single parents and families in circumstances of hardship with nursery fees. The ceiling is £25 per week per family. The borough is committed to maintaining its current level of provision for the rest of the financial year.

**Further information**

For details on day nurseries, childminders and playgroups:
Social Services Department
42 York Street
Twickenham TW1 3BW
Tel: (081) 891 1411 × 7513

For details on nursery schools, units and classes:
Education Department
Regal House
London Road
Twickenham TW1 3QB
Tel: (081) 891 1411 × 7513

## MORTLAKE DAY NURSERY

Sheen Lane
London SW14 8LP
**Tel:** (081) 876 7294

**Owner:** Richmond-upon-Thames Social Services
**Manager:** Aly Carroll, NNEB
**Type:** Social Services day nursery offering full- and part-time places
**Children:** 16mths–5yrs. 35 places. 35 on register
**Hours:** 8am–6pm
Open 52 weeks a year (excl bank holidays)
**Status:** State nursery. Part fee-paying, part non fee-paying
**Number of years open:** 11
**Meals:** Mid-morning milk, lunch, tea
**1992 fees:** No fees unless in full-time work, then minimal. Means tested
**Waiting list:** All admissions are dealt with by the Day Care Advisor for the Borough
**Registered by:** London Borough of Richmond-upon-Thames SS

**Premises** Housed in an old courthouse with a small forecourt for parking, the nursery consists of two children's rooms, staff room, office, parents' room, kitchen, laundry and toilet facilities. The main nursery for the 2½- to 5-year-olds is the former courtroom itself – spacious, with high ceilings and dark wood panelling on the lower half of the walls. Windows along two sides make it airy, bright and welcoming. Tired decor is brought to life by a wonderful panoramic mural showing children of all nations and imaginative children's artwork. Younger children, from 16 months to 2½ years, have a smaller, homelier room. Each children's room has direct access to a large play area equipped with a range of fixed outdoor climbing equipment and toys. The children have their own garden to tend. The nursery is next to Mortlake railway station and off Sheen Lane, a friendly high street, with a village atmosphere. Opposite, there is a large playground, used mainly in the summer.

**Manager & staff** At the time of our visit, there had been a complete change of management. Aly Carroll, NNEB, is the new manager and her deputy is Jeanie Crennell, NNEB.

Prior to staff changes, much of the day-to-day running of the nursery had been in the efficient, capable hands of Anne-Marie Pallister, acting deputy, normally third-in-charge. Currently there are eight full-time staff, the majority NNEB qualified. The full complement is nine, but due to local authority cutbacks, one post has been frozen and fewer children admitted to compensate for the lack of staff. A keyworker system operates, and staff keep detailed ongoing records of each child's development. More formal reviews are conducted every six months when every aspect of a child's progress is discussed, from health to relationship with parents and staff. Staff meetings are held once a month, and informal discussions every day. Five students each year assist and follow their practical training here. Staff have many years' experience working with children with disabilities and special educational needs. A well-established support system enables them to call on local authority psychologists, community welfare officers, doctors and other professionals when necessary. The community welfare officer visits once a month and sees up to five children at a time. She carries out the 18-month and 3-year developmental checks and other special check-ups.

**Children & parents** All admissions are dealt with by the Borough's day-care advisor, who assesses each family and their needs. Priority is given to children with special educational needs or disabilities or from working single-parent families with social and emotional problems. Some children are on the at-risk register, while others are in danger of abuse or are from backgrounds with a history of drug or alcohol difficulties. Predominantly working class, most parents do not pay fees, as many are on low incomes and receiving benefits. Those in work are means tested and some contribute a small, daily rate. Children with disabilities are counted as filling two places each. The staff/child ratios are excellent, allowing much individual attention. New children are phased-in gradually and parents are encouraged to stay with their child to settle in. Parents' and staff meetings are held once a term. Children sometimes stay for short periods during a family crisis.

**Curriculum & activities** The nursery follows the High Scope programme. There is a highly structured routine based on a 'plan, do and review' system. Children choose whichever activity they wish to pursue and are encouraged to share their experiences with the group, guided by their keyworker. All progress is carefully monitored. Rather than formal teaching of reading or writing, the nursery concentrates on the acquisition of social skills in preparation for school. Children are divided into age groups – Tigers, the youngest, have their own room and keyworkers and cover similar activities to the main nursery but in a less structured format. Encouraged to abandon nappies at their own speed, they move into the main nursery once they are potty-trained. Older children are divided into three groups of mixed ages, each with a keyworker. Activities are varied and equipment plentiful: cooking, gardening, building and construction, art and craft, puzzles, imaginative play and looking after pets (a goldfish and gerbils) form part of the curriculum. Food is prepared and cooked by two full-time kitchen staff. Special dietary and religious needs are catered for. Regular outings for children and parents include a picnic in Richmond Park, an away-day at the seaside, farm visits and train journeys. Multicultural festivals are celebrated regularly and there is a puppet show at Christmas.

**Remarks** Dedicated, friendly and motivated staff, experienced in dealing with stressful family situations. There is a genuine sense of teamwork, despite recent staff upheavals. The nursery has no control over the allocation of places or influence over the waiting list. A safe haven offering limitless love and understanding for some of the most needy children in the community. Demand far outweighs the number of available places.

# NOAH'S ARK DAY NURSERY

Christ's School West
Queens Road
Richmond
Surrey TW10 6HW
**Tel:** (081) 332 1597

**Owner:** Christ's School West and London Borough of Richmond
**Principal:** Anna Stevenette, Mont Dip
**Type:** Day nursery offering full-time places
**Children:** 2–5yrs. 21 places. 28 on register

**Hours:** 8am–6pm or 9.30am–3.30pm
Open 49 weeks a year
**Status:** Voluntary organisation, fee-paying
**Number of years open:** 1
**Meals:** Lunch, tea, snacks
**1992 fees:** £80 per week full-time (8am–6pm)
£55 per week full-time (9.30am–3.30pm)
**Waiting list:** Long. Early registration advisable
**Registered by:** London Borough of Richmond SS

# ORLEANS COMMUNITY NURSERY

Hartington Road
St Margarets
Twickenham TW3 3YU
**Tel:** (081) 477 2333 × 2536

**Owner:** Orleans Community Nursery Management Committee
**Headteacher:** John Thwaites, MA (Hons), PGCE
**Type:** Community nursery offering half-day sessions. No full-time places
**Children:** 3–4yrs 8mths. 24 places. 40 on register
**Hours:** Morning session 9.15am–12 noon
Afternoon session 1pm–3.15pm
Open 38 weeks a year
**Status:** Fee-paying, non profit-making
**Number of years open:** 2
**Meals:** Lunch (from the infant school, by request)
**1992 fees:** £7 per morning session
£6.50 per afternoon session
£1 for lunch plus 80p for lunchtime supervision
**Waiting list:** Minimal
**Registered by:** London Borough of Richmond-upon-Thames SS

**Premises** The ground floor of an old school building next to Orleans Infant School in a quiet, residential part of Twickenham. The nursery was originally the school's woodwork room. Inside, it feels like a large school classroom. It is not homely or cosy, but definitely geared towards the young children it caters for. Almost everything is at child height and the large space is divided into smaller, more manageable, child-size areas for art, computing, imaginative play, messy play, table-top activities and quiet reading. The room is cheerful and light, with a high ceiling and big windows. Few of the windows are low enough for children to look out, but there is so much to do inside that this hardly matters. There is a bathroom area at the back of the classroom. Everything in sight is clearly labelled so that children begin to understand that words have meaning. There is a wonderful art area, with paper, paint and collage materials easily reached and also clearly labelled. The nursery was started on a low budget, but equipment is plentiful and well maintained, including a computer and television. The infant school playground is next to the nursery and must be quite noisy at playtime. Nursery children use a smaller area for their outside play – part grass, part concrete. As yet there is no fixed outdoor equipment and the area needs refurbishment. A seven-stage plan to transform it awaits funding.

**Headteacher & staff** The headteacher John Thwaites, MA, PGCE, has a degree in anthropology and is a qualified early years teacher. A warm, friendly young man, he worked originally as a film-maker and explored the way children from different cultures perceive the world around them in his films. He is laid-back and relaxed and appears to be disorganised, although he isn't. The nursery staff comprise two qualified early years teachers, each responsible for her own group of children. Parent volunteers help in the classroom on a rota basis. There is also a special needs helper, funded by the local authority, for a particular child. Staff meetings are held once a week. There is no training policy or budget. Staff expertise includes French, Spanish, music, information technology and special needs. Good staff/child ratio of 1:7.

**Children & parents** Strongly middle-class with little mix of race or culture. Most children come from the suburban streets of St Margarets, lined with rows of three-bedroomed, terraced houses. Children with special educational needs are particularly welcome. John Thwaites believes that as nursery children come from very similar backgrounds, the integration of children with disabilities brings a richness to the nursery, otherwise lacking. Most children go on to Orleans Infant School, although a nursery place does not guarantee a place at the school. Children in the Borough of Richmond start main school gradually, with morning sessions only. The nursery helps working parents by collecting their children at lunchtime and keeping them for the afternoon session. Parents are very active and involved at Orleans – in fact, the nursery was set up by a group of teachers and local parents with very limited resources. Parents take up the majority of places on the management committee and are influential in every aspect of nursery life. They assist at curriculum meetings and help with fund-raising events.

**Curriculum & activities** Children work at play in this nursery school, following the High Scope method of plan, do and review. During each session there is also a carefully structured group activity, which involves number, letter and pre-reading games and tasks. The day begins with songs and a strum on John Thwaites's guitar. Children then divide into groups – owls, bears or dolphins – for a relaxed exchange of news and views, each child being encouraged to contribute. They are then given total freedom to choose their activities. Each child has a card with his/her name written on it and two Velcro tabs at the back. When they choose an activity area, they stick their names on the board for that area and once it is full, no more children can choose that particular activity for the time being. This limits the number of children in each area and avoids argument. When children have completed their activities, they tidy up and come together with their teacher to review what has been done and achieved. Themes and topics are covered and changed regularly. Artwork and craft reflect the current topics. Music is used every day and outdoor play is an important part of the curriculum. Visits are planned – the local hospital was a recent success – and visitors are invited to talk about their jobs. Parents come in to share particular skills and interests. The school does not set out to teach reading and writing, but concentrates on pre-reading and pre-writing skills. Children become familiar with Letterland characters and recognise their own and each other's names. There are close links with the primary school. Each day children are offered computing, construction, junk modelling, water and sand play, painting, books, cooking and music-making. Despite a restricted budget, equipment is varied and in good condition (annual budget £1000).

**Remarks** An impressive, relatively new nursery school with very reasonable fees.

Friendly, confident children, who respond positively to having a male role model leading their activities. John Thwaites's enthusiasm is infectious. A good school for parents who want to be actively involved and support their child's nursery education. All teachers are early years trained and qualified. The nursery has ambitious and exciting plans for the future.

# RUSSELL NURSERY

The Russell School
Petersham Road
Petersham
Richmond TW10 7AH
**Tel:** (081) 940 1446

**Owner:** Richmond-upon-Thames LEA
**Headteacher:** Toni Richards, MA, Cert Ed and management diploma.
**Nursery Teacher:** Julia Welchman, Cert Ed
**Type:** Nursery class in state primary school offering half-day sessions
**Children:** 3–5yrs. 25 places. 50 on register
**Hours:** Morning session 9am–11.30am (4–5yrs) Afternoon session 12.45pm–3.15pm (3–4yrs) Open 38 weeks a year
**Status:** State nursery class
**Number of years open:** 21
**Meals:** Fruit or biscuits and milk. 50p per week
**1992 fees:** No fees
**Waiting list:** Very long. Preference to siblings. Overall priority to children with disabilities or special educational needs
**Registered by:** London Borough of Richmond-upon-Thames LEA

**Premises** South-facing, single-storey, purpose-built unit in the grounds of the Russell School. Beautiful surroundings alongside the River Thames, including playing fields, woods, a music garden, pond, nearby farm and the whole of Richmond Park. The nursery exploits its stunning rural setting fully, and walks and nature studies are high on the list of priorities. Inside, the open-plan classroom is welcoming, comfortable, well used and well maintained. Walls are decorated with colourful children's art and topic work. There is a separate quiet room with a piano and other instruments for music, bookwork and storytelling. The nursery is self-contained, with its own kitchenette. Double doors from the main classroom lead into a very large play area, part of which is covered. Here there is an excellent selection of outdoor equipment including a play house and trampoline.

**Nursery Teacher & staff** Julia Welchman, Cert Ed, has taught at the Russell for nine years. Her teaching experience and organisational skills are extensive, but it is her ability to communicate effectively with children, staff and parents that is exceptional. Determined and charming, she teaches the class with the help of Cheryl Rowe, a bright and cheerful NNEB who has been at the nursery for three years. Together the two women make an enterprising team, devoted to their work. They exchange views and ideas with staff from other nurseries whenever possible and respond enthusiastically to offers of help from outside. Parents, nannies, grandparents, students and childminders are all welcome to come and help on an ad hoc basis. The nursery is run independently from the primary school, but liaises with the headteacher, uses some school facilities and enjoys good relations with the school.

**Children & parents** The nursery is a genuine neighbourhood school, with children from the local community – all classes, every nationality. There is no automatic transfer from nursery to primary school, separate applications are required for each, and the waiting list is huge. Priority is given to children with special educational needs – Judy Fry, special needs co-ordinator from the main school, advises, although they are under the care of Julia and Cheryl. Introductory sessions are held for new children, private meetings for parents with the teachers and general parents' evenings termly. Julia and Cheryl also make home visits to help extend the nursery as a place for the family, not just the children. There is an active open-door policy which parents respond to well. Lunches, picnics, concerts, Nativity plays all bring morning and afternoon session parents together. Nursery parents are also invited to main school events. Many parents are glowing in their praise of staff and the nursery.

**Curriculum & activities** Children are divided into peer groups – the older children attend the morning sessions, and the 3- to 4-year-olds the afternoon sessions. Julia Welchman believes children are more alert in the mornings and more able to sit and concentrate on table-top activities. Morning children sometimes take part in main school activities such as assembly. The nursery philosophy draws on the Froebel method and aims to provide a safe, stimulating environment for independent and collaborative play. The priority is to enable children to enjoy a happy transition period between home and school, over five terms. With strong home links, the school guides children to gain the confidence and motivation to make the best use of their school lives. There is no formal timetable although a general framework for playtime, storytelling and break exists. Each day different activities are set out on tables and children move freely from one to another. One teacher concentrates on a particular activity, working with the children in small groups to encourage self-help and finding creative ways of including language and writing in the activity. The National Curriculum per se is not used, but is aimed at through a formal checklist. If a child shows interest he/she may take home a folder of work related to that day's activity. There is no formal teaching of reading or writing, but most can manage their names by the time they leave. Plenty of outdoor activities throughout the year make full use of the nursery's lovely setting. Options include wildlife studies, nature walks, fruit picking. Strong community links with visits to local farm, village and church expeditions and recitals from local musicians. Music and singing are enjoyed daily, dance and movement weekly. Children share main school festivals, plays and concerts.

**Remarks** A terrific nursery, making the most of its beautiful rural surroundings. Well-paid, qualified and dedicated enthusiasts working independently and as a team, to cover all the children's nursery needs. Happy children, and involved and very satisfied parents, who could not praise this nursery highly enough to us. Sadly, the nursery is unable to offer places at 3 years old to all children who live locally and want to come, due to its huge waiting list. Equally sadly, those who do secure a place can only benefit for 2½ hours a day. There is no guarantee of a place in the primary school either; a separate application is required.

## STUDIO MONTESSORI SCHOOL

25 Kew Gardens Road
Richmond
Surrey TW9 3HD
**Tel:** (081) 948 0319
(081) 940 0064 (answering machine)

**Owner/Principal:** Kim Simpson, Mont Dip, Counselling Psychotherapy Dip
**Type:** Montessori nursery school offering mainly morning sessions, plus full-time places for 4–5yr-olds
**Children:** 3–5yrs. 30 places. 30 on register
**Hours:** 9.30am–12.30pm 5 mornings
9.30am–3pm 3 days a week
Closed Fridays. Open 39 weeks a year
**Status:** Private, fee-paying
**Number of years open:** 19
**Meals:** Juice and biscuits. Packed lunches for full-timers
**1992 fees:** £400 per term for 4 morning sessions a week
£8 per afternoon session
Sibling discounts
£50 registration fee plus £50 part-refundable deposit
**Waiting list:** Very long. Priority to siblings
**Registered by:** London Borough of Richmond-upon-Thames SS

**Premises** Large, detached family home close to Kew Station and just a few hundred yards from Kew Gardens. Spacious, carefully manicured garden. Inside there are three large classrooms filled with Montessori equipment. Newly decorated throughout, with impressive high ceilings and original cornices. The atmosphere is homely, relaxed and comfortable. Children move freely between the three rooms. The Nest is mainly for new children, cosy, friendly and containing the more basic Montessori equipment. The Working Room has practical life apparatus and messy play – water, paint and play dough. The Pink Room is where most of the traditional Montessori equipment is kept. A corner of the hall has been set aside as a brick corner for non-Montessori construction and building sessions.

**Principal & staff** Kim Simpson, Mont Dip, is a dedicated, experienced woman in her early 50s. Devoted 100 per cent to the Montessori principles and philosophy, she holds strong views on individual liberty and believes passionately in 'the goodness of children'. She lectures widely and writes on pre-school education and psychotherapy. Of her team of three teachers, one is NNEB qualified, another Mont Dip and the third a Montessori student. All are quiet, thoughtful and caring towards the children but clearly take their lead from Kim Simpson.

**Children & parents** Professional parents, with a small number of working mothers. Nationalities include French, Finnish, Czech and British. Most children live locally or come from surrounding leafy suburbs of Richmond, Chiswick or Putney. Very popular school, with long waiting list. Eager parents and Montessori afficionados have been known to travel from the West End to bring their children here. Parents are invited to the Christmas Nativity play and summer music and movement concert. Also in the summer they organise their own open day in the garden with food reputed to be of banqueting proportions. Children move to private prep and pre-prep schools, and a few also go to the local Church of England school.

**Curriculum & activities** All children attend four mornings a week, with the 4- to 5-year-olds staying all day. On some mornings children begin 'work' as soon as they arrive, while on others they start with a group session of news and conversation around topical themes. At work time, children are free to choose the room they want to be in and the equipment or activity they desire. Teachers will demonstrate the apparatus, but will never tell a child what to do. Older children help the younger ones. Children are left to go about their business quietly, while observant staff ensure that each child covers every aspect of the three rooms over a period of time. Kim Simpson believes parents are wrongly obsessed with early reading and any psychological pressure at this age is likely to damage future reading skills. 'Caring for the books in the book corner is more important than learning to read at this age,' she says adamantly. Although this is a very traditional, old-style Montessori school, there is enough flexibility to allow drama, movement, singing and games to take place regularly. Topics are popular – a topic on Harvest Festival included children making a harvest festival soup which they then shared with their parents. Occasional walks or outings are undertaken to nearby Kew Gardens and

Syon Park. French will be added to the timetable when a suitable teacher has been found. Each child has a folder to put his or her work into each day, which is then taken home on Thursdays. Afternoon sessions offer the older children the opportunity to prepare for the 3Rs. Packed lunches are eaten with some ceremony, including a candle and prayers. Children are uncannily quiet and beautifully behaved whatever they are doing. The atmosphere is relaxed and happy but very serious.
**Remarks** Highly popular, very traditional Montessori nursery, carefully and closely following the theories and principles of Dr Maria Montessori. Strong principal with very clear beliefs about what she aims to achieve, and an unshakable commitment to the individual freedom of children. The quiet, hushed mood of the nursery would not suit all. Many may prefer a more bustling, fun atmosphere. Children are beautifully behaved and appear happy with the very serious business of attending this nursery.

## SUNFLOWER MONTESSORI SCHOOL

8 Victoria Road
Twickenham
Middlesex TW1 3HW
**Tel:** (081) 891 2675

**Owner/Principal:** Joy Colbert, Adv Mont Dip, MRAD
**Type:** Nursery school offering half-day sessions, and some full-time places for over-4s
**Children:** 2–7yrs. 27 places. 49 on register
**Hours:** 9am–3pm Mon–Thurs
9am–12 noon Fri (for full-time children only)
Morning session 9am–11.45am Mon–Thurs (under 4yrs)
Afternoon session 1pm–3.30pm Mon–Thurs (under 4yrs)
Wed pm 1hr introductory session with parents (2–2½yrs)
**Status:** Private, fee-paying
**Number of years open:** 2
**Meals:** Snacks. Packed lunches
**1992 fees:** £764.50 per term for 4½ full days
£423 per term for 4 sessions
£10 registration fee
**Waiting list:** Small. Preference to siblings
**Registered by:** London Borough of Richmond-upon-Thames SS

## TWICKENHAM PARK DAY NURSERY

Cambridge Road
Twickenham
Middlesex TW1 2HW
**Tel:** (081) 892 0872

**Owner:** Carol Cuthbertson, B Ed, NNEB
**Officer-in-charge:** Rae Farmer, NNEB
**Type:** Private day nursery, offering full- and part-time places and half-day sessions
**Children:** 1–5yrs. 44 places. 50 on register
**Hours:** Full-time 8am–6pm
Morning session 8am–11.30am
Afternoon session 2.30pm–6pm
Open 51 weeks a year
**Status:** Private, fee-paying
2 local authority subsidised places
**Number of years open:** 11 on present site. 11 on previous site
**Meals:** Breakfast, snacks, lunch, tea
**1992 fees:** £14.50 per day full-time
£5.75–£6.50 per session
**Waiting list:** Variable – usually 3mths wait
**Registered by:** London Borough of Richmond-upon-Thames SS

# Southwark

Southwark spends £10.5 million a year on education and care for its 10,000 under-5s. Forty per cent of 3- and 4-year-olds receive part-time nursery education; there are also some full-time places. In order to save the nine Social Services day nurseries from closure, due to budgetary cuts, they are to broaden their entrance criteria and run on 'mixed economy' lines. A third of places will continue to be for high-priority children, a third will go to single working parents and the rest will be sold on the open market at a rate of around £40 per week. All early years services are now part of the Education Department. At last, one telephone enquiry covers all services, including voluntary and private facilities. The private sector includes 13 day nurseries and ten workplace nurseries, mainly in educational institutions for the use of students and staff.

## Further information

For details on all types of childcare and education for under-5s and booklets 'The First Step – Under Fives in Southwark' and 'Early Education in Southwark':

Education Department
Early Years Section
1 Bradenham Close
off Albany Road
Walworth SE17 2QA
Tel: (071) 525 5000 × 5178/5193

## DULWICH COLLEGE PREPARATORY SCHOOL

Nursery Department
Gallery Road
London SE21 7AB
**Tel:** (081) 693 4341

**Owner:** Dulwich College Preparatory School
**Headmistress:** Susan Metzner, Cert Ed (Froebel)
**Type:** Nursery school offering full-time places only
**Children:** 3–5yrs. 96 places. 96 on register
**Hours:** 9am–3pm
Open 36 weeks a year
**Status:** Private, fee-paying
**Number of years open:** 57
**Meals:** Milk and lunch
**1992 fees:** £1055 per term
£30 registration fee
**Waiting list:** Long. Children registered at birth. All prospective entrants interviewed
**Registered by:** Dept for Education and Science

**Premises**  Single-storey, purpose-built, wooden building with its own large playground in the grounds of the main prep school. Although not particularly elegant, it provides four large, light and agreeable classrooms, an assembly hall, cloakrooms and a kitchen, all opening off a long central corridor. Everything in this school has been extremely carefully thought out, down to the teddy bears placed on each armchair in the headmistress's office. The playground offers endless possibilities for running around, climbing ladders, making dens and playing in a large sandpit under the verandah leading off the two first-year classrooms.

**Headmistress & staff**  Susan Metzner, Cert Ed, has been headmistress of the nursery school at Dulwich Prep (known as DCPS) for five years. She is a mature, precise, and impressive woman, with strong views and a very direct manner. She has worked in education in London for many years. Her deputy, Helen Strange, PGCE, LRAM, LRCM, Mont Dip, has been at the school for 15 years and teaches music – a very important element of the curriculum – to all children each day, class by class. The ten other staff are all qualified: four teachers, five NNEBs and one nurse. There are also two cooks, two cleaners and from time to time NNEB students from either Croydon or Southwark colleges. There are curriculum meetings once a week, attended by teachers only, and full staff meetings every fortnight. All staff get together for a few minutes each morning before school starts to exchange information. Each teacher is in charge of one classroom, assisted by a nursery nurse, who changes class at the end of every term. Teachers are known to children by their full names and nursery nurses by their Christian name.

**Children & parents** Highly motivated, high-earning, professional, South London parents who want their children to be achievers from an early age. There is one intake a year, in September, and children are interviewed during the spring and summer terms on a one-to-one basis. The interviews with Susan Metzner last for about 20 minutes. Between two and three children are seen for every place available and only the most able are chosen. The school's catchment area is enormous and children come from as far away as Bromley, New Malden and Blackheath. From the age of 5 upwards DCPS is boys-only. Consequently girls are a minority at the nursery school, although numbers fluctuate – most in fact are siblings. Children are predominantly British, although there are other European nationalities and some Americans and Indians. Girls transfer to James Allen's (JAPS), Sydenham High and Streatham High.

**Curriculum & activities** Parents have high expectations and so inevitably does the school. The children are being primed for a life of high academic achievement, and this is reflected in the school's approach to every aspect of the curriculum. Susan Metzner told us that although a disabled child would not automatically be excluded, she would consider very carefully whether the child would be able to cope and keep up with the other, extremely able, confident and articulate children. Year One children pursue a less structured version of the Year Two curriculum, which is based on four core subjects: English, maths, science and music. The difference is obvious as you walk around the school – the younger children are occupied in a variety of different ways, some playing, some doing tablework with their teacher, others painting, while the older children are in a much more structured, working environment with a classroom feel to it. Susan Metzner is looking for 'child-centred learning and good teaching practice' from her staff and aims to 'use all a child's good points as a starting point'. We were shown examples of children's paintings, which were terrific and very artistic. Children are only provided with red, yellow, blue and white paint. However, they succeed not only in mixing every tint and hue imaginable, but in creating tasteful and attractive colour combinations. All classes meet together in the hall at 9.45 each day for assembly, which is Christian-based and includes prayers and a topical discussion. Each class spends a further 25 minutes in the hall every day for a music session of singing, instrument playing and rhythm. Reading and writing are not forced upon the children, but form an important part of the curriculum. Children take home two books each day, one for parents to read to them and the other for the child to look at or read. Reading schemes are not used, but there is a huge supply of books. Most children are copy-writing well and reading to at least some degree by the time they leave the nursery school. Parental pressure for faster results is apparently enormous. Susan Metzner is adamant that such pressure is counter-productive and she is quite prepared to confront the issue head on when necessary. The school keeps a file on each child's development and teachers are responsible for putting together record books, like scrapbooks, which include dated examples of a child's work as well as photographs and drawings. This provides an instant picture of a child's progress and is passed on to parents when the child leaves. Reports are sent out halfway through the spring term and at the end of the summer term. Parent/teacher interviews take place at the end of the autumn term. Children eat lunch in their classrooms supervised by one half of the staff, while the other half have their lunch in the staff room.

**Remarks** A school that sets its standards high and has a justifiably high opinion of itself. Children are hand-picked at 3 to benefit from an environment that is designed to cater for the crème de la crème. For the chosen few who can afford it, DCPS nursery school is the first important rung on the ladder to success.

# MOTHER GOOSE BABY NURSERY

54 Linden Grove
Peckham
London SE15 3LF
**Tel:** (071) 277 5956

**Owner/Principal:** Krish Brown, Mont Dip, BTEC
**Type:** Baby nursery offering full- and part-time places
**Children:** 0–2½yrs. 18 places. 20 on register
**Hours:** 8am–6pm
Open 50 weeks a year
**Status:** Private, fee-paying
**Number of years open:** 4
**Meals:** Lunch, tea, snacks
**1992 fees:** £410 per month full-time
£307 per month – 3 days per week
£206 per month – 2 days per week
**Waiting list:** Kept at 10 max, so all will be offered a place in time. Early registration advisable
**Registered by:** London Borough of Southwark LEA
**Under same ownership:** Mother Goose Nurseries in Waveney Avenue, Peckham, Everlina Road, Peckham, Upland Road, E Dulwich

**Premises** A three-storey, Victorian, terraced house, with converted outhouse attached. Front access off a busy road, but there is a quiet side street for safe parking. A mixed residential area. Inside decorations are good, the atmosphere cheerful and warm, and there is plenty of natural light. The nursery consists of the Ladybird Room for play and rest-time; a messy-play room with washroom facilities where children keep their toothbrushes and flannels; the Snowdrop Room (for babies not yet walking) with six cots, a soft-activity area and nappy-changing facilities. Play areas are carpeted throughout for babies at the crawling stage. Children may not move from room to room without adult supervision. Safety gates are used at all times and the kitchen and toilet facilities are well fitted and spotlessly clean. Fire safety is checked regularly, and health and hygiene procedures followed strictly. The outside covered play area has plastic resin flooring for safety, a small area for children to grow seeds and bulbs, and a large selection of quality equipment, including a small Wendy house. The local park is used frequently in summer.

**Owner/Principal & staff** Krish Brown, Mont Dip, BTEC, has had a varied career, starting as a dispensing chemist, followed by a period managing the family travel business. She gained her Montessori Diploma in 1990 and opened the first Mother Goose Nursery, with one child. She now has four nurseries catering for over 100 children up to 5 years old. It is a family business; her mother is in charge of the baby unit and her husband steps in whenever necessary. There are six full-time nursery workers, all women, and one part-timer. Four are qualified – NNEB, PPA, Mont Dip. Unqualified staff include a former registered childminder and a worker with 12 years' nursery experience. There is a strong staff training policy and a budget of £1000 for first-aid training and other relevant courses. Cover for absenteeism is provided by staff from other nurseries in the group. The staff/child ratio is 1:3 or better at all times. Some nursery nurses have been in their posts since the nursery opened. A happy, multicultural team, full of enthusiasm and representing a refreshing range of ages, social backgrounds and nationalities, including Turkish and Asian.

**Children & parents** One of very few nurseries in the area catering solely for babies, and there is always a waiting list. Children come from a range of professional backgrounds – doctors, teachers, lawyers – and a mix of cultures. Many move on to other nurseries in the group when they turn 2½. The majority then progress to private prep schools, including Dulwich College Prep. The company offers discretionary discounts to some parents struggling to pay their fees. Parents are warmly welcomed at the nursery, provided they give advance notice. Phasing-in is done gently, with a flexible approach. Parents must be available for the first two weeks of entry, in case their child needs them. Parents are invited to join the nursery for festival celebrations.

**Curriculum & activities** A curriculum based on Montessori principles and equipment. The priority is to create a safe and homely environment, a good nutrition and health programme and educational play and activities. Equipment is simple but stimulating. Building blocks, first puzzles, games and books and lots of bright, plastic toys. Children spend periods of up to half an hour at 'heuristic' or discovery play, in which they sit on the floor surrounded by 'treasure baskets' full of interesting, but safe, everyday objects such as clothes pegs, pot scourers, hair curlers, large pebbles, corks, feathers, walnuts and fir cones. Staff quietly observe as the babies become more and more absorbed in exploring and discovering whatever is in their basket. There are strong daily programmes of music, dance, movement and singing. Painting is encouraged, with plastic overalls provided for protection. Circle time each morning includes stories, songs and finger play. Outdoor play is safe for crawlers, and art and craft activities often take place outside. Frequent rests and sleep are fitted in according to each child's needs. Plenty of affection and cuddles; no child is left to cry. Full details of intellectual development and progress are recorded monthly. Parents receive a report twice a year. A book records each child's physical milestones, to which parents have access. Outings are limited because of the high staff/child ratio required, but there are buggy trips to the park, shops and market stalls. Food is prepared by a cook, and the menus are appetising, nutritious and varied, with all special and religious diets catered for.

**Remarks** High-quality baby care. Clean, friendly and comfortable – a very homely environment. Enthusiastic, experienced and gentle staff team. The nursery offers some continuity, as children are able to move on to other Montessori nurseries in the group.

# Sutton

Two local authority nursery schools and 24 nursery classes attached to primary schools. 36 per cent of 3- and 4-year-olds receive a morning or afternoon nursery place. Two independent schools have nursery classes with fees starting at around £500 per term, rising to £700. Full-time daycare is in short supply. 450 registered childminders, charging between £1.50 and £2 per hour, and 13 private day nurseries, with fees of up to £95 per week, are the main suppliers. Sutton has an Under Fives Development Officer with a direct line for queries and information. Parents are encouraged to ring him directly for advice, although, despite repeated attempts, we never managed to get through to him. Very few day nurseries and nursery classes responded to our questionnaire.

**Further information**

Under Fives Development Officer
Civic Offices
St Nicholas Way
Sutton SM1 1EA
Tel: (081) 770 4497

Information on Sutton's childcare and quality guidelines can be contained from:
The Sutton Childcare Information Centre
Times Square Shopping Precinct
Sutton High Street
Tel: (081) 770 6000

# JACKANORY NURSERY

21 Hawthorn Road
Wallington
Surrey SM6 0SY
**Tel:** (081) 669 2988

**Owner:** Gaye Whitwam
**Supervisor:** Lynne Stott, NNEB, CPQS
**Type:** Day nursery and nursery school offering full- and part-time places and half-day sessions
**Children:** 18mths–5yrs. 38 places (25 full-time). 56 on register
**Hours:** 8am–5.30pm
Morning session 9am–12.15pm
Afternoon session 1.30pm–5.15pm
Day nursery open 51 weeks a year
Nursery school open 46 weeks a year
**Status:** Private, fee-paying
**Number of years open:** 3½
**Meals:** Lunch, tea, snacks
**1992 fees:** *Day nursery*
£85 per week full-time
£74 per week for 4 days
£60 per week for 3 days
£21 per day (min 2 days a week)
*Nursery school*
£47.50 per week for 5 morning sessions
£21 per week for 2 morning sessions
£45 per week for 5 afternoon sessions
£20 per week for 2 afternoon sessions
£25 registration fee
10–15% sibling discount for 2 or more children
**Waiting list:** None
**Registered by:** London Borough of Sutton SS

**Premises** Large detached Edwardian house in a street close to Wallington town centre. Ample car parking space in front and to the side. The entire ground floor and some of the first floor are given over to the nursery. The remainder is the home of the owner, Gaye Whitwam, and her family. Everything is child-centred, safe, attractive and fun. There is a new purpose-built porch, with tiled floor and cubby holes for dozens of pairs of little wellies. Beyond that, in the hallway are shelves holding dozens more brightly coloured storage boxes for each child, used for posting notes to parents and any work the child may be taking home. In the hall is a wall of framed photos of each member of staff showing their names and job titles, and huge home-made and brightly coloured posters of Mickey Mouse, Thomas the Tank Engine and others. There are three main rooms for the children, all extremely well stocked with equipment, sinks and book corners with carpet and beanbags. There is also a messy-play room, a pristine and extremely well-equipped kitchen, a cosy office, staff room, a staff cloakroom and little loos with a mini urinal for the boys, special temperature-control taps, and a clown's face cut into the end of the sink unit with a gaping-wide mouth for used paper towels. Two-thirds of the garden has been fenced off for use by the children and holds a rabbit hutch and large wooden Wendy house. At the end of the garden is the gym, used by the gym instructress who comes in once a week to lead sessions on tumble gym equipment and a trampoline. Soundproofed and heated, it also doubles as a winter play area when the weather is too bad for outside play.

**Owner, Supervisor & staff** Gaye Whitwam is clearly a doer. She has built her nursery up from scratch and in three years filled all her places. She has taken a PPA Foundation course, and various other courses including a High Scope introductory course. The rest of her time is spent cooking, administering the nursery and caring for the children during their lunch hour. She has a highly qualified and extremely friendly team of nursery staff; Lynne Stott, NNEB, CPQS, the nursery supervisor, is in charge of the day-to-day running of the nursery and deals with parents. She also spends much of her time with the full-time children. Debbie Selby, NNEB, is in charge of the older, pre-school full-time children and Lucy Roberts, NNEB, has responsibility for the sessional nursery school, known as the pre-prep section. There are three further NNEB-qualified members of staff, and specialist teachers come in once a week to teach gym, ballet and music. Staff meet at least once a month for planning sessions and to discuss progress, although Gaye Whitwam admits that they 'need to do a bit more planning' and will be meeting more frequently in the future. The staff/child ratio is 1:5.

**Children & parents** Children are mainly local and many parents also work locally. Reasonable social and cultural mix, with some Chinese and Indian children, others with single parents. The local authority sponsors one place. A good number go on to state schools when they leave. The children are relaxed, busy and chatty and all of the day-care children appeared to be completely at home in their surroundings. The day nursery and nursery school children generally remain in their separate groups and do not mix, but the older full-timers, who have their own pre-school room, join up with the younger ones at certain times of day. Different groups sometimes meet in the garden, but Gaye Whitwam feels that smaller groups are best, even outside. A keyworker system has operated since the nursery opened. It is most evident at lunch time when each group eats with its particular keyworker; the keyworker notes who has eaten what and how much, and posts the information on a noticeboard in the hall for parents to read. Settling-in is taken seriously and parents are expected to stay for at least two introductory sessions with their child. If a longer period is required, a settling-in programme is arranged and a good-bye routine carefully worked out.

**Curriculum & activities** Gaye Whitwam has made every effort to supply a complete range of equipment in her nursery, from dressing-up clothes and messy-play areas to a computer with word and number games. Children arrive at the nursery between 8 and 9am and have discussion time with their keyworker before embarking on free-play for younger children and pre-reading, writing and arithmetic for older children. The Stagecoach system – a comprehensive reading, writing and arithmetic course – is used mainly, but Letterland is also available and they are just starting with the Ginn system. Children start with Stagecoach from around $2\frac{1}{2}$, once they have mastered basic motor skills such as sorting and sequencing and learnt shapes and colours. There is an abundance of messy equipment for the 2-year-olds. Parents do not at present receive any written reports, but children have folders which they take home every month or six weeks. The nursery is still considering what type of reports to provide and may opt for High Scope observation records (report on conceptual awareness). Parents' evenings will be starting soon. There is a strong emphasis on helping each child help him or herself to become independent; table manners, managing a knife and fork, pencil control, taking time to tie shoe laces before going out, are all important activities. Food is a serious business and meals a special event at this nursery. Gaye Whitwam plays a major role in the kitchen, doing some of the cooking herself. The nursery prides itself on being awarded a place in Sutton's *Cleaner Food Guide*. Special dietary needs are catered for.

**Remarks** A delightful home from home with a real family feeling. Gaye Whitwam is an excellent administrator and manager and has built up a loyal and impressive team over the last three years. She says the nursery is 'in its last stage of development' now. Solid foundations suggest it has a strong future. High-quality care with developing educational programmes.

# Tower Hamlets

A borough committed to expanding daycare and nursery education. Tower Hamlets is near the top of London's league table for nursery education, and has increased provision by a substantial 25 per cent over the last two years. The majority of places are full-time. The borough is at the forefront of bilingual teaching, with many Bengali as well as English teachers. Nearly three-quarters of the under-5s in the area are of Bangladeshi origin. There is great demand for affordable daycare, with 200 names on the waiting list for places at the nine Social Services day nurseries. Childminders, playgroups and 20 private nurseries provide places for a further 1000 children.

### Further information

'Starting School', a brochure published in English, Bengali and Somali, is distributed to all schools, libraries and the borough's seven neighbourhood centres.

For the Directory of Services and all information on education, contact:
Pupil Services

Tower Hamlets Education Department
Mulberry Place
5 Clove Crescent
London E14 2BG
Tel: (071) 512 4200

Under-8's supervised activities and daycare provisions are dealt with in each of Tower Hamlet's separate Neighbourhoods. Contact the Neighbourhood Under Eight's Registration Officer at:

*Bethnal Green* Neighbourhood
Tel: (071) 377 6080

*Bow* Neighbourhood
Tel: (081) 980 1812

*Globe Town* Neighbourhood
Tel: (081) 980 8067

*Isle of Dogs* Neighbourhood
Tel: (071) 987 6966

*Poplar* Neighbourhood
Tel: (081) 980 7111

*Stepney* Neighbourhood
Tel: (071) 790 1818

*Wapping* Neighbourhood
Tel: (071) 987 9200

# Waltham Forest

A borough committed to maintaining and developing services for under-5s. Over 40 per cent of 3 and 4-four-year-oids receive a part-time place in one of four nursery schools and 32 nursery classes. At the beginning of the financial year the leader of the Council wrote to all departments declaring his intention to protect early years services, despite budget cuts. His letter points out that it is known that children learn most in their first few years of life. 'Lack of facilities must be a national scandal,' he says. There is a large voluntary sector, including 39 playgroups, some supported by local authority grants. The five Social Services day nurseries are not exclusively for children in need. Places are marketed at £60 per week for full-time places, and waiting lists are long. Twelve private day nurseries charge an average of £80 per week, or £17 per day and there are 550 registered childminders. No nursery schools or day nurseries in Waltham Forest responded to our requests to be considered for inclusion in this book.

**Further information**

For details on day nurseries, childminders, playgroups and general advice:
Under-Eights Service Manager
Children and Families Division
604 High Road
Leyton E10
Tel: (081) 539 5577

For information on nursery classes:
Tel: (081) 531 6970
Telephone advice and information any morning. An answering machine will take your query in the afternoons, and your call will be returned promptly.

'Link Up' booklets and a 'Primary Education Guide' are available at:
Walthamstow Public Library
High Street
Walthamstow
London E17 7JN
Tel: (081) 520 3031

# Wandsworth

Wandsworth's early years resources have been channelled into pursuing the council's policy of part-time nursery education for every child rising 4 in the borough. The number of Social Services day nurseries and centres for children with special needs has been cut back drastically, from 18 in 1991 to eight currently, although four new centres are in the pipeline. There is very little affordable full-time provision for parents on average or low incomes. Cash cuts to Education and Social Services budgets are unlikely to improve the situation. The private sector has expanded rapidly over the last few years, and there is plenty of choice for those who can afford it. Fees range from £300 to £1000 per term for nursery schools and up to £140 per week for full-time day care. The borough is now looking at ways to provide after-school care. 51 schools have nursery classes and there are 3 borough nursery schools.

**Further information**

From the Registration Unit:
On day nurseries, playgroups, play schemes and childminders, tel: (081) 871 6332

Or by area:
West: (081) 871 8811
Central: (081) 871 8833 N. East: (081) 871 8833
S. East: (081) 871 8844

For local authority nursery schools and classes:
Schools Admissions Section
Education Department
Wandsworth Town Hall
London SW18 2PU
Tel: (081) 871 7962 or 871 8266

Under Eights Directory available from libraries or telephone (081) 871 7962

## BALHAM NURSERY SCHOOL

72 Endlesham Road
London SW12 8JL
**Tel:** (081) 673 4055

**Owner:** London Borough of Wandsworth LEA
**Headteacher:** Ann Douglas, Cert Ed (Froebel Cert)
**Type:** Local authority nursery school offering half-day sessions (no part-timers) and limited full-time places
**Children:** 3yrs–5yrs 3mths. 75 places (12 full-time). 75 on register
**Hours:** 9am–3.15pm
Morning session 9am–11.30am
Afternoon session 12.45pm–3.15pm
Extended day 3.15pm–6pm
Open 38 weeks a year
**Status:** State nursery school
**Number of years open:** 60
**Meals:** Lunch, tea and milk

**1992 fees:** No fees
£20 per week for extended day care
95p per day for lunch (free for those on income support)
**Waiting list:** Very long. Over 80 for Sept '93. Children should be registered by May for Sept
**Registered by:** London Borough of Wandsworth LEA
**Under same ownership:** Somerset Nursery, Battersea; London Eastwood Nursery, Putney

**Premises** Balham Nursery School is the oldest of Wandsworth's three state nursery schools and has occupied the same premises since it opened in 1933. It was bought by public subscription and donations were received from Queen Mary, Major and Mrs Clement Atlee and Lady Megan Lloyd-George. The school was opened by Lady Nancy Astor. Other famous names were added to its list of friends when the school was evacuated to the Macmillan country home for two years during the war. Close to Balham tube and rail stations, the school is in a detached house with a large back garden. There are two main classrooms; a reading room full of books, comfortably furnished for quiet concentration; and an art and craft area. Upstairs are the offices, a large and comfortable parents' room which is also used for music sessions and indoor play in wet weather, and a kitchen where parents can make themselves tea and coffee. Both classrooms open on to the garden, which is vast by London standards. It provides a beautiful copper beech tree, a sandpit, a climbing frame, lots of push/pull and pedalling equipment, seesaws and some rather thin grass. There are plans to improve the play area and extend the soft surface.

**Headteacher & staff** Ann Douglas, Cert Ed, has been headteacher for the last eight years and is only the fifth person to have held the post. Her deputy is Judith Seymour, Cert Ed. Anne Flanders is the third qualified teacher. There are four NNEB nursery nurses and a fifth NNEB part-timer. The ancillary team includes a part-time primary helper, two meal supervisors, one part-time extended day worker, a part-time premises officer and a secretary. The head and two teachers have complete responsibility for those in their care. There is a weekly staff meeting, and five INSET days in the year. A speech therapist visits once a week. Students sometimes visit from a local dance college to give music and movement sessions. Ann Douglas, who plays the piano, takes two main music sessions each week in the parents' room, although there is musical content to every day.

**Children & parents** A complete cross-section of the local community, from barristers' children to the unemployed on income support. There is a rich cultural mix. Priority is given to those living closest to the school, those who will be going on to a primary school with no nursery class, and referrals from Social Services. Most transfer to Holy Ghost (RC) School, Fircroft and Alderbrook. Very few go to independent schools. Children are normally given a place at the beginning of the academic year in which they are 4, and admission is staggered through the autumn term. The process starts with a registration day, which deals with the formalities, and then parents and children make social visits, getting to know the nursery and its staff. Parents are welcome at any time and are encouraged, through the Parent Staff Friends Association, of which they are all automatically members, to take part in activities and outings on a regular basis. Some come into the nursery regularly to read stories, help to mend equipment or run the book club. Others do laundry at home or make dressing-up clothes or goodies for fund-raising. There is an annual charity event at Christmas. Special needs children are welcome and special provision can be made for those with severe disabilities.

**Curriculum & activities** Children are divided between two classrooms, but each group contains a range of ages and abilities. Both classrooms are divided into clearly defined areas, each supporting a different part of the curriculum. There is an office area with telephone directories, calendars, writing implements, sticky tape and a typewriter, where many skills can be acquired through copying and pretend play; a science corner where children learn about weights, measures, magnets, springs, wheels; a home corner for domestic play; a computer for matching and word games, which even allows children to compose their own tunes. The art and craft area, a covered way between the two classrooms with a glass roof, is always available and children have free access to the garden after the first half-hour of the morning. Each class has group time at the end of a session. The huge selection of books in the reading room amounts to a small library. Reading and writing are encouraged throughout the nursery and children borrow books to take home. Most children are counting well and reading ready by the time they transfer to their next school. Frequent outings are made to back up themes and projects. Food is supplied by the kitchens at Fircroft Primary and delivered by van. Children eat in their classrooms with a member of staff, and are encouraged to help serve and clear up. Special dietary needs can be catered for.

**Remarks** A wonderful nursery, where staff are doing a fantastic job. A broad and balanced curriculum, close relationships with parents and well-qualified, motivated teachers and carers. The only nursery in the area providing combined free state education and extended day care.

## BLUNDELL'S TRADITIONAL TEACHING NURSERY

The Old Court
194-196 Sheepcote Lane
London SW11 5BW
**Tel:** (071) 924 4204

**Owner/Principal:** Susan Stevens, NNEB, Mont Dip
**Type:** Day nursery offering full-time places and half-day sessions
**Children:** 2–5yrs. 47 places. 38 on register
**Hours:** 8am–6pm
Morning session 8am–1pm
Afternoon session 2pm–6pm
Open 52 weeks a year
**Status:** Private, fee-paying
**Number of years open:** 1¾
**Meals:** Lunch, tea
**1992 fees:** £82.50 per week full-time
£55 per week for 5 morning sessions
£44 per week for 5 afternoon sessions
£20 per term for ballet
**Waiting list:** Places available
**Registered by:** London Borough of Wandsworth SS

**Premises** Relatively new nursery in a beautifully and expensively converted old court house, with large, spacious, light rooms on two floors. The old courtroom, renamed the Rainbow Room, is used for art, craft, music, ballet and group activities. Children are based, according to age, in three other rooms.

**Owner/Principal & staff** Susan Stevens, NNEB, Mont Dip, comes from a family of childcarers – her mother has been running a nursery in London for 40 years – and is a former teacher. A driving force, she works a minimum 12-hour day and managed to purchase, convert and register the nursery within three months. Two-thirds of the staff are qualified NNEB or Mont Dip, but the rest, perhaps too many, are trainees (some male) or students. All wear smart but institutional mint-green uniforms. The children also wear overalls. Susan Stevens describes herself as a 'workaholic committed to childcare'. She says, 'I hope we are an extension of the family. Pressure to do well is not necessary. So much more can be achieved by learning with friends in a friendly, loving environment. Instruction, encouragement and lavish praise work every time.'

**Children & parents** The children of middle-class, working parents from diverse cultures. The nursery also subsidises a small number of places for low-income families, who would not otherwise be able to afford the fees. They are nominated by local health visitors and their identity is known only to the principal. Parental involvement is encouraged and there is an open day every three months for parents to view work-in-progress and talk to staff. Most children start on a sessional basis and gradually build up to a full day. Phasing-in is generally done without parents present, as this is considered less disruptive.

**Curriculum & activities** Children learn through play and have *fun*, but there are regular periods set aside for schoolwork in line with the National Curriculum. Some Montessori equipment is used for teaching. We liked the strong emphasis on 'conversation and communication', with older children helping the younger ones. All age groups eat together *and* clean their teeth after meals – this is the first nursery we visited which takes dental hygiene seriously.

**Remarks** Amazingly good value for a private nursery in central London at just over £80 per week. This nursery is a rare commodity – it has available places. It is too early for Blundell's to have built up a strong reputation, or acquired a list of satisfied customers, but it seems to have laid some solid foundations.

## BUSY BEE NURSERY SCHOOL

19 Lytton Grove
London SW15 2EZ
**Tel:** (081) 789 0132

**Owner/Principal:** Lucy Lindsay, Mont Dip
**Type:** Nursery school offering part-time places and half-day sessions
**Children:** 2½–5yrs. 30 places. 30 on register
**Hours:** Morning session 9.30am–12.30pm
Afternoon session 1.15pm–3.30pm
Open 36 weeks a year

**Status:** Private, fee-paying
**Number of years open:** 8
**Meals:** Milk and biscuits
**1992 fees:** £370 per term for 5 morning sessions
£250 per term for 3 morning sessions
£7 per afternoon session
£10 registration fee
**Waiting list:** Very long. Registration advisable before child is 5mths
**Registered by:** London Borough of Wandsworth SS
**Under same ownership:** The Bees Knees, London SW15

# GARDENS NURSERY SCHOOL

The Gardens Tennis Club
343 Wimbledon Park Road
London SW19 8NP
**Tel:** (081) 788 3807

**Owner/Principal:** Sarah Bokaie, NNEB
**Type:** Nursery school offering part-time places (2 or 3 sessions per week) and half-day sessions
**Children:** 2–5 years. 32 places. 55 on register
**Hours:** Morning session 9.30am–12.15pm (3–5yrs)
Afternoon session 1pm–3pm
Open 36 weeks a year
**Status:** Private, fee-paying
**Number of years open:** 5
**Meals:** Mid-morning snack
**1992 fees:** £350 per term for 5 sessions a week
£250 per term for 3 sessions a week
£200 per term for 2 sessions a week
**Waiting list:** Moderate. Main intake in Sept
**Registered by:** London Borough of Wandsworth SS

**Premises** Described by the owner/principal as 'very shabby and uncared for', this nursery operates from a dilapidated, single-storey, Edwardian, weatherboard tennis clubhouse, which in spite of its lack of paint retains a certain charm. It is set back from Wimbledon Park Road down a short driveway with parking for three or four cars. There is a long raised verandah running the length of the building above the three tennis courts. A fourth, unkempt, unused grass court is used as an outside play area. The nursery school/tennis club is near Southfields rail and tube stations and a few hundred yards from the entrance to the All England Tennis Club. The interior of the building has recently been decorated, but there is still room for improvement. The toilet area has not been painted and gives some impression of how bad things were previously. There are adult loos only and a small old-fashioned kitchen providing juice, snacks and the finished products of regular cookery classes. There is neon strip lighting throughout the clubhouse, but plenty of daylight coming in from the verandah. It all seems remarkably clean, considering it's used as a beer-swilling bar by club members in the evenings. It's also surprisingly peaceful, surrounded by tree-lined streets of terraced houses with gardens backing on to the tennis courts.

**Owner/Principal & staff** Sarah Bokaie's enthusiasm for her school, staff and children is totally infectious. The staff are so enthusiastic and motivated that they more than compensate for the shoddy building. The fact that many of them (three out of five) are unqualified also seems irrelevant, as they are so obviously loved by the children. Sarah Bokaie herself has an NNEB and the team does include an SRN and a Mont Dip. Staff turnover is no problem and staff are happy to divide up the day's chores democratically. Ballet, music/singing and art are taught by visiting teachers each week.

**Children & parents** This is, inevitably, a middle-class nursery school in a culturally diverse (South African, German, Swedish, Chinese, Indian) middle-class neighbourhood. Sarah Bokaie explains that 'we're terribly bossy and make sure that less outgoing children are involved by encouraging parents to invite them round to tea outside the nursery environment'. Children are accepted before they are potty-trained, although it is made clear that as the youngest ones only attend for two hours in the afternoons, nappies will be changed only if they are 'offensive'. Children with special needs are particularly welcome. The much adored peripatetic music teacher is herself severely physically handicapped. Approximately one third of the mothers work, but only a few have nannies. About 50 per cent of the children go on to private schools in and around Wimbledon – others go to St Michael's, the local state C of E school.

# HONEYWELL NURSERY CLASS

Honeywell Infants School
Honeywell Road
London SW11 6EF
**Tel:** (071) 223 7359

**Owner:** Wandsworth Education Dept
**Principal:** Stella Fleming, B Ed
**Type:** Nursery class in state primary school offering full-time places and half-day sessions
**Children:** 3yrs 1mth–3yrs 11mths. 39 places. 52 on register
**Hours:** 9.15am–3.30pm full-time
Morning session 9.15am–11.45am
Afternoon session 1pm–3.30pm
Open 36 weeks a year term-time only
**Status:** State nursery class
**Number of years open:** 17
**Meals:** Milk, lunch
**1992 fees:** No fees
**Waiting list:** Apply after child's 2nd birthday. Places allocated the following year. Preference to siblings
**Registered by:** London Borough of Wandsworth LEA

**Premises** A pleasantly shabby, homely and welcoming, single-storey, purpose-built classroom in a separate area of the infant school grounds. The main entrance is on Honeywell Road and there is access at the rear into the school's very own and much fêted nature reserve, which has been the sole recipient of PTA-raised funds for the last year or two. It boasts a pond, bird house, dozens of newly planted trees and other environmental attractions. The nursery building is flanked on either side by lawn and trees and in front by a tarmac playground which offers a climbing frame (with safety surface), small wooden house and a range of outdoor equipment. Most of the building is open-plan and is filled with an amazing jumble of equipment, furniture, books and toys. Not particularly attractive, but it does give the place a comfortable, well-used feel. There are two extensions off the main room – one used for quiet time and reading, the other fitted out as a child-size play kitchen. Cloakroom, kitchen and loos are at the rear. The main classroom is rather stuffy and has large, very dirty windows looking out on three sides. The ceiling is tangerine orange broken up by white roof supports and strip lighting.

**Curriculum & activities** The philosophy here is one of learning through structured play, and there is a large amount of equipment to assist this task: a wigwam, climbing frames, tricycles, a trough filled with lentils and dried peas for pouring, a book corner and a huge cupboard filled with equipment. Montessori methods and aids are not used as Sarah Bokaie feels they do not encourage group awareness. Although there is no particular 'work time' or structured learning, each session follows a pattern of playtime, group-time, music and singing, and special projects. The older children have workbooks and by the time they move on to primary school, they can generally write their names and recognise them, tell the time, hold a pencil and use scissors. Morning sessions (3 years +) are divided into three groups: Ladybirds (youngest), Butterflies and Parrots (oldest). Parrots stay on and eat a packed lunch on Wednesdays to help prepare them for a full day at school. The children are divided into these groups by age and ability, although the older children are encouraged to help the younger ones. Each group is led by a different member of staff on different days, using a rota system. The project work is imaginative and wide-ranging. At the time of our visit, a world project was well under way with a large hand-drawn map of the world covering one wall; one country in each continent was highlighted for closer study, Ethiopia being the current focus of attention. Outdoor play and activities are very important and the nursery offers excellent opportunities for the athletic. The wide verandah, an unused grass court and two newly resurfaced hard courts are all available for outside play. A tennis-playing member of staff teaches short tennis to small groups, and rounders is also popular. Outings include weekly library visits (in groups of six) and ambitious termly expeditions. Preparations were being made to visit the Pirate Exhibition at Greenwich and the Cutty Sark via Charing Cross and a river boat.

**Remarks** Very impressive, loving staff, brimming with enthusiasm. Ignore the shabby building and lack of facilities and feel the warmth and friendship. Sarah Bokaie is expanding to open a second 30-place nursery about two miles away in St George's Park. She should have no difficulty filling it.

**Principal & staff** Stella Fleming, B Ed, has been running the class for four years. Intelligent, committed, energetic and an able manager, she teaches full-time and is a teacher-governor of the school and teachers' rep on the PTA. Her deputy, Brenda Priestley, a BTEC nursery nurse, is calm and capable. Between them they can deal with most situations. They also have an unqualified primary helper to assist them. Stella Fleming is in control of her own budget. At the time of visiting, staff were anticipating a planned increase in numbers of 50 per cent, from 26 to 39 places, with some apprehension. The nursery has recently adopted a keyworker system to help staff monitor each child's development and are looking at ways to adapt the timetable to cope with an additional 13 children.

**Children & parents** A refreshingly representative mix from the local community, living mainly in the immediate locality. Places are allocated within a specific catchment area, which may alter each year, according to numbers. Priority is given to siblings. The current register includes two Down's syndrome children (plus part-time special needs staff to look after them), and others with learning difficulties and speech problems. The school's reputation extends far and wide and many hopeful parents, living way beyond the Borough boundaries, put their children's names down. There is an energetic and vociferous PTA and a rota of parent volunteers, who help out in the class during specific sessions. Some come in to play music, others to cook or read to the children. Each parent is provided with a list of all parents' names and addresses to promote sociability and also to speed up SOS messages in times of crisis.

**Curriculum & activities** There is no formal timetable at present. Children have complete freedom of choice and are not forced into anything they would rather not do. Free play begins indoors, until the doors into the playground are opened at 9.45. There is a ten-minute milk break at 10.30 and stories and songs at 11.30, but outside this general framework the system is very flexible. Structured learning is planned in advance at a weekly staff meeting and specific topics suggested. All the children we saw were extremely busy, working at a range of activities in twos and threes. The National Curriculum per se is not used, but it is aimed at, and although children are not formally taught to read or write, most can manage their names by the time they move on to the reception class. The class has the use of the infant school hall twice a week for music and movement (to a guitar played by the primary helper) and occasionally the children join in the school's main assembly, but only when the topic is suitable for 3-year-olds. The nursery has its own piano and an 'art gallery' of children's work. Equipment and books are plentiful. Full-time children, some preparing for primary school, others with single or working parents, have lunch brought down from the main school. At the end of the school year parents receive a Wandsworth Early Years Report on their child. It concentrates on language development and maths and science, but also covers what the child most enjoys doing and physical development.

**Remarks** A happy and homely nursery offering high-quality stimulation and care. Every local authority should strive for similar provision. However, the planned 50 per cent increase in numbers means that Honeywell will almost certainly never be the same again. Provided the staff can maintain their high levels of energy and commitment, the nursery will continue to be a model of its kind and the envy of many. The one major disadvantage is that entry is at 3-plus only and could come to an abrupt halt at the 4th birthday, if a place cannot be found in the reception class.

# LION HOUSE NURSERY SCHOOL (formerly Rainbow Nursery School)

Old Methodist Hall
Gwendolen Avenue
London SW15 6EH
**Tel:** (081) 780 9446

**Owner/Principal:** Jane Luard, Mont Dip, TEFL diploma
**Type:** Nursery school offering some full-time places for older children. Co-ed, pre-prep school for 5-8yr-olds. After-school club also available
**Children:** 2½–5yrs. 30 places. 45 on register
**Hours:** Morning session 8.30am–12.30pm
Afternoon session 1pm–4.30pm

After-school club 3.30pm–6pm
Open 38 weeks a year
**Status:** Fee-paying, non profit-making
**Number of years open:** 8
**Meals:** Lunch, juice and biscuits
**1992 fees:** £475 per term full-time
£7–£8.50 per session
£35 registration fee plus deposit of ½ term's fee
**Waiting list:** Moderate. Early registration advisable
**Registered by:** Dept for Education

**Premises** Not just another church hall. Lion House Nursery School has taken full control of its premises, with a ten-year lease from the church, and has completely redecorated the interior. The days of dingy paintwork and distemper are gone for ever; in their place are glowing, newly sanded parquet floors, light yellow walls and stencilled friezes. They now have the whole church hall, on two floors, including a spacious lobby, two downstairs classrooms, an office, loos, a kitchen and upstairs a huge and incredibly airy hall, even on a wet and blustery November day. There are windows on two sides of the room and a high-vaulted, newly painted ceiling to add to the feeling of spaciousness and light. There is more than enough room for every kind of activity. An art room, with sink, opens on to the hall and is used for messy work, painting, sticking and modelling. There is a stage with the regulation dark red velvet curtains, used for the Christmas show and as a dumping ground for the rest of the year. The hall has a home corner, a reading corner with carpet mats to sit on and masses of mainly Montessori equipment housed on open-shelved bookcases round the sides. Small movable partitions divide up the space and are decorated with children's artwork. There is a narrow outdoor play area with a hard surface. A slide and other equipment is used in dry weather.

**Owner/Principal & staff** Jane Luard, Mont Dip, has been principal and owner for eight years, through its previous incarnation as Rainbow Nursery School, and has masterminded the transition to nursery school and pre-prep. She is gentle, unflappable and intelligent. She spent some years teaching English as a foreign language at an international sixth form college before starting up her nursery venture. Her background means she is at home with the international clientele at Lion House, including children with little English and some with additional learning difficulties. Her deputy, Jackie Vernal, Mont Dip, has been with her for four years. Between them they are responsible for the day-to-day running of the school and the discussions concerning children's progress and activities. There are four other full-time staff and three part-timers, five of whom are qualified (four Mont Dip). Teachers are affectionate and well informed. Students attend from time to time, but Jane Luard prefers to use parents when she needs an extra pair of hands. Staff meetings are held once a fortnight.

**Children & parents** A multinational school, with 12 different nationalities and children from every corner of the globe. Strong efforts are made to ensure that the children all learn about each other's cultures. Parents are urged to help in this and also take an active role in outings. Jane Luard feels strongly that 'English schools have a tendency to shut their doors in parents' faces', something she abhors and which her well-off overseas parents will not tolerate. A PTA has recently formed, which meets every other term for nursery parents and every term for pre-prep parents. Parents are welcome to come into the nursery and take part, on the understanding that 'if they come in they muck in'. New children and their parents attend an introductory session for an hour the morning before they start, where a goodbye routine is worked out for the following day. If there are initial problems with leaving a child, parents are encouraged to stay. Children are divided into groups by age and ability and stay with their group teacher for one or two terms before moving on. Roughly one-third go on to local state schools, mainly church schools. In the past two-thirds have gone on to private schools in Putney, Sheen and Wimbledon, but in the future many will be staying on at Lion House. Pre-prep pupils wear a practical and attractive uniform of navy shorts or skirts and an emerald green sweat-shirt. Although not required to wear uniform, most nursery school children wear the green sweat-shirt over their own clothes.

**Curriculum & activities** The curriculum is general: a long-term programme starting with pencil control, cutting and learning to put things away, and progressing gradually on to pre-reading and pre-number work. Most of the equipment at Lion House is Montessori, although Jane Luard does not want her school to be labelled a 'Montessori' nursery school. When they are ready, children move on to phonic letters and numbers from one to ten using Montessori equipment. By the time they leave most are 'reading-ready'. Some are using the New Way and Ginn schemes which are also used by the pre-prep children. All children have music and movement classes. Some do short tennis, gym and French (by Club Frère Jacques) as extras. The extra-curricular activities take place in the afternoon and some interlink with the after-school club, which is available for local children from 2½ to 8 years old. Parents are supplied with written reports covering reading, numeracy, art and social skills at the end of each school year. Creative work includes painting and a range of handicrafts. Cookery is ever popular. Activities are designed to be fun, with the accent on learning through practical demonstration.

**Remarks** Lion House took an ambitious step forward in September '92 when it expanded from just a nursery to become a pre-prep taking 70 children up to 8 years old. A brave move in the middle of a recession. The well-established nursery remains the bedrock, offering interesting, stimulating, pre-school education. Exciting indoor space, disappointing outdoor area.

# LITTLE RED ENGINE

Church of the Nazarene
2 Grant Road
London SW11 2NU
**Tel:** (071) 738 0321

**Owners/Principals:** Annie Richardson, NNEB, RSH (Norland)
Caroline Sloan, NNEB, RSH (Norland)
**Type:** Nursery school offering part-time and sessional places
**Children:** 2½–5 years. 25 places. 15–20 on register
**Hours:** 9am–12 noon
12 noon–3pm Wed & Thurs (older children)
Open 36 weeks a year
**Status:** Private, fee-paying
**Number of years open:** 4
**Meals:** Juice and biscuits
**1992 fees:** £400 per term full-time
£350 per term for 3 sessions a week
£320 per term for 2 sessions a week
£15 registration fee
**Waiting list:** 9 average per term on list. No one yet turned away
**Registered by:** London Borough of Wandsworth SS

**Premises** This is not the smartest part of Battersea. The nursery is housed on the ground floor of a modern, hexagonal, concrete church, between the Grant Road exit of Clapham Junction and the Falcon Road estate. The building has clearly been built on the cheap and is remarkably ugly, but in good repair. Recently added, architect-designed iron railings enclose a small, grassy area and playground. From here you look up to one of the platforms of Europe's busiest railway junction. The main room used by the nursery in the centre of the building is also hexagonal. Painted a rather dark, gloomy beige colour, it has only two strip lights which are barely adequate. Four classrooms surround the main room, two of which are used by Little Red Engine. With all the doors open, a reasonable amount of light comes in. There is a kitchen where snacks are prepared and cookery lessons take place. There is a very active Sunday School and youth group at the church, which means the nursery has to clear everything away on Mondays and Fridays. New, stringent parking restrictions around Clapham Junction prevent all but a brief stop to drop off and pick up children.

**Owners/Principals & staff** Annie Richardson and Caroline Sloan, both NNEB & RSH (Norland), have worked as nannies and in a variety of London nurseries, since qualifying. They share a flat nearby and are close friends. The third member of staff, who is unqualified but very experienced with children, is also a close friend. Annie and Caroline agree that recruitment is best done by word of mouth. All three girls are demonstrably caring and loving. Children enthusiastically and happily climb in and out of their teachers' laps to give and receive warm hugs, praise and encouragement. Annie Richardson plays the guitar for fun and a pianist visits once a week for dance and movement sessions.

**Children & parents** The majority of children live locally, although some travel from Fulham and even from Balham. Most have professional parents and many are cared for by nannies. State-school fans try to secure a place at Honeywell, but the majority go on to the private sector – Eaton House, Thomas's, Putney High and the Lycée. Both principals feel that all the children should mix together as much as possible, so they are divided by age and ability only for work-time, which lasts for half an hour each morning before break. Much socialising takes place outside school hours and children develop firm friendships. A reward system operates – stars are given for being tidy, producing neat work, etc, and prizes for the children with most stars. Great care is taken to ensure that every child wins at least one prize during the year.

**Curriculum & activities** Each day follows a set routine of play for half an hour, register and diary, class-work, break, art and craft or cookery, music and story-telling. Older children stay till 3pm on Wednesday and Thursday, to prepare them for school. Staff assess children carefully to be sure they are ready for a longer day. Annie Richardson was keen to point out that all children work at their own pace and all have time and space for play. A large proportion of the plentiful toys and equipment has been donated by parents. The only Montessori equipment used is sandpaper letters. Phonetic reading and flashcards are used for school-time, and flashcards are taken home to help with learning new words. A short prayer is said each morning, although there has been some parental opposition to this. Music is a strong feature, with use of tapes as well as a Radio 5 music and movement programme. There is an annual outing to the local fire station to spray the hoses and try on helmets, and the police pay friendly visits, sometimes on horseback.

**Remarks** A very cosy, warm and loving atmosphere, despite the dingy accommodation. Much fuss over birthdays, and during illness cards are sent out and phone calls made – children will become a member of an extended family here.

## MINNOWS DAY NURSERY

30 Dents Road
London SW11 6JA
**Tel:** (071) 924 1919

**Owner:** Early Days Childcare Ltd
**Principal:** Marilyn Dooley, NNEB, CPQS
**Type:** Day nursery and nursery school offering full-time places and half-day sessions
**Children:** 2–5yrs. 52 places. 59 on register
**Hours:** 8.30am–5pm
Extended hours 8am–6pm available
Morning session 8.30am–12.30pm
Afternoon session 1pm–5pm
Open 50 weeks a year
**Status:** Private, fee-paying
**Number of years open:** 2
**Meals:** Breakfast, lunch, tea, snacks
**1992 fees:** £130 per week full-time
£30 registration fee plus £130–£260 refundable deposit
**Waiting list:** Places available
**Registered by:** London Borough of Wandsworth SS

## MOUSE HOUSE NURSERY SCHOOLS

2A Mallinson Road
London SW11 1BP
**Tel:** (071) 924 1893 or 924 5325

**Owner/Principal:** Amanda White-Spunner, Mont Dip
**Type:** Montessori nursery school, offering morning sessions, and afternoon sessions subject to demand
**Children:** 2½–5yrs. 56 places. 56 on register
**Hours:** Morning session 9.15am–12.30pm
Afternoon session 1.15pm–3.30pm on demand
Open 36 weeks a year
**Status:** Private, fee-paying
**Number of years open:** 5
**Meals:** Juice and biscuits or fruit
**1992 fees:** £600 per term for 5 morning sessions a week
£580 per term for 3 morning sessions a week or less
£360 per term for 3 afternoon sessions a week
£25 registration fee

**Waiting list:** Huge. 30 upwards on list for each term. Early registration advisable
**Registered by:** London Borough of Wandsworth SS

**Premises** The nursery school has been divided between two premises, both church halls, round the corner from each other on the west side of Wandsworth Common. However, at the time of writing both schools are about to move to new premises in a nearby converted warehouse at 2A Mallinson Road. This means that the school will be able to make use of wall space and set up permanent displays for the first time. Children will still be divided into two groups, and each school will occupy one floor. In addition, the owner is starting up a class for 2- to 3-year-olds called the Mouse Hole. There will be five morning sessions a week in the church hall at 2a Mallinson Road, vacated by Mouse House Two. No staff changes are anticipated although numbers may increase slightly in the future.

**Owner/Principal & staff** Amanda White-Spunner, Mont Dip, generally known to parents and children as Miss Moo (her nickname since childhood), is vivacious, enterprising and motivated. She oversees the friendly team of seven Montessori-qualified staff from her home next door to the Mouse House. She spends four mornings a week at the school, and Fridays are devoted to showing new parents round. Loulou Alexander, Mont Dip, and Kathy Parker, Mont Dip, are in charge in Miss Moo's absence. Two or three students from St Nicholas and the London Montessori Centre are regularly on hand and new members of staff tend to be selected from among their number. Outside teachers visit for ballet and music lessons. French is taught at least once a week by Miss Bronwen, and Miss Diana plays her guitar to all the children each week. Staff turnover has been a problem in the past, but salary increases have now stopped teachers moving on.

**Children & parents** Very middle-class school in a very middle-class area of Battersea between the commons. Miss Moo says, 'Sadly, we serve just one community.' Last year one child went on to the local primary school, Honeywell, and all the rest to the private sector – Broomwood Hall, Finton House, Thomas's, Hornsby House, and others. Nearly all the children live within walking distance although a few come from over the river. The majority are dual-income families, but parents are expected to take part in school life as much as possible. Parents' evenings are held every term, and parents are encouraged to spend 'work-time' with their child whenever possible. Written reports are produced at the end of the year, despite Miss Moo's feeling that 'reports can be a dangerous thing at this stage'. She ensures that they express only the positive, and considers their only real worth is for the child 'to show his/her fiancé in 20 years' time'. Close liaison and regular conversations with parents.

**Curriculum & activities** This is a Montessori nursery school, but pleasantly relaxed. There is a pleasing hum of activity as the children go about their individual business. The only strict rule in operation is that no child can choose any piece of equipment that hasn't first been demonstrated to them. There are family groupings throughout which are subject to experiment – in one class a group stays with one teacher, in the other the teachers change around each term. The two schools only come together for special events, but both are run in exactly the same way and have the same plentiful Montessori equipment and an excellent selection of books. Parents are given no choice between the two schools and places are offered where and when they become available. The day starts with book time and a story. Children then move into their groups and embark on their choice of work. Miss Moo points out that 'not everyone is ready to learn A is for apple at 10am on Monday morning', and consequently the children choose for themselves and are encouraged to help the younger ones with their work. Towards the end of the week concentration on Montessori exercises often lapses and work-time is shortened. Break is followed by projects, which can go on for several weeks if enough interest is generated, and French. Children then go to the park and end their session with circle time, songs, and rhymes. Reading and numeracy are taught the Montessori way, using sandpaper letters and the pink, blue and green card system. Children are not introduced to this until they are ready, which means some may not have started before they leave. A few of the local private schools are opposed to introducing children to reading schemes at nursery school, but New Way and Bangers & Mash are available for those who are motivated and ready. A workbook is used for pencil control and writing. Outings take place as often as possible – to Battersea Police Station, the police stables, Knightsbridge Barracks, Windsor Safari Park and other places of interest.

**Remarks** Cosy, friendly and happy schools with committed, approachable and well-qualified staff. Children are confident, independent and considerate. More expensive than other nursery schools in the area. A member of Wandsworth Independent Nursery Schools Association, listened to by Wandsworth Social Services. Infinitely long waiting list, with preference to siblings.

## NOAH'S ARK NURSERY SCHOOL

St Mark's Church Hall
Boutflower Road
London SW11 1EJ
**Tel:** (071) 228 9593

**Owner/Principal:** Sarah Chandor
**Type:** Christian nursery school offering half-day sessions (afternoon sessions for youngest children only)
**Children:** 2½–5yrs. 32 places.
**Hours:** Morning session 9.15am–12.15pm (3¼–5 yrs-old)
Afternoon session 1.15pm–3.15pm (2½–3¼yrs-old)
Open 34 weeks a year
**Status:** Private, fee-paying
**Number of years open:** 6½
**Meals:** Snacks
**1992 fees:** £410 per term for 5 morning sessions a week
£300 per term for 5 afternoon sessions a week
**Waiting list:** Long. Early registration advisable
**Registered by:** London Borough of Wandsworth SS

**Premises** Brick-built church hall, just off Battersea Rise. Not very attractive outside, but the church has recently been refurbished and a major extension of four purpose-built classrooms is about to begin. Hopefully this will transform these disappointing premises. The school currently consists of shoulder-high partitions dividing up half the hall into three 'classrooms', one of which is on a balcony at the back of the hall, up a short flight of stairs. Equipment is kept in roll-front, lockable cupboards. There is a rudimentary kitchen and the loos and washbasins are in a rented Portakabin squeezed in just outside the front door. Although this is not an ideal arrangement (the children have to be escorted to the toilet as the doors are kept locked), they are perfectly clean and pleasant. A perspex canopy covers the distance between the front door and the loos. There is a Council-run, dog-free, grassy area surrounding the church which serves as a playground. The hall is also used by Boy Scouts (in the unpartitioned end) and a Sunday school, which uses the nursery area, but not the equipment.

**Owner/Principal & staff** The principal, Sarah Chandor, is a committed Christian and this is very much a Christian nursery school. Although she has no formal qualifications, she has worked with under-5s for over 15 years. She has a strong, but friendly and welcoming personality and is clearly dedicated to her school and the children. She teaches the youngest group in each session. Her staff of two Montessori teachers are also active Christians and recruited through the Church (Holy Trinity, Brompton). The staff are close friends and hold daily discussions about the progress of each child. There are five school governors, including Sarah Chandor, also recruited through the Church.

**Children & parents** Children are predominantly white, middle-class and from practising Christian families in the area. Many come to the school through St Mark's or other local churches. Children with special needs are welcome and happily integrated into the life of the school. There are no formal parents' meetings, but there is an open and relaxed attitude towards parental involvement. Parents often come in to help out when the nursery is short-staffed or to assist on outings. Sarah Chandor feels strongly that she would like to open up the nursery to a wider group of parents, especially when the expansion plans are completed and the number of places increases. She would like more children from ethnic minority backgrounds and some from the neighbouring Peabody Estate. This will need subsidy, and she is considering approaching parents, past and present, and probably the Church, to set up a bursary for assisted places.

**Curriculum & activities** Children are divided by age (and ability) into three groups for school work and creative play. The youngest children (2½–3¼-year-olds) come to school in the afternoons and their programme is very much geared towards play. Activities include art and craft, sand and water play, play dough, construction toys, a home corner, stories, songs, music and cooking. There is a reasonable amount of equipment including Montessori equipment, although not much evidence of children's work on the walls. At about 3¼ years, the children move up to the morning session, where there is some structured learning. They start on shapes and colours and gradually build up towards letters, numbers and writing. Most are reading and writing quite well by the time they leave. Sarah Chandor explains, 'We use Christian principles throughout our time with the children and we aim to show them God's love and acceptance of each child as an individual. We believe discipline to be very important and we approach this with love and firmness, encouraging them to make right choices.' Children are taught to know and love God through daily Bible readings, prayer and the singing of hymns. There is a piano as well as a tape recorder, and music and action games take place on Fridays.

**Remarks** Noah's Ark will look and feel more like a nursery school, and less like a church hall, when the new extension is completed. However, it is a popular, unpressurised and non-competitive school for practising Christians. Expanding to meet a clear demand in the area.

## THE PARK NURSERY SCHOOL

St Saviour's Church
351 Battersea Park Road
London SW11 4LH
**Tel:** (071) 627 5125
(081) 749 1256/5 (School Office)
**Owner:** Bringing Up Baby Ltd
**Principal:** Alison Dady, NNEB (Princess Christian)
**Type:** Nursery school offering full- and part-time places and half-day sessions
**Children:** 2½–5yrs. 30 places. 45 on register
**Hours:** 9.15am–3.30pm
Morning session 9.15am–12.15pm

Afternoon session 1pm–3.30pm
Open 36 weeks a year
**Status:** Private, fee-paying
**Number of years open:** 7 (under previous owner)
**Meals:** Snacks and juice
**1992 fees:** £520 per term for 5 sessions a week
£25 registration fee
**Waiting list:** Places available. Early registration advisable
**Registered by:** London Borough of Wandsworth SS
**Under same ownership:** Camden Day Nursery, Camden; Shepherd's Bush Day Nursery & Annexe, Shepherd's Bush (see listings)

## NODDY'S NURSERY SCHOOL

Trinity Church Hall
Beaumont Road
London SW19 6SP
**Tel:** (081) 785 9191

**Owners:** Sarah Edwards, NNEB, Mont Dip
William Edwards
**Principal:** Sarah Edwards, NNEB, Mont Dip
**Type:** Day nursery and Montessori nursery school offering full- and part-time places and half-day sessions (min 3 sessions a week)
**Children:** 2–5yrs. 48 places. 48 on register
**Hours:** 8am–6pm
Morning session 8am–12.45pm
Afternoon session 1.15pm–6pm
Open 51 weeks a year
**Status:** Private, fee-paying
**Number of years open:** 8
**Meals:** Breakfast, lunch, tea, snacks
**1992 fees:** £390 per month full-time
£11 per session
£35 registration fee plus refundable deposit
**Waiting list:** Long
**Registered by:** London Borough of Wandsworth SS
**Under same ownership:** Noddy's Nursery School, London SW15 6EH

# PROSPECT HOUSE SCHOOL

75 Putney Hill
London SW15 3NT
**Tel:** (081) 780 0456

**Owners:** Mr & Mrs A Gerry
Mr & Mrs P Eley
**Headteachers:** Hermione Gerry, SRN, B Sc, M Sc
Sarah Eley, B Ed
**Type:** Nursery class in co-ed prep school offering morning sessions only
**Children:** 2yrs 10mths–4yrs 11mths. 30 places. 30 on register
**Hours:** 9am–12 noon
Open 36 weeks a year
**Status:** Private, fee-paying
**Number of years open:** 19 (2 in present premises)
**Meals:** Juice and biscuits
**1992 fees:** £570 per term for 5 morning sessions a week
£35 registration covering upper and lower schools
**Waiting list:** Very long. 1997 list already started
**Registered by:** Dept for Education

**Premises** Large, detached, Victorian house at the top of Putney Hill in a quiet cul-de-sac close to the A3. The building, originally divided into flats, has been completely refurbished to provide sparkling, bright classrooms on four floors, a beautiful, well-equipped gym with doors into the garden, a separate nursery section and a three-quarter-acre garden at the back. The nursery class is at the rear of the building and consists of one main room with two smaller classrooms partitioned off it. The reception class for rising-4s is just next door, so that children who move up are not thrown into a totally strange environment. Serious thought and hard work have gone into the design and decoration of the premises and serious money has been spent. The nursery school's previous location was in Hermione's own home in Barnes, where three rooms were used. For the sake of continuity, the new nursery area also consists of three rooms and although relatively small, the space is well used. The large garden is mainly grass but there is an area of hard surface with climbing frames.

**Headteachers & staff** Hermione Gerry, SRN, B Sc, M Sc, has been running Prospect House Nursery School for 19 years. She started at home, and now with Sarah Eley, B Ed, an ex-deputy head of the junior school at Putney High, has achieved her ambition of setting up a school for 170 3- to 11-year-olds. They are both highly competent, mature and experienced teachers who have known one another for many years. Hermione is head of the lower school and Sarah of the upper school, but they make sure there is some overlap in their roles by sharing an office and working very closely together. Most of the nursery staff moved with the nursery to the new premises and Sarah Buckley, an experienced NNEB, has worked at Prospect House for almost 19 years. Other members of staff, all very experienced, have a range of relevant qualifications.

**Children & parents** Almost without exception, the children are the middle-class offspring of professional parents. The catchment area spreads from Wimbledon and Barnes to Fulham and Hammersmith, and the school's fast-growing reputation ensures that all places are taken. So far all children have gone on to the main school. The waiting list is very long, and in fairness to babies born in the summer months, a ballot system is used to allocate places once siblings have been placed. At present, three-quarters of the children in the nursery class are siblings of older children at the school. Hermione makes sure that she and her team stay in close contact with parents, and verbal communication is preferred to sending out written reports on each child. Parents come in with their children for a trial morning or two the term before a child starts and are welcome to stay with their child until they are settled. Hermione feels that it can be very illuminating and helpful for staff to see how parents and children relate to each other.

**Curriculum & activities** Each day's curriculum is planned in advance. During her many years of experience Hermione has developed a broad, child-centred curriculum which borrows from a variety of different philosophies. It is a low-key approach based on learning through play, which leads cumulatively to a wide knowledge of many subjects, good motor control and, most importantly, a desire to learn. The day starts with free play, followed by news time, when children sit in a semi-circle and chat, sing songs and experience group activities. They are then split into small groups, based on ability and level of concentration, for table time. This period concentrates mainly on motor skills – pencil control, cutting, sticking, etc – but also incorporates pre-reading and pre-writing, counting, shapes and colours. One or two particular colours, letters, numbers and shapes are highlighted each week within a particular topic. 'Kitchens' had been a recent topic. Children learnt about cooking, the dangers of fire and to understand hot and cold and other opposites. The day we visited, they were making trumpets out of loo rolls and tissue paper. Having completed that exercise, they were each given a turn at blowing a real trumpet. A fantastic selection of books – almost as good as a bookshop. Most children are emergent readers by the time they move on to the reception class. A qualified music teacher visits once a week for music and movement with the nursery class, which has its own piano. There is another piano in the gym. Notes are kept on each child's development, covering the school curriculum, level of understanding and emotional and social development. Children are highly motivated and communicate well with each other and the staff.

**Remarks** Years of battling to find the right property have finally paid off for the Gerrys. Ideal premises and highly qualified staff ensure the very best of everything for the privileged few who manage to secure a place. Good luck in the ballot is needed by anyone brave enough to join the hundreds on the waiting list!

---

# RED BALLOON NURSERY SCHOOL

St Mary Magdalene Church Hall
Trinity Road
London SW17 7SD
**Tel:** (081) 672 4711

**Owner/Headmistress:** Tamsin Millington-Drake, Mont Dip
**Type:** Nursery school offering half-day sessions.
**Children:** 2½–5yrs. 40 places morning session. 30 places afternoon session. 70 on register
**Hours:** Morning session 8.45am–12.15pm
Afternoon session 1.30pm–4pm
Open 36 weeks a year
**Status:** Private, fee-paying

**Number of years open:** 6½
**Meals:** Mid-morning snack, tea
**1992 fees:** £550 per term for 5 morning sessions a week
£530 per term for 5 afternoon sessions a week
£5 registration fee
£25 per term for swimming
**Waiting list:** Huge (4 years). Entry Sept. only
**Registered by:** London Borough of Wandsworth SS

**Premises** An unattractive, red brick church hall on a busy road crossing Wandsworth Common. Access is straight off the main road – it is just possible to stop briefly to drop off children. Parking is a real problem, but buses pass the front door and Wandsworth Common station is a five-minute walk away. Inside, the entrance hall, kitchen and disabled loo are all newly painted white and the kitchen has been recently refurbished. The main hall is light, and pleasantly spacious. Walls are off-white and in a reasonable state; the floor is fairly worn parquet. There is a stage at one end with shabby red curtains. It is furnished simply and sparsely, with three sets of tables and chairs grouped together. Equipment is kept in cupboards around the walls. A second room, leading off the main hall, seems more friendly as it has grey wall-to-wall carpeting and a reading corner with beanbags. There is no outside play area, but Wandsworth Common is about 100 yards away.

**Owner/Headmistress & staff** Tamsin Millington-Drake, Mont Dip, has been teaching for ten years. She teaches the afternoon session and enthuses staff and children with a bubbly personality and reassuring, friendly manner. Her six Montessori-qualified teachers are particularly lively and noticeably well-bred. There is tangible warmth and friendliness between staff and children, and also between the children themselves. The staff ratio is 1:8 in the mornings and 1:6 in the afternoons. All staff are known to the children as Miss Tamsin, Miss Abigail, etc.

**Children & parents** This is a middle- to upper-class nursery school, though not totally by design. Tamsin Millington-Drake claims she would love to have children from a greater variety of backgrounds, but the catchment area is mainly Bellevue Village, home to TV personalities, actors, and a high proportion of professional, high-earning parents. There have been different nationalities in the past, including Indian children and a Japanese child. But on the whole, pretty smocks and Liberty prints predominate and there are upper-class accents wherever you turn. The vast majority go on to smart prep schools in the area. There is no induction or phasing-in period for parents or children – they are thrown straight into the school five days a week, as, they say, 'generally it works out best this way'. At the beginning of each year parents are provided with a list of names and addresses of all nursery families, and interaction outside school is encouraged as much as possible.

**Curriculum & activities** Tamsin Millington-Drake and her staff believe that the most formative years of a child's life are from 2½ to 5 years, and that each child should be allowed to develop at his or her own pace. Each session begins with assembly. Morning children are divided into two groups for this (cubs and bears). The register is taken, and they discuss their news with the group, sing a song and do a weather board. Then they go off into smaller groups, divided by age and ability for 'school time'. A blackboard is used in schoolroom fashion and children are taught reading, writing, the time, addition and subtraction. Some Montessori equipment is available, but is used collectively rather than individually. Other equipment includes Breakthrough, Fletcher and Galt puzzles and toys. Painting, drawing, modelling, collage and handicrafts are available all the time and a limited amount is displayed in the walls. Regular activities include music, ballet, swimming and some French conversation. Cooking tends to be done in the winter instead of visits to the park. There are two outings a term to art galleries, exhibitions (they visited the modern art exhibition at the Royal Academy), museums or the theatre. Regular visitors to the school to talk about their jobs have included representatives from the nursing profession, fire brigade, police force and library services.

**Remarks** Despite its uninspiring and limiting church hall home, this is a very popular school in the area. Tamsin Millington-Drake obviously has a following – as her four-year waiting list testifies. Safe, conventional, but warm and compassionate.

# REDFORD HOUSE NURSERY

Froebel Institute College
Grove House
Roehampton Lane
London SW15
**Tel:** (081) 878 4745

**Owner:** Roehampton Institute
**Managed by:** Richmond, Twickenham & Roehampton Health Authority
**Nursery Co-ordinator:** Lynne Bartholomew, Froebel Teaching Cert and Multi-Professional Diploma in Early Childhood Studies
**Type:** Workplace nursery offering full- and part-time places and half-day sessions. Outside places available
**Children:** 3–5yrs. 35 places. 34 on register
**Hours:** 7.15am–6pm
Morning session 7.15am–1pm
Afternoon session 1pm–6pm
Open 52 weeks a year
**Status:** Private, fee-paying
**Number of years open:** 4
**Meals:** Breakfast, lunch, tea, snacks
**1992 fees:** £1.50–£2 per hour depending on income
Outside places £12.50 per session
**Waiting list:** Minimal. Priority to full-time places
**Registered by:** London Borough of Wandsworth SS

**Premises** At the far end of the large and beautiful grounds of the Roehampton Institute, housed in the former piggery and stables – almost rural. A single-storey, not very attractive building, but with older and more attractive parts surrounding the courtyard, which is used as a play area. This is an Aladdin's cave of a nursery – so child-centred it is almost overwhelming. There is a Blue Room with a kitchen in one corner and an eating area, used as a play area on wet days. The Red Room is the nerve centre of the day's activities and houses every kind of equipment, from boxes full of junk to large water and sand troughs, a graphics corner and a reading corner. But best of all, the Beige Room (each room is named after the colour of lino on the floor) houses a fabulous and imaginative home corner, like a bedouin tent, suspended from the ceiling and made from swathes of brightly coloured fabric held together with clothes pegs. There is a jungle area complete with snake charmer's basket, a tissue paper tree and hammock; a music corner with a wide selection of instruments from tambourines and xylophones to noisy African shakers made from nutshells. At the far end is an area sectioned off with wooden blocks behind which is a 'beach' with shells, colanders and dumper trucks. This is all surrounded by hardboard panels which are painted, stencilled, hand-daubed and splattered with a stunning array of primary colours. The courtyard boasts an old (specially purchased) water butt with a pump on top, used to teach pump priming and other elementary laws of physics, as well as climbing frames, steps and other outdoor equipment. The nursery has free use of the College's extensive and beautiful grounds used for tree climbing, duck feeding and nature studies.

**Co-ordinator & staff** Lynne Bartholomew, Cert Ed, the nursery co-ordinator, is open, honest, intelligent and very welcoming. She is a graduate of the Froebel Institute, part of the Roehampton Institute, and now lectures there on Early Childhood Studies; she is also about to publish a much needed book on child record-keeping. Lynne is the mature and enthusiastic leader of an equally motivated and well-qualified team, including deputy, June Byne, NNEB, CPQS, and three other members of staff (all NNEB). The team has worked hard to create a happy family atmosphere in the nursery and all muck in to do whatever needs to be done, such as driving up to the College kitchens each day in an old van to collect lunch.

**Children & parents** Lynne opened the nursery four years ago for staff and students from the College and neighbouring Queen Mary's Hospital, but it is now open to anyone on a sessional basis. The nursery has a catchment area of about 50 miles and the children come from a wide variety of backgrounds; their parents may be distinguished academics or hospital cleaners. About eight a year transfer from the baby nursery at the hospital. Lynne regrets that there is little parental involvement in the nursery, but since all parents are in fulltime work, many doing shifts, it is understandable that they do not take part in many activities. There are parents' evenings each term and comprehensive notes on each child's development, which are accessible to all – parents are encouraged to add their own observations to them. Children are divided into family groupings which a particular member of staff is then responsible for supervising, although most of the time children tend to work and play in 'friendship groupings' instead. This is based on the theory that they will learn more successfully if they are with children they feel comfortable with and with whom they share common interests. All age groups and friendship groups come together at least twice a day for story sessions and meals. Most children move to state schools.

**Curriculum & activities** The curriculum in this nursery is deliberately unstructured and fluid since many of the children do not attend every day. The governing philosophy here (which applies to almost everything that happens at the nursery) is based on the teachings of Froebel, with much influence from the modern Froebelists Tina Bruce and Chris Athey. There is a conscious determination to move away from a 'content-centred' curriculum. Teachers do not decide or dictate which project or activity children will do. Instead they carefully watch each child's current pattern of behaviour and try to identify its underlying meaning or obsession. They then group children with similar behaviour patterns – or 'schemas' in Froebel jargon – and provide materials, equipment and activities that will support and extend their particular interests, likes and obsessions at that time. Interesting and often inspired results come out of this seemingly random but completely child-centred approach. We were shown books made and written by children, trees made from plastic bottles, twigs and scraps of fabric and endless examples of self-motivated, child-led creativity. Reading and writing are not taught per se, but children are ready for both by the time they leave. They begin with letter recognition and learning their names. Art, graphics, dressing up, arithmetic, technology, physics, chemistry, biology and countless other subjects are all taken in. The child's natural inquisitiveness is allowed free rein in a carefully controlled environment, and nurtured with unlimited praise and cuddles.

**Remarks** A truly constructive, child-centred atmosphere. Real, imaginative learning experiences for the children in a spacious setting and beautiful grounds. We loved it, and so do children, parents and staff. Watch the waiting list grow now that the nursery is open to outsiders.

# SCHOOLROOM NURSERY SCHOOL

St Simon's Church Hall
Hazlewell Road
London SW15 6LU
**Tel:** (071) 931 7079

**Owner/Principal:** Judy Alexander, Mont Dip
**Type:** Nursery school, offering full-time places, plus a few part-time places for younger children
**Children:** 2½–5yrs. 20 places. 23 on register
**Hours:** 9am–12.15pm
Open 36 weeks a year
**Status:** Private, fee-paying
**Number of years open:** 15 (3 in present site)
**Meals:** Juice and biscuits
**1992 fees:** £360 per term full-time
£28 per term for French
**Waiting list:** Reasonable. Early registration advisable
**Registered by:** London Borough of Wandsworth SS

**Premises** Attractive and well-maintained small church hall built on to the side of the priest's house. This is a quiet and affluent area of tasteful, tree-lined streets and substantial Edwardian detached houses, close to Upper Richmond Road and Putney High Street. Parking is a problem, but fortunately there is space for cars to pull in off the street, to pick up and drop off children. Many children live in adjoining streets and walk to the nursery. The school is housed in one fairly small room, but what it lacks in size is made up for by a really lovely, absolutely huge garden to the rear, running the length of the church hall, the priest's house and the church as well. There is a wide grassy area, a willow tree to play under and various attractive hollows and groves to make dens in – there are so many natural play areas in the garden that there is no real need for any outdoor play equipment. The schoolroom is painted white with pretty mint green curtains and windows overlooking the garden. There is a newly installed door which leads straight into the garden. The floor has been sanded recently and now has a glowing, waxed surface which is striking and homely. There is a small kitchen, partitioned off in one corner with a cooker and some units. The nursery has been in this building for two years; previously it was run from two rooms in a private house nearby. Every lunch time all the equipment has to be locked up in cupboards as other groups use the room. Substantial and well-built, the nursery is in perfect decorative order inside and out.

**Owner/Principal & staff** Judy Alexander, Mont Dip, obtained her qualification in 1966 and has worked in several nursery schools in the area, as well as having a family of her own. She is assisted by one other Mont Dip member of staff, recently appointed, her predecessor of six years having left to have a baby. Other, unqualified, staff come in as required. Numbers are slightly down at present due to the recession and to the fact that about four new private nurseries have opened in the area in the last two years. When we visited, the staff ratio was a generous 1:4. Judy Alexander is a fastidious and caring principal, who runs a well-organised, disciplined school. It does in fact feel like a classroom. The children are kept fully and quietly absorbed in their work and 'are not just allowed to run around'. Club Frère Jacques visits once a week to give French lessons which take place in the vestry (across the garden in the main church building). About half the children attend these lessons.

**Children & parents** The children are a prosperous bunch and many live in adjoining streets. Parents are professional and well-off; generally the mothers do not work outside the home. Most children go on to local private schools, such as Putney Park and Putney High. Since many of them are local, out-of-school socialising is popular. The children each have a file for their work which is taken home at half-term and the end of term, so that parents can inspect work and monitor their progress. Parents are welcome to visit the principal by appointment any day at 9.30, or prior to the end of a session at around 11.30.

**Curriculum & activities** The day starts with group time between 9 and 10.30, although this may go on a little longer if the weather is bad. The children divide themselves between a maths table, an art table and a letters and reading table and are free to move on to the next table when they choose. Each day a new letter is presented, which is then worked on the following day by using sandpaper letters and drawing relevant pictures. The school uses abundant Montessori equipment and aims to teach good pencil control as well as hundreds, tens and units by the time a child is 4½. The children do most of their work in exercise

books. Work time is followed by a break, then there is a group lesson, where they learn the days of the week, months of the year, colours, etc. This is followed by a story during which there is 'absolutely no fidgeting'. After that they have their juice and biscuits and then (around 11.30), weather permitting, they are taken in a line into the garden and allowed to run around and play with balls, skipping ropes, etc. Rainy days mean inside play with toys, a round of musical bumps or other action games.
**Remarks** Possibly the most attractive of the church hall nursery schools visited and certainly the best garden, where children have complete freedom to explore. The School Room offers a varied curriculum within a disciplined, structured timetable. Your child will learn self-control as well as pencil control; good manners along with literacy and numeracy skills.

## SQUARE ONE NURSERY SCHOOL

12 Ravenna Road
Putney
London SW15 6AW
**Tel:** (081) 788 1546

**Owners/Joint Principals:** Deirdre King, Cert Ed
Valerie Tate, Mont Dip
**Type:** Nursery school offering morning sessions, plus 2 afternoon sessions for older children
**Children:** 2½–5yrs. 36 per session. 48 on register
**Hours:** Morning session 9.30am–12.15pm
Afternoon session 12.15pm–3pm
Open 36 weeks a year
**Status:** Private, fee-paying
**Number of years open:** 22

**Meals:** Snacks, packed lunches
**1992 fees:** £375 per term for 5 sessions a week
£75 per term for one extra afternoon
**Waiting list:** Very, very long. Priority to siblings
**Registered by:** London Borough of Wandsworth SS

## THOMAS'S KINDERGARTEN

St Mary's Church
Battersea Church Road
London SW11 3NA
**Tel:** (071) 738 0400

**Owner:** Thomas's London Day Schools
**Principals:** Mr & Mrs David Thomas
**Headmistress:** Sally Wakefield, NNEB
**Type:** Nursery School offering morning sessions. Children may stay on for afternoon activities (short tennis, gym, music or ballet) twice a week
**Children:** 2½–5yrs. 50 places. 33 on register
**Hours:** Morning session 8.45am–12 noon
Lunch/afternoon activities 12 noon–2 or 3pm
Open 38 weeks a year
**Status:** Private, fee-paying
**Number of years open:** 1
**Meals:** Juice and biscuits, packed lunches for those staying for afternoon activities
**1992 fees:** £615 per term for 5 morning sessions a week
£475 per term for 3 morning sessions a week
£390 per term for 2 morning sessions a week
£115 per term for afternoon activity club
£15 registration fee
**Waiting list:** Long. Early registration advisable
**Registered by:** London Borough of Wandsworth SS
**Under same ownership:** Thomas's Kindergarten, Westminster (see listing)

# Westminster

At the time of writing, Westminster City Council's policies towards nursery care and education are in a state of total reorganisation. No one is entirely clear which direction either Social Services or Education will finally take. So far, there are plans to turn three of the City's ten day nurseries into family centres and market-test the remaining seven, to see if the private or voluntary sectors are interested in taking them over. Budget cuts have meant that staff posts have been frozen and lengthy waiting lists have built up in some areas. There are 21 playgroups and 49 private nurseries. Most of these are open during school term-time only, offering sessional places to over-2s. Fees can be high – £1200 per ten-week term from 9am to 3.30pm at a Montessori nursery school is not uncommon. More reasonable facilities are available in the grant-aided voluntary sector, including nine excellent nurseries run by the Westminster Children's Society, a local charity. Over 100 registered childminders, 55 of whom are paid by the council, cater mainly for children under 2. Thirty per cent of Westminster's 3- and 4-year-olds receive nursery education. There are three nursery schools and 24 nursery classes, with plans to open a further four. Parents are advised to register early.

## Further information

For enquiries about daycare services, playgroups, nurseries, childminders:
Social Services Department
Tel: (071) 798 2245

For details on nursery schools and classes:
Education Department
Tel: (071) 798 1816/7

For details and publications covering all types of early years provision:
One Stop Services
First Floor
Westminster City Hall
Victoria Street
London SW1E 6QP

## ABERCORN PLACE SCHOOL NURSERY

28 Abercorn Place
London NW8 9XP
**Tel:** (071) 286 4785

**Owner:** Abercorn Place School PLC
**Principal:** Andrea Greystoke, BA (Hons)
**Type:** Nursery school offering half-day sessions
**Children:** 2½–4yrs. 20 places. 27 on register
**Hours:** Morning session 8.45am–11.45am
Afternoon session 12.45pm–3.45pm
Open 34 weeks a year
**Status:** Private, fee-paying
**Number of years open:** 6
**Meals:** None
**1992 fees:** £955 per term for 5 sessions a week
**Waiting list:** One year
**Registered by:** Dept for Education

## LONDON MONTESSORI CENTRE NURSERY SCHOOL

18 Balderton Street
London W1 1TG
**Tel:** (071) 493 0165

**Owner:** Leslie Britton, B Ed
**Principal:** Martina Furness, Mont Dip
**Type:** Nursery school offering full-time places, plus full-day holiday playscheme (2½–9yrs)
**Children:** 2½–5yrs. 30 places. 30 on register
**Hours:** 9.30am–3.30pm
Open 36 weeks a year
**Status:** Private, fee-paying
**Number of years open:** 22
**Meals:** Lunch, snacks
**1992 fees:** £1200 per term full-time
£100 per week for holiday scheme
**Waiting list:** First come first served
**Registered by:** City of Westminster SS

# THOMAS'S KINDERGARTEN

14 Ranelagh Grove
London SW11 8PD
**Tel:** (071) 730 3596

**Owner:** Thomas's London Day Schools
**Principals:** Mr & Mrs David Thomas
**Headmistress:** Arabella Plunkett, Mont Dip
**Type:** Nursery school offering half-day sessions. Children may stay on for afternoon activities (short tennis, gym, music or ballet) twice a week
**Children:** 2½–5yrs. 65 places. 57 on register
**Hours:** Morning session 8.45am–12 noon
Afternoon session 1pm–3pm
Open 38 weeks a year
**Status:** Private, fee-paying
**Number of years open:** 22
**Meals:** Juice and biscuits, packed lunch for those staying for afternoon activities
**1992 fees:** £615 per term for 5 morning sessions a week
£475 per term for 3 morning sessions a week
£390 per term for 2 morning sessions a week
£475 per term for 4 afternoon sessions a week
£15 registration fee
**Waiting list:** Very long. Early registration advisable
**Registered by:** City of Westminster SS
**Under same ownership:** Thomas's Kindergarten, Battersea (see listing)

---

# WESTMINSTER CHILDREN'S SOCIETY CHIPPENHAM MEWS NURSERY

Beauchamp Lodge
2 Warwick Crescent
London W2 6NE
**Tel:** (071) 289 3131

**Owner:** Westminster Children's Society
**Manager:** Maria Freeman, NNEB
**Type:** Day nursery offering full-time places
**Children:** 2½–5yrs. 20 places. 20 on register
**Hours:** 8.30am–5.30pm
Open 51 weeks a year
**Status:** Fee-paying. Registered charity
**Number of years open:** 4 at current address. 10 at previous

**Meals:** Lunch, tea, snacks
**1992 fees:** £47.50 per week full-time (+ £6.50 for lunches) maximum
Reduced fees available on sliding scale
**Waiting list:** Long. Only 4 places for 2yr-olds. Priority to children living in Westminster
**Registered by:** City of Westminster SS
**Under same ownership:** There are 9 other WCS nurseries in the borough. For information contact Westminster Children's Society, 121 Marsham Street, London SW1P 4LX.
Tel: (071) 834 8679

**Premises** A large, once grand, but now very dilapidated building in a prominent position, overlooking the canal at Little Venice – an exclusive, beautiful and very up-market district on one side, and the M40 flyover on the other. The nursery occupies two rooms on the ground floor of Beauchamp Lodge, which also contains facilities for disabled workers, the homeless and the Gingerbread organisation for one-parent families. The main room has a large bay window, with a windowseat, overlooking the houseboats on the canal and the attractive Rembrandt Gardens. It is crammed full of equipment, toys and furniture and every inch of wall space is used for the display of children's work or notices. The quiet room, which also acts as office and kitchenette, is as full of equipment as the main room and provides television and video, computer and a quiet/reading corner on a raised landing with storage below. Beyond this is a corridor used for hanging coats and the loos. There is a small, well-fenced, outside patio area, facing the canal, with a slide and other outdoor equipment.

**Owners/Manager & staff** The Westminster Children's Society, a registered charity, was established in 1903. The Society is non profit-making and all its income is derived from fees, donations, fund-raising and a grant from Westminster City Council. Maria Freeman, NNEB, has worked in WCS nurseries for the last ten years. She joined the Chippenham Mews nursery just over four years ago and was responsible for the move to the new premises. She leads a team of five full-time NNEB nursery nurses. Her deputy, Sue Sweet, NNEB, and other members of the team have also transferred from other WCS nurseries. All work shifts to cover the nursery opening hours. BTEC and NNEB students attend for work experience, supervised by members of staff. A music teacher comes in once a fortnight for a session of music, movement and mime, using a tape recorder. Staff lead a similar session in the intervening week. Formal staff meetings are held once every four to six weeks. WCS organises managers' and deputies' meetings, and staff frequently exchange ideas with workers from the other nurseries. A health and safety officer makes regular visits.

**Children & parents** A truly multicultural group, although the majority are Afro-Caribbean. Most are from low-income families and live close to the nursery, usually within walking distance. The sliding fee scale means that children from all social backgrounds attend. Although most go on to local primary schools, some transfer to the private sector. Children are divided into four colour groups, each with a keyworker, and when all children are present there are five in each group. Within each colour group there are five shapes, so that each child can be individually identified by a colour and shape. This encourages independence as children are able to recognise their own coat peg, mattress and table place by picking out the correct colour and shape. Most parents work outside the home, but willingly participate in the fund-raising activities that are vital to the nursery's survival – sponsorship, raffles, events and securing corporate donations. They receive a monthly newsletter and are invited on outings and to parents' evenings. There is a daily exchange of information about each child and six-monthly assessments, when parents are formally invited to discuss their child's progress. Parents are encouraged to visit at any time of day. Children with disabilities and special educational needs are integrated.

**Curriculum & activities** Learning through play is the governing philosophy. Each day is planned around an ongoing theme, but the programme is kept deliberately flexible to allow for spontaneity and new ideas. The nursery makes every effort to provide equipment and activities which 'take into account the child's religious, cultural, racial and linguistic background as well as age and stage of development'. Themes are planned in advance at staff meetings and are drawn into every possible aspect of the daily routine and outings. Sand, water and paint are freely available during the day. Imaginative play is encouraged in the large and well-equipped home corner and dressing-up box. Kitchen utensils are changed every few weeks to chopsticks and bowls, or Indian dishes and plates. Pre-school work includes learning colours and shapes, reasoning games, puzzles and teaching the children to recognise their names. Children come together every day for circle time and stories, when they are expected to sit absolutely still and quiet. This is a time when children take the lead and staff let them do most of the talking. There is at least an hour of outdoor play every day, weather permitting. Lunch, prepared in the café upstairs, is a social event, and each week children are chosen as servers, to set the tables, take orders during lunch and help clear up. There are fortnightly outings to Paddington Library and frequent other outings. WCS has a mini-bus and children are taken as far as Gloucestershire to see lambing, and to the seaside.

**Remarks** A vital community service and a life-saver for many low-income parents in the area, although open to all backgrounds and nationalities. Professional, high-quality, innovative care and education at an affordable price.

## YOUNG ENGLAND KINDERGARTEN

St Saviour's Hall
St George's Square
London SW1V 2HP
**Tel:** (071) 834 3171

**Owner/Principal:** Kay King, Mont Dip
**Type:** Nursery school offering half-day sessions
**Children:** 2½–5yrs. 50 places morning session. 25 places afternoon session. 75 on register
**Hours:** 9am–12.30pm Mon–Fri (3–5yrs)
1.45pm–3.45pm Mon, Wed, Fri (2½–3½yrs)
Open 36 weeks a year
**Status:** Private, fee-paying
**Number of years open:** 30
**Meals:** Juice and biscuits
**1992 fees:** £635 per term for 5 morning sessions a week
£390 per term for 3 afternoon sessions a week
£25 registration fee plus £250 refundable deposit
£50 per term for swimming or ballet
**Waiting list:** Long. Registration forms not sent out until parents have visited school
**Registered by:** City of Westminster SS

**Premises** An unattractive, but reasonably well-kept, brick-built hall next to St Saviour's Church on the edge of St George's Square gardens, a stone's throw from Pimlico tube station. The hall is large, long and light, with a stage at one end used mainly for storage, two smaller rooms used for quiet concentration, a kitchen and recently refurbished loos. The most striking features are a sea of pale green lino which has obviously stood up to years of wear and tear and small mobile cupboards dotted about the room to break up the space, each painted a different bright colour. There is an extensive selection of toys and equipment. The school was started 30 years ago in this hall by Mr and Mrs Young and has been through two subsequent changes of ownership. The hall is leased from the church next door; the vicar, an ex-teacher himself, is supportive. The church uses the hall when the school is closed. The gardens in St George's Square are open to the public and the school uses them regularly.

**Principal & staff** Kay King, Mont Dip, has been sole owner and principal of Young England since 1988. For ten years before that she jointly owned the school with Vicky Richardson, who has now set up an exclusive children's clothes shop nearby. The shop shares its name with the Kindergarten, but that is the only link between the two. Kay King is assertive, very organised and very talkative. She presides over her school from a desk at one end of the hall and calls rowdiness to order with the use of a handbell. Her role is mainly administrative and she delegates most of the teaching and caring to the rest of her team and in particular her deputy, Angela Oliver, NNEB, who has worked at the nursery for 20 years and has a mature, gentle and smiling presence. There are nine other members of staff, four full-time and five part-time. Seven of them are qualified – mostly Montessori, but some NNEB. Although this is not a strictly Montessori school, Kay King strongly favours a Montessori bias among her staff as she feels that 'the Montessori training is one of the very best for this age group'. One afternoon and two mornings a week, Jane Nevett, B Mus, LRAM, arrives to play the piano for a music and movement session. Other staff members include Olive, who is described by Kay King as 'general dogsbody', and cooks lunch for the staff who are staying all day. Young England's most famous former nursery assistant is the Princess of Wales, although no evidence of her time here remains today.

**Children & parents** The school draws in children from a wide area. In the past there have been such large groups from up-market Holland Park, Kensington and south of the river that school buses have been arranged. However, many are local and there is a strong American contingent. At the most, one child a year goes on to a state primary school, while all the others are destined for private schools, such as Eaton House, Frances Holland, Thomas's, Garden House. Kay is always present at the school and expects parents to discuss any problems with her at picking-up time. Parents and nannies come right into the hall to deliver children and to collect them at the end of a session, so there is always the opportunity for a chat. Many mothers work, but Kay emphasises that she is never afraid to call a mother if there is a real problem. A parents' open day is held once a term and reports are sent out at the end of the year or in the term that a child is leaving. Parents of new children are invited to attend the nursery with their child the term before entry, so that they have adequate time to prepare for nursery school.

**Curriculum & activities** The morning session for 3- to 5-year-olds starts with an hour of free play. This is a time for making friends and getting used to the mêlée of a school playground. Children have the use of a climbing frame, bikes and trikes, a trampoline, a quiet corner for imaginative play and a colouring table. At 10.00 a bell is rung to signal tidying-up time, and children are expected to help. The register, hand shaking and milk and biscuits – good manners are expected – are followed by a group activity such as singing, dancing, percussion band, acting, agility games, storytime or a visit to the garden or library. The last part of the morning is set aside for drawing, painting, handicraft, modelling and collage work, educational and memory games and messy play. Older children are introduced to phonetic reading and number work, taught in small groups offering individual attention. Elements of the Montessori teaching philosophy and some Montessori equipment are used. Children also have exercise books. There is no regular written assessment, but a short yearly report on each child's progress is sent home at the end of the summer term. Twice-yearly display of work is put on, and a concert or play, with the chance for parents to discuss any problems with staff. Excellent art and craft. When we visited, children were painting and decorating fantastic, huge Christmas trees on paper. Weekly ballet classes are held at the Chelsea Ballet School and swimming at Latchmere Pool. The three afternoon sessions are for younger children – 2½ to 3½ years in a smaller group of approximately 25, with a higher ratio of staff to pupils. Activities are similar but more relaxed and less structured. There is greater opportunity for free play. Music is taught to all children.

**Remarks** Discipline and manners, instilled by the formidable Kay King and her handbell, are among the priorities. This is one of the most expensive and exclusive nursery schools in London. Nevertheless, affluent SW1 parents are queuing up for places. Children leave well prepared for the competitive rigours of pre-prep and public school life.

# MANCHESTER

## Bolton

Bolton offers mainly part-time places to 41 per cent of 3- and 4-year-olds. There are waiting lists in some districts, but the inner, urban areas are reasonably well supplied. Funds permitting, the borough hopes to include a nursery unit in a proposed new school. There are fewer enquiries for daycare in the 26 private nurseries, due to the recession. Four Social Services day nurseries have merged to form three units, with the loss of 60 places. Many parents use the area's 400 registered childminders and support the 61 active playgroups.

### Further information
For a list of day nurseries, childminders and playgroups:
Registration and Inspection Unit
Park House Cottage
Laurel Street
off Chorley New Road
Bolton BL1 4RB
Tel: (0204) 365119

For information and advice on all types of childcare in the area:
Under Fives Forum
Children's Centre
Devonshire Road
Bolton BL1 4NS
Tel: (0204) 842886 or 497947

A register of nursery classes, childminders, playgroups and crèches will soon be available for public inspection in 150 different locations, including libraries and local authority offices, and will be updated every six months.

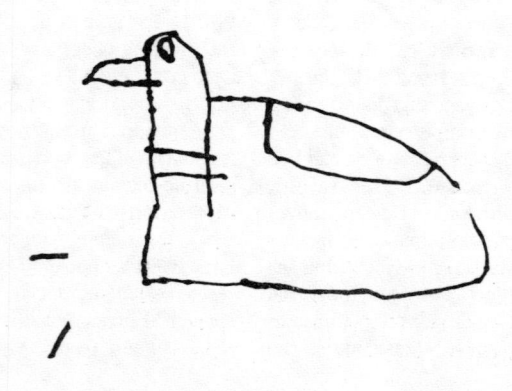

# ELMS NURSERY SCHOOL

717/719 Blackburn Road
Astley Bridge
Bolton BL1 7JJ
**Tel:** (0204) 304258

**Owners:** Brian and Dorothy Wrigley
**Principal:** Dorothy Wrigley, Cert Ed (McMillan Early Years Specialist Teacher)
**Type:** Day nursery offering full- and part-time places and half-day sessions
**Children:** 6wks–5yrs. 50 places. 75 on register
**Hours:** 8am–6pm
Morning session 8am–1pm
Afternoon session 1pm–6pm
Open 50 weeks a year
**Status:** Private, fee-paying
**Number of years open:** 3
**Meals:** Breakfast, lunch, tea
**1992 fees:** £60 per week full-time
£42.50 per week for 5 morning sessions inc lunch
£36.50 per week for 5 afternoon sessions excl lunch
£14.50 per day
£10 per morning session
£9 per afternoon session
**Waiting list:** 17. Mainly for baby places
**Registered by:** Met Dist of Bolton SS

**Premises** The ground floor of two large, Victorian, red-brick, semi-detached houses, knocked into one, situated on the main Bolton to Blackburn road, to the north of the city centre. The owners live upstairs. The nursery occupies six rooms, all large, colourful, beautifully furnished and extremely well decorated. A stimulating place for young children. A toilet block and conservatory, to extend the toddlers' play space, have been added on. Outside, in the large, mature garden, there is a hard area for riding tricycles. The lawn is soon to be re-planned, to increase the range of activities available outdoors. The laundry, store room, workshop and staff room are all downstairs in what were once the cellars.

**Owner/Principal & staff** Over the past 20 years, Dorothy Wrigley, Cert Ed, has taught the whole of the primary age range. From 1988 to 1992 she was head of Sharples CP School, which has a nursery class and unit for visually impaired children. A specialist in early years teaching and tireless campaigner for nursery education, she has brought a wealth of experience to the planning, resourcing and staffing of the Elms nursery. Her husband, Brian, is responsible for administration. Dorothy Wrigley gave up her full-time headship last year, and is now fully involved in the day-to-day running of the nursery. 'My role is team-builder, leader by example, motivator, decision-maker, planner and trainer,' she says. She clearly relates well to her staff of eight full-time and two part-time workers, mainly qualified NNEB nursery nurses, and to the children who shower her with questions and tell her their news from home whenever she appears. Each room in the nursery has a nursery nurse in charge. The senior nursery nurse has particular experience of special needs children. Four students are accepted on work experience and spend a month in each room. An additional helper comes in once a week to work with a Down's syndrome baby on a one-to-one basis. Staff/child ratios average 1:3 in the baby room, 1:4 for toddlers, and 1:5 or 6 in the pre-school room. Induction programme for new staff, in-house training and monthly attendance at talks given by the Bolton branch of the British Association of Early Childhood Education.

**Children & parents** Socially mixed children from families with two working parents, some professional, some blue-collar workers and some single parents. A few of the children come simply for the pre-school education, part-time, and have mothers who do not work outside the home. Parents are welcome at any time and are kept informed via a regular newsletter. Babies are sent home each day with a completed form showing details of their sleep, food, toileting and drinking patterns during the day. Most of the children transfer to state primary schools. The children are polite, happy and busy. The nursery is able to take children with special educational needs. Parents settling-in new children are invited in with their child for about an hour a week for some weeks prior to starting at the nursery. A room is available for mothers wishing to come in and breast-feed.

**Curriculum & activities** Full of bright, new, gleaming equipment – a stimulating place for any child. In Dorothy Wrigley's words, 'The emphasis here is on learning through play, with children given access to a range of activities, planned and structured to develop all areas of their physical, social, emotional and intellectual skills.' Children are always offered opportunities for free expression and there was a very lively and messy session of finger painting in progress when we visited. Children are grouped by age, and each group has a wide variety of appropriate toys, books and equipment. They participate daily in music and singing and have weekly dance, movement or PE sessions. They also attend swimming lessons. The pre-school group do pre-reading, pre-writing and pre-number work and, when they are ready, are introduced to books from Link Up and the Oxford Reading Tree. Individual children's needs are recognised and encouraged accordingly. There is no formal religious content, but the children sometimes enjoy hymn singing. Meals are prepared and cooked by the nursery's trained cook in an immaculate kitchen. Staff and children eat together, and special diets are catered for. All children clean their teeth after meals.

**Remarks** Care and education of a very high standard. Places in the baby rooms are very much in demand and need to be booked early. Dorothy Wrigley has been a member of the British Association for Early Childhood Education for many years and, despite her move into the private sector, is still committed to the fight for state nursery education for every child whose parents want it. First-class value for money. If this standard of care is to continue unsubsidised, then we suspect fees will have to increase for the nursery to survive. 'I consider it a privilege to be entrusted with the care and education of young children during their most formative years,' the owner told us.

## HIGHVIEW NURSERY

off Belmont Road
Sharples
Bolton BL1 7DZ
**Tel:** (0204) 595315

**Owners:** Colin and Lesley Sobey
**Principal:** Lesley Sobey, NNEB
**Type:** Day nursery offering full- and part-time places, plus after-school and holiday scheme for 5–11yr-olds
**Children:** 0–5yrs. 50 places. 70 on register. 25 places for after-school and holiday service
**Hours:** 8am–6pm
Open 50 weeks a year
**Status:** Private, fee-paying
**Number of years open:** 6
**Meals:** Lunch, tea
**1992 fees:** £70 per week full-time
£16 per day
£10 per morning
£9 per afternoon
**Waiting list:** Long for baby places – around 100 a year are turned away
**Registered by:** Met Dist of Bolton SS

**Premises** The ground floor of the owner's large, early Victorian, detached house in the village of Sharples, three miles north of Bolton. The stone-built house stands well back from the road, in large lawned gardens and a paved area. There is ample parking and all children are brought by car. The nursery consists of seven rooms plus a kitchen and two toilet blocks. Everywhere is light, cheerful and spotlessly clean. The rooms are decorated annually. Babies have their own day room opening on to a patio, and a sleep room with a fleet of Silver Cross prams and a four-poster cot. Mobiles are everywhere and plenty of baby toys as well as a soft play area. The toddler room has children's paintings on the walls, large toys and a big slide. The 3-year-olds have a tremendous range of toys and a messy-play room for art, craft, water and sand play which opens on to an outdoor all-weather play area. A pre-school room for the oldest age group is divided into a classroom and a play area. Walls reveal colourful examples of the children's considerable artistic talent.

**Owners/Principal & staff** Lesley Sobey, NNEB, and her husband Colin opened Highview in 1988 when their daughter Grace was 18 months old. Both have three children from previous marriages, and a wealth of childcare experience between them. Lesley is a young grandmother and has been a foster mother for 20 years. She has worked with children with special educational needs and designed games for children with learning difficulties. As the supernumerary principal, she keeps a watchful eye on all that goes on and organises special outings and themes. The staff of 18 includes ten qualified NNEBs. Of the remaining eight, most have had some relevant childcare training and all have completed a first-aid course. Staff are members of the Private Nursery Association, which holds evening training sessions every two months on various topics – such as HIV, the asthmatic child, child abuse and speech therapy. There is good teamwork and a mixture of ages. Staff seem outgoing and responsive, and have warm relationships with the children. The nursery takes NNEB students on practical placements. Staff/child ratios are 1:3 for babies and toddlers and 1:5 or 1:6 for older children.

**Children & parents** 'Very privileged children', is Lesley's description. Most have two working parents, mainly in the professions. All are English-speaking, although a few are of Italian, Polish or Chinese descent. Children are very happy, responsive to visitors and busy, divided into five age groups, with relevant activities for each. Some go on to state primaries in Belmont and Egerton, others to the private sector – Beech House, Clevelands or Highfield. The nursery offers a 'settling-in trial period', free of charge to all new parents. The door is always open and parents are encouraged to call in whenever they wish. Observation books are completed daily in the baby room for parents to read at the end of each day. The nursery welcomes children with special needs such as asthma, hearing impairment and epilepsy, backed up by Social Services support when necessary.

**Curriculum & activities** Apart from the babies, all age groups have a structured day, which includes free play, art and craft work, outdoor play or indoor physical activities, songs, stories and some pre-reading, pre-writing and pre-number work for shorter periods. Children also watch a limited amount of television and the older ones use a computer to develop their keyboard skills. Reading is not taught, but books are plentiful. During the final year the emphasis is on pre-school education, but in a low-key manner. In Lesley's view, 'Above all else, a child needs to be happy and well cared for, without pressure.' The nursery owns a 16-seater mini-bus, which is used for outings. Children are taken to weekly pre-school gymnastics and on outings to parks, museums and places of special interest. Puppet shows and musicians come in to entertain the children. Photographs are taken on birthdays and other special occasions and given to parents. Children are regularly assessed and parents informed of their progress. The hotpot with cabbage served for lunch on the day we visited was freshly cooked, looked delicious and was enthusiastically devoured.

**Remarks** A high-quality service, with no expense spared and no corners cut. This is reflected in the cost – the highest in the Bolton area. The nursery is deservedly popular and always full. Parents are advised to plan their childcare well ahead of birth to stand any chance of securing a place.

## MOORLANDS CHILDREN'S NURSERY

342 Chorley New Road
Horwich
Bolton BL6 5PS
**Tel:** (0204) 669518

**Owner/Principal:** Denise Hunt, NNEB
**Type:** Day nursery offering full- and part-time places and half-day sessions
**Children:** 0–5yrs. 40 places. 50 on register
**Hours:** 7.45am–6pm
Morning session 7.45am–1pm
Afternoon session 1pm–6pm
Open 51 weeks a year
**Status:** Private, fee-paying
**Number of years open:** 4
**Meals:** Lunch, tea, snacks
**1992 fees:** £75 per week full-time
£52 per week for 5 morning sessions
£47.50 per week for 5 afternoon sessions
£21 per day
£11.50 per morning session
£10.50 per afternoon session
£50 refundable deposit
Sibling discounts
**Waiting list:** None
**Registered by:** Met Dist of Bolton SS

**Premises** Opened in September 1989, the first purpose-built nursery in the area. An attractive, brick, single-storey building, specifically designed to provide a safe, secure and happy environment. The nursery also owns the church next door and eventually hopes to expand into it when funds are available for refurbishment. Every safety aspect has been considered, including electric sockets and door handles out of children's reach, double glazing throughout and safety surfaces in the outside play area. It is situated off busy Chorley New Road, parking is not a problem and the bus service runs nearby. The nursery comprises three children's rooms. The baby room, half lino, half carpet, includes a changing area and separate pram area. The toddler room, with a lino floor and washable rugs, has a fish tank; tables and chairs and fold-up mattresses for naps; and a slide, ride-on toys and floor toys. The classroom has lino floor with a carpeted book corner, desks for table-top games, puzzles, sand, water, a train set and a piano. Other facilities include a fully-fitted kitchen and laundry room, office, storeroom and staff room. There are four children's toilets and washbasins, and facilities for the disabled. Inside and out, the nursery is in excellent condition. Attractive hanging baskets of flowers, window boxes and pretty curtains create a homely atmosphere. Each of the children's rooms has its own outside play area with separate access, and with appropriate toys, impact-absorbing safety surface and a secure fence.

**Owner/Principal & staff** Moorlands is 'a dream come true,' says Denise Hunt, NNEB. She gained her 25 years' experience working with both nursery and infant children for Bolton Education Authority and working abroad as a nanny. She is involved daily in every aspect of the nursery and believes that the pre-school years are the most important years of a child's life. Her staff team comprises 13 women, 11 full-time and two part-time. Eight are qualified (six NNEB, two SRN) and three unqualified (one trained and two training). All NNEBs have life-saving and first-aid qualifications. Staff include an experienced special needs worker and a dance expert. Denise says she has been trying to employ a male member of staff for three years and finally has a trainee whom she hopes will stay on. 'He is marvellous, much loved by both children and parents,' she says. Low staff turnover is attributed to good pay and working conditions. Four members of staff are more mature, others in their early 30s. All staff wear a uniform which makes them look like nurses. Qualified staff wear blue and trainees wear a tabard. The relationship between staff and children is visibly warm and caring. No staff training policy or budget.

**Children & parents** Reasonable social mix of children, with parents including teachers, nurses and dentists, painters, decorators and factory workers, though since the recession the majority have been professionals. The children travel from a wide area, including Manchester and Preston. Most stay for full-day sessions. Moorlands also accepts children up to 8 years old during school holidays, if they attended the nursery before entering primary school. Children with special needs are welcome and there are facilities for wheelchairs and a disabled toilet, though there are none at present. Phasing-in of new children is according to the needs of individuals. Parents are allowed to phone at any time during the day and the door is always open to parents. They are invited to open days, but there are no parents' evenings, plays, sports days or concerts and no parental involvement in the running of the nursery. At present one child is subsidised by a local company.

**Curriculum & activities** The philosophy is 'learning through play in a richly resourced educational environment'. The facilities at Moorlands are excellent – there are areas for quiet relaxing moments; creative play with paint, clay and dough, sand and water; beautiful books and educational toys and a music corner with a yellow piano – all stimulating, child-orientated and excellent quality. Children are divided into peer groupings, not family groupings. Denise believes children learn more this way. 'Different ages have different needs,' she says. However, some time is spent all together – in free play, storytime or perhaps music and movement. Although there are no written programmes or timetable, the children learn early concepts of number and pre-reading and writing skills and are encouraged to write their own name before going on to 'big' school. Written records are kept – parents have access if they wish. Library visits are every eight weeks, the local park weekly if possible, and dance and movement are also weekly. The nursery invites different people in for topic work, such as the local ambulance crew and the fire brigade. One mother, who is a nurse, visited and put the children's arms and legs in plaster! Lunch is prepared in the spotless, well-equipped kitchen by a cook and includes plenty of fruit and well-balanced, nutritious food. Staff do not eat with the children. Every attention is paid to hygiene and safety throughout.

**Remarks** Professional nursery, offering safe, happy care and some education. Excellent provision for babies and toddlers. Enthusiastic staff who get stuck in. One NNEB recently spent the day dressed as a clown, painting children's faces for a weekly topic on circus life. The owner hopes that one day the nursery will be profitable. This is unlikely, as her priority is always to invest any spare funds in even better facilities for staff and children.

## MOSS LEA PRIVATE NURSERY SCHOOL

14–16 Moss Lea
Sharples Park
Bolton BL1 6PL
**Tel:** (0204) 300195
**Owners:** Bob and Pat Gleaves
**Officer-in-charge:** Pat Gleaves, NNEB
**Type:** Day nursery offering full- and part-time places
**Children:** 6wks–5yrs. 30 places. 38 on register
**Hours:** 8am–6pm
Open 50 weeks a year
**Status:** Private, fee-paying
**Number of years open:** 6
**Meals:** Breakfast, lunch, tea, snacks
**1992 fees:** £65 per week full-time
£15 per day
£9 per half-day
**Waiting list:** Minimal. All children on waiting list are guaranteed a place
**Registered by:** Met Dist of Bolton SS

**Premises** The ground floor of the owner's impressive detached country house, in half an acre of gardens, on the north side of Bolton, hidden down a private road which is difficult to find. The original house has been extended and a conservatory added, and it is light and well decorated inside and out. The pretty baby room is airy and carpeted throughout. It contains high chairs, soft toys and a drawer for each baby's belongings. The toddler room is cheerful, part carpeted and full of displays of children's art and craftwork. The conservatory has been turned into a rough-and-tumble space and adjoins the pre-school room used for more formal learning activities. Furniture and toys are high quality (annual equipment budget £2000). Outside there is a large paved area for ride-on toys and a covered area, where babies sleep in their prams. Barlow Park is adjacent and children often go to the children's playground or on nature walks.

**Owner/Officer-in-charge & staff** Pat Gleaves, NNEB, owner and officer-in-charge, sees her main duties as training, administration and supervision of staff. Although not directly involved in the day-to-day care of children, she is always in and out of the nursery and often works alongside the staff in the baby room. She devotes much of her time to parents. The friendly, young staff have complementary skills and regularly change from one group of children to another so they all know each other well. The nursery operates a keyworker system. There are seven full-time nursery workers and one part-timer. All have been at the nursery for over two years. Five staff members have childcare qualifications, two NNEB, two City & Guilds and one BTEC. There is no early years teacher on the team. No formal training programme. The staff/child ratio is generally 1:4 overall. Sixth-formers, hoping to study childcare, come for work experience, and are always under supervision.

**Children & parents** The children come from a wide variety of backgrounds, with parents who are lawyers, dentists, bankers, skilled manual workers and some recently unemployed. No ethnic diversity. Staff are anxious for parents to see them as 'friends who care for their children', and to know that they are always welcome at the nursery. Parents of new children are encouraged to bring them before their formal start date for a couple of hours at a time on a regular basis, so that they can get to know staff and the other children. The children we saw seemed very happy – laughing, smiling and busy, busy, busy! Some transfer to Walmsley and High Lawn CP Schools, others into the private sector, such as Beech House and Clearlands Prep School. Children with disabilities and special needs are welcome, though there were none on the register when we visited.

**Curriculum & activities** The nursery grew out of a playgroup, held in the neighbouring cricket club pavilion. The children learn through play, based on the PPA philosophy, within a structured framework which varies according to age. 'Play with a purpose' is the aim. Staff take an active part in all play, including rough and tumble and dressing up. There is a strong emphasis on artwork and role playing. On a typical morning, there is a free-play session when children arrive, then at

9.15am they split into small groups for artwork or baking. After a mid-morning snack they watch *Playbus* on television, followed by role play, play dough, art and craft or music before lunch. Most then have a sleep. Older children then enjoy an hour's rough and tumble followed by 'school work' and projects. There is a wide variety of good-quality equipment and toys for all ages. Children are not taught to read and write and there is no qualified teacher on the staff, but they do pre-reading, pre-writing and pre-number work, learn numbers and recognise and write their own names. Some are encouraged to read, if they seem ready. There are weekly swimming lessons and twice weekly visits to the library. The park is used most days. Children's progress and development are monitored monthly by their keyworker and discussed with parents. The nursery is strong on safety and security, with electronically operated security gates to deter unwelcome visitors and a monitoring system when children are sleeping. There are safety surfaces for outdoor play equipment, smoke alarms throughout the house and no stairs.

**Remarks** Quality childcare, based on the PPA philosophy of learning through play, though it may not suit parents looking for more high-powered, formal education. Warm, safe and homely facilities, where adults and children are one big family. Good staffing ratios. Pat Gleaves tells parents, 'We never forget we cannot be you, but we aim to be the next best thing.'

# Bury

The two nursery schools and 29 nursery classes offer part-time sessions to 29 per cent of 3- and 4-year-olds. Priority goes to the socially deprived, children with special needs or those with unemployed parents. The remaining few places are allocated on a first come first served basis. This year's round of spending cuts has knocked £320,000 off the nursery education budget. There has been increased demand for private nursery places and the number of facilities has expanded from 14 to 19 over the last three years. There are two local authority day nurseries. After re-registration in October 1992, the number of childminders fell from 480 to 360, but applications are beginning to come in again. The area also offers 45 playgroups, five crèches and six after-school care schemes.

**Further information**

For details on day nurseries, childminders and playgroups:
Under Eights Unit
Department of Social Services
18 St Mary's Place
Bury BL9 0DZ
Tel: (061) 705 5491

For details on nursery schools, units and classes:
Pupil and Student Services
Education Department
Market Street
Bury BL9 0BN
Tel: (061) 705 5000

# Manchester

Manchester is politically committed and enthusiastic about developing all forms of childcare provision. They believe that children have a right to comprehensive services and parents the right to choose facilities best suited to their needs. However, funding is a serious problem. There are 24 local authority day nurseries, which are used as workplace nurseries by City Council employees, local businesses and individuals, as well as providing care for Social Services referrals. There are also six pioneering Children's Centres offering a range of care and education for all children and families, including baby places and after-school and holiday playschemes. 25 were originally planned, before final cutbacks. The private sector is expanding, with 28 day nurseries, double the number of two years ago, 570 childminders, with more applying for registration all the time, and 98 playgroups. Nanny agencies are also increasing in number. The LEA provides seven purpose-built nursery schools, providing education from 2 years old, and one nursery class in every primary school (a total of 39). There are full- and part-time places available. Primary schools in the city take children from 4 years old. Despite some of the best provision in the country, with 55 per cent of pre-school children in education, demand still exceeds supply in all sectors and there are waiting lists almost everywhere.

## Further information

For details on all forms of childcare and nursery education:
Children's Services
Cumberland House
Crown Square
Manchester M60 3BB
Tel: (061) 234 7203 or (061) 237 7212

## BIRCH GROVE DAY NURSERY

126 Dickenson Road
Rusholme
Manchester M14 5HT
**Tel:** (061) 225 0766

**Owners:** Ruth Holland, Dip Ed
Clare Garvey, SRN, HRCEA
June Clayton, Dip Ed
**Officer-in-charge:** Jean Moore, NNEB, CPQS
**Type:** Day nursery offering full- and part-time places and half-day sessions
**Children:** 6mths–5yrs. 5–8yrs after school hours and during school holidays. 35 places. 45 on register
**Hours:** 8am–6pm
Morning session 8am–1pm
Afternoon session 1pm–6pm
Open 51 weeks a year
**Status:** Private, fee-paying
**Number of years open:** 3
**Meals:** Breakfast, lunch, tea, snacks
**1992 fees:** £411 per month full-time – under 2½
£390 per month full-time – over 2½
**Waiting list:** None. Places available
**Registered by:** Manchester City Council SS
**Under same ownership:** Higher Downs Day Nursery, Altrincham, Trafford (see entry)

## BURNAGE CHILDREN'S CENTRE

Broadhill Road
Burnage
Manchester M19 1AG
**Tel:** (061) 443 1668

**Owner:** Manchester City Council
**Co-ordinator:** Kate Kavanagh, NNEB
**Type:** Day nursery offering full- and part-time places, plus after-school care and mother and toddler sessions 4 times weekly
**Children:** 6mths–5yrs. 50 places. 64 on register
**Hours:** 7am–7pm

Open 51 weeks a year
**Status:** State children's centre
**Number of years open:** 4
**Meals:** Breakfast, lunch, tea, snacks
**1992 fees:** All subsidised on a sliding scale from £10 up to £50 max. Free to parents on income support
**Waiting list:** 50
**Registered by:** Manchester City Council SS

**Premises** Excellent, purpose-built, single-storey, brick nursery, only four years old and superbly equipped inside and out. There are six warm and cheerful playrooms, each with its own toilet facilities and outside play area. In addition, there is a kitchen, a laundry room and a central play area used by all. The centre is set in spacious grounds, in a Manchester suburb, and there is easy parking, although most parents walk to the nursery. All outside play areas are well fenced and there is a large amount of colourful and stimulating outdoor adventure-play equipment, used daily. Children visit the nearby park every two weeks.

**Co-ordinator & staff** Kate Kavanagh, the centre co-ordinator, qualified as an NNEB over 20 years ago in Liverpool and has worked in nursery schools and classes in Manchester since then. She has managed and administered Burnage since it opened and is actively involved with the trade unions in promoting the professionalism of qualified nursery nurses. She reports to a management committee, which meets four times a year. Virtually all staff are NNEBs. They are a happy, friendly, mixed cultural and social group, mainly in their 20s. There are two male nursery workers. One is a qualified residential care worker, the other a sessional worker, who looks after the children who attend after school. All take keen advantage of relevant training offered and paid for by the City Council. Students come in for work experience and the nursery is able to call on LEA peripatetic teachers, when necessary. The centre receives regular visits from a doctor, audiologist, educational psychologist, health visitor and the dental health team.

**Children & parents** A truly multicultural nursery, with children from the whole community. Some of the children, and staff, have English as a second language. The children appear happy, busy and very well supervised. The staff work in close partnership with parents, who are represented on the management committee. The children's centre is a community resource, with a small number of places (five at present) reserved by local companies. It operates a keyworker system within family groupings; the nursery believes that children and their parents need an individual member of staff to relate to. Most children go on to St Bernard's RC or Green End CP School, both state primaries. The nursery will take children with special needs and can call on any additional services supplied by the City Council.

**Curriculum & activities** Children spend most of the time in their family group, but twice a week they have open play sessions. Every conceivable activity is on offer to meet all individual needs. The annual equipment budget is enormous. There is almost limitless daily opportunity for self-expression and creativity. Children experience a structured day, with caring and learning operating hand-in-hand. The aim is for children to leave for school confident and assertive, with high self-esteem. Children are not taught to read and write, but they participate in pre-reading and pre-writing activities. A research project has indicated that children who attend Manchester City Council's Children's Centres are academically well advanced. Dance, movement and music sessions take place two or three times a week and there are weekly swimming and library visits. Children are regularly taken to museums, adventure playgrounds, restaurants and mosques and to Chinatown at Chinese New Year. Other religious festivals are celebrated and there is a dedicated multicultural approach with occasional visits from Indian dancers and musicians, steel bands, 'Circus Sensible' and puppeteers. Dishes from around the world are freshly cooked on the premises by the cook-in-charge and an assistant. All special diets are catered for. Meals are a time for socialising and conversation, and staff eat with the children.

**Remarks** Splendidly equipped nursery which offers subsidised, high-quality childcare for anyone lucky enough to secure a place. It provides a loving and stimulating, but very safe environment for young children and has the advantage of being able to draw on the wide range of expertise of the City Council health and education departments. A superb community facility and a wonderful start for any child.

# Oldham

The recession has affected Oldham badly. Of the 940 registered childminders listed in 1991, only 490 have re-registered and there are vacancies in some areas. Numbers are expected to rise again, to about 600 this year, as a backlog of applications is processed. Average charges range from £45 to £50 per week. Fees in the 11 private day nurseries are between £40 and £65 per week. There are also eleven Social Services nurseries with places only available to high-priority children. There has always been a demand for part-time places, because of the seasonal nature of some of the local industries. Demand has increased during the recession, as women find it easier to obtain part-time jobs than their unemployed partners. Part-time places are available in the 52 nursery classes, providing education for 37 per cent of children over 3 years old. Social Services told us, 'In 1991 there were 90 enquiries for our booklet on how to set up a private nursery. In 1992 there were none.'

**Further information**

For day nurseries, private nursery schools, childminders and playgroups:
Registration and Inspection Unit
Department of Social Services
Wellington Buildings
Hobson Street
Oldham OL1 1DA
Tel: (061) 620 5034

For local authority nursery schools, units and classes:
Education Department
Old Town Hall
Middleton Road
Chadderton
Oldham OL9 6PP
Tel: (061) 678 4260

# Rochdale

The private sector is still expanding and the number of private day nurseries has increased from 15 to 21 since 1991. Nearly 150 childminders have fallen by the wayside since the 1989 Children Act came into force, and 11 playgroups have closed. There is huge demand for baby places, but few nurseries are registered to take under-2s. The area's eight, mainly part-time, nursery schools and 20 nursery classes in primary schools come under budgetary threat every April, and so far ten places have been lost. The inner, urban areas are reasonably well supplied, the outer suburbs not so. Just under 50 per cent of Rochdale's under-5s will receive some form of nursery education before they enter primary school. The education authority admits, 'If you don't fit into a special needs category and you live in certain areas of Rochdale, the only option is private nursery education.'

**Further information**

For a list of nurseries, childminders, playgroups, nursery schools and classes:
Children's Officer
Education Department
Municipal Offices
Smith Street
Rochdale OL16 1XG
Tel: (0706) 47474

## APPOLLO DAY NURSERIES LTD

The Rookeries
Market Street
Whitworth
Rochdale OL12 9BE
**Tel:** (0706) 359768

**Directors:** Terry and Kath Duffy
**Senior Officer-in-charge:** Judith Dudgeon, NNEB
**Type:** Day nursery offering full- and part-time places and half-day sessions
**Children:** 6mths–5yrs. 37 places. 60 on register
**Hours:** 7.30am–6pm
Morning session 7.30am–1pm
Afternoon session 1pm–6pm
Open 51 weeks a year
**Status:** Private, fee-paying
**Number of years open:** 2½
**Meals:** Breakfast, lunch, tea, snacks
**1992 fees:** £62 per week full-time – under 2s
£60 per week full-time – over 2s
£7.75 per morning session – under 2s
£7.50 per afternoon session – under 2s
£7.25 per morning session – over 2s
£6.75 per afternoon session – over 2s
**Waiting list:** None
**Registered by:** Met Dist of Rochdale SS
**Under same ownership:** For information on other nurseries please contact Judith Dudgeon on (0706) 359768

# Salford

One of the top providers of nursery education in the country. Only seven of the 80 primary schools are without a nursery class. Waiting lists in most areas are manageable. Children with special needs attend one of the three Social Services day nurseries, eight family centres, seven children's centres or 37 local authority sponsored childminders. Salford's children's centres, run as a partnership between Social Services and Education, are among the first of their kind to be established in the country. The private sector provides 2000 places, including 300 registered childminders. Current financial restraints (nearly £800,000 cut from the Social Services budget this year) prevent the local authority from increasing its genuine commitment to childcare in the community.

### Further information

For general lists of day nurseries, childminders and playgroups:

Inspection and Registration Unit
Department of Social Services
Turnpike House
631 Eccles New Road
Salford M5 2AZ
Tel: (061) 737 0551

For specific enquiries:
Under Eights Unit
Department of Social Services
Avon House
Avon Close
Little Hulton M26 6LA
Tel: (061) 799 1829

For details on nursery schools, units and classes:
Admissions Unit
Education Department
Chapel Street
Salford M3 5LT
Tel: (061) 832 9751

# Stockport

The number of nursery schools and classes has increased steadily over the last few years, catering for approximately 50 per cent of the area's pre-school children. They receive three terms of part-time nursery education before starting school at 4½ years old. Demand far exceeds supply, and waiting lists are long. However, new nursery classes are scheduled to open, including three this autumn. Priority is given to children in need, irrespective of their catchment area. The private sector is also growing, with 19 private day nurseries and applications continuing to come in. Numbers of registered childminders (850) are also on the increase. Social Services fund one day nursery, six family centres and a day-fostering scheme for children with special needs. Over 100 playgroups provide part-time play activities.

### Further information

For details on day nurseries, private nursery schools, childminders and playgroups:
Department of Social Services
Ponsonby House
Edward Street
Stockport SK1 3UR
Tel: (061) 474 4631

For details on nursery schools, units and classes:
Education Division
Town Hall
Stockport SK1 3XE
Tel: (061) 474 3926

## 0-2-5 NURSERY

22-24 Thornfield Road
Heaton Mersey
Stockport SK4 3JT
**Tel:** (061) 442 1112

**Owners:** Paul, John and Maureen Stark
**Officer-in-charge:** Katherine Waudby, B Ed
**Type:** Day nursery offering full- and part-time places and sessions
**Children:** 3mths–5yrs. 53 places. 74 on register
**Hours:** 7.45am–6.30pm
Morning session 7.45am–1pm (inc lunch)
Afternoon session 1.30pm–6.30pm
Open 52 weeks a year
**Status:** Private, fee-paying
**Number of years open:** 2
**Meals:** Breakfast, lunch, tea, snacks
**1992 fees:** £92 per week full-time
£20 per day
£11.50 per session
**Waiting list:** Early registration advisable
**Registered by:** Met Dist of Stockport SS

## ORCHARDS DAY NURSERY & NURSERY SCHOOL

20 Tatton Road South
Heaton Moor
Stockport SK4 4PF
**Tel:** (061) 432 1994

**Owners/Principals:** Sylvia Graham, Cert Ed
Anna Shanley, SRN
**Type:** Day nursery and nursery school offering full-time and some part-time places
**Children:** Day nursery 6mths–2½yrs
Nursery school 2½yrs–5yrs
50 places. 52 on register
**Hours:** 8am–6pm
Open 51 weeks a year
**Status:** Private, fee-paying
**Number of years open:** 2
**Meals** Breakfast if required, lunch, tea
**1992 fees:** £335 per month full-time – under 2
£315 per month full-time – over 2
£80 per week full-time – under 2
£75 per week full-time – over 2
£50 refundable deposit, sibling discounts
**Waiting list:** For babies only
**Registered by:** Met Dist of Stockport SS

**Premises** Situated about a mile north of Stockport town centre, close to the main road and rail routes into Manchester. Two large Victorian semis, converted into one substantial property in which the nursery occupies the whole of the ground floor. The kitchen, staff room, staff toilets, laundry and nursery office are in the basement. The rooms above ground level have been converted to six flats, which are rented out. Separate facilities are provided for babies, toddlers and pre-school children. Decorations are bright, clean and new, and children's art and craft work is displayed in every room. The baby activity room leads out on to a newly constructed covered verandah. Babies have their own nappy-changing room, while older children use the toilet block, where each keeps a personal towel, sponge and toothbrush. Nursery school children, from age 2½, have a carpeted quiet room for pre-school learning, full of books and a BBC master computer with relevant software; a rumpus room with large toys for more physical play; and a dining room which doubles as a messy-play area and houses the home corner. There is a large safe garden, including grassed and safety-surfaced play areas, and furnished with plenty of ride-on toys, sand and water play and a large, expensive climbing frame. A pet rabbit lives on the verandah. Heaton Moor Park, a quarter of a mile away, is visited for summer picnics.

**Owners/Principals & staff** The babies and small toddlers are in the care of Anna Shanley, a State Registered Nurse with extensive experience as a midwife and health visitor. She is the mother of four children and fully aware of the needs of young children and working parents. Sylvia Graham, Cert Ed, is responsible for the older toddlers and pre-school nursery class. A well-qualified teacher with many years' experience teaching children of nursery and primary school age. Before starting Orchards, she was deputy head of a Manchester school. Anna Shanley and Sylvia Graham, long-time close friends, have a well-chosen, qualified staff team of eight full-time NNEBs and a Montessori-trained teacher, all with first-aid qualifications. One nursery nurse has an ESL (Teaching English as a Second Language) qualification and special needs certificate. There have been no male applicants for jobs so far, but both principals have sons who help in the nursery from time to time.

Staff/child ratios are 1:3 for under-2s, 1:4 for over-2s and 1:5 for pre-school children. No peripatetic teachers visit. NNEB students in their final year at Stockport College come in on six weeks' placement. Staff meetings are held every two weeks, with staff encouraged to have open and frank discussions about policies, procedures and problems. There is no training budget at present, but staff take advantage of some Social Services courses – the most recent was on child abuse. The staff wear uniforms of red sweatshirts.

**Children & parents** Little social or ethnic mix. The fee level means that the nursery is used by middle wage earners – teachers, bank staff, doctors, middle and upper management – and the mothers mostly work. The phasing-in policy for new children depends on age and individual requirements. There are no children with special needs at the moment, but a ramp has been built for wheelchair use. A proportion of the children go on to private education – Oriel Bank School, Stockport Grammar and St Ambrose – and the others to local state schools, such as St Winifred's, Norris Bank and Didsbury Road. A happy, chatty, well-supervised group. There is an open-door policy and parents are invited to open days, concerts and sports days. Comments on the running of the nursery are welcomed and parents are encouraged to help and become involved. Good relationship between staff and parents, with one of the principals always available at the beginning or end of the day.

**Curriculum & activities** No one particular philosophy, but the nursery aims to develop self-esteem, confidence and independence. 'We want to prepare children for school by using pre-reading, pre-writing and numeracy schemes, but we also want them to be safe, happy and secure,' Mrs Graham told us. Although there are separate facilities for each age group, all inter-connecting doors are open for at least the first hour of every session, to encourage a family atmosphere. The daily programme is varied, with plenty of free choice and free play. Messy play and painting are available at all times. Pre-school children are taken into the quiet room in small groups to practise letter, sound, number and language skills. They each spend time on the computer. Staff guide and support, rather than direct, but make sure children, particularly the few not at the nursery all week, cover a range of activities. A keyworker system operates. The principals are currently working on full written programmes and policies (this is still a new nursery), but full records are kept on each child. Equipment is high quality (£2000 annual budget), stimulating and age appropriate. There is a good supply of quality books, toys, educational games and musical instruments. The curriculum has no religious content, but the nursery is hot on equal opportunities and multi-culturalism. Children are taught about various cultures and celebrate a number of different festivals. There is outdoor play, music every day, and monthly outings – to farms, the theatre, the airport or shopping. Dance and movement, library visits, PE and games are undertaken twice a week.

**Remarks**  Dedicated, qualified staff with two strong experienced managers at the helm. Excellent combination of care, freedom and pre-school education. Relatively new nursery still building a reputation.

# Tameside

Tameside Education Authority tries to ensure that as many 4-year-olds as possible are offered a one-year part-time place (total places, 2600) in one of the area's four nursery schools or 41 nursery classes. Any places left over may be allocated to 3-year-olds, resulting in 40 per cent of pre-school children receiving nursery education. On the daycare front, the number of local authority child and family centres has increased from ten to 12 and private day nurseries have doubled in number, to a total of eight. The number of childminders and playgroups have remained stable. In some areas childminders have had no work for 12 months, in others, mothers are clamouring for them, especially to look after babies as there is little alternative care. 'There has been an increase in demand for nursery places for babies, but because the baby/staff ratios are high, nurseries prefer to take toddlers,' says a Social Services spokeswoman.

### Further information

For lists of day nurseries, private nursery schools, childminders and playgroups visit the Town Hall, local libraries or contact:
Under Eights Unit
Denton Town Hall
Market Street
Denton M34 2AP
Tel: (061) 336 9621

For details on nursery schools, units and classes:
Admissions Section
Education Department
Council Offices
Wellington Road
Ashton-under-Lyme
Tameside OL6 6DL
Tel: (061) 342 3214

# Trafford

The number of private day nurseries has increased from 23 to 33 in the last two years, but numbers have remained static for other types of provision. There are six local authority day nurseries, but cuts are expected this year. There are 600 registered childminders and 60 playgroups. Trafford has no nursery schools, but is actively trying to increase the number of nursery classes. Currently, 32 per cent of 3- and 4-year-olds receive some part-time nursery education. Four new nursery classes are due to open this autumn, and there are plans for four or five new, purpose-built classes every year until there is one in every primary school.

**Further information**

For details on day nurseries, childminders and playgroups:
Quality and Inspection Unit
Department of Social Services
Stratham House
Talbot Road
Stretford M32 0FP
Tel: (061) 872 2101 × 4732

For details on nursery units and classes:
Education Department
Town Hall
PO Box 19
Tatton Road
Sale M33 1YR
Tel: (061) 872 2101

## HIGHER DOWNS DAY NURSERY

Kings Pyon
Cavendish Road
Bowden
Altrincham NA14 2NX
**Tel:** (061) 928 7581

**Owners/Officers-in-charge:** Ruth Holland, Dip Ed
Clare Garvey, SRN, SCM, HV Cert
June Clayton, Dip Ed
**Type:** Day nursery and nursery school offering full and part-time places and half-day sessions, plus after-school care and holiday playschemes
**Children:** 6mths–5yrs. 5–11yrs after school hours and during school holidays. 60 places. 58 on register
**Hours:** 8am–6pm
Morning session 8am–1pm
Afternoon session 1pm–6pm
Open 51 weeks a year
**Status:** Private, fee-paying
**Number of years open:** 6
**Meals:** Breakfast, lunch, tea, snacks
**1992 fees:** £413 per month full-time – under 2½
£384 per month full-time – over 2½
£10 per session – under 2½
£9 per session – over 2½
Childcare vouchers accepted
**Waiting list:** Early registration advisable for under-2s. Places available for older children
**Registered by:** Met Dist of Trafford SS
**Under same ownership:** Birch Grove Day Nursery, Rusholme, Manchester (see listing)

**Premises** Large Edwardian detached house in a third of an acre of grounds, situated in a quiet side street, with easy parking, in the most prosperous of Manchester's suburbs. A large nursery with ten rooms on two floors. The babies' and toddlers' rooms, kitchen and office facilities are on the ground floor. Upstairs there is a pre-school room, messy-play room and classroom. Rooms are light and well decorated, with lively pictures and displays and plenty of suitable furniture and equipment. The large, walled garden has swings, a climbing frame and a paved area for all-weather outdoor play. In summer, older children visit the nearby park twice a week.

**Owners/Officers-in-charge** The partners who own this nursery and one other in Manchester are all working mothers with years of knowledge and understanding of pre-school children between them. June Clayton, Dip Ed, and Ruth Holland, Dip Ed, are experienced, qualified teachers and Clare Garvey, SRN, SCM, HV Cert, is a trained midwife and health visitor. They divide the responsibilities: June looks after finance, Ruth bookings and purchasing, and Clare staff and training. They employ a deputy manager and a senior nursery nurse to take charge of day-to-day care of the children. There are 15 full-time staff and three part-time. Eight staff are NNEB qualified, five are taking BTEC training. A qualified dance teacher and a fine arts graduate help with the after-school group. The team also includes a fully trained reception class teacher. The nursery takes YTS, City & Guilds, NNEB and BTEC students on work experience. There is a training policy and generous training budget. The partners step in to cover for sickness and holidays. Two staff members were made redundant last year due to falling numbers, because of the recession. An excellent staff handbook clearly laying out all the nursery's policies and procedures is a document other nurseries could benefit by copying.

**Children & parents** The children come from middle- to upper-class families. Many are doctors, solicitors, teachers or run their own businesses. Some mothers send their children part-time so that they can have a break and their children can socialise. There are three parents' evenings a year and parents help with fund-raising events and attend sports days and pantomime trips. Parents can be as involved in the nursery as they like. Children are grouped according to age. Brothers and sisters in different groups can visit each other during the day. Children transfer to local state primaries and schools in the private sector such as Altrincham, Bowdon and Hale prep schools. Children with special needs are accepted. No child is ever turned away if places are available.

**Curriculum & activities** The main priority is happy children. Learning is through carefully monitored play, to ensure that each child has experiences that will help every aspect of his/her development. All age groups follow a planned day, starting and ending with an hour and a half of free-play activities and interspersed with circle songs and rhymes, music, outdoor play, television and a structured learning period each session. Babies and young children sleep during the day according to their needs and home routine. The toys and equipment are plentiful (annual budget for the two nurseries £5000), stimulating and in good condition. Cuddles are considered to be as important as anything else. There are daily sessions of dance, art and craft and a member of staff will often take a child out for a lunchtime walk. Two annual outings – a summer visit and a Christmas pantomime. Children are not taught to read and write, but the pre-school group learn pre-reading, pre-writing and pre-number skills. Individual children are encouraged to start reading if they are ready. Fine motor and large motor skills, language and social ability are monitored regularly. Toys are colour-coded and used by each room on a four-day rota. Care is taken to offer children appropriate equipment for their stage of development. For example, when a baby can bang on the table spontaneously, he/she may be given drums, a xylophone and hammer toys to encourage more precise co-ordination of hands and eyes. Themes and accompanying wall displays are changed every two months. Staff plan the week's activities in advance, detailing in writing the aims of the week, the planned and free-play activities and what each is to achieve.

**Remarks** Happy, safe and homely, despite its size. A highly organised, meticulously planned nursery with a strong management team. This nursery provides a flexible, quality service for busy working parents. At the top of the price range for the area.

# Wigan

Over the last two years, the number of registered childminders (600) and playgroups (89) has not changed, and they supply the main childcare provision in the district. Children on the 'alert' register may secure a highly sought-after place in five Social Services day nurseries. There are 15 registered private day nurseries for parents who can afford fees. Waiting lists are long for pre-school education in many of the 29 nursery classes attached to primary schools. 25 per cent of 3- and 4-year-olds are catered for. There are no plans to increase provision in the area, or to cut the number of existing places, despite this year's round of spending cuts.

## Further information

For a Children's Directory listing day nurseries, childminders and playgroups, look in GPs' surgeries, health centres and libraries, or contact:

Under Eights Office
Department of Social Services
Civic Centre
Millgate
Wigan WN1 1YD
Tel: (0942) 44991

For details on nursery schools, units and classes:

Education Department
Gateway House
Standishgate
Wigan WN1 1AE
Tel: (0942) 44991

## GREENFIELDS DAY NURSERIES

School Street
Gin Pit Village
Astley
Tyldesley
Manchester M29 7DL
**Tel:** (0942) 875985

**Owners:** Heather Dakin, Cert Ed
Ronald Dakin
**Officer-in-charge:** Charlotte Lewis, NNEB
**Type:** Day nursery offering full- and part-time places, plus after-school care
**Children:** 3mths–5yrs. 5–10yrs after-school care. 65 places. 75 on register
**Hours:** 8am–6pm
Open 51 weeks a year
**Status:** Private, fee-paying
**Number of years open:** 8
**Meals:** Breakfast, lunch, tea
**1992 fees:** £58 per week full-time
£30.50 per week for 5 morning sessions
£30.50 per week for 5 afternoon sessions
**Waiting list:** Long for babies – book a year ahead. Minimal for over-2s.
**Registered by:** Met Dist of Wigan SS
**Under same ownership:** Greenfields Day Nursery, Leigh, Wigan

**Premises** A former village school, built at the turn of the century, in a small pit village, surrounded by fields. It is well maintained inside and out, with a large tarmac playground and Astroturf all-weather area. The nursery occupies three rooms on two floors, with the main playroom colourfully divided into two separate age groups. Each half is part carpeted and has plain walls with bright child-centred decorations. The baby room has a separate nappy-changing area and is well furnished. Pre-school children and those who come for after-school care use the upstairs room, a comfortable, cheerful place filled with stimulating things to explore. There is also a library/quiet room which doubles as a staff room.

**Owners, Officer-in-charge & staff**
Heather Dakin, Cert Ed, and her husband jointly own and run two nurseries. Heather makes sure that she spends some time every day at each of them. A trained teacher, with special needs experience, she takes all major

decisions in conjunction with senior staff, who are responsible for the day-to-day organisation. All nursery workers are qualified NNEBs and are encouraged to participate in Social Services training and development sessions, as well as in service training. Staff ages range from 18 to 40. They are a friendly, polite group, concerned to create a homely atmosphere. Heather Dakin's husband, Ronald, takes the children to weekly swimming sessions. The nursery cook is also male. Nursery policy is to promote from within in order to offer nursery nurses some career structure. There is also a comprehensive staff appraisal system, to help identify training and development needs and encourage staff to work together in a happy and professional environment.

**Children & parents** The majority of children have working parents, though a few come simply for the advantages of pre-school care and education. Parents are interested in the benefits of nursery education and supportive of the nursery. There is usually a good cultural mix. Noticeboards in the entrance hall keep parents informed of nursery events, and staff set aside time to talk to them at the beginning and end of the day. Children appear to be talkative and well supervised, with plenty to interest them. Each has a keyworker. Virtually all go on to local state primary schools. There are no children with special needs at present. Parents attend curriculum evenings and parents' evenings by appointment to discuss their child's progress and are active in the PTA.

**Curriculum & activities** The nursery aims to give children broad, balanced experiences which will prepare them for school, both socially and intellectually. There is a structured day, with directed activities interspersed with free-play sessions and plenty of scope for free expression. Programmes and timetables for each group are carefully planned in advance and written down. Babies have frequent cuddles and look content and secure. They are exposed to a wide variety of experiences during the week. Pre-school children are taught basic numeracy and literacy skills and some go on to start reading. There is a computer with several children's software programmes for children. Weekly sessions of swimming, French (a specialist teacher comes in), dance and movement and visits to the library. Music sessions take place three times a week and outings every term. Visitors come to talk to the children about their specific skills or knowledge. Every year there is an annual sports day. Each member of staff is responsible for developing a particular area of the curriculum: the environment, play, music (vocal and instrumental), movement and dance, art, number development, language and cookery. Children's progress is monitored on an individual basis and written record sheets are kept. Parents can view and discuss records by appointment. An after-school care programme is available for children from 5 to 10 years old.

**Remarks** Carefully thought out, well-planned nursery, and reasonably priced. Cheerful, welcoming and stimulating. Good staff training programme and appraisal system. As chairwoman of Wigan's private day nursery association, Heather Dakin says she would like to see a closer relationship between the public and private sectors. Parents highly recommend this nursery.

# MERSEYSIDE

## Knowsley

There are nursery class places, on a part-time basis, for 39 per cent of 3- to 4-year-olds. Waiting lists are often long, and arrangements need to be made well in advance. Nearly all primary schools now have nursery units attached, but demand far outstrips supply. Social Services maintain eight full-time day nurseries for children with special needs, but £500,000 cut from this year's budget has affected daycare. There are 18 private day nurseries, some catering for babies, and 107 registered childminders. A small number of part-time playgroups are also available. Questionnaires were sent out to nurseries and nursery schools in this district, but none were returned.

**Further information**

For details on day nurseries and playgroups:

Registration and Inspection Unit
Department of Social Services
Municipal Buildings
Archway Road
Huyton L36 9YY
Tel: (051) 443 3442

For details on nursery schools, units and classes:

Education Department
Huyton Hey Road
Huyton L36 5YH
Tel: (051) 443 3262

For a list of childminders:

Save the Children Fund
Knowsley Training and Resource Centre
St Mark's Church Hall
Brookhey Drive
Kirby L33 9TE
Tel: (051) 548 0289

## Liverpool

Six nursery schools and 93 nursery classes, providing places for 47 per cent of 3- and 4-year-olds, about a third of which are full-time. There are also a number of nursery schools for children with special needs. Liverpool offers better daycare services than many local authorities, with 17 Social Services day nurseries. Despite 47 private day nurseries, 300 childminders and 77 playgroups, there are still not enough affordable places in the city to meet demand.

**Further information**

For details on day nurseries, childminders and playgroups:

Department of Social Services
26 Hatton Garden
Liverpool L3 2AW
Tel: (051) 225 3779

For details on nursery schools, units and classes:

Education Department
14 Sir Thomas Street
Liverpool L1 6BJ
Tel: (051) 227 3911

# KELTON DAY NURSERY

Park Avenue
Mossley Hill
Liverpool L18 8BT
**Tel:** (051) 724 5802

**Owner:** Kelton Nursery Parents Association
**Officer-in-charge:** Linda Jones, NNEB, CPQS
**Deputy:** Jean Mayne, NNEB
**Type:** Day nursery offering full-time places
**Children:** 6wks–5yrs. 90 places. 102 on register
**Hours:** 8am–6pm
Open 51 weeks a year
**Status:** Fee-paying registered charity
**Number of years open:** 9
**Meals:** Breakfast, lunch, tea
**1992 fees:** £305 per month full-time
£50 registration fee
**Waiting list:** Moderate, but longer for babies
**Registered by:** Liverpool City Council SS

**Premises** An attractive bright red sign welcomes the visitor to Kelton Day Nursery. It is a very large, Victorian, semi-detached house, with a coach house and outbuildings, set in an up-market residential area. Nursing homes and university halls of residence are nearby. Outings and picnics to the duck ponds at the halls of residence are very popular with children and staff. Parking in the drive is only for staff, or parents who have two or more children or children with disabilities. Otherwise, parking is on the road. Some parents walk, others who work in the city use the train. The top floor of the house is used by an after-school group, but the rest of this four-storey house is used by the nursery. It comprises nine rooms, milk kitchens, main kitchen, cloakrooms, laundry, and offices. The building is airy and colourful with pictures on the walls and windows and bright attractive curtains. A special feature is the soft-play room with ball pool, tunnels, tents and soft play shapes and they have just invested in a parachute. Outdoors, the very large garden can accommodate all the children at once and contains a good selection of outdoor equipment, all on safety surfaces.

**Officer-in-charge & staff** Linda Jones, NNEB, CPQS, has been qualified for 19 years. She had experience in special needs education in nursery schools and residential childcare, and ten years in Social Services, before joining Kelton two years ago. Her experienced deputy, Jean Mayne, NNEB, is doing DPQS training. They complement each other well and pride themselves on their approachability to parents and members of staff. Nursery nurses are given the flexibility to organise their own rooms and routines. There are regular staff meetings and social gatherings outside work. Linda reports to a committee of 12 parents, who are elected annually. The 21 full-time staff are all qualified NNEB or City & Guilds in childcare. NNEB and BTEC students are also trained here. Ancillary staff include a bursar/bookkeeper, a cook, two kitchen assistants, a driver/handyman and laundress/cleaner.

**Children & parents** The children are predominantly English; ten per cent are Jewish and there is a small Asian and Chinese contingent. Most are from professional families in the local area, or as far afield as Cheshire and Lancashire. No formal parents' evenings are held, but there is good communication between parents and staff, with an open-door policy and regular newsletters. Several short visits are encouraged prior to a baby or child starting at Kelton. They also have home-nursery books, and parents and staff contribute to these. The children move to a wide variety of primary schools, both state and private. Kelton also runs an after-school club for children who have attended the day nursery. Their own minibuses provide a daily pick-up service from about 20 local private and state schools.

**Curriculum & activities** The Kelton philosophy is 'caring and sharing'. The nursery aims to offer a good grounding in all the pre-school skills to prepare children for infant school. Linda and Jean keep abreast of new developments in nursery education by attending courses and visiting other nurseries. There is an annual training bursary of £7500. They belong to the new Private Day Nurseries' Owners Association, which gives support with implementing the new Children Act and provides training opportunities. Religious content includes grace before meals, and the celebration of major festivals from all faiths. Frequent outings by mini-bus are arranged. All rooms have home corners, sand and water, large construction toys and games, sit and ride toys and table-top toys. Art and craft, stories, singing and dance take place regularly. There is a central resource area for the big, expensive equipment and extra dressing-up clothes. The pre-school children have access to a BBC computer. Children are divided into peer groupings, and every member of staff is keyworker to a small group. Each age group has detailed written programmes and timetables. Keyworkers monitor their children's progress and records are available to parents. By the time they move on, children can name primary and usually secondary colours, identify basic shapes, count and recognise numerals to ten and follow a sequence of pictures in a book and they are familiar with concepts of early maths. Self-awareness, social skills and good communication and language are also a central part of the day. There is no formal teaching of the 3Rs. The wonderful soft-play room is used each day. Outdoor play in the large garden takes place every day and outings as often as possible.

**Remarks** A lovely, caring environment, run by dedicated professionals, all of whom regret that the nursery is only available to those who can afford to pay fees. High-quality daycare rather than formal education. As a registered charity, any profits are ploughed back into the nursery. The popular after-school scheme means the nursery can satisfy the needs of working parents with children from 6 weeks to 10 years old. A large number of children, with over 100 on the register. The numbers may be reduced in the light of Children Act guidelines.

# MCVS NURSERY

Mount Vernon Green
Hall Lane
Liverpool L7 8TF
**Tel:** (051) 708 8432

**Owner:** Merseyside Council for Voluntary Services (MCVS)
**Manager:** Linda Hardy, NNEB, DPQS
**Type:** Workplace nursery offering full- and part-time places
**Children:** 6wks–5yrs. 50 places. 50 on register
**Hours:** 8am–6pm
Open 50 weeks a year
**Status:** Fee-paying registered charity
**Number of years open:** 5
**Meals:** Breakfast, lunch, tea, snacks
**1992 fees:** £60 per week
£60 non-refundable deposit
**Waiting list:** Minimal – for babies
**Registered by:** Liverpool City Council SS

**Premises** An old secondary school has been converted for the use of MCVS, and the lower ground floor at the rear of the building has been adapted to form a sunny, self-contained nursery. Formerly solely a workplace nursery for students on MCVS training schemes, it is now available to anyone living and/or working in the area. Very close to Liverpool city centre, and the universities, the area is a mix of modern office blocks and Victorian terraced houses. Entry is via a car park, so parking is no problem. The safety of the children is of prime concern, as there are several doors from the building into the nursery. A bell rings to alert staff as you enter. The nursery consists of three rooms: a baby room, a toddler room and a pre-school room. The facilities have recently been updated to include a milk kitchen and a spotless cloakroom with small loos and washbasins for the toddler and pre-school room. Direct access outside to the garden area, but no permanent fixed climbing frames, slides or swings, although there is a vast array of outdoor toys. The facilities are on one floor, and include ramps and wide-opening doors into all rooms for wheelchair access.

**Manager & staff** The manager, Linda Hardy, gained her NNEB qualifications six years ago as a mature student, after settling her three children into school. Her fourth child is at present in the baby room. She passed her DPQS last year. Her wide experience covers playgroups, parent and toddler groups and toy libraries. Both she and her deputy obviously understand the worries and problems of working parents. She leads a team of eight qualified NNEB nursery nurses (including one man), and ancillary staff. Students on placement from NNEB or other courses and sixth-form work-experience students are all somehow assimilated into the team. The staff go about their work in a quiet, caring but firm manner. A rather unfortunate, white nurse-style uniform gives them an institutional, medical feel. There is a small training budget, and staff are encouraged to attend courses and develop fresh ideas.

**Children & parents** The children come from very varied backgrounds. Some live locally, while others travel long distances. All work or study in the area, and many are single parents. Parents are always invited to anything special or interesting that the children do, such as puppet plays, harvest festival and Christmas entertainment. There is an open-door policy at the nursery and parents can ring or visit as often as they wish. Children with disabilities are particularly welcomed and catered for. Virtually all the children move on to state primary schools.

**Curriculum & activities** Learning is through play, with the emphasis very much on play. The routine is flexible in the baby room, with feeding and sleeping on demand and a variety of toys. In the toddler and pre-school room, a limited amount of more formal work involves pencil control, colours and number recognition. The curriculum appears to be very vague, and staff see themselves as qualified carers not teachers. There are no written programmes or schemes. Painting, craft, songs, music and stories take place daily, and occasionally children are allowed to watch television. We felt that there could have been more toys and equipment freely available for children to choose from and that not enough was at child height or easily accessible. The nursery's annual equipment budget is £600.

**Remarks** A very popular nursery. Qualified and uniformed nursery nurses, who provide high-quality care, but opportunities for more formal learning are limited. Strong relationships between staff, children and parents. The nursery is currently anticipating a serious change of character. Fifty per cent of children have single parents on employment training schemes – their childcare at MCVS subsidised by the government. The government is now phasing-out this childcare subsidy. These children will be forced to leave, to be replaced by private full-fee-paying customers.

# MONKTON NURSERY SCHOOL

16 Elmsley Road
Mossley Hill
Liverpool L18 8BB
**Tel:** (051) 724 4500

**Owner/Principal:** Susan Poole, B Ed, MA
**Type:** Day nursery school offering full- and part-time places and half-day sessions
**Children:** 1–5yrs. 48 places. 74 on register
**Hours:** 8.15am–5pm
Morning session 8.15am–1pm
Afternoon session 1.15pm–5pm
Open 46 weeks a year
**Status:** Private, fee-paying
**Number of years open:** 13
**Meals:** Snacks, lunch, tea
**1992 fees:** £72 per week full-time
£41 per week for 5 morning sessions
£38 per week for 5 afternoon sessions
£50 registration fee
10% sibling discount
**Waiting list:** 20+, mainly for toddlers. Some afternoon places available for older age groups
**Registered by:** Liverpool City Council SS

**Premises** The ground floor of the owner's family home, a beautiful, well-maintained Victorian detached house. It is surrounded by well-kept gardens which are very child-centred, with slides, climbing frames, swings, play house and other outdoor toys. This is a smart area with a mix of large houses and smaller semis. The nursery is a few minutes' walk from Mossley Hill Mersey Rail Station into Liverpool Lime Street, but most parents use their cars, parking outside on the road. Inside there are two main classrooms: the playroom for younger children, and the schoolroom for the older ones. In addition there is a rumpus room with sand, water, trampoline and climbing frames, also used for dance and gymnastics, and a small quiet room for stories, games and rests. An industrial kitchen, child-sized loos and washbasins, and store cupboard make up the rest of the nursery. Both classrooms are partially carpeted, welcoming and colourful, with the children's own work decorating the walls.

**Owner/Principal & staff** Susan Poole, B Ed, MA, is at present working towards her Ph D. She is enthusiastic, devoted to the children in her school and much appreciated by her parents. There is a warmth and friendliness between staff and children, with masses of cuddles and individual attention. The deputy, Elaine Williams, NNEB, is in charge of the playroom for 1-year-olds until they are potty-trained at 2-plus. Susan's husband is supportive and joins in with all the activities when his work schedule permits. There are nine full-time nursery nurses, three NNEBs and one Cert Ed. Six staff are unqualified, but Susan Poole says, 'I have trained them myself and they have all worked for me for more than four years. Two of them also have children of their own.' Susan would welcome a male staff member as she thinks it would benefit the children. A specialist teacher comes in once a week for Science and Technology and a professional guitarist to take singing and music. The cook works from 9am to 1pm. Staff turnover has never been a problem, and many return after maternity leave. A loyal and flexible team.

**Children & parents** The children come from professional, middle-class families in which both work full or part-time. There are some one-parent families, whom the nursery itself subsidises by offering discounts on the fees. Good communication with parents is considered crucial. The nursery has an open-door policy – parents may ring or visit whenever they wish and visitors are always welcome. It aims to involve parents as much as possible, sending out invitations to open days, plays and concerts at Christmas and in the summer, regular parents' evenings. Parents are also asked to contribute to a Suggestion Box. Every newsletter exhorts them to comment and offer ideas for improvements at the nursery. Susan Poole has a close personal relationship with many of the parents. New parents and children are encouraged to visit before they start. The keyworker system is employed until a child settles. A women's group meets at weekends. Mothers can share their experiences and problems and the nursery provides childcare facilities.

**Curriculum & activities** Children are divided by age into two groups: the playroom for the youngest and the school room for the oldest group. The playroom programme is geared towards structured play. It has a collection of early educational equipment – jigsaws, books, construction and counting games, as well as large play equipment, farms, fire stations, garages and a Wendy house. A carefully written timetable charts which toys and activities should be used each day and at what times. In the schoolroom, play continues, but children also begin more formal learning through schemes of work developed by Susan Poole over the years. There are very comprehensive written programmes of structured work for number, reading, writing and language skills. Children work through them individually at their own pace, supervised by a carer. Once their concentration span is long enough to listen to stories and work in a one-to-one situation, the children move into the schoolroom. Each day, there is a period of one-to-one teaching in number, reading and writing activities for every child. The Ginn 360 Reading Scheme is used and the Ginn Maths Scheme, in conjunction with Susan Poole's own programmes. Comprehensive written records on each child's progress are kept, with a copy given to parents on transfer to school. The wide range of daily activities includes art and craft, music, singing, drama, movement, early sciences, baking and sand and water play. Limited television viewing of educational programmes is allowed. The rumpus room, filled with boisterous-play equipment, is used for gymnastics on Fridays – children follow the BAGA pre-school gymnastics and movement programme and gain Jumping Joey awards. In the quiet room small groups enjoy looking at books, storytime, and quiet board games. After lunch, all the children rest. A grounding in the Christian religion, with short prayers, hymns and grace before meals. Food is fat-free, low-sugar, with no additives. Outings are held in summer only, but there is garden play daily, weather permitting.

**Remarks** Very popular, well-organised nursery, with highly structured and detailed plan of work, tailored to individual needs. Without any apparent pressure, children gradually work through a mountain of pre-reading, pre-writing and number work and transfer to their main school thoroughly prepared and well ahead of many of their peers. The nursery will need some upgrading of toilet facilities to comply with the new Children Act, and the numbers may also be reduced.

# OAK HOUSE CHILDREN'S NURSERY

Oak House
17 Aigburth Hall Road
Aigburth
Liverpool L19 9BN
**Tel:** (051) 427 2870

**Owner/Manager:** Patricia Hawley
**Type:** Day nursery offering full- and part-time places and half-day sessions
**Children:** 2–5yrs. 20 places. 27 on register
**Hours:** 8am–6pm (Mon–Fri)
9am–1pm (Sat)
Open 51 weeks a year
**Status:** Private, fee-paying
**Number of years open:** 4
**Meals:** Lunch, snacks
**1992 fees:** £50 per week full-time (inc meals and nappies)
£14 per day
£7 per session
£6 session Sat morning
**Waiting list:** Short
**Registered by:** Met Dist of Liverpool SS

**Premises** The owner's home, a listed, mid-19th-century stone house on a corner site in a quiet residential area. There is parking space in the drive and public transport nearby. The nursery is in the converted basement flat with its own entrance. There is a large main room, divided in two by a safety gate. It uses strip lighting, but has large windows at each end, which let in plenty of natural light. The walls are covered with examples of children's artwork. The sleep room is very small and has no natural light, but is attractively decorated with mobiles and wall friezes. There is also a carefully thought out toilet area with child-height fittings. The owner's kitchen is used. Outside, there is an area of hard surface for riding bikes and trikes, and the 'dell', which is a pretty garden, secluded and surrounded by an established shrubbery. Outdoor play equipment is carried down from the nursery when required. Local parks are not visited, 'as the risks outweigh the benefits', but there is ample outdoor space at the nursery.

**Owner/Manager & staff** Owner and manager, Patricia Hawley, has no childcare qualifications, but decided to set up the nursery so that she could combine work with caring for her two young children. She does not pay herself a salary, but is present in the nursery throughout the day, with a team of two full-time NNEB nursery nurses and two other full-time nursery workers with City & Guilds qualifications. All are young and friendly and have an easy, relaxed rapport with the children. Formal staff meetings are only held two or three times a year, but in such an intimate nursery the staff are able to exchange information and discuss problems on a daily basis. There is no staff training policy or budget, nor are there any peripatetic teachers or students.

**Children & parents** The children are nearly all white and English, many of them with mothers in full-time employment. Many of the parents are professional – dentists, teachers, vets, office workers and civil servants. Most transfer to local primary schools, particularly St Austin's RC School and Booker Avenue Primary. Very few stay in the private sector. Children are not divided into age-related groups; instead, they spend most of their time all together. There is a similarly loose arrangement for parents, who are free to come in at any time and chat with the owner or a member of staff. There is no particular encouragement for them to become involved in the day-to-day running of the nursery, but parents are invited to open days and the Christmas play.

**Curriculum & activities** A completely unstructured programme. 'The day is as it comes,' explains Patricia Hawley. The children are provided with plenty of brightly coloured furniture, climbing equipment, water and sand trays, Duplo and construction toys, a dolls' house, garage and a huge selection of other toys (annual equipment budget £1500). They choose from regular activities, such as painting, collages, play dough and table-top toys. There is dancing and singing to cassettes or the recorder, played by a member of staff. There is quiet time for at least half an hour each day, when children settle down to look at books or concentrate on pre-writing exercises. Parents are kept informed of the level their child has reached in pre-school work, so that they can provide appropriate back-up at home. There are no reading schemes and no structured pre-school work, but most children know their primary colours and can read their names, and some can write them by the time they leave.

Patricia Hawley says, 'It is more important that children should be prepared socially and emotionally for primary school, rather than pressured into pre-school work.' Children are encouraged to learn right from wrong and there is strong emphasis on cleanliness and hygiene. The nursery believes discipline is important, 'because with discipline comes security'. There are daily sports and games, indoors and out, occasional outings and twice-termly visits to the library. Meals are cooked on the premises, in the owner's kitchen by a cook. Snacks are either a biscuit or fresh fruit, morning and afternoon. No written records, timetable, procedures or policies at present, although plans are underway to introduce some record-keeping.

**Remarks** A small, cosy and homely nursery, not far from the city centre. Warm atmosphere and lovely garden. Children obviously stimulated, contented and well-behaved. Unstructured programme may not suit parents wanting their children to spend more time on formal pre-school work.

# Sefton

A third of the area's 2500 3- and 4-year-olds attend nursery classes part-time. Good provision for children with special needs, including facilities in ordinary primary schools, plus a special educational needs Support Scheme. There are six local authority day nurseries and 20 run by private suppliers. 300 registered childminders and 83 playgroups offer further services. Overall, provision is reasonably good and cash sums have been increased for 1993/4.

**Further information**

For details on day nurseries, childminders and playgroups:

Department of Social Services
Burlington House
Crosby Road North
Waterloo
Liverpool L22 0PF
Tel: (051) 934 3705 or 3747

For details on nursery schools, units and classes:
Education Office
Town Hall
Bootle L20 7AE
Tel: (051) 922 4040

## GRIFFIN NURSERY (KIDS UNLIMITED)

The Grange – Stonyfield
Sefton
Bootle
Merseyside L30 0QS
**Tel:** (051) 931 1853

**Owner:** Kids Unlimited
**Nursery Manager:** Margaret Griffiths, NNEB
**Type:** Day nursery offering full- and part-time places and half-day sessions
**Children:** 6mths–5yrs. 25 places. 31 on register
**Hours:** 8am–6pm
Morning session 8am–1pm
Afternoon session 1.15pm–6pm
Open 52 weeks a year (excl bank holidays)

**Status:** Private, fee-paying
**Number of years open:** 3
**Meals:** Breakfast, lunch, tea, snacks
**1992 fees:** £65 per week full-time
£6.50 per morning session
£1 for lunch
**Waiting list:** None. Places available
**Registered by:** Met Dist of Sefton SS
**Under same ownership:** 22 in total across the country. For further information contact: Kids Unlimited, 126 Gravel Lane, Wilmslow SK9 6EG. Tel: (0625) 527400

**Premises** A purpose-built former infants' school in the middle of a reasonably well-maintained council estate. A quiet position, with a canal behind where ducks and swans swim and a grassy play area on one side reached through the main playroom. It is completely fenced in by a metal fence. Due to its open position next to a main pathway through the estate, litter is an ongoing problem in the play area. There is no fixed play equipment – all outdoor apparatus is carried out from the building at playtime. There are no parks nearby, but outings by public transport or hired mini-bus are regular. Car parking is available for parents. Old Roan railway station is a 12-minute walk away. The rooms are light, well decorated and spotlessly clean, and the plain, pale blue walls covered with children's pictures. The staff room is small and cramped.

**Nursery Manager & staff** Margaret Griffiths is NNEB qualified and holds a Community Development Diploma. Twenty years ago, she set up a toy library in the area, which then became a mobile toy library and has now developed into a network of organised playgroups, run by parents throughout the borough. She was also employed by Save the Children Fund for ten years, working with families and young children. 'I like to keep admin to a minimum and spend my time on the shop floor as much as possible. Team meetings and one-to-one discussions with staff and parents are very important,' she says. There are five nursery workers in the team – four are NNEB qualified, one is a male worker and particularly popular with the boys. There are no trained nursery teachers on the staff. All staff work their way through a comprehensive training manual (over-long and full of jargon) and video supplied by the company. Their ages range from early 20s to mid-50s. Staff and students wear a uniform of grey and black tee-shirts, plus leggings or skirts. Turnover is low and nursery workers relate well to the children, listen to what they say and respond warmly. Staff meetings are difficult to organise, but usually take place after lunch when children are resting or have free play. After-hours meetings are not popular. Students are accepted on placement.

**Children & parents** The children come from a broad variety of backgrounds and from a wide catchment area. When they leave, they move on to a fairly even mix of state and private schools. Each member of staff is key-worker to a group of five children and charts their progress. Children with special educational needs are welcome and there is good back-up from Social Services. There is an open-door policy and parents are welcome to visit at any time. They are sent a written report on their child's development every three months. Phasing-in is done slowly, according to the needs of each child. Parents are represented on the management committee, which meets approximately six times a year.

**Curriculum & activities** Learning through play, with many different activities prepared and supervised each day. Staff have a written weekly activity schedule, planned in advance. Themes and projects are followed and regularly changed. The large playroom is divided into different areas: a home corner for imaginative play, a book corner and a physical-play area with a large indoor climbing frame. Computers are due to be delivered soon. The toddler room is well equipped with puzzles, games and pushing and riding toys (annual equipment budget £1500), all easily accessible so that children can choose their own activities. There is very limited formal teaching and no reading schemes. Music is twice a week, dance and movement fortnightly. Library visits and outings take place once a month. Each child has a named pouch hanging around the walls, where all his/her artwork is put, to be taken home from time to time. Lunch is prepared by a resident cook. Children help to prepare their own teas.

**Remarks** Efficient, friendly nursery, with a good relationship of mutual respect between staff and children. The location in the middle of a housing estate is not particularly stimulating and there are no trees, flowers or parks for nearby walks. Good record-keeping and plenty of different activities. A qualified nursery teacher on the staff would be a benefit.

# JEAN JESSOP DAY NURSERY

Mornington Road
Southport
Merseyside
PR9 0TT
**Tel:** (051) 934 2705

**Owner:** Southport College
**Manager:** Jane Condall, B Ed (Hons)
**Type:** Day nursery offering full- and part-time places. Half-day playgroup sessions also available
**Children:** 0–5yrs. 27 places. 35 on register
**Hours:** 8.15am–5.30pm
Morning session 9am–12 noon (playgroup)
Afternoon session 1pm–4pm (playgroup)
Open 51 weeks a year
**Status:** Private, fee-paying, non profit-making
**Number of years open:** 3
**Meals:** Breakfast, lunch, tea, snacks
**1992 fees:** £65 per week full-time, 8.15am start
£60 per week full-time, 8.30am start
£6 per session playgroup
**Waiting list:** 15 names
**Registered by:** Met Dist of Sefton SS

**Premises** The main playroom, kitchen and staff toilets are housed in a Victorian Methodist church hall near the town centre with good parking and public transport. Three adjoining Portakabins are used for the baby room, playgroup room, staff room and bathroom. The bright baby room is warm and cosy, with pretty curtains and pictures. The wood-panelled, carpeted quiet room is rather gloomy, without sufficient light, but well furnished and full of books at child-height and a large fish tank. The big playroom has two carpeted areas, with tables and chairs, a messy-play area and a home corner. The plain walls are covered with pictures and collages and all the toys are easily accessible to children and of good quality. Despite its proximity to the town centre, the outside area is both secluded and peaceful, part paved, part grass, with a shed to store ride-on toys and equipment.

**Manager & staff** Jane Condall, B Ed, the nursery manager, has 25 years' experience of childcare and lecturing to student nursery nurses. She reports to the principal of Southport College and holds regular meetings with her staff and termly meetings with parents. The eight female staff are all qualified NNEB, and include a proficient musician, who sings and plays keyboard. Another nursery nurse has substantial experience of dealing with special needs children. All work closely with the families and each member of staff is keyworker to four or five children. There is a good age range and staff all appear to be lively and interested in their work. Some are currently completing language courses so that French, Spanish and Italian can be introduced into the curriculum. The nursery is a high-quality training centre. NNEB, BTEC and NVQ students are always present on work experience and are trained by a designated member of the qualified team. There is no staff turnover. Salary rates are good – comparable with local authority education scales. The college provides an annual budget for staff training and development. A comprehensive staff appraisal scheme operates. The official staff/child ratio is 1:2 for babies, 1:3 for under-2s, 1:4 for 2- to 3-year-olds and 1:8 for 3- to 5-year-olds. However, the nursery is overstaffed, frequently offering better ratios than this.

**Children & parents** Children of professionally qualified, working parents. Some are lecturers or students at the college, others are doctors, business owners or bank employees. Four places are sponsored by Midland Bank. Some parents travel more than 25 miles to the nursery each day. College lecturers and students pop in to see their children whenever they like during the day. Two parents and two staff members form a working party, to discuss nursery policy and fund-raising. They also write a regular newsletter to keep parents informed. Children are very sociable, constantly chatter to staff and visitors and appear busy and well supervised. Daily diaries are kept in the baby room, and taken home by parents at the end of the day. Children transfer to a mix of state and private schools. The nursery is willing to take children with special needs and is supported by Social Services and the LEA as necessary.

**Curriculum & activities** After an early morning free play session, each day is broken up into components and the children have a choice of activities, often following a theme. They are encouraged to make their own choices, usually between pencils/crayons/paper, water and sand, puzzles, construction toys, games, art and the home corner. Imaginative play is generally around the current theme. Children are encouraged to tidy up before moving on to a new activity and there are cuddles on demand. Collage making or baking and outside play are done every day, and musical instruments and music and movement once a week. Older children learn pre-literacy skills through their everyday activities and any child who is ready is encouraged to start reading. There are no formal educational programmes. In summer, small groups of children go by public transport to Hesketh Park, two miles away, and there are regular outings to Southport beach, the zoo, and the aquarium. Children are also taken to any appropriate activities happening in the college. Meals are important social occasions, where staff and children sit down together. The demands we heard for seconds suggest that the food tastes as good as it looks.

**Remarks** A lively, loving and stimulating nursery, interested in quality of service rather than profit and offering excellent childcare at a reasonable price. College students usually have subsidised places. A recently opened playgroup in one of the adjoining Portakabins offers similar facilities without meals. The high staff ratio guarantees individual care for each child's needs. Strong parental involvement. Professional, dedicated staff and an impressive staff development policy. Nursery has links with a select group of childminders who care for babies on the waiting list until a nursery place is available.

# St Helens

A part-time nursery school for 35 per cent of all 3- and 4-year-olds, although provision is patchy, with some areas devoid of any nursery education and others with long waiting lists. Full daycare is left entirely to the private and voluntary sectors. This year's £3.4 million Social Services budget cut has resulted in the closure of the only local authority day nursery. There are eight private day nurseries, 420 registered childminders and 38 playgroups. Three-quarters of under-5s in St Helens have no form of childcare open to them. Demand for inexpensive provision is insatiable.

**Further information**

For details on day nurseries, childminders and playgroups:

Under Eights Section
c/o Inspection Unit
14 Rainford Road
St Helens WA10 6BS
Tel: (0744) 24028

For details on nursery schools, units and classes:

Education Department
Century House
Hardshaw Street
St Helens WA10 1RN
Tel: (0744) 24061

## ST HELENS COLLEGE NURSERY

St Helens College
Brook Street
St Helens
Merseyside W10 1PZ
**Tel:** (0744) 33766 (× 363)
**Owner:** St Helens College
**Officer-in-charge:** Carol Thompson, NNEB
**Type:** Workplace nursery and college crèche offering full- and part-time places
**Children:** Nursery: 3mths–5yrs. 20 places.
Crèche: 2–5yrs. 20 places
56 on register

**Hours:** Nursery 8am–6pm
Open 51 weeks a year
Crèche 9am–5pm (must collect child for lunch)
Open 36 weeks a year
**Status:** Part private fee-paying, part college-funded
**Number of years open:** Crèche: 5
Nursery: 2
**Meals:** Breakfast, lunch, tea, snacks (crèche, snacks only)
**1992 fees:** £14 per day for nursery
£1.45 per hour for crèche
Some crèche places fully subsidised
**Waiting list:** None for nursery. Sometimes for crèche
**Registered by:** Met Dist of St Helens SS

# Wirral

Twenty-five per cent of 4-year-olds spend two terms in a state nursery class before entering school. There are very few full-time places in the three nursery schools and 37 classes. Social Services fund six full-time day nurseries and a sponsored childminding scheme for children with special needs. Most parents seeking full-time care use one of 300 registered childminders. Private day nurseries contribute approximately 500 places. There are part-time playgroups throughout the district. £500,000 has been cut from the overall Social Services budget for 1993/4. Despite sending out questionnaires to a range of nurseries in the area, none were returned to us.

**Further information**

For details on day nurseries, childminders and playgroups:
Inspection and Quality Assurance Unit
St Mary's Building
235a Leasowe Road
Wallasey L45 8RE
Tel: (051) 691 2292

For details on nursery schools, units and classes:
Education Department
Hamilton Buildings
Conway Street
Birkenhead L41 4FD
Tel: (051) 666 2121

# Norfolk

Norfolk has 33 private day nurseries, with fees generally out of the reach of the average earner. Salaries are not high in the county. The local authority provides no day nurseries, and although there are four nursery schools, none offers full-time places. Only five per cent of the county's 3- and 4-year-olds receive nursery education, putting Norfolk virtually at the bottom of the league table. Working mothers rely on childminders, but many would prefer to offer their children the chance of pre-school education, rather than just somewhere to play. Private providers complain of unnecessary bureaucracy. 'I have tried to open up several day nurseries, but have failed to get planning permission. The Council seems more concerned about the noise the children may make, than the desperate need for childcare in this area,' says one nursery owner who hopes to expand. Of a total of 18 questionnaires sent out, only two were returned.

## Further information

For details on day nurseries, childminders and playgroups:
Department of Social Services
County Offices
Martineau Lane
Norwich NR1 2DH
Tel: (0603) 222141

For details on nursery schools, units and classes:
Education Department
County Hall
Martineau Lane
Norwich NR1 2DL
Tel: (0603) 222146

## PARK HOUSE DAY NURSERY

Mallow Road
Cloverfields
Thetford
Norfolk IP24 2YD
**Tel:** (0842) 752757

**Owner:** Park House Nursery Ltd
**Manager:** Rebecca Bourne, NNEB
**Type:** Day nursery offering full-time places and half-day sessions, plus after-school club and holiday playscheme.

**Children:** 2–5yrs. 50 places. 180 on register
**Hours:** 8.30am–5.30pm
Morning session 8.30am–12.30pm
Afternoon session 1.30pm–5.30pm
Flexible hours
Open 50 weeks a year
**Status:** Private, fee-paying
**Number of years open:** 3
**Meals:** Lunch, tea, snacks
**1992 fees:** £55 per week full-time
£5.50 per session
**Waiting list:** Moderate. Places available
**Registered by:** Norfolk County Council SS

## PLAYHOUSE DAY NURSERY

Manor View
The Street
Long Stratton
Norfolk NR15 2XJ
**Tel:** (0508) 30790

**Owner/Principal:** Peggy Sanderson, SRN, SCM, Mont Dip
**Type:** Day nursery offering full-time places and half-day sessions
**Children:** 0–5yrs. 18 places (4 for 0–2yrs). 51 on register
**Hours:** 8am–6pm
Morning session 8.30am–12.30pm
Afternoon session 1.30pm–5.30pm
Flexible hours
Open 49 weeks a year
**Status:** Private, fee-paying
**Number of years open:** 2
**Meals:** Breakfast, lunch, tea and snacks
**1992 fees:** £80 per week full-time – under 2
£64 per week full-time – over 2
£8 per session
**Waiting list:** Very short. Places available
**Registered by:** Norfolk County Council SS

**Premises** A detached, red-brick house built in the 1930s and surrounded by a half-acre of grassy garden. Long Stratton is a rapidly expanding village half-way between Norwich and Diss. The Playhouse is situated on the busy A140 and access is through a complex system of gates. Cars are only allowed on to the premises in emergencies. The nursery occupies six rooms on two floors. On the ground floor are an activity room where children eat meals and spend much of their day, a conservatory which is used as the messy room and a carpeted quiet room, equipped with a good supply of books, puzzles, quiet toys and beanbags for afternoon sleeping. The baby rooms are on the first floor, equipped with cots and including a playroom well stocked with toys. There is also a kitchen, child-sized loos and full clothes-washing facilities. The garden is split into two areas: a natural habitat at the back and a play area in front with outdoor play equipment.

**Owner/Principal & staff** Peggy Sanderson, SRN, SCM, Mont Dip, the enthusiastic and dedicated owner/principal of the nursery, has extensive experience nursing children and is also a registered midwife. Because of Peggy's training, the nursery will accept children from birth. She employs three full-time staff, two job-sharers and one part-time. Two are NNEB qualified, one City & Guilds and one has done the PPA Foundation course. Her deputy is Donna Visiers, NNEB. When recruiting, Peggy looks not only at experience and qualifications, but also age and background in order to ensure a well-balanced team. She makes a point of being available to parents at all times, providing them with her home telephone number. Staff wear nurse-like uniforms and a pink pinafore.

**Children & parents** Most are middle-class children of professional, working parents although a few have been referred by Social Services or health visitors. Two places are subsidised, one by Social Services and one by the principal herself. Children transfer to a number of different schools, some local primaries, others private and a few to special needs schools. The growing population in and around Long Stratton means increased diversity, and Peruvian, Anglo-Chinese and Canadian families use the nursery. Many parents come from as far away as Norwich and Diss and one works in Ipswich. Peggy is happy to take children with physical, as well as mental disability or learning difficulties. She has in the past accepted children in 'temporary crisis' through Social Services. The children are happy, confident and polite. The nursery has a flexible attitude towards working parents, and at the time of writing the first child arrives each day at 6.40am. The nursery is hoping to increase its numbers this year as demand increases.

**Curriculum & activities** The mornings and afternoons are broken up into six sessions lasting from 20 minutes to a maximum of one hour each. They include free play, theme work, table games, outdoor play, music/tapes/television, stories and songs. Children learn through play, and older children (3½ upwards) do some pre-writing and pre-number work in groups twice a week. Reading is not a major feature of the pre-school curriculum because the children are going on to such a wide variety of schools, each with different methods and reading schemes. Peggy feels that 'care is of primary importance in a day nursery' and she lets the children set the pace for the learning process. Staff meet once a week for planning and discussion. The nursery provides a wide range of toys and games as well as water and sand play, home corner, drawing and painting materials and outdoor play equipment. The annual equipment budget is £3500. The garden is used as much as possible and there are occasional outings to a local field centre. The nursery operates a keyworker system, although it is really only applied rigidly for the babies. Parents are encouraged to visit with their children prior to enrolling. Older children spend most of their time together and meals are always eaten with staff. Food is fresh and cooked on the premises.

**Remarks** In a county where pre-school care is virtually non-existent, this relatively new nursery is a bright star on the horizon. There are plans to increase places for all age groups. A particularly well-qualified and approachable principal, with well-trained staff, but no qualified or experienced early years teacher. Access off the busy A140 is not ideal. The secure gates had unfortunately been vandalised when we visited.

# Northamptonshire

Lack of funds is the reason given by Northamptonshire County Council for poor pre-school provision. A mere 17 per cent of the county's under-5s secure a place in a nursery school or nursery unit, and there are only 74 full-time places. There are seven nursery schools, but no new ones have been built since the late seventies. The last one had foundations laid, but was never finished. The private sector is inadequately served, with only 59 day nurseries, one with a long waiting list of nearly 200.

**Further information**

For details on private nurseries, childminders and playgroups:
Department of Social Services
Northampton House
Northampton NN1 2LJ
Tel: (0604) 236082

For details on nursery schools, units and classes:
Education Department
Northampton House
Northampton NN1 2LJ
Tel: (0604) 236268

## OLD RECTORY DAY NURSERY

Church Lane
Little Billing
Northampton NN3 4AF
**Tel:** (0604) 407740

**Owner/Principal:** Sue Hartley, B Ed
**Type:** Day nursery offering full- and part-time places and half-day sessions
**Children:** 2–5yrs. 60 places. 136 on register
**Hours:** 8am–6pm
Morning session 8am–1.10pm
Afternoon session 1.15pm–6pm
Open 51 weeks a year
**Status:** Private, fee-paying

**Number of years open:** 9
**Meals:** Lunch, tea
**1992 fees:** £47.50 per week full-time
£25.50 for 5 morning sessions per week
£25 for 5 afternoon sessions per week
£11 per day
£6 per morning session
£5.50 per afternoon session
50p for music and movement
£2 for swimming
**Waiting list:** Very long. 150+ (whole new Sept intake)
**Registered by:** Northants County Council SS

**Premises** Beautiful, 18th-century, stone-built rectory. The owner lives in the front of the house, and the nursery is housed at the rear on two floors. A recent extension provides children's toilets and cloakrooms. The rectory is next to a church, at the heart of the old village, which has now developed into a large residential suburb of Northampton. The one-acre garden is a paradise for children, with shrubberies, grottoes, lawns, swings and a tarmac drive for bike riding. Part is securely fenced off for the very youngest. There is a local bus service and restricted parking. Inside a total of seven spacious rooms are allocated to children, who are divided into groups of 20. There is an indoor rumpus room for wet playtimes. A kitchen and staff room complete the accommodation. Bright painted murals and examples of children's work are everywhere. Each room has a carpeted and a vinyl floor space for clean and messy work, with spotlights in the carpeted areas and fluorescent lighting in the messy-play areas.

**Owner/Principal & staff** Sue Hartley, B Ed, is a cheerful, outgoing, sporty person who was a middle-school teacher for ten years before opening the Old Rectory. She teaches the oldest children upstairs in the mornings, leaving the afternoons free for administration. She also works the late shift to enable other staff to go home. Of the ten full-time nursery nurses, seven are qualified NNEBs. The unqualified staff are all experienced and include a mother of eight children. Sue Hartley meets weekly with her two deputies, who are in charge of the toddlers and the middle group, and holds full staff meetings once a term. Children treat staff more as teachers than companions. Students come for work experience and there are also regular visits from speech therapists and physiotherapists. A well-organised experienced team, augmented by a full-time cook and a cleaner.

**Children & parents** Very wide, lively, social and ethnic mix, covering a 15-mile radius. The children come from many different cultural backgrounds, and ethnic minority festivals are recognised and celebrated. About half come from families with both parents working. They transfer mainly to state schools – about 26 different schools across the county. Sue Hartley liaises closely with the LEA and the Social Services department. Children in Northampton start school in the September of the year in which they are 5, so the whole of the top nursery group leave together each July. There is an open-door policy towards parents. A monthly newsletter keeps them informed of the staff rota. A daily diary is kept on each child, so that staff can refer to it and ensure continuity when shifts change. No open days or parents' evenings. Parents stay to phase in new children.

**Curriculum & activities** The emphasis is on care, but there is solid educational input. Each session is divided into periods of free play, supervised structured pre-school work or art and craft, group stories and singing. Painting and sand and water are always available. There is plenty of child-sized furniture and good equipment, with huge stocks of jigsaws and educational toys thoughtfully organised and stored. Annual equipment budget averages £4000. Inside each room, the atmosphere is more like a happy bustling classroom than a homely living room. The layout of the building is not ideal. Staff and children usually stay in their separate areas in different rooms on different floors, but meet together in the garden, at birthday parties or for outings. Reading is not taught, but children practise many pre-reading and writing skills. Progress is monitored every six months; there are no written programmes. The 30 older children are taken swimming weekly by coach with five staff. They swim in small groups, using the adjacent playground to wait their turn. Music and movement is also weekly. The nearby Aquadrome is a popular place for summer outings. Theatre trips and an annual Fun Day are also part of the busy timetable.

**Remarks** A first-class nursery offering quality full-time daycare, with some educational input. Organised and experienced staff. Wonderful mix of children. The large numbers and noisy, lively atmosphere might be too challenging for some 2-year-olds. Very good value for money – fees are fairly low for the quality of facilities offered. The Hartleys are continually ploughing money back into the nursery.

# SOUTHBROOK EARLY EDUCATION UNIT

Southbrook Infant School
Hawke Road
Daventry
Northants NN11 4LJ
**Tel:** (0327) 703440

**Owner:** Northants County Council LEA
**Head of School:** Dulcie Ogilvy, Cert Ed, MA
**Teacher-in-charge:** Ann Hill-Towers, Teachers' Diploma, Post Grad, Cert Infants Nursery Teaching
**Type:** Nursery unit attached to state infant school offering full-time places and half-day sessions
**Children:** 3yrs–4yrs 11mths. 30 places per session plus 12 full-time special educational needs places. 72 on register
**Hours:** Morning session 9am–11.30am
Afternoon session 12.50pm–3.10pm
Open 36 weeks a year
**Status:** State nursery class
**Number of years open:** 15
**Meals:** Sandwiches provided for full-time children
**1992 fees:** No fees
**Waiting list:** 34 names. Only a few will be offered places
**Registered by:** Northants County Council LEA

**Premises** Modern, architect-designed, brick and glass building, with large windows and pitched roof. The nursery unit shares the site with Southbrook primary and secondary schools. Inside is one big open-plan classroom, with central toilets and washroom area, also open-plan. There is a tiny mezzanine, a staff room and a small glassed-in office. The brick walls are painted in pale yellow, and there are hessian pinboards for exhibits. The huge windows and lack of internal walls limit the amount of children's work on display. There is tough carpet in most areas and vinyl in the art room and cloakrooms. The class has its own separate playground, safely enclosed by a high brick wall (with brightly coloured mural) and high gates. It is partly roofed for wet playtime, and there is a safety surface under the climbing frames. Attractive, flagged paths and low fences divide it into small gardens and sandpit areas.

**Teacher-in-charge & staff** Ann Hill-Towers, a friendly, easy-going Scotswoman, is an experienced primary and nursery school teacher. She has a teachers' diploma and post-graduate certificate in infant and nursery teaching. Four years at the nursery, she heads a team of three mature, experienced, qualified teachers (one a specialist in special needs teaching) and two young NNEB assistants. Staff are frequently supplemented by NNEB and teacher-training students on work-experience placements, plus two mothers of former pupils. The head of the infant school, Dulcie Ogilvy, Cert Ed, MA, has overall responsibility for the nursery, but delegates the day-to-day running to Ann. She and the governors remain relatively detached. There are two weekly staff meetings, one jointly with the school, the other for nursery unit staff only, where themes, projects and activities are discussed and children's progress monitored. High morale and good team spirit are apparent. Staff seem very cheerful and many are long-serving – two have been here since the nursery opened 15 years ago. Continuity is particularly helpful for the children with special educational needs. The staff/child ratio is 1:8. Training is considered important, with the LEA providing a budget and regular inset courses.

**Children & parents** The children come mainly from working-class families, some with professional parents; there is no ethnic mix. Places are strictly allocated: 27 from Southbrook estate, 23 from Daventry and surrounding villages, ten Social Services priority children from the area, 12 children with disabilities or special educational needs. Approximately half the class transfer to Southbrook Infant School, on the same site, others to local state schools. The children seem very well settled and integrated, especially since when we visited many had only been in the class for a few weeks. Parents are given a warm, enthusiastic welcome and involved in all nursery activities. There is a 'welcome' day on the first Friday of each month for prospective parents and children. They come with younger brothers and sisters and join in the play. Phasing-in is done slowly at the beginning of term. Each group teacher introduces two new children per session every week, so that there is time for each child to receive individual attention.

**Curriculum & activities** Southbrook follows the High Scope philosophy. Children are divided into groups, led by a keyworker. Staff keep a low profile, ensuring that all the equipment and play activities are well laid out and easily accessible and that children have freedom of choice. The open-plan arrangement is subdivided into home bases and work areas, where different activities take place. The High Scope method strongly encourages independence. It allows children to choose, collect their equipment, make, paint or play with what or who they like and tidy up, before re-grouping to talk about their achievements. There is plenty of good equipment and materials, heavily used. Formal teaching of reading or writing does not occur, but children practise pre-reading and manipulative skills at their home bases. Music and songs daily, dance and movement two or three times a week. Outings are usually once a term. Children use the garden throughout the day and can always choose outdoor play as an activity. They meet together for songs and rhymes each day after tidyup time.

**Remarks** Happy, busy, well-equipped nursery with mature and experienced staff. A stable, secure environment. Children with disabilities and special educational needs are very successfully integrated and benefit from the freedom of the High Scope method. The only real weakness is the lack of space, especially storage space. Strong, positive links with the primary school, which is also planning a workplace crèche and after-school care for children of staff.

# WINCHESTER HOUSE PRE-PREP NURSERY CLASS

70 Manor Road
Brackley
Northants NN13 6EE
**Tel:** (0280) 703070

**Owner:** Winchester House School Trust
**Headmistress:** Ingram Lloyd, Teachers' Cert
**Nursery Teacher:** Chris Banks, Cert Ed
**Type:** Nursery class in pre-prep school, offering full-time places and half-day sessions
**Children:** 3yrs–4½yrs. 20 places. 15 on register
**Hours:** Morning session 9am–12 noon
Afternoon session 1.30pm–3.30pm
Open 34 weeks a year
**Status:** Private, fee-paying
**Number of years open:** 11

**Meals:** Snacks. Lunch in prep school for children staying all day
**1992 fees:** £810 per term full-time
£410 per term for 5 morning sessions a week
£310 per term for 5 afternoon sessions a week
£25 registration fee
**Waiting list:** None
**Registered by:** Dept for Education

**Premises** Edwardian house, with large reception rooms, now used as classrooms, plus one very big modern classroom, built on six years ago. The nursery class, very much a part of the pre-prep school, has its own spacious classroom and cloakrooms. Children share all the pre-prep school facilities – including use of the main hall, library/television room and modern classroom. Bright, informative friezes and children's work decorate the walls. Large French windows lead out into the garden. Generous-sized school grounds, with tarmac playground, lawns, climbing frames.

**Headmistress, Nursery Teacher & staff** Ingram Lloyd is the charming, mature, yet youthful headmistress. Froebel-trained, she taught in infant schools for many years before transferring to a nursery, when her own children were small. She came to Winchester House seven years ago and quickly rose to become headmistress of the whole pre-prep school. She divides her teaching time between the reception class and the nursery class. Day-to-day running of the nursery is the responsibility of Chris Banks, Cert Ed, who is assisted by a qualified NNEB nursery nurse. Children attend two half-hour music sessions a week in the main school. BTEC and work experience students help from time to time. The staff/child ratio when we visited was a good 1:6.

**Children & parents** Upper middle-class, some titled, professional families, including Brazilians and Americans. Upper Heyford airbase is close by. Children are being carefully groomed for the public school system. Winchester House is one of the top prep schools in the country, feeding some of the leading public schools. Although the nursery is part of the pre-prep, there is no obligation to move up through the school, although most children do. The children are bright, articulate and confident. As the class is so small – 15 on the morning we visited – children benefit from regular individual tuition. They mix with pre-prep school children (up to 8 years old) at assembly, mealtimes and playtime. Parents are invited to open days and parents' evenings, and staff operate a home liaison programme.

**Curriculum & activities** The atmosphere is surprisingly unpressured, considering most children are preparing for examinations and boarding school entry at 8 years old. The school philosophy is that every child should give as much as he/she can and gain pleasure and satisfaction. The week's work is based on topics, and the activities emphasise or complement the topics. Each session follows a structured plan including registration, free play, group activities and outdoor play with older children from the main school. Sand and water play, painting and the home corner are always available. Small groups work with a teacher in turn, practising letters, sounds and colours. The Letterland phonic reading scheme is used throughout the school. Most of the children are reading by 4½. They come to the teacher's table individually or in pairs to do number work and writing, in their own specially designed workbooks. Music and drama are an important part of the nursery timetable. Using the home corner in a variety of roles from hospital to shop, children improvise aspects of the current topic. Ideas are developed, polished and often performed for the whole school during assembly. Wet playtimes and assemblies take place in the large modern classroom used by Group 1 (the reception class), so nursery children feel quite at home when they finally move up – usually after three terms in the nursery. Children's progress is carefully monitored by staff, on a daily basis if necessary.

**Remarks** Small, exclusive nursery class, attached to a pre-prep and prep school with an impressive reputation. Very well-qualified staff; carefully planned and thought-out curriculum, which challenges children without pushing them. Not 'glamorous' by current standards, but the premises are homely and welcoming. Part of a first-class educational package for consumers of the British public school system.

# Northumberland

A high provider of nursery education by British standards, with 39 per cent of 3- and 4-year-olds receiving a part-time place. Recent expansion has been rapid. However, serious budget cuts this year will affect children's services and education in Northumberland. 138 playgroups, many of them reported to be excellent, offer part-time sessions. The only local authority day nursery, located in Blyth, caters for children in need. In the private sector, daycare facilities appear to meet demand. There are 14 day nurseries and 630 childminders (more in the process of registration). Many childminders report vacancies.

**Further information**

For details on day nurseries, childminders and playgroups:
Department of Social Services
Inspection Unit
Wansbeck House
Hepscott Park
Morpeth NE61 6NF
Tel: (0670) 505086

For details on nursery schools, units and classes:
Education Department
County Hall
Morpeth NE61 2EF
Tel: (0670) 533000

## MEADOWS DAY NURSERY

Nafferton Farm
Stocksfield
Northumberland NE43 7XD
**Tel:** (0661) 836266

**Owner/Principal:** Margaret Taylor, NNEB
**Type:** Day nursery offering full- and part-time places and half-day sessions
**Children:** 2–5yrs. 24 places. 72 on register
**Hours:** 8am–6pm
Morning session 8am–12.30pm
Afternoon session 1.30pm–6pm
Open 51 weeks a year
**Status:** Private, fee-paying
**Number of years open:** 3
**Meals:** Lunch, snacks
**1992 fees:** £86.40 per week full-time
£18.75 per day
£11.64 per session (inc lunch)
£8.64 per session (excl lunch)
**Waiting list:** Long. About 50 names
**Registered by:** Northumberland County Council SS

**Premises** A stone-built Victorian farmhouse in an isolated, rural setting, surrounded by open countryside. Newcastle and Corbridge are both 15 miles away. The farmhouse doubles as a nursery and family home, with children occupying the ground floor and part of the first. Downstairs there is a large playroom with areas for art and craft, wet sand, water and a purpose-built play shop. Attractive country murals, depicting sheep, rolling hills, tractors and farms, cover the walls. There is a carpeted quiet room full of books and providing cosy, soft seating. The kitchen, shared with the owner and her family, is pristine and well equipped. There are also children's cloakrooms, an office and a staff room. Everywhere is spotless, comfortable and welcoming. Outside, there is ample parking space and a fenced-off play area with Wendy house, slide and swings.

**Owner/Principal & staff** Margaret Taylor, NNEB, has 17 years' experience working in nursery schools and in a children's psychiatric unit. She has also completed a two-year business and management course. She works a 50-hour week in the nursery, with the help of five full-time nursery workers, all women. Three are NNEB qualified, one is PPA trained and another has a City & Guilds Childcare Diploma. They offer a good combination of personalities and ages. Some are motherly and mature, others calm and unflappable. All are enthusiastic and motivated. Nursery workers wear tabard-style tunics bearing the Meadows logo. Staff meetings are held weekly. There is no training policy or budget. The staff/child ratio is 1:4.

**Children & parents** The nursery has a good reputation and attracts children from a 20-mile radius. The parents are middle-class and generally well-off. There is no cultural mix in the area. Most mothers work outside the home and a number also employ nannies or au pairs. The children mainly go on to various state primary schools, and ten per cent to independent schools. They are all confident and outgoing, friendly to visitors and happy to show off their achievements.

**Curriculum & activities** Children work in small groups and are encouraged to rotate round the various activities laid out. The first part of the session is spent at cookery, craft, fun activities and free play, followed by milk and snacks. The session continues with music, dance and movement and a daily farm walk. Monthly themes are planned in advance and parents are notified of all aspects of the curriculum, so they can support it at home. Equipment is high quality and nearly new. Pre-reading and pre-writing skills are developed with the older children, mainly using worksheets. Letterland is used for phonetic work and reading, and the children react enthusiastically to it. Detailed records are kept, and parents are shown their children's work on a regular basis. Outings are difficult, due to the nursery's out-of-the-way location, but nature trails, picnics and country walks are an integral part of the timetable.

**Remarks** A very popular nursery, which has rapidly built up a good reputation. Children benefit from the wonderful rural setting, although the isolated location makes it difficult for the nursery to foster community links. The staff are professional and caring. Strong emphasis on quality care rather than educational programmes.

# SWIFTDALE CLOSE DAY NURSERY

Swiftdale Close
Bedlington
Northumberland NE22 7LF
**Tel:** (0670) 530477
**Owner:** Nomad Housing Group Ltd
**Officer-in-charge:** Susan Dixon, NNEB, CPQS, Mont Dip
**Type:** Day nursery offering full- and part-time places and half-day sessions
**Children:** 3mths–5yrs. 40 places. 57 on register
**Hours:** 7.30am–6pm
Morning session 7.30am–1pm
Afternoon session 1pm–6pm
Flexible hours
Open 50 weeks a year
**Status:** Private, fee-paying
**Number of years open:** 3
**Meals:** Breakfast, lunch, tea, snacks
**1992 fees:** £80 per week full-time
£16 per day
£8 per session
Housing Association residents half price
£5 reduction per week for siblings
**Waiting list:** Minimal – 10 names
**Registered by:** Northumberland County Council SS

**Premises** Situated in a new housing development, owned and maintained by the Nomad Housing Association, the nursery was purpose-built two years ago. It is a single-storey building, designed in a V shape, with offices and cloakrooms at the apex of the V. Inside is spacious and light, with a jolly colour scheme (pink and lemon walls, raspberry red carpets). Recently redecorated throughout. It is easy to find, only half a mile from the town centre and well served by public transport. There is parking for seven cars outside the building. The securely fenced garden, used daily, has a climbing frame, slide and a tyre swing, set on safety surface, but is otherwise not particularly child-friendly with immaculately weeded rosebeds and carefully manicured borders. The nursery's original accommodation of one main playroom has recently been expanded to include the use of a second room, shared with the residents' association.

**Officer-in-charge & staff** Susan Dixon, NNEB, CPQS, Mont Dip, the officer-in-charge, is well qualified and has wide experience in Social Services day nurseries, hospitals, special schools and Dr Barnardo's nurseries. She reports to a management committee, chaired by the Nomad housing manager. The staff team comprises five full-time and seven part-time young, female nursery nurses. Seven are qualified, NNEB, CPQS, City & Guilds, and five are unqualified. Certificates are held in first aid, life-saving and basic sign language. A staff development and training policy is in place and workers attend Social Services courses. The nursery would welcome a male member of staff, as many children come from single-mother homes. None applied when the last post was advertised.

**Children & parents** The children are from a variety of backgrounds, but there is no ethnic diversity. At the time of our visit, the majority were under three years old. Children with disabilities are well supported and integrated, and there are disabled loos and wheelchair access. The lunch we observed was very well supervised, with 13 children attended by six nursery workers. The staff/child ratio is 1:3 for the youngest group; 1:4 for the over-2s. Most of the parents are in full-time employment and find it difficult to visit the nursery for any length of time, although they are always welcome. Christmas parties and nursery outings are well attended.

**Curriculum & activities** All the equipment is nearly new, well cared for and appropriate for under-3s (annual budget £1000). The officer-in-charge has control of the equipment budget. Water, sand and art materials are available at all times. Toys are changed every hour, unless children are particularly absorbed. Basic pencil skills, numbers, colours and shapes are taught, but no reading or writing. Music, storytime, songs and cookery take place every day. A written report is sent home every six months. A message book passes between home and nursery each day, detailing routines, feeding and toileting habits, activities and anything else of interest about the child. Parents and keyworkers fill it in and discuss the entries at the beginning or end of the day. Outings are organised as often as possible. A large garage space is used regularly in wet weather and as a verandah, with the doors open on good days. Meals are an important social event, where children are encouraged to feed themselves and progress from high chair to table as smoothly as possible.

**Remarks** High-quality childcare in sparkling, purpose-built premises. Limited educational programmes, but most of the children are still very young. Qualified, experienced nursery nurses. Reasonable fees for full daycare of such quality.

# North Yorkshire

England's largest county, and a predominantly rural area, has no local authority nurseries. Private day nurseries accommodate 1600 children, but most parents rely on relatives or childminders, of whom there are over 1000. The 300 or so playgroups are also a popular choice for part-time, occasional cover. North Yorkshire is committed to nursery education, but limited by a lack of government funding. However, the LEA is just embarking on a five-year development programme to target rural areas and update provision in urban areas. Depending on resources, they plan to open two new nursery classes every year until 1997. Currently some 20 per cent of the county's under-5s receive part-time places. Four of the 46 nursery classes are peripatetic, providing half-day sessions in outlying villages, which otherwise would have no nursery education. Generally, services are patchy and over-subscribed. 'Facilities-wise, the best place to live is slap-bang in the middle of the garrison at Catterick. Army provision is good,' a local authority worker told us.

### Further information

For details on day nurseries, private nursery schools, childminders and playgroups:

Customer Relations Unit
The Old School
East Road
North Allerton
North Yorkshire DL7 1NQ
Tel: (0609) 779999

For details on nursery schools, units and classes:

Education Department
Racecourse Lane
North Allerton
North Yorkshire DL7 8AE
Tel: (0609) 780780

## HCAT NURSERY

Harrogate College of Arts & Technology
5 Victoria Avenue
Harrogate
N Yorkshire HG1 1EL
**Tel:** (0423) 505269

**Owner:** N Yorkshire County Council
**Supervisor:** Emma Hinchcliffe, NNEB
**Type:** Workplace nursery offering full- and part-time places and half-day sessions to HCAT staff and local community
**Children:** 6mths–5yrs. 24 places. 45 on register
**Hours:** 8am–5.45pm
Morning session 8am–1pm
Afternoon session 12.45pm–5.45pm
Open 50 weeks a year
**Status:** Private, fee-paying
**Number of years open:** 2½

**Meals:** Snacks, packed lunches. Parents provide baby feeds
**1992 fees:** £74 per week full-time – under 2
£54 per week full-time – over 2
£16 per day – under 2
£13.80 per day – over 2
£7.95 per session – under 2
£6.95 per session – over 2
£2.35 per hour – under 2
£1.70 per hour – over 2
**Waiting list:** 6 months for under-2s. None for over-2s. Priority to HCAT staff.
**Registered by:** N Yorkshire County Council SS

**Premises** The basement of a large, grey stone, late Victorian, listed building, housing the College of Arts & Technology. Situated on a dual carriageway in a business area, five minutes from the town centre. In common with most architecture of this period, the rooms are large and light despite being in the basement, with plenty of space for play. The nursery occupies four rooms and has two toilets plus a changing room equipped with a sink, nappy-changing area, washing machines and rubbish bins. Babies and toddlers have a day room with carpeted play area and small tables and chairs, where older children can paint, draw or model. They rest in a comfortable sleep room. Three- to five-year-olds have a 'classroom', well stocked with books, games, toys and equipment, and an 'artroom' with copious evidence of high artistic achievement. The nursery has no garden or outside play area. Each day children are taken in groups to play in the nearby park, or to Valley Gardens, where there are swings and a paddling pool. In summer, there are nature walks and picnics in a favourite area of pine woods. Children also visit the library two or three times each term and occasionally go to the supermarket, in small groups.

**Nursery Supervisor & staff** Emma Hinchcliffe, NNEB, is young and friendly and firmly committed to a career in childcare. She is now studying for a teaching qualification to enable her to train NNEB students and holds an NNEB diploma in supervisory management. She heads a team of seven, plus occasional NNEB students. All the staff hold childcare or teaching qualifications, NNEB or Montessori, and all have passed at least a GCSE or O-level in art. A very high standard of children's creative work is on display in the nursery. The nursery workers are a young, enthusiastic team, who harmonise together well and look smart, if rather clinical, in their navy uniforms – the supervisor and deputy wear green. Staff meet once a month to discuss the day-to-day running of the nursery. They make themselves available to parents daily to talk about progress or discuss problems. Free training is available through the college, although only the supervisor has taken advantage of this. A male nursery nurse employed in the past was not voted a success, but the supervisor would certainly consider future male applicants. No staff turnover. Emma Hinchcliffe reports to a management committee, which includes parent representatives. The staff/child ratio is 1:3.

**Children & parents** The children's families are largely from professional business backgrounds. A third of the nursery's places are reserved for the children of Midland Bank employees. Due to pressure of places, some children attend other private nurseries on different days of the week. The nursery relies on word of mouth from satisfied parents to fill places. Children arrive from a wide geographical area – most have parents who work in Harrogate. The leavers transfer mainly to state schools. The nursery is willing to take children with special needs, but cannot cope with wheelchairs due to the position and layout of the premises. New parents are encouraged to spend trial sessions at the nursery, when they can see for themselves how their child settles down and participates in nursery activities. Time spent at the nursery is built up gradually. Babies' progress is monitored daily and a 'baby book' is sent home each night in the child's bag with comments and developmental milestones – eg 'crawled for the first time today'. Files charting older children's achievements are available to parents and can be passed on to new schools. There is an open-door policy and parents are always welcome.

**Curriculum & activities** Art is clearly a very strong force here. Children are encouraged to use all sorts of materials to produce creative and stunning work, helped by their imaginative nursery nurses. There is no formal teaching; the nursery operates on the learn-through-play principle, including normal pre-school activities – number work, colour and shape recognition, letter recognition and pencil control. Small groups of children rotate through various activities each day, coming together for stories, musical movement and free play. Daily activities are planned and laid out in advance, ready for the children when they arrive. Children work in groups of six, supervised by their keyworker. Older children explore projects, associated with chosen themes. Each child has a drawer marked with a picture to keep their workbooks and drawings in. The nursery is very well funded and extremely well equipped with toys and games for constructive and imaginative play. There appears to be no limit to the equipment budget – whatever is needed is supplied.

**Remarks** A happy nursery with young, well-motivated and qualified staff. Outstanding artwork, which is mainly adult led. Future plans include the provision of a much needed outdoor play area – a space has already been set aside – and outdoor toys. Lack of a hot meal for full-time children is a distinct disadvantage. Fees offer excellent value for such a quality service.

## JOSEPH'S NURSERY

The Pavilion
Rawcliffe Lane
Clifton
York YO3 6NP
**Tel:** (0904) 651767

**Owner:** York Childcare Ltd
**Manager:** Rosemary Flanagan, NNEB
**Type:** Day nursery offering full- and part-time places and half-day sessions
**Children:** 2mths–5yrs. 38 places. 67 on register
**Hours:** 8am–6pm
Morning session 8am–1pm
Afternoon session 1pm–6pm
Open 51 weeks a year
**Status:** Fee-paying registered charity
**Number of years open:** 2½
**Meals:** Lunch, tea, snacks
**1992 fees:** £87.50 per week full-time – under 2
£85.00 per week full-time – over 2
£23.10 per day – under 2
£18 per day – over 2
£9–£13 per session
**Waiting list:** Long. Priority to lone parents and corporate clients
**Registered by:** N Yorkshire County Council SS

**Premises** A converted sports pavilion, grade II listed and unusually picturesque, with dormer windows set in a steeply sloping roof and exposed oak beams inside. The nursery, built by Joseph Rowntree, was originally thatched, but severe fire gutted the building last year. It has now been completely rebuilt and refurbished to a very high standard. The children moved back in, two days before our visit. There are two floors in use. Babies are upstairs in a main room, with nappy-changing facilities and a separate milk kitchen nearby. Toddlers and pre-school children have a large playroom downstairs, with a dining area, home corner and book corner. Toilets, kitchen, staff room, offices and utility room are also provided. Everywhere is newly decorated and vibrant. There is smart green cord carpeting throughout, with vinyl flooring in the wet areas. With windows on three sides of the building, there is plenty of natural light. Outside, there is a large, secure, grassy area, divided into two by a wooden fence. The garden perimeter is carefully planted with a beech and privet hedge. Homestead Park, a quarter of a mile away, is visited two or three times a week. The nursery is in a quiet residential area, close to main bus routes and a mile from the outer ring road.

**Manager & staff** Rosemary Flanagan, NNEB, is an experienced playgroup supervisor, who ran her own nursery prior to joining Joseph's. She heads a team of ten female nursery nurses, eight full-timers. Two are unqualified, and the rest have NNEB qualifications. All staff have first-aid certificates and four are Makaton trained. At present, there is one male supply teacher; more male workers would be welcome. BTEC students are accepted on placement. Staff are encouraged to attend training and information courses. The nursery has a small training budget. A strong reputation tends to attract good staff, and turnover has been minimal since the nursery opened. Only two nursery workers have left, unable to cope with the trauma of the fire.

**Children & parents** Interesting mixture of social and economic backgrounds, with several children from ethnic minority backgrounds. All are English-speaking. The nursery was originally set up to provide high-quality care so that parents in the York area, particularly lone parents, could return to work. There is an assisted places scheme for single parents and reserved places, at a discount, for local companies. York Childcare Ltd is a non-shareholding partnership between York City Council, York Health Authority, North Yorkshire County Council, local private companies and nursery parents. The company set up Joseph's Nursery with the help of a £100,000 grant from the City Council. Parents are encouraged to become active in the running of the nursery, attend committee meetings, open evenings and outings and help with fund-raising activities. They are asked not to visit the nursery unannounced after 10am or before 3.30pm, as constant visitors are disruptive to the routine and upset the children. Parents phase-in new children, if their employment commitments allow. Children with special educational needs and Social Services referrals are successfully integrated.

**Curriculum & activities** High Scope is gradually being introduced. The philosophy is based on encouraging children to become responsible for their own decisions (within the limits of safety and hygiene), ensuring that they are confident with their peers. A huge amount of new equipment and toys has been bought to replace the total loss in the fire. 'There is a basic plan for each day, but flexibility is the name of the game,' explains Rosemary Flanagan. Children and parents are welcomed at the beginning of each session, and the children have free choice of art and craft activities, sand and water play and construction toys. After a snack at 9.30am, there are stories and rhymes, outdoor play, walks and visits. Children take part in planning their own activities and discuss what they have achieved with their carers after each task is completed. Art and craft are always available and music and movement and outdoor play once a day. Swimming, library visits, cookery and gardening are part of the busy timetable. Rosemary Flanagan says that, 'Care and education are run in parallel, with support and encouragement given to children who appear ready for more formal, structured pre-school work.' Most children can read by the time they leave. Outings take place once a term to farms, museums, small-holdings and local places of interest. Developmental progress is monitored once a month by nursery officers. All written reports are available to parents. The nursery is buzzing with activity of all kinds.

**Remarks** High-quality day nursery, with a wide variety of activities and busy, stimulated children. Assisted places scheme ensures a good social mix. Despite the terrible trauma of seeing their nursery burnt to the ground, staff have remained loyal. The nursery has survived a major upheaval, but is now back in its original home, stronger and more enthusiastic than ever. York Childcare continues to campaign for more nursery provision in the area and is actively seeking funding for future partnership initiatives.

## LISVANE

Scarborough College Junior School
Sandybed Lane
Scarborough YO12 5LJ
**Tel:** (0723) 361595

**Owner:** Scarborough College
**Principal:** Elizabeth Kitching, Cert Ed
**Type:** Nursery class in junior school offering full- and part-time places and half-day sessions
**Children:** 2yrs 8mths–4yrs 11mths. 16 places. 22 on register
**Hours:** 9am–3.30pm
Morning session 9am–12 noon
Afternoon session 12.30pm–3.30pm
Open 34 weeks a year
**Status:** Private, fee-paying
**Number of years open:** 3
**Meals:** Packed lunches, snacks
**1992 fees:** £5.88 per session
£20 registration fee
**Waiting list:** 17 names. Early registration advisable
**Registered by:** Dept for Education

## ST PAUL'S NURSERY SCHOOL

12 St Paul's Square
Holgate Road
York YO2 4BD
**Tel:** (0904) 622291

**Owner:** N Yorkshire County Council LEA
**Headteacher:** Gillian Chalk, NNEB, Cert Ed, Adv Dip Ed
**Type:** Nursery school offering half-day sessions. No full-time places except in special circumstances
**Children:** 3–5yrs. 50 places per session. 100 on register
**Hours:** Morning session 9am–11.30am
Afternoon session 12.40pm–3.10pm
Open 36 weeks a year
**Status:** State nursery school
**Number of years open:** 56, of which 46 under LEA control
**Meals:** Lunch, snacks
**1992 fees:** No fees
**Waiting list:** Very long – over 200 names. Places cannot be guaranteed
**Registered by:** N Yorkshire County Council LEA

**Premises** The nursery occupies a large, 200-year-old house on the corner of a quiet garden square in the centre of York. The building was donated by a trust in 1936, so that a nursery could be set up for children with unemployed fathers. Since then, it has had many additions and modifications and now provides three main activity rooms, a kitchen, dining room, staff room which doubles as a library, toilets and offices. Outside there is a large garden with a sandpit, play house, and a pets' corner with four guinea pigs. A split-level area of tarmac creates a bike and truck racetrack and playground. There is a good supply of outdoor apparatus – climbing frames, a swing, slide and tunnels. A shed houses an impressive collection of outdoor toys. Indoors, children divide their time between the Active Room, where they can play in the home corner, shop or telephone box, build with bricks and construction toys, or listen to music. The Creative Room is kitted out for art and craft of all kinds and sand and water play. The Quiet Room is used for table activities, games and looking at books. The dining room doubles as an extra activity room where older children work on pre-school activities or have cooking sessions and stories. Parents' coffee mornings are also held here. The nursery is light and sunny, with plenty of windows, well heated and ventilated. Decoration in fairly good condition. Annual equipment budget £1600.

**Headteacher & staff** Gillian Chalk, Cert Ed, Dip Ed, formerly a lecturer in child education, has been headteacher at St Paul's for three years. She controls her own budget and is responsible for the day-to-day running of the nursery and its maintenance. She reports to the Support Body, made up of herself and another member of staff, LEA representatives and parents. They meet once a term to discuss nursery policy. Gillian Chalk heads a team of six women, all qualified, one teacher and five NNEB nursery nurses. The staff have had many years' experience and range in age from mid-30s to mid-50s. Extra qualifications include special needs training, Makaton course certificates and first-aid. Ancillary staff include a cook, caretaker, secretary and dinner supervisors. Students and parents help out. Staff are well motivated and long-serving. The staff/child ratio is 1:10.

**Children & parents** The children come from a variety of backgrounds and income brackets. The parents represent a genuine social mix – including university professors and unemployed single parents. The school is extremely popular, with places filled by word of mouth or Social Services placement. Children include some with special needs – social, developmental or medical. The majority of the children go on to different state primaries, some to special needs schools and one or two to private prep schools. Parents are invited to open days, parents' evenings and meetings and are encouraged to take an active part in nursery life, helping out with activities or outings. Comments and complaints are encouraged. Parents fill three places out of eight on the Nursery Support Body and have a positive say in how the nursery is run. Parents of new children stay for one session or more until their child is settled. They are welcome to phone for progress reports at any time. The admission policy is to take the oldest applicants first. Parents and children can find out everything they need to know about the nursery in an excellent policy and curriculum document on the school, provided by the local authority.

**Curriculum & activities** The children are divided into four groups of 12 to 14 with one member of staff taking responsibility for each group. The groups come together each day for a story and the group leader monitors and records their progress. The nursery operates a learn-through-play policy, giving children plenty of stimulation and encouragement to develop their skills and imagination. Morning and afternoon sessions are structured and well organised to include an almost bewildering number of activities – dressing up, role-playing, construction, art and craft, woodwork, listening to audio tapes, working on the computer, using apparatus to develop dexterity – to say nothing of the outdoor play, free play, stories, games and music. Older children follow the accepted pre-school curriculum in preparation for their next schools. Gillian Chalk places great importance on a holistic approach to each child and his/her family. The nursery sets out to provide a familiar, safe environment where each child can develop, encouraged by interested adults. She worries about the fact that the popularity of the nursery means children often cannot be offered places when they reach the age of 3. About a third of the children stay for a free lunch each day – either at the end or beginning of their session.

**Remarks** An extremely well-organised nursery providing a huge variety of different and stimulating activities. Staff would like to see the nursery school expand to meet the huge demand in the area and stay open longer to cater for the needs of working parents. Qualified, experienced, long-serving staff who all told us, 'It's great to go to work!'

# WESTFIELDS INFANTS SCHOOL – NURSERY UNIT

Askham Lane
Acomb
York YO2 3HP
**Tel:** (0904) 798033

**Owner:** N Yorkshire County Council LEA
**Teacher-in-charge:** Jenny Rice, BA (Hons), PGCE in Early Years Education
**Type:** Nursery unit in state infants school offering half-day sessions. No full-time places
**Children:** 3yrs 6mths–4yrs 10mths. 40 places each session. 80 on register
**Hours:** Morning session 9.05am–11.20am Afternoon session 12.50pm–3.05pm
**Status:** State nursery class
**Number of years open:** 17
**Meals:** None
**1992 fees:** No fees
**Waiting list:** Long. Apply as soon as possible after child's 2nd birthday
**Registered by:** N Yorkshire County Council LEA

**Premises** Ideal. A purpose-built single-storey building, within the grounds of a suburban infant and junior school complex, with access to school playing fields and playground. Children play and work in one large room, with an annexe acting as a quiet/computer room. The nursery has its own toilets and washbasins, plus a shower room. The main room has non-slip flooring with a carpeted home corner. The annexe is fully carpeted. Everywhere is brightly decorated in white and yellow, with plenty of children's artwork displayed on the walls. Big windows let in streams of sunshine and natural light. The nursery has its own large grassy, partly paved play area well equipped with climbing frames, ride-on toys, tunnels, tyres, ropes and a trampoline.

**Teacher-in-charge & staff** Jenny Rice, BA, PGCE, heads a team of four – two teachers qualified Cert Ed and two NNEB nursery nurses – ranging in age from their 20s to 40s. She reports to the Head of the infant school. NNEB students and sixth formers also work at the nursery as part of their courses. Parents help with some activities. Staff turnover is low and supply staff are available to cover for holidays and sickness. Staff meetings for the whole school are held fortnightly; nursery staff also meet weekly to plan for the following week. They seem a happy, relaxed team, with a good relationship with the children. The staff/child ratio is 1:10. Ongoing training is considered vital. Staff have access to a full range of LEA courses and constantly review and assess their class work.

**Children & parents** Children come from nearby working communities – an established local authority housing estate and lower- and middle-income private housing. The majority move on to the infant school, with a few transferring to other nearby state primaries. Children with special needs are welcome but wheelchairs cannot be accommodated because of the layout of the nursery. Parents are encouraged to take an active interest in the nursery. Open days, plays, concerts and sports days are held throughout the year. Parents are invited to join the first hour of each session to help out and contribute. They can also phone the nursery at any time to check on their child's progress. Children visit with their parents before starting. No more than two new pupils join per session, so that enough staff are available to provide one-to-one support, if necessary. Priority is given to children coming from the school's catchment area, or children referred by Social Services. A regular newsletter tells parents which topics and projects will be covered each term, to encourage discussion and reinforcement at home. An excellent school brochure sets out every aspect of nursery life.

**Curriculum & activities** A broad philosophy, based on the experience and formal training of the staff. Priorities are social and emotional development, independence, language development, creative and intellectual growth and aesthetic awareness. Each week is carefully planned in advance, with a theme and a special area of interest. The week we visited, the theme was 'Christmas' and the special interest subject 'bells'. Tables and floor are set out with different activities covering seven main areas: natural materials, including sand and water and clay; art and craft with easels for free painting and tables for sticking and cutting; construction – stickle bricks, Duplo, Lego, bricks, jigsaws, threading cubes, etc; pre-school work including a pre-number and pre-reading table with dominoes, lotto, number boards, colours and shapes; listening corner with tapes, music and stories; a writing centre for colouring, tracing and drawing and the computer; the seventh area children cover each day is environmental studies. This includes looking after the nursery guinea pig and rabbit, nature studies and outdoor activities. Music, songs, rhymes and finger games are done every day. Time is also set aside daily for group activities – stories and talking time. Dance and movement are done every week. The home corner takes on a different role each half-term – recently it has been a café, fire station and baby clinic – offering opportunities for imaginative role playing and focused art and craft. Books and games can be borrowed from the nursery to use at home. There is no formal teaching of reading, but children are ready to read when they reach the primary school next door. Outings are undertaken ad hoc, often relating to themes. Visitors from the local community frequently arrive to talk about their jobs. The nursery shares some assemblies with the infant school and has a special birthday assembly on Fridays. Staff and children light candles and sing Happy Birthday to anyone who has had a birthday that week.

**Remarks**  An excellent, well-equipped nursery with a sound understanding of the educational needs and development of pre-school children. Experienced, trained and caring staff, meticulously planned curriculum and activities. Lack of space excludes the possibility of expansion, so the long waiting list will remain.

# YORK COLLEGE NURSERY

York College of Further & Higher Education
Dringhouses
York YO2 1UA
**Tel:** (0904) 704141 × 205

**Owner:** York College of Further & Higher Education
**Supervisor:** Karen Bartlett, NNEB
**Type:** Workplace nursery, offering full- and part-time places to college staff and students, Midland Bank employees and local community
**Children:** 2mths–5yrs. 31 places. 72 on register
**Hours:** 8.15am–5.45pm
Morning session 8.15am–12 noon
Afternoon session 1pm–5.45pm
Flexible hours
Open 50 weeks a year
**Status:** Private, fee-paying, non profit-making
**Number of years open:** 3½
**Meals:** Lunch, tea, snacks
**1992 fees:** £72 per week full-time for outside community
*Students*
£50 per week full-time – under 2
£38 per week full-time – over 2
*College staff*
£60 per week full-time – under 2
£55 per week full-time – over 2
**Waiting list:** 21 names. Priority to students
**Registered by:** N Yorkshire County Council SS

**Premises**  On the campus of York College of Further and Higher Education, the nursery consists of a converted ground floor area of the Business Studies block, originally a bike shed and caretaker's office. There are two activity rooms with toilets and cloakrooms, and a kitchen. Decorations are adequate and walls are covered with children's art and craft work. The large, carpeted main room has a small kitchen area at the far end, strip lighting and windows down two sides. A recently created baby room, off the main room, contains cots, changing mats and a fridge for milk feeds. The outside play area is used daily and is fully enclosed. There is a variety of outdoor equipment including a brightly coloured wooden play house and slide. Limited parking is available in the college. Park-and-ride buses to the station and city centre stop directly opposite.

**Supervisor & staff** Karen Bartlett, NNEB, has been the supervisor for three years. Her past experience includes work in the paediatric wards of a hospital and a spell in the nursery class of an infants school. She has recently passed an A-level in psychology. The nine full-time nursery workers comprise five qualified NNEBs, three YTS students and an unqualified nursery assistant. Supplementary qualifications include four staff with first-aid certificates. Two are learning sign language. Carers are all young and friendly and mix socially outside work. Students from the college come on a regular placement – catering students help with the preparation and serving of nursery meals. There is a generous training policy and budget. Staff may attend relevant courses in and out of the college.

**Children & parents** The children and parents come from a wide social spectrum and different cultural backgrounds. Approximately half are the children of students, the remaining places being taken up by staff from various colleges in York, Midland Bank employees and the general public. Children play in family groupings, although the three babies stay in their own room for most of the day. All children meet together at mealtimes and for free play indoors and out. Parents are asked to take an active role in open days, parents' evenings and outings. There are four parent representatives on the management committee. Parents are discouraged from visiting their children during the day, as the nursery feels this can be upsetting. Phasing-in over three sessions is advised, but is frequently impractical as parents often begin their college courses at the same time as their children begin at the nursery.

**Curriculum & activities** A relaxed atmosphere, where children's primary needs are looked after – nappy changing, toileting, feeding and sleeping – and where they can enjoy stimulating play experiences. Daily activities include art, craft, sand and water play, music and singing. Dance and movement sessions take place three times a week. Pre-reading and pre-writing skills are encouraged on an informal basis. Pencil holding, cutting, glueing and drawing are regular supervised activities. The National Curriculum is kept in mind, but no child is ever required to do anything unless he/she is interested and wants to. Language development, social interaction, physical and emotional development are most important. There are ample supplies of age-appropriate equipment and materials (annual budget £2500). Children garden regularly and bake once a fortnight. Library visits and outings to the shops or around the college campus are frequent. There is a close and fertile relationship with the college – drama students entertain the children with pantomimes and puppet shows; fashion students use them as models for their children's wear designs; an engineering student is designing a collapsible room-divider for the activity room. Staff monitor children's progress as a team, on a termly basis. There are no reading schemes and no qualified teacher on the staff.

**Remarks** A much needed and appreciated workplace nursery, offering friendly and safe childcare. Close and beneficial relationships with the college. The principal credits the nursery with 'humanising' the campus, and claims vandalism and aggressive behaviour have decreased markedly since it opened. Extremely reasonable fees for the quality of service provided.

# Nottinghamshire

The second-largest provider of pre-school education in the country, with half of all 3- and 4-year-olds receiving a part-time nursery place. Despite budget cuts, the Council has kept early years education a priority. Provision for working parents comes mainly from the county's 1700 registered childminders many of whom serve the rural areas. There are 13 Social Services day nurseries and four family centres, targeting children with special needs, which also offer limited places to low-income and single parents. The private sector is expanding rapidly. 60 private day nurseries, many taking babies, charge £50-£90 per week. 260 playgroups, with charges ranging from 20p per session to £2, offer over 6000 part-time and some full-time places. The local authority estimates that one in five of all pre-school children has access to some form of nursery care or education. Nottinghamshire Education and Social Services Departments did not co-operate with our research. We were unable to acquire lists of under-5s provision and only sent out questionnaires to seven nurseries, which were recommended by National Childbirth Trust members.

**Further information**

For details on day nurseries, childminders and playgroups:
Under Eights Unit
Lindens
379 Woodborough Road
Nottingham NG3 5GX
Tel: (0602) 857745

For details on nursery schools, units and classes:
Education Department
County Hall
West Bridgford
Nottingham NG2 7QP
Tel: (0602) 823823

## ARBORETUM NURSERY SCHOOL

Arboretum Street
Nottingham NG1 4JA
**Tel:** (0602) 789190

**Owner:** Notts County Council LEA
**Headteacher:** Ann Crampton, B Ed
**Type:** Nursery school offering 5 half-day sessions a week
**Children:** 3-5yrs. 40 places per session. 80 on register
**Hours:** Morning session 9.15am-11.45am
Afternoon session 12.45pm-3.15pm
Open 39 weeks a year
**Status:** State nursery school
**Number of years open:** 16
**Meals:** Milk and snacks
**1992 fees:** No fees
**Waiting list:** Very long. No places guaranteed. Visits welcome
**Registered by:** Notts County Council LEA

## CROFT FAMILY CENTRE

Family First Ltd
Albert Road
Alexandra Park
Nottingham NG3 4JD
**Tel:** (0602) 620772

**Director:** Graham Wright
**Manager:** Gill Keyse, NNEB, CSS
**Type:** Family centre offering full- and part-time care for 2-5yr-olds, plus toddler groups accompanied by parent from birth to 5yrs and after-school care for 5-8yr-olds
**Children:** 2-5yrs. 30 places. 45 on register
Toddler group 10 places
After-school care 10 places
**Hours:** 8am-5.30pm (hours flexible)
Toddler group 2pm-3.30pm Mon & Wed
3.15pm-5.30pm after-school care
Open 49 weeks a year
**Status:** Voluntary organisation funded mainly by local authority

**Number of years open:** 18
**Meals:** Breakfast, lunch, tea
**1992 fees:** £10–£1.85 per day (sliding scale depending on level of benefits)
**Waiting list:** Early registration advisable. Priority to special needs and single-parent families
**Registered by:** Notts County Council SS

## MAPPERLEY PLAINS PRIMARY SCHOOL NURSERY

Central Avenue
Mapperley
Nottingham NG5 5LD
**Tel:** (0602) 670251

**Owner:** Notts County Council LEA
**Headteacher:** Randall Lewis, B Ed, Cert Ed, Dip Ed
**Nursery Teacher:** Kay Wallis, Teachers' Cert
**Type:** Nursery class offering 5 half-day sessions a week
**Children:** 3½–5yrs. 40 places per session. 80 on register
**Hours:** Morning session 9am–11.30am
Afternoon session 1pm–3.30pm
Open 39 weeks a year
**Status:** State nursery class
**Number of years open:** 15
**Meals:** Milk, fruit
**1992 fees:** No fees
**Waiting list:** Very long. Registration from 2yrs old
**Registered by:** Notts County Council LEA

## STATION HOUSE DAY NURSERY

211 Station Road
Beeston
Notts NG9 2AB
**Tel:** (0602) 259898

**Owners/Officers-in-charge:** Elizabeth Cox, NNEB
Sheile Kempsey, NNEB

**Type:** Day nursery offering full- and part-time places and half-day sessions
**Children:** 6wks–5yrs. 28 places. 30 on register
**Hours:** 7.30am–5.30pm Mon–Thurs
7.30am–5pm Fri
Morning session 7.30am–1pm
Afternoon session 1.30pm–5.30pm
Open 51 weeks a year
**Status:** Private, fee-paying
**Number of years open:** 13
**Meals:** Breakfast, lunch, tea
**1992 fees:** £65 per week full-time
£15 per day
£7.50 per half-day
**Waiting list:** 20 names. Early registration advisable for baby places. First come first served
**Registered by:** Notts County Council SS

## VAL MARY'S DAY NURSERY

3 Robinson Road
Mapperley
Nottingham NG3 6BA
**Tel:** (0602) 604259

**Owner/Head of Nursery:** Val Daikell, NNEB
**Type:** Day nursery offering full- and part-time places, plus after-school hours and holiday sessions for 5–10yr-olds
**Children:** 1–5yrs. 25 places. 50 on register
**Hours:** 8am–6pm
Flexible hours
Open 51 weeks a year
**Status:** Private, fee-paying
**Number of years open:** 4
**Meals:** Breakfast, lunch, tea, snacks
**1992 fees:** £75 per week full-time
£20 per day
£10 per half-day
**Waiting list:** Long. Early registration advisable
**Registered by:** Notts County Council SS
**Under same ownership:** Val Mary's II, Nottingham

# Oxfordshire

Oxfordshire continues to increase its early years education budget, which currently enables 17 per cent of 3- and 4-year-olds to attend a nursery school or class part-time. The council is also committed to providing a nursery unit each time a new primary school is built, and there are several in the pipeline. Daycare provision is left to the private and voluntary sectors. Social Services provide just one family centre for children in need. The majority of full-time places come from the county's 1700 registered childminders. The voluntary sector contributes 284 playgroups, offering part-time sessional places only. Oxfordshire Social Services have pioneered a partnership scheme with the private sector, helping providers to find premises and assisting with setting-up costs, in return for subsidised and priority places. Private nurseries have increased rapidly in number, although many have waiting lists and parents report acute shortages in certain areas.

### Further information

For a list of private nurseries, childminders, playgroups, nursery schools, nursery units in primary schools and area daycare advisors:

Childcare Co-ordinator
County Hall
Oxford OX1 1ND
Tel: (0865) 810816

---

## BANBURY SCHOOL – CLIPPER DAY NURSERY

Ruskin Road
Banbury
Oxon OX16 9HY
**Tel:** (0295) 256400

**Owner:** Alex Lawrie Factors Ltd and Banbury School
**Supervisor:** Andrea Brooker, NNEB
**Type:** Day nursery offering full- and part-time places to Alex Lawrie and Banbury School employees and local community
**Children:** 6mths–5yrs. 18 places. 34 on register
**Hours:** 8am–5.30pm; flexible hours
Open 50 weeks a year
**Status:** Private, fee-paying, non profit-making
**Number of years open:** 4
**Meals:** Snacks, lunch
**1992 fees:** £65 per week full-time – under 2
£60 per week full-time – over 2
£2.60 per hour, for up to 5 hours – under 2
£2.40 per hour, for up to 5 hours – over 2
**Waiting list:** Long. Priority to Alex Lawrie and Banbury School employees. Limited community places
**Registered by:** Oxfordshire County Council SS

**Premises** Tucked away in a corner of the large Banbury School campus, the nursery has been converted from two ground-floor classrooms. It is sited next door to the first-year secondary school class. Full-length metal-framed windows down one side of the building provide a bright, cheerful environment. Children are divided into two groups – under-2s in one room and 2- to 5-year-olds in the other. The baby room has a sleeping area full of new wooden cots, a kitchen and a carpeted play area with cushions spread around. The over-2s space is rather cramped, with activities and equipment everywhere. The toilet facilities are due for an upgrade. There is a spacious fenced garden area with outdoor equipment. The nursery also has access to the secondary school gym and hopes to start using the drama rooms – this will provide much needed additional indoor space. The campus is used for regular walks.

**Supervisor & staff** Supervisor Andrea Brooker, NNEB, looks after the over-2s and her deputy is responsible for the babies. The staff are young, competent and keen. All are qualified NNEBs. There are five full-timers, with part-timers occasionally to cover for sickness and holidays. Andrea is given a free hand to structure the day, recruit staff and liaise with parents. Students and sixth formers from the school are often present on placement. Staff training is subsidised by Banbury School. The staff ratio is 1:3 for babies, 1:6 for over-2s.

**Children & parents** Children travel from Banbury and outlying villages. Priority subsidised places are reserved for Alex Lawrie employees, and teachers and staff at Banbury School. Places for the outside community are limited, and full fees are charged. Despite the social mix, there is little ethnic diversity. A parents' committee meets once a term to discuss the needs of the nursery, and parents are invited to social evenings twice a year. The nursery welcomes parents and tries to communicate with them as much as possible. Phasing-in is done with parents present. Parents requiring flexible hours are accommodated as much as possible.

**Curriculum & activities** A structured routine which provides a variety of activities throughout the day. Children are allowed to choose what they want to do within the limits of a cramped space. Time is set aside for water and sand play, painting and play dough. Both rooms have a quiet time after lunch, with under-2s sleeping in their cots and quiet activities – jigsaws, books and puzzles – for any of the older children who decide not to sleep. The school gym is used for music and movement twice a week. Specialist staff from the school are available from time to time. As the ethnic mix of the nursery is limited, a special effort is made to introduce children to various cultures through projects and topics on multicultural customs, festivals and ceremonies. There is no formal teaching of reading or writing and no written programmes. Letter formation, pre-reading and pre-number work may be introduced in a limited way, if a child appears ready. Artwork in progress during our visit was adult led, but children were enjoying the activity and receiving one-to-one attention. Theme work drives the activities which are changed regularly. Written developmental checks are given to parents every three months which monitor their child's progress.

**Remarks** Young, qualified group of nursery nurses who maintain a relaxed atmosphere. Children appear calm, confident and happy. Positive parental involvement through parents' committee. Nursery is rather cramped, especially the provision for over-2s.

# THE CLOSE NURSERY SCHOOL

14 Prospect Road
Banbury
Oxon OX16 8HH
**Tel:** (0295) 256726

**Owner/Headteacher:** Hazel Croft, Cert Ed
**Type:** Nursery school offering part-time places and half-day sessions. Some full-time places
**Children:** 3–5yrs. 26 places per session. 130 on register
**Hours:** 9am–3.30pm
Morning session 8.45am–11.45am
Afternoon session 12.30pm–3.30pm
Open 36 weeks a year
**Status:** Private, fee-paying
**Number of years open:** 35 (9 in current form)
**Meals:** Snacks, packed lunches
**1992 fees:** £4 per session
**Waiting list:** Places available at some sessions
**Registered by:** Oxfordshire County Council SS

**Premises** Purpose-built, cedar-wood building in the garden of the owner's detached, 17th-century house. Spacious and cheerful, the space is divided into two main areas, one for painting, creative and messy activities, the other for table-top work. A separate carpeted area is used for singing, stories and quieter activities. The safe, enclosed gardens are accessible from two different sides to ease parking congestion. One side leads on to a quiet road close to the town centre, the other, reached by recently constructed steps and gates, to a nearby car park. Activities and children spill over into the owner's house, where at present the toilets are situated. The living room is used for selected television programmes and the dining room becomes the special schoolroom for serious work for the pre-schoolers. Plans are underway to extend the main building in the garden to include toilets and further classroom space.

**Owner/Headteacher & staff** Hazel Croft, Cert Ed, is an experienced nursery and infant school teacher who has spent many years in local authority schools. She is enthusiastic and dedicated, with firm views on preparing children for school and high expectations. She teaches four days a week at the nursery. Her staff of eight are all part-timers to provide maximum flexibility. Continuity is not a problem, as many of the children are also part-time. The all-woman team includes one NNEB, two Cert Eds and some very experienced, mature, motherly assistants. The staff/pupil ratio is 1:8. Students from local schools and colleges also come for work experience. There is no in-house staff training policy or budget. All dealings with the children are quiet and calm. The warmth of the carers' is obvious.

**Children & parents** The children all appeared calm and content, clearly enjoying the routine of their day. The families are mainly middle-class British, from the immediate area and outlying villages and Banbury. The day we visited a Thai boy had just arrived, who spoke no English. The care and attention he received was understanding, encouraging and thoughtful. Parents are welcomed into the nursery to collect their children after each session and to discuss any problems with the staff. They are also recruited to help on outings and invited to the Christmas play held in the local primary school and to open days. Children with disabilities are integrated and helped to take part in all activities.

**Curriculum & activities** There is an old-fashioned feeling about the approach to work. Children are encouraged to take a pride in their achievements and older ones are treated as special and taken into the house to do elementary writing and reading work. Due to the diversity of schools to which the children move on, the 3Rs are kept at a basic level, although high achievers can forge ahead at their own pace. Social skills are as important as academic success. Most important of all is a loving, caring atmosphere where children feel safe and inspired. The daily routine is based around a weekly theme. Where possible, stories, songs, artwork, puzzles, games and toys reflect the topic of the week – ranging from seasonal activities such as holidays or snow, to bird recognition and serious subjects such as road safety. Artwork is a good mix of adult guidance and execution by the child, and is proudly taken home each day. Rooms are pre-prepared with activities before each session so that a child's interest is immediately attracted. A few children stay all day, but the majority come for a range of different sessions. Change-over time each day is well organised and calmly handled. Outdoor play is frequent, with a homemade Wendy house the favourite piece of equipment. The school motto is 'learning is fun'.

**Remarks** A friendly, busy nursery where each child is able to learn at his/her own pace and level. A firm routine provides the platform and stability to grow in confidence. Staff are mature and caring and ensure each child has individual attention every day.

## FAIR MILE DAY NURSERY

Fair Mile Hospital
Reading Road
Nr Wallingford
Oxon OX10 9HH
**Tel:** (0491) 651281 × 4071

**Owner:** West Berkshire Health Authority
**Nursery Manager:** Ruth Wilkinson-Smith, NNEB
**Type:** Workplace nursery offering full- and part-time places to hospital staff and local community
**Children:** 3mths–5yrs. Up to 9yrs at weekends. 20 places. 35 on register
**Hours:** 6.50am–8.10pm
Open 7 days a week, 52 weeks a year
**Status:** Subsidised workplace nursery, non profit-making
**Number of years open:** 5
**Meals:** Breakfast, lunch, tea, supper, snacks
**1992 fees:** £6–£11 per session according to hospital salary
25% sibling discount
**Waiting list:** 2-year waiting list for baby places
**Registered by:** Oxfordshire County Council SS

**Premises** The ground floor of a converted house on the edge of the psychiatric hospital campus. The children's rooms are divided by a corridor lined with their own artwork. The babies have a separate playroom and sleep room; the over-2s have access to a messy-play room and a spacious classroom, also used for large-group activities. Everywhere is bright and welcoming, with coloured curtains, murals, stencils and children's art and craft covering the walls. At the time of our visit a redecorating programme had just begun and new art display boards were being put up throughout. There is half an acre of safely fenced garden with further access to an orchard and extensive hospital grounds beyond. The garden is better equipped than most public playgrounds, with robust colourful outdoor equipment and generous space for letting off steam. A huge car park nearby enables parents who work at the hospital to park conveniently.

**Manager & staff** Ruth Wilkinson-Smith, NNEB, has managed the nursery since it opened five years ago and has been influential in creating the friendly atmosphere and smooth-running routines. The all-female care team comprises six qualified NNEB nursery nurses and two experienced unqualified carers. The nursery is open from 6.50am to 8.10pm seven days a week, and requires a complicated shift system to fit in with the hospital shift patterns worked by parents. It appears to work efficiently, but means a large fluctuation in the numbers of children and staff at various times of the day and week. Weekend working has proved unpopular when nursery staff are being recruited, and staff turnover has been a problem – five workers had left in the two years prior to our visit. Staff are all first-aid trained and attend many other training courses throughout the year, run by the hospital or local Social Services. Pay scales are in accordance with the Whitley Nursing Scale.

**Children & parents** Wide social and racial mix, with high turnover of children. The parents are often seconded to the hospital for 18 months, for psychiatric nursing experience. Flexibility of hours and all-year opening (including Christmas Day if required) is exactly what parents working long hours at the hospital need. Children can spend from breakfast to bed-time at the nursery and a relaxed, caring routine is essential. The age range at weekends is often from three months to nine years, depending on which shift is in operation or whether a family has one parent off-duty. Parents are from all levels of the hospital hierarchy, from consultants to porters. The nursery fees are earnings-related, with a subsidy from the Health Authority for the lower-paid. The nursery was set up to help retain female staff, many of whom left the hospital when they had children because there was no childcare in the area. Most people living locally work at the hospital, although there are four places set aside specifically for non-hospital parents from the community. A close relationship exists between staff and parents, with a total open-door policy. 'We are here to help the parents all we can,' says Ruth Wilkinson-Smith. There is frequent liaison, regular communication and a real effort on the part of staff to follow parents' preferred routines for each individual child. Children with disabilities and special educational needs integrate happily into nursery life and are particularly welcome.

**Curriculum & activities** The week operates around a topic, and each activity will, at some time in the week, reflect that theme. Staff select a suitable subject and inform parents in advance so that they can bring in relevant materials, puzzles, books or toys. There is no formal educational content within the timetable. Nursery policy is that children should be stimulated and looked after with love and care, not taught the 3Rs. However, pencil control, scissor work, dot joining, tracing etc are everyday activities. The large playroom is used for daily singing and music and self-expression, which are topic-related when appropriate. Outings are difficult to organise because of the shift systems, but regular visits to the village, library and local parks fit into the timetable, especially at weekends.

**Remarks** Open 365 days a year, and over 12 hours a day – offering friendly, flexible care from energetic qualified nursery nurses. Fair Mile is a workplace nursery which successfully caters for the complicated shifts and working patterns of hospital workers. Since the nursery opened, staff turnover at the hospital has declined, although it has been a problem at the nursery itself due to long hours and weekend working. High-quality childcare has enabled the hospital to retain valuable staff. Only four places set aside for non-hospital employees and very little alternative nursery provision in the area.

# MANOR NURSERY

The Manor House
Horspath
Oxford OX31 1RU
**Tel:** (0865) 874895

**Owner/Principal:** Birte Milne
**Type:** Day nursery offering full- and part-time places
**Children:** 2yrs 3mths–5yrs. 20 places. 28 on register
**Hours:** 8am–5pm
Flexible hours
Open 52 weeks a year

**Status:** Private, fee-paying
**Number of years open:** 2
**Meals:** Snacks, packed lunches
**1992 fees:** £1.75 per hour
**Waiting list:** Small, but growing. Preference to working mums and siblings
**Registered by:** Oxfordshire County Council SS

**Premises** The first floor of a stunning 16th-century manor house in the centre of Horspath, a village on the outskirts of Oxford. The owners live in the remainder of the manor. The nursery is spacious, light and recently decorated and refurbished. Accommodation includes a large playroom, a combined dining room/creative play area, a messy room for sand and water play and painting, a reading room and a quiet room for rest time, plus kitchen, toilets and office. The rooms are carpeted, with lino in the messy-play room; the atmosphere is friendly – despite the grandeur, very much like home. A large turfed and paved outside garden offers scope for strenuous physical activity. Parking is limited, but the nursery is in a quiet cul-de-sac, so picking up and dropping off is not a problem. There are local authority playing fields a short walk away and the animals at Shotover Park are within easy reach.

**Owner/Principal & staff** Birte Milne has had first-hand experience of the difficulties many working mothers face when they try to find a suitable nursery. 'I had to make do with two days in one nursery and three mornings in another, a solution which was neither satisfactory to me nor my son, but there was just not enough choice,' she says. Birte Milne decided to increase the choice in South Oxfordshire and, with the help of a trained NNEB, opened the Manor two years ago. Although unqualified, she is currently following a childcare diploma course. Her three full-time staff are NNEB qualified and the two part-timers experienced, mature carers. Staff work together well as a team, sharing all tasks equally without any obvious hierarchy. A quiet, efficient atmosphere. Staff to child ratio is 1:4 for under-3s and 1:5 for over-3s.

**Children & parents** Nursery provision is a scarce commodity in this area and parents travel in from all over south Oxfordshire. Preference is given to working mums and siblings. The parents are predominantly busy professionals requiring flexible childcare arrangements, and the nursery is popular with dons at the university. As its reputation spreads parents are beginning to travel in from even further afield. No parents' evenings are held – parents tend to have a quite formal relationship with the nursery, and many are too busy to be actively involved.

**Curriculum & activities** Children move from room to room during the course of the day, to ensure they experience a range of different activities. When we visited, the home corner had become a shop, the dressing-up room was extremely busy and other small groups of children were absorbed with puzzles, toys and in the messy-play room. Children are divided into family groupings, but come together as one big group at various points of the day for juice, stories, singing and music. Pre-school activities such as pencil control and scissor work are well supervised, but specific educational input is limited unless requested by parents. There is no reading scheme and no formal teaching. Artwork is strongly encouraged and a well-balanced mix of adult-led and child-oriented and executed. No written programmes or formal monitoring of children. Any child who can read is supported and listened to. Older children are given individual attention to help prepare them for school. Safe, stimulating and well organised. Outings once a month and full use made of the beautiful manor grounds full of wildlife for nature study.

**Remarks** A relatively new nursery still finding its feet. It is very much at home in its grand 16th-century manor house, but with the disadvantage of being on the first floor. However, children are always supervised on the stairs and doors securely bolted. High-quality childcare with stimulating and well-organised activities in a dream house. The waiting list is unlikely to remain small.

# RAINBOW CORNER DAY NURSERY

Icknield School and Community Centre
Love Lane
Watlington
Oxon OX9 5RB
**Tel:** (0491) 613923

**Owner:** Icknield Community Management Committee
**Nursery Supervisor:** Debbie Hemmins, PPA
**Type:** Day nursery offering full- and part-time places and half-day sessions
**Children:** 3mths–5yrs. 15 places. 45 on register
**Hours:** 8.15am–4.30pm
Morning session 8.30am–12 noon
Afternoon session 1pm–4.30pm
Open 45 weeks a year
**Status:** Community nursery, non profit-making
**Number of years open:** 8
**Meals:** Juice and biscuits. Packed lunches, microwave available
**1992 fees:** £70 per week full-time – under 1
£65 per week full-time – over 1
£13 per day
£6.70 per session
**Waiting list:** Long. Priority to staff at Icknield School and employees of Oxfordshire County Council
**Registered by:** Oxfordshire County Council SS

**Premises** An old further education room, with kitchen and toilets, based in the centre of Icknield Community Secondary School. Glass partitions overlook the school dining room. Space is at a premium. A small curtained-off area of the main room is used for sleeping. Hoards of equipment is piled high in wall cupboards, as there is not enough open shelf space in the room itself. Toilet facilities need some upgrading to comply with Children Act regulations – new fund-raising initiatives are required to deal with this problem. Children's art and craft work covers every available wall and ceiling space. A bright home corner and comfortable book area are somehow crammed into the room. The nursery is justifiably proud of a new, safely fenced outside play area, which is part grass, part paved, and has an extravagant log cabin. Nursery children also have access to the school playing fields.
**Supervisor & staff** The nursery was launched eight years ago on a shoestring by two local mums – Debbie Hemmins, PPA, a registered playleader and now the nursery supervisor, and her deputy Maureen Walker, PPA – on the initiative of the headmaster of the secondary school. They raised all the money and then painted and converted the nursery themselves in the evenings and at weekends. Within six months the nursery was full, with a growing waiting list. Staff paid themselves 'pocket money' in the early days, and still receive extremely modest salaries in order to keep fees affordable. There are four full-time nursery workers and one part-timer, all PPA trained. The atmosphere is warm and homely, despite the cramped premises. Staff are long-serving, down to earth, mature, motherly figures and very affectionate with the children. Students from Henley College are accepted on placement and pupils from the school often attend morning sessions or take the children for walks (supervised by staff) to learn about childcare. Parent helpers are also appreciated. The nursery nurses are well motivated and take advantage of as many Social Services training courses as possible – usually about eight a year. The staff/child ratio is an excellent 1:3. The nursery is run by a six-member management committee, comprising representatives from the school, staff and parents.
**Children & parents** Priority is to children of teachers at the school and employees of Oxfordshire County Council, but places are available to the local community. Children also attend from outlying rural villages. Hours and sessions are flexible; about six children stay all day. Virtually all transfer to state primary schools in the area. Each morning the over-3s are taken from the nursery into a different wing of the school for pre-school work, play and physical activities. Relations with the local primary school are excellent and children visit for plays, events and sports day. Parents play a crucial role, and without their exhaustive fund-raising efforts, the nursery would be forced to close. They provide over £1000 a year for essential equipment. Each pays a £7 membership fee on joining the nursery, which contributes to nursery funds. Staff salaries are covered by the fees. There is a 'hardship fund' for any family in difficulty and a 33 per cent discount for a second child. An open-door policy exists, a termly newsletter and a busy programme of events to involve parents.

**Curriculum & activities** Learning through play following the PPA philosophy. The nursery is literally bursting with equipment. Under-2s have an activity-packed morning while the older children practise some pre-school skills in the youth wing of the school. Glueing, painting, collage work, cutting, simple model-making and bubble blowing are popular morning tasks. Themes and topics are followed and regularly changed. Sunflowers, Autumn and Windmills have recently been explored. Time is set aside for free play and imaginative games. The play house has become a space ship, hospital, hairdresser's and post office. There is also a pretend shop. There are huge piles of books for every age, from material and board books for the babies to story books for older children. Sand and water play is always available. Music, songs and outside play take place daily, and cookery weekly. Children learn numbers and letters through rhymes, games, educational puzzles and construction toys and bricks. Children and staff bring packed lunches which can be heated in the microwave. Despite the lack of fresh cooked meals, lunch is a happy, social event, with children and nursery workers sitting and talking together. Children's progress is discussed daily with parents. No written development records are kept. Regular nature walks and visits are related to topic work.

**Remarks** A real family atmosphere – warm and friendly, with a team of sensible, down to earth, motherly figures, firmly in control. The quality of the relationship between staff and children, and a generous supply of good-quality equipment, more than compensate for the cramped premises. Run on a shoestring, it is dependent on fund-raising by parents, so that fees can be kept to a minimum. Long waiting list, with priority to teachers and County Council employees.

# ST NICHOLAS GARDEN SCHOOL

273 Greys Road
Henley-on-Thames
Oxon RG9 1QS
**Tel:** (0491) 575833 (answering machine)

**Owner:** Mrs E Bushell
**Principal:** Jennifer Sanderson, B Sc (Economics)
**Type:** Nursery school offering morning sessions only
**Children:** 2½–5yrs. 34 places. 32 on register
**Hours:** 9am–12 noon
Open 36 weeks a year
**Status:** Private, fee-paying
**Number of years open:** 27
**Meals:** Biscuits and milk
**1992 fees:** £300 per term for 5 morning sessions
£240 per term for 4 morning sessions
£120 per term for 2 morning sessions
£5 registration fee
**Waiting list:** Small. Less than 5 names usually
**Registered by:** Oxfordshire County Council SS

**Premises** Don't be put off by the premises, which are well past their sell-by date, because this is a happy nursery. The building is old – housing the nursery for the last 27 years – and there has never been enough money left over for refurbishment or new equipment. Known as 'Mrs Bushell's place' (she has now retired but is still the owner), it is familiar to everyone in Henley-on-Thames, where its reputation is very good. An extension of Mrs Bushell's home, it consists of two large rooms, one a conservatory-style shed. Space is limited, but everything has its place and the walls are crammed with bright, colourful children's artwork. The garden area is enormous and safely enclosed. Mrs Bushell still lives next door.

**Principal & staff** Jennifer Sanderson, B Sc, took over three years ago. Her deputy has a B Sc in physics. Due to the new Children Act, both women are preparing to take formal childcare qualifications (NVQ). The remainder of the staff is made up of a full-time nursery nurse, NNEB, and a team of part-time helpers, mainly local mums and friends. A mature, intelligent and very caring group, many of whom go back a long way.

**Children & parents** The children and their parents are very mixed socially and culturally. Some travel great distances, while others are local. Parents we intercepted at the gate admitted there was a dearth of nurseries in the area. All proclaimed themselves very happy with 'Mrs Bushell's', citing their support for the excellent balance between structured learning and play. 'All you need to do is see how happy, engrossed and stimulated the children are,' one said.

**Curriculum & activities** Children are grouped by age for the structured part of the morning, which lasts 30–40 minutes. There are three groups in all, divided between the shed and the main room, which is sectioned off by a curtain. Younger children work on colours, shapes, eye/hand co-ordination, colouring, construction and puzzles. Those in the middle age group do more advanced number and letter work, usually using worksheets. The children in the top group sit individually at old-fashioned school desks working through number, writing and reading exercises. The approach to reading is phonetic and 'look-and-say'. A number of different reading schemes are used and go home with the children at lunchtime. Each session includes specific fun activities including cookery, art and craft, free play, sand and water and outdoor games. The teaching methods are old-fashioned, the results good. There is a Nativity play at Christmas, followed by drinks and mince pies for the parents and an open day in the summer. Outings are avoided due to lack of transport, escorts and time.

**Remarks** Very traditional teaching of the 3Rs in a building which has certainly seen better days. However, welcoming, mature and dedicated staff and visibly engrossed, happy children. There is very little choice if you live in this area and are looking for a nursery with a formal teaching programme.

# VALLEY ROAD NURSERY SCHOOL

Valley Road
Henley
Oxon RG9 1RR
**Tel:** (0491) 573784

**Owner:** Oxfordshire County Council LEA
**Headteacher:** Ann Wilson, B Ed (Hons)
**Type:** Integrated county nursery school with special needs assessment unit, offering half-day sessions. No full-time places
**Children:** 3–5yrs. 23 places (+ 8 special needs places). 58 on register
**Hours:** Morning session 9am–12 noon
Afternoon session 1pm–3.30pm
Open 36 weeks a year
**Status:** State nursery school
**Number of years open:** 4½
**Meals:** Snacks
**1992 fees:** No fees
**Waiting list:** Long. Many more names than places. First come first served
**Registered by:** Oxfordshire County Council SS

**Premises** Specially adapted nursery unit alongside Valley Road Primary School which it was part of until 1988. There are two classrooms and two small side rooms. Space is tight and one of the two classrooms is little more than a lobby. However, there is still enough space for a messy-play area with painting and play dough, a home corner, water and sand trays, a book corner and construction toys. There is a toy and book library from which children can borrow on a regular basis and take toys and books home. The nursery school has its own grassy garden where children plant seeds and bulbs and take part in watering and weeding. The nursery has just won a £3000 prize in a competition, and it plans to use the money to landscape the garden. There are two sheds full of outdoor equipment. Children also care for a rabbit, a hamster, several fish and some stick insects.

**Headteacher & staff** Ann Wilson, B Ed (Hons), is headteacher of the primary school and the nursery. She is responsible for the three nursery staff, but not for special needs staff, who work with the eight children in the assessment class. They are the responsibility of Bishopswood School in Sonning Common, which provides additional staff and resources for their needs. The nursery team is made up of two part-time qualified teachers and one full-time NNEB nursery nurse, plus other part-time, voluntary helpers, parents, and occasionally students from Chiltern and Henley Colleges. The assessment unit has a similar number of staff and a speech therapist for one day a week. One of the teachers plays the piano and guitar. Training is considered vital at this nursery and staff attend INSET days at least once a term, as well as other early years courses run by the local authority.

**Children & parents** A complete cross-section of the local community attends the school, from Bosnian refugees to the children of affluent local professionals. All but a small percentage go on to local state primaries, which have a strong reputation in the area. Nursery and assessment unit children with special needs mix together throughout the day, and it is almost impossible to distinguish between them. Although the two units are nominally separate, staff and children interact easily and the happy mêlée is divided up for storytime only. Parents of children at the nursery automatically become members of the Valley Road School Parents' Association. This encourages them to take part in meetings and fund-raising activities. The school aims to form a partnership with parents. Ann Wilson emphasises, 'There is no them and us at this school, and parents are welcome to stay and help out at any time.' Most are very supportive and become actively involved.

**Curriculum & activities** The nursery curriculum is based on nine areas of learning and experience – aesthetic and creative, human and social, linguistic and literary, mathematical, moral, physical, scientific, spiritual and technological. Themes and 'centres of interest', which last for a term, are planned in advance and designed to incorporate each of these areas in relevant ways to the children's experience. A recent project was a study of clothes and fastenings. This included visits from spinners, weavers and knitters, dressing up and fashion shows, learning to put on and take off clothes, packing a suitcase, sorting fibres, footprint and sole matching, removing stains, studying fastenings and washing clothes. Although very structured, the nursery aims to ensure that each child is given as much individual scope as possible. 'Every child comes into the nursery bringing his own world with him . . . our objective is to build on this,' says Ann Wilson. The children's names feature on their coat pegs and drinking cups and they quickly learn to read and eventually to write their names. Reading and writing are encouraged through making books, lists, labels and maps and by allowing children to label their own work. The nursery library is a focal point and children take books home regularly. A strong emphasis is placed on language development and conversation. A local puppy walker from Guide Dogs for the Blind visits regularly and in return children collect aluminium cans and bottle tops for their fund-raising. Dance and movement sessions are held twice-weekly and music daily. Parents and staff together develop a written profile on each child, detailing progress, achievements, strengths, likes, dislikes and personality. Children take their profiles with them when they leave.

**Remarks** A happy, relaxed if rather cramped nursery school where children of all backgrounds and abilities, some with severe disabilities and special needs, are allowed to grow and learn together. The well-planned curriculum offers genuine equal opportunities and responds to the educational needs of all the children lucky enough to be offered a place.

## WESTFIELD HOUSE NURSERY SCHOOL

Westfield House
Bampton Road
Aston
Oxon OX18 2BU
**Tel:** (0993) 850758

**Owner:** TJ & GA Hook
**Headmistress:** Hilary Mills, Cert Ed
**Type:** Day nursery and nursery school offering full- and part-time places and half-day sessions (min 2 sessions a week)
**Children:** 2–5yrs. 64 places. 140 on register
**Hours:** 8.30am–5.45pm
9am–5pm (nursery school)
Sessions also available
Open 50 weeks a year
**Status:** Private, fee-paying
**Number of years open:** 5

**Meals:** Lunch, snacks. Packed teas after 5pm provided by parents, microwave available
**1992 fees:** £90 per week full-time
£18 per day inc lunch
£9 per session
5% sibling discount
£20 registration fee
**Waiting list:** Places available for some sessions
**Registered by:** Oxfordshire County Council SS

**Premises** The nursery is in a small village on the edge of the Cotswolds and serves a huge surrounding rural area. It is housed in the School House, a stone-built Victorian institutional building made up of four separate self-contained nursery units, each with its own entrance, classrooms and staff toilet facilities on the ground floor – less intimidating for small children than access to the whole school. The main front door opens into a bright, spacious hall which gives on to each of the units and doubles as an indoor play area on wet days, a resource store and a singing hall. Each nursery caters for a different age group – Swifts (green), 2- to 3-year-olds, Swallows (blue), 3- to 3½-year-olds, Wrens (yellow), 3½- to 4-year-olds and Robins (red), 4- to 5-year-olds. Original features have been retained where possible, including elegant full-length curtains in one unit. Each area has its own messy-play space, with easily cleaned, non-slip flooring and carpeted areas. The whole building was modernised in 1988. The two acres of mature grounds, with a fenced area surrounding a swimming pool, include a stone-built play house, large areas of grass, a hard play area and ample parking facilities. The garden is well stocked with outdoor play equipment, trikes, bikes and toys and is used whenever possible.

**Headmistress & staff** Hilary Mills, Cert Ed, has been headmistress since the school opened in 1988. A strong-willed, somewhat overwhelming woman, she is an experienced primary school teacher, adored by the children. The nursery operates peer groupings, each group with its own supervisor and staff, with Hilary responsible for the overall organisation. The 15 full-time staff and five part-timers have a wide mixture of qualifications between them including NNEB, Mont Dip, Cert Ed, PPA, Open University Diploma. Others are actively following in-service training courses. Training is considered important and encouraged. A budget is set aside each year specifically for training, and the nursery works closely with the local Social Services in-service training department, hosting many of their lectures and seminars. Staff are recruited locally and are generally young, enthusiastic and supportive. Peripatetic teachers come in for weekly ballet and music.

**Children & parents** The children come from a wide catchment area, up to 20 miles from the school. Public transport is available, but all the children are brought by car. Their parents are relatively affluent. Half the children move on to the state sector, half to independent schools. Parents can stay to help settle in and can phone at any time. A parents' meeting is held once a year for each unit and there are several different events each term. Problems and queries can be raised with the unit supervisor at any time, or by appointment. Children with disabilities and special educational needs are welcome and are well integrated.

**Curriculum & activities** Activities in each unit are based on the age of the children. The youngest group concentrate on socialising skills with activities aimed to build their confidence. The oldest group spend time learning correct letter formation and pre-school skills. This includes learning to dress themselves, message-taking and registration. Worksheets are used and each child has a folder for completed work. Any duplicates or spares are proudly carried home. Phonics are taught by the use of Letterland characters, colours, shapes and numbers. Children have frequent opportunities for pre-reading and reading on an individual basis, but there is no pressure to learn to read. Educational input is carefully planned, with written timetables for each unit. Rather than one particular philosophy of childcare or education, there is a willingness to take the best from all of them and to try new ideas. Continuous staff appraisal and monthly monitoring of children's development are undertaken. The day is extremely busy but well organised. French conversation, ballet, music, dancing, free play, discovery learning, and singing are all offered. The equipment is plentiful, carefully looked after and in good condition. Children are allowed the freedom to direct their own artwork. All the children come together for outside play and lunch in one of the

units, and staff take turns to eat with the children. Grace is said before meals.
**Remarks** Friendly nursery providing much-needed quality provision. Considered expensive for the area, but well run by professional, experienced staff. Carefully thought-out mix of care and education to stimulate children and thoroughly prepare them for infant school. Genuine commitment on the part of owners and headmistress to make this one of the best nurseries in the area. Limited places available for certain sessions, but a full-time place can usually be found when required.

# WILLOW COTTAGE NURSERY & KINDERGARTEN

Dyleys Farm
Cumnor Road
Farmoor
Oxford OX2 9NS
**Tel:** (0865) 865206

**Owner:** Mrs Grady, B Sc, PGCE
**Headmistresses:** Mrs Grady, B Sc, PGCE
Mrs Green
**Type:** Full-time day nursery and term-time kindergarten
**Children:** 6mths–5yrs  48 places (24 full-time, 24 term-time). 45 on register
**Hours:** *Day Nursery*
8am–6pm
Open 50 weeks a year
*Kindergarten*
Morning session 9.10am–11.50am
Afternoon session 12.30pm–2.50pm
Open 36 weeks a year
**Status:** Private, fee-paying
**Number of years open:** 2 at present site
**Meals:** Lunch, tea
**1992 fees:** £2.50 per hour – under 2
£75 per week full-time – over 2
£15 per day
£7.50 per session
£1 per day for lunch
**Waiting list:** 20 names approx
**Registered by:** Oxfordshire County Council SS

# WILLOWS NURSERY SCHOOL

41 Witney Road
Eynsham
Oxford OX8 1PL
**Tel:** (0865) 880504

**Owner/Principal:** Hilary Kendall, PPA (Foundation)
**Type:** Nursery school and day nursery offering full-time places and half-day sessions
**Children:** 2–5yrs. 36 places per day. 81 children on register
**Hours:** 8.15am–5pm
Morning session 8.15am–12 noon
Afternoon session 1pm–5pm
Open 50 weeks a year
**Status:** Private, fee-paying
**Number of years open:** 3
**Meals:** Snacks, lunch
**1992 fees:** £15 per day inc lunch
£7.50 per session (+ £2 inc lunch)
**Waiting list:** Places available
**Registered by:** Oxfordshire County Council SS

**Premises** Purpose-built extension on the side of the owner's detached house. About 100 yards from the main Witney road, the nursery is at the bottom of a single-track lane with parking for a number of cars. Eynsham is a quiet village in rural Oxfordshire, but accessible by bus from Witney and Oxford (20 minutes away). The nursery comprises a large, open-plan area with solid-wood room dividers, covered with beautiful art and craft displays, creating different areas for different activities. The premises are well cared for and loved. Children's work is carefully mounted, named, dated and titled by a member of staff before it is displayed. The room is awash with colour and activity – dressing-up clothes, home corner, a telephone box, dolls' house, painting easels, tables set up with different activities. Even the windows have children's paintings on them. The owner's kitchen is used for preparing meals, and she has a small office in her house. Outside, a large, well-kept garden, overlooking open fields, is stocked with fruit trees to climb, slides, swings, a Wendy house and a rabbit and guinea pig. Although there are no plans to increase the number of children at the nursery, she would like to open an extra classroom upstairs, above the nursery.

**Owner/Principal & staff** Hilary Kendall started Willows in 1989, when her own children went to school. A quiet, refreshingly unopinionated woman, she had no qualifications, although she has since done the PPA Foundation Course. The only other pre-school provision in the area is a state-run playgroup in the grounds of the village school. She works three days a week, shopping, cooking, organising, and talking to parents and does not pay herself a salary. Hilary Kendall is full of praise for the help and support she has received from the local community and West Oxfordshire District Council. Staff are selected for their nurturing qualities as much as for their qualifications. There are two full-time qualified NNEB nursery nurses, a full-time PPA assistant, a part-time qualified nursery school teacher (Cert Ed) and a part-time assistant. Staff appear friendly, talkative and loving towards the children and each other. The nursery has a good ratio for sessional care of 1:5. Hilary Kendall promotes teamwork and delegation. There are monthly staff meetings where new ideas are encouraged and discussed. The highly organised staff constantly try to improve their performance and the quality of their service. There is a rota for cooking, preparing activities and supervising and carrying out projects.

**Children & parents** Parents drive in from surrounding villages, some from as far as Oxford and Headington, while others walk from Eynsham itself. The majority use the nursery for sessions only; there were only five full-time children when we visited. Parents are from a wide range of backgrounds, but predominantly middle-class. There is no racial mix, which reflects the immediate catchment area. The children are bright, lively, confident and chatty. There are many siblings. Parents are welcome to stay with their children. Hilary Kendall is always available to talk to parents, and is eager to be flexible and respond to their needs. The children move on to local village schools, and some to the private sector.

**Curriculum & activities** The daily routine is packed with activities. Morning and afternoon sessions follow the same routine. As children arrive, they can choose a table-top activity – drawing, construction, puzzles, etc. The session proper begins with registration and talking, in a circle. Verbal communication is very important here – everything is discussed and children are encouraged to express their views. Separate activities are organised for under-4s and rising-5s, initiated by the member of staff responsible for that week's theme. All craft, artwork, projects, games etc will relate to the theme of the week, eg Road Safety, Princes and Princesses, Weddings. Rising-5s are taken in small groups, or on a one-to-one basis, to a sectioned-off corner of the room to work with the nursery teacher. They start on worksheets and, as they get older, graduate to exercise books. From 4 years onwards, children visit the teacher regularly for pre-number work, number games, talking and pencil control. There is no reading scheme. A daily file is kept on each child's work – parents may inspect. At each session, work and activities stop for half an hour for milk, biscuits and storytime, then continue for a further 45 minutes. Singing and music are taught by the staff. Outside play occurs every day in the beautiful garden. Gardening is a popular activity. There is no dance and only infrequent outings though more are being planned for the future. The nursery is closely involved with the local community – they mount a float at the annual carnival, arrange flower displays for the church and take part in various aspects of village life.

**Remarks** Relaxed, happy village nursery with loving, friendly, well-organised staff. Given the almost total lack of nursery provision in the area, parents are very lucky to live near Willows. The owner/principal is still building up the school, so it should continue to thrive and become even better.

# Shropshire

Poor nursery education provision, with only 12 per cent of 3- and 4-year-olds attending a nursery school or class, and long waiting lists everywhere. One new church-aided nursery school and family centre opened this spring, offering an additional 60 part-time places. Daycare is also disappointing. There are no local authority day nurseries and fees at the 33 private nurseries are out of the reach of low-income families. The majority of working parents use 1000 registered childminders. Playgroups are plentiful, but only offer two or three sessions a week. This year's cuts mean that all services are at a standstill.

### Further information

For details on day nurseries, childminders and playgroups:
Department of Social Services
Registration and Inspection Unit
Shirehall
Abbey Foregate
Shrewsbury SY2 6ND
Tel: (0743) 253771

For details on nursery schools, units and classes:
Education Department (address as above)
Tel: (0743) 254364

## CHAPEL NURSERY
Stafford Road
Oakengates
Telford
Shropshire TF2 6JN
**Tel:** (0952) 617548

**Owner:** Maureen Horton, City & Guilds, NNEB trainer and assessor, NVQ
**Officer-in-charge:** Sue Saxelby, Infant Teacher – Early Years
**Type:** Day nursery offering full- and part-time places and half-day sessions
**Children:** 12wks–5yrs. 50 places. 100 on register
**Hours:** 7.30am–6pm
Morning session 7.30am–1pm (inc lunch)
Afternoon session 1pm–6pm
Open 51 weeks a year
**Status:** Private, fee-paying
**Number of years open:** 5
**Meals:** Breakfast, lunch, tea
**1992 fees:** £72 per week full-time – under 2
£70 per week full-time – over 2
£14.50 per day – under 2
£14.25 per day – over 2
£7.50 per morning session – under 2
£7 per afternoon session – over 2
**Waiting list:** Babies usually registered 9–12mths in advance, otherwise no waiting list kept
**Registered by:** Shropshire County Council SS

## HALESFIELD DAY NURSERY SCHOOL
Halesfield 22
Telford
Shropshire
TF7 4QX
**Tel:** (0952) 583848

**Owner:** Marcelle Hitchin, B Ed
**Nursery Supervisor:** Donna Smith, NNEB
**Type:** Day nursery and nursery school offering full-time places and half-day sessions, plus holiday care for children under 6yrs
**Children:** 1–5yrs. 51 places (inc 6 for under-2s). 65 on register
**Hours:** 7.45am–5.45pm
Morning session 7.45am–12.30pm
Afternoon session 1.30pm–5.45 pm
Open 52 weeks a year
**Status:** Private, fee-paying
**Number of years open:** 4½
**Meals:** Mid-morning snack, lunch, tea
**1992 fees:** £65 per week full-time
£57.50 per week, max 6 hours per day
£37.50 per week for 5 sessions
£14.50 per day
£8.50 per session (excl lunch)
**Waiting list:** Minimal. All will get places
**Registered by:** Shropshire County Council SS

**Premises** On a large industrial estate just off the main A442 through Telford, with access by car only. Single-storey brick building built by National Coal in the 1930s and used originally as offices. Set on a half-acre site, the nursery has ample parking space and a large, enclosed, outdoor playground with a lawn, tarmac area and two brick sandpits. From the outside the nursery inevitably looks like an industrial unit, but the interior has been transformed and decorated with huge, cheerful, brightly coloured Disney characters painted by one of the nursery nurses. The two main day nursery rooms (one for under-3s and the other for over-3s) lie at either end of a long central corridor. In between are two baby rooms, a soft ball play room, loos, an office, a kitchen and a dining room. This is a very spacious, well-equipped nursery. Although it will never be a home from home, the atmosphere is warm and lively.

**Owner, Supervisor & staff** Marcelle Hitchin, B Ed, the owner, has never been involved on a regular daily basis. An energetic, bubbly, working mother, she lectures in higher education and spends up to ten hours a week on the nursery administration, decision-making and policy. Day-to-day supervision is left to the nursery supervisor, Donna Smith, NNEB, a cheerful, welcoming, experienced nursery nurse. There are 13 carers in all (the majority qualified): five NNEB, one B Ed, three BTEC and City & Guilds. The staff/child ratio is 1:2 for babies and 1:5 for over-2s. There are several older, motherly figures among the predominantly young, female team. The nursery takes NNEB students on placement and is always keen to accept male students. A happy, well-organised team, who are firm but loving with children.

**Children & parents** Apart from a small number of Japanese children whose parents are on a tour of duty with local Japanese firms, the rest are Caucasian. Most have two working parents. Some of the parents are professional, but many are office workers in Telford. At least half of the children attend full-time and a further third for three or more days. A minority of parents, who live in isolated rural areas, use the nursery to help their children develop socially. The children are well behaved and the older group are extremely confident and inquisitive. Virtually all, except the Japanese, go on to a wide range of state primary schools. Most parents are busy and overworked; once their children have settled in they are content with minimal involvement in nursery activities. Babies often spend two or three days a week at the nursery and are cared for by grandparents for the remainder of the week. The lack of parents' evenings, open days, plays, concerts and outings is compensated for by a strict parental reporting policy. Staff talk to parents in detail at the end of each day about their child's progress and achievements, behaviour and eating. Parents are encouraged to develop a strong relationship with their child's keyworker.

**Curriculum & activities** No particular philosophy of education or care predominates. The nursery aims to be as flexible as possible to the needs of individuals and to treat all children with love and respect. A keyworker system operates, and much of the day is spent in a family group with the same carer. Under-2s play in the mornings and sleep for some of the afternoon. The 2- to 3-year-olds are offered generous and frequent periods of free play and more directed group activities like art and craft with their keyworker. Groups come together regularly during the day for songs, rhymes, stories, limited television viewing and conversation. There is always large, fixed, play equipment and a play house available, and a quiet reading corner with a dangerously comfortable sofa. Older children are offered more educational activities in small groups. Pre-writing and number skills are encouraged, but not pre-reading. There is no reading scheme, no written educational programmes, no formal developmental checks or written reports. The requirements of the National Curriculum are taken into consideration, and there is daily outdoor play, regular afternoon dance, music and PE. The ball play room is used frequently, with great enthusiasm. Mealtimes are considered important occasions – staff eat with children, and good table manners and eating habits are firmly instilled.

**Remarks** Solid reliable care for working parents in a happy, stable and comfortable environment. Limited pre-school education for the older age group. Well equipped and reasonably priced for average earners.

# THE MOUNT NURSERY SCHOOL

Calcutts Road
Jackfield
Telford
Shropshire TF8 7LH
**Tel:** (0952) 882121

**Owner/Principal:** Heather Fraser, BA, Cert Ed
**Type:** High Scope nursery school offering part-time places and half-day sessions (min 3 sessions a week). Full-time care available on demand
**Children:** 3yrs–4yrs 9 mths, but slightly flexible. 15 places. 35 children on register
**Hours:** Morning session 8.30am–12.30pm
Afternoon session 1pm–5pm
Open 44 weeks a year
**Status:** Private, fee-paying
**Number of years open:** 5
**Meals:** Mid-morning snack, lunch, afternoon snack
**1992 fees:** £65 per week full-time
£15.50 per day
£9 per session
**Waiting list:** Not encouraged. Names taken during term prior to starting
**Registered by:** Shropshire SS

**Premises** Single-storey, brick building, adjoining the owner's large Victorian detached house set in an acre of well-kept gardens, just above Ironbridge Gorge. On arrival there was a warm welcome and we immediately felt at home. The main activity area is through a small, but very well-stocked and organised art/craft room. Everywhere is light, busy and easily accessible to children – an important aspect of the High Scope approach, which the nursery follows. The furniture and stained-wood walls are a little dull, but brought to life with excellent theme-work collages made by the children. Outside is a large yard and a grassed area with swings and climbing frame. The sandpit and play house are under cover for all-year-round use. A sitting room in the owner's house is available for quiet, directed activities. The premises feel friendly, caring and stimulating.

**Owner/Principal & staff** Heather Fraser, BA, Cert Ed, is a former secondary school history teacher who changed direction after having her own children. She is warm, gentle, thinking and enthusiastic about the possibilities of the High Scope approach to learning. She is currently taking time out to study the way young children learn, with a view to completing a further degree at Birmingham University. The Mount is now run as a co-operative, with the three other staff members encouraged to contribute observations and ideas. They work well as a team, all with relevant but different qualifications. They are young, lively and sensitive to each child's needs. Relationships with the children are loving but firm, with lots of cuddles.

**Children & parents** Happy, confident and spontaneous, the children are definitely at home in their environment. Some travel considerable distances to the nursery and most attend part-time. They come from mainly middle-class, professional families, with mums who work part-time. There are several Japanese children, some of whom started with no English, and one or two others from different cultural backgrounds. Parents are encouraged to join in, whenever they can contribute to particular themes through their own experiences. Heather Fraser emphasises that parents must, first and foremost, trust the nursery. The parents tend to have varying needs and require a flexibility not met by the rigid part-time local authority provision in the area. Most children go on to a variety of state primary schools, many to small village schools. The nursery is willing to take special needs children and has particular experience of Down's syndrome children and children with English as a second language. Heather Fraser herself has a child with learning difficulties.

**Curriculum & activities** The Mount embraces the High Scope approach to early-years learning. It is active, practical, 'hands on' learning, where success brings confidence and a positive attitude to the learning process. A typical session begins with each child choosing for him/herself three or four different activities for the first hour and a half – ranging from looking at books to woodwork or playing outside in the sandpit. Older children often plan and complete projects. At the end of this period, everyone comes together to review the activities and talk about what has been achieved. Staff observe and assist. There is no pressure, only encouragement and praise. After break comes news, an educational TV programme and outside play. The session ends with directed work in three small groups, each working on different aspects of the same theme, with the emphasis again on doing and reviewing. For example, a recent Early Technology group project was based on a long-term study of the development of frogspawn via tadpoles to frogs. When the frogs finally tried to leave their bath, each group was asked to decide what would be the best thing for the frogs. One group constructed a tight netting to stop them jumping out and a built-in feeding system to tempt them to stay. Another group wanted the frogs to leave as easily as possible and constructed a path of rocks in the bath, a boat for them to ride in and a ramp to help them jump down. The different ideas were thought through, discussed and reviewed. Most important – the children had come up with, and implemented, the ideas themselves. Sessions end with everyone coming together for a lively activity like songs, dance or music. Reading and writing are not taught per se, but evolve naturally from other activities. Early science and technology feature strongly. Good use is made of local museums and libraries, and frequent visitors are welcomed where they are relevant to theme work. Lunch is an important social occasion for staff and children. It is prepared in Heather Fraser's kitchen by a local caterer, who supplies and prepares a range of nutritious fresh and frozen meals.

**Remarks** Although expensive for the area, this High Scope nursery provides high-quality, flexible childcare and stimulating education. The hardworking and caring staff, led by an intelligent, motivated principal, ensure that children leave with confidence, independence and all the basic skills needed for school. A positive learning experience.

# Somerset

Second only to Gloucestershire at the bottom of the league table for nursery education. The county provides no nursery schools, and part-time places in nursery classes for just 2 per cent of the county's 3- and 4-year-olds. A further four or five classes are due to open in the next financial year, targeted on schools in areas of high social need. There are two Social Services day nurseries for children with special needs. A small number of the 33 private day nurseries cater for babies and toddlers under 2. In many parts of the county, registered childminders are the only form of childcare available to working parents. The local authority subsidises some childminding places and approximately 1600 playgroup places. Somerset parents report that in certain areas there is an acute shortage of affordable daycare, particularly for children under 2 and low-income families.

### Further information

For details on day nurseries, childminders and playgroups:
Department of Social Services – Children & Families
County Hall
Taunton TA1 4DY
Tel: (0823) 333451 or 255150

For details on nursery units and classes:
Early Years Officer
Education Department
25 Priory Avenue
Taunton TA1 1XX
Tel: (0823) 333451 or 255150

## ST JOHN'S (VC) INFANTS' SCHOOL – NURSERY CLASS

Glastonbury
Somerset BA6 9DR
**Tel:** (0458) 832085

**Owner:** Somerset County Council LEA
**Headteacher:** Sandra Bradshaw, BA
**Nursery Teacher:** Shirley Wiggins, Teachers' Cert
**Type:** Nursery class in state primary school
**Children:** 3–5yrs. 20 places. 40 on register
**Hours:** Morning session 9am–11.45am
Afternoon session 1pm–3.05pm
Open 39 weeks a year
**Status:** State nursery class
**Number of years open:** 1
**Meals:** Snacks
**1992 fees:** No fees
**Waiting list:** Long. Early registration advisable
**Registered by:** Somerset County Council SS

## SOMERSET MONTESSORI NURSERY SCHOOL

Norton Fitzwarren
Taunton
Somerset TA2 6RQ
**Tel:** (0823) 337107

**Owner/Principal:** Sue Fancourt, NNEB, Mont Dip
**Type:** Montessori nursery school offering full-time places and half-day sessions
**Children:** 2yrs 9mths–5yrs. 18 places. 25 on register
**Hours:** 8.30am–3.15pm
Morning session 8.30am–12.30pm
Afternoon session 1.30pm–3.15pm
Open 36 weeks a year
**Status:** Private, fee-paying
**Number of years open:** 3
**Meals:** Packed lunches, snacks
**1992 fees:** £540 per term for 3 full days and 2 mornings a week
£350 per term for 5 mornings a week
£150 per term for 2 mornings a week
**Waiting list:** None. Places available
**Registered by:** Somerset County Council SS

**Premises** Attractive, purpose-built, pre-fabricated, wooden building, surrounded by trees and grass, in a sleepy village a few minutes' drive from Taunton. There are two classrooms, connected by an entrance lobby and cloakroom, with toilets and washbasins. The classrooms are spacious, wonderfully light, clean and full of interesting pictures and displays. The main room has small tables and chairs and shelves lined with Montessori equipment, all at child height. It looks like a grown-up primary school classroom. Fresh flowers on all the tables make it more homely. The second room is sparsely furnished, but has lovely murals painted by one of the helpers. Art and craft materials and project work for the day are set out. There is a small office to one side. Children all keep wellies at school for use in the garden, where there is a climbing frame for summer play. Parking is a serious problem. The nursery is located at the end of a path, off a very busy, winding country road, and there are no parking spaces outside. The nearest car park involves walking children along a narrow, twisty and dangerous country road, with fast cars and no pavement.

**Owner/Principal & staff** Sue Fancourt, NNEB, Mont Dip, the young, Chiltern-trained owner, has wide experience of working with small children in nursery schools and hospitals. She has also worked in a school for children with special educational needs, and spent time at the Peto Institute in Hungary. Sue teaches full-time in the school. There are three teachers in all, two Montessori trained and one NNEB, currently following a Montessori correspondence course. An additional teacher comes in weekly to give music and French sessions. The staff/child ratio at all times is 1:6 or better.

**Children & parents** The children are noisy, talkative and outgoing, but well behaved. Most have middle-class, professional parents, who are very supportive of the nursery. There is a variety of nationalities. Parents can visit, talk to staff and see their child's workbooks whenever they wish. New children are kept in a small group with the same member of staff for the first half-term. Children move on in equal numbers to the private and state sectors. Children with special needs integrate happily. At present there are a number of children with speech difficulties. Sue Fan-

court is always available to speak to parents and they all have her home telephone number, if they need her help outside school hours.
**Curriculum & activities** The school follows the approach to education developed by Dr Maria Montessori. Children develop and learn within a structured framework and a carefully prepared environment, using equipment and apparatus specially designed by Montessori. The emphasis is on treating children as individuals. Children choose their first activity of the day from a good range available. At 9.15am they are split into three groups of six children, and staff work with each individual child using Montessori equipment during the next hour. Then comes tidy-up time, followed by break, the weather board and a story. Half an hour of outside play is next, with traditional songs and games. Then comes project time, with all children contributing to the project display. Each project usually lasts one or two weeks. Recent examples include Frogs, the Desert and the colour pink. The morning ends with rhymes and a story, usually from a book that one of the children has brought from home. Lunchtime is a quiet time and is followed by another group session of games, I-Spy, telling the time or colours. Each child chooses an activity, often junk modelling, play dough, Lego or puzzles. The day ends with outside play, a drink and storytime. The timetable is always flexible and is adjusted to accommodate weekly music, French and dance and movement. There are plenty of opportunities for free expression, though limited time for free play. Some children go on to read using the New Way scheme, but there is no pressure to do so. The nursery has an impressive collection of expensive Montessori equipment and an annual equipment budget of £1500.
**Remarks** A select, intimate group. Although registered to take 24 children, the owner prefers to stay small. Friendly, caring staff. Well organised and disciplined, with the emphasis heavily on 'school'. It is very much like walking into a schoolroom. A serious educational environment, which might benefit from at least some frivolous toys and play things. The lack of parking is a serious drawback.

# TAUNTON SCHOOL KINDERGARTEN & NURSERY

Weirfield
Staplegrove Road
Taunton
Somerset TA1 1DW
**Tel:** (0823) 272502

**Owner:** Taunton School
**Nursery Teacher:** Louise Vincent, Cert Ed, Kindergarten Dip (New Zealand)
**Type:** Nursery unit attached to independent co-ed school offering full-time and sessional places and half-day sessions
**Children:** 2yrs 11mths–3yrs 11mths. 21 places. 23 on register
**Hours:** 8.30am–3.30pm
Morning session 8.45am–11.45am
Afternoon session 1pm–3.30pm
Open 36 weeks a year
**Status:** Private, fee-paying
**Number of years open:** 7
**Meals:** Lunch, snacks
**1992 fees:** £635 per term full-time
£415 per term for 5 mornings a week
£25 registration fee
**Waiting list:** Long. Early registration advisable
**Registered by:** Dept for Education

**Premises** Just off the busy main road into Taunton, a purpose-built, pre-fabricated building set in the vast and impressive grounds of Taunton Junior Girls' School. A high wire fence surrounds the grounds, and open countryside stretches beyond. The nursery consists of one big room, overflowing with equipment. There are two carpeted areas, one a book corner furnished with child-size sofa and chairs, and the other a space for floor toys, building blocks, cars and puzzles. There is also a home corner and a painting and craft area. Children's cloakrooms are off the main room. It is a bright and jolly place, with children's artwork covering the walls and hanging from the ceiling. The outside area is vast, safe and securely fenced. It contains a patio and a climbing frame, with wood chippings for safe landings, seesaw, bikes and trikes. There is also a grass meadow with a wooden playhouse, slide and plenty of space for running wild.
**Nursery Teacher & staff** Louise

# SOMERSET

Vincent, Cert Ed, came to this country from New Zealand 18 years ago. She is extremely experienced and has set up two nurseries of her own in the past. She has sole charge of the day-to-day running of the nursery, but the school holds the purse strings and makes the major spending decisions. There are two other full-time members of staff, both NNEB qualified and experienced. A mature, motherly part-timer works mornings only. NNEB students from a local college train at the nursery. There is no budget or policy for staff training and development. The staff/child ratio is 1:7.

**Children & parents** The nursery is only open to children who will be staying on at Taunton School, many until they are 18. Parents come from the professional middle classes. There is an open-door policy, an active parents' association and two social events a year. Most communication between parents and staff takes place at the beginning and end of the day. The school has a good reputation in the area, and there is strong demand for places. All children wear a school uniform.

**Curriculum & activities** The nursery day unfolds in an informal and flexible way. During morning and afternoon sessions, there is a choice of activities. The curriculum covers art, craft, news, stories, modelling, collage, dance and imaginative play and free play, indoors and out. Younger children watch appropriate television programmes. Time is set aside for pre-reading, pre-writing and number work to open the way for a smooth transition into the kindergarten and its more structured timetable. Workbooks are used and the Ginn reading scheme, levels 1 and 2. Children are only taught to read when they are ready and willing. Approximately a third of the children will be using Ginn level 2 by the time they move on. Workbooks and records on reading ability and developmental progress are shared with the parents. Children take home their reading books and word tins. The emphasis is on learning through experience.

**Remarks** A delightful nursery for those who will be progressing through Taunton School. Well equipped, relaxed and friendly, with the staff visibly working as a team. The outside play area and beautiful setting are as stimulating as the classroom.

# WYVERN NURSERY

Lyngford Park School
Bircham Road
Taunton
Somerset TA2 8EX
**Tel:** (0823) 336175

**Owner:** Somerset County Council LEA
**Manager:** Stephanie Jenkins, NNEB, RSH, BA
**Type:** Workplace nursery offering some part-time places and half-day sessions, plus holiday playscheme for 5-10yr-olds. Places available to Somerset County Council employees and Midland Bank employees at present
**Children:** 3mths–5yrs. 26 places. 37 on register
**Hours:** 8am–5.45pm
Open 49 weeks a year
**Status:** Private, fee-paying, non profit-making
**Number of years open:** 3½
**Meals:** Lunch and tea
**1992 fees:** £72.50 per week pre-booked
£75.50 per week temporary use
£15.10 per day
£7.55 per session
£1.30 per day supplement – under 2
**Waiting list:** 20 on list. Places cannot be guaranteed
**Registered by:** Somerset County Council SS

**Premises** Single-storey, pre-fabricated building in the grounds of Lyngford Park School. Difficult to find, it is tucked away down a cul-de-sac in the middle of a housing estate. There are two playrooms, a kitchenette and an office/staff room. The main playroom for over-2s, known as the Sunshine Room, is well equipped with toys, a home corner, a book corner, a quiet area and children's artwork on the walls. Leading off it is a small, but attractive, tiled dining area full of plants and mobiles. The baby room, known as the Rainbow Room, is equally brightly decorated with paintings and collages. It is light and airy, full of toys and six cots, with each child's sleeping preferences carefully noted. There is a nearby kitchenette, used for heating bottles and drinks. A small outside covered play area provides sand and water play and a Wendy house, used nearly every day. The school playing fields are available during the summer.

**Manager & staff** Stephanie (Stevie) Jenkins, NNEB, RSH, BA (OU), has been working with children for 30 years. She is friendly and extrovert, and was a Woman of Today finalist for the South West in 1992. She has a staff of five full-time NNEB nursery nurses and two PPA assistants who job-share. Two relief workers stand in during sickness and holidays. A male volunteer comes in for 1½ days a week – he originally came on student placement and liked the nursery so much that he has continued on a voluntary basis.

**Children & parents** There is a good social mix, but no cultural or racial diversity, reflecting the local community. At present, places are available to children whose parents work for either Somerset County Council or the Midland Bank (six places). Consequently there is a wide catchment area and children go on to state schools in Taunton, Yeovil, Wellington and other neighbouring towns. Children stay in colour-coded family groups – they use a particular colour of cup or plate which helps everyone to know who relates to whom. Each child is allocated a keyworker. The nursery operates an open-door policy towards parents.

**Curriculum & activities** The curriculum is based on the High Scope programme, which encourages children to make decisions for themselves and to explain their actions once they have completed an activity. During 'work time' each child plans an activity with the adult in their group. Once this has been done and any problems thought through, the child goes off and completes his/her activity under unobtrusive supervision. The children are then brought back together to share their successes and failures with the group. They then tidy away their activities themselves. There is also time for children to play in small groups and for the whole nursery to come together for stories and outdoor play. Pre-number and pre-writing skills are taught and most children can recognise and write their names by the time they transfer to primary school. Records on each child are regularly updated and available to parents. Food is prepared at the Moorhaven Elderly Care Centre and delivered to the nursery ready to serve. A holiday playscheme for 5- to 10-year-olds operates from 8.30am to 5pm during school holidays and half-terms. One of Stevie's ambitions, to link or twin with a nursery in France, has just been achieved. She also aims for the nursery to become a training establishment for the High Scope curriculum, which she has recently introduced.

**Remarks** An excellent workplace nursery providing a much-needed service in an area where there is almost no provision for under-2s. Highly professional and very experienced staff. The nursery went independent in 1993 so no further subsidies will be forthcoming from the council. If numbers fall as a result of higher fees, Wyvern will offer places to the local community.

# SOUTH YORKSHIRE

# Barnsley

With no local authority day nurseries and only four small private ones, there is growing demand for childminders. 129 have re-registered so far, and there is a backlog of applications waiting to be processed. The provision of nursery education is good (48 per cent), but unequally distributed around the district, with a number of the 51 classes concentrated in certain areas and none in others. The LEA estimates that just over 60 per cent of children will have had one or more terms of nursery education before they start school.

**Further information**

For details on day nurseries, childminders and playgroups:
Registration and Inspection Unit
Department of Social Services
Dearne Town Hall
Goldthorpe
Rotherham S63 9EJ
Tel: (0709) 888355

For details on nursery units and classes:
Education Department
Berneslai Close
Barnsley S70 2HS
Tel: (0226) 770770

## SUMMERLANE DAY NURSERY

Chamber of Commerce Training (Barnsley) Ltd
Industry House
Summer Lane
Barnsley S70 2NY
**Tel:** (0226) 733838

**Owner:** Kirklees & Wakefield Chamber of Commerce and Industry Ltd
**Nursery Manager:** Jane Chapell, NNEB
**Type:** Workplace nursery offering full- and part-time places and half-day sessions to Chamber of Commerce and Midland Bank employees and local community
**Children:** 6mths–5yrs. 35 places. 74 on register
**Hours:** 8am–6pm
Flexible hours
Open 52 weeks a year (excl bank holidays)
**Status:** Private, fee-paying, non profit-making
**Number of years open:** 2½
**Meals:** Breakfast, lunch, tea
**1992 fees:** £63.50 per week full-time
£13.75 per day

**Waiting list:** Growing. Long for babies, moderate for over-2s
**Registered by:** Met Dist of Barnsley SS

**Premises** A large, modern, four-storey building near Barnsley town centre. Converted from an old textile mill and used as an adult and youth training centre. The nursery occupies the self-contained ground floor, and has been totally refurbished. This is a busy part of town with no parking, but there is a dropping-off area at the side of the building. There are regular bus and rail services. Inside, the children's rooms are light and colourful. Newly decorated white walls display cheerful nursery pictures and carefully chosen examples of children's work. The large main playroom, with a separate craft area, offers wide scope for creativity – sand, water, play dough and clay – and a good selection of table and floor activities. The home corner is tastefully carpeted and filled with good-quality, solid wood furniture – kitchen, sink, telephone kiosk, bedroom, tables and chairs. The quiet room, soon to be converted into a baby room, has a large selection of books, television, comfortable bean bags, rocking chairs and cushions. One room is used as a gym and physical playroom containing non-slip flooring and quality climbing equipment. It is used frequently, as outside play facilities are meagre. The small grass and concrete area, due to be resurfaced, is dull and uninteresting, completely enclosed by buildings and brick walls. The nearest park is over a mile away – too far to visit.

**Manager & staff** Jane Chapell, NNEB, has been at the nursery since it opened. She has many years' Social Services and private nursery experience in senior positions. She reports to the Chamber of Commerce. Her all-woman team comprises a deputy (NNEB), nursery officer (NNEB) and six nursery assistants (five NNEB, one City & Guilds). It is a young group, with similar backgrounds and a range of experience, including special needs and nannying. Two are fresh from college. All have worked at the nursery since it opened. They are friendly, flexible and work as a team. There is no qualified nursery teacher on the staff. Jane spends at least 15 hours a week with the children and says, 'I like to be where the action is.' NNEB students visit for four days every fortnight, supervised by the deputy manager. The staff/child ratio is 1:3 for babies, 1:5 for over-2s. Training is an important feature and an ongoing process. Staff attend on-site health authority and Chamber of Commerce courses.

**Children & parents** Wide social and cultural mix – most children are from Barnsley, but a few from Sheffield. The immediate catchment area is industrial. Some parents are professional, some trainees and others employees of the Chamber of Commerce. The Midland Bank reserves six places. About a third of the children are from single-parent families. Special needs children are welcome – at present there is a child with cerebral palsy and one requiring speech therapy. There are regular parents' meetings, and parents are encouraged to help out, as well as comment or complain. They can telephone at any time of day for news of their child. New parents come in with their children for an hour a day two or three weeks prior to their start date. There are staggered dropping-off and collecting times, because of the parking problems. Some children wear a sweatshirt with the nursery logo but it is not compulsory. The nursery carries a large stock of clean clothing in case of accidents.

**Curriculum & activities** Jane says, 'My aim is to provide good, well-balanced care for all our children – treating each child as an individual.' The equipment and toys are plentiful, of high quality and stimulating. Some of the attractive wooden furniture is made by trainees on carpentry courses in the building. The nursery says, 'Play is the business of childhood,' and believes that everything is learnt through play. The curriculum revolves around monthly themes, which are planned annually in advance – examples are 'Shapes and Numbers', 'Farms and Animals', 'Springtime' and 'Winter'. Children work in small, age-related groups and spend time all together each day at mealtimes or watching television. The staff ensure that the children cover all activities during the course of the nursery day – free play, gym, painting and craft, planned activities, music, topic work and more structured learning. Literacy and numeracy are encouraged but not pushed. Children can read or recognise several words by the time they leave. The Usborne First Learning scheme is used and there are piles of picture and first books. Basic science, cookery, modelling and dance and movement fit into the weekly timetable. Occasional outings to the library, pet shop or to buy birthday presents are undertaken, and there are regular visits from the police, fire brigade and hospital nurses to talk about their jobs. Meals are prepared in the restaurant upstairs by catering trainees. Developmental and progress reports are kept; children are formally monitored once a year.

**Remarks** High-quality care and flexible hours for working parents. Modern, clean building, with excellent equipment and indoor facilities. Austere, confined outdoor space and no nearby park. Limited spaces for the local community.

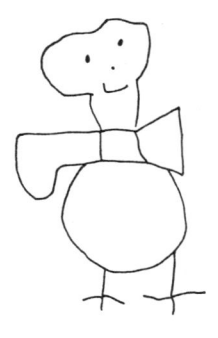

# Doncaster

Large-scale unemployment in the area has resulted in a fall in demand for full daycare. Three private day nurseries have closed, leaving 11 private and two hospital trust nurseries. Social Services have one day nursery for high-priority placements. The 206 childminders have vacancies. Doncaster has a good record for nursery education, with over half the area's 3- and 4-year-olds attending part-time. However, there is some expansion. There are 60 nursery classes, and a few have increased their numbers from 30 to 40.

## Further information

For details on all types of local authority childcare and education:

Education Services
The Council House
College Road
PO Box 266
Doncaster
Tel: (0302) 737204/05

For details on private nurseries:

Inspection Unit
Rosemeade Centre
May Avenue
Balby
Doncaster DN4 9AE
Tel: (0302) 850921

# Rotherham

With only one private nursery, offering 12 places, and no local authority day nurseries, parents in Rotherham rely on relatives and childminders. There are 331 registered childminders and the number is still rising. Small signs of improvement are evident – three private nurseries are in the process of registration and three colleges of further education provide full daycare for the children of staff, students and Midland Bank employees. A recent survey by the Child Information Line showed an increase in demand for full-time care, as more women return to work. The education authority offers some 4-year-olds the opportunity of a part-time place in a nursery class for two or three terms before they turn 5 and begin school. Provision is uneven, with long waiting lists and most places concentrated in areas of high population. There are currently three nursery schools and 47 classes attached to primary schools, one of which opened this autumn. The LEA is keen to open new units, but lacks funds. One idea being pursued is to reduce numbers in existing classes and create new places in areas with no facilities. More than half of the area's 17,800 under-5s have no access to any form of childcare provision.

## Further information

For further information on all types of childcare:

Rotherham Under Fives Together
Durlston House
5 Moorgate Road
Rotherham S60 2EN
Tel: (0709) 369537

# RAWMARSH NURSERY SCHOOL

Barbers Crescent
Rawmarsh
Rotherham
S Yorkshire S62 6AD
**Tel:** (0709) 710123

**Owner:** Rotherham LEA
**Headteacher:** Judith Shelley, Cert Ed
**Type:** Local authority nursery school offering half-day sessions. No full-time places
**Children:** 3yrs 4mths–4yrs 11mths. 160 places. 140 on register
**Hours:** Morning session 9am–11.30am Afternoon session 1pm–3.15pm Open 38 weeks a year
**Status:** State nursery school
**Number of years open:** 53
**Meals:** None. Hot or cold milk
**1992 fees:** No fees. £1 per term for baking
**Waiting list:** Long. 231 names. All children on list guaranteed some attendance. Early registration advisable
**Registered by:** Met Dist of Rotherham LEA

**Premises** Wide, symmetrical, 1940s building, all on one floor, set in extensive, attractive grounds. A reasonable standard of decoration inside and out. There are two open-plan nursery 'bases', one on each side of the building – each a mirror image of the other. Each classroom is an exciting voyage of discovery, laid out in different, well-resourced activity areas: a quiet area with shelves of books and beautiful patchwork cushions made by the staff; a home corner, furnished with child-sized wooden furniture and hand-knitted 'food' including ice cream melba and cauliflowers, again the handwork of staff. There is time set aside for woodwork, collage and model-making and a tactile table with clay, dough and potting compost. There is a non-slip wet area, with sand (wet and dry), water and painting and a brick and construction base. The imaginative play area offers dressing-up clothes, shop, hospital, hairdresser's, cooker and two guinea pigs. Cloakrooms and toilets are off the main classrooms. The nursery also has a community room used by parents, local pensioners, health visitors and the school nurse. The headteacher's office doubles as a quiet room for stories. There is also a general office for administration. The outside area is a delight – a huge grassy expanse, with a paved area, imaginatively laid out with a sandpit, paths, flowers, shrubs and mature trees. The nursery was awarded a grant from Children in Need four years ago, and spent it on landscaping this area. Two large huts are brimming with outdoor equipment. The whole area is safely enclosed with chain fencing and hedging. Parking is available either in the grounds or on a quiet side road. Bus services from all directions.

**Headteacher & staff** Judith Shelley, Cert Ed, has been headteacher for six years. Prior to this, she was deputy head of an infant and junior school. Her particular subjects are art and music. The team consists of a deputy head (Cert Ed), class teacher (Cert Ed) and four nursery nurses (all NNEB). There are also two non-teaching assistants for special needs children (one is NNEB and the other has done a childcare course). Staff meet daily, before sessions. Staff turnover is minimal – only one person has left over the last two years. Ages range from 20s to 50s and they are a friendly, united team, who have lunch together between sessions. Judith Shelley spends about 25 hours a week teaching – a job she loves. There are two pianists and two guitar players among the staff and a piano in each nursery base. They are also skilled in arts and crafts. Five days a year are devoted to staff training and development. Students attend from time to time. Parent volunteers are welcome. The staff/child ratio is 1:10.

**Children & parents** Families must live within the borough of Rotherham, a steel and mining area with high unemployment. They are mainly white, but very mixed socially. About a quarter of the children come from one-parent families. Children with language and communication problems, and developmental delays, are not uncommon and there is regular contact with speech therapists. The children move on to local state schools. When a place becomes available, parents are invited to new-parents' meetings, to look round the nursery and meet staff. This is followed by a visiting day for children and parents. There is an open-door policy towards parents. Informal coffee mornings are held and termly newsletters sent out.

**Curriculum & activities** Rawmarsh has a detailed curriculum document entitled 'Working Hard at Playing'. Children are not grouped (ex-

cept for administration purposes) and have complete freedom to choose to play wherever they wish, inside or out. Teachers follow the children and guide, teach or supervise, as appropriate. Judith Shelley says, 'We favour a child-centred approach, where the provision is well structured, but children have free choice. They are encouraged to be independent learners, with the support of the staff. We encourage children to think for themselves, and make their own decisions; not simply to follow instructions.' The curriculum is structured and carefully planned. There is an abundance of stimulating, child-oriented equipment (annual budget £2500) and games – all of excellent quality and well maintained. Strong emphasis on art and music. Informal dancing, games and music daily, baking once a week and a school lending library twice a week. No reading schemes, but in the majority of cases children can read and write their own name when they leave. The foundations of every academic subject – maths, science and nature, language and literacy can be found in the range of activities. Children are busy, talkative and working hard at playing. Each child has a drawing and painting file for their work. Records are kept on progress and development, and all files are available to parents. Full use is made of the lovely garden and plentiful outdoor equipment.
**Remarks** Quality pre-school education for older children. Experienced and talented staff and spacious, well-resourced facilities. Successful integration of children with special educational needs. A very popular school, which welcomes parental involvement. Because of the pressure on places, many children can only be offered two or three sessions a week.

# Sheffield

There has been rapid growth in the private sector here over the last five years. In 1991, there were 15 private day nurseries, and now there are 32 – the majority in the affluent south-west of the city. The more deprived north-east suburbs contain most of the 11 local authority day nurseries, but demand far outstrips supply. The 750 registered childminders are still the most popular providers of childcare, especially for babies, as most private-sector nurseries take children only from 2 years old. Sheffield provides nearly 6000 places in 75 education authority nursery schools and classes for 44 per cent of 3- and 4-year-olds. The council is actively looking for new ways to increase childcare provision, through partnership with the voluntary and private sectors. Initiatives include encouraging businesses to buy places at a premium in community-run nurseries thus subsidising fees for local children. Another plan is to sell off council property for a housing development and to build a new children's centre with the revenue. Overall there is not enough adequate, accessible or affordable childcare. A spokeswoman for the city's Children's Information Line says, 'The biggest change has been in the increased employment of nannies and how they are used. They are no longer regarded as Mary Poppins figures, who live in and can only be afforded by the rich. In fact, if you have two or more children, they can be cheaper than a childminder, and far more families are sharing nannies.'

### Further information

For a detailed computer print-out covering all services for under-5s:

Children's Information Line
14-18 West Bar Green
Sheffield S1 2DA
Tel: (0742) 756699

# ENDCLIFFE CHILDREN'S NURSERY

The Rise
Endcliffe Rise Road
Sheffield S11 8RU
**Tel:** (0742) 663230

**Owner:** Fred Farrant, Meadowbank Nursery Services Ltd
**Supervisor:** Kath Johnson, NNEB
**Type:** Day nursery offering full- and part-time places
**Children:** 6mths–5yrs. 40 places. 83 children on register
**Hours:** 8am–6.30pm
Morning session 8am–1pm
Afternoon session 1pm–6pm
Flexible hours
Open 52 weeks a year
**Status:** Private, fee-paying
**Number of years open:** 4
**Meals:** Lunch, tea, snacks
**1992 fees:** £45 per month for 1 session a week – under 2
£40 per month for 1 session a week – over 2
Discounts for full-time attendance
**Waiting list:** Variable, depending on age. Easier for over-2s
**Registered by:** Sheffield City Council SS

**Premises** Large, stone, detached, Victorian house in its own grounds, about a mile from the university. The nursery occupies six rooms on four floors, including a basement used for the over-2s. A reception area, dining room, babies' room and kitchen are on the ground floor. The baby sleep room, office, staff room and sluice are on the first floor, with further offices in the attic. There are toilet facilities on each floor. The children's rooms have a homely atmosphere, with numerous comfortable sofas and large, open shelves filled with equipment. The babies' play room has an activity gym, camp beds and baby bouncers; the walls are covered with collages and paintings. Over-2s have a room for messy play in addition to their main playroom, with sofa, easy chairs, television, home corner and piles of toys and games. The enclosed garden includes grass and gravel areas, as well as beds for the children to grow flowers and vegetables. There are log seats, a climbing frame, a sandbox and two sheds crammed with play equipment.

**Owner, Supervisor & staff** The owner, Fred Farrant, has no involvement in the day-to-day running of the nursery, but is responsible for the building and resolving any major problems, if they occur. The supervisor, Kath Johnson, NNEB, worked as Fred Farrant's nanny for seven years before taking over the nursery when it opened. She has additional typing and computer skills. She and her deputy report to the owner regularly, to discuss future plans and finance. The 11 full-time and two part-time nursery nurses range in age from 19 to 54. Seven are qualified, six unqualified. There is no teacher on the staff. They create a happy and relaxed atmosphere. There is normally one carer to three children – a generous ratio, which means that there is always in-built cover for absences. Unqualified staff are experienced and have been childminders or care assistants, or have brought up large families of their own. Students come for work experience, and a speech therapist and special needs helper visit weekly.

**Children & parents** The nursery serves a very large catchment area, with the children coming from as far as Stockport, Huddersfield and Derbyshire. A small number of children are from one-parent families and there are some from West Indian, Japanese, Pakistani and mixed-race families. Most have professional working parents. Parents are encouraged to bring new children for short trial periods. There is an open-door policy and flexible start and finish times to fit in with parents' work patterns. Children are grouped according to age and appear happy, busy and talkative. There are special needs children with autism and cerebral palsy attending at present. Children transfer to a wide number of state primary schools. Those who remain in the private sector go on to independent schools such as Birkdale, Westbourne and Ashdell.

**Curriculum & activities** Children learn through play in a structured environment. There are daily opportunities to participate in construction, art and craft, imaginative play, sand and water, jigsaws, table-top play, home corner, looking at books, storytime, physical activities, dancing and music. We also observed lots of cuddles and spontaneous affection between children and staff. Older children are introduced, informally, to pre-reading, pre-writing and pre-number skills, only if they are interested. Most leave able to read and write their own names. There are no reading schemes or formal teaching, but a full record-keeping procedure is followed. Children are taken on outings when staffing allows, but this is sometimes difficult to arrange because of the widely differing hours of attendance. Equipment is plentiful and of good quality (annual budget £1000–£2000). There is an emphasis on music and singing games, which are done at least twice a day. Role-play with creative dressing-up clothes is popular. Staff and children eat together to create a social, family gathering.

**Remarks** A happy, homely, well-equipped nursery, offering high-quality care with excellent opportunities for children to learn through different play experiences. Flexible hours to cater for the needs of working parents. A good staff/child ratio overall offers scope for one-to-one relationships. No qualified teacher to plan educational programmes.

## FULWOOD PLAY CENTRE

Hallam Methodist Church
Nether Green Road
Sheffield S11 7EG
**Tel:** (0742) 304681 (owner's home)
**Owner/Principal:** Tina Powell-Wiffen, Mont Dip
**Type:** Nursery school offering 5 morning and 2 afternoon sessions a week
**Children:** 2yrs 4mths–5yrs. 40 places. 94 on register
**Hours:** 8.30am–3.30pm
Morning session 8.30am–12.30pm
Afternoon session 12 noon–3.30pm
Open 38 weeks a year
**Status:** Private, fee-paying
**Number of years open:** 13 (6 in current premises)
**Meals:** Snack, packed lunches
**1992 fees:** £315 per term for 5 morning and 2 afternoon sessions a week
£235 per term for 5 sessions a week
£132 per term for 2 sessions a week
**Waiting list:** Variable. Most will secure places eventually
**Registered by:** Sheffield City Council SS

**Premises** The basement of a stone-built, late-Victorian Methodist church in a socially mixed residential area with a high student population. The spacious, but rather characterless premises, rented from the church, are enlivened by displays of the children's artwork. Toilet facilities have recently been upgraded. The main playroom has a home corner, table-top activities, scope for artwork on a one-to-one basis, a book trolley, numerous tables and chairs and a piano. The smaller playroom, for messy play, doubles as a cloakroom. There is a large sports hall for boisterous physical play, equipped with slide, bikes, trikes and large building bricks. Two further rooms, used for church activities, are also available as quiet teaching areas. There is a kitchen for preparing snacks and cookery sessions. An adequate, enclosed grass area provides for outside play, with equipment taken out when required. Endcliffe Park is within easy walking distance and children are sometimes taken there.

**Owner/Principal & staff** Tina Powell-Wiffen, Mont Dip, originally set up her nursery school in a much smaller building, and moved to the current premises six years ago. Her deputy has worked with her for ten years and other staff are equally long-serving, with a good mix of ages and social backgrounds. Seven are qualified teachers or nursery nurses, four are unqualified but experienced. One has strong artistic talents and another is a qualified nurse. A peripatetic music teacher visits for 12 hours a week. A speech therapist and special needs tutor come to help children with special needs. Five YTS trainees also assist. Staff participate in PPA training courses to keep up to date with childcare practice. There is a good staff/child ratio of 1:5 or better.

**Children & parents** Mostly local and from very mixed backgrounds. Many are the children of foreign students attending the university from South Korea, Germany, France, Mauritius, Egypt and Eastern Europe. Roughly half have parents who both work, one usually part-time. Parents' comments and views are welcome and staff are approachable and accessible. New children are phased-in slowly, with sessions gradually increasing to three hours. Children are grouped by age, with one member of staff acting as keyworker to five children. They work busily and happily in small, well-organised groups. Children with speech problems, sight impairment, autism, mild behavioural problems and some degree of disability can all be integrated. 70 per cent of children go on to state primary schools such as Nether Green and Hallam Infants. In the private sector, boys go to Birkdale and Westbourne and girls to Ashdell and Brantwood.

**Curriculum & activities** Some Montessori teaching equipment is used and children are encouraged to develop a sense of independence and self-confidence, with education and care running in tandem. The first part of the morning is devoted to free play, from a wide choice of activities, including art and craft. After break comes music, singing and dancing, and children end the morning in small groups supervised by their keyworkers. Each child works at his/her own level within the group. There is a different topic each week – 'triangles' when we visited. Older children are encouraged to develop pre-literacy skills and, when they are ready, start to read using look-and-say flashcards. Afternoon sessions are similar, but without the more formal group work. There are termly outings to places of interest such as Whirlow Farm Trust, and small groups of older children visit museums and parks. Some teaching of French and other European languages is imminent, as several nursery workers have foreign language skills. Children are monitored regularly and written progress reports are kept.

**Remarks** A good standard of care and teaching and a strong, diverse staff team. Reasonably priced, considering the high staffing ratios and the opportunities for children to work in small groups. The premises are not ideal, as the church hall and warren of rooms attached to it do not easily lend themselves to a homely, child-centred environment.

# MONTESSORI NURSERY SCHOOL

137 Psalter Lane
Sheffield S11 8UX
**Tel:** (0742) 552626

**Owners:** Tony and Judy Fearnehough
**Principal:** Judy Fearnehough, NNEB
**Type:** Montessori nursery school offering full-time places and half-day sessions
**Children:** 2–5yrs. 75 places. 200 on register

**Hours:** 9am–3.15pm
Morning session 9am–12 noon
Afternoon session 1pm–3.15pm
Open 32 weeks a year
**Status:** Private, fee-paying
**Number of years open:** 21 (6 under present ownership)
**Meals:** Milk, packed lunches
**1992 fees:** £420 per term full-time
£321 per term for 5 morning sessions a week
£187 per term for 5 afternoon sessions a week
£155 per term for 1 full day a week
**Waiting list:** Variable
**Registered by:** Sheffield City Council SS

**Premises** Large, detached, stone-built house in a middle-class suburb of Sheffield. Parking is permitted on the nearby main road, but can be difficult close to the school. The spacious, colourful nursery, with grass-green carpets throughout, occupies nine rooms on two floors, with a lean-to recently converted into a permanent art room. Children are divided into six different groups, according to age. Each group has its own well-equipped room, with interesting displays of work. There is also a music room with a piano, where children staying all day have lunch. The kitchen is immaculate. The large, well-designed outdoor play area includes swings, climbing frames, bridges, sandpit, portable water play tunnels and a slide.

**Owner/Principal & staff** Tony and Judy Fearnehough took over the nursery school six years ago, when the previous owner retired. Judy Fearnehough, NNEB, had already been teaching at the school for three years. She and her deputy lead a united and very enthusiastic all-female team of 11 full-time and nine part-time nursery workers. With a wide age range and an excellent mix of training and experience. All have either teaching or nursery nurse qualifications. Staff wear a smart uniform of red jumpers with black skirts or trousers and openly demonstrate their love of children. There is plenty of humour and witty repartee. The five qualified NNEBs are also Montessori trained. There are monthly staff meetings and regular 'in-house' training. A peripatetic music teacher visits for five hours a week and YTS trainees help out four days a week. The staff/child ratio is 1:5.

**Children & parents** Mainly local, white and middle-class, with a small number of children from Greek, Afro-Caribbean and Indian families. The children are talkative, busy and polite. Approximately five attend full-time, increasing to 75 per cent in the summer months, just before they go on to school. The rest are part-timers. Children under 2½ years old are considered for a full-time place only under exceptional circumstances. Parents are welcome and stay until new children settle. They are invited to plays and concerts and are encouraged to comment or complain whenever necessary. A Down's syndrome child attends at present; any requests for special needs places are considered individually.

**Curriculum & activities** Staff follow the Montessori method of teaching. There is a large selection of Montessori educational toys and teaching aids and constant praise and encouragement for each child. Good manners, self-discipline, concentration and consideration for others are considered important. Children are split into small groups, usually by age. A normal morning session begins with half an hour of free play, followed by project work – painting, numbers, letters, cooking – in small groups; then milk time and picture books, jigsaws and garden play. At 11am children form two larger groups for music, movement and singing. All children are read a story before they go home. Afternoon sessions are slightly shorter and less structured, with a more flexible timetable. Children are introduced to pre-literacy skills, though they are not formally taught to read. They learn to read and write their own names, and each is encouraged to progress and achieve according to his/her capabilities, without stress or strain. Home reading schemes are supported. Older children are taken to parks and on nature walks in small groups, and visitors come in frequently to talk about their jobs and work; the dentist, the fire officer and a local farmer are regular guests.

**Remarks** A long-established Montessori nursery school, which has built up a deservedly high reputation in the area. Abundant equipment and good premises. The nursery workers offer an excellent range of teaching and childcare qualifications and experience. Excellent care and pre-school education for parents who can afford it. Fees can be paid in stages in cases of hardship. A personal and friendly service in spite of the large numbers.

# Staffordshire

A part-time nursery place for 24 per cent of 3- and 4-year-olds. Many schools have waiting lists, especially in urban areas. Social Services provide 14 day nurseries for families in need. The private sector offers working parents the choice of 105 day nurseries and 1600 registered childminders. However, high unemployment means that the real need in this county is for more affordable provision. There are over 300 part-time, sessional playgroups, unevenly spread across the county, most with waiting lists. Many more are needed.

**Further information**
For details on day nurseries, childminders and playgroups:
Department of Social Services
Inspection Services
3a Chapel Street
Stafford ST16 2BX
Tel: (0785) 224804

For details on nursery schools, units and classes:
Education Department
Under Fives Team
Tipping Street
Stafford ST16 2DH
Tel: (0785) 223121

# LANGDALE NURSERY SCHOOL

Earls Drive
Clayton
Newcastle
Staffs ST5 3QH
**Tel:** (0782) 617110

**Owner:** Staffs County Council LEA
**Headteacher:** Gill Hampton, Cert Ed, LRAM, LGSM
**Type:** Nursery school offering 5 half-day sessions a week
**Children:** 3yrs 9mths–4yrs 10mths. 40 places. 80 on register
**Hours:** Morning session 9am–11.30am
Afternoon session 1pm–3.30pm
Open 39 weeks a year
**Status:** State nursery school
**Number of years open:** 26
**Meals:** None
**1992 fees:** No fees
**Waiting list:** Registration after 2nd birthday
**Registered by:** Staffs County Council LEA

# LITTLE ANGELS DAY CARE NURSERY

The Weeford Centre
Weeford
Staffs WS14 0PW
**Tel:** (0543) 481778

**Owners/Managers:** Erica Beeching, Mont Dip
Stephanie Sadler, Mont Dip
**Type:** Day nursery offering full- and part-time places
**Children:** 2–5yrs. 24 places maximum. 41 on register
**Hours:** 7.30am–6.30pm
Open 51 weeks a year
**Status:** Private, fee-paying
**Number of years open:** 2½
**Meals:** Breakfast, lunch, tea, snacks
**1992 fees:** £50 per week full-time
£10 per day
£1 per day for lunch
**Waiting list:** None
**Registered by:** Staffs County Council SS

**Premises** The nursery shares a solid-looking, modern, former infant and junior school building with the Council's agricultural department in an isolated rural area, close to the A5 and A38 near Lichfield. Students come in a few times a week to plant shrubs and to do general gardening practice. The exterior is cold and unappealing, with the nursery entrance at the side, badly signposted. Inside is more welcoming, well decorated and light. There are three children's rooms, kitchen, loos and a lean-to cloakroom. Children have a room for messy and water play, with paint and easels (aprons available). There is a carpeted main room with play house, tables, storage shelves and cupboards full of equipment as well as a quiet room, also carpeted, for rest, stories and reading. Shelves here are lined with a good selection of books. Outside, the garden is well fenced, but has limited equipment – it is mainly a space for running around.

**Owners/Managers & staff** Erica Beeching, Mont Dip, and Stephanie Pugh, Mont Dip, own the nursery. Erica also runs a part-time Montessori nursery in the next village which is open two mornings a week, and Stephanie used to work for her. They both teach 3½ days a week at Little Angels and share the day-to-day running of the nursery. At the time of our visit, a full-time NNEB was being recruited. Two further part-time staff are qualified, one NNEB and the other PPA, and one part-timer is unqualified. A specialist music teacher visits once a week. All staff are young, adaptable and team-spirited. There is emphasis on good communication, especially with parents.

**Children & parents** The children come from families that are generally middle-class career-minded, although some parents are struggling to pay the fees. Social Services pay for two places for children from their lists. No public transport is available – all travel by car, some from as far away as Cannock. About 70 per cent of the mothers work. Parents are encouraged to take part in Christmas activities at the nursery, but otherwise their involvement is minimal. There are no parents' evenings. Children are an equal mix of boys and girls, but there are not many 4- to 5-year-olds. Leavers tend to come back for school holiday care. The nursery potty-trains, but waits until parents initiate the process to ensure back-up at home. The majority of the children go on to state primaries; one or two have gone on to private

school in the past. Interested parents ring for a prospectus and are invited to visit at any time.
**Curriculum & activities** Each day children are offered a variety of art and craft activities, with messy sand and water play a permanent fixture. There is a generous supply of construction sets and table-top activities. Time is set aside each day for a Montessori-based education programme for the older children. They practise pencil control and pre-reading and writing skills in special workbooks compiled by their teachers. There is no reading scheme, but a desire to read is encouraged. Letters and phonic sounds are taught with Montessori sandpaper letters. A good knowledge of numbers – both recognising their shapes and understanding the concept – is achieved by everyone. Basic addition and subtraction are taught, but only if and when a child is ready. Staff and children eat together. After lunch the smaller ones sleep, while the older children peacefully work on their books or use Montessori apparatus to develop their concentration. Outdoor play takes place on demand, provided someone is free to supervise. There is strong emphasis on gaining independence. Children are encouraged to feed and dress themselves and to do as much as possible without adult intervention. The older ones help the younger ones – children are grouped vertically (mixed ages), specifically to foster a caring attitude. Storytimes are considered very important. Weekly or fortnightly themes are explored through artwork, conversation, stories, songs and pictures. Dance and drama are once a week. There are no regular outings – only on special occasions.
**Remarks** High-calibre staff in a relaxed, loving atmosphere. Quality of care and the curriculum make Little Angels very good value for money. A relatively new nursery which needs time to build up a reputation. Plans to operate a separate baby unit are underway at the time of writing.

# WILLOWS COUNTY PRIMARY SCHOOL – NURSERY UNIT

Anglesey Road
Lichfield
Staffs WS13 7NU
**Tel:** (0543) 251338

**Owner:** Staffs County Council LEA
**Teacher-in-charge:** Jill Hassall, qualified teacher
**Type:** Nursery unit in state primary school offering half-day sessions
**Children:** 3yrs 6mths–4yrs 11mths. 60 places. 120 on register
**Hours:** Morning session 9.45am–11.35am Afternoon session 12.45pm–3.15pm Open 40 weeks a year
**Status:** State nursery class
**Number of years open:** 16
**Meals:** Milk and biscuits mid-session
**1992 fees:** No fees. 50p per day voluntary contribution for snack
**Waiting list:** Moderate. Priority given to children who will attend Willow County Primary. Places allocated to almost all on list, but only for 1 or 2 terms prior to primary school
**Registered by:** Staffs County Council LEA

**Premises** A self-contained, single-storey brick building to the rear of Willows County Primary School. Dull and uninspiring from the outside, it is dominated by two high-rise tower blocks only a few hundred yards away. The school is on the north side of Lichfield and serves all young families living on this side of town. The fenced play area outside – available at all times to children – has a large concrete area with bikes and trikes, a sandpit and a grassy, landscaped area. The interior is a large, airy, L-shaped room, with the open-plan part divided into four carpeted areas. These act as home base for the four groups into which the 60 children are divided and can be curtained off for privacy. It is cheerful, bright and welcoming, with myriad activities set out on tables and the floor, imaginative mobiles spinning from the ceiling and attractive artwork displayed on the walls (though much of it done by adults). The room nevertheless shows signs of the constant wear and tear to which it is subjected. A large verandah on the side of the building has recently been enclosed, conservatory-style, and this serves as a noisy, all-weather playroom. Large play equipment like the climbing frame lives here, along with the nursery guinea pig, conspicuously ignored, and a wet sand tray. There are two cloakroom areas with coat pegs and toilets, a staff room and separate staff loo. Everywhere you turn there is something creative and new to look at. No child could possibly be bored here.

**Headteacher & staff** Jill Hassall is the qualified teacher-in-charge, having set up the nursery unit 16 years ago. She is a friendly, mature, down-to-earth woman, with extraordinary energy. She has tremendous teaching experience and a grown-up family – parents and children listen to her with respect. As well as being involved in every aspect of running the nursery, she is responsible for her own particular group of 15 children. There is one other qualified teacher and two qualified NNEBs. Each session has four staff members. One of the NNEB posts is job-shared – one assistant working mornings, the other afternoons. There are absolutely no staff turnover problems – in fact, this nursery team qualifies for a long-service award. The head has been here for 16 years, the other teacher 14 years and one of the NNEBs 14 years also. A solid, stable group, which has built up excellent relationships with local families, seeing several children from the same family pass through the school. Student teachers and NNEB students are frequent visitors and help improve the staff-child ratio of 1:15.

**Children & parents** Priority is given to local children who will attend Willows County Primary. The children come from a variety of social backgrounds and income brackets. Some mothers work, but those who do not are encouraged to join a rota of parents who help in the nursery regularly. The children are predominantly white, but from time to time there are also children from Chinese, Bangladeshi and West Indian families. Before children start at the nursery their parents are invited to a meeting where the nursery philosophy is explained. In particular, Jill Hassall emphasises that the nursery is for the benefit of children, not their parents. Parents can stay with their children to settle in, but staff prefer them to leave as soon as possible.

**Curriculum & activities** A noisy, extremely busy nursery, where children have an enormous variety of choice each day. The emphasis is on confidence-building, making own choices, self-organisation and self-reliance. Apart from group times – storytime, singing and pre-reading and writing – children are free to be self-directional, and are guided only if totally aimless. On the morning of our visit, the 60 children present were busy and totally absorbed almost all the time. Similarly, staff were watching and working with the children all the time. Children, without exception, were treated with respect and love, and all responded positively and responsibly. Music is a daily part of the curriculum; the head plays the guitar and there is a piano. There is time set aside for pre-reading and pre-writing work. However, priority is given to physical, emotional, social and developmental progress, rather than academic achievement or the 3Rs. Any surplus from the voluntary contribution for mid-morning snacks goes towards equipment or to replace worn-out toys.

**Remarks** Successful and popular nursery unit with long-serving, dedicated teachers and nursery nurses. A nursery where little has changed over the years. An excellent preparation for school, and children graduate to primary school self-motivated and independent. Unfortunately, because of the pressure for places, only available to children for one or two terms.

# Suffolk

Just 26 day nurseries for the whole county and only one of them is local authority owned. There is virtually no provision for babies or toddlers under 2, even in the private sector. No full-time places in the 64 nursery classes attached to primary schools, and only six full-time places in the one nursery school. Only 16 per cent of the county's 3- and 4-year-olds receive any nursery education. In the villages and coastal areas, 1600 registered childminders provide the flexible hours required by many part-time working mothers.

**Further information**
For details on day nurseries, childminders and playgroups:

Department of Social Services (Early Years)
17 Tower Street
Ipswich IP1 3BE
Tel: (0473) 210641

For details on nursery schools, units and classes:
Education Department (Pupils' Services)
St Andrew's House
County Hall
Ipswich IP4 1LJ
Tel: (0473) 230000

## LINDA EVANS CHILDREN'S DAY CARE CENTRE

The Old Chapel
65a The Street
Capel St Mary
Ipswich
Suffolk IP9 2EG
**Tel:** (0473) 310767

**Owner/Principal:** Linda Evans, Hons Dip Mothercraft and Child Welfare, OU Cert for Pre-School Child
**Type:** Day nursery offering full-time places and half-day sessions
**Children:** 6mths–5yrs. 23 places per day (inc 4 under-2s). 46 on register
**Hours:** 8.15am–5.30pm
Morning session 8.15am–1pm
Afternoon session 1pm–5.30pm
Flexible hours
Open 48 weeks a year
**Status:** Private, fee-paying
**Number of years open:** 11
**Meals:** Breakfast, lunch, tea
**1992 fees:** £85.50 per week full-time – under 2
£71.75 per week full-time – over 2
Part-time fees scaled according to hours
**Waiting list:** Long
**Registered by:** Suffolk County Council SS

**Premises** Converted chapel in the heart of a pleasant, active village. Every inch of space in the long, narrow building is utilised. A raised level at one end is divided into the baby room and a quiet room for books and play. An abundance of play materials and equipment is stored and displayed around the main room at child height. Though space is limited, children move freely from one activity to another, mindful of each other's needs. Colourful decorations and a warm, snug atmosphere. There is a new kitchen for preparing meals and recently redesigned cloakroom and toilets allow children free access. Outside are a rubberised play area with imaginative climbing apparatus, a large sandpit, a Wendy house and a trike and bike path.

**Owner/Principal & staff** Linda Evans is principal and decision-maker, having bought and converted the building ten years ago in response to local demand. Linda has experience as a nanny, childminder and nursery worker and has slowly built up the nursery. She is a valued member of the village community. When we visited there were two full-time qualified staff (NNEB) and eight part-timers – mainly unqualified assistants. Unqualified staff attend short playgroup and first-aid courses. Co-operation and efficiency are priorities.

**Children & parents** This is very much a nursery for the village community, but because of the total lack of nursery care for under-2s in the area, children also come from far and wide. The majority of mothers work full-time. Family backgrounds are diverse, but predominantly middle class and professional. A strong, very active Parents' Association organises fund-raising events and helps with outings and visits. Parents play an active role in the nursery and are always welcome. Many continue their support long after their children have left the centre. Unusually good communication between parents, nursery, local primary school and local education authority.

**Curriculum & activities** There is no timetable, nor any written programmes or policies. However, the day is firmly structured. Games and activities help recognition of number, shape and colour but no actual teaching is done. Daily cutting, sticking and making activities develop manipulative skills. Storytelling is a part of every child's day and speech. Social skills and independence are encouraged. There is no division into age groups and no special educational programmes for the pre-schoolers. The stated aim is to provide a home-like environment and routine, where children mix and play in a caring and friendly atmosphere. Art and craft work is largely produced by the children themselves with staff encouragement. Lack of space limits activities – there is no large space for musical games, movement and mime, dressing up or extensive messy play. However, the atmosphere is warm and caring. There are lots of cuddles and the relationship between staff and children is close.

**Remarks** Warm, loving childcare in a safe, efficient environment, offering flexible hours for working parents. Does not aspire to strong educational programmes or a stimulating learning environment. Would benefit from more space and possibly more qualified staff.

# SWEET BRIAR NURSERY SCHOOL

Gatehouse Farm
Syleham Road
Hoxne, Eye
Suffolk IP28 4LZ
**Tel:** (0379) 75480

**Owner/Principal:** Sarah Buckley, Cert Ed
**Type:** Nursery school offering morning sessions
**Children:** 4–5yrs. 18 places. 34 on register
**Hours:** 9.30am–12 noon
Open approx 34 weeks a year
**Status:** Private, fee-paying
**Number of years open:** 4
**Meals:** Mid-morning milk and biscuits
**1992 fees:** £4 per session
**Waiting list:** Approx 12 months. Priority to siblings
**Registered by:** Suffolk County Council SS

**Premises** A single-storey brick building converted from a cattle barn, in the yard of the owner's 15th-century farmhouse. The entrance to the school is through the children's outside play area, which is securely fenced off from the rest of the yard. Parents can drive into the yard. The school itself is one large room decorated with children's work. The nursery is bright and warm, with windows the length of the south-west-facing wall. There is a variety of equipment ranging from construction toys to book and home corners. From the classroom children can observe farm life. The outside play area is easily accessible, but would benefit from some fixed climbing equipment.

**Owner/Principal & staff** Sarah Buckley, Cert Ed, owns the nursery and teaches every day. She has 16 years' teaching experience, having worked in London and run her own nursery school in Singapore. She employs five qualified teachers/carers and one experienced, but unqualified assistant, all on a part-time basis. There is a high ratio of staff to children for sessional care (1:5) and they work closely together throughout the morning. Teachers are recruited for their imaginative and lively approach. Between them they play a variety of musical instruments; music forms an important part of the morning's activities.

**Children & parents** Children who attend come from the surrounding farms and villages. As this is a rural area, there is a good social mix. Children start at the nursery in the term of their 3rd birthday and, as the majority go on to their village primary school, most stay until they are 5 years old. The interaction between the different ages is very good as the children all work and play together as one group. The school does not have open days but parents are encouraged to make comments and enquire about their child's progress. They are also strongly advised to spend a morning at the nursery before they register.

**Curriculum & activities** The school has a weekly theme which is discussed each morning after the register has been taken. The theme is developed during the morning's activities, which include art and craft work and nature study. There are no formal groupings and children are encouraged to choose their own activities. They are taught number and letter recognition, together with pencil control, but there is no emphasis on teaching them to read. On Wednesdays some children bring a packed lunch and stay for a music lesson, at extra cost. The rural location enables children to observe farm animals and the workings of a farm at close quarters. Short sessions of PE and gym are held on wet days, dancing and yoga on an informal basis. No formal monitoring of progress or written reports.

**Remarks** An extremely friendly, small, family nursery school with a relaxed atmosphere. Sarah Buckley's aim is to provide a stimulating environment where children can develop their social, emotional and intellectual needs. An unpretentious, caring nursery in an area with poor provision for the under-5s.

## WEST SUFFOLK COLLEGE NURSERY

Out Risbygate Street
Bury St Edmunds
Suffolk IP33 3RL
**Tel:** (0284) 701301 × 242

**Owner:** West Suffolk College
**Principal:** Gill Roney, NNEB
**Type:** Day nursery offering full-time places to West Suffolk College staff and students and Midland Bank employees and local community
**Children:** 0–5yrs. 23 places (inc 6 under 2)
**Hours:** 8.30am–5.30pm. Open 51 weeks a year
Flexible hours
**Status:** Private, fee-paying
**Number of years open:** 2½
**Meals:** Lunch and tea
**1992 fees:** £17 per day
£2.50 per hour
£1 per day for lunch
**Waiting list:** Long. Priority to college staff and students and bank employees
**Registered by:** Suffolk SS

**Premises** Tucked away in a quiet, sheltered corner of the college grounds, in a wooden, pre-fabricated building. Big sunny windows look on to a grassy play area, which is bordered on one side by a high brick wall that originally enclosed a kitchen garden and is well fenced on the other sides. The nursery is on one level, thoughtfully designed and furnished. It is divided into three areas by low partition walls, for under-2s, 2- to 5-year-olds and a quiet play and library area. A separate room accommodates cots for babies. A further room, catering for 2-year-olds, is planned to open this year. All is brightly decorated with children's art and craft work and gay curtains. The entrance hall is lined with named folders for children's work and messages for parents. A pleasant hum of activity prevails. A wooden shed outside shelters outdoor play equipment. Neat hutches and runs house the nursery pets – a rabbit and guinea pig. There is generous space for prams with sleeping babies and for children to play.

**Principal & staff** Gill Roney, NNEB, the nursery principal, is an energetic mother of teenage children. A no-nonsense, capable person with a gentle, sympathetic approach to children, she has ten years' nursery experience, including a year running her own nursery. She has eight staff, all qualified NNEB, four of whom are full-time. The week's programme and projects are decided at a weekly staff meeting when the ideas and needs of individual children are discussed. All staff are involved in the day-to-day running of the nursery, although it is Gill who has the final say. She reports at regular intervals to the college governors. Building alterations and major policy changes take place at their discretion. Gill has constant and helpful communication with the college through its Services Officer. There are nearly always extra helping hands, as the college runs an NNEB and BTEC nursery course, and students use the nursery to gain practical experience under the supervision of the principal.

**Children & parents** The nursery was started in 1990 by West Suffolk College and Midland Bank as a result of college policy to bring in more mature students and female teachers. The nursery is open to families not connected with the college, although priority is given to college staff, and five subsidised places are held for students. Midland Bank at present holds three places. There is a cultural mix of children, but they are predominantly white and from middle-class backgrounds. Nearly all of the children are there because their mothers work. The children are divided into age groups for some activities, but the partitions are open for much of the day. Older children are encouraged to help with smaller ones and take responsibility for certain tasks – this is something they obviously enjoy. Parents come in at all times of the day to collect their children and there is always a member of staff available to discuss problems and progress. There is a parents' committee which helps with fund-raising activities, and parents are invited to attend nursery functions, such as summer picnics, birthday parties and a Christmas Nativity play which involves all the children.

**Curriculum & activities** The day is structured, providing the security of routine. There are abundant play materials and equipment of all kinds. Older children who are ready form small groups and participate in number work, pre-reading and pre-writing activities. They also visit the library once a week. There is ample space for messy play, artwork and large-group activities, and the sand tray and water trough are always out. A large dressing-up box is available for imaginative play and weekly cookery classes are held for all but the babies. Music is greatly encouraged and enables all the children to come together each morning for singing and playing musical instruments. Gill Roney is the piano player and musician. A quiet corner is available at all times. The atmosphere is relaxed, and children can choose from a huge selection of educational and fun activities, helped and supervised by high-quality staff. Meals are an important social occasion. Lunch is prepared in the college canteen, and children and staff sit down together for conversation; good table manners are encouraged. Outdoor play takes place in a large, well-equipped play space. The children look after nursery pets and plant bulbs and seeds in a gardening plot.

**Remarks** High-quality, full-time nursery catering primarily for the children of working parents. Intelligent balance between care and education, with well-qualified, professional staff. The only nursery in the area to accept babies under 2 years of age. Children of diverse ages and abilities, from contented babies to grown-up 4-year-olds, are all happily and busily stimulated.

# Surrey

Access to provision varies considerably. Those who live in the more populated areas in the north of the county have some hope but parents in the rural south have little choice. Nursery education is available to only 11 per cent of 3- and 4-year-olds. A mother in Surbiton thoroughly recommends her local state nursery school, while another in Epsom Downs reports, 'There is no state provision at all for the under fives in this area. Playgroups are plentiful and vary considerably in quality.' In recent years, all local authority day nurseries have been closed and replaced by a network of family centres, targeted at children in greatest need. The private sector has grown rapidly. 72 private nurseries offer places for a range of age groups, with flexible hours and varying costs. Virtually all have waiting lists. Childminders are also in great demand, with 2600 already registered and more going through the process. The Surrey Pre-school Playgroups Association boasts that it is the single largest provider of pre-school services in the UK. They have 332 members, catering for over 18,000 children. Again waiting lists can be long. The council is currently promoting 'out of school' provision and holiday playschemes.

**Further information**

For details on day nurseries, childminders and playgroups:
Department of Social Services
AC Court
High Street
Thames Ditton
Surrey KT7 0QA
Tel: (081) 541 8704

For details on nursery schools, units and classes:
Education Department
County Hall
Penrhyn Road
Kingston
Surrey KT1 2DJ
Tel: (081) 541 9501

For additional information on playgroups:
Surrey Pre-school Playgroups Association
The Regional Office
Neale House
Moat Road
East Grinstead
West Sussex RH19 3LB
Tel: (0342) 312553

## CARING DAYCARE

Pitfold House
Woomer Hill
Haslemere
Surrey GU77 1QA
**Tel:** (0428) 661960

**Owner:** Veronica Craig
**Manager:** Sarah Walton, NNEB
**Type:** Day nursery offering full- and part-time places and half-day sessions
**Children:** 3mths–5yrs. 43 places. 78 on register
**Hours:** 8am–6pm
Morning session 8am–1pm (inc lunch)
Afternoon session 1pm–6pm
Open 51 weeks a year
**Status:** Private, fee-paying
**Number of years open:** 4

**Meals:** Breakfast, lunch, tea, snacks
**1992 fees:** £437.35 per month for 5 days a week
£24.15 per day
Non-refundable registration fee 10% of 1 mth's fees
£2 for ballet
£1.45 for swimming
**Waiting list:** None
**Registered by:** Surrey County Council SS

## SWANSMERE SCHOOL (formerly AMBLESIDE FIRST SCHOOL)

Ambleside Avenue
Walton-on-Thames
Surrey KT12 3LL
**Tel:** (0932) 227494
**Owner:** Surrey County Council LEA
**Head of Nursery:** Hazel Craig, ARAM, Dip Ed
**Type:** Nursery class in primary school
**Children:** 3–4½ yrs. 80 places. 78 on register
**Hours:** Morning session 8.55am–11.45am
Afternoon session 1pm–3pm
Open 40 weeks a year
**Status:** State nursery class
**Number of years open:** 18
**Meals:** None
**1992 fees:** No fees
**Waiting list:** Apply after child's 2nd birthday. A few places reserved for special needs
**Registered by:** Surrey County Council LEA

## TEDDY'S NURSERY SCHOOL

Sandhurst Pavilion
Yorktown Road
Sandhurst
Surrey GU17 8BJ
**Tel:** (0252) 879151
**Owner/Nursery Supervisor:** Heather Geens, NNEB, AMRSH, PCN, Mont Dip
**Type:** Nursery school offering full- and part-time places and half-day sessions
**Children:** 3–5yrs. 20 places. 21 on register
**Hours:** 9.15am–3.30pm Tues, Wed, Thurs
Morning session 9.15am–12.15pm Mon–Fri
Afternoon session 1pm–3.30pm Tues, Wed, Thurs
Open 36 weeks a year
**Status:** Private, fee-paying
**Number of years open:** 5
**Meals:** Snacks, packed lunches
**1992 fees:** £325 per term for 5 morning sessions a week
£260 per term for 4 morning sessions a week
£195 per term for 3 morning sessions a week
£150 per term for 3 afternoon sessions a week
£10 registration fee
**Waiting list:** Places available
**Registered by:** Berkshire County Council SS

## WILLOW TREE NURSERY

c/o Salfords First School
West Avenue
Salfords
Redhill
Surrey
*Postal Address*
Crutchfield Lane
Hookwood
Surrey RH6 0HT
**Tel:** (0737) 774275 and (0293) 768268
**Owner/Principal:** Gundela Kerfante, Cert Ed, Mont Dip
**Type:** Montessori day nursery offering full- and part-time places
**Children:** 2½–5yrs. 25 places. 44 on register
**Hours:** 8.30am–4.30pm
Open 50 weeks a year
**Status:** Private, fee-paying
**Number of years open:** 3
**Meals:** Lunch, snacks
**1992 fees:** £230 per month full-time
£96 per month for 2 days a week
£120 per month for 5 half-days a week
£74 per month for 3 half-days a week
**Waiting list:** Long. 94 names
**Registered by:** Surrey County Council SS

**Premises** A single-storey, 20-year-old, brick-built annexe to Salfords County First School, conveniently close to Reigate, Redhill, Crawley and Horley. There are two spacious school rooms and an outside playground, exclusively for nursery use. Each room has small tables and chairs and low, open shelves allowing children access to all the Montessori equipment. One room is designed for practical life exercises, such as transferring objects and water from one container to another, cleaning shoes, silver and brass, laying the table, sewing, playing with magnets, keys and locks and cutting out. The second room, for sensorial play, has natural brick walls covered with educational pictures and houses a book corner and Montessori equipment for children to learn about shapes, colours, textures and numbers. Outside there is a grass area with slides, sandpit, roundabout and a hard playground with painted-on game layouts, clocks and other activities. There are also playhouses, a climbing frame and outdoor water play.

**Owner/Principal & staff** Gundela Kerfante, Cert Ed, Mont Dip, completed her training in Germany, where she ran a small kindergarten. When she moved to England, she opened the nursery in her own home, before moving to the present premises rented from Salfords First School. She plans to expand to become a Montessori centre, which will also take older children. She works at the nursery full-time, assisted by a calm, friendly, female staff of four. All the nursery workers are Montessori trained and qualified. Two are currently studying for an international diploma, and Gundela and her deputy are beginning a course on children with special needs. Staff attend Saturday seminars at the Montessori Centre. Peripatetic teachers come into the nursery to teach French and German. Students are accepted on work experience. Teachers speak enthusiastically about a former male student who was 'absolutely marvellous' and everyone, including the children, hopes that he will not be the last.

**Children & parents** The children come exclusively from middle-class families and several are non-British and bilingual. They are visibly and unusually kind to one another, and talk quietly and politely among themselves as they go about their different activities. The atmosphere is calm, the noise level uncannily low. Parents are able to talk to staff at any time; there are monthly parents' meetings and regular open evenings, social events and newsletters. Parents' comments are listened to and frequently acted upon. Older children help new ones to settle in, creating good peer group bonding from the start. Some children transfer to state primaries, such as Wraycommon and South Nutfield, and others to private schools such as Micklefield or Reigate. Special needs children are welcome, provided they do not require nursing care. A Montessori teacher, trained to help dyslexic children, has recently been recruited. Gundela Kerfante is willing to subsidise some children whose parents would not otherwise be able to afford the fees.

**Curriculum & activities** Learning through play, firmly based on Montessori principles. Montessori teaching equipment is used throughout to develop the five senses and for mathematics, writing, reading and an understanding of music. Children learn independence and self-awareness. The environment is very carefully prepared and all equipment has its own special place which never changes. Children return apparatus when they have finished using it. The staff are quiet observers, allowing children to explore and discover for themselves and guiding only when they judge it necessary. Children are encouraged to be considerate to one another and orderly. There are opportunities for self-expression through art, craft, dancing, music and movement and a daily discussion group, when the whole group get together to share their news. Children are taught French and German. Those who are ready are encouraged to read via the Montessori method using sandpaper letters, movable alphabet and word boxes. Regular outings are organised and parents assist. Visitors come in to share experiences or to entertain. Children receive an ample supply of cuddles and comfort and, above all, praise and encouragement. Detailed written assessments on each child are completed regularly.

**Remarks** A first-class example of a Montessori nursery school. A dedicated owner and committed, trained staff. Excellent selection of Montessori equipment and teachers who know how it should be used in a carefully prepared environment. Long waiting list, but there are active plans for expansion.

# TYNE & WEAR

## Gateshead

Gateshead is working progressively towards providing some form of educational experience for all 3- to 5-year-olds. Currently about 35 per cent of 3- and 4-year-olds receive a part-time place in a nursery class. The LEA plans to open at least one new nursery unit each year, and wherever there is surplus capacity in existing primary schools, accommodation is adapted to provide nursery facilities. Gateshead has completed its statutory review of services, and publishes a comprehensive up-to-date list of all provision for under-5s – care and education. There is one large, 62-place day nursery for children with a range of special needs and another sizeable pre-school centre for Social Services referrals. Six family centres are situated in social priority areas. They are highly staffed and involve parents and the community. Out-of-school clubs are promoted, and a special scheme matches babies and toddlers to childminders and pays the fees when necessary. There are also 11 private day nurseries which cater for babies. The 45 registered playgroups take children from 3 years only.

**Further information**

For details on day nurseries, childminders and playgroups:
Department of Social Services
Under Eights Section
Civic Centre
Regent Street
Gateshead NE8 1HH
Tel: (091) 477 1011

For details on nursery schools, units and classes:
Senior Officer for Primary Education
Education Department
(address and telephone as above)

## Newcastle-upon-Tyne

Forty-three per cent of 3- and 4-year-olds have some experience of life in a nursery class before they start school and nearly all primary schools have a nursery class attached. Full-time daycare is less well provided, with five Social Services day nurseries taking high-priority children and only 11 private day nurseries registered. Most working mothers rely on families or childminders. Five of the 70 playgroups are funded by the local authority.

**Further information**

For details on day nurseries, private nursery schools, childminders and playgroups:
Social Services Under Eights Section
1 Osborne Terrace
Newcastle-upon-Tyne NE2 2NE
Tel: (091) 212 1057

For details on nursery schools, units and classes:
Education Department
Civic Centre
Barris Bridge
Newcastle-upon-Tyne NE1 8PU
Tel: (091) 232 8520

## ASHFIELD NURSERY SCHOOL & PARENTS' CENTRE

97–99 Elswick Road
Newcastle-upon-Tyne NE4 8DD
**Tel:** (091) 273 5587

**Owner:** Newcastle City Council LEA
**Headteacher:** Joan Lister, Cert Ed
**Type:** Nursery school offering full-time places and half-day sessions
**Children:** 2½–4½yrs. 104 places. 130 on register
**Hours:** 8.50am–3.15pm
Flexible hours
Open 36 weeks a year
**Status:** State nursery school and family centre
**Number of years open:** 60
**Meals:** Lunch
**1992 fees:** No fees
**Waiting list:** Very long. Full till '94/95
**Registered by:** Newcastle City Council LEA

**Premises** A listed, stone mansion nearly 200 years old, originally a family home and given to the local authority in 1932 on condition it was used 'for the well-being of children and families'. The outdoor play area is a stunning walled garden, almost like a park, developed by the parents' group and imaginatively designed and equipped. The area is plagued by vandalism. Cars must be parked in front of the building, in sight of security cameras, and ugly metal spikes deter unwanted visitors from climbing the perimeter walls. Ashfield is said to have been the first nursery school in the Northeast and is enormous, with 130 children on the register. Inside, the many different classrooms need redecoration, but shabbiness is cleverly hidden behind wonderful art and craft displays. The rooms are light, organised and clean.

**Headteacher & staff** Joan Lister, Cert Ed, has been headteacher for 20 years. She has seen the nursery school 'rise again' as a modern nursery after it was gutted by fire in 1974. She is a distinguished early years educator who has spent most of her teaching life with the youngest age range. A past chairwoman of the National Association for Primary Education, she is deeply committed to state nursery education. In 1989 she was made an honorary fellow of the Royal College of Preceptors for her services to young children. The co-writer of material on child protection, when she retires she plans to write about her pioneering work on parental and community involvement and flexible approaches to nursery education. There are eight full-time members of staff: four Cert Ed qualified teachers and four NNEB nursery nurses. Joan Lister says, 'They work together as a close team, a teacher and nursery nurse side by side. They are totally dedicated and under great stress at the moment. They all deserve medals the size of frying pans.' Due to local authority cuts this year, the school has lost six members of staff. The community teacher who used the school as a base has also gone and the extended daycare facility has been cut. Numbers have been reduced from 130 to 104. Each teacher is responsible for a designated area of the curriculum. Care and education go hand in hand. A male teacher is employed part-time by the parents' management committee as a counsellor and playgroup worker. A special needs helper attends three afternoons a week and an ESL (English as a Second Language) teacher, mainly for the Asian children, three hours a week. There are five staff training days a year.

**Children & parents** The children come from the neighbouring housing estate in an area of considerable social deprivation and high unemployment. There is a high ethnic minority representation, particularly Asian. Some children have little or no English when they join. All transfer to local state or church primary schools. Good provision for children with special educational needs and more would be taken if additional financial support were available. The children are happy, friendly and eager to join in. They are well supervised as they move about the building. Parents share in the management of the nursery and are genuine partners in nursery life. Parents' meetings and events are held during daylight hours, as the streets have proved unsafe at night. There is an open-door policy towards parents, who have their own centre in the building which they maintain themselves. It includes a mother and toddler room, drop-in room, baby-changing area and kitchen. All children start on a part-time basis until parents and staff agree that they are ready for a full day.

**Curriculum & activities** The broad-based curriculum aims to provide quality pre-school education in partnership with parents and the wider community. The weekly timetable is carefully planned in advance to offer children the choice of many different and challenging activities. There is creative play, with paint, junk, sand and water, crayons and pencils, dough and clay. There is also imaginative play in the home corner, with dressing-up clothes, the farm and the zoo. The construction toys – table bricks, Duplo, stickle bricks – develop motor skills. Table activities include computer time, puzzles, sorting and matching games, Lego, pegs and mosaics. Outdoor physical activities, songs, music, dance and movement all feature in the daily timetable. Small groups visit the swimming pool on a rota basis. The children are taught to read and write when they are ready. They can recognise simple words and names when they leave, and the more capable ones can manage a sentence. Each child has a personal action plan, with an individual programme based on detailed assessments made every three weeks. Children can develop at their own pace. There are frequent outings, in small groups, in the nursery minibus to museums, farms and places of interest related to projects. Puppeteers and theatrical groups visit from time to time, and negotiations are under way for a musical entertainment by the Northern Sinfonia. Full developmental and progress reports are kept on each child. An industry/education project between the nursery and a local brick-and-cement factory was initiated in 1990. All children, in groups of 12, visited the brick works to watch the brick-making process, made their own bricks and, together with staff, made paving stones for the nursery garden. This link has led to a series of other imaginative projects between nursery and community.

**Remarks** A large and remarkable nursery school with a strong character and identity. It is an outstanding example of partnership between children, parents, teachers and the community. Love, security and education are provided for the children who need them most. This year's round of local authority spending cuts has seriously damaged the service.

# GOSFORTH PRIVATE DAY NURSERY

4–6 Harley Terrace
Gosforth
Newcastle-upon-Tyne
NE3 1UL
**Tel:** (091) 285 6006

**Owners:** Juan and Elizabeth Villalobos
**Principal:** Elizabeth Villalobos, Cert Ed
**Type:** Day nursery offering full-time places and half-day sessions
**Children:** 2–5yrs. 50 places a day. 114 on register
**Hours:** 8am–5.30pm
Morning session 8am–12 noon
Afternoon session 1pm–5.30pm
Open 52 weeks a year
**Status:** Private, fee-paying
**Number of years open:** 13
**Meals:** Lunch, tea, snacks
**1992 fees:** £75 per week full-time
£16 per day
£9.75 per session (inc lunch)
£9.25 per session (excl lunch)
**Waiting list:** Moderate
**Registered by:** Newcastle City Council SS

**Premises** Two adjoining, three-storey, Victorian terraced houses in a densely populated, middle-class area of Newcastle. The owners live on the top two floors of one house, and the ground floor is used as a nursery classroom by 2½- to 3-year-olds. There are two similar classrooms for older children next door. The playrooms are light, colourful and warm, with displays of children's work everywhere. Each has a messy-play area, tables and chairs, computer and television. The younger children have home and pets' corners. There is a small art and craft room on the first floor, used for three-dimensional work such as clay modelling, box modelling and papier mâché. It also doubles as the French classroom. The top floor accommodates an immaculate kitchen, the staff room and the storerooms. Outside there is a small grassy garden at the front and a slightly larger area at the back with an all-weather safety surface. The nursery has a plentiful supply of outdoor and PE equipment.

**Owners/Principal & staff** Elizabeth Villalobos, Cert Ed, trained as a teacher and, after gaining qualifications in business and accounting in New York, set up her own nursery when she returned to Britain in 1979. She has been involved in the full-time running of the nursery ever since. 50 per cent of her young staff of 15 nursery nurses are NNEB qualified. They are a friendly, reliable and dedicated team. Peripatetic teachers visit for two hours of French and an hour of mini-aerobics every week. NNEB and BTEC students come in for work experience – male students are regular visitors and popular with the children. Training courses run by local Social Services, the PPA and other agencies are available to staff on a limited basis. Staff wear a sporty navy blue uniform, and a matching uniform is available to children who want it.

**Children & parents** The intake reflects the local population – mainly middle-class professionals, with a small number of bilingual children. The children appear happy, well mannered and sociable, treating staff with respect. They are divided into three classes by age. About 40 per cent progress to the private sector. Parents are encouraged to discuss their child's progress at any time. No formal parents' evenings are held; the principal says they would cause traffic problems. Family social events – picnics with entertainment or sponsored events to raise money for charity – are occasionally arranged. At the moment there are no children with special educational needs or disabilities attending the nursery. When a child leaves, parents are asked to complete a 'standards and quality assurance questionnaire' detailing their views and comments on the quality of the nursery.

**Curriculum & activities** Children are offered a planned programme of play activities which aims to develop their imagination, manipulative skills, language, reasoning and self-confidence. Learning through play is the philosophy and messy play – in the form of sand, water, paint, clay and papier mâché – is on offer at all times. All classes have periods of free play, but as the children grow older the programme is more structured, to include pre-reading, pre-writing and pre-number work. There is no formal teaching of reading. Children can recognise and write the letters of the alphabet and their own names by the time they leave. Children's progress is recorded in writing weekly. Assessment tick lists are completed once a term. Parents receive an annual report. Early science and nature study are regular features of the curriculum. There is daily singing and dancing, and twice-weekly music sessions, with staff frequently accompanying on piano, keyboard or clarinet. Once a week there is mini-aerobics and French for everyone. Children are introduced to computers and become familiar with keyboards. Twice-yearly theatre visits and occasional outings to a park or farm also take place. There are many varied and interesting projects, and relevant visitors are invited to come and share their experience with the children. Mothers brought in newborn babies for children to bathe, change and feed during a recent project on 'babies'.

**Remarks** A well-established, popular nursery offering a good balance of quality care and pre-school education. Secure, homely environment which would, however, benefit from a larger outside play area. Good standard and quantity of equipment, including computers and a varied, plentiful supply of books.

# HEATON NURSERY SCHOOL

38 Heaton Grove
Heaton
Newcastle-upon-Tyne NE6 5NP
**Tel:** (091) 265 6427

**Owner/Principal:** Jean Brown, Cert Ed
**Type:** Day nursery offering full-time and half-day sessions
**Children:** 6wks–4+yrs. 33 places. 33 on register
**Hours:** 8am–5.30pm
Morning session 8am–1pm
Afternoon session 1pm–5.30pm
Flexible hours
Open 51 weeks a year
**Status:** Private, fee-paying
**Number of years open:** 23
**Meals:** Breakfast, lunch, tea
**1992 fees:** £78 per week full-time – under 2
£70 per week full-time – over 2
£45 per week for 5 sessions
£17 per day – under 2
£15 per day – over 2
**Waiting list:** For babies only
**Registered by:** Newcastle City Council SS

**Premises** A 1930s, terraced house, attractively painted, with large Disney characters in each window. Situated in a quiet road, with little through traffic, ten minutes from the city centre and with easy access to all areas. Parking would only be a problem if everyone arrived at the same time. There are plenty of buses and Metro stations nearby. The nursery has recently been completely refurbished inside and out. It occupies all three floors of the house, and the garage and storeroom have been converted to provide a self-contained baby unit. The nursery is divided into three distinct areas, according to children's ages. The baby unit has two rooms – one for sleep, another for play and feeding – and an adjoining bathroom for nappy changing. The floor is carpeted, and there are plenty of stimulating pictures, mobiles and soft toys, but limited natural light. Also on the ground floor, toddlers play in a long room full of toys and equipment with home corner, play house, piles of books and walls covered with children's creativity. Natural light is restricted here, too, as there is only one window in this room. Upstairs there is an L-shaped classroom for older children, with a big blackboard, well-stocked bookshelves, television, video and computer. Examples of children's art, craft and drawing are everywhere. It is a bright, stimulating room with facilities for imaginative and creative play. The toilets have brightly coloured curtains instead of doors for privacy. The staff room and office are on the second floor, and a small kitchen is downstairs. A small backyard is full of pot plants. Directly opposite, a safely fenced, grass playground, with colourful outdoor equipment, overlooks the railway. Heaton Park, a short walk away, is visited occasionally in summer.

**Owner/Principal & staff** Jean Brown, Cert Ed, was the first person in the area to open a private nursery, 23 years ago. She also launched, and is chairwoman of, the National Private Day Nursery Association in Tyne Tees. A warm, outgoing woman who has been involved in teaching and childcare all her working life, she commands a loyal staff team, some of whom have worked for her for over 18 years. Currently there are six full-time nursery nurses – five NNEB and one City & Guilds. They work closely together and meet socially outside work. All have first-aid qualifications and a range of different talents including art and craft and sign language. In the past, the nursery employed a male YTS student, who was extremely popular. A visiting dance teacher takes children over 1 year old for weekly movement, expression and deportment. Staff/child ratios range from 1:3 for babies to 1:8 for over-3s. Jean Brown is an assessor for the new NVQ training course and trains staff herself in-house. There is no specific budget allocated for training. Staff meetings are held once a week. Staff are noticeably calm and quiet-spoken. They never raise their voices with the children.

**Children & parents** The children come from reasonably well-off, dual-income families, with some ethnic diversity (Nigerian and Chinese). Most people come through recommendation. Jean Brown offers parents flexibility and is prepared to change opening hours to fit in with their needs. Parents have open days, parents' evenings and the chance to help out or turn up whenever they wish. New parents visit two or three times with their child, prior to starting, but do not stay once a child has begun. There are no children with special educational needs – the nursery has never been asked to take them. The children we observed were well supervised, cheerful and disciplined. They transfer to a variety of state and private schools in the area.

**Curriculum & activities** A planned combination of care, play and structured learning. The emphasis is on good manners, social skills, confidence and respect for each other and teachers. There is a written timetable for pre-school children, which includes play activities – glueing, painting, drawing, construction toys, musical instruments, imaginative play, dough and sand – interspersed with periods of more formal learning, such as computer work, project work, pre-reading, pre-writing and stories. The blackboard is used in traditional fashion to encourage children to sit and listen. Time is spent each day in the library corner. Flashcard work is done every day, with the Ginn reading scheme for those who are ready. Most children can recognise and write their own name and read simple books by the time they go to primary school. There is continual assessment of all children, from babies upwards, and written developmental records. Staff are imaginative and creative and prepare many materials themselves to stimulate children – folders, pictures, mobiles. Plenty of colourful, appropriate equipment for all ages. Music is done daily, dance and movement and library visits weekly. French will be introduced, when a teacher is found. The hour a day that is set aside in the timetable for television viewing seems rather excessive. There are outings for children over 2 year olds – theatre, wildlife park, a Christmas treat. A short prayer is said before meals and care is taken to talk about different religions and cultures.

**Remarks** Homely, friendly day nursery with a solid traditional, educational element to each day. Dedicated and enthusiastic staff and a principal who is a qualified teacher with years of childcare and nursery management experience.

# NEWBURN MANOR NURSERY SCHOOL

Townfield Gardens
Newburn
Newcastle-upon-Tyne NE15 8PY
**Tel:** (091) 267 6065

**Owner:** Met Dist of Newcastle-upon-Tyne LEA
**Headteacher:** Marjorie Swailes, Cert Ed
**Type:** Nursery school offering full- and part-time places
**Children:** 2½–5yrs. 78 places. 80 on register
**Hours:** 8.30am–3.30pm
Open 39 weeks a year
**Status:** State nursery school
**Number of years open:** 21
**Meals:** Milk, lunch
**1992 fees:** No fees
**Waiting list:** Long. Full for 1993
**Registered by:** Met Dist of Newcastle-upon-Tyne LEA

**Premises** An old 1930s, single-storey, brick building that is a converted village infants' school. It is situated next to Newburn Manor First School, which was 100 years old last year. On the other side is Newburn Motor Museum. There is no through traffic past the school, which is in a semi-rural area and faces on to a common, with fields behind. It is easily accessible by bus or car. The nursery uses a central hall, which is divided into four classes with an experienced, qualified teacher in each. The nursery has wooden floors throughout with carpeted areas, high ceilings and light paintwork, generally in good condition. There is a small office for the headteacher and secretary plus a staff room and toilets, all very clean. The building feels spacious and is heated by large, old-fashioned radiators. The school yard is divided into two, by growbags in summer, – to create a car park for teachers and a play area. Rather cracked concrete and uneven slabs, although more in the parking lot than the playground. There is a broad, grassy area on two sides of the building. Part of this is being developed with bushes and logs to provide an area for playing hide-and-seek and making dens. There is a tunnel through a grassy mound, and the whole area is fenced with a safety catch on the gate. A wooden hut, without a door, is used as a play house.

**Headteacher & staff** Marjorie Swailes, Cert Ed, has been headteacher at Newburn for 12 years, having previously taught in primary and secondary schools in England and Scotland. Before coming to the nursery, she took further nursery qualifications. She is a non-teaching head, responsible for the curriculum and day-to-day running of the nursery. Staff are experienced, well qualified and long-serving – all her original appointees are still at their posts. The seven female members of staff are all full-time and qualified – three NNEB and four Cert Ed or B Ed. They are mature women, with a sound knowledge of child development. One has a B Ed in special needs, another is expert in relating to special needs children and their families. Marjorie Swailes employed a male teacher for two years, but he moved on to a county headship. There is a talented musician, and all NNEBs have first-aid certificates. At the moment, staff are being trained in basic computer skills. Students, both graduates and nursery nurses, come to Newburn as part of their training. Staff meetings are held once a week. The staff/child ratio is 1:13.

**Children & parents** Wide social and cultural mix, from unemployed to professional families and including a local MP's child. There is a high proportion of single-parent families and half the children are eligible for free school meals. Two children, one Norwegian and one Chinese, are learning English. Four gypsy children attend, in winter only. Children with special educational needs are welcome and integrate successfully. Children transfer to the state system – some to local first and primary schools and others to Roman Catholic schools. Each teacher, assisted by a nursery nurse, has responsibility for 26 children and their families.

Most children stay at the nursery all day. The teacher visits a child at home before he/she starts, and the child then visits the nursery three or four times with a parent. Physical contact is important, and there is a warm, close relationship between children and staff. There is also a very close relationship between staff and parents. 'We don't have to work at it. We see parents as our equals and they are encouraged to contribute. The staff care about the children, and parents know that we listen to them.' Parents help out at the nursery and attend open days, plays, concerts and sports day.

**Curriculum & activities** The nursery follows the National Curriculum for pre-school children, preparing them for school. Priorities are 'academic education, social skills, physical skills, aesthetic appreciation and confidence both to achieve and fail'. Children are taught in family and peer groupings, but spend time all together once a day for registration and occasionally for singing and games. The teaching process promotes self-expression through various subjects. Children make choices within different activity areas and are given the opportunity to learn the difference between writing and drawing. They sort objects into groups or sets and practise matching and ordering. There is cookery and sand and water play to introduce the concept of weight, volume, balance, capacity and shape recognition. Plants and animals are studied and visits are made to local farms and parks. No reading scheme is followed, but there are plenty of books, story reading and tapes. Language and listening skills are developed and conversation is of great importance. There is no formal teaching of the 3Rs, but they underpin all activities. Activities always available include painting, collage, clay, cutting and using pencils and crayons. The annual equipment budget is £1400. Detailed records are kept of each child's progress in self-help and social skills. 'We try to pick up on any special needs,' Marjorie Swailes says. More detailed records of language, writing, maths and reading skills are kept on the older children. A final report goes with the child to their next school.

**Remarks** Experienced, qualified and enthusiastic teaching staff providing a sound educational grounding in all skills. Happy and fulfilled children. Good provision for children with special educational needs. The long waiting list will leave many families disappointed and frustrated at missing out on this excellent pre-school provision.

# North Tyneside

A caring, innovative local authority, which began a policy of providing and expanding nursery education in the 1970s. The continuing programme, which has put them at the top of the league for nursery education, has been held back by central government cuts. There are three nursery schools and 46 units attached to primary schools. Over half the area's 3- and 4-year-olds attend nursery. The local authority believes in close co-operation between education and Social Services departments. A recently set-up 'Childcare Function Unit' implements a policy of matching and complementing the work of the two departments for the benefit of consumers. The local authority actively promotes and publishes its childcare services, which include nine day nurseries, registered childminders, a management scheme to help employers set up workplace nurseries, a mobile crèche for conferences and meetings, a nanny service and a recently initiated after-school scheme in primary schools.

**Further information**

For information and advice on all forms of childcare and nursery education:
Jacky Doughty
The Childcare Shop
Station Mews
Tynemouth Station
North Shields NE30 2TF
Tel: (091) 296 2111

# CHILDCARE BATTLE HILL

Bromsgrove Close
Battle Hill
North Tyneside NE28 9SA
**Tel:** (091) 263 4393

**Owner:** Childcare Enterprise/North Tyneside Met Council
**Manager:** Julia Lee, SRN, RM, NNEB
**Type:** Day nursery offering full- and part-time places and half-day sessions
**Children:** 4mths–4yrs 11mths. 40 places. 69 on register
**Hours:** 7.15am–6pm
Morning session 7.15am–12.30pm
Afternoon session 12.30pm–6pm
Flexible hours
Open 52 weeks a year
**Status:** Social Services day nursery, fee-paying. Some subsidised places based on need
**Number of years open:** 3
**Meals:** Breakfast, lunch, snacks
**1992 fees:** £218.75 per month full-time
£10.50 per day
£5.25 per session
**Waiting list:** Long
**Registered by:** North Tyneside Met Council SS
**Under same ownership:** Norham, North Shields; Shiremoor, North Tyneside; Wideopen, Newcastle; Wallsend (see entry); 2 further nurseries opening 1993

**Premises** A prefabricated Portakabin with three separate nursery rooms, two kitchens, staff room, office, laundry and toilet facilities. The three nursery rooms make up the baby room, toddler room and pre-school room. The rooms are mainly carpeted, but a quarter of the area is laid with washable tiles for art and craft, messy play and mealtimes. In each room, there is an alcove for imaginative play with a play house, hospital, home corner and dressing-up clothes. The children are particularly fond of their pets – a hamster, a rabbit and a tank full of fish. There are parking facilities just off the main road (most children arrive by car) and a frequent bus service. The nursery is in a large complex of mixed council and private housing estates. The outside play area is part paving, part grass and perfectly safe.

**Manager & staff** Julia Lee, SRN, RM, NNEB, has been manager for two years, following a varied career first in a bank and then in nursing. She is also a qualified midwife. A Geordie born and bred, she has a good understanding of the neighbourhood and relates naturally to children and staff. All seven female nursery workers are NNEB qualified. Three hold first-aid certificates, and all, including the cook have the basic Food and Hygiene Certificate. They form a well-organised, friendly team, all in their 20s. Since Julia took over as manager, there have been no staff changes, and some carers have worked at the nursery since it opened. Generous staff development training is provided by North Tyneside Council. Students attend regularly on placement. A pre-school advisory teacher visits regularly. There are 25 children present at any one time and seven nursery nurses. A keyworker system operates.

**Children & parents** A good mix of children from different social and cultural backgrounds, all English-speaking. Virtually all transfer to state schools in the district. They appeared to be happy, chatty and active. Children with disabilities and special educational needs integrate successfully and there is excellent back-up from health visitors and speech therapists. The nursery operates an open-door policy and parents can arrive at any time. Phasing-in is done gently over a two-week period. Two of the children are subsidised by Midland Bank, and some by Social Services. Parents are invited to all nursery activities and there is a formal complaints procedure if required. Parents talk to their child's keyworker at the beginning and end of the day.

**Curriculum & activities** The nursery sets out to provide a safe, stimulating environment with a flexible, structured timetable, tailored to suit individual needs. The owners, Childcare Enterprise, believe in learning through play. Activities are carefully planned in advance around themes and written down. Equipment and educational toys and games are plentiful – the annual budget is a generous £3825. Every opportunity is given for the child to develop through imaginative play, painting, modelling, construction, stories and music and dance, but there is no formal learning. Older children are taken by their keyworker to Battle Hill Nursery School for sessions every afternoon. Most children can recognise and write their own names and a certain number of other words by the time they leave. A developmental progress booklet is kept on each child, regularly updated, and taken home when a child leaves. Babies are included in as many activities as possible. They have an indoor paddling pool to sit in and enjoy sand and water play. We watched one baby on his keyworker's knee, with a plate of jelly to play with and feel. Outings, related to topics, are a regular feature – the Metro Interchange was visited recently as part of a project on transport. Library visits take place once a month. Fresh food is cooked on the premises by a full-time cook. Staff eat with the children, encouraging good table manners and stimulating conversation.

**Remarks** High-quality daycare at a very reasonable cost. The cheerful, friendly staff have a close relationship with children and good communication with parents. The long opening hours meet the needs of working parents. The premises lack a cosy, homely feel and the outside play area needs some refurbishment. Although it is brightly decorated with children's art and craft, the main playroom remains rather too large an open space for very young children. The nursery hopes to move to better premises in the future.

# CHILDCARE WALLSEND

Wilson Street
Wallsend
Tyne and Wear
NE28 8RS
**Tel:** (091) 262 3839

**Owner:** Childcare Enterprise/North Tyneside Met Council
**Principal Officer:** Freda Patterson, NNEB
**Type:** Day nursery offering full- and part-time places
**Children:** 3mths–4yrs 6mths. 50 places (30 places subsidised by local authority, some free places for priority families). 63 on register
**Hours:** 7.30am–5.45pm
Open 52 weeks a year
**Status:** Social Services day nursery, fee-paying. Some subsidised places based on need
**Number of years open:** 53
**Meals:** Breakfast, lunch, tea
**1992 fees:** £218.75 per month full-time
**Waiting list:** Long
**Registered by:** North Tyneside Met Council SS

**Under same ownership:** Norham, North Shields; Shiremoor, North Tyneside; Wideopen, Newcastle; Battle Hill, North Tyneside (see entry); 2 further nurseries opening 1993

**Premises** Pre-fabricated building erected 53 years ago when the nursery opened, with an additional Portakabin used for pre-school children. A quiet street in a working-class area on the edge of town. Easy access by bus or Metro and plenty of parking space. The large baby room is divided into sleep, play and eating areas. The latter doubles as a messy-play area for paint, sand and water. A colourful and stimulating environment with mobiles, low mirrors, soft things to crawl on and piles of toys. The toddlers have separate but similar rooms, part carpeted, part vinyl, and a cosy sleep area with mattresses and soft low chairs. Windows and walls are decorated with children's work and there is a generous amount of suitable equipment, in good condition (annual budget £2300). One whole room has been set aside as an imaginative home corner, complete with clothes rack full of dressing-up clothes and a pet hamster. There is a small television room and each age group has separate bathrooms and toilets. The pre-school children in the Portakabin have a cloakroom area, bathroom, toilets and a large, sunny and very colourful play room with a television and quiet corner, messy play, construction area and table-top activities. Each age group has its own safe outside play space and all children visit the nearby park frequently.

**Principal Officer & staff** Freda Patterson, NNEB, is an approachable, caring, mature woman with years of childcare experience in playgroups, maternity wards, families and day nurseries. Her young staff of 15, including two male workers, are a happy, friendly and outgoing team, who all work enthusiastically together. All are NNEB qualified and many have been at the nursery for some years. They are experienced in all areas and can work with any age group. A close relationship between children and staff, based on mutual respect, is evident. Staff do not raise their voices, and children listen and respond positively. Nursery nurses are innovative and artistic. There are examples around the nursery of toys and equipment, which they have created and made themselves, using everyday items to provide stimulating activities at little cost. NNEB and BTEC students come for work experience.

Staff training and development has suffered from local authority cut-backs. The staff/child ratios are 1:3 for babies; 1:4 for toddlers; 1:6 for pre-school children.

**Children & parents** The children come from a wide catchment area and very different social backgrounds, but there is minimal ethnic diversity. Parents include professionals, manual workers, single parents, the unemployed and students. The nursery has an open-door policy. Any parent can telephone or visit at any time and there are parents' evenings every term. Each child has a keyworker and new children are introduced over a two-week period. Parents fill in a detailed child profile form to provide staff with maximum information. Children are visibly happy and settled into the routine. There are cuddles for all. Most children move on to state primary schools. There are two special needs children at present. The nursery has direct access to local authority support services.

**Curriculum & activities** Stimulation and learning through play. Children discover and learn in a comfortable, homely environment which values and treats them as individuals. Much of the nursery's philosophy is based on research and guidelines drawn up by the National Children's Bureau. Each day begins with free play until 9am. For the remainder of the day children are split into four age-related groups, for activities which change daily. They include art and craft, construction, investigation, water play with bottles, role play, listening to stories or music, physical play, looking at books, planting seeds, outside play and a group activity such as finger rhymes or singing. There are pets to look after, children's television and meals, which are looked on as a social occasion. Children are introduced to pre-school literacy skills, but reading is not taught. There is no nursery teacher on the staff, but many of the NNEBs are experienced with pre-school children. Local walks and shopping trips, visits to the beach and occasional outings to museums and country centres are all undertaken. The nursery shares a seven-seater mini-bus with the nurseries owned by Childcare Enterprise at Wideopen and Norham. Detailed written developmental records are kept on each child; parents have full access.

**Remarks** Long-established nursery, offering high-quality care at a very reasonable cost, with subsidised places for low-income families. Loving, dedicated and skilled nursery workers, who display an imaginative enthusiasm for innovation. Strong relationship with parents. Warm, friendly atmosphere, despite the age of the building.

# South Tyneside

One of the best records in the country, with 90 per cent of all 3- to 5-year-olds receiving part-time nursery education for a year before they attend primary school. Social Services fund six full-time day nurseries and four family centres and register two private day nurseries. A copy of South Tyneside's review document listing all under-5s services in the region is available from public libraries and schools. Unfortunately no local authority nursery schools or classes responded to our questionnaire.

**Further information**

For details on day nurseries, childminders and playgroups:

Department of Social Services – Under Eights
South Tyneside House
Westoe Road
South Shields NE33 2RL
Tel: (091) 427 1717

For details on nursery schools, units and classes:

The Education Office
Town Hall and Civic Offices
Westoe Road
South Shields NE33 2RL
Tel: (091) 427 1717

## VICTORIA PRIVATE TEACHING NURSERY

84 Victoria Road West
Hebburn
Tyne and Wear NE31 1LR
**Tel:** (091) 430 1643

**Owners:** Moira and Jean Taylor, both Cert Ed
**Type:** Nursery school offering full- and part-time places and half-day sessions
**Children:** 2–5yrs. 48 places. 47 on register
**Hours:** 8.30am–4.30pm
Morning session 8.30am–12 noon
Afternoon session 1pm–4.30pm
Open 48 weeks a year
**Status:** Private, fee-paying
**Number of years open:** 22
**Meals:** Lunch, snacks
**1992 fees:** £46.25 per week full-time
£9.25 per day
£3.67 per session
**Waiting list:** 24 names
**Registered by:** South Tyneside Met Council SS

**Premises** Large, brick, Victorian, terraced house in a residential area, with easy access by car, bus and Metro. The nursery occupies the whole building and comprises a free play room, classroom, gym, art and craft room, 'dramatic' playroom with a home corner and dressing-up clothes, kitchen and bathroom, all clean, well equipped and cheerful. A different colour predominates in each room, and there are Disney characters on the walls and stencils on the windows. The atmosphere is intimate and homely. Other decorations include items collected by the owners on various trips abroad, ranging from a Chinese dragon to light switches and mobiles from Disneyland. Much use is made of the television, video, cine and slide projectors. The rather small, narrow, enclosed garden is disappointing. It is used daily and has some outdoor equipment, which is stored in the garage.

**Owners & staff** Moira and Jean Taylor, both Cert Ed, are sisters who trained as teachers and taught children with learning difficulties prior to setting up their own nursery school over 20 years ago. They are 'of the old school' – obviously adore the children, devote enormous time and energy to their nursery, but have very definite views about pre-school education. They like things to be done 'their way'. They prefer to train their young staff of 3 themselves. Most of the staff have no recognised childcare qualification; Moira and Jean Taylor believe that character is more important than qualifications. Relationships with the children are warm and loving and children are relaxed, but very respectful and polite. There is a great deal of affection and physical contact, hand-holding and cuddling. The staff/child ratios vary depending on the age of the children. Extra help is used when necessary.

**Children & parents** The majority of the children have professional parents or parents who run their own businesses. Some have both parents working full-time. They come from within a 25-mile radius. The children are articulate and self-assured, without being pushy or precocious. This is one of the few nurseries where our researcher was shown round by children, two 4-year-olds, along with the principals. The children were instructed to call her by her full name, when they addressed her. Most children start in September and are phased-in over a six-week period. They are put into different groups for each activity, so that they have the opportunity to get to know each other well. If any child is obviously unhappy, then the sisters suggest to their parents that they 'leave it for a little while and try again later'. A quarter of the children go on to schools in the private sector, such as Newlands Preparatory School. No children with special needs have ever been enrolled at the nursery, although they would be welcome.

**Curriculum & activities** An organised and disciplined nursery school, where children experience a structured day or session with some flexibility for individual needs. They begin in the free-play room and then divide into small groups of eight for activities in different rooms. There is a diary system in each room, to ensure that children do not participate in the same activity twice in quick succession. Moving between rooms, before the appointed time, is discouraged. Children play in each of the rooms during a session, experiencing art and craft, physical play, imaginative and role play, free play and structured learning. They learn pre-literacy skills, but reading is not taught. All learn to recognise and write their own name. Children are encouraged to be proud of 'good work'. There is a quieter and more genteel atmosphere than in many nursery schools, but even the most boisterous children seem relaxed, open and responsive to staff. Birthday parties can be held at the school. Clowns and magicians entertain and mothers bring balloons, crisps and birthday cake.

**Remarks** A very long-established nursery school that has been caring for children in the same inimitable way for the last 20 years. Moira and Jean Taylor have created a warm and homely, but organised and disciplined environment. Children appear happy, articulate and very polite. A slightly old-fashioned approach, but popular with parents. Places are always full, though the waiting list is manageable. Outside play facilities could be improved.

# Sunderland

Sunderland provides one nursery centre, run in partnership with the Education Department, and four family centres, offering the equivalent of 150 full-time daycare places. It also offers five facilities for children with special needs. The aim is a 'home from home' nursery service which involves local parents and the community. 38 per cent of the county's 3- and 4-year-olds benefit from state nursery education. There are just three registered private day nurseries. In 1990, the National Children's Bureau was funded to research the county's pre-school needs. One of the results has been the development of community nursery schools, modelled to meet the needs of individual neighbourhoods. A lively, caring authority.

## Further information

For details on day nurseries, childminders and playgroups:
Under Eights' Section
Department of Social Services
3 The Esplanade
Sunderland SR2 7BQ
Tel: (091) 510 2998

For details on nursery schools, units and classes:
The Primary Advisor
Education Department
Broadway Centre
Springwell Road
Sunderland SR4 8NW
Tel: (091) 511 0333

## CORK STREET NURSERY CENTRE

Cork Street
Hendon
Sunderland SR1 2AN
**Tel:** (091) 567 4191 or 565 8787

**Owner:** Sunderland Met Council LEA and Social Services
**Headteacher:** Jill Sansom, Cert Ed
**Nursery Officer:** Denise Maddison, NNEB
**Type:** Children's centre offering full- and part-time places. All children referred by Social Services
**Children:** 0–5yrs. 50 places. 70 on register
**Hours:** 8am–5pm Mon–Thurs
8am–4pm Fri
Open 51 weeks a year
**Status:** State children's centre
**Number of years open:** 12

**Meals:** Breakfast, lunch, tea
**1992 fees:** No fees. £1 per day for those not on Family Support Income
**Waiting list:** Long. Not all can be guaranteed places
**Registered by:** Sunderland Met Council SS

**Premises** Purpose-built bungalow with a flat roof in a run-down inner-city area with high levels of unemployment. People are moved here from all over Sunderland. The surrounding council housing is mainly depressingly drab blocks of flats. The nursery is a rabbit warren of rooms leading off narrow corridors. Beautifully decorated throughout, with carpets, attractive wallpaper and borders, wall and table lamps and music playing in the corridors and areas used by parents. Staff do their utmost to provide an attractive environment for the many children who come here from deprived backgrounds. There is a welcoming and comfortable parents' room, with sofas, kettle, coffee and magazines. Particularly well-equipped playrooms for different age groups, each with a home corner and children's work lovingly mounted and displayed. Ramps for wheelchairs. Waterproof coats and wellies are provided for wet weather play in the huge, well-designed and constantly used garden. Most children attending have no outside play space at home and are encouraged to play outdoors as often as possible. They plant bulbs in the raised flower beds.

**Headteacher & staff**  Jill Sansom, Cert Ed, has been head of the Centre for three years. A trained early years teacher with experience in support teaching, youth leadership and counselling, she reports to a sustaining advisory committee, with representatives from both Social Services and the Education Department, and leads a team of 14 qualified and experienced workers, all flexible, open-minded and receptive to new ideas. A mix of teachers and nursery nurses, they are relaxed with each other, work well together and support the children and their families. They all have the art of listening. A peripatetic teacher helps children with hearing impairment, and social workers visit when necessary. NNEB students come for work experience. Male students are particularly welcome. The staff/child ratio is an excellent 1:4. A training and staff development policy and budget is in operation. Ancillary staff include cooks, domestics and a clerk.

**Children & parents**  The children are predominantly high-priority Social Services referrals from all corners of the city. Many have lone parents or parents who are unemployed and depressed. A number of children come from high-income families, but all are in need of help and support. Some live with grandparents or foster parents, others are in residential care. There are children with language problems, hearing impairment, delayed physical or emotional development, epilepsy or hyperactivity and children on very special diets. Some of the families have suffered traumatic experiences, and staff at the centre support not only the child, but the whole family. Parents can drop in for meals. Courses on beauty, cooking and parenting skills are organised, in addition to regular 'socials'. All children transfer to state schools in the city.

**Curriculum & activities**  The timetable is carefully planned according to each child's individual needs, with special emphasis on language development. Rooms are set out workshop-style and children work in small groups. The High Scope method of 'plan, do, review' in small groups is followed. Each child chooses and works through different activities at his/her own pace, to promote self-discipline, independence and confidence. Positive behaviour is promoted by constant reinforcement and praise. The nursery is wonderfully well equipped (annual budget £5272), and ordinary, everyday things such as cups, phones and cutlery are used during activities whenever possible. There is no pressure to read or write, but pre-reading and pre-writing skills (mark-making) are practised. There are exciting opportunities for self-expression. Art, craft, music and outdoor play are always available. The garden is still developing and a vegetable plot has just been created. In summer, lessons and picnics are held in the adjacent 'meadow'. Children are taken on regular outings to the coast, airport, library, shops and markets. There are also toy and book libraries. A full range of records is kept on each child. Wonderful food is cooked on the premises, including special medical diets as required.

**Remarks**  Marvellous care and support for young children and their families in an area of very great need. This is an exciting and unique collaboration between Education and Social Services departments – a glowing example of what can be achieved when funds are provided. More centres like this one are desperately needed.

## HETTON-LE-HOLE NURSERY SCHOOL

Brewery Field
Hetton-le-Hole
Tyne & Wear DH5 9DG
**Tel:** (091) 526 2221

**Owner:** Sunderland Met Council LEA
**Headteacher:** Maureen Ainsley, Cert Ed, SRN
**Type:** Nursery school offering full- and part-time places and half-day sessions
**Children:** 3yrs–3yrs 11mths. 42 places per session. 84 on register
**Hours:** Morning session 9am–11.30am (12.30pm inc lunch)

Afternoon session 1pm–3.30pm
Open 39 weeks a year
**Status:** State nursery school
**Number of years open:** 48
**Meals:** Milk. Lunch by arrangement
**1992 fees:** No fees. 70p per day for lunch. 50p per term for milk
**Waiting list:** Priority to children with special educational needs
**Registered by:** Sunderland Met Council LEA

## MILL HILL NURSERY SCHOOL

Saint Court
Doxford Park
Sunderland SR3 2LE
**Tel:** (091) 528 7191

**Owner:** Sunderland Met Council LEA
**Headteacher:** Gloria Simpson, Cert Ed
**Type:** Nursery school offering part-time places and half-day sessions. Full-time places only in cases of special need
**Children:** 3–5yrs. 60 places. 120 on register
**Hours:** 9am–3.15pm
Morning session 9am–11.30am
Afternoon session 1pm–3.15pm
Open 41 weeks a year
**Status:** State nursery school
**Number of years open:** 17
**Meals:** Snacks, lunch

**1992 fees:** No fees
**Waiting list:** Very long. 153 for Sept '93. 62 for Sept '94
**Registered by:** Sunderland Met Council LEA

## USWORTH COLLIERY NURSERY SCHOOL

Manor Road
Washington
Tyne & Wear NE37 3BL
**Tel:** (091) 416 3050

**Owner:** Sunderland Met Council LEA
**Principal:** Margaret Brabban, NNEB, Cert Ed
**Type:** Nursery school offering half-day sessions. Full-time in special circumstances
**Children:** 3yrs–4yrs 11mths. 156 places (max 10 full-time). 156 on register
**Hours:** Morning session 9am–11.30am
Afternoon session 1pm–3.30pm
Open 39 weeks a year
**Status:** State nursery school
**Number of years open:** 19 in current premises (60 in total)
**Meals:** Milk (lunch for full-time children)
**1992 fees:** No fees
**Waiting list:** Long. Apply after child's 2nd birthday. First come first served, although special needs may take priority
**Registered by:** Sunderland Met Council LEA

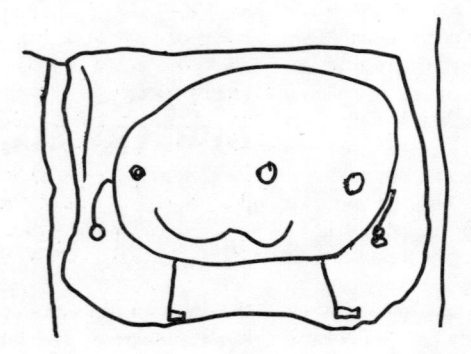

# Warwickshire

Seventeen per cent of 3- and 4-year-olds have access to part-time nursery education. Priority is given to Social Services referrals and, in some areas, to local authority employees. Demand far outweighs supply and there are long waiting lists in the council's nine nursery schools and 23 classes. The 178 playgroups, offering inexpensive, sessional care, are extremely popular. Nearly 1000 childminders (more are in the process of being registered) provide the most common form of childcare for working parents. There are 46 private day nurseries, many of which have opened in the last two years. This is one of the few counties to have increased its Social Services and Education budgets this financial year.

**Further information**

For details on day nurseries, childminders and playgroups:
Department of Social Services
Shire Hall
Warwick CV34 4SR
Tel: (0926) 410410

For details on nursery schools, units and classes:
Education Department
22 Northgate Street
Warwick CV34 4SR
Tel: (0926) 412266

## ALCESTER NURSERY SCHOOL

Town Hall
Alcester
Warwickshire B49 5QW
**Tel:** No telephone at premises
Leader's tel no (0789) 762029

**Owner:** Town Hall Committee
**Leader:** Debi Tilley, PPA
**Type:** Community nursery offering part-time places and morning sessions (min 2 sessions a week). Member of PPA
**Children:** 3–5yrs. 45 places. 72 on register.
**Hours:** 9.15am–12 noon
Open 38 weeks a year
**Status:** Self-funding charity
**Number of years open:** 8
**Meals:** Mid-morning snack
**1992 fees:** £2.25 per session
**Waiting list:** 40. All will be allocated a place
**Registered by:** Warwickshire County Council SS

**Premises** A 350-year-old stone-built town hall, in a quiet area near the centre of Alcester, a five-minute walk from the main car park. The nursery school is on two floors, with two main playrooms, two kitchens, a storeroom and toilet facilities. The rather dismal decor is brightened up by children's pictures and the building is in good repair considering its age. The downstairs playroom, with kitchen facilities at the far end and adult-size tables and chairs, is used for messy play and cookery classes. Upstairs, a wonderful, large, beamed playroom, with sprung wooden floor, is ideal for dance and other physical activities on the climbing frame or trampolines. The nursery has plenty of books and equipment but there is no outside play area. The equipment has to be put away every day as the hall is used by others. Moorfields Park is three minutes away and the children visit it about six times a year.

**Nursery Leader & staff** Debi Tilley, PPA, is a lively, energetic leader, in her early 30s, with two sons at secondary school. She has completed an Open University Course on 'the pre-school child' as well as several PPA courses and spent four years as an assistant in the reception class of a local infant school. She is ably assisted by a staff of four, all qualified in teaching or nursing or as nursery nurses. One worker has particular experience with special needs children. The women are all in their 30s or early 40s, friendly and enthusiastic. There is excellent communication between staff and children and a wide variety of skills and interests among staff. The nursery school takes a range of students including nursing students on work experience. A management committee of 15 mothers takes overall responsibility for the nursery. Debi has a 'hands on' role, taking decisions about day-to-day organisation, but can always call a committee meeting if there are any serious problems. The staff/child ratio is 1:8.

**Children & parents** The children are mainly local or from villages within five miles of Alcester. Most come from middle-class professional families with mums at home. Some children are brought by nannies or au pairs. A minority come from one-parent families or have parents who are unemployed. In cases of severe hardship the nursery will provide subsidised places. Parents are actively encouraged to attend parties, plays and outings. Many help with fund-raising and are kept informed via a regular newsletter. The children are chatty, polite and well behaved, with hardly time to say good-bye to mum as they rush off to become involved in their chosen activities. One or two children a year go on to the Croft private school in Stratford-upon-Avon, and the rest transfer to state primaries in and around Alcester. The nursery is willing to take special needs children. At present they have a child with brittle bone disease and several with sight problems. A special needs worker comes in regularly to assist.

**Curriculum & activities** After free play on arrival, children are registered at 9.30am and then split into two groups according to age. For the next hour, the downstairs group do painting, glueing, clay modelling, cooking or play with water and sand. Those upstairs do pre-writing, pre-reading or number work, supplemented by a choice of free-play activities. After break at 10.30am the two groups swap floors until clearing-up time, when everyone helps. All the children join together for songs and storytime to end each session. Dance and movement feature daily and children make their own music, with staff bringing in keyboards. Musical efforts are often recorded on tape. There is no formal teaching of reading, but the children are introduced to Letterland, which is used in the local primary schools. They leave the nursery able to form letters, write their name and recognise some words. Children go out twice weekly to help buy fruit for their snacks and there is a big trip each term. Staff keep written records on each child's progress.

**Remarks** Friendly and very happy stepping-stone from home to school. Staff and children having fun and enthusiastically learning together. Premises are not ideal – high rent, shared use, over two floors and no outside play area – but the quality of the relationship between staff and children more than compensates. Nursery workers were genuinely interested in listening to what children had to say. Active fund-raising by parents and small donations from local business help to keep the school going. Very reasonable cost, with further help for anyone in real need.

## BINSWOOD NURSERY SCHOOL

52 Binswood Avenue
Leamington Spa
Warwickshire CV32 5RX
**Tel:** (0926) 314036

**Owner/Principal:** Edwina Lightfoot
**Type:** Day nursery and nursery school offering full- and part-time places and half-day sessions
**Children:** 2–5yrs. 32 places. 66 on register
**Hours:** 8.15am–6pm
Morning and afternoon sessions flexible hours
Open 50 weeks a year
**Status:** Private, fee-paying
**Number of years open:** 7
**Meals:** Lunch, tea, dinner, snacks
**1992 fees:** £1.80–£2.25 per hour depending on child's age
**Waiting list:** Reasonable
**Registered by:** Warwickshire County Council SS
**Under same ownership:** Binswood Bunnies Crèche, Leamington Spa

**Premises** The light and spacious basement of a large Georgian house, in a smart tree-lined street off one of the main roads into Leamington Spa. The nursery comprises a large, generously equipped playroom, colourfully decorated with children's artwork; a workroom for older children, with a blackboard, computer and well-stocked book corner; a television and music room; a cosy, comfortable quiet/rest room; and sparkling clean toilets where each child has a toothbrush, mug and toothpaste.

Outside there is a well-maintained garden full of mature trees with a Wendy house, rope ladder, trampoline, swings and a 'secret' garden area.

**Owner/Principal & staff** Edwina Lightfoot, a former ophthalmic nurse, founded the school six years ago when she moved to Leamington Spa and failed to find a suitable nursery for her son. From an initial register of four, the nursery has grown steadily to its current 32 places, filled by over 60 full-time and part-time children each week. There are 18 members of staff, who work five hours a day, morning or afternoon shifts. Nine are qualified NNEBs, and two are Norland-trained nursery nurses. Unqualified staff are experienced playgroup workers or school assistants. There is no qualified nursery teacher. Edwina Lightfoot has a policy of not employing girls under 30 and prefers experienced nursery workers who have had children of their own. There is a visiting male music and drama teacher, an educational psychologist, who when we visited was playing the guitar and holding singing practice with the children for a forthcoming concert. Turnover is low and staff are happy and dedicated. 'People ask to be employed here,' says Edwina. Staff mix socially and often go out together to discuss nursery policy. Formal staff meetings are held every six months.

**Children & parents** A complete social mix. Children transfer to a wide range of schools in the private and state sector. Each member of staff is allocated a particular group of children and stays with them as they grow. Children each have their own file and progress folder, which is updated weekly and is available to be discussed with parents. Parents are welcome at any time, except lunchtimes. Edwina makes a point of meeting parents daily. Staff and parents are on first-name terms. Parents are invited to regular open days and concerts and also help with outings. They visit with their child on the first occasion, but after that children stay without their parents as staff feel they settle in more quickly on their own. Most parents hear about the school through the local grapevine.

**Curriculum & activities** The nursery believes that discovery-learning is the key to self-confidence and knowledge for young children. A wide range of activities is available at each session, including painting, handicrafts, modelling, music and musical instruments, drama, songs and dance. There are no written programmes or timetable, but a more structured programme is available to older children, who practise pre-reading and pre-writing skills, oral self-expression, numbers, colours and shapes. A strong emphasis is placed on music, from Mozart to pop; it is often played in the background during activities, and there are also frequent music-making sessions. Well-maintained and high-quality equipment (annual budget £1000) throughout. Children use the computer from an early age. Edwina Lightfoot says, 'Primary schools like ex-Binswood children, because they have been well prepared for school.' Ladybird and Ginn reading schemes are used and progress is monitored weekly on each child's reading card. Hygiene is considered of paramount importance and great care is taken to teach good habits. Children clean their teeth after meals and wash their hands regularly. The school is spotlessly clean.

**Remarks** High-quality care in a safe, homely, hygienic environment. Strong musical content to every day. No qualified nursery teacher on board. Light and spacious facilities and a large, attractive garden for outdoor play. Babies from 3 months to 2½ years are cared for separately at nearby Binswood Bunnies Crèche.

# PRIORY DAY NURSERY

8 Priory Road
Kenilworth
Warwickshire CV8 2LL
**Tel:** (0926) 59138

**Owner/Principal:** Barbara Smith, NNEB
**Type:** Day nursery offering full- and part-time places and half-day sessions, plus after-school and holiday playscheme for 5–8yr-olds
**Children:** 3mths–4½yrs. 26 places. 65 on register
**Hours:** 8am–6pm
Morning session 8am–1.30pm (inc lunch)
9am–12 noon (excl lunch)
Afternoon session 1.30pm–6pm (inc lunch)
1.30pm–4pm (excl lunch)
Open 51 weeks a year
**Status:** Private, fee-paying
**Number of years open:** 4
**Meals:** Breakfast (for babies only), lunch, tea
**1992 fees:** £85 per week full-time
£10 per morning session
£6.50 per morning session (excl lunch)

£9 per afternoon session
£5.50 per afternoon session (excl lunch)
**Waiting list:** Reasonable
**Registered by:** Warwickshire County Council SS

**Premises** The ground floor of a large, 1960s, chalet-style bungalow. The owner lives upstairs. There is a tarmac forecourt for easy access and parking. At the back is a good-sized, fenced garden, well maintained and full of large, brightly coloured toys. Inside there are three main rooms used for children's activities – the 'school room' for the over-3s, the 'tweenies room' for the 2-year-olds and the 'baby room'. The baby room is cosy and warm, with bean bags, mirrors, a baby bouncer and well-stocked with toys. The school room and tweenies room are more practical, with tables, chairs, equipment and toys for pre-school activities, including a computer. The rest of the accommodation includes a sleep room, spotlessly clean kitchen, changing room, bathroom and staff rest room. The nursery is not smart, but has been kept as homelike as possible. Although rather cluttered, it is clean and safe. Stair gates are used to prevent children from moving from one area to another without supervision and the outside door has both a low and a high latch to deter escapees.

**Owner/Principal & staff** The nursery is owned and managed by Barbara Smith, a Chiltern-trained NNEB, with varied experience in childminding, work in a special school and nurseries. There are nine female staff, six full-time and three part-time. Seven are qualified NNEB, one City & Guilds and one PPA Foundation. No member of staff has nursery teaching experience or qualifications. Arrangements for the care of under-2s reflect Barbara Smith's strong belief that a nursery should be as close as possible to home life. Each baby has one carer only, so that a special relationship develops. Barbara is actively involved in the day-to-day care of the children. A caring and friendly person, she has a loyal team of nursery nurses. Ancillary staff include a cook, cleaner and washing-up assistant. Staff training policy includes first-aid courses for all staff and access to a range of short courses, usually PPA-run. The nursery nurses frequently socialise together after work. The staff/child ratio averages 1:4.

**Children & parents** The children come from middle-class families, reflecting the location of the nursery. There is no ethnic diversity. Some assisted places are available through the local authority and local charitable organisations. Interaction with parents is strongly promoted. No parents' evenings are held, but a newsletter detailing current topics and activities is sent out every six weeks and there is an open door policy. New children build up attendance slowly and parents can stay with them for as long as they wish. There are regular 'granny days' when grandparents are invited to spend the afternoon at the nursery. Children are confident, busy and talkative. Most transfer to state schools. Excellent facilities for children with disabilities and special needs. The nursery cares for two babies who require gastric tube feeding and one child with cystic fibrosis. Two children from a local special school attend once a week for an integrated session at the nursery.

**Curriculum & activities** The nursery philosophy is 'learning through free play' with staff nearby to guide and encourage. The children are separated into three groups twice a day, according to age, for different activities. This is interspersed with collective activities, such as singing, storytime, playtime in the garden and meals. No formal reading or writing is taught, although pre-school skills such as memory games, sorting, matching and pencil control are covered in tweenies and the school room. There are no written educational programmes or timetable, nor is there a formal structure to the day. There are, however, substantial supplies of educational toys and equipment and plenty of painting, play dough, messy play in the sandpit and water play area, and some cooking for older children. A qualified piano teacher attends once a week for music and there are regular weekly trips to the park, library, swimming pool and soft play centre. Frequent outings to the local woods or into town. Annual sparkler and Christmas parties and a trip to see Santa Claus. Each spring, a bottle-fed lamb takes up residence for six weeks. Nursery pets include rabbits, fish and gerbils.

**Remarks** Cosy, friendly and home-like. Caring, qualified nursery nurses and confident, polite children. Stimulating nursery where children enjoy enormous freedom and have fun. Not a structured, formal learning environment for the over-3s, but your pre-school child will come home happy, healthy and dishevelled.

# WEST MIDLANDS
# Birmingham

A nursery place for 34 per cent of 3- and 4-year-olds, with about half offered full-time education. The Education and Social Services departments plan to work together to expand this number, as soon as resources allow. Birmingham has the highest number of local authority day nurseries in the country – 33 – with priority to children in need. The private sector provides 85 day nurseries and 2000 registered childminders – although the cost of places is often outside the scope of low-income families. Most of the 300-plus playgroups have waiting lists. With the city's current high unemployment, the greatest need is for affordable full-time daycare.

**Further information**

For details on day nurseries, childminders and playgroups:
Department of Social Services
44 New Hall Street
Birmingham B3 2PA
Tel: (021) 235 2946

For details on nursery schools, units and classes:
Education Department
School Management Support Division
304 Portland Road
Birmingham B17 8LR
Tel: (021) 235 2620/2259

## CELANDINE NURSERY

8–10 Glastonbury Road
Yardley Wood
Birmingham B14 4DR
**Tel:** (021) 474 2995

**Owners:** Linda Jones, Cert Ed, Mont Dip
Vanessa Sutton, Mont Dip
**Principal:** Linda Jones
**Nursery Manager:** Jennifer Lanfermeijer-Russell, NNEB
**Type:** Day nursery offering full- and part-time places and half-day sessions
**Children:** 3mths–5yrs. 40 places. 60 on register
**Hours:** 7.30am–5.30pm (late collection by arrangement)
Morning session 7.30am–1pm
Afternoon session 1pm–5.30pm
Open 49 weeks a year
**Status:** Private, fee-paying
**Number of years open:** 7
**Meals:** Packed lunches, drinks, snacks
**1992 fees:** £70 per week full-time
£15 per day
£7.50 per session
**Waiting list:** Places available
**Registered by:** Met Dist of Birmingham SS

**Premises** After serving the community as a church and church hall for 50 years, the building is now skilfully converted to a day nursery. It provides three playrooms for different age groups, kitchen, toilets and office, all on one floor. A heated summer house makes a useful staffroom. All playrooms are brightly decorated and cheerful, with plenty of space to play and lots of good equipment, toys and books. Babies have a large play mat; for toddlers there is enough room to run about. The oldest, pre-school group have sand and water, a nature table with fish tank, television and video. Outside there is a hard area for trikes and ride-on toys and a lawn with rope ladder, swings, obstacle course and climbing frames. Fixed equipment is set on a safety surface. The nursery is on a quiet road in a former council estate where most residents are now owner/occupiers. It is also close to a new housing development. There is plenty of parking space at the front and a railway station nearby. The local park has a splendid duckpond regularly visited by Canada Geese and nursery children.

**Owners/Principal, Manager & staff** Jennifer Lanfermeijer-Russell is a mature, experienced NNEB, who has worked in nurseries, hospitals and residential homes for over 30 years in the Birmingham area and also in Amsterdam. A friendly, outgoing woman, she has kept up to date through extensive in-service training. The present owners of the nursery, sisters Linda Jones and Vanessa Sutton, rely on her for the day-to-day running of the nursery. Vanessa helps three or four mornings a week, opens the nursery each day and greets parents. Linda works on three afternoons, attending to paperwork and fees. The staff of 14 female nursery nurses and teachers represent a variety of different cultures and backgrounds. They include two Cert Eds, nine Montessori-trained teachers and two NNEBs. One teaches French and another dance. Vanessa is trained in British sign language. All nursery workers have first-aid certificates. Two or three YTS students attend on placement. The annual training budget is small at £300. Formal staff meetings are held once a term. The day of our visit, there were 25 children and 15 members of staff. A keyworker system is in operation. Staff/child ratios are 1:3 for babies and 1:4 for toddlers.

**Children & parents** Mainly English-speaking children with professional parents. About half transfer to state schools, the rest to the private sector. Celandine provides individual, specialised care for children with special needs and currently has one Down's syndrome child, one toddler with impaired hearing and deaf parents and one with a muscle-wasting disorder. New children are introduced to the nursery by attending a brief session with a parent. The nursery holds open days and parents' evenings. Parents are invited to call in to see what is going on at any time, except during the rest period from 1pm to 2.15pm. Two children are subsidised by their local authority.

**Curriculum & activities** A safe, happy environment, where parents can leave their children and go to work with a clear conscience. The timetable loosely follows the Montessori approach and many teachers are Montessori trained. Every child works with a variety of equipment, some of it Montessori. The emphasis is on learning to socialise with other children and adults, to become independent and to develop motor skills – pencil control, handling paintbrushes, cutlery, crayons and scissors. There is good-quality equipment and a large selection of books available, including Ladybird reading books. Reading is not normally taught, unless a parent particularly requests it. Children learn their numbers and letters and most build up a reading vocabulary of about ten to 20 words, learnt from flashcards. There is a regular weekly outing to the library for storytime, and 50 books a term are borrowed from the library. Painting, dough, sand and water play are always available. Nature studies and daily music are also part of the curriculum. Activities centre around themes and topics, and visitors or visits are arranged to complement them. Topics relating to road safety and safety in the home feature regularly. There are outings and theatre trips for the older children. On Thursdays there is a 'Take a Tumble' gym session, for which parents pay extra. Children use the kitchen area to cook and help make their own sandwiches. They bring packed lunches which can be re-heated if necessary. Older children go to the supermarket once a week to help with shopping for the nursery. Children's progress and development are monitored by group leaders, but no written reports are kept.

**Remarks** Happy, relaxed children, eager to talk about their activities and interests. Very good balance between quality care and educational programmes – staff qualifications and experience reflect this balance. The team has strong teaching abilities.

## EDGBASTON PARK NURSERY

65 Rotton Park Road
Edgbaston
Birmingham B16 0SG
**Tel:** (021) 454 2833

**Owner/Principal:** Kathy Hartley, BA
**Type:** Day nursery offering full- and part-time places and half-day sessions
**Children:** 6wks–5yrs. 30 places. 27 on register
**Hours:** 7.30am–6pm
Morning session 7.30am–1pm
Afternoon session 1pm–6pm
Open 52 weeks a year (excl bank holidays)
**Status:** Private, fee-paying
**Number of years open:** 2½
**Meals:** Breakfast, lunch, tea, snacks

**1992 fees:** £70 per week full-time
£15 per day
£10 per session
Registration fee of half of first week's fees
**Waiting list:** None, although some baby places reserved in advance
**Registered by:** Met Borough of Birmingham SS

**Premises** A 1930s detached, corner house, overlooking Edgbaston Reservoir at the back. Easily recognisable by the Disney characters stuck on windows, the nursery is located in a select and peaceful area of detached houses about two miles from the centre of Birmingham, close to main bus routes to and from the city. There are three main rooms for the children: one a large room for babies from 6 weeks old, overlooking the garden at the rear, furnished with an array of travel cots, a tunnel for crawling through, baby walkers and many recently purchased toys. Still downstairs is a bright and well-lived-in toddler room with colourful window paintings of familiar characters and children's work decorating the walls. The Green Room, for 18-month-olds onwards, is more an activity room with water play, play dough and other equipment for messy play. Children have their own bathroom opening off this room. The older children also have a quiet room for less rowdy games, for stories or for quietly getting on with a project. In addition, there is a staff room, a well-equipped kitchen and a changing room for babies. The nursery is well worn but not tatty. The fenced-in back garden provides a patio and large grassy area, with play house, rabbit hutch and other outdoor toys. Summerfield Park is a ten-minute walk away, and is visited reasonably often, but Edgbaston Reservoir is used more frequently for walks and duck-feeding expeditions.

**Owner/Principal & staff** Kathy Hartley, BA, is calm, placid and approachable and spends most of her time in the nursery. She describes herself as a Jack-of-all-trades, in charge of the smooth running of the nursery and liaison with parents. The nursery manager is Paula Whitehouse, NNEB. She and her BTEC-qualified deputy work together with Kathy on all aspects of the day-to-day organisation of the nursery. There are three further qualified members of staff, two NNEB and one BTEC. Other unqualified assistants are called in when necessary. There are two Asian members of staff, reflecting the local community, one of whom speaks Punjabi. Only one care worker has left in the last 2½ years, and the nursery is able to call on an 'emergency group', some qualified, to cover for staff holidays and sickness. Peripatetic teachers for various subjects such as music have been considered, but because most children are part-timers many of them would miss out on a regular class, so the idea has been dropped. On the day of our visit the staff/child ratio was a generous 1:3 and usually averages 1:4.

**Children & parents** Children come from a wide variety of cultures, with large numbers of Irish, Asian and Afro-Caribbeans reflecting the cultural mix within the locality. Many have full-time working mothers – teachers, nurses, social workers – and the nursery operates an open-door policy for communication and reassurance. Kathy reflects that the guilt working mothers feel generally means they need a lot more reassuring than their children. About 75 per cent of the children go on to local state schools, while those who choose the private sector favour Edgbaston High School and Holy Child.

**Curriculum & activities** The nursery has a positive but unstructured approach to pre-school activities. Children are divided into different groups by age and move from room to room as they grow older. All children come together each day first thing in the morning and again at the end of the day. All, except the babies, do a different activity each day such as clay modelling, painting, cookery, etc, as well as learning pencil control, numbers and the alphabet. There is a small quiet room for concentration, where pre-number and pre-writing work, quiet play and reading take place. There is also a wet-play room for messy activities. The Small World reading scheme is used together with videos, posters and many, many books. By the time children leave – some going into the private sector leave as early as 3 for their next school – they are generally able to recognise letters and numbers and have mastered most of the fine motor skills. They are also adept at telling the time, colour recognition and can recite familiar nursery rhymes. A good range of toys, books and equipment, many purchased new within the last year, but best of all and very noticeable, there are lots of cuddles. Staff and children are all very tactile. Notes on progress are kept for each child, but because the nursery is fairly small, direct communication with parents is considered the best way to keep them informed. A daily diary shows what a child has eaten, how much, and how often nappies were changed, etc. Children are taken on library visits, and outings to the swimming pool. Parties are a popular feature – birthdays, Hallowe'en, and summer and Christmas events where parents are invited to join in.

**Remarks** Comfortable, lived-in atmosphere and not a miserable child in sight. Good-quality care in a well-planned, well-placed nursery that sets out to be a home from home. Longer-than-average opening hours and an unusually high staff ratio make this nursery ideal for full-time working parents who need reassurance and peace of mind. Not a glamorous nursery, but a secure, stimulating environment with loving staff.

# Coventry

An uneven spread of provision across the city, with waiting lists for most services, except childminders. Part-time nursery education is available to 25 per cent of 3- and 4-year-olds. Social Services provide 14 day nurseries for children in need, but this does not satisfy demand in an area with a high percentage of lone parents and ethnic minority groups. Negotiations are underway to close some facilities following this year's budget cuts. There are 35 private day nurseries and five more in the process of registration. Nearly 800 registered childminders provide most of the full-time daycare available.

**Further information**

For details on day nurseries, childminders and playgroups:

Department of Social Services
Stoke Under Fives Unit
57 Ribble Road
Stoke
Coventry CV3 1AW
Tel: (0203) 636035

For details on nursery schools, units and classes:

Education Department
New Council Offices
Earl Street
Coventry CV1 5RS
Tel: (0203) 831622/3

## ST OSBURG'S PRIMARY SCHOOL & NURSERY

Upper Hill Street
Coundon
Coventry CV1 4AP
**Tel:** (0203) 227165

**Owner:** Met Dist of Coventry LEA
**Headteacher:** Ann Bunt, Cert Ed
**Type:** Nursery class in primary school offering half-day sessions. No full-time places
**Children:** 3–4yrs. 32 places. 60 on register
**Hours:** Morning session 8.55am–12 noon
Afternoon session 1.10pm–3.30pm
Open 36 weeks a year

**Status:** State nursery class
**Number of years open:** 17
**Meals:** None
**1992 fees:** No fees
**Waiting list:** Too long. Places cannot be provided for all who apply
**Registered by:** Met Dist of Coventry LEA

**Premises** A purpose-built, single-storey, brick building, detached from the main school, originally put up in the 1960s to house two infant classes. Both large, light classrooms are now used by the nursery unit – one for physical activities, well equipped with slide, climbing frame, bikes and television, and the other for concentrating on puzzles, construction toys, the home corner and a generously stocked book corner. Opening off the first classroom is an office which houses the cooker used during the weekly cookery session. The school is close to the Coventry Ring Road and easily accessible by public transport. There is a large, grassy and sturdily fenced playground outside. All outdoor play equipment is stored in the main building and brought out when weather permits. Nearby Nauls Mill Park is rarely visited, generally only in autumn for nature studies.

**Headteacher & staff** Ann Bunt, Cert Ed, has been headteacher of the school for the last four years. She is a key link in local community care projects, dealing with child abuse and learning difficulties in particular. She recently detected hearing difficulties in a child who had suffered from behavioural problems for years. There are two full-time members of staff in the unit, one a qualified teacher, the other an NNEB nursery nurse who has worked at the school for eight years. There is generally one student from a local college on work experience, sometimes male. Ann Bunt visits the nursery every day and spends two days teaching in different parts of the school. The school secretary is the official first-aider. Staff meet formally every fortnight and, after so many years together, work as a very close team. Staff training is important, with in-house and local authority INSET days provided, and, depending on the budget, some short outside courses. The basic staff/child ratio is 1:16. Not generous enough, but helped by the presence of a student and visits from the headteacher.

**Children & parents** St Osburg's is the nursery class closest to the centre of Coventry, and consequently children come from a wide variety of backgrounds. The majority live in council or rented accommodation, often high-rise. 'We feel it is vital to build up good relationships with parents,' says Ann Bunt, and parents are encouraged to become involved in the nursery and to feel they are welcome to take part in all the activities. Parents' evenings are held once a term. The school often acts as a help-link for families who need extra support. No particular method of grouping children is used, although they are divided between different activities during each session. New children are visited at home prior to starting at the nursery and are phased-in over the first three weeks of term in small groups of four.

**Curriculum & activities** Children learn through play and the school provides a huge supply of educational games, construction toys, puzzles, climbing frames, sand and water, paints, home corner and books. Half-termly topics are built into the programme and provide the basis for much of the curriculum. There is plenty of free playtime, but children are also encouraged to sit down and concentrate on a particular subject, in preparation for what will be expected of them at primary school. Books and pre-school exercises, such as tracing letters, numbers and their names, are an important part of the curriculum. The Letterland reading scheme is available, although children are not generally ready for this by the time they move up to the reception class. Cookery classes are held weekly. There is regular swimming in the school pool, which parents may also use. The library is only visited twice yearly, but libraries visit the school more frequently. Limited contact with the main school.

**Remarks** Described by the head as 'an oasis in a concrete jungle', the nursery class provides a much needed social centre for children and families living in inner city high-rise blocks. The school would like to improve its outside play area, to provide the best possible space for children who have no garden at home. Caring and understanding staff take as much interest in the parents and families as they do in the children. Huge demand for places, with many left unsatisfied.

# Dudley

Four thousand of the district's 19,000 under-5s receive some part-time or full-time nursery education. A 'rising-fives policy' allows many 4-year-olds to attend primary school full-time. The Education Authority is committed to expanding the number of nursery classes, as funds permit. Currently certain areas have excellent provision, and others long waiting lists or no provision at all. There are no local authority day nurseries. All full-time daycare is provided by the private and voluntary sectors. 19 private day nurseries cater mainly for children over 2 years old, and their fees exclude low-income families or parents with more than one child. Working parents with babies use the borough's 425 registered childminders.

**Further information**

For details on day nurseries, childminders and playgroups:
Children's Daycare Officer
Inspection and Quality Audit Unit
Social Services Department
8 Ednam Road
Dudley DY1 1HL
Tel: (0384) 456000

For details on nursery schools, units and classes:
Education Department
Westox House
1 Trinity Road
Dudley DY1 1JB
Tel: (0384) 456000

## PRIORY PRIMARY – NURSERY UNIT

Limes Road
Dudley
West Midlands DY1 4HN
**Tel:** (0384) 255505

**Owner:** Dudley Metropolitan Council LEA
**Headteacher:** Mike Millman, B Ed
**Teacher-in-charge:** Marjorie Fernihough, Cert Ed
**Type:** Nursery class in primary school offering half-day sessions. No full-time places
**Children:** 3yrs 3mths–4yrs 9mths. 60 places. 120 on register
**Hours:** Morning session 9.05am–11.30am
Afternoon session 1pm–3.25pm
Open 39 weeks a year
**Status:** State nursery class
**Number of years open:** 55
**Meals:** Milk mid-session
**1992 fees:** No fees. 25p per week voluntary contribution to school funds
**Waiting list:** 80
**Registered by:** Dudley Metropolitan Council LEA

**Premises** Purpose-built, single-storey, school building in front of the main school, screened from the road by a shrubbery. The school serves the Priory council estate. The nursery unit consists of one large main classroom, which can be divided into two by sliding doors; two long corridors, kitchen, cloakroom, storeroom and four small rooms used as a staff room, office and library. The emulsioned walls are enlivened by children's paintings and craftwork. Equipment is plentiful and very well used (annual equipment budget £1600). All furniture is in the process of being replaced. The main room incorporates a messy-play area, small tables and chairs, and a home corner. The library has been newly created with £1000 spent on books, which children are allowed to take home. Outside is a lawn with ancient climbing frame, and sloping garden bed leading to a turreted castle for children to play in. There is also a tarmac playground for ride-on toys. Priory Park is a brisk walk away – children are taken twice-termly.

**Teacher-in-charge & staff** Marjorie Fernihough, Cert Ed, the teacher-in-charge, has run the nursery class for the last five years. She originally taught reception class infants, but after leaving the profession to have children, she returned initially to teach English as a second language. She reports directly to the headteacher of the primary school and is responsible for the day-to-day running of the nursery. The team consists of Marjorie and four NNEB nursery nurses. One, in her early 50s, has been at the unit for 15 years, the others are in their 20s. A speech therapist visits one day a week to work with children with language problems and the nursery takes NNEB students for work experience. The staff/child ratio is 1:12 on average, but can be 1:15 at times. The local authority does not provide as many training opportunities as staff would like.

**Children & parents** The children are predominantly from low-income families. Many have unemployed or single parents; most live on the Priory council estate. Many of the parents also attended the nursery. A number are of mixed race. The majority of parents are caring and interested but some children lack motivation and stimulus at home and as a result have difficulty communicating. They need extra help in this area. The nursery does not take children assessed as having special educational needs, although some are identified as such once they have started. Outside help is sought and available when necessary. The majority are busy, talkative amongst themselves and well supervised. A pre-nursery group, the Priory Pandas, operates in a community room in the main school. Parents help to organise it, and children over 2½ sometimes visit the nursery. Most children move on to Priory Primary School. The nursery has an open-door policy towards parents. They come into the classroom to help, talk to staff each day and are invited to open days and parents' evenings.

**Curriculum & activities** Learning through play, with the emphasis on language development. As a number of the children have communication problems, staff create many situations in which children are encouraged to talk and listen. Activities are chosen to stimulate their language development. The nursery nurses monitor social behaviour and skills and reactions to other children and adults. Good behaviour is emphasised. Sessions start with registration and free play, including messy play, construction toys, home corner and puzzles. Children are free to choose their activities. After a break for milk, songs and stories, they divide into four small groups for more structured activities including pre-writing and reading skills. The Letterland scheme is used. Most leave familiar with letters, but only a few start to read. Those who are ready are introduced to the Oxford Reading Tree. There is a weekly session of PE in the school hall, plus swimming and cookery classes. One mum or dad helps at each session with painting, modelling and craft work – rolling up their sleeves and writing names on pictures. We observed lots of cuddles and holding hands. Staff are treated very much as mother substitutes. All children help to clear up after activities. There are termly visits to a nature reserve and a grand summer outing with parents, which last year filled five coaches. Every Christmas there are visiting clowns. Written records are kept on each child's social behaviour and inter-personal skills. A detailed report is prepared for the next school when children leave.

**Remarks** Now into its second generation of children, this very long-established nursery is an institution on the Priory Estate. In 55 years, it has built up a strong, well-deserved reputation, providing care and pre-school education vital to the local community. Children are taught how to learn and how to behave. Excellent organisation in a busy, loving atmosphere. A lower staff/child ratio would be a distinct advantage.

# Sandwell

Sandwell offers good nursery education provision, with 56 per cent of 3- and 4-year-olds attending classes part time. There are three nursery schools and 75 nursery classes. No local authority day nurseries are available. The Council sponsors places in the private and voluntary sectors for children in need. The 17 private nurseries charge reasonable rates in order to attract customers. 328 registered childminders offer flexible hours and affordable places. There are no waiting lists anywhere. In an area of high unemployment and some considerable poverty, many people use the unofficial, unregulated childcare network of family, friends and neighbours. The provision of local authority day nurseries, available to low-income families, would be warmly welcomed by many.

**Further information**

For details on day nurseries, childminders and playgroups:
Department of Social Services
Hollies Family Centre
Coopers Lane
Smethwick
Warley B67 7DW
Tel: (021) 558 1382/5

For details on nursery schools, units and classes:
Education Department
Shaftesbury House
402 High Street
West Bromwich B70 9LT
Tel: (021) 525 7366

# Solihull

No nursery schools, but the 31 nursery classes offer part-time places to 34 per cent of 3- and 4-year-olds. Provision is patchy, with waiting lists in many areas. There are no local authority day nurseries. Children in need receive sponsorship within the private and voluntary sectors. 24 private day nurseries (more in the pipeline), two workplace nurseries and nearly 500 registered childminders provide full-time daycare, but demand exceeds supply. Most services have waiting lists and parents frequently complain that there are no local vacancies for the type of care they require. Certain areas of the borough are particularly hard-hit by unemployment and need more affordable care and state education provision. 'Daycare is very expensive if you are on a low income. Having my two children with a childminder costs 80 per cent of my wages,' one mother complained.

**Further information**

For details on day nurseries, childminders and playgroups:
Under Tens Centre
6 Craig Croft
Chelmsley Wood
Birmingham B37 7TR
Tel: (021) 770 8850

For details on nursery schools, units and classes:
Education Department
Council House
Solihull B91 3QU
Tel: (021) 704 6656

# GREEN LANES PRIMARY SCHOOL

Tamar Drive
Chelmsley Wood
Birmingham
B36 0SY
**Tel:** (021) 748 2360

**Owner:** Solihull Met Council LEA
**Headteacher:** Vanessa Ward, B Phil Ed, Cert Ed
**Teacher-in-charge:** Shirley Bryars, Cert Ed
**Type:** Nursery class in primary school offering half-day sessions. No full-time places
**Children:** 3yrs–4yrs 11mths. 30 places. 60 on register
**Hours:** Morning session 9am–11.30am Afternoon session 12.45pm–3.15pm Open 40 weeks a year
**Status:** State nursery class
**Number of years open:** 15
**Meals:** Snacks, milk
**1992 fees:** No fees. Voluntary contribution of £1 per week
**Waiting list:** Variable
**Registered by:** Solihull Metropolitan Council LEA

**Premises** Detached building, purpose-built 15 years ago, in the grounds of Green Lanes Primary School. The school is on a council housing estate, with high-rise blocks of flats, in a working-class area of Solihull, with high unemployment. The main, spacious, L-shaped classroom has large windows and an excellent array of children's work. It also incorporates a quiet area, with carpeted floor and comfortable seating. Leading from this are a well-furnished home room, a small cheery cloakroom covered with posters and friezes, a tiny kitchen, toilets and a boxed-in verandah with slab floor, housing sand and water play, a dolls' house and guinea pigs in their hutch. The verandah opens out on to an outside play area, including grass, paving and asphalt surfaces, used each session, weather permitting.

**Teacher-in-charge & staff** Shirley Bryars, Cert Ed, is the qualified teacher-in-charge of the nursery class. She stopped teaching when her own children were born, but returned some four years ago and has run the nursery class for the last two years. She loves children and has unlimited energy. She liaises skilfully with parents and is firmly in control of the class – in a relaxed, friendly way. She reports once a week to the headteacher of the primary school, who also herself visits the nursery twice a day. In addition there are two energetic young NNEBs, one particularly good at art. They work as a team, helping each other and interacting closely with the children. All staff take advantage of the range of relevant LEA training opportunities available.

**Children & parents** The intake covers many nationalities, from a broad social spectrum. Some children live in tough working-class areas of high unemployment, others in the better-off suburbs, the children of white-collar workers. Some parents are very supportive, while others have no involvement with the nursery. All are visited at home by Shirley Bryars before their child starts nursery so that she can introduce herself, see the child in his/her own environment and answer any questions. Parents are invited to the nursery regularly for coffee mornings, plays and concerts and are free to speak to staff whenever they wish. At present there are two special needs children who are well integrated and making excellent progress. All children move on to state primary schools, many to Green Lanes itself.

**Curriculum & activities** The nursery philosophy is 'to provide a stable, happy and stimulating environment to assist social, emotional, physical, spiritual and intellectual development'. The children learn through play and enjoy a wide range of activities, including art, craft, music, singing, storytime, cooking, growing plants and tending animals. Staff ensure that each child participates in every activity and when children need extra help with a task they are given individual attention. Social training is considered important and children are well mannered and responsive. There are lots of cuddles and much encouragement. Each week there is a 45-minute dance session in the school hall. Children are not taught to read, but the topic work – colour, shape, weather – involves developing all the skills they need in order to settle quickly and successfully into full-time infant classes. There is a summer outing every year. Written records are kept on each child, for the school and the local authority – parents have access to both.

**Remarks** Impressive all-round nursery care and education, serving a community with more than its fair share of social problems. Loving staff, who relate well to the children and command their respect. Responsive, happy children, who obviously benefit from their nursery environment.

## ST ALPHEGE (C of E) INFANT SCHOOL – NURSERY UNIT

New Road
Solihull
West Midlands B91 3DW
**Tel:** (021) 705 0443

**Owner:** Solihull Met Council LEA/Diocese of Birmingham
**Headteacher:** Elaine Winterbottom, Cert Ed
**Teacher-in-charge:** Jane Sims, Cert Ed (from Sept '93)
**Type:** Nursery class in state primary school offering half-day sessions. No full-time places
**Children:** 3yrs–4yrs 11mths. 30 places. 60 on register
**Hours:** Morning session 8.55am–11.25am
Afternoon session 12.55pm–3.25pm
Open 40 weeks a year
**Status:** Church-aided state nursery class
**Number of years open:** 18
**Meals:** None
**1992 fees:** No fees. Voluntary contribution of £3.50 per term for cookery and incidentals
**Waiting list:** Long. Not all will be offered places. Places allocated to the children of practising Anglicans, in Sept following their 3rd birthday
**Registered by:** Solihull Met Council LEA

**Premises** Purpose-built, 12-year-old, single-storey, brick nursery, set in spacious grounds, two minutes' walk from the centre of Solihull. The large lawned area at the back has lovely views overlooking the rector's garden, which is used for sports day each summer. The nursery unit consists of one large playroom with a small, carpeted, almost separate reading area. Leading off are the toilets, kitchen and an office, also used for one-to-one teaching. Crammed with child-oriented equipment and furniture (annual budget £2000), the main room is a little cramped. Plans are underway to enclose an existing veranda area to provide extra space for wet play and large equipment. The school is only 100 yards from Malvern Park, which children visit at least once a term.

**Teacher-in-charge & assistants** At the time of our visit, Margaret Maund, Cert Ed, the teacher-in-charge, was about to retire after 12 years in the post. Her replacement from September '93 is Jane Sims, Cert Ed. The two nursery assistants are qualified NNEB nursery nurses. One is artistic and creative, the other skilled and experienced in working with children with disabilities, especially hearing impairment. The staff are happy and friendly, all older women who have worked together as a team for the past 12 years. There is a rota of parent helpers and students on practical placement. The annual budget for staff training is £1000. The teacher-in-charge reports to the infant school head and the Board of Governors. The staff/child ratio is 1:10.

**Children & parents** Mainly middle-class, but with a good ethnic mix. Professional practising Anglican families – teachers, doctors, nurses and solicitors. A number of priority places are set aside for children with special educational needs, disabilities and social problems. At present there are hearing-impaired children, epileptics and children with severe learning difficulties, all successfully integrated. Most transfer to the infant school. Strong relationship with parents and regular contact, as staff consider this 'the most important part of our job'.

**Curriculum & activities** A church-aided school based on Christian principles. Nursery sessions begin with a short assembly, including prayers, simple Bible stories and hymns. All children participate in each of the activities available during a session. These range from construction equipment and board games to painting, play dough, sand, water and the home corner. They are encouraged to participate in large group activities and are also taken out individually for pre-reading, pre-writing and pre-number work, on a one-to-one basis. Most learn to recognise words and letters and are introduced to the Oxford Reading Tree in preparation for school. There are always singing games and action rhymes followed by outdoor or indoor physical play depending on the weather. Each session ends with storytime. Cooking, music, dance and movement and PE (in the main school hall) are weekly events. In summer children spend most of their time outside. Occasional visits relate to topic

work. Visitors to the infant school include theatre groups and a man who brings in animals – birds, snakes and other small reptiles. The nursery class joins in, if the subject is suitable.
**Remarks** A long-established nursery class offering a broad-based curriculum in a caring, happy environment. Experienced, patient staff. Links with the main school will become even closer as the new teacher-in-charge, Jane Sims, has responsibility for co-ordinating all early years learning in the nursery and school reception class.

# Walsall

The best nursery education provision in the West Midlands, with eight nursery schools and nursery classes attached to the majority of primary schools. 58 per cent of 3- and 4-year-olds receive a part-time place. 26 playgroups offer part-time, part-week provision and a travelling nursery mini-bus visits areas which lack other facilities. The local authority runs four family centres, three jointly funded with the Children's Society charity, and two day nurseries catering for families in need. There are waiting lists in some areas. Of the 500 childminders (more in the process of registration), 90 are sponsored by the council. There are two private day nurseries and a further three awaiting registration. The real need in this densely populated borough with high levels of unemployment is for less expensive, subsidised full-time care.

## Further information

For details on day nurseries, childminders and playgroups:
Department of Social Services
Children's Daycare Team
106 Essington Road
New Invention
Willenhall WV12 5DT
Tel: (0922) 710751

For details on nursery schools, units and classes:
Education Department
Civic Centre
Darwall Street
Walsall WS1 1DQ
Tel: (0922) 652350

# Wolverhampton

A borough which prides itself on being at the forefront of nursery education provision. With ten nursery schools and 57 nursery classes, nearly 60 per cent of 3- and 4-year-olds receive a part-time place before starting school. Waiting lists are long in some areas. There are also at least five private nursery schools in the district. Social Services provide five day nurseries, exclusively for children in need. 70 playgroups are well distributed geographically, and many report vacancies. There are 275 registered childminders, plus others in the process of registration. Some have vacancies. 12 private day nurseries, mainly in the south-west of the borough, charge from £40 to £85 per week.

**Further information**

For details on local authority day nurseries, childminders and playgroups:
Under Eights Team
South West Division
Sheldon House Flat
Lord Street
Chapel Ash
Wolverhampton WV3 0QU
Tel: (0902) 21089 or 21317

For details on private/voluntary nurseries:
Social Services Department
Registration and Inspection Unit
49 Waterloo Road
Wolverhampton WV1 4QJ
Tel: (0902) 313466

For details on nursery schools, units and classes:
Education Department
Civic Centre
St Peter's Square
Wolverhampton WV1 1RR
Tel: (0902) 27811 × 4176

# West Sussex

Some excellent playgroups, but very little nursery provision for working parents in search of full-time daycare. There is virtually nothing for the under-2s. The county's 43,000 under-5s have no Social Services day nurseries, and only four local authority nursery schools. The six nursery classes attached to primary schools in the county all have huge waiting lists and offer part-time places only. The number of registered private day nurseries has increased to 60 over the last few years, and fees of £100 per week are common.

**Further information**

For details on private nurseries, childminders and playgroups, contact your local social services area office:
Bognor Regis (0243) 826711
Chanctonbury (0903) 745331
Chichester (0243) 752999
Crawley (0293) 535381
East Grinstead (0342) 316333
Haywards Heath (0444) 453141
Horsham (0403) 264872
Littlehampton (0903) 717341
Midhurst (0730) 816721
Shoreham (0273) 463551
Worthing (0903) 700870

For details on nursery schools, units and classes:
Education Department
County Hall
West Street
Chichester PO19 1RF
Tel: (0243) 777100

## BODY SHOP CHILD DEVELOPMENT CENTRE – KIDS UNLIMITED

Watersmead Business Park
Littlehampton
W Sussex PO21 3TS
**Tel:** (0903) 731848

**Owner:** Kids Unlimited
**Nursery Manager:** Jan Brockhurst, NNEB, SEN
**Type:** Workplace nursery offering full- and part-time places to Body Shop employees, Midland Bank employees and if possible, the local community
**Children:** 3mths–5yrs. 50 places. 61 on register
**Hours:** 7.45am–6pm
Morning session 7.45am–1pm (inc lunch)
Afternoon session 1pm–6pm
Open 51 weeks a year
**Status:** Workplace nursery
**Number of years open:** 3
**Meals:** Lunch, tea, snacks
**1992 fees:** On a sliding scale for Body Shop employees according to salary
**Waiting list:** 20 names, all for baby places. Waiting list operates on a Body Shop points system. Employees must register when 3 months pregnant
**Registered by:** W Sussex County Council SS
**Under same ownership:** 22 in total across the country including Griffin Nursery, Merseyside (see entry)

## BROADWATER MANOR NURSERY DEPARTMENT

Broadwater Manor School
Broadwater Road
Worthing
W Sussex BN14 8HU
**Tel:** (0903) 201123

**Owner/Head of Department:** Kim Woodley, Cert Ed
**Type:** Day nursery attached to co-ed prep school, offering full- and part-time places and half-day sessions, plus separate mother & toddler group for 2 sessions a week
**Children:** 2–3yrs mother and toddler group. 30 places. 37 on register
3–5yrs. 100 places. 114 on register
**Hours:** 9.00am–3.30pm
Morning session 9.15am–12 noon
Afternoon session 1.30pm–3.30pm
Mother and toddler group 1.45pm–3.15pm Mon/Thurs or Tues/Fri
Open 40 weeks a year
**Status:** Private, fee-paying
**Number of years open:** 11
**Meals:** Lunch, juice and milk
**1992 fees:** £370 per term for 5 morning sessions a week
£310 per term for 5 afternoon sessions a week
£230 per term for 3 morning sessions a week
£190 per term for 3 afternoon sessions a week
£85 per term for 2 afternoon mother & toddler sessions
Sibling discounts
**Waiting list:** None
**Registered by:** Dept for Education

**Premises** Broadwater Manor Nursery inhabits an entire wing of the main Broadwater Manor Preparatory School – a large, gracious manor house dating back some 400 years in parts (mentioned in the Domesday Book). Set in beautiful grounds, the nursery also has its own safely fenced, grass play area full of equipment in prime condition. Entry is via a hallway to the left of a stunning conservatory – the painting room, known rather pretentiously as the Design Realisation Room. Everywhere is light, colourful and active. Walls and ceilings are crowded with ambitious examples of children's work, information charts and friezes. The entrance hall leads to a spacious reception area – shelves, at child height, are full of well-kept equipment and books. At the back, a door leads to the two large classrooms – one for younger children, the other for the older age group. Light streams through large windows and skylights in all rooms. There is equipment everywhere, and cupboards and shelves full of books, puzzles and toys. Loos and washbasins are located in a large, spotless room, with warm-air hand-driers for hygiene (and fun). The decor and carpeting throughout are in prime condition, but most of all this is a well-ordered environment, where children come first. The nursery also has use of the main school gym, assembly hall and playing field.

**Head of Department & staff** Energetic and passionate about preparing children for school, Kim Woodley, Cert Ed, has the advantage of being a member of the family which owns the business. She became a partner in the school when her father retired in 1987 after 27 years as headmaster. She had set up and opened the nursery department six years earlier. Kim has total responsibility for running and organising the department and teaches all age groups full-time, apart from Thursday mornings which are kept free for showing parents round and administration. A warm, demonstrative person, children are her main concern and they showed great affection for her as we toured the classrooms. Kim Woodley has a loyal, long-serving team of qualified staff (staff have left only because of pregnancy, retirement or relocation). There are three qualified teachers (Cert Ed), two nursery nurses (NNEB), one with a BTEC (Nursery Nursing Diploma) and one with a PPA diploma. They are mature in years and in experience. Students are also a regular part of the scene – boys from Lancing College, girls from schools in Brighton and Worthing. Non-teaching staff include a cook, cleaner and secretarial help.

**Children & parents** Mainly white, middle class with most arriving by car from chic enclaves up to five miles away. The owners regret the narrow social and racial mix. The majority of children attend a half-day session per day. A mother and toddler group takes place twice a week for children between 2 and 3 years old accompanied by mum, dad or carer, in preparation for joining the nursery school at 3 years old. A handful of children attend all day, but only for two or three days a week at most. Kim Woodley believes nursery complements what happens at home, therefore parents have a strong input and their co-operation is vital. The nursery attracts upwardly mobile parents with high expectations, who choose it for its strong educational programmes and good results – the emphasis is unequivocally on preparation for school (mainly the highly competitive world of public school) both socially and academically. Children call staff by their full names – Mrs Woodley, Mrs Humphries, etc – both as a token of respect and because this is the way of big school. Polite, confident and articulate children. All parents co-operate in the nursery's early learning system: each child has a 'work bag' which goes home each day with specific homework – books, words to learn, games, tasks, etc. for parents to do with them. Also in the bag is a book for parents to write their comments, problems or worries.

**Curriculum & activities** Each session commences with 40 minutes of free play – Lego, puzzles, dressing up, Wendy house, home corner. During this time, a teacher will spend some time with each child on a one-to-one basis, discussing their previous day's homework in the work bag. Group activity follows – writing or number skills or a logic activity designed to develop powers of reasoning and observation. Groupings are age-related. The Ginn maths scheme is used, and reading books include Through the Rainbow picture books and some Ladybird. Each child has his/her own individual programme aimed to develop all spheres – intellectual, creative, social and physical – at his/her own pace. At least once a week children use the school gym, with its wall bars, climbing frame, slides, trampolines, mats. Kim Woodley plays the guitar and there is singing every day. Painting, sand and water, model making, woodwork and other creative activities take place in the conservatory. The project work is exciting – at the time of our visit a circus project had taken over an entire classroom – clowns, elephants, jugglers, on windows, walls and ceiling space. Annual sports day, Christmas play, regular open evenings. The majority of children go on to Broadwater Pre-Prep, and 25 per cent to local primary schools.

**Remarks** Wonderful, caring nursery with strong educational programmes. Dependent on enthusiastic, dedicated head and active, co-operative parents.

# DAVISON CRÈCHE & UNDER FIVES CLUB

Davison High School
Selbourne Road
Worthing
W Sussex BN11 2JX
**Tel:** (0903) 820260

**Owner:** Davison CE High School
**Crèche Co-ordinator:** Pauline Jackson, PPA
**Type:** Day nursery offering full- and part-time places and half-day sessions, plus after-school care, to Davison High School employees, W Sussex education workers and Midland Bank staff
**Children:** 2mths-5yrs. 24 places (inc 8 babies). 31 on register

**Hours:** 8am–6pm
Morning session 8am–1pm
Afternoon session 1pm–4pm
Flexible hours available after 4pm
Open 52 weeks a year
**Status:** Workplace nursery
**Number of years open:** 4
**Meals:** Lunch, tea
**1992 fees:** £60 per week full-time
£7.50 per morning session
£4.50 per afternoon session
£1.50 per hour after 4pm
Fees kept deliberately low
**Waiting list:** Horrific
**Registered by:** Local education property – registration not required

**Premises** Converted single-storey classroom huts in the corner of the playing fields of a large, all-girls, state comprehensive school. There is a spacious, grassed and paved outside play area, well fenced. The building is not the best feature of this nursery and space is a problem, although there is talk of possible expansion. A partitioned corner of one of the classrooms serves as a kitchen for babies' milk and food preparation, staff drinks and morning snacks. Meals are brought over from the school kitchens. There is no separate kitchen and no staff room. Loos and washbasins are sandwiched between the two rooms. The lack of an ideal building is, to some extent, compensated for by the fact that the nursery has full use of all Davison High School's generous facilities. These include a leisure centre, swimming pool, tennis and netball courts, gym, conservation area and music rooms. Nursery children regularly attend plays, concerts and presentations at the school.

**Co-ordinator & staff** Pauline Jackson, PPA, a warm, homely mother figure, leads her qualified team (all NNEB, PPA, BTEC and City & Guilds) with calm efficiency. She believes the quiet, friendly atmosphere at the Davison Crèche is achieved by 'praise, encouragement and thanks'. Her seven staff (including two deputies) cover a wide age range and are all happy and long-serving. The nursery also acts as a learning resource centre for pupils at the school studying for GCSE Child Development and the National Association for Maternal and Child Welfare Certificate. Girls come to the nursery in groups of four and, under the supervision of nursery staff, put into practice the childcare skills they have been taught in the classroom.

**Children & parents** Priority is given to teachers (male and female) at the school. The Midland Bank has five places reserved for their employees and the rest are open to 'anyone in education in West Sussex'. Nursery provision generally in the area is poor, and parents travel long distances to bring their children here. All work in the area. Pauline Jackson says that parents are sometimes demanding. 'They are very busy people under a lot of pressure, but they are very trusting. If their children are happy, then the parents are happy.' There is very little parental involvement (the Christmas play is videoed for working mums to see) and no demand for parents' meetings, although parents are welcome to visit at any time. Mothers at the school frequently pop in to breast-feed between classes. Children are bright, articulate and busy. Virtually all move on to state primary schools.

**Curriculum & activities** The nursery follows the aims and philosophy of the PPA (Pre-Schools Playgroups Association) – that children learn through play. There is no formal learning, but there is a wide range of play equipment to teach the child to develop mentally, socially, physically and emotionally. Painting and craft, songs, music and dance take place every day. Children are allowed to watch television (*Playbus*) in the mornings. Activities and outings are plentiful and imaginative. Once a term, children from a local school for the handicapped come to play for the afternoon. Children here are not pushed in any way. The emphasis is on creating a happy, family atmosphere where they learn to develop relationships, make friends and build up the confidence and maturity to cope with school.

**Remarks** An oasis in the childcare desert of West Sussex! Davison Crèche owes its existence to the dynamism and campaigning spirit of Sheila Wallace, the headmistress of Davison High School. As a working mother struggling with two small children, she recognised the importance of reliable, affordable childcare provision in attracting and keeping high-quality teaching staff. One of the first things she did when she took over as head was to set up the nursery. Her example has now been successfully copied by several other schools in this local authority area.

# FIRST STEPS DAY NURSERY

Chichester College of Technology
Westgate Fields
Chichester
W Sussex PO19 1SB
**Tel:** (0243) 532043

**Owner:** Chichester College
**Manager:** Jacqueline McCulloch, NNEB
**Type:** Day nursery offering full- and part-time places and half-day sessions to college staff, students and local community
**Children:** 3mths–5yrs 11mths. 25 places. 50 on register
**Hours:** 8am–6pm
Morning session 8am–12.30pm
Afternoon session 1pm–6pm
Open 51 weeks a year
**Status:** Private, non profit-making
**Number of years open:** 3
**Meals:** Lunch, tea, snacks
**1992 fees:** £97 per week full-time – under 2
£88 per week full-time – over 2
£93 per week for staff/sponsored places – under 2
£85 per week for staff/sponsored places – over 2
£11.50 per session – under 2
£11 per session – over 2
20% sibling discount
**Waiting list:** None
**Registered by:** W Sussex County Council SS
**Other nurseries under same ownership:**
Second Steps Day Nursery, Royal Wessex Hospital, Chichester

**Premises** A single-storey, wood-clad, converted classroom on the college campus. Access is through the main entrance of the college, with parking in front. Bus and train stations are close by. In all, there are eight bright, freshly painted rooms, decorated with mobiles, nursery pictures and children's art. Carpets cover the floors in the smaller baby rooms, and washable, non-slip vinyl in the activity and eating areas. The large main room holds a piano, computer, carpeted home corner, books and a bed, plus tables and chairs for table-top games and activities and a popular dressing-up corner. Babies under 2 have a separate air-conditioned suite, with a good range of activities, mobiles, collages on the wall, changing facilities and their own kitchen. Children use the main kitchen for cookery classes, and meals are sent over from the college. Finally, there is a small office, staff room, storage and toilet area. A strong emphasis is placed on health and hygiene. Outside is a large, fenced, grassy garden and play area with safety surface. The impressive equipment includes climbing frame, Wendy house, see-saw, trampolines and push-and-ride toys. There are two parks nearby with no main roads to cross, which are used frequently.

**Manager & staff** Jacqueline McCulloch, NNEB, has 20 years' childcare experience, including work with physically and mentally handicapped children. She is a full-time manager and reports to the vice-principal of the college. The staff team comprises six full-time staff and three part-time staff. All are qualified NNEB, one is Montessori trained, and the assistant manager is a qualified infant teacher. Some are young girls at the beginning of their careers, others more mature mothers who have returned to nursery nursing. A male helper, employed as a part-time casual worker, tidies up and serves tea. Staff turnover is not a problem – only one carer has left since the nursery opened. Staff meetings are held once a fortnight, and communication between staff and managers is relaxed. Staff mix socially, but largely in their own age groups – there is a wide age range. Staff/child ratios are good: 1:2, under 12 months; 1:3, 12–23 months; 1:5, 2–3 years; 1:8, 3–5 years. All staff are encouraged to attend training courses once or twice a year. NNEB students from the college assist as part of their practical training.

**Children & parents** The nursery is available to college staff and students and the wider community. Midland Bank and the DSS subsidise places at the nursery for the children of their employees. There is a broad social mix and some ethnic diversity. Children with disabilities and special educational needs are welcome but there are none at present. The nursery has an open-door policy to parents, and holds three open days a year. There are quarterly parents' evenings as well as plays, concerts, a sports day and regular newsletters. Parents are asked to become involved in phasing-in, outings and nursery activities and are represented on the management committee. Children transfer to both state and private schools at rising-5.

**Curriculum & activities** Jacqueline McCulloch believes that they have developed their own methods and philosophy. Some Montessori equipment is used. The nursery operates around a flexible daily timetable, beginning with free play and registration, followed by a planned activity – string painting, cookery, printing, gardening. After drinks, snacks and outside play, the children divide into smaller groups – the younger ones for another planned activity, usually relating to the current topic, and the older children for more formal work time. There is no set reading scheme, but Letterland is used. A peripatetic French teacher visits two or three times a week. No clear distinction is made between care and education, play and learning. Everything is considered to be learning. Equipment is plentiful, bright and stimulating (annual budget, a huge £6000). Singing, music and movement, with percussion instruments, storytime and walks take place daily. There is a computer, painting, modelling and sand and water play are always available. Swimming takes place at the local leisure centre once a week, library visits fortnightly and an outing once a month to a farm, sea-life centre or local places of interest. Once a week, children are taken to the college for gymnastics, pottery and woodwork. Staff monitor children's progress and record their observations in writing each week. Parents are given regular profile reports.

**Remarks** Efficient, professional nursery providing everything a child could possibly want, in a happy, homely atmosphere. A busy and interesting timetable. High calibre of staff and good staff/child ratios. Costs are very fair for the quality of service offered. During our visit, the telephone rang constantly with parents enquiring about places.

# LITTLE ORCHARD DAY NURSERY

Penthorn
Clay Lane
Fishbourne
Chichester
W Sussex PO19 3PX
**Tel:** (0243) 775274

**Owner/Supervisor:** Margaret Bellhouse, NNEB, RSH, Mont Dip
**Type:** Day nursery and nursery school offering full- and part-time places
**Children:** 2–5yrs. 18 places per day. 58 on register
**Hours:** 8.30am–5.30pm
Open 49 weeks a year
**Status:** Private, fee-paying
**Number of years open:** 3
**Meals:** Lunch (or packed lunches), tea, snacks
**1992 fees:** £1.55 per hour
£1.30 per day for lunch if required
**Waiting list:** Minimal
**Registered by:** West Sussex County Council SS

**Premises** A specially designed extension to the owner's brick-built, 1930s house in a quiet lane. A middle-class, rural part of town, five minutes from the centre with good parking. Warm, cheery and airy, with plenty of natural light from windows, sky-lights and half-glass roof. The nursery school has its own separate entrance and consists of a large playroom which opens directly on to the garden, a quiet room, cloakroom and toilets. It is decorated and equipped to a high standard with toys and games easily accessible to the children. Outside they have the freedom of a large, safe, fenced-in garden, which has a climbing frame and slide. On the well-maintained patio area children can handle rabbits and guinea pigs and play with the family cat.

**Owner/Supervisor & staff** Margaret Bellhouse, NNEB, RSH, Mont Dip, is a down-to-earth and aware manager, sensitive to the needs of staff, children and parents. She creates a calm, family atmosphere and is totally involved with both staff and children. She is particularly experienced with special needs children and works directly with them. Single mothers at the nursery say they often turn to her for sympathy and advice. Margaret oversees all activities and leads the loyal team in an easy and relaxed way. There are two full-time and two part-time staff. Three are NNEB qualified including a teacher. The unqualified worker is studying for a PPA qualification. Margaret's husband, who works away from home, is actively involved when he is between jobs, and the children love to see him. A professional musician visits for four hours a week for music sessions with instruments. NNEB students from Chichester College come for practical training and fifth-form students from Chichester High School for work experience.

**Children & parents** Children come from a wide mix of backgrounds. Parents include shopkeepers, nurses, teachers, lawyers, single-parent families and others referred by Social Services. Margaret Bellhouse always makes herself available to talk to parents and is keen that they should discuss any worries or problems as soon as they crop up. The children appear very happy and well-mannered and show a great respect for each other unusual at such a young age. They are busily occupied and interested in visitors. Most move on to local state schools, Fishbourne and Central School, Chichester. There are several children with special educational needs – hearing and speech difficulties, a Down's syndrome child and a child with cerebral palsy. They mix easily with the other children and make excellent progress. The nursery is an important step for them towards integration in a main school.

**Curriculum & activities** The aim is to provide stimulation and education in a welcoming environment. The curriculum is loosely based on Montessori methods, and uses some Montessori equipment. The children are free to choose from a wide range of activities and to move from one to another at will. There are lots of cuddles and abundant opportunities for creativity and self-expression. Painting, play dough, cutting and sticking, pottery and sewing take place regularly. During the week each child will do some more formal learning on an individual basis: reading, writing, colour, shape and number work. No one is ever pushed beyond his/her concentration level. Older children have a reading card and a folder for special work. At the end of term this is made into a 'book' for parents. For those ready to read, the Ladybird Read with Me scheme is used. Children come together for meals and songtimes and are taken on nature walks and to visit the local horses in a nearby field. Music is considered very important, and, helped by a professional musician each week, the children enjoy making their own music. Special entertainers, clowns and magicians visit at Easter and Christmas. Staff are known by their Christian names and do not wear uniforms. Meals are an important social event – children sit chatting quietly and eat their food in a civilised manner.

**Remarks** Quality pre-school care and education in a homely environment. Little Orchard deserves its high reputation in the area. Lack of space is soon to be solved by the addition of a further extension. Emphasis on individual care and attention, with skilled and loving integration of children with special needs. A very happy nursery and excellent value for money.

## MILLAIS DAY NURSERY

Millais School
Depot Road
Horsham
West Sussex RH13 5HR
**Tel:** (0403) 270398

**Owner:** Millais School/W Sussex County Council
**Manager:** Sherry Wood, NNEB
**Type:** Workplace nursery offering full- and part-time places and half-day sessions. Half the places go to local community and half to teachers
**Children:** 6mths–5yrs. 23 places. 26 on register
**Hours:** 8am–6pm
Morning session 8am–1pm (inc lunch)
Afternoon session 1pm–6pm (inc tea)
Open 51 weeks a year
**Status:** Workplace nursery, non profit-making
**Number of years open:** 2
**Meals:** Breakfast, lunch, tea, snacks
**1992 fees:** £82 per week
£10 registration fee
**Waiting list:** Extremely long. Full until 1995
**Registered by:** W Sussex County Council SS

## POPPINS DAY NURSERY

231 Min Road
Southbourne
Emsworth
Hants PO10 8JD
**Tel:** (0243) 377711

**Owner:** Denise Bowen
**Supervisors:** Zena Payne, PPA
Mary Evans, NNEB
**Type:** Day nursery offering full- and part-time places, plus after-school care, holiday playscheme and nanny agency
**Children:** 3mths–5yrs. 33 places (5 babies). 38 on register
**Hours:** 8am–6pm
Flexible hours
Open 51 weeks a year
**Status:** Private, fee-paying
**Number of years open:** 4
**Meals:** Lunch, tea, snacks
**1992 fees:** £65.50 per week full-time
£14 per day
£2.05 per hour
**Waiting list:** Small
**Registered by:** W Sussex County Council SS

**Premises** A very attractive modern medical centre, built five years ago in the style of a Sussex barn, with low sloping roof and dormer windows. The area is primarily residential. Southbourne Medical Centre occupies half the building, the nursery the remainder. The accommodation consists of ten rooms, over two floors. Light streams in through numerous windows, and children's artwork is everywhere – the atmosphere is sunny and bright. Carpets are a practical mottled grey and everything you see looks new and in mint condition. The nursery rooms include a long, carpeted play area; an art and craft room; projects room; a library with TV, video and computer; a separate baby unit for 'Poppets', with its own sleep room, playroom and changing area. Staff have a rest room and upstairs the older children are allocated a schoolroom for more formal learning. The large L-shaped garden is fenced and mainly grassed, with a small tarmac area. Outdoor equipment includes a Wendy house, sandpit, climbing frame, swings, boat and ride-on toys. Nursery pets are a guinea pig and a rabbit. Babies have a separate fenced area to themselves.

**Owner, Supervisors & staff** The owner, Denise Bowen, is a physiotherapist, her husband a doctor at the medical centre. She manages the nursery and runs a range of other childcare services, including after-school care, holiday playschemes and a nanny/babysitting agency. She delegates the day-to-day running of the nursery to two supervisors, Zena Payne, PPA, and Mary Evans, NNEB. Their staff include an NNEB deputy supervisor, two qualified nursery officers and four assistants, all PPA trained. There is no qualified teacher on the staff. Ancillary workers consist of a cook, cleaner, gardener and students from Highbury and Chichester College. A male trainee was employed for a short time, but was not well received by mothers. Staff are recruited for their qualifications and experience, but an outgoing personality and a sense of humour are also required. They have a warm, open relationship with each other and relate well to the children. Staff cover is provided through Denise Bowen's nanny agency, when required.

**Children & parents** The children come from various backgrounds, mainly lower middle and middle-class families from rural, agricultural areas. Most are followers of the state system, particularly the local primary school, Bowne School. A few children transfer to local private preps – Oakwood, Northgate House or Glenhurst in Havant. As the nursery is part of a medical centre, children with disabilities or special educational needs are particularly well served. Down's syndrome children, children with dyslexia and speech impediments and a profoundly deaf boy have all happily and very successfully integrated with the other children, supported by the doctors, nurses and health visitors on the premises. Children are phased-in gently, with their parents and according to individual needs. A close relationship with parents is promoted by daily contact, open days twice a year, an annual parents' evening and frequent invitations to plays and concerts. At the time of our visit, children were rehearsing a Nativity play. All were concentrating hard and appeared a well-motivated, happy group. We observed some impressive staff supervision, offering consistent praise and reassurance to the nervous performers.

**Curriculum & activities** No particular philosophy prevails, but an interest in books is encouraged and word and letter recognition skills practised from an early age. Older children, known as Squirrels, practise number work and more structured activities in the mornings and early afternoons. The emphasis is on preparation for primary school – acquiring independence, social skills and some basic learning tools, mainly through play. Free expression flourishes through readily available painting, craftwork and model making. There are musical instruments, a percussion band and weekly movement and dance. A BBC computer is regularly loaded with age-appropriate software. Furniture and equipment (annual equipment budget approx. £4000) are plentiful and regularly replenished. There is limited record-keeping on each child – progress is passed on verbally – and no written programmes of work or activities.

**Remarks** High-quality childcare and good facilities. A caring and efficient team. Low-key educational programmes; no one with teaching experience on the staff. An excellent support system, provided by the medical centre, makes this nursery ideal for the integration of children with special needs. The day of our visit, a distressed mother arrived to tell Denise Bowen that her husband had been made redundant and they could no longer keep their child at the nursery. She was immediately assured that the nursery would waive the fees and sponsor the child until her circumstances changed.

# THREE BRIDGES FIRST SCHOOL – NURSERY CLASS

Gales Place
Crawley
West Sussex RH10 1QG
**Tel:** (0293) 524076

**Owner:** W Sussex County Council LEA
**Nursery Teacher:** Susan Holford, Cert Ed, NNEB
**Type:** Nursery class in state primary school offering half-day sessions. No full-time places
**Children:** 3–5yrs. 26 places. 52 on register
**Hours:** Morning session 8.55am–11.45am
Afternoon session 12.30pm–3pm
Open 38 weeks a year
**Status:** State nursery class
**Number of years open:** 21

**Meals:** Milk, juice, snacks
**1992 fees:** No fees
**Waiting list:** Very long. Full till 1995. Early registration advisable
**Registered by:** W Sussex County Council LEA

**Premises** Attached to Three Bridges First School, in a long, low, white building, typical of many buildings built in the early '60s. Well decorated inside and out. The two main classrooms have been subdivided into different activity areas, featuring different themes. The larger of the two is equipped with climbing apparatus and bright boxes of toys, old and new – many donated by parents. The second room contains computers, worktables, sand and water play and equipment for art and craft work. There is a pets' corner, a home corner and two pretend telephone kiosks, complete with phone books. Some areas are carpeted, with a quiet area and book corner. Coats and shoes are left in the entrance hall; toilets and washbasins are also in this area. There is a paved patio outside for riding bikes, and a grassy area with a play house and logs to climb on. A small field with a secure wire fence will soon be available for more boisterous play. Parking is available in the road outside the school grounds, and there is a safe pathway to the nursery.

**Nursery Teacher & staff** Susan Holford is an NNEB and a qualified teacher. She taught in a primary school before deciding to specialise in nursery teaching. There are two other full-time members of staff and a succession of NNEB, BTEC and other students who are under supervision and are welcome as extra pairs of hands. Gay Withington, an experienced NNEB nursery nurse, specialises in working with hearing-impaired children. A multilingual assistant comes in for six hours a week to help to settle children from the Asian community and to teach them English. There are at least two full-time staff and two students with the 26 children at any one time. 'Some training is available, but not enough that is relevant to NNEBs,' says Susan Holford.

**Children & parents** Over half the children come from the local area, which is socially and culturally very mixed. Others are referred by Social Services, including those with disabilities and special educational needs. A working-class, urban area with a very large Asian population – mainly Sikh, but some Muslim families. Many of the children are bilingual, while others have little or no English. Staff encourage as much contact as possible with parents. There are regular parent helpers, particularly for activities such as cooking. Parents also supply and mend dressing-up clothes, paint equipment and help generally with maintenance. Parents' meetings are often poorly attended, as Asian women in particular find it difficult to get out in the evenings. Most of the children transfer to Three Bridges First School or other local state schools.

**Curriculum & activities** The timetable is kept flexible. Children are encouraged to vary their activities so that they cover a range of experiences at each session. Pre-reading skills, numbers, colour recognition and other pre-school topics are available. The nursery uses some of the ideas from the High Scope method. This encourages greater independence and means structured play for each child. Children are not expected to learn to read or write while they are in the nursery class, although cursive writing is taught if a child is ready, and they are allowed to take books home. Children join in main school activities whenever possible, attending plays and assemblies and presenting their own assembly each term. They use the main school hall for music and movement. There is close liaison with the primary school. Once a year, a puppet show comes to the area and the nursery children join with the school to watch it. Small groups of children go on outings and short walks to the library for storytime. They also visit an old people's home for singsongs or to deliver harvest gifts. There are occasional train journeys to Horsham or Crawley. Staff respond warmly to children, offering support and affection. Furniture and equipment are well used, but carefully looked after. The annual budget for replenishment is small at £300. Children's progress and development are monitored regularly and records kept.

**Remarks** Very popular, over-subscribed nursery class. An excellent preparation for school, run by professional, well-trained staff who have a clear commitment to the educational needs of pre-school children. Good facilities for teaching children with English as a second language.

# WEST YORKSHIRE

# Bradford

Only enough childcare places in Bradford to meet the needs of two-fifths of the current under-5s population. 117 part-time playgroups provide 62 per cent of places. The county's 650 registered childminders are regarded as a valuable resource by Bradford parents, with charges ranging from £1.25 to £2 per hour, but one-third of available places are currently vacant. In the last 18 months the number of registered day nurseries has doubled, bringing the total up to 41 with nine run by the local authority. LEA nursery schools and classes only offer part-time education. Over half the children in Bradford receive no nursery education before entering school. Bradford provides a Child Care Information database, available in schools, health centres, housing departments and community centres.

**Further information**

For details on all services for under-8s:
Bradford Childcare Information Service
Olicana House
Chapel Street
Bradford BD1 5RE
Tel: (0274) 757503

or look out for their signpost logo in public service agencies.

## ABC DAY NURSERY

490 Halifax Road
Buttershaw
Bradford BD6 2LM
**Tel:** (0274) 677595

**Owner:** Mrs C A Feehan
**Officer-in-charge:** Kath Whittel, NNEB
**Type:** Day nursery offering full- and part-time places and half-day sessions
**Children:** 6wks–5yrs. 33 places. 44 on register
**Hours:** 8am–5.30pm
Open 51 weeks a year
**Status:** Private, fee-paying
**Number of years open:** 5
**Meals:** Breakfast, lunch, tea
**1992 fees:** £336.87 per month – under 2
£245 per month full-time – over 2
£82.50 per week full-time – under 2
£60 per week full-time – over 2
£19 per day – under 2
£16 per day – over 2
£10 per morning session – under 2
£9 per morning session – over 2
£9 per afternoon session – under 2
£7 per afternoon session – over 2
£25 registration fee
**Waiting list:** Reasonable. Mainly for babies
**Registered by:** Bradford City Council SS

**Premises** A large, stone, end-of-terrace, two-storey Victorian house with a single-storey stone extension. It faces a busy main road but the entrance is through a door at the back, where there is parking for three cars. The main door leads into a large reception cum cloakroom with red wallpaper, a fish frieze done by the children and a rogues' gallery of photos of the staff, seen through the eyes of the children. Up a short flight of stairs to a little landing (a minstrels' gallery), and there are two children's rooms for the 2- to 3½-year-olds. The baby room is on the first floor, fully carpeted, with its own kitchen, and a room (still awaiting decoration) for the oldest age group. Up even more stairs to the staff room and storage area. A new kitchen in the basement can only be reached by going outside – in fact, the building does not easily lend itself to use as a nursery. There is a medium-sized garden, largely grassed, facing the main road, with an extra large wooden climbing frame, sandpit and small paved area for bikes and trikes. Two parks with swings and lakes are within walking distance.

**Officer-in-charge & staff** Kath Whittel, NNEB, has worked in day nurseries for the last 14 years and has been at ABC since it opened five years ago. She feels her nursery is small enough to be run as a home with the children as part of the family. The previous nursery she worked in had over 100 places! Her philosophy is to treat the children as if they were her own. She likes to be involved with them as much as possible, reads to them and cuddles them. The all-female workforce of seven full-time and three part-time carers includes four NNEB qualified nursery nurses. The remaining staff are unqualified but experienced. A qualified teacher comes in to teach the older toddlers each morning. Turnover is minimal, usually for maternity leave and then staff often return. Calm, friendly atmosphere.

**Children & parents** The children come mainly from middle-class families but not entirely. Some parents commute from Leeds, Barnsley and Huddersfield to work in Bradford. There are also some mums who do not work outside the home but who bring their child for one or two sessions a week. A number of parents have moved their children here because they have been dissatisfied with other nurseries in the area. Parents treat staff as friends and often come in to help out.

**Curriculum & activities** The staff ratios are 1:3 for under-2s and 1:6 for over-2s. Children come together as a large group during the day for stories, singing, lunch and outdoor play. Other activities are done in their separate age-related rooms. There is no strong philosophy of care or education and no strict timetable nor any written programmes or curriculum. Children play and learn in peer groupings. The emphasis is on art and craft activities – finger and string painting, clay modelling, collage work, sticking and cutting. Importance is attached to good manners, speech training and table manners. The quiet area is used for reading, television watching and one-to-one conversation. Weekly library visits are undertaken, and a special visit to the local supermarket when a project or colour theme requires. Children perform a concert for parents at Christmas. There is no pressure to achieve academically, and large chunks of the day are given over to free play. Written developmental records are not kept, although at

the time of our visit staff were assessing various options in preparation for the introduction of some form of record-keeping.
**Remarks** Happy, confident children in a friendly, unpressured and homely atmosphere. The premises are badly laid out and do make life awkward at times. Nothing remarkable or unusual but a happy, welcoming nursery nevertheless.

# AIREDALE GENERAL HOSPITAL DAY NURSERY

Airedale General Hospital
Skipton Road
Keighley
West Yorkshire BD20 6TD
**Tel:** (0535) 652511 × 4091

**Owner:** Airedale NHS Trust
**Senior Nursery Nurse:** Lynne Briggs, NNEB
**Type:** Day nursery offering full- and part-time places and half-day sessions to hospital staff and local community (2–5yr-olds only)
**Children:** 2mths–5yrs. 40 places. 85 on register
**Hours:** 7.15am–5.15pm
Morning session 7.15am–12.15pm
Afternoon session 1.15pm–5.15pm
Flexible hours
Open 52 weeks a year
**Status:** Workplace nursery
**Number of years open:** 22
**Meals:** Lunch, snacks
**1992 fees:** £12 per day – under 2 (inc lunch)
£9.25 per day – over 2 (inc lunch)
Half-day sessions approx half full-day fee
Small discount for children of hospital staff
**Waiting list:** Moderate. Priority to hospital staff
**Registered by:** Exempt till recently. Currently registering with Bradford City Council SS

**Premises** A single-storey, brick building – once a social club – in the grounds of Airedale General Hospital, surrounded by lovely countryside. The building is divided into three rooms, plus toilets and staff room. Babies under 1 year have a room to themselves, furnished with bouncing cradles, high chairs, prams and playmats. The room is heated by safety radiators. The 1- to 2-year-olds' room is divided in half with non-slip flooring on the art and crafts area and carpet on the play area. Furniture includes tables and chairs, play cushions and a climbing frame. The older group have the largest room, with a Wendy house, a hospital corner, story corner and dressing-up box. All the rooms are light, with big windows, and are well decorated and spotlessly clean. There are six toilets and washbasins, plus a specially adapted toilet for disabled children. Outside there is an excellent play area – with safety surface for ride-on toys and bikes and a lawn for games. Children can clamber around on a climbing frame and on swing bars hanging from a big tree. The hospital is surrounded by open countryside, and children see wild rabbits in the nursery garden and springtime lambs in neighbouring fields.

**Senior Nursery Nurse & staff** Lynne Briggs, NNEB, has worked at the nursery for 20 years, and has been the Senior Nursery Nurse for seven. She is no longer involved with the daily routine of the nursery, but after so many years there is not much she doesn't know about it. She is backed by a deputy and five nursery workers – all NNEB qualified. Students, nurses or YTS trainees help out from time to time. A voluntary helper comes in during the morning to supervise playtime. All staff hold first-aid certificates and one member is experienced in work with special needs children. A training policy and budget are in operation.

**Children & parents** A broad social and ethnic mix. The majority are children of hospital employees (baby and toddler places are *all* taken by hospital staff). Most of the children go on to local state primaries, one or two to prep schools. Places for 2- to 5-year-olds are available to the local community. New entrants visit with parents before starting at the nursery. Parents are encouraged to stay with their child – gradually leaving earlier and earlier. Parents can talk to staff about their children on a daily basis. With most parents on the premises and welcome to drop in at any time, there is a very relaxed and informal atmosphere.

**Curriculum & activities** Very laid-back attitude, developing pre-school skills, but with no formal learning. The nursery is particularly anxious not to cause confusion by starting reading schemes that may be out of step with the child's next school. There is lots of free play, art and craft, constructive and imaginative play with guidance from staff, music, stories and games. The aim is to provide a happy, safe environment where a child can develop at his/her own pace and build up social and communication skills. There has been good feedback from primary schools taking children from the nursery. Written records are kept of babies' progress and achievements, but none are kept for older children – staff keep parents up-to-date on a day-to-day basis. There is a good amount of educational equipment and toys, and a generous annual equipment budget of £5000. A hot lunch is provided daily by hospital caterers; all dietary needs can be catered for. Some children bring packed lunches.

**Remarks** Organised, friendly day-care centre, with a very relaxed approach. Ideal for children with disabilities or special educational needs, as all necessary medical facilities are on site. Long flexible hours and very reasonable fees make the service attractive to all grades of hospital staff. Any profits are returned to the nursery to be spent on more toys and equipment.

# ELIM CHURCH DAY NURSERY

Wakefield Road
Bradford
BD4 7AF
**Tel:** (0274) 305528

**Owner:** Elim Church
**Principal Officer:** Doreen Bonham, NNEB
**Type:** Christian day nursery offering full- and part-time places and half-day sessions
**Children:** 2–5yrs. 35 places. 32 on register
**Hours:** 7.45am–5.45pm
Morning session 7.45am–1pm
Afternoon session 1pm–5.45pm
Open 51 weeks a year
**Status:** Private, fee-paying, non profit-making
**Number of years open:** 21
**Meals:** Breakfast, lunch, tea
**1992 fees:** £55 per week full-time
£45 per week for 5 morning sessions
£41.66 per week for 5 afternoon sessions
£12 per day
£10 registration fee
**Waiting list:** Minimal
**Registered by:** Bradford City Council SS

**Premises** The nursery forms part of the Elim church and was purpose-built in 1972. Modern-looking, but the blue and white paintwork needs renewing. It is situated next to a dual carriageway, half a mile from the city centre. Parents have to pull into a lay-by with double yellow lines in front of the church. However, the nursery has verbal assurance that traffic wardens will turn a blind eye to parents picking up and dropping off. Entry is with a key card, as the door is kept locked. There is a small council estate behind the church, but the surroundings are mainly industrial – factories or derelict land. Leading directly off the entrance hall is a small meeting hall, which is used by the nursery for sleep and has rows of little camp beds with pillows and blankets. The nursery consists of two rooms which are separated by a partition, but can be used as one big room at certain times. Washable carpet tiles are on the floor. There is a separate toilet and washroom and a newly renovated kitchen and utility room. Both rooms have access to the outside via patio doors. High wire fencing surrounds large grass and tarmac areas with a garage for outdoor toy storage. There are few fixed outdoor toys – the climbing frame was vandalised and swings have been taken down. There is all-weather safety matting down in this area which also doubles as the church car park at weekends. The playground runs parallel to the dual carriageway, but is screened by shrubs.

**Principal Officer & staff** Extrovert and full of fun, Doreen Bonham, NNEB, has been the principal officer for 13 years. Bursting with enthusiasm, she is always looking for fresh ideas. When we met, she had recently been inspired by a seminar at Bradford University on the National Curriculum and 4-year-olds. She worries that nursery workers in the private sector are not offered the same opportunities to keep up with the latest developments in their field as their counterparts in the public sector. She is constantly trying to persuade Bradford Social Services to provide more training for nursery nurses. Doreen sees herself as a catalyst, exciting the staff and helping to trigger off their own ideas. She has an all-female team of four full-time staff, NNEB qualified, and two part-timers. The two unqualified staff have at least two years' childcare experience and one has completed a two-year care course. The ethos of the nursery is Christian and all staff are required to be committed, practising Christians. Doreen herself attended theological college. Students are welcome on placement. A part-time cook prepares a two-course lunch every day. Doreen Bonham is responsible for day-to-day decisions and sits on a nursery committee, which meets every six to eight weeks to oversee the running of the nursery. Although much of her time is spent on administration, she still takes the morning register and listens to the children's news. The staff/child ratio is 1:6.

**Children & parents** Genuinely multicultural – Asian, Afro-Caribbean, Eastern European, English. The children come from a wide catchment area – one commutes in from York – and from a mixture of working-class and professional families. There are no children with disabilities or special educational needs at present. Parents are welcome at the nursery, but by appointment if possible, and are invited to regular 'fun days', special church events, plays and concerts. When work commitments allow, they help on outings and make the costumes for nursery plays. They also discuss their child's progress with staff on a regular basis. New parents visit the nursery with their child as often as possible to familiarise them and make the transition to nursery life as smooth as possible. Parents feel at home at Elim, which welcomes the whole family. Staff are prepared to become very involved with families and their problems if requested. Virtually all the children transfer to state schools.

**Curriculum & activities** Learning through play, in a Christian environment. Elim aims to offer the all-round development of physical, social, emotional and intellectual skills. The nursery teaches Christian principles; there is a Bible story each morning, and children and staff pray together daily. Christian songs are sung, grace is said at mealtimes and religious poems, decorate the walls. Weekly themes include 'Caring People' and 'Different Religions' and often contain a religious content. Good artwork, adult and child led, with collages and friezes displayed throughout. Children are divided into two groups by age, but come together for meals, playtimes, stories and music – one nursery nurse plays the piano and the accordion. Activities, educational equipment, games and toys are laid out and children move from task to task at will. Varied choice of equipment (annual budget £1500). Reading and writing are not taught formally, and there are no written programmes. The home corner is a constant source of inspiration and has even been turned into a 'swimming pool' by the children with pretend showers, lockers and diving board. The book and tape corner has a cassette player, which all children have been shown how to use, so they can listen to a story or music by themselves, whenever they wish. There is weekly dance, movement and music, monthly library visits and a Christmas Nativity play and party. Visits take place to the local railway and bus stations, shops and primary school. The day of our visit, children had baked parkin for bonfire night. Regular formal monitoring of children's progress is not yet in place, but was under discussion at the time of writing.

**Remarks** A happy, caring church nursery, with a positive Christian influence. Dedicated and immensely likeable principal officer, bursting with ideas, and committed Christian nursery workers. Poor location, surrounded by factories and derelict land. Very reasonably priced for the area and for the quality of care provided.

## HIRST WOOD NURSERY SCHOOL

Clarence Road
Shipley
Bradford BD18 4NJ
**Tel:** (0274) 584368

**Owner:** Bradford City Council LEA
**Headteacher:** Diane Clayton, Cert Ed
**Type:** State nursery school offering full-time places and half-day sessions
**Children:** 3–5yrs. 60 places. 75 on register
**Hours:** 9am–3.30pm
Morning session 9am–11am
Afternoon session 1.30pm–3.30pm
Open 39 weeks a year
**Status:** State nursery school
**Number of years open:** 60
**Meals:** Lunch
**1992 fees:** No fees
**Waiting list:** 2 years min. Names go down at birth. 300 names on list
**Registered by:** Bradford City Council LEA

**Premises** Conveniently situated near the main Bradford/Keighley and Leeds roads, in a quiet suburban street next to the model mill village of Saltaire, the canal, parks and wooded hillsides of Shipley Glen. The building is U-shaped, around a large play quad. In front is a huge grassy slope with trees running down to the road; to the side is another large patch, in development, but planned as a children's garden and conservation area. Inside there is a long corridor following the shape of the U, filled with displays, exhibits, artwork, parents' information and notice boards. Leading off the corridor are three classrooms, cloakrooms, staff room, office, parents' room, library and kitchen. The cloakroom and toilet areas need refurbishment – and are now near the top of the list of priorities.

**Headteacher & staff** Headteacher Diane Clayton, Cert Ed, is enthusiastic, very amusing and passionate about nursery education. She copes calmly with a dozen things at once and has been responsible for many improvements during the nine years she has been in charge of the nursery. Her team consists of three qualified teachers and three NNEB-qualified helpers. There is also a care assistant assigned to one of the children with disabilities. Staff turnover is not a problem, although two staff left recently, one after 37 years' service, the other after 18 years. Support staff include a caretaker, cleaner, cook, assistant cook, kitchen helper and two dinner supervisors. Training is considered important and a budget set aside for it. All staff have been on special needs and language courses and continually update skills and expand their areas of expertise.

**Children & parents** The children's families are a complete cross-section of the local population, from textile mill workers to hospital consultants. There is no real cultural or racial mix – only two Asian and two Chinese children when we visited – reflecting the immediate catchment area. The majority of children transfer to local state primary schools. The enormous waiting list means there is little chance of places becoming available. Places are allocated on a first come first served basis, with priority to children with special educational needs and disabilities referred by their GP, health visitor or a social worker. Good parental involvement. There is a long introduction period for new children, starting with an hour in the classroom with their parent and slowly building up to a half-day session on their own.

**Curriculum & activities** There is a rhythm to the day rather than a specific timetable. Children stay in their own classrooms for most of the time. There is one class for 15 4- to 5-year-old full-timers and another for five 3- to 4-year-olds, who attend morning or afternoon sessions. The children learn through play, with activities and projects set out on tables supervised by a teacher and assistant in each class. The morning begins with the register, followed by free play inside or outside, with the freedom to move between classes. Each class is full of equipment (equipment budget £2000 per annum), a piano, a selection of musical instruments, messy sand and water play, a woodwork corner, home and book corners and a creative area for painting. There is also a tactile table and always a seasons table with a display. Each room also contains a small office area, with an old typewriter rather than a word processor, and a writing area. Conversations and language are important, with teachers and children discussing topics and themes in groups and on a 1:1 basis. There is no formal teaching of reading or writing, but children are encouraged to use the book corner regularly and the nursery has its own lending library. Storytime takes place every day for all children and music and musical instruments are always available. Diane Clayton says that there is less formal instruction than there used to be. 'Teachers no longer spend most of their time telling children what to do, instead we talk to children about what they're doing. They are so motivated, and can do so much for themselves.' The nursery is full of good ideas. For example, outside in the playground large cardboard wallets hang from the wall, one containing maps for make-believe adventure games, the other sheets of paper for children to draw their own maps. Records of children's progress are compiled daily, assessed weekly and reported to parents termly.

**Remarks** A very happy, busy, self-contained school, led by an inspiring headteacher. The waiting list, as with all popular state nursery schools, is hundreds of names long and names need to be put down at birth.

# MOORFIELD NURSERY SCHOOL

Bramham Road
Bingley
West Yorkshire BD16 4HP
**Tel:** (0274) 566945

**Owners:** Stephen Hopkins, M Ed
Lynne Hopkins, BA (Hons), PGCE
**Matron:** Lynne Hopkins, BA, PGCE
**Type:** Nursery school offering full- and part-time places and half-day sessions
**Children:** 2–5yrs 11mths. 50 places. 130 on register
**Hours:** 9am–4pm
Morning session 9am–12 noon
Afternoon session 1pm–4pm
Open 46 weeks a year
**Status:** Private, fee-paying
**Number of years open:** 10
**Meals:** Lunch, snacks
**1992 fees:** £62.50 per week full-time
£12.50 per day
£5 per session
£2.50 per lunch hour inc meal
**Waiting list:** Long. Min 1 year
**Registered by:** Bradford City Council SS

**Premises** A large, rather austere, detached Victorian house, in a quiet residential area. The nursery school occupies four rooms plus toilets, kitchen, staff room and store room. Children use a large playroom, well stocked with toys, games and musical instruments including a piano, Wendy house, television and video. An activity room and craft room are used for creative work and play of various kinds and there is a quiet room for pre-school work. The small reception area, furnished with squashy beanbags, is used for storytime. The rooms on the ground floor are spacious, with plenty of natural light coming in through large windows. Those on the garden floor (the house is built on a slope) are smaller, with less light, but still acceptable. The interior is adequately decorated with a light colour wash and furnished with well-used child-sized wooden tables and chairs. The garden provides a tarmac area equipped with a slide, seesaw and ride-on toys – it is fairly small for the number of children and not big enough for boisterous games. A larger, grassy area for good weather play is equipped with a trampoline. An outdoor shed holds equipment and toys and the whole area is securely enclosed.

**Owner/Matron & staff** Lynne Hopkins, BA, PGCE, took a degree in fine arts and then moved into post-graduate teaching. When she decided to combine work with a family, she set up the nursery school, in one room, with 15 children. Nine years later, the school has grown to its present size entirely through recommendation. Matron has never advertised. She employs a staff of five qualified teachers, three NNEB nursery nurses and five unqualified but experienced assistants. One teacher holds a Dip Ed, specialising in teaching special needs children, another has music qualifications and plays the double bass, guitar and piano. All staff have first-aid training. They cover a wide age range and, unusually for a nursery school, include two men, who teach reading and writing to the older children. One is the joint-owner, Stephen Hopkins, M Ed. The staff seem compatible and relaxed and the children well organised and happy.

**Children & parents** The children are from solid middle-class backgrounds and move almost exclusively to private schools. The nursery maintains good links with local prep schools and prepares children to fit in with their different reading schemes. The children we talked to were well disciplined, polite and talkative. Parents are welcome to discuss their child's progress with the matron at any time. A regular newsletter goes out and parents' evenings are held. New children come for a series of pre-visits and then parents attend sessions with their child, gradually leaving earlier and earlier. Only one new child is introduced each session. All children are accepted and those with special needs and disabilities can be integrated.

**Curriculum & activities** An organised, structured approach to teaching, when the child is considered ready to learn. Children are split into colour-coded groups according to age and development. They start in the red group age 2-plus, move into yellow at about 3 and then into the green pre-school group. Many children wear sweatshirts in their group colour, but there is no formal uniform. Daily activities for all children include music, art and craft, constructive play, imaginative play, group work, games, stories, singing and news. With smaller children, the emphasis is on play and creating a quiet, organised atmosphere, where they gradually become able to listen and concentrate. Older children work through various reading schemes, writing skills, number work and topic-related activities. All children leave either reading or well on the way. The nursery is particularly well stocked with toys, games, equipment and books (annual equipment budget £2000). Children have exercise books which they take home. Written records are kept on developmental progress. Outings are not considered necessary. The nursery pets are a cat, two guinea pigs and a red canary.

**Remarks** A popular nursery, geared towards preparing children for entry into local private schools. Strong educational programmes, with five qualified teachers on the staff. Relaxed, disciplined and organised.

# SEVERN LODGE PRIVATE NURSERY

Severn Road
Bolton
Bradford BD2 4LS
**Tel:** (0274) 637425

**Owners:** Sandra & Rodney Hardy
**Matron:** Sandra Hardy, NNEB
**Type:** Day nursery offering full- and part-time places and half-day sessions
**Children:** 3mths–5yrs. 38 places. 75 on register
**Hours:** 8.15am–5.45pm
Morning session 8.30am–12 noon
Afternoon session 1pm–4.30pm
Open 50 weeks a year
**Status:** Private, fee-paying
**Number of years open:** 7
**Meals:** Lunch, tea, snacks
**1992 fees:** £60–£80 per week full-time, depending on age and hours
£13.75–£17 per day
£5.50–£8.50 per session
£5 registration fee
**Waiting list:** Minimal
**Registered by:** Bradford City Council SS
**Under same ownership:** Dracup Lodge Private Day Nursery, Great Horton, Bradford

**Premises** A pleasant, detached, Victorian stone villa in a leafy suburb three miles from city centre. Situated in a cul-de-sac which it shares with one other building and the entrance to a school for children with special educational needs. Parking is no problem. There is good access as the entrance is just off the inner ring road and 50 yards from major bus routes. A heavy wrought-iron gate, with a bolt placed at high level, leads into a walled garden with a very large paved area for ride-on and push-pull toys, swings and a slide on the lawn. There is lots of room to run around and let off steam. A quiet room for pre-school work leads off the compact entrance hall. The owners live above the nursery. The 3- to 5-year-olds spend most of their time in a large, light through-room with water play, sandpit, play house, table and chairs. Babies have their own area with cots, sleep mats, a separate nappy-changing room and a kitchen for preparing milk and feeds. There is a protected outdoor pram verandah so that they can sleep in the fresh air. The 2- to 3-year-olds are housed across the yard in a converted stable block with their own toilets and nappy-changing facilities. Peel Park is across the main road, with gardens, woodland, a lake, wildlife, a playground and occasional fairs and circuses, all frequently visited by the children.

**Owner/Matron & staff** Sandra Hardy, NNEB, ran a children's-wear shop before gaining her NNEB as a mature student. She is on the selection committee for the BTEC, NNEB course at Bradford & Ilkley Community College and is studying for an Advanced Diploma in hygiene and catering. Calm in temperament, she believes in doing things by the book. 'There are no short cuts where children are concerned,' she says. Staff ratios are 1:3 for under-2s, 1:5 for over-2s. There are nine full-time staff and one part-timer. Five are NNEB qualified, and the remainder have approximately four years' experience working at the nursery under Sandra Hardy's supervision. No staff training policy or training budget. Two students – YTS and BTEC – assist the nursery nurses. A back-up of part-time helpers cover for sickness and holidays. This is a family concern, with Sandra's husband and joint owner Rodney regularly joining in activities and helping with the children. Sandra's mother, Marjorie Butcher, is matron of their second nursery, Dracup Lodge.

**Children & parents** A wide social and cultural mix, including children of professional business people, single parents, Sikhs, Hindus, Jehovah's Witnesses, Mormons and Social

Services referrals. Some travel up to 30 miles to the nursery because their parents work in Bradford. Most go on to local state schools, with approximately 30 per cent continuing in the private sector. The nursery has an open-door policy towards parents. Problems are dealt with and solved as they arise. No formal parents' meetings or evenings are held but Sandra and her staff are available at all times to discuss progress or deal with queries.

**Curriculum & activities** Learning through play. Days are structured, but with long periods of free playtime. After registration at 9am, the emphasis is on language development. The group exchanges news, talks about the weather and discusses the current topic or theme. There are set art and craft activities each day, based on the theme of the week, and a story and music session every morning and afternoon, including traditional songs and rhymes. All the toys and books are openly displayed at child height and labelled so that children can help themselves and put things back. Older children are taken into the pre-school quiet room in groups of four or five for more concentrated work. Letter recognition is taught through alphabet cards, jigsaws, an alphabet board and simple flashcards. Number concepts and pre-reading exercises are practised. Name recognition is encouraged with the extensive use of labels throughout the nursery. If a child is ready, he/she can progress to simple word and sentence copying. No reading or maths schemes are followed. Each child's progress and development are constantly monitored and discussed. Star charts on the wall and work folders record achievements. There are weekly visits to the local library (children walk there and catch the bus back), and other visits linked to specific projects. The nursery enjoys strong links with the nearby special school and an old people's home across the road, and joint visits and activities are common. Children take something home every day.

**Remarks** A friendly, family-run nursery with happy, busy children. Emphasis on play and project work in a relaxed caring atmosphere. Dedicated staff. The joint-owner, Rodney Hardy, provides a welcome male role model in the predominantly female environment. Good location, with lovely parkland nearby. Staff undaunted by taking large groups of children on regular outings.

# Calderdale

Calderdale is an area where women have traditionally worked outside the home, turning to the family first and then to the 300-plus childminders, to solve their childcare problems. Over 100 childminders have dropped off the register in the past year, due to the stricter regulations of the Children Act. There are no workplace nurseries. An increase in the number of professional families moving into the region without immediate family support has led to a recent rapid increase in private day nurseries – more than twice the national average. However, recession has taken its toll and three of the 29 facilities have closed in the last year. Currently offering 65 per cent of over-3s a part-time place in one of 37 nursery classes, the LEA plans to continue opening new nursery classes every year, as it has done for the past three years. The view of one under-5s development officer we talked to is typical of many parents and childcare workers in the area. 'Parents do want nursery education, but full-time, not part-time. Part-time is useless for the working parent. In one area, relatively well supplied with nursery classes, numbers have fallen because parents have opted for private daycare.'

## Further information

For details on all types of daycare, nursery schools, childminders and playgroups:

Under 5s Development Officer
Northgate House
Northgate
Halifax HX1 1UN
Tel: (0422) 357257

Or:

Principal Officer – Early Years
Department of Social Services
Horsfall House
Skircoat Moor Road
Halifax HX3 0HJ
Tel: (0422) 363561

## PELLON & DISTRICT COMMUNITY DAY NURSERY

Pellon & District Community Centre
Church Lane
Mount Pellon
Halifax HX2 0JG
**Tel:** (0422) 363321

**Owner:** Pellon & District Community Association
**Supervisor:** Donna Flynn, NNEB
**Type:** Community nursery offering 20, 30 or 40 hours of care per week
**Children:** 3mths–5yrs. 59 places. 59 on register
**Hours:** 7.45am–5.15pm. Open 49 weeks a year
**Status:** Fee-paying, non profit-making
**Number of years open:** 10
**Meals:** Lunch, snacks
**1992 fees:** £34.32 per week, 20 hrs – under 18mths
£29.12 per week, 20 hrs – over 18mths
£40.04 per week, 30 hrs – under 18mths
£35.36 per week, 30 hrs – over 18mths
£46.80 per week, 40 hrs – under 18mths
£41.60 per week, 40 hrs – over 18mths
£2 sibling discount per full day
**Waiting list:** Minimal
**Registered by:** Calderdale Met Council SS

**Premises** Community centre in a former Infant & Junior school, built in the mid-1800s out of Yorkshire stone. Apart from the nursery and a pensioners' session once a week, other community activities such as badminton and Scouts take place in the evenings. The building looks dilapidated; there is graffiti on the outside of the doors, and the huge gothic-style windows have metal grids to deter vandals. The railings round the school playground are rusting. Paint is peeling off the single-storey '60s-style extra classroom, which is attached to the main school by a short, covered passageway. Inside there are two large, light rooms, one for children up to 2½ years old, the other for 2½- to 3-year-olds. Both have Disney character murals on the walls, painted by the probation service, together with children's artwork. The small kitchen and separate toilets are covered with more colourful art to brighten up the shabby walls. Across in the main school, there is a large classroom for the 3- to 5-year-olds and, up a short flight of stairs, the main school hall and kitchen. At the far end is another, smaller hall, which is used for gym and games sessions. Continuing up the stairs, brightened by paintings of flowers done by the staff, you finally reach the baby room. A large, cheerful room, its prams, cots and toys are donated by parents. The outside play area is spacious and safely fenced, with grassed and paved sections. There are splendid views across the valley to the moors. Throughout, the signs of underfunding are clear. Equally clear is the determination to overcome financial problems and make the very best of the nursery. The warm, friendly atmosphere is palpable.

**Supervisor & staff** Donna Flynn, NNEB, leads a team of six full-time staff and nine part-timers. She has been at the nursery for ten years and has gathered a friendly, dedicated team around her, who share the chores, trust each other and work together as friends. Many are unqualified – there is not enough money to pay highly trained staff. Donna says, with some force, 'You can't teach someone to like and care for children. You need natural ability and talent. I'd rather take on someone with a natural flair who loves children and encourage them to take a PPA certificate, than a qualified nursery nurse who is efficient but distant with the children.' She frankly admits that at times staff turnover has been a problem, due to financial constraints. Extra help is provided by three YTS students, one NNEB student, a cook and a book-keeper. Donna herself spends as much time as possible working in the baby room.

**Children & parents** The children come from predominantly working-class families, some professional and a proportion of single parents. All are in full-time employment. The local community spans a mixture of council estate (mainly owner-occupiers), private semis and stone terraces. Some travel from Leeds and Cleckheaton, approximately 20 miles away, to work in Halifax. Most of the children transfer to local state primary schools. Parents are always welcome and are encouraged to stop for coffee and a chat at either end of the day. They are also heavily involved in fund-raising activities. The nursery is very dependent on their results.

**Curriculum & activities** The nursery's primary purpose is to provide care, rather than education, in a stimulating environment, and to help children socialise with their peers and develop as individuals, at the same time keeping them safe and happy. The nursery offers a great deal of space and a good selection of toys and equipment, although not as much as it would like. There are no written programmes, but a loose structure to the day. As children and staff arrive in the morning they 'clock in', factory-style, so accurate records of numbers can be kept each day. Children are then free to play all together until 9am when they split into peer groups and move to their separate rooms for free play, songs and an activity. They all have access to sand and water, painting materials, climbing frames, books and a range of table-top toys. Music lessons are daily, dance and movement weekly. Art and craft activities are frequent. Colour, letter and word recognition are taught through games and craft activities. Outings are very rare, as the cost of extra insurance is prohibitive, and the extra staff needed are not available. However, they receive regular visitors – 'Mr Tufty' teaches road safety, 'Wellephant' represents the fire brigade, and the police are frequent guests. Children hold their birthday parties at the nursery – a popular event. There is a pre-school room for the oldest children. The maximum number in the group is eight, which enables the two staff to give more individual attention to prepare children for school. There is no formal teaching of reading or writing, but staff ensure that children are well prepared to deal with the demands of whichever primary school they transfer to. Meals are happy social occasions, freshly prepared by a cook on the premises. Staff eat with the children.

**Remarks** Fantastic amount of space inside and out. Friendly staff and a large range of play activities. Long-established nursery offering a much-needed service to the community at very cheap rates. Emphasis on care rather than education. It is run on a shoestring, and the lack of funds is evident, and the whole building needs complete redecoration. The supply of equipment and toys is totally dependent on fund-raising and the goodwill of parents. One of the few day nurseries within the means of working parents on low incomes.

ent content that is

# Kirklees

Kirklees is committed to a long-term programme aimed at offering a part-time nursery school place to every child who wants one, during the term in which he/she turns 4. There are five Social Services nurseries for priority children and 41 private day nurseries. 600 registered childminders are the most popular option for parents, who are also actively involved in organising over 100 playgroups.

**Further information**

For details on nurseries, nursery schools, childminders and playgroups:
Early Years Service
Oldgate House
2 Oldgate
Huddersfield HD1 6QW
Tel: (0484) 422133

## ASPLEY DAY NURSERY

Kirklees & Wakefield Chamber of Commerce & Industry Ltd
Commerce House
Wakefield Road
Aspley
Huddersfield HD5 9AA
**Tel:** (0484) 426591 × 245

**Owner:** Kirklees & Wakefield Chamber of Commerce & Industry Ltd
**Manager:** Deborah Blakey, NNEB
**Type:** Workplace nursery offering full- and part-time places and half-day sessions
**Children:** 2mths–5yrs. 33 places. 45 on register
**Hours:** 8am–6pm
Open 52 weeks a year (excl bank holidays)
**Status:** Private, fee-paying, non profit-making
**Number of years open:** 4
**Meals:** Breakfast, lunch, tea
**1992 fees:** £62.50 per week full-time
£13.50 per day
£7.80 per morning session (inc lunch)
£6.80 per afternoon session (excl lunch)
**Waiting list:** Long for baby places
**Registered by:** Kirklees Met Council SS

**Premises** Self-contained area on the ground floor of a two-storey modern industrial factory unit. Built of brick and steel, this is the headquarters of the Kirklees and Wakefield Chamber of Commerce. It is five minutes' walk from the town centre, on one side of a six-lane dual carriageway. The large windows of the nursery are painted with pictures of happy children. Inside, there is one large, light room with other rooms leading off it. The over-2s spend their time in this open-plan area, with a reading corner, home corner, sandpit, water play and messy-play area sectioned off, a piano and a soft area with mats for a climbing frame and slide. Equipment is plentiful and well laid out. Other rooms include a large playroom for under-2s decorated in primary colours, with children's art at child height below a dado rail. It is fully carpeted, and so a large plastic sheet is laid out for messy play; the room contains a wooden slide with holes and tunnels to crawl through and a number of soft big plastic shapes to climb on. There is also a separate kitchen with toy storeroom behind; toilets and washrooms, brightly decorated with Postman Pat characters; a babies' sleep room and an office. Outside is a generous, well-fenced play space, part grassed, part paved, with attractive outdoor play equipment and picnic tables. The immediate neighbours are more modern factory units and a KwikSave supermarket. The nearest park is a ten-minute bus ride away.

**Manager & staff** Deborah Blakey, NNEB, believes in teamwork and has tried to gather a multicultural staff group around her. She has employed male staff in the past and was disappointed that there were no male applicants for the last post she advertised. There are seven full-time staff – five qualified NNEB, and two unqualified but experienced. Additional staff skills include musical ability and one member with an excellent knowledge of Punjabi. Extra assistance comes from NNEB students, a catering assistant and a cleaner. The nursery operates a keyworker system, with each member of staff responsible for five or six particular children. Deborah tries to spend as much time as possible with the children, but if she is in the office, her door is always open. Often a child will wander in and sit on her knee or at the other side of the desk to do some crayoning. A staff training policy is in operation, and staff attend relevant courses during the year. Full staff meetings are held once a term, and individual meetings with nurses more frequently. The nursery follows a comprehensive equal opportunities policy drawn up by the Chamber of Commerce. Staff wear navy sweatshirts with the nursery logo on the breast pocket over a blue and white striped shirt.

**Children & parents** The children come from a mixture of backgrounds – professional families, single parents on training courses, workers from any company that is a member of the Chamber of Commerce, Midland Bank employees and parents from the community. A comprehensive social and racial mix, reflecting the immediate catchment area. The nursery has a very close relationship with parents and an open-door policy.

**Curriculum & activities** The nursery follows the learning-through-play philosophy of the PPA (Pre-school Playgroups Association). Themes are planned months ahead and used to bind different areas of learning together. Each lasts about a week and covers science, water play, stories, songs and artwork. Recent themes have included food, weather, transport, colours and 'people who help us'. Parents are encouraged to contribute, bring in relevant items and reinforce theme work at home. There is daily music (a piano in each room) and weekly dance and movement. The nursery is strong on art and craft, and creative activities are available at all times and are encouraged. Children choose their activities and are free to go to any part of the room. Equipment and activities are laid out everywhere at all times. Gentle encouragement from staff ensures they participate in a wide range. Outings are a problem and are rare as there are few places of interest nearby. A weekly walk is undertaken to the local library, Early Learning Centre and local supermarket. There is no formal teaching of reading or writing and no pressure. Key-workers monitor their key children's progress and report back regularly to parents and the rest of the staff team.

**Remarks** High-quality care in a warm, caring atmosphere, with stimulating activities. Although the location leaves something to be desired, the nursery is extremely well equipped, with excellent outdoor facilities and a friendly staff team. No pressure on children to perform academically. One of few private nurseries where children from different backgrounds and cultures are able to interact with one another. Strong nursery relationship with parents. Money does not appear to be a problem. Subsidies from the business community make this all-day care excellent value for money. Situation next to a six-lane dual carriageway is not ideal.

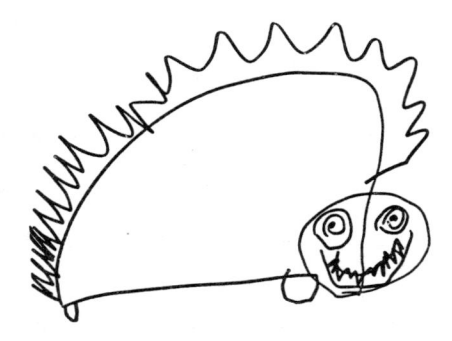

# Leeds

Leeds has a positive approach to childcare and aims to achieve a good balance between the public and private sectors. There are three nursery schools and 133 nursery classes providing places for 43 per cent of 3- and 4-year-olds. It is well supplied with local authority day nurseries, compared to the rest of the county, with 34 family nursery centres. There are 35 private day nurseries, over 200 playgroups and one travelling playbus. Childminders, over 1200 of them and numbers still rising, are the most popular choice. Some businesses in the city are looking at ways to retain their trained female employees by providing crèches, childcare vouchers and workplace nurseries. The Under Eights Unit says the main demand, still to be met, is for full-time baby places. 'Two years ago a career mother might stay at home for a year or so. Now we are getting calls from mothers trying to find places for babies as young as four weeks. This is often because their partner has been made redundant and they must find work.' The area's Under Eights Unit is one of the most helpful and responsive we contacted.

### Further information

For details on all types of provision for under-8s, including nannies and babysitters, from a computer database updated weekly, and referral to professional advisors if necessary. Contact:

Under Eights Unit
Civic Hall
4th Floor
Leeds LS1 1UR
Tel: (0532) 474386

## GROVE NURSERY SCHOOL

28 Grove Road
Headingley
Leeds LS6 4EE
**Tel:** (0532) 751471

**Owner/Principal:** Anne Sneideris, Cert Ed
**Type:** Day nursery offering full- and part-time places
**Children:** 3mths–4yrs 11mths. 43 places. 53 on register
**Hours:** 8.15am–5.30pm
Open 48 weeks a year
**Status:** Private, fee-paying
**Number of years open:** 23
**Meals:** Lunch, tea, snacks
**1992 fees:** £100 per week full-time – under 2
£80 per week full-time – over 2
£50 per week part-time (3 full days)
£10 registration fee
**Waiting list:** For babies only
**Registered by:** Leeds City Council SS

**Premises** A large, stone, Victorian semi, standing in a third of an acre of land in a quiet, suburban part of town. The nursery is on the ground and half the first floor. The owner and her family live in the rest of the house. The premises comprise five rooms plus toilets, kitchen and storeroom. Babies are cared for in a large room which operates as a separate unit. Half is carpeted as a play area, and the rest used for feeding and sleeping. Washing and nappy-changing facilities open off the room and there is a secure courtyard area for play and outdoor naps. Older children have a large, airy playroom for games in wet weather or free play. It is equipped with a Wendy house, large toys, a slide and ride-on toys. The messy-play room has sand and water play, painting, cooking, modelling and craft. It doubles as a dining room at midday. A quiet room is set aside for storytime, news, quiet play – jigsaws, railway and car tracks, dolls' houses, etc – and for looking at books. The fifth room is equipped as a classroom with small tables and chairs. The older children work here on early learning skills, under the guidance of a qualified teacher. Children can move freely from one room to another after informing staff. The nursery has recently been redecorated and is heated throughout by gas fires fitted with safety guards. The big, secluded garden is a definite plus. It has a tarmac area for trike riding and games and a large lawn for romping around and picnics in the summer. Surrounded by mature bushes and trees, good for hide and seek.

**Owner/Principal & staff** Anne Sneideris, Cert Ed, has been at the nursery for seven years, the last four as principal. She employs a staff of 13, ten full-time and three part-time. Ten are qualified, NNEB, Cert Ed, B Ed, BTEC. Three are unqualified – two mothers and one with playgroup experience. Only two members of staff have first-aid certificates. Due to prompting by Anne Sneideris, the local college has started a refresher course in child care, which staff attend. All staff recently attended a child protection course, run by the NSPCC. Students help out from time to time on block release courses or placements. A former male student comes in for half a day each week as a volunteer. Anne Sneideris is keen to employ a full-time male member of staff. Nursery workers meet every five weeks to discuss nursery policy, but talk informally on a daily basis. Anne Sneideris handles the overall management of the nursery but believes in maintaining close contact with children, staff and parents and will help out in any area – including nappy changing – if needed. Staff cover a large age range and a variety of talents. They have a happy, caring relationship with children. At the time of our visit, we counted 15 staff, including two students, to 43 children.

**Children & parents** The children come from diverse backgrounds and a variety of ethnic groups, including Asian, Afro-Caribbean, Nigerian and different European countries. Some are bilingual, one with English as a second language. The vast majority have two working parents. Half the children go on to private education at local prep schools and half to state primaries. The catchment area is large, with many children travelling long distances to the nursery. Children are divided into peer groups for work and play, rarely coming together because of numbers. Larger groups join together for news time and singing games. The nursery welcomes children with special needs but cannot cater for those needing extra carers or one-to-one attention. A speech therapist helps two children with speech and language difficulties. Regular parents' evenings and open days are held, and parents can talk to staff at the beginning and end of each day. Phasing-in new children is done gently, with parents present.

**Curriculum & activities** A structured but relaxed approach towards learning. Children leave well prepared for school, having acquired pre-reading skills – letter shape and sound recognition – pencil control, number work, colour and shape recognition. The older children work on pre-school activities in the classroom from 9.30am to 12 noon. Each day, all children take part in art and craft, music, dance and movement, news time and storytime. There is plenty of free play and outdoor games. Progress and developmental milestones are charted and each child leaves with a certificate of achievement to pass on to the next school. Good-quality, stimulating equipment, suitable for each age group (annual budget £1000). The playroom has a home corner, dressing-up clothes, dolls and prams for imaginative play. There are also large cubes for hiding in and climbing on and ride-on toys. Paint, glue, play dough, plasticine and sand and water are available in the messy room. Books are plentiful, augmented by 30 library books changed monthly. The garden is used regularly for nature studies. The nursery pet is a hamster. Few outings are undertaken, but regular visitors come to the nursery, including an urban farm and a puppet show. A bouncy castle is hired three times a year. Meals are freshly prepared in the nursery kitchen by the cook and vegetarian alternatives available.

**Remarks** Long-established, popular nursery, providing good-quality care and education. Children have freedom to express themselves within a structured framework. Emphasis on music, conversation, books and nature studies. Qualified teachers ensure good grounding in the 3Rs. There are never enough baby places to meet demand. The spacious, secluded garden is an added bonus.

# ROSE COURT PREPARATORY SCHOOL – NURSERY CLASS

Leeds Girls' High School
Headingley
Leeds LS6 1BN
**Tel:** (0532) 744000

**Owner:** LGHS/LGS Grammar School Foundation
**Head:** Anne Pickering, B Ed (Hons)
**Type:** Nursery class attached to prep school, offering half-day sessions. No full-time places
**Children:** 3–4yrs. 16 morning places, 12 afternoon places. 28 on register
**Hours:** Morning session 8.55am–12.20pm
Afternoon session 1.20pm–3.20pm
Open 36 weeks a year
**Status:** Private, fee-paying
**Number of years open:** 73
**Meals:** Milk and snacks
**1992 fees:** £741 per term for 5 morning sessions a week
£651 per term for 5 afternoon sessions a week
**Waiting list:** None. Entry by selective interview according to ability
**Registered by:** Dept for Education

**Premises** A 19th-century, detached stone villa, which has been extensively modernised and developed. It is a listed building, surrounded by lovely, spacious gardens. There are plans to extend Rose Court to provide extra classroom space, a new nursery and a larger hall. The nursery shares the building with the prep school, and includes a very well-stocked library and assembly hall. The nursery classrooms, on two floors, are light and roomy, the walls covered with pictures and charts and shelves filled with educational equipment. The large garden offers swings, a climbing frame and open grassy spaces for letting off steam. There is good public transport from the city centre, 1½ miles away, but limited parking. The school is situated on the main route north from Leeds.

**Head & staff** Before coming to Leeds in 1990, the head, Anne Pickering, B Ed, was deputy head of an infant school in Newcastle for five years. She has had many years' experience in church and state schools. A music specialist, she is involved in all the prep school and nursery productions. The nursery teacher is NNEB qualified and holds a Teachers' Certificate. She is assisted by an ancillary teacher, one of a rota of four, who are on duty throughout the day. All staff hold a Red Cross certificate and are encouraged to attend in-service training sessions. The annual training budget is £2500. Teachers make a half-day visit each term to another school, to exchange ideas and see different methods. The staff/child ratio is 1:8 in the morning and 1:6 in the afternoon, when the average age is slightly younger.

**Children & parents** Children come from within a 30-mile radius of Leeds. Entry is selective. Each child is interviewed individually and assessed for maturity, ability to listen and concentrate, language and comprehension, observancy and readiness. In 1992, over 140 children were interviewed for 47 places, some in the nursery class. Virtually all the girls progress from the nursery to the preparatory school and then on to Leeds Girls' High School. The boys go on to the prep school and then have to move on at 8 to either Leeds Grammar School or other private schools in the area. They are a happy, well-disciplined, motivated group of bright children who have a good rapport with their teachers. A full record is kept of each child's development, to which parents have ready access. Parents are involved as often as possible in events and activities and are encouraged to make comments and suggestions on the running of the nursery.

**Curriculum & activities** Primarily an educational establishment, preparing children for the academic challenges ahead as they move up through the school. Every possible effort is made to offer children a wide variety of experiences, to learn through practical work and play. Pre-reading and pre-numeracy skills, baking, basic computing, dance, drama, music, and art and craft are all on the timetable. There is an excellent supply of books and the nursery is extremely well equipped with constructive learning materials. Toys and free play are not seen as an important part of the comparatively short school session. Leeds Girls' High School is a school which values academic excellence, and children are encouraged to achieve their full potential from an early age. The curriculum of the nursery includes science and environmental studies, information technology, computing, design technology, history and geography, religious education, PE, games and gymnastics. A variety of reading schemes are used, depending on the individual child and their readiness – New Way, 1-2-3 and Away, Story Chest, and the Oxford Reading Tree. At 4 years old, children move into the kindergarten, where they attend for 4½ days a week. The nursery class has regular outings in the school mini-bus to local farms and places of interest. The many visitors to the class include theatre groups, puppet theatres, a dental hygienist, Save the Children Fund, road safety officers and the Leeds Hedgehog Sanctuary.

**Remarks** Ideal for parents who want their daughters to progress through the school and on to higher education. A good preparation for boys aspiring to Leeds Grammar and other independent schools. Competitive entry ensures hand-picked, bright, confident, well-motivated children. Progressive head, full of ideas, and experienced nursery teacher.

## SPRINGWOOD NURSERY SCHOOL

3 Springwood Road
Roundhay
Leeds LS8 2QA
**Tel:** (0532) 659345

**Joint Owners:** Julia & Graham Watt
**Principal:** Julia Watt, B Sc, PGCE
**Type:** Day nursery offering full- and part-time places
**Children:** 2–5yrs. 30 places. 21 on register
**Hours:** 8.30am–5.30pm
Flexible hours
Open 52 weeks a year
**Status:** Private, fee-paying
**Number of years open:** 47
**Meals:** Lunch, snacks
**1992 fees:** £280 per month full-time
£35 per week for 5 morning sessions
£14 per day
£7 per afternoon session
£20 non-refundable deposit
**Waiting list:** None
**Registered by:** Leeds City Council SS

# Wakefield

Wakefield is trying hard to meet the demand for nursery education with five nursery schools, 64 nursery classes and 39 'pre-5s' classes. 49 per cent of 3- and 4-year-olds are in mainly part-time nursery classes. It is now council policy to incorporate a nursery class when a primary school is built or refurbished, and another three nursery classes have recently become available. Daycare facilities are inadequate to meet demand. There are only 40 places available for high-priority children at the three local authority day nurseries. Social Services use childminders and buy places in the 15 private nurseries. The LEA says, 'Overall, we have nearly enough nursery school places to meet the demand, but because Wakefield district is made up of small communities, parents are reluctant to take up a place in a school a mile away when their local school is over-subscribed.'

## Further information

Registration Section
Department of Social Services
87 Northgate
Wakefield WF1 3DA
Tel: (0924) 297770

For details on nursery schools, units and classes:

Research and Planning Office
Physical Resources
Education Department
County Hall
Wakefield WF1 2QL
Tel: (0924) 295588

# Wiltshire

Wiltshire County Council blames lack of resources for the complete absence of local authority nursery provision in the county: no day nurseries, no nursery schools and only 624 part-time places in nursery classes for the county's 39,000 under-5s. One workplace nursery in Swindon offers places to local authority employees. They make an annual grant of £250,000 to the Pre-school Playgroups Association to help support some 350 part-time playgroups. There are 23 private day nurseries in the county, some with waiting lists up to two years long. 'If you want a place in our nursery, you must put your child's name down the minute you conceive,' one private nursery owner advises parents.

### Further information

For details on day nurseries, private nursery schools, childminders and playgroups:

*Salisbury*
Department of Social Services
Salt Lane
Salisbury SP1 1DU
Tel: (0722) 327551

*Swindon*
Department of Social Services
Clarence House
Clarence Street
Swindon SN1 2HH
Tel: (0793) 531131

*Trowbridge*
Department of Social Services
County Hall East
Bythesea Road
Trowbridge BA14 8JQ
Tel: (0225) 777792

For details on nursery schools, units and classes:
Education Department – Under Fives Advisor
County Hall
Bythesea Road
Trowbridge BA14 8JG
Tel: (0225) 774626

For details on all early years provision:
Children's Resource Centre
53 Rutland Crescent
Trowbridge
Tel: (0225) 752198

## HOPSCOTCH NURSERY SCHOOL

Willow Barn
Stanley
Chippenham
Wilts SN15 3RF
**Tel:** (0249) 658380

**Owner/Principal:** Zabé Viner, Cert Ed
**Type:** Nursery school offering full-time places
**Children:** 3–5yrs. 18 places. 18 on register
**Hours:** 9am–2.30pm
Open 39 weeks a year
**Status:** Private, fee-paying
**Number of years open:** 4
**Meals:** Packed lunches, snacks
**1992 fees:** £11 per day
£20 deposit
**Waiting list:** Early booking advisable
**Registered by:** Wiltshire County Council SS

## STEPPING STONES NURSERY SCHOOL

Oakhill Farmhouse
Froxfield
Near Marlborough
Wilts SN8 3JT
**Tel:** (0488) 681067

**Owners/Principals:** Sue Corfield, NNEB (Norland)
Audrey Vertannes, NNEB

**Type:** Nursery school offering full- and part-time places and half-day sessions (min 2 morning sessions a week)
**Children:** 2yrs 10mths–5½yrs. 36 places. 75 on register
**Hours:** 9am–3pm Mon–Thurs
Morning session 9am–12.30pm
Afternoon session 12pm–3pm (excl Fri)
Open 38 weeks a year
**Status:** Private, fee-paying
**Number of years open:** 3
**Meals:** Juice and biscuits. Children bring packed lunches. Microwave available
**1992 fees:** £11 per day
£6.50 per morning session
£5.50 per afternoon session
**Waiting list:** Full till '95. Early registration advisable
**Registered by:** Wiltshire SS

**Premises** Two renovated barns in the picturesque village of Froxfield, fringed by a small artificial lake on one side and by lush, rolling hills on the other. There are two identically equipped classrooms separated by a large, covered courtyard – one with original, exposed beams and wooden doors, and the other newer and more clinical. In addition, there are cloakrooms, loos and a small kitchenette. The outside play area is fenced off in part of a field, with a large collection of outdoor play equipment.

**Principals & staff** Audrey Vertannes and Sue Corfield, both NNEB and former nannies, own and run Stepping Stones. Close friends, they are mature, confident and energetic. They run a classroom each and share administration. Other members of staff include one full-timer and three part-timers – all but one (who is a local mother) are qualified (PPA, City & Guilds and NNEB). In contrast to Audrey and Sue, the rest of the staff are quieter and more low-key, but they all work well together and relate closely to the children. A ballet teacher visits twice a week.

**Children & parents** None of the children are from Froxfield village at present – they have all left and gone off to school. Most come from other villages. The mothers are mainly at home during the day, and some fathers commute daily to London. They come from mixed social backgrounds, and all are at the nursery because of its reputation. Parents like the informal, relaxed atmosphere and young, easy-going staff. Children have to be potty-trained before they start and they stay until they go on to school (rising-5 in the local state schools). Only ten children – the oldest – stay all day, to prepare for school.

**Curriculum & activities** The morning begins with free play, as children arrive at any time between 9 and 9.30am. Activities, including construction, puzzles, painting and a Wendy house are available. Registration and juice and biscuits follow in each classroom and then outdoor play, weather permitting. At 11am serious work time begins. Each classroom is set up with three tables. When we visited, one was laid out with sticking exercises, choices of colouring worksheets and a shapes template. Another had puzzles and a simple mix and match worksheet. The third table requires most concentration. Here Sue and Audrey, with the help of another teacher, take children through letter and number work, either on worksheets or in exercise books. Reading is also heard at this table. All children spend time at each table every day. The Ginn and 1,2,3 & Away reading schemes are used, as these are the schemes followed by local schools. Reading books are only introduced when a child knows at least 75 per cent of his/her letters and can build up words. Worksheets are carefully selected, graded and made into workbooks, which can be taken home. The academic progress is impressive, with children concentrating easily and happily. There is enjoyment everywhere – teachers frequently have to persuade children to stop work when it's time to go home. Before the end of a session, all children come together for songs, music and movement or percussion, with Sue Corfield at the piano. The nursery puts on a Nativity play and a summer concert in the village hall each year, and has a very close and warm relationship with the village community. There are two outings a year – spring lambing at a local farm and a summer coach trip.

**Remarks** Well-organised, fun nursery with a deservedly strong reputation. Impressive academic preparation for school and every penny of profit is pumped back into buying equipment for the children. The extremely limited nursery provision in the area makes this an even more vital and reasonably priced resource.

## TIDWORTH CLARENDON INFANT SCHOOL – NURSERY CLASS

Ordnance Road
Tidworth
Wilts SP9 7QD
**Tel:** (0980) 43381

**Owner:** Wiltshire County Council LEA
**Nursery Teacher:** Karen Somerville, B Ed (Hons)
**Type:** Nursery class in primary school offering half-day sessions. No full-time places
**Children:** 3–5yrs. 26 places. 52 on register
**Hours:** Morning session 9–11.30am
Afternoon session 12.45pm–3.15pm
Open 39 weeks a year
**Status:** State nursery class
**Number of years open:** 2½
**Meals:** Snacks
**1992 fees:** No fees
**Waiting list:** Long. Over 100 names, but place guaranteed for at least 1 or 2 terms before entering primary school
**Registered by:** Wiltshire County Council LEA

**Premises** A purpose-built, chalet-style, single-storey building in the grounds of a primary school, with its own garden and access to school playground. Inside there is one large classroom, carpeted except for an area for messy play; a small book room, a staff room and child-sized toilets and washbasins. The nursery is new, smartly decorated and full of art, craft and interesting objects to look at – evidence of strong imaginative and creative powers at work. The large home corner changes its appearance regularly – on the week of our visit it had been turned into a huge Noah's ark of paper and cardboard, an ambitious project carried out by staff, helped by the children. The book room was in the process of being turned into a stable for the animals! The entrance lobby, where children hang their coats, was an under-sea world of fish and seaweed. The nursery has been generously endowed by Wiltshire County Council and is enviably well furnished and well provided with toys, books, games, art and craft materials and other necessary equipment. The initial equipment budget for setting up was £10,000, and the annual replenishment budget is £800. Outside there is a garden and the perennial children's favourite, a den, underneath the steps to the nursery. In wet weather, children use the hard-surfaced school playground for games and trike riding. The whole nursery, inside and out, has been designed for easy access and use by children and adults with disabilities.

**Nursery Teacher & staff** Karen Somerville, B Ed, is a powerhouse of enthusiasm and creative ideas, which is reflected in the atmosphere of the nursery. Given excellent backing by her deputy, Val Colley, NNEB, and part-time teacher, Janet Stanford, B Ed, she provides an exciting and stimulating environment for children to learn in. Karen Somerville actively encourages parental involvement and provides parents with detailed reports on their child's activities. Some children arrive at the school from a local homeless resettlement programme, which uses empty army houses. Often with very young, inexperienced parents and brought up in deprived circumstances, some children have language difficulties. Karen Somerville and her team work closely with children and parents to overcome these problems. 'A lot of parents are nervous about coming into a school and talking to a headteacher,' says Karen 'They see the teacher as an authority figure. We like them to come in and work with their child – see what we're doing.' Karen Somerville is planning to set up a mother and toddler group at the nursery and hopes to extend the building to include a parents' room. The staff/child ratio varies from 1:10 to 1:13. Staff tap into the main school staff training programme and attend any other specific nursery courses that will enhance their skills.

**Children & parents** Located in the middle of a huge complex of army camps and service quarters, it is not surprising that the nursery's intake is 70 per cent from army backgrounds. The nursery was established in recognition of the particular needs of service families. Of the 30 per cent civilian intake, most are from former homeless or temporarily rehoused families. There is a high turnover of families. Children come and go as their parents are posted away, or rehoused. Few spend more than two or three terms at the nursery. They are well motivated, cheerful and chatty and plainly love the time they spend at the nursery. Children with special educational needs and disabilities integrate happily.

**Curriculum & activities** The nursery follows a learning through play philosophy but, as interpreted by Karen Somerville, this is a real voyage of discovery. Using the National Curriculum attainment targets as guidelines, Karen and her team weave an intricate pattern of activities around a specific topic. The topic when we were there, Noah's Ark, was used to introduce ideas on music, maths, history/geography, science, drama, technology, art and craft and for plenty of imaginative play. Children are encouraged to move from one activity to another, with an element of free choice and guidance when needed. A strong emphasis is placed on language development. There is music and computers daily, dance and movement twice a week, and the timetable also includes cookery and gardening, library visits and an outing each term. It is a child-centred, active-learning approach, encouraging investigation and exploration. Staff monitor each child continuously, looking for any difficulties or problems and recording achievements meticulously. Written reports are updated termly and sent home for parents' comments, invaluable to parents frequently having to enter their children into new schools.

**Remarks** It's hard not to eulogise over this nursery. Excellent facilities and resources and wonderful staff – particularly the nursery teacher, Karen Somerville. It is probably enough to say that it is absolutely first-class and the children who attend are very lucky indeed.

# Northern Ireland

Northern Ireland lags behind the rest of the country, with only 13 per cent of 3- and 4-year-olds offered access to nursery education. Some full-time places are available, but the majority are three-hourly sessions. There are no local authority day nurseries. Playgroups are the prime source of care and education in the province. The Northern Ireland Pre-school Playgroups Association (NIPPA) has 800 members, covering playgroups, parent and toddler groups and 100 full-time day nurseries. The private sector is fast-growing, although demand far exceeds supply, and there is virtually no provision for after-school care or holiday playschemes. Fees vary from £40 to £75 per week for a full-time nursery place, and from 50p to £2 per session for part-time facilities. Playgroups are grant-aided by their local Education and Library Boards. Funding varies from £300 to £5000 per playgroup per year. This year, grants have increased by three per cent. Most children are offered a playgroup place for at least a year before starting school. Many groups rely heavily on volunteers, and a yearly intake of 'A' Scheme trainees (similar to YTS), and are open during school term-time only. Private day nurseries are expensive and out of the reach of most parents. Northern Ireland has the highest number of childminders per head of population in the United Kingdom. 4000 are currently registered. Vacancies depend on area. In and around Belfast, there are waiting lists for all forms of childcare. By tradition, the province is family orientated, and relatives are popular and frequent carers. The Children Act, known in Northern Ireland as the Children's Order, is still in draft form and at the consultation stage. Implementation is due to take place at the end of 1994.

## Further information

For details on all forms of childcare and early years education contact your local Education and Library Board

Eastern Board
North & West Belfast (0232) 327156
South & East Belfast (0232) 790703
North Down (0247) 818518
Down & Lisburn (0846) 665181

Northern Board (0266) 653333

Southern Board (0762) 336611

Western Board (0504) 860086

# ASHGROVE NURSERY SCHOOL

23 Chestnut Grove
Newry BT34 1JT
**Tel:** (0693) 63355

**Owner:** Southern Education and Library Board
**Principal:** Dorothy McMillan, B Ed
**Type:** Nursery school offering half-day sessions. No full-time places
**Children:** 3–4yrs. 25 places. 45 on register
**Hours:** Morning session 9am–11.30am
Afternoon session 12.30pm–2.45pm
Open 39 weeks a year
**Status:** State nursery school
**Number of years open:** 20
**Meals:** Snacks
**1992 fees:** No fees
**Waiting list:** Long. 60-plus names
**Registered by:** Southern Education and Library Board

**Premises** Ashgrove Nursery School started life in 1970 as a private playgroup. A local builder custom-built it for his wife. The local authority bought the building three years later and converted it into a nursery school. From the outside, it looks like all the other bungalows on the private housing estate. In excellent condition, it has large picture windows and rooms flooded with light. The classroom is open-plan and divided into work, play and storage areas by low shelving. It is bright, cheerful and welcoming. Walls are covered with photographs of the children, mobiles hang from the ceiling and there is children's art and craftwork to be seen on every surface. There is also an office, kitchen, cloakrooms, toilets and indoor storeroom. Two separate, fenced, well-equipped outdoor play areas, one tarmac, the other grass, are available at all times.

**Principal & staff** Dorothy McMillan, B Ed, is an experienced, efficient teacher. She reports to the board of governors, who are responsible for the overall management of the school. They meet a minimum of three times a year. Two nursery assistants, one a qualified nurse, help run the class. A supply teacher comes in one day a week, to allow Dorothy McMillan to catch up on administration. Staff relate well to each other, meeting informally each day before class and once a month for a formal staff meeting. The staff/child ratio of 1:13 is not generous, but an extra helper is allocated for children with special educational needs. Training and development are difficult to arrange, as most courses are held during the day, when staff are unable to attend.

**Children & parents** A good social and religious mix. Children progress to 11 different primary schools in the area. The nursery passes an assessment of each child to its next school. Primary school teachers visit the nursery in June, to meet their future pupils. New parents meet their children's teachers the first time during a home visit. They then visit the nursery to observe the class in action, and for a further two evening meetings. Regular parents' meetings to discuss progress and development are currently being planned. Parents visit the nursery class to give talks about their work. Recently the home corner was turned into a pretend-hospital and a parent who is a nurse displayed her skills using the children as patients. Farmers bring in lambs, new mothers their babies. Parents donate useful equipment and help to maintain well-used apparatus. There are several parent-representatives on the board of governors. Children with disabilities and special educational needs integrate successfully.

**Curriculum & activities** The nursery follows the Southern Education and Library Board's guidelines, which encourage learning through play, with emphasis on outdoor play. They recommend at least an hour of outside physical activity each day, weather permitting. Doors are left open so children can move in or out as they wish. Nursery education guidelines define the curriculum as 'the creation within the school of a flexible, developing, learning environment, in which the child will actively pursue his interests with the guidance and support of adults'. Activities are provided and children choose from a wide range – painting, clay, dough and craft activities for creativity; and sand, water and construction for toys, early maths and scientific concepts. There is imaginative play in the home corner and dressing-up box, and language development through stories, rhymes, talking and listening. Music appreciation comes from daily songs and percussion instruments. Large indoor and outdoor equipment is used for physical play. The nursery is well-resourced, with an annual equipment budget of £1200. Other activities include dance, movement and gardening. No outings are held. There is no teaching of reading or writing. The ethos is structured play, planned in advance, around monthly themes – Colours, Seasons, the Senses, Special Events. Record keeping is to be improved. The headteacher is currently working on more detailed curriculum planning, an individual assessment scheme and a prospectus for parents.

**Remarks** Flexible, thorough grounding, which prepares children physically, emotionally and intellectually for their first school. A holistic approach in a happy, lively school. The cosy bungalow looks and feels like a home from home. Strong relationships between staff, children and parents, with a supportive board of governors. Long waiting list, as nursery provision in the area is inadequate. There are three nursery units for a town population of 20,000.

# CASTLEREAGH NURSERY

Clonduff Drive
Belfast BT6 9NR
**Tel:** (0232) 704539

**Owner:** South Eastern Education and Library Board
**Principal:** Maureen Fryer-Kelsey, B Ed, ACE, DASE
**Type:** Nursery offering 3 sessions a day
**Children:** 3yrs 1mth–4yrs 1mth. 75 places. 75 on register
**Hours:** 9am–1.30pm (inc lunch)
9am–11.30am
12 noon–2.30pm
Open 38 weeks a year
**Status:** State nursery school
**Number of years open:** 15
**Meals:** Lunch, snacks
**1992 fees:** No fees. 90p per day for lunch
**Waiting list:** Enrolment commences in Jan for following Sept
**Registered by:** South Eastern Education and Library Board

# COZY CORNER PLAYGROUP

The Community Centre
The Square
Crossmaglen
Northern Ireland BT35 9AA
**Tel:** (0693) 861949

**Owner:** Committee for the Handicapped, Crossmaglen
**Playgroup Leader:** Anne McShane, NIPPA
**Type:** NIPPA playgroup offering part-time places
**Children:** 3–5yrs. 20 places per session. 20 places. 39 on register
**Hours:** Morning session 10am–1pm
Afternoon session 12 noon–3.30pm
Open 40 weeks a year
**Status:** Northern Ireland Pre-school Playgroups Association
**Number of years open:** 9
**Meals:** Snacks
**1992 fees:** £5 per week for 5 sessions
**Waiting list:** Early registration advisable. Special needs have priority
**Registered by:** Northern Ireland SS

# DOWNSHIRE NURSERY SCHOOL

Primrose Gardens
Banbridge
Co Down BT32 3EN
**Tel:** (08206) 25195

**Owner:** Southern Education and Library Board
**Principal:** Eithne Hamilton, Cert Ed, Nursery Dip
**Type:** Nursery school offering 3 sessions a day
**Children:** 3yrs 2mths–4yrs. 45 places. 150 on register
**Hours:** 9am–1.30pm (inc lunch)
9am–11.30am
12.30pm–3pm
Open 38 weeks a year
**Status:** State nursery school
**Number of years open:** 13
**Meals:** Lunch, snacks
**1992 fees:** No fees
**Waiting list:** Very long. 130 names. First come first served
**Registered by:** Southern Education and Library Board

# DUNGANNON NURSERY SCHOOL

Circular Road
Dungannon BT71 6BE
**Tel:** (08687) 22689

**Owner:** Southern Education and Library Board
**Principal:** Laura Adair, Cert Ed, Adv Cert Nursery Ed
**Type:** State nursery school offering half-day sessions
**Children:** 3–5yrs. 70 places. 69 on register
**Hours:** 8.45am–1.40pm
Morning session 8.45am–11.30am
Afternoon session 12.25pm–3pm
Open term-time only
**Status:** State nursery school
**Number of years open:** 15
**Meals:** Lunch
**1992 fees:** No fees
**Waiting list:** Very long. Over 200 names
**Registered by:** Southern Education and Library Board

**Premises** Set well back from the town's Circular Road and difficult to find. Red-brick, purpose-built and single-storey, the nursery looks conventional and rather institutional. Inside is definitely more inspiring and attractive. The two large, light classrooms are completely child-orientated, with every available space dedicated to play, enjoyment and stimulation. Each classroom has its own set of child-size toilets, with low doors and partitions, and every child has his/her own towel. Children await collection in a small, cosy library, where they sit on the carpet listening to stories, music or looking at books. The building also has an office, staff room (with washing machine and tumble dryer) and an impressive catering-style kitchen. Outside there is a terrific covered play area, with new safety flooring, a spacious tree-lined playground full of good-quality outdoor equipment and a grassed area with swings, slides and climbing frames.

**Principal & staff** Principal, Laura Adair, Cert Ed, Adv Cert Nursery Ed, was head of a local infant department before taking up her position at Dungannon 15 years ago. She is busy, efficient, friendly and, most important, fantastic with the children. She leads a team of four – vice-principal Mrs Dosey, Cert Ed, and three qualified NNEB nursery nurses. There have been no staff changes since the nursery opened 15 years ago. Two of the staff are trained in special educational needs; there is also a part-time special needs assistant. The nursery employs a cook and cleaner.

**Children & parents** A complete cross-section of local children, admitted on a first come, first served basis. All transfer to a variety of state schools in the area. Every year the nursery is required to accept a minimum of six children with disabilities or special educational needs. Laura Adair strongly believes in integration and has successfully taught children with Down's syndrome, cerebral palsy, autism, hearing impairment and developmental delay. She teaches the older children (4- to 5-year-olds) from 9am to 1.30pm; the younger children are divided into a morning and afternoon group of 25 children each session. Parental involvement is low and the nursery does not operate an open-door policy as they find it disruptive. Parents are invited to concerts and a few social evenings, the most popular is when videos of the children are shown. New children start in September and are phased in in groups of three over a ten-week period. By Hallowe'en, the school is fully operational.

**Curriculum & activities** Laura Adair has written her own comprehensive teaching manual. The curriculum is highly organised and structured, with three-weekly themes, each carefully designed to develop a different skill area – creative, language, scientific, rhymes, games. When we visited they were just finishing 'myself' and all activities were related to this theme. Children had painted self-portraits, made face plates, completed hand-prints, traced their footprints (beautifully displayed around the walls) and made biscuits, which they had iced with faces. All the rhymes, songs, games and books were also relevant. At the same time, they were learning the colour 'blue'. Blue paint, dough and water were in use and a blue table covered with familiar objects all coloured blue. The atmosphere is very relaxed and children move freely from one activity to the next at will. The nursery has a vast amount of equipment (an annual equipment budget of £6000) and its use is carefully planned, on a rotating basis, changing every month. No formal teaching of reading or writing is done, but pre-reading, writing and number skills are taught. Intellectual development is promoted through stories, rhymes and picture discussion. Graded equipment is used in the water tray to teach size, weight, capacity and displacement. Sorting, matching, ordering and predicting are practised. There is a huge variety of tabletop toys – Duplo, Lego, dominoes, matching cards and games, sorting, stringing and problem-solving toys. The nature table encourages an awareness of the environment, and observing the weather leads to discussing the theme of 'clothes'. Imaginative play is encouraged in the home corner, and pretend hairdresser's, hospital and shop, also through junk-modelling, bricks, painting and craftwork. Safety is taught at a weekly Tufty lesson. The spacious covered outside play area ensures physical development whatever the weather. There is daily music for all children.

**Remarks** This is what a nursery school should be like – every corner is packed with stimulation and activity. Interested, happy children are supported by encouraging but unobtrusive, qualified teachers. The relaxed, play-orientated atmosphere disguises the very careful planning and structure that has gone into the curriculum. Masses of equipment of every kind. This is the only nursery school in Dungannon. It is hardly surprising that the waiting list is over 200 names long.

# KIDS & CO

Tullynure Lodge
Donaghmore
Dungannon
Co Tyrone BT70 3PQ
**Tel:** (08687) 61182

**Owner:** Alison McCague, B Ed
**Type:** Day nursery offering full-time places and half-day sessions. After-school pick-up service
**Children:** 2mths–5yrs. 20 places. 23 on register
**Hours:** 8am–6pm
Flexible hours
Open 48 weeks a year
**Status:** Private, fee-paying
**Number of years open:** 2
**Meals:** Breakfast, lunch, snacks
**1992 fees:** £50 per week full-time
£1.50 per hour
10% sibling discount
**Waiting list:** Minimal
**Registered by:** Southern Health and Social Services Board

**Premises** An old, converted barn set amid beautiful countryside, well back from the road, behind a large country house. The owner, Alison McCague, lives in the house and the nursery adjoins it. The nearest town is ten minutes' drive away. The nursery cannot be reached by public transport. The whole nursery complex including a grassed play area is contained within a walled yard. Parents enter by ringing a bell on a wooden gate. The two-storey barn is small, but every inch is utilised. Downstairs the under-2s' room is homely and warm, furnished like a living room. There is also a small, well-equipped kitchen, changing room and staff toilet and babies' sleeping area. On the upper floor, there are two playrooms and a bathroom/cloakroom with childsize toilets and washbasins.

**Owner & staff** Alison McCague, Cert Ed, an efficient, engaging woman, heads a team of six full-time staff, all NNEB qualified, and a part-time cook. Two of her four children attend the nursery. She has 11 years' experience as a home economics teacher and her knowledge is evident in the insistence on good fresh food and exemplary standards of hygiene. Kids & Co was the 1992 winner of the Avon PPA (Pre-school Playgroup Association) Award for high standards in daycare, a prestigious childcare award which reflects the quality of the nursery. The staff/child ratio is 1:3 and numbers are strictly limited in order to maintain this ratio. Staff offer spontaneous hugs, kisses and cuddles and a great deal of individual attention.

**Children & parents** Parents travel long distances to bring their children here. Nursery provision in the area is non-existent. Kids & Co is the only facility within a 14-mile radius. The majority of parents are professional, working families. Alison McCague believes that good care must be a partnership, and she is very open to ideas and suggestions from parents. She also liaises with parents on matters of discipline and tries to ensure that nursery care is as close to parents' care as possible. The nursery also helps working parents by collecting children after school.

**Curriculum & activities** The nursery follows the PPA philosophy of learning through play. In addition, staff are currently undergoing training in High Scope. Children are allowed to choose their own play activity and there is a strong emphasis on the natural world. The nursery's rural setting is an ideal location for this – its private lane leads to a picturesque lake. Nature rambles, walks to look at birds' nests, collecting leaves and examining wildlife are a regular part of the timetable. Art and craft work is much in evidence, often linked to weekly themes, which are planned at the monthly staff meetings. Play dough, sand and water play, cooking, stories, rhymes and movement are included in the programme. Outings include visits to the library and dentist. Kids & Co is a member of the Royal Society for the Prevention of Accidents, and a special gravel area in the grounds is used for road safety practice. Pre-school children are given a grounding in the basics of education totally free from academic pressures. The aim is to make learning fun and encourage a love of books. The nursery has its own library. Mealtimes and break times are social occasions and times for practising table manners. Food is high fibre and low sugar. The cook always uses fresh vegetables and there is fruit available whenever a child wants it. Children under 2 years old receive a daily written report card detailing what they have eaten and drunk and how they have slept and played throughout the day. Kids & Co prides itself on extremely high standards of hygiene. The nursery is spotless. Each baby has his/her own cot and bed linen, and no sharing is allowed. There is even a travel cot in the corner of the babies' changing room so if an emergency arises or the telephone rings in mid-chang the baby can be left in a safe place. Children are encouraged to be as independent as possible, which means learning to tidy up, and regular toileting, washing hands, setting the table for lunch and getting dressed.

**Remarks** An excellent nursery, wholly deserving of its award, and a valuable asset for working mothers in the area. Despite its isolated rural location, it is building up a strong reputation. The high staff/child ratio ensures quality care and stimulation. It is difficult to see how Alison McCague can break even when charging only £50 a week, certainly she herself admits to taking a very small salary.

# LISBURN CENTRAL NURSERY UNIT

Lisburn Central Primary School
52-56 Hillsborough Road
Lisburn
Northern Ireland BT28 1JJ
**Tel:** (0846) 665527

**Owner:** South Eastern Education and Library Board
**Headteacher:** Helen Pollock, Cert Ed
**Type:** Nursery class in state primary school offering half-day sessions
**Children:** 3–4yrs. 50 places. 100 on register
**Hours:** Morning session 9am–11.30am
Afternoon session 12.15pm–2.45pm
Open 36 weeks a year
**Status:** State nursery unit – two classes
**Number of years open:** 6
**Meals:** Snacks
**1992 fees:** No fees
**Waiting list:** Long – over 150 names
**Registered by:** South Eastern Education and Library Board

**Premises** Situated in a large park, adjacent to a leisure centre. Parents stop in the leisure centre car park and walk along a pathway to the school. It is a traditional red-brick, 1930s building with high ceilings and long, echoing corridors. The nursery unit, in one wing of the primary school, was renovated and modernised before it opened six years ago. Completely self-contained, it has two classrooms, a staffroom, toilets and stores. Although the building is rather austere, the classrooms are bright, cheerful and colourful, decorated with art and craft work. The outside play area is a sectioned-off part of the primary school playground, without grass. The outdoor equipment is brought inside each day because of vandalism. The children sometimes visit the soft play area in the leisure centre for parties.

**Headteacher & staff** Helen Pollock, Cert Ed, is a calm and caring headteacher, who went to great lengths to show us round and answer our questions. She reports directly to the head of the main school. The staff team consists of two qualified nursery teachers, two classroom assistants and an NNEB qualified nursery nurse. Staff meet regularly to plan future programmes and attend training courses provided by the Education Board.

**Children & parents** 50 children attend the nursery each session, divided between the two classrooms. A teacher and nursery assistant are responsible for each group. The Education Board allocates six children with special educational needs to the unit annually. Children come from many different backgrounds and religions; priority is given to children who will progress to the main school (generally about 50 per cent). The nursery has a close relationship with parents – there are open days, parents' evenings and concerts – and parents are encouraged to come into the classroom at the beginning and end of each session. Parents and grandparents regularly join in with the children and bring in lambs, kittens, puppies as well as newborn babies for discussion. Written reports on each child's progress are kept by teachers, but passed on verbally to parents.

**Curriculum & activities** The nursery follows guidelines set down by the education authority and is subject to regular inspectors' visits. The curriculum is highly organised and selected themes are systematically worked through each month. Everything is written down and carefully planned in advance, constantly revised and updated by the headteacher. The aim is to develop the whole child – emotionally, intellectually, socially and physically. There is no formal teaching of the 3Rs, but strong emphasis on language development. 'If children lack the primary skill of language, they will be slower to develop in all other areas,' Helen Pollock believes. Each theme is explored through a range of different activities, designed to improve knowledge of science, language, motor skills and social skills. No activity is undertaken without a clear idea of its educational purpose. There is a colour table, where children can touch, feel and smell different items of the same colour. They experiment with shapes using dough. Environmental studies are an important part of the curriculum and an impressive natural science display is set up in the entrance hall. Children bring in creatures and plant seeds and bulbs throughout the year. The nursery provides snacks and turns them into a learning experience, offering different types of bread and a variety of fruits. Cookery classes are popular, with scones and popcorn the favourites. There is daily music and outings once a term. Staff work closely with children, praising and talking to them. They are careful to encourage and extend play rather than direct it.

**Remarks** Excellent pre-school nursery providing desperately needed provision. Despite a population of 80,000, Lisburn has just four nursery schools. Close links with the primary school ensure a smooth transfer for the 50 per cent of children who move over. Impressive, very experienced, helpful headteacher and detailed, highly organised, child-centred curriculum. Rather daunting, austere building and uninspiring play area.

## SCALLYWAGS PRIVATE PLAYGROUP

5 Jubilee Road
Newtownards
Northern Ireland BT23 4YH
**Tel:** (0247) 815356

**Owner/Principal:** Helen Robinson, Cert Res Childcare, PPA Foundation, City & Guilds
**Type:** Playgroup offering morning sessions
**Children:** 2yrs 6mths–5yrs. 24 places. 30 on register
**Hours:** 9am–12 noon
Open 38 weeks a year
**Status:** Private, fee-paying
**Number of years open:** 11 (5 in current premises)
**Meals:** Snacks
**1993 fees:** £3 per session. £10 contingency fee per year
**Waiting list:** 20 names. First come first served
**Registered by:** Eastern Health and Social Services

## SQUIRRELS MONTESSORI NURSERY CENTRE

Rossorry Church Road
Enniskillen
**Tel:** (0365) 325904 (owner's home)

**Owner/Principal:** Catherine Whitley, Certificat d'Aptitude Pédagogique, Mont Dip, BA
**Type:** Montessori nursery school offering half-day sessions
**Children:** 2yrs 9mths–4yrs 11mths. 16 places. 25 on register

**Hours:** Morning session 9.15am–12.15pm
Afternoon session 1.30pm–4.30pm
Open 41 weeks a year
**Status:** Private, fee-paying
**Number of years open:** 9
**Meals:** Snacks only
**1992 fees:** £3.30 per session
50p per extra hour
**Waiting list:** Long. 50 names. Enrol at birth
**Registered by:** Western Health and Social Services

**Premises** Mobile classroom, next to a supermarket, in a largely residential part of the town. Parking is in the supermarket car park. The nursery is surrounded by wooden fencing, with a small gravel play area containing a slide and some huge concrete pipes for children to sit on and crawl through. The light nursery room is filled with Montessori equipment and apparatus on low, open shelves. The floors are vinyl, with carpeted areas for the book and story corners and plenty of space for children to sit on the floor and use the Montessori apparatus.

**Owner/Principal & staff** Catherine Whitley is French, a qualified nursery and primary teacher, who has lived in Enniskillen for 12 years. She arrived, after spells in France and America, to take conversation classes in schools, married a local man, and now has two young sons. She has a Montessori diploma and psychology degree. Close friends with many of her parents, she dispenses advice and reassurance with a lively sense of humour. PPA assistant, Carolyn Maguire, is young, reliable and committed. Two NNEB students a term attend on placement. Staff meetings are held daily. The staff/child ratio is 1:8. There is no staff training policy or budget.

**Children & parents** The children come from a variety of social backgrounds and religions. Most move on to primary schools in the town. Children with special needs are welcome and a Down's syndrome child currently attends. Parents play a vital role in the life of the school. They have a chance to talk with staff at the beginning and end of each session, are invited to plays and concerts at least twice a year and occasionally help out in the classroom or on outings. New parents visit in June and attend an open day each August, where Catherine explains the Montessori approach to education and demonstrates the apparatus. Settling in is done with parents present, if their work commitments allow. Parents receive detailed written reports on their child's progress in December and June. There is weekly developmental monitoring of all children.

**Curriculum & activities** The nursery believes in 'adapting the Montessori curriculum to the demands of the environment of today's children'. The approach is flexible, but time and space are structured. Children move freely within the carefully prepared room, using their initiative to choose different activities, guided by staff, but encouraged to be independent. There is a full range of Montessori equipment–sensorial, practical life, mathematical, language and environmental. We watched children having great fun using chopsticks to lift pieces of sponge. Children interact well with staff, individually, in small groups and all together. 'We listen to each child's interests and try to build up their experiences, never underestimating their abilities,' says Catherine. Last year a parent visited China and children made colourful Chinese masks, rickshaws and and a huge costumed dragon. Stories, movement, games and music play an important part in the programme; children always come together in one group for these activities. French is weekly. They learn rhymes, songs, dances, counting, animals and the parts of the body. Art is central to nursery life, but is directed, with emphasis on motivation and the creative process rather than the end result. Walls are left deliberately uncluttered, only displaying work which is relevant and essential to what children are currently exploring. Reading and writing are only taught if a child shows enthusiasm and ability. Outings include trips to the park, local pet shop and farms and an annual boat ride to Devenish Island.

**Remarks** A first-class, small Montessori school. Dedicated, loving staff, offering structured activities adapted to individual needs. Different from other pre-school provision in the area and very popular.

# SCOTLAND

## Borders

This is not a good area for childcare, even for those who can afford private fees. There are no local authority nursery schools and only 12 nursery classes offering part-time, part-week places to 20 per cent of 3- to 4-year-olds. Peebles, a market town with a population of 6000, has no state nursery provision. No local authority day nurseries in the region either. The private sector contributes only 12 facilities, with limited baby places. The majority of the 220 registered childminders are concentrated in and around Peebles, within commuting distance of Edinburgh. Part-time, sessional places are available at reasonable cost in 62 voluntary playgroups. Neither the Social Work nor the Education Department responded to our letters or phone calls asking for information, and the questionnaires we sent out to two nurseries in the region were not returned.

**Further information**

For details on all types of childcare:
Regional Headquarters
Newtown St Boswells
Melrose TD6 0SA
Tel: (0835) 23301

## Central

The regional council provides full-time daycare in seven local authority day nurseries and two family centres. A further four family centres, in areas of particular social deprivation, are grant-aided and voluntary run. 53 childminders are sponsored by the council. Eight private day nurseries, all opened in the last four years, offer 240 places, and most take babies. Almost 45 per cent of 3- and 4-year-olds receive a part-time place in the region's 11 nursery schools and 34 nursery classes. The Education Department hopes to maintain its commitment to opening two new nursery classes every year.

**Further information**

For details on day nurseries, childminders and playgroups:
Social Work Department
Langgarth
Stirling FK8 2HA
Tel: (0786) 442000

For details on nursery schools, units and classes:
Education Department
Viewforth
Stirling FK8 2ET
Tel: (0786) 442000

## ST ANNE'S NURSERY

Stirling University
147 Henderson Street
Bridge of Allan SK9 4RG
**Tel:** (0786) 467188

**Owner:** Stirling University
**Childcare Supervisor:** Mary Fowler, NNEB
**Type:** Day nursery offering full- and part-time places and half-day sessions to university students and staff and local community
**Children:** 3mths–5yrs. 42 places. 55 on register
**Hours:** 8.30am–6pm
Morning session 8.30am–1pm (inc lunch)
Afternoon session 1pm–6pm
Open 50 weeks a year
**Status:** Workplace nursery, fee-paying, non profit-making
**Number of years open:** 2 as day nursery 14 as playgroup
**Meals:** Snacks, packed lunches
**1992 fees:** £85 per week full-time – under 2
£75 per week full-time – over 2
£19 per day – under 2
£15 per day – over 2
£11 per session – under 2
£9 per session – over 2
Subsidised rates for staff and students
**Waiting list:** Early registration advisable, especially for 2–3yr-olds
**Registered by:** Central Region Social Work Department

# Dumfries & Galloway

No nursery schools and restricted hours in the 21 nursery classes. A taste of nursery provision for just over 23 per cent of 3- and 4-year-olds. 78 playgroups also offer part-time places, opening only a few days a week. There are no local authority day nurseries and only a tiny number of baby places among the eight private day nurseries. Childminders (119), nannies and relatives are the only childcare option for the majority of women returning to work. Of the five questionnaires we sent out to nurseries in the region, none was returned.

### Further information

For details on day nurseries, childminders and playgroups:
Social Work Department
5 Gordon Street
Dumfries
Tel: (0387) 60898

For details on nursery units and classes:
Education Department
30 Edinburgh Road
Dumfries DG1 1JQ
Tel: (0387) 61234

# Fife

Despite high unemployment and a history of supportive, extended families, there is increasing demand in Fife for more affordable childcare facilities. 50 per cent of the area's 3- and 4-year-olds receive part-time nursery education – making it the highest provider in Scotland. There are four nursery schools, run jointly with Social Work departments, offering full-time places for younger children with special needs. The council also funds two day nurseries for working parents in the Dunfermline district. Most playgroups operate five days a week, but the bedrock of provision in the region comes from 750 registered childminders. There are only seven private day nurseries. Rural areas are covered by peripatetic teachers, but because they are often shared among small village schools, children in outlying areas can receive as little as two sessions a week of nursery education. One parent wrote to us raving about the part-time nursery class attended by her 4-year-old, where she is one of only two pupils! Of the nine nurseries we sent questionnaires to in the region, none responded.

**Further information**

For details on day nurseries, childminders and playgroups:

Social Work Department
Ling House
29 Canmore Street
Dunfermline KY12 7NU
Tel: (0383) 735502

For details on nursery schools, units and classes:

Education Department
Fife House
North Street
Glenrothes KY7 5LT
Tel: (0592) 754411

# Grampian

Grampian has eight nursery schools and 72 nursery classes offering part-time places to over 30 per cent of 3- and 4-year-olds. Provision includes 260 full-time places. There are four local authority day nurseries and three family centres for children in need. In the private sector there are 65 day nurseries, over 700 registered childminders and more than 200 playgroups.

**Further information**

For details on day nurseries, childminders and playgroups:

Social Work Department
Woodhill House
Westburn Road
Aberdeen AB9 2LU
Tel: (0224) 682222

For details on nursery schools, units and classes:

Education Department
(address and telephone as above)

## ALBYN SCHOOL FOR GIRLS INFANT NURSERY DEPT

17–23 Queen's Road
Aberdeen AB9 2PA
**Tel:** (0224) 322408

**Owner:** Albyn School for Girls
**Headmistress:** Jeanette Blease, Dip CE (Prim Ed) Aberdeen
**Type:** Nursery school offering half-day sessions only. No full-time places
**Children:** 3–5yrs. 30 places. 36 on register
**Hours:** Morning session 8.45am–11.45am
Afternoon session 1.45pm–3.45pm
Open 36 weeks a year
**Status:** Private, fee-paying
**Number of years open:** 30+
**Meals:** Snacks only
**1992 fees:** Dependent upon length of term. Approx £28.50 to £30 a week
**Waiting list:** None
**Registered by:** Grampian Regional Council

**Premises** The nursery department of a long-established, well-known Aberdeen independent girls' school. It is housed in the Oliver wing, a separate, purpose-built, two-storey building – the well-equipped nursery classroom is upstairs with a primary classroom below. It is a large, light room with big windows and a southerly aspect. The floors are part-carpeted, part-covered with linoleum allowing for a variety of different activities. The outdoor play area is the spacious asphalt school playground – completely secure and private and used by the nursery children at a different time from the rest of the school. They have their own outdoor equipment, which is kept under cover and taken out when required. As the children are in school for only mornings or afternoons, outings are rarely made to the nearby park.

**Headmistress & staff** The headmistress of the Lower School, Jeanette Blease, Dip CE (Prim Ed), IM, Froebel trained, is ultimately responsible for the nursery and spends several hours a week with the children and staff. The day-to-day running of the class is in the hands of Eileen Presly, Dip CE (Prim Ed) Aberdeen, an imaginative and enthusiastic teacher. There are two NNEB teachers and a visiting specialist music teacher. A friendly, highly professional team.

**Children & parents** Many of the children's parents are in oil or oil-related industries, culturally but not socially mixed. Boys leave when they reach the age of admission to primary school; most go to Robert Gordon's College. Virtually all the girls continue up through the school. Some of the families have two working parents and all are solidly middle class. Nannies, au pairs or grannies collect at the end of each session. No one is allowed to stay in the school over the lunch break. Approximately 26 children attend in the mornings, with a staff of four, and ten children in the afternoons with a staff of three. There are excellent staff/child ratios for sessional nursery education. The 3-year-olds are assessed before acceptance and invited back with their parents to prepare them before entering the school. No uniform is worn, although many wear a green checked gingham pinafore, which girls can continue to use in the lower school.

**Curriculum & activities** There is no formal instruction in reading or writing as this is frowned upon by the local authority, but it is obvious from the quality of decoration on the classroom walls that highly imaginative work goes on. At our visit, the current themes were 'Movement' and 'Hallowe'en', and the children were busy making pumpkin pies for the Hallowe'en party, the following day. The air was filled with the delicious smell of baking. Windows were decorated with large cut-out pumpkins and the children were making orange drawings of them. They proceeded to play a singing game with a pumpkin theme with great enjoyment and assurance. One day is regularly set aside as Toy Day and children bring in a special toy or book to show and share with the rest of the class. Storytime is popular and occasionally a video is shown as a special treat. The nursery aims first and foremost to make its pupils happy and secure – helping children to know themselves and share with others, at the same time building up self-confidence and self-discipline. From time to time the class ventures into the main school, usually to take part in assembly. There are music lessons every week, and two or three outings a year.

**Remarks** Happy, relaxed nursery class with professional, imaginative staff. Impressive teaching with very favourable staff/pupil ratios – 1:3 in the afternoon, 1:6.5 in the morning. Children receive a thorough grounding, in a family atmosphere.

# GREENBURN NURSERY

Greenburn Road North
Bucksburn
Aberdeen AB2 9UA
**Tel:** (0224) 715212

**Owner:** Greenburn Nursery Ltd
**Co-ordinator:** Carol Wood, NNEB
**Type:** Workplace nursery offering full- and part-time places to Rowett Research Institute employees and local community
**Hours:** 8.15am–5.45pm
Open 50 weeks a year
**Status:** Private, fee-paying, non profit-making
**Number of years open:** 2
**Meals:** Breakfast, lunch, tea
**1992 fees:** £260–£360 per month
15% sibling reduction
**Waiting list:** Long especially for baby places. 20 names approx.
**Registered by:** Grampian Regional Council

**Premises** Located in a traditional, Victorian, semi-detached Aberdeen granite house on a quiet, private road in the grounds of the Rowett Research Institute in Bucksburn on the north-western outskirts of Aberdeen. The house was converted in 1991 for use as a nursery, with separate accommodation upstairs for babies, and downstairs for pre-school children. The atmosphere is warm, cheerful and fresh. There is a good variety of toys and educational materials as well as pleasant, sensible furniture and furnishings. Behind the house is a lovely, sheltered, completely secure garden with attractive outdoor equipment and a large grassy area where the children can play, accessible by French windows from the playroom. Just down the road is one of the experimental farms belonging to the Rowett Institute, where there are not only sheep and goats in the fields, but also a herd of llamas. It is well off the beaten track, with no convenient public transport, but there is plenty of room for staff and parents to park in front of the nursery.

**Co-ordinator & staff** Carol Wood, NNEB, the co-ordinator, has 15 years' professional childcare experience. Her team includes two qualified NNEB nursery nurses and two experienced, but unqualified, assistants, plus a part-time cook and a cleaner. The senior nursery nurse, Katy Broadfoot, spent many years working in the Special Care Baby Unit at Aberdeen Royal Infirmary before joining Greenburn. The nursery is run by the staff as a co-operative. They have voting rights at the AGM and make decisions collectively. They are a strong team, actively supported by parents and Rowett Institute staff.

**Children & parents** The nursery is isolated in the countryside, and children have to be brought by car from all directions. Their parents are mostly professionals from a range of different cultures – many overseas students work at the Institute. The nursery was originally set up in 1991 by a group of staff who were concerned by the lack of full-time nursery facilities in the area. Many of the initial planning group were working mothers faced with the problem of finding a safe, happy environment for their children. Parents still play a full and active part in the running of the nursery and are encouraged to make suggestions and put forward ideas. There is a management committee with representatives of nursery staff, parents (Rowett and non-Rowett) and Rowett personnel. Parents are expected to take time off work to settle their children in when they start. Breast-feeding mothers are welcome at any time. The nursery enjoys a positive, close relationship with parents. The children all move on to state primaries covering a wide area.

**Curriculum & activities** No particular educational philosophies predominate. Children learn through play, provided with stimulating and challenging materials. The regime is orderly but relaxed, and quite unstructured. The 3Rs are not taught formally, as local primary schools strongly disapprove of this practice. However, by the time children leave, they can recognise most letters of the alphabet, write and recognise their own names and have some idea of numbers. Their art, craft, language and social skills are well developed too, so that they arrive at primary school independent and confident. The youngest children – up to 2 years – play, rest and sleep in a large open-plan area upstairs, partitioned off by a low fence so that babies can roll and crawl around safely, but within sight of the toddlers. Older children enjoy monthly library visits, twice-weekly music and daily dance and movement. Swimming is about to be added to the timetable. The country setting and nearby farm offer freedom and endless opportunities for nature, wildlife and animal studies. Art is imaginative and plentiful. An eye-catching display of colourful footprints, of all sizes, is the first sight to greet visitors. As nutrition is one of the special fields of study at the Institute, particular attention is paid to meals and food. Parents have access to specially drawn-up nursery guidelines on feeding pre-school children and a weekly menu is displayed. Anti-social behaviour is dealt with by firmly removing the child from the situation or by distraction. No punishments are sanctioned.

**Remarks** Happy and homely, with warm, friendly staff. Rather isolated, but this is the only full-time nursery care for children under 3 years old for miles around – hence the long waiting list for baby places. Unusually close cooperation between staff and parents, with parents taking an energetic and committed part in all aspects of nursery life. Would benefit from more space, so that places could expand to meet the demand. The area also desperately needs some after-school provision, which Greenburn would like to be able to provide.

# THE KINDERGARTEN

196 Westburn Road
Aberdeen AB2 4LT
**Tel:** (0224) 633803

**Owner/Headmistress:** Una Tod, Dip Ed, DPSE
**Type:** Day nursery offering full- and part-time places
**Children:** 3–5yrs. 16 places. 34 on register
**Hours:** 8.15am–5.15pm
Open 50 weeks a year
**Status:** Private, fee-paying
**Number of years open:** 3
**Meals:** Breakfast, lunch, snacks
**1992 fees:** £80 per week full-time
£50 per week for 5 morning sessions
£37 per week for 5 afternoon sessions
**Waiting list:** Minimal
**Registered by:** Grampian SS

**Premises** Ground floor of a traditional Aberdeen granite, semi-detached villa, built at the turn of the century. There is a small garden in front and a slightly larger one behind, which has a paved area for riding trikes and a grassy patch with climbing frame and sand tray. Not much room for running about and no privacy, just a low wooden fence between the garden and a quiet side street beyond. The school is situated on a busy road radiating out from the city and carrying heavy traffic. Cars can park briefly at the gate to drop off and pick up children, but two side streets nearby are used for longer stays. The nursery is open-plan and well decorated, with one end carpeted for quiet games and activities, the other covered in vinyl for messy play. The hallway is used for reading to small groups – space is at a premium. There are good parks within walking distance, but children are not taken there on a regular basis. The headmistress and her daughter live on the top two floors of the building.

**Owner/Headmistress & staff** Una Todd, Dip Ed, DPSE, is well qualified with diplomas in education and special education and 15 years' teaching experience in state primary schools. A woman with strong views and a sensible no-nonsense approach, she is herself the daughter of a headmaster and headmistress. This is very much a family concern, with three generations of Tods working in the nursery and all experienced in childcare. Una's mother, now retired, does all the cooking for the children – they call her Nana – and Una's daughter, NNEB qualified, is a full-time nursery worker. The staff complement is three full-time qualified nursery workers and two part-timers. There is always a young trainee, employed for a year to gain practical experience before starting an NNEB course. The staff/child ratio was a generous 1:3 on the day we visited. The mother of one of the children is French and comes in once a week to give French lessons. This is unlikely to have a lasting effect, however, as there is no foreign language teaching in the Scottish primary system.

**Children & parents** Most children are local Scots, with working mothers from varying social backgrounds. Some come from as far as 15 miles away and are dropped off in the morning as parents drive into the city for work. All move on to local state primary schools. Parents are encouraged to talk to staff on a daily basis. More formal interviews with the headmistress can be arranged at any time and social events take place regularly.

**Curriculum & activities** No particular educational philosophy prevails, nor is formal instruction in reading or writing given, as local primary schools do not encourage this. However, by the time children leave, they recognise most of the letters of the alphabet, can write their own names and have some understanding of numbers. The headmistress and staff are well qualified to provide an interesting and challenging environment. The children are allowed to learn through play experiences, with help and praise from an adult when needed. Discipline is good, and the day is carefully structured. A detailed timetable is prepared in advance. Each day children experience a range of table-top activities and messy play which they choose for themselves. Group time, including some pre-school work, is done for half an hour in the morning and afternoon. Games, including Kindergym, musical games, ball games and exercises, and outdoor play also take place twice a week. Swimming is available twice weekly for all pupils at no extra cost. Skating is an optional extra, and there is daily music and weekly dance and movement. Outings take place every two or three months to the theatre, local farm and other places of interest. The school rooms are well equipped with all the things you would expect to find in a good nursery school, although there were not many books to be seen on the rack when we visited. Staff sit with children and talk to them during meals. There is a good variety of food, including plenty of fruit, and a sensible approach to who eats what.

**Remarks** Small, family-run, homely nursery with experienced, qualified staff. Would benefit from more space or a covered outdoor area for year-round use. Impressive, down-to-earth headmistress ensures individual attention for all children and is particularly qualified to teach children with special emotional needs.

# MORAY STEINER SCHOOL KINDERGARTEN

Drumduan House
Forres
Morayshire IV36 0RD
**Tel:** (0309) 676300

**Owner:** Moray Steiner School Ltd
**Principal:** All teachers collectively
**Type:** Kindergarten – part of Steiner primary school – offering 5 morning sessions and 3 afternoon sessions a week
**Children:** 3½–6½yrs. 30 places. 23 on register
**Hours:** 9am–12.30pm Mon, Fri

9am–3pm Tues, Wed, Thurs
Open 34 weeks a year
**Status:** Private, fee-paying, non profit-making charity, assisted by Steiner School Fellowship
**Number of years open:** 6
**Meals:** Packed lunch, snacks
**1992 fees:** By individual agreement according to circumstances. Average fees £90 per month
**Waiting list:** Short. Places available
**Registered by:** Grampian Regional Council

# ROSEBRAE SCHOOL – KINDERGARTEN

Rosebrae Farm House
Spynie Road
Elgin
Morayshire
**Tel:** (0343) 544841

**Owner:** Rosebrae Educational Trust Ltd
**School Headteacher:** Christeen Bell, Dip Ed
**Head of Kindergarten:** Margaret Young, qualified nursery nurse (Primary Cert in Residential Care)
**Type:** Kindergarten attached to prep school, offering full-time places and half-day sessions
**Children:** 2½–5yrs. 27 places. 30 on register
**Hours:** 9.15am–3.15pm
Morning session 9.15am–12.30pm
Afternoon session 1.45pm–3.15pm (2½yr-olds only)
Open 36 weeks a year
**Status:** Private, fee-paying
**Number of years open:** 26
**Meals:** Lunch, snacks
**1992 fees:** £281 per term (2½–4yr-olds)
£318 per term (4yr-olds)
**Waiting list:** Minimal.
**Registered by:** Scottish Education Dept

**Premises** A typical old Morayshire farmhouse, adapted for use as a school in 1967. It is situated in the middle of the rolling fields and meadows of the Laigh of Moray, three miles from Elgin, the nearest town. The kindergarten has recently been expanded into a series of Portakabins, providing a large, open-plan classroom, built on to the original two-storey farmhouse. Windows look north and south, with stunning, uninterrupted views across miles of undulating countryside to the sea. In front of the house there is a walled garden, where children play safely on a stretch of rough grass. An interesting collection of climbing frames, rope ladders and other wooden adventure equipment is set out beside the house. The property is well maintained inside and out. Located just off the A96 Inverness–Aberdeen trunk road, a few miles west of Elgin. No public transport; a car is essential.

**Headteacher, Head of Kindergarten & staff** The school headteacher, Christeen Bell, Dip Ed (Aberdeen), has been at Rosebrae for nine years. Her previous teaching experience includes schools in Somerset and local authority schools in Scotland. She teaches in the preparatory department and visits the kindergarten regularly, takes prayers once or twice a week, and knows all the children. The head of the kindergarten is Margaret Young, a nursery nurse who trained at Moray College of Further Education, and who has also worked at Rosebrae for nine years. She is assisted by two other nursery nurses. One is a registered playgroup supervisor, and the other a science graduate with particular responsibility for organising projects.

**Children & parents** Children from 3 to 5 years old attend morning sessions. The afternoons are reserved for the 2½-year-olds on their own. Parents, mainly from the local farming and business communities, bring their children by car from up to 20 miles away. The children move up through the school or transfer to local private and state schools. Parents attend open days, parents' evenings and an annual outing and are welcome to talk to teachers whenever they wish. There is a friendly, working relationship between parents and staff.

**Curriculum & activities** A flexible approach to learning, with emphasis on developing language and numeracy skills. Self-expression is encouraged through creative play. Projects are chosen each term. At our visit, the theme was 'Weather'. Workbooks, drawings and models were all based on the theme. Experiments with weather vanes, rain gauges and thermometers were in progress. Because of the position of the nursery, children are able to watch different types of weather approaching from miles away. The open-plan classroom is divided into colour-coded areas for different activities, with large circular tables where children sit and work. Pre-reading, pre-writing and number work are done here, with a teacher guiding and helping at each table. Children move freely from activity to activity. There is a messy-play and art area, a dressing-up corner and racks of interesting clothes and a home corner. Books are everywhere and stories read and told at each session. Children appear happy and spontaneous, reading well to staff and each other. Their environment is bright and stimulating, with a good supply of resources.

**Remarks** Happy, friendly and recently expanded nursery class in a spectacular position, surrounded by miles of open countryside. Sessions for 2½-year-olds on their own. Caring, impressive teachers provide a good preparation for both the Scottish private sector and the primary school system.

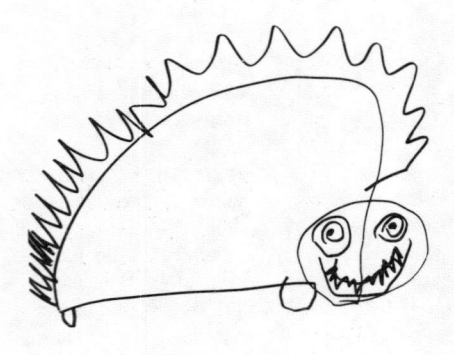

# Highland

At the bottom of the Scottish league table for nursery education, with one nursery school and 21 nursery classes, offering part-time and often part-week places only. Just over 15 per cent of 3- and 4-year-olds experience nursery education before school. Although provision has increased over the last few years, Highland still lags behind the rest of Scotland. When places are allocated, priority is given to children in the immediate catchment area. This creates long waiting lists in certain areas, particularly Inverness. 195 playgroups, many oversubscribed, offer additional part-time backup. There are only three private day nurseries in the region. Most working parents find willing relatives or choose one of the 314 registered childminders. Despite sending out questionnaires to a range of providers in the region, none responded.

**Further information**

For details on day nurseries, childminders and playgroups:
Social Work Department
Kinmylies Building
Leachkin Road
Inverness IV3 6NN
Tel: (0463) 702000

For details on nursery schools, units and classes:
Education Department
Regional Buildings
Glenurquhart Road
Inverness IV3 5NX
Tel: (0463) 702000

# Lothian

Lothian recognises the pressing need to expand nursery education in the region and plans are underway to guarantee every 4-year-old a part-time nursery class place and improve the situation for 3-year-olds. Nearly 50 per cent of 3- and 4-year-olds are in nursery education. Local authority daycare provision is restricted to children's centres in areas of social deprivation, and waiting lists are long. Working parents must rely on the private sector, where the average cost of a full-time place is £70–£80 per week. Of the 67 private day nurseries, 55 are in the city of Edinburgh. Childminders are the most popular and affordable option; Lothian registers 2000 of them.

**Further information**

For details on day nurseries, childminders and playgroups:
Community Care
Registration and Inspection Services
128/130 East Claremont Street
Edinburgh EH7 4LD
Tel: (031) 556 6787

For details on nursery schools, units and classes:
Education Department
40 Torphichen Street
Edinburgh EH3 8JJ
Tel: (031) 229 9166

# CARGILFIELD NURSERY

Cargilfield School
37 Barnton Avenue West
Edinburgh EH4 6HU
**Tel:** (031) 336 4472

**Owner:** Cargilfield School
**Headteacher:** Elizabeth Ford, DCE, NFF
**Type:** Nursery class in co-educational prep school offering morning sessions
**Children:** 2yrs 9mths–5yrs 3mths. 27 places. 25 on register
**Hours:** 8.30am–12 noon
Open 36 weeks a year
**Status:** Private, fee-paying
**Number of years open:** 11
**Meals:** Mid-morning snack
**1992 fees:** £415 per term
**Waiting list:** Varies in length. Places cannot be guaranteed although some currently available
**Registered by:** Lothian Regional Council

**Premises** In the western suburbs of Edinburgh, close to the A90 as it leads towards the Forth Road Bridge and Fife, Barnton is an exclusive area of wide, tree-lined avenues, large houses and huge gardens close to Cramond and the Firth of Forth. The nursery class is housed in a purpose-built, prefabricated building in the grounds of Cargilfield School. There is just one main room divided into different areas for various activities. It is close to the school entrance and there is ample parking space. The school grounds are immaculately tended, with freshly painted flower tubs on display, even in the middle of winter. Children are able to make use of an extensive outdoor space furnished with climbing frames, slides, swings and a bird table. The grounds are also used for rambling and nature walks.

**Headteacher & staff** Elizabeth Ford, DCE, NFF, has been headteacher of the nursery class for the last six years. She oversees a part-time staff of three, all with teaching or Montessori qualifications. Jill Preston, DCE, is in charge of the nursery on a day-to-day basis. They are a talented team; one is an artist in her own right, another excels at PE and the headteacher plays the piano and supervises music and movement sessions with the children. The school governors are keen on academic qualifications when looking for new staff, but Elizabeth Ford says, 'I'm also looking for experience with young children and a caring attitude.' She has no objection to employing a man, but does not see it as a priority. 'Few children at this nursery come from single-parent families,' she says. Staff meet daily for a short exchange of information and weekly for more detailed planning sessions. The staff/child ratio of 1:7 is excellent for a sessional nursery class.

**Children & parents** Without exception these are the children of affluent, professional parents – bankers, lawyers, doctors – many with nannies. There is comparatively little cultural or racial mix in Edinburgh and this is reflected in the group attending the school. Most will go on to Cargilfield pre-prep and prep, although the school clearly states that entry into the nursery does not guarantee a pre-prep place. It is a small, friendly nursery and children have no difficulty in building relationships with the three members of staff. Parents are invited to an open day before being offered a place. Once a place has been secured, parents and children are invited to look round and to attend sports day.

**Curriculum & activities** The emphasis is on learning through play, and children mix freely, taking part in water and sand play, construction games, drawing and painting, home corner, snack corner, book corner and craftwork. There are no dressing-up clothes, and no computers. Time is set aside for older children, when they are ready and able, to concentrate on pre-reading and counting exercises as well as pencil control. However, the nursery does not advocate a structured learning programme as Elizabeth Ford feels not all the children are ready for it at this stage and she is against any form of pressure. In line with educational policy throughout Scotland, reading is not taught to this age group, although children learn to recognise letters and numbers in preparation for formal instruction in the 3Rs in the pre-prep school. The school keeps records on each child covering language development as well as social and emotional behaviour, which parents may ask to see. There are no written reports, but parents are kept informed of their child's progress by staff on a regular basis. Nursery outings in the school mini-bus include the zoo, Botanic Gardens, butterfly farm and the city farm.

**Remarks** A cosy, caring introduction to one of Scotland's best-established traditional prep schools. Well-qualified staff and a good staff/child ratio. Stimulating and safe. Neither complacent nor progressive.

# CASTLE NURSERY

Franchise Village
Curiosity Street
Craigpark
Newcraighall Road
Edinburgh EH15 3RD
**Tel:** (031) 669 9200

**Owner:** Bruce D Smith
**Manager:** Margaret Woodrow, Dip Ed
**Type:** Day nursery offering full- and part-time places
**Children:** 0–5yrs. 50 places. 44 on register
**Hours:** 8am–6pm Mon–Fri
9am–6pm Sat & Sun
Open 52 weeks a year
**Status:** Private, fee-paying
**Number of years open:** 3
**Meals:** Breakfast, lunch, snacks
**1992 fees:** £411.66 per month full-time – under 2
£325 per month full-time – over 2
**Waiting list:** Short waiting list for under-2s
**Registered by:** Lothian Regional Council

**Premises** The first purpose-built, independent day nursery in Scotland, set in a new, two-year-old shopping and leisure park on the east side of the city. The entrance is through the shopping mall and over a small artificial bridge. This is no normal neighbourhood. Instead of houses, buses, schools and trees, there is a large car park surrounded by megabowl, cinema, discount stores and neon lights. The nearest serious blade of grass is a quarter of a mile away. Children do have access to a large, enclosed outside play area, with wood-chip safety surface, wooden climbing frame, rubber tyres and fixed ride-on toys. Inside, the rooms are well decorated and equipped. Children's work is displayed throughout. There are three rooms for different age groups: a baby room with sleep room off it; a toddlers' playroom and separate rest area; and the main nursery room, with a messy-play area, doubling as a dining room. The nursery feels spacious and modern, but not very homely.

**Owner, Manager & staff** The owner, Bruce Smith, has no childcare qualifications, but started the nursery because he wanted a school for his young son, and the lease of the building was available. He is responsible for the cooking and cleaning of the nursery and runs another business by phone from the nursery. Staff all agree, 'It's good to have a man about.' Margaret Woodrow, the manager, has a diploma in education and has always worked with under-5s. She has completed courses on organisation, play and child development and has had 15 years' experience in pre-schools. She enjoys excellent relations with the owner and says the Castle Nursery is great compared with others she has worked in. There are ten members of staff, eight of whom are NNEB qualified; one has a university degree. A YTS trainee, hoping to gain her NNEB qualification, assists. Most staff have a first-aid qualification, and one has a drama diploma. Students, including trainee nurses, are accepted on placement at certain times of year. The staff/child ratio is 1:3 for under-2s, 1:5 for over-2s. The day we visited there were 24 children and ten nursery workers. Staff training has in the past been through Lothian Regional Council Play Forum, but this has now been scrapped due to local authority cutbacks.

**Children & parents** There is no particular catchment area for the nursery, because of its unusual location. Children are dropped off by parents on their way to work. It is a mixed group. Generally both parents are working, mainly in professional, white-collar jobs. The door is always open to parents. They are invited to spend a morning working in the nursery, talk to staff any time (there is a key-worker system) and spend time phasing-in new children. Because many are working full-time, this can be difficult. There is a parents' gathering at least once a term, a summer barbecue and Christmas songs from the children. To date, most children have transferred to the state system, but many children now in the nursery are heading for private schools. Children with special needs integrate well. There is wheelchair access and specialist support staff available to visit, when necessary.

**Curriculum & activities** No one particular philosophy predominates, but the general belief is that 'play should be both fun and educational'. Equipment and furniture are child-oriented and of good quality. Weekly themes are worked on by the 3- to 5-year-olds, with all activities relating in some way to the theme. A recent road safety theme involved, among other things, relevant stories, books and rhymes; cooking traffic light biscuits; jumping and stopping on the trampoline; a traffic lights game; constructing roads and houses;

building fences to keep farm animals safe; walking safely to the shops; and foot painting a large wall display of feet on the edge of a pavement. Art and craft, woodwork, music and movement, dressing-up and storytime are a regular part of each day. There is no formal instruction in reading, writing or maths, as the local schools do not approve. Pre-school work is minimal. Children are encouraged to recognise numbers and letters through their different play experiences, matching, sorting, looking at books. Local outings by bus take place once a month to Princes Street Gardens, a butterfly farm, local parks. There is a whole day outing in the summer.

**Remarks** Friendly, down-to-earth, well-qualified manager and continuity of care from trained staff. High standards of hygiene and spacious facilities. The nursery lacks a homely touch and the location in an out-of-town shopping centre is a real drawback. Still not full after two years, Scotland's first purpose-built, independent nursery may be feeling the effects of the recession. Alternatively, parents may be nervous about sending their children to such an artificial setting.

# EDINBURGH ACADEMY NURSERY CLASS

Denholm Green
Arboretum Road
Edinburgh EH3 5PL
**Tel:** (031) 552 3981

**Owner:** The Edinburgh Academy
**Nursery Head:** Elinor Denholm, Teachers' Cert, INSC
**Type:** Nursery class in independent school offering full-time places and half-day sessions
**Children:** 3–5yrs 6mths. 30 places (inc 15 full-time). 45 on register
**Hours:** 8.45am–3pm
Morning session 8.45am–12 noon
Afternoon session 1pm–3pm
Open 37 weeks a year
**Status:** Private, fee-paying
**Number of years open:** 9
**Meals:** Lunch, snacks
**1992 fees:** £565 per term full-time
£340 per term for 5 morning sessions a week
£225 per term for 5 afternoon sessions a week
85p per day for lunch
£50 non-refundable deposit
**Waiting list:** Long, but many on list do not take up places
**Registered by:** Lothian Regional Council

**Premises** Located in the attractive, modern prep-school building of the prestigious Edinburgh Academy, surrounded by extensive, well-kept grounds, close to the Botanic Gardens. The nursery consists of an entrance hall, cloakroom with three toilets and one large, sunny classroom. The main classroom was originally used as a music room before it was totally refurbished as a nursery. A bright, colourful room, it has been imaginatively divided into a maze of small, well-equipped play areas. There is a cooking area, pet's corner, messy play area, reading and book corner and music area. Direct access into a large, fenced-off, safe garden and play area, with swings, climbing frames, sandpit and a hut crammed full of outdoor equipment. Children also enjoy their own flower and vegetable garden. The outside area, used daily, is particularly valuable as the classroom provides no real space for running about and letting off steam.

**Nursery Head & staff** Elinor Denholm has a Primary School Teaching Certificate and the Infant and Nursery Endorsement (INSC), as well as nearly ten years' teaching experience. Appointed head in October 1989, she it ultimately responsible for most decisions concerning the running of the nursery. Her two full-time assistants are qualified NNEB nursery nurses with many years' experience at this nursery. A pool of relief staff cover absenteeism, and the school nurse administers any necessary medical care during nursery hours. Occasionally, students taking the one-year post-graduate teaching course at Moray House College are placed for four weeks at the nursery. A happy, established and well-qualified staff team, who work well together. Salaries are above the national average and staff are paid a special Academy allowance. In-service training and continuous critical examination of their work enables staff to develop their skills and keep up with new developments in nursery education. There are regular weekly staff meetings and informal discussions daily. The staff/child ratio is 1:10.

**Children & parents** The children come from mixed cultural backgrounds and affluent middle-class homes. Boys generally progress to the Edinburgh Academy, although a nursery place does not guarantee entry into the prep school. Most of the girls transfer to St George's or St Margaret's. There is no real catchment area; children travel in from all over the city. Parents are encouraged to discuss their children with staff at any time and to take advantage of the open-door policy. There is an annual open day and a social evening, and parents are invited to help with outings. The nursery aims to achieve a close working relationship between parents and staff.

**Curriculum & activities** Learning through play in a warm, caring and happy environment. The nursery wants each child to develop as a whole and at his/her own rate. Children are carefully observed and their individual interests and abilities extended and challenged to their full potential. There are no formal classes in reading, writing or number work, but activities are provided to stimulate interest in these subjects. A strong emphasis is placed on language and communication skills – staff take time to talk and to listen. Children move from area to area and choose freely from a wide range of activities and educational equipment (annual budget £1635). There is messy play with sand, water, clay and paint and construction with bricks, scrap materials, wood and cardboard. Scientific interests are encouraged and environmental studies pursued in the garden and beautiful school grounds. Music and dance and movement sessions are held every day. Drama and imaginative play, art, drawing and cookery enable children to express themselves freely. Regular outings in the school mini-bus take place, often related to special interest topics being studied in the nursery. There is no formal written programme and no timetable. Children's progress is formally monitored twice yearly, after staff discussions. Details are recorded in writing and available to parents.

**Remarks** A well-established nursery class in one of Edinburgh's most famous schools. Experienced, qualified staff, who seem genuinely happy in their work. Lively, confident children, clearly having fun. An excellent introduction to school for the privileged. There is very little nursery provision in this area, particularly local authority nursery schools or nursery classes.

# THE EDINBURGH NURSERY CRÈCHE

13 East London Street
Edinburgh EH7 4BN
**Tel:** (031) 557 9014

**Owner:** Karen Fairlamb
**Acting Manager:** Caroline Ingram, NNEB, deputising for Elizabeth Walker, NNEB, who is on maternity leave
**Type:** Full-time day nursery offering part-time places
**Children:** 3mths–2yrs. 18 babies per day. 28 on register
**Hours:** 8am–5.45pm
Open 51 weeks a year
**Status:** Private, fee-paying
**Number of years open:** 3
**Meals:** Packed lunches, tea, snacks
**1992 fees:** £347.25 per month full-time
**Waiting list:** Moderate
**Registered by:** Lothian Regional Council
**Under same ownership:** The Edinburgh Nursery; The Edinburgh Nursery Annexe; The Edinburgh Nursery School

**Premises** The ground floor and basement of a typical late-Victorian, central Edinburgh tenement building. It is part of a commercial terrace in a mainly residential area, with shops on the ground floor and flats above. The street is wide and fairly quiet. Five minutes from the city centre, with good public transport. Short-term parking is not a major problem. There is a secure, walled garden accessed through French windows from the main playroom. As most of the children are not yet walking, the garden is only used in the summer, when they can sit on the rather patchy grass. Children are taken to a local park two or three times a week throughout the year. Inside, in the basement, there is a spacious, brightly decorated playroom, divided into three areas for messy play, soft play and active play, a separate sleep room and a nappy-changing room. Brightly coloured and well lit, but little natural light. On the ground floor there is a sparkling clean kitchen which is also used as a staff room, and on both floors reception areas with office, telephone, notice boards and a meeting place for parents.

**Owner, Manager & staff** The owner, Karen Fairlamb, has no childcare qualification and does not look after the children herself, though she will cover in an emergency. She takes charge of administration, organises staff and parents' meetings and generally oversees the smooth running of her four separate facilities. Each nursery has a manager and senior nursery nurse who report back to the owner. Any member of staff can suggest topics or issues for discussion; each nursery works to a budget and can make its own decisions on what equipment and materials to buy. Both the manager, Elizabeth Walker, at the time of writing on maternity leave, and the acting manager, Caroline Ingram, are NNEB trained and have worked at the nursery for over four years. There is a staff of seven in the Crèche, the majority NNEB qualified and mainly in their twenties. One is Dutch, another has specialised in working with handicapped children and one is a gifted artist, responsible for the outstanding paintings on the playroom walls. The staff ratio is 1:3. Students are accepted on placement. Permanent staff wear nursery sweatshirts, while students do not. When we visited there were 12 children, two full-time members of staff and two students which is a real ratio of 1:6 – students do not count as full staff members. Staff are encouraged to attend short training courses regularly; recent ones include first-aid, health and hygiene and child abuse.

**Children & parents** Most of the full-time children have professional, working parents. Students and some who are self-employed take up part-time places. The nursery operates an open-door policy; parents, including fathers, are invited to come in to feed their children at lunchtime as the nursery is very near the city centre. Breast-feeding mothers call in regularly. Full written records are kept for each child, charting their progress, feeding and sleeping patterns. Parents have ready access to all records. Parents' evenings are held three times a year, and there are also fund-raising activities, and in the summer a picnic outing which parents take a day off work to join.

**Curriculum & activities** Learning through play with plenty of good, soft play equipment and baby toys (annual budget £1500). Every encouragement is given to take part in all kinds of messy play: sand and water, play dough and painting – including full body painting where the child rolls in the paint and then prints his/her entire body on paper. There is a paddling pool, which is used indoors in winter, filled with warm water. Children are taken on outings to the Zoo, the Botanic Gardens, pet shops or the trampoline centre and pushed to the nearest park in double buggies. Daily charts are posted on parents' noticeboards in reception, detailing activities, food and each child's sleep and toileting routine. Stair gates are secure and in use. The kitchen and nappy-changing areas are cleaned regularly throughout the day. Soiled nappies are triple-sealed and put in storage bins to await commercial waste collection.

**Remarks** Small, family unit specifically for babies and toddlers up to 2 years. The first nursery in the city to take babies. Ideal for career mothers returning to work after maternity leave. Enthusiastic, professional carers. Children can progress from the crèche to other nurseries in the group. A businesslike and friendly organisation.

# Orkney

No local authority day nurseries or nursery schools. The five nursery classes attached to primary schools cater for only 18 per cent of the islands' pre-school children, and offer part-day/part-week places only. Working parents rely on their close-knit families to help with childcare needs. Two private day nurseries are in the pipeline and the number of registered childminders, currently 30, is expected to expand. We sent questionnaires to all the islands' five nursery classes, but none responded.

**Further information**

For details on day nurseries, childminders and playgroups:

Social Work Department
Registration and Inspection Unit
The Bungalow
St Colm's Centre
Pickaquoy Road
Kirkwall KW15 1PB
Tel: (0856) 876445

For details on nursery units and classes:
Education Department
Council Buildings
Kirkwall KW15 1NY
Tel: (0856) 873535

# Shetland

Council policy is, 'Where need has been demonstrated and a classroom is available, nursery education will be provided.' However, overall provision is still inadequate. 360 of Shetland's 1590 under-5s receive a part-time nursery place. There are no local authority or private day nurseries, and no state-funded nursery schools. Traditionally, Shetlanders are part of an extended family network, living in tight-knit, rural communities, all within three miles of the sea. Relatives provide most of the childcare. Incomers, without such in-built support, have few options open to them. Working mothers juggle playgroups, nursery classes, childminders (35), friends and family. 19 parent and toddler groups and a very part-time crèche, open 1½ days a week in a Lerwick church, have been set up in response to local demand.

**Further information**

For details on childminders and playgroups:
Social Work Department
92 St Olaf Street
Lerwick ZE1 0ES
Tel: (0595) 3535

For details on nursery classes:
Education Department
14 Market Street
Lerwick
Tel: (0595) 3800

# SANDWICK JUNIOR HIGH SCHOOL – NURSERY CLASS

Sandwick
Shetland
ZE2 9HH
**Tel:** (09505) 454

**Owner:** Shetland Islands Education Dept
**Headteacher:** Brian Wishart, MA
**Primary Assistant Head:** Patricia Ash, DCE Senior Teacher
**Nursery Teacher:** Senga Leslie, DCE Nursery Endorsement
**Type:** Nursery class attached to junior high school offering half-day sessions. No full-time places
**Children:** 3–5yrs. 20 places. 36 on register
**Hours:** Morning session 9.15am–11.30am
Afternoon session 12.45pm–3pm
Open 40 weeks a year
**Status:** State nursery class
**Number of years open:** 3
**Meals:** Milk and fruit
**1992 fees:** No fees. £1 voluntary contribution for snacks and cookery
**Waiting list:** Minimal – places available for all 3yr-olds
**Registered by:** Shetland Islands Council LEA

**Premises** A new building, set in open countryside, not far from the sea. The primary department takes children from Sandwick parish, and the secondary school from the whole South Mainland of Shetland. For many children, SJHS is the only school they will ever attend. The warm, bright and airy nursery classroom is in the primary department. There is an amazing, colourful selection of equipment, play house, building blocks and books. Outside the classroom, the small outdoor play area is rarely used. The wind is often fierce enough to blow adults away and far too dangerous for young children. In good weather, children have sole use of another, more protected, area with a climbing frame and sandpit.

**Primary Assistant Head & staff** Patricia Ash, DCE, a gentle, friendly woman, is primary assistant head and administers the primary school, including the nursery class. She is one of a small group of senior teachers in the school and her special interest is children from 3 to 6 years old. The nursery class has one nursery teacher, Senga Leslie, DCE, assisted by a nursery nurse. There is also a YTS trainee. The staff/child ratio is 1:10. A staff development and training budget allows the team to take five days' training each year, plus first-aid courses. There are no staff turnover problems; there were 57 applicants when the nursery nurse post was advertised three years ago.

**Children & parents** Children are from rural communities and all social backgrounds, the majority Shetlanders. They are collected by bus and brought to school, which means that parents have limited contact with the classroom and staff. However, parents are welcome to visit if they can, and are invited to open days, sports day, the Christmas play and parents' evenings. They do not assist in the classroom, but will soon be helping at swimming lessons, when a new community pool opens next door to the school. Settling in new children is done with parents in attendance for the first few visits, according to need. Children with special educational needs are welcome and have priority. Auxiliary help is available to aid integration.

**Curriculum & activities** Children learn through play and structured activities. Equipment and materials are generous and age-appropriate (£2000 annual budget). Language skills are encouraged through discussion, describing, listening and recalling. Pre-reading and pre-writing are taught but there is no formal teaching of reading. Children become familiar with the printed word, seeing their names on their paintings and work. Clear labelling is used throughout the class. Books for reference and storytelling are plentiful. Early numeracy is developed by sorting, matching, selecting and ordering with materials such as sand, water, bricks and glue. The standard of artwork is high – mobiles, lanterns and paintings hang everywhere. There is weekly dance and movement and music daily, as well as visits to the local library each week and occasional other outings linked to projects. Good standards of behaviour and social graces are taught and expected, and opportunities for self-expression exist through imaginative play and outdoor activities including PE. The nursery class has regular contact with the main school. Children are monitored monthly. Those leaving receive a report at the end of the year.

**Remarks** A cosy, lively place with caring staff. Children receive an excellent grounding for school and avoid any transition problems, as the nursery is very much part of the larger school complex. Children are brought in by bus from rural areas, which means parents miss out on daily contact with the classroom and teachers.

# Strathclyde

Strathclyde has 137 nursery schools and 73 nursery classes attached to primary schools, offering 30 per cent of 3- and 4-year-olds a nursery place, including 1300 full-time places. There is no provision in Argyll and Bute. The council also funds 64 day nurseries, five play groups and a number of children's centres, catering for families with special needs. The bulk of provision is centred in Glasgow, but demand far exceeds supply. With a population of almost 150,000 children under 5, there are waiting lists in most places. Many working parents turn to the private sector, which has grown rapidly over the last few years and offers 161 day nurseries and 2053 childminders on the register.

### Further information

For details on all types of childcare in the region:
Education Department
Pre-Fives Services
Dalian House
350 St Vincent Street
Glasgow G2 4PS
Tel: (041) 249 4176

## ACORN PARK NURSERY

20a Woodside Terrace
Glasgow G3 7HX
**Tel:** (041) 332 2461
**Owner/Principal:** Mary McDonald, NNEB
**Type:** Day nursery offering full- and part-time places and half-day sessions
**Children:** 2mths–5yrs. 52 places. 70 on register
**Hours:** 8am–6pm
Open 50 weeks a year
**Status:** Private, fee-paying
**Number of years open:** 6
**Meals:** Lunch, snacks
**1992 fees:** £85 per week full-time – under 2
£75 per week full-time – 2–3yrs
£70 per week full-time – over 3
£18 per day – under 2
£16 per day – 2–3yrs
£15 per day – over 3
**Waiting list:** Moderate – places cannot be guaranteed
**Registered by:** Strathclyde Regional Council SS

**Premises** The lower ground floor of a private junior girls' school in a rather grand Victorian terrace, not far from the city centre. It is surrounded by offices and commercial properties, so parking after 8.30am is difficult. The nursery is reached by fairly steep, railed, area steps down to a patio with big tubs of plants. A private car park across the road, which is safe and well kept, is used for outside play. In bad weather, the nursery is allowed to use the school gymnasium. There are four nursery rooms: a baby room, a messy-play and physical-play room, a toddlers' quiet room with home corner and library, and a similar room for the 'tweenies'. The nursery feels warm, safe and secure with good-quality equipment and stimulating decorations.

**Owner/Principal & staff** Mary McDonald, NNEB, owns and runs Acorn Park. An experienced mother and childminder, with a keen sense of mischief, she is actively involved in every aspect of the nursery, which she organises in a firm but gentle manner. She has warm, motherly relationships with the children who eagerly accept her hugs and kisses and offer the same in return. The majority of the 14 female staff are qualified NNEB nursery nurses in their mid-20s and work well as a team. We observed much talking, listening and physical contact between staff and children. A ballet teacher comes once a week and male teachers take music and French sessions. The nursery takes students for work experience and employs a full-time domestic worker. Staff training courses are attended at Jordanhill College of Education.

**Children & parents** Most children come from high-income, career families with parents in professional or managerial positions. There is very little social or cultural mix, although six free places are available to single parents, who would not otherwise be able to afford the fees. The majority of the children go on to state primary schools. Parents stay to settle new children in, but after this they are not encouraged to pop in, as the nursery feels it often unsettles children and makes them think it is time to go home. A regular newsletter keeps parents informed of nursery activities. The nursery will take selected children with special needs, provided they are confident that they can integrate them successfully.

**Curriculum & activities** Learning through play in a structured framework. Not everything is available all the time, but a good selection of activities are set out during each session. Children start the day with free play and staff join in only if invited. At 9.30am, they meet together to share news and choose a theme to draw. Most of the day, they are split into small groups according to ability and undertake a variety of activities including number work and pre-reading and pre-writing exercises for older children. Programmes are planned monthly in advance and written down. Diaries are kept of all group activities, and each child's progress is carefully recorded. Parents have free access to written notes. A strong emphasis is placed on music and art, with a weekly formal music lesson from a much adored male music teacher. Children join together each day for songs and after lunch for a quiet time. Ballet is also offered for boys and girls. A French teacher visits fortnightly. Reading is not taught, in accordance with Scottish primary school policy, although books and stories play a vital part and time is set aside each day for children to enjoy books. There are outings every two months to a variety of places – the airport, the zoo and the countryside. Visitors relevant to particular themes like 'those who help us' come to talk. Pre-prepared frozen lunches are produced by an outside catering company and reheated in the nursery microwave. The corned beef hash we saw did not look particularly attractive. Staff eat with older children.

**Remarks** Quality care in a homely and relaxed atmosphere. Dedicated staff, who offer praise and encouragement. The pre-prepared frozen meals are disappointing in a nursery of this standard.

# BARRACHNIE CHILDREN'S NURSERY

19a Barrachnie Road
Garrowhill
Glasgow G69 6HB
**Tel:** (041) 771 8331

**Owner:** Mrs A Kaya
**Nursery Head:** Claudia Danielle, NNEB
**Type:** Day nursery offering full- and part-time places and half-day sessions
**Children:** 6wks–5yrs. 70 places. 130 on register
**Hours:** 8am–5.30pm
Open 52 weeks a year
**Status:** Private, fee-paying
**Number of years open:** 3½
**Meals:** Lunch, snacks
**1992 fees:** £70 per week full-time – under 18mths
£57 per week full-time – over 18mths
**Waiting list:** Minimal
**Registered by:** Strathclyde Regional Council

**Premises** A U-shaped, rose-pink building with a bright blue door. A former factory, it has been extended and converted into a very large day nursery occupying six rooms, all on one floor. The area is residential, socially mixed and next to a small shopping parade. The youngest children, Baby Blossoms (6 weeks–18mths), rest and play in their own room. There are six cots on one side, large soft cushions on a carpeted play area, a fridge for baby bottles and a nappy-changing area off the main room. Gentle music provides a homely background. Toddlers (18 months–2½ years) are in the Sunshine Room. There is both carpet and vinyl flooring for messy and dry play, a video, a settee and comfortable chairs. The Rainbow Room is home to 15 children aged

2½–3 years. A large pinboard on wheels, which can act as a room divider, is covered with named photographs of all the children. Pre-school children, the Busy Bees, have a large, light room, with lino floor, which doubles as a dining room, and is equipped for work and play, with small tables and chairs. There is a physical-play room with large play equipment and a painting room for messy activities. Walls are brightly decorated with displays of adult-led children's art and friezes. All rooms, including kitchens and toilets, are spotlessly clean. The outside area is tarmac only, and equipment is moved outside as and when required. The nearest park is a good 15-minute walk away and is visited only occasionally in summer. The nursery is screened from the main road outside and securely enclosed by a brightly painted, high mesh fence.

**Nursery Head & staff** Claudia Danielle, the lively young head, is an NNEB who feels she has finally found her niche and would like to stay at Barrachnie until she is 50. She is in charge of the day-to-day running of the nursery, but the owner, Mrs Kaya, visits every day bringing supplies, usually in time to meet parents when they drop off or collect children, prompting them to ask questions or make suggestions. There are ten NNEB nursery nurses on the full-time staff, all young local girls, and two full-time unqualified assistants as well as additional part-time helpers. The staff/child ratios are 1:3 for babies, 1:5 for 2- to 3-year-olds and 1:8 for the oldest group. On the day we visited, there were 55 children attending. The nursery is registered to take up to 70 children, but with that number it would certainly begin to feel like an institution. Holidays and staff absences are covered from within. There is no policy or budget for staff training. Staff wear a uniform of blue overalls.

**Children & parents** A predominantly working-class area, but the nursery attracts a wide social range of working parents. Most children transfer to state primary schools. No formal parents' evenings or meetings are held, but the occasional newsletter is sent out. Parents are welcome to come in and chat at any time. Each child has a group leader, who is responsible for monitoring his or her progress and discussing it with parents. Phasing-in is 'played by ear', according to parents' and children's needs. Some parents stay with their children, while others do not.

**Curriculum & activities** Learning through play, with child-oriented and stimulating equipment. Staff follow the basic programme they were taught during their NNEB training. Equipment and toys are good-quality, sturdy and clean, and the games are educational and well maintained (annual equipment budget £2000). Gross motor skills and free expression are encouraged in the painting and physical rooms. Singing, dancing and music are daily activities. Each member of staff is responsible for initiating different activities during the day. As numbers are so large, children cannot all meet together. Pre-school children (4 years plus) practise writing patterns and learn to recognise their names before they leave. Reading is not taught and formal number work is minimal in line with Scottish nursery education policy. There are no reading schemes, no written educational programmes and no detailed written records on children's progress. Babies and toddlers play together with a lively selection of toys in a safe 'soft' environment. Outings in small groups relate to current themes, or to the library. There are annual outings of the whole nursery to Butlins. Meals are not a strength – children are given convenience food such as fish fingers or tinned spaghetti hoops, and no fresh vegetables or home-made meals. The excuse given was that children prefer convenience food.

**Remarks** A good standard of care from qualified nursery nurses, in one of the less affluent areas of the city. High-quality premises and facilities and carefully thought-out organisation. Children were in very large groups, and we would have liked to see some evidence of the mess of creative, busy activity – everywhere was far too tidy. We hope the nursery will reconsider its policy of convenience foods and offer home-cooked meals with fresh fruit and vegetables.

# RIVERBANK KINDERGARTEN & DAY NURSERY

2 Citadel Place
Ayr KA7 1JN
**Tel:** (0292) 268014

**Owner:** Penelope Kilpatrick
**Headteacher:** Marjorie Fullerton, B Ed
**Type:** Day nursery and nursery school, offering full- and part-time places and half-day sessions
**Children:** 2–5yrs. 100 places. 275 on register
**Hours:** 8am–6pm
Morning session 9am–12 noon
Afternoon session 12.30pm–3.30pm
2–3yr-olds daily 1pm–2.30pm and 2.30pm–4pm
Open 52 weeks a year
**Status:** Private, fee-paying
**Number of years open:** 9
**Meals:** Mid-morning snack, tea. Children bring packed lunches
**1992 fees:** £11 per day
£3.65 per session
**Waiting list:** Fairly long. 50 names on list
**Registered by:** Strathclyde Regional Council SS

**Premises** Large, detached, red sandstone, Victorian villa on a corner site, close to the centre of town. A car park in front of the house is used mainly by staff. Parking can be a problem outside the nursery if a number of parents arrive at the same time, but traffic wardens apparently turn a blind eye to short-term use. The kindergarten has four light, warm classrooms. There is also a quiet room with leather armchairs, a television, play kitchen and good supply of books and Lego, as well as a rumpus room, with tartan carpet, climbing frames, Wendy house, rocking horse, trampoline and two slides. The day nursery has its own separate wing. There are loos and a nappy-changing area on both floors, as well as facilities for the disabled. An immaculate kitchen is used only for preparing snacks. The garden room was added on last year. It has the same tartan carpet and white walls as elsewhere and is equipped with a Wendy house, art materials and a dressing-up box. The garden is small compared to the spacious interior. There is a paved, fenced-in side patio and the asphalt car park in front where children use bikes and trikes. Daily visits to the nearby park are made in good weather.

**Owner, Headteacher & staff** The owner, Penelope Kilpatrick, is an ex-stockbroker who started the kindergarten when she was unable to find nursery provision for her own child. Beginning with a handful of 2-year-olds, the kindergarten has now expanded into a large and growing concern with plans to open a second facility. Marjorie Fullerton, B Ed, the headteacher, is a mature, ex-primary teacher, who has responsibility for the educational side of the kindergarten. Ann Johnson is the nursery manager. There are 22 members of staff; four are NNEB nursery nurses and six are qualified primary school teachers. Only six work full-time, all the rest are part-timers. Twelve of the staff – a higher proportion than usual – are unqualified; they are mainly middle-class mothers with school-age children. It is an all-female team. Marjorie Fullerton says, 'We would consider a male, but he would have to be very special. Mothers are very wary of strange men being in contact with their young children.' Staff work well together, always a minimum of three to a room. No staff training policy or budget.

**Children & parents** A typical prosperous county town. Most of the children are white and middle-class. There are a few single parents and some mothers working simply to earn the nursery fees. There is some cultural mix and a handful of bilingual French, Spanish, Finnish, Italian and Chinese children. Most go on to local state primaries such as Doonfoot and Alloway, but a few transfer to independent Wellington. There are currently two children with Down's syndrome and there have been children with disabilities and special educational needs in the past. Wheelchair access and a disabled toilet are available. Children are divided into groups by age, with three members of staff to each group. The day nursery generally stays separate from the kindergarten, although the two have close links. Kindergarten children can use the day nursery service, provided a place has been booked in advance, although in emergencies every effort is made to find a space. Day nursery children join kindergarten children for classes and then return to the sanctuary of their area for the rest of the day. The door is always open for parents to talk to nursery workers. There are regular parents' evenings.

**Curriculum & activities** The 2-year-olds, known as Teddies, attend for short, 1½-hour sessions twice a week or more. They learn to share and take turns, and develop their social skills through play. The emphasis is on songs, stories, rhymes, painting and glueing. The 3-year-olds, known as Juniors, learn to develop their fine motor skills and co-ordination, as well as their imaginations. Themes are introduced as vehicles for learning colours, opposites, numbers, shapes and manipulative skills such as sorting, matching, cutting and drawing. Pre-school teaching for 4-year-olds is more structured and aims to prepare for school. Themes and projects are still used, but in greater depth and include simple science, maths, pre-reading, pre-writing and name recognition. As in all other Scottish nursery schools, reading is not taught, partly because the children are going on to so many different schools, but mainly because primary schools feel this is their job. However, most are ready to read by the time they leave Riverbank. Staff keep records of classwork, but not individual records of children's progress. The lack of a hot meal every day for full-timers is a disadvantage – the children bring packed lunches. These are returned unemptied, so that parents know exactly how much has been eaten. The outdoor play area is disappointing, but there are frequent outings to the park, harbour and beach, and visits to the post office and toy shop. Ballet is held in the hall next door.

**Remarks** A thriving, busy concern with a large number of children, in an area where childminders are the only alternative. Spacious, comfortable indoor facilities and caring, committed staff. Very reasonable fees.

# SOMERSET NURSERY I

8A Somerset Place
Glasgow G3 7JT
**Tel:** (041) 331 1111

**Owners:** Laura Adams
Rae Black
**Principal:** Laura Adams, NNEB
**Type:** Day nursery offering full-time places for babies
**Children:** 3mths–2yrs. 18 places max. 15 children on register
**Hours:** 8am–6pm
Open 52 weeks a year (excl bank holidays)
**Status:** Private, fee-paying
**Number of years open:** 5½

**Meals:** Lunch, snacks
**1992 fees:** £82 per week – under 2
**Waiting list:** Minimal
**Registered by:** Strathclyde Regional Council
**Under same ownership:** Somerset II, Glasgow, for 2–5yr-olds

**Premises** Lower ground floor of a Victorian terrace in the Park area of the city centre. The building is old, but newly converted and in good condition. Parking is impossible and illegal double parking often the only choice. Somerset I is the baby unit. Children over 3 years old are accommodated in Somerset II, a recently opened similar basement nursery, two minutes' walk away. Tiny babies have a small, but soft, playroom with a good variety of play and activity equipment – scatter cushions, babysoft mats, wall mirrors, mobiles and two 'sit and swing' frames. There are plenty of stimulating colours and pictures. A nappy-changing area is off their room. The toddlers and crawlers' room is larger, freshly painted and spacious enough to allow children to practise their motor skills without bumping into or falling over each other. A third activity room was out of use when we visited. A tiny office area, small kitchen and children's toilets and washbasins complete the plan. As this is a basement, artificial lighting is necessary at all times. The building is old and the floors very uneven. A small outside paved area, below street level, offers limited access to fresh air. The large, private garden square opposite (key entry) is used daily.

**Owner/Principal & staff** The co-owner and principal, Laura Adams, NNEB, runs Somerset I with the help of six full-time NNEB nursery nurses. The staff/child ratio is 1:3. Staff are young, bubbly and cheerful. When we were there they were down on the floor playing, talking, laughing and cuddling the children, and obviously enjoying themselves. Students are accepted on placement throughout the year. Staff at the two nurseries mix together regularly, sharing skills and covering for each other during holidays or sickness. We were surprised by the strength of Laura Adams' reluctance to consider male applicants for nursery jobs. 'Because of toileting, I think the mothers feel happier knowing it's all female staff. If anything happened, God forbid, the finger would be pointed at the male,' she says. Staff receive occasional in-house training and attend short courses. Co-owner Rae Black acts as administrator, housekeeper and cook. Staff wear pin-striped overalls with white collars and cuffs and look very much like student nurses.

**Children & parents** The children come from middle-class, professional families working in the city centre – accountants, vets, lawyers, business executives. There is no ethnic mix and no children with special needs, although a few have attended in the past. Children transfer in equal numbers to the state and private sectors. Older siblings at Somerset II visit their baby brothers and sisters during the day. A keyworker system is in operation, but staff are encouraged to build up a good relationship with all children. Parents are always welcome – some pop in at lunchtime to feed their babies. A regular newsletter is sent out, with all staff, including students, contributing. Settling-in is done gradually over a week. An annual cheese and wine party is held for parents and staff.

**Curriculum & activities** Learning through play, with a wide selection of well-used, high-quality equipment and furniture. Stimulating mobiles, mirrors, pictures, activity centres and lots of 'soft experiences'. The emphasis is on health and safety and emotional and physical security. Children are played with, talked to, cuddled and picked up frequently. No baby is left to cry. There are regular rest times during the day and outings to the park, library and swimming pool. The staff/child ratio for swimming is 1:1. Dance and movement are done weekly. Themes are planned in advance and changed fortnightly. Recent topics have included colours, shapes, nature study, 'people who help us', the seasons and Hallowe'en. Pre-reading and pre-writing skills are introduced in the toddler room, but never pushed. There is no structured learning. Social skills and preparation for school are the main priority. Painting, modelling, sand and water play are always available. Children help to make a fresh batch of play dough each week. Healthy, home-cooked food is prepared in the tiny kitchen. No written programmes or reports on child development are prepared, but the nursery keeps a register, accident book, medicine forms and child profiles. Older children visit art galleries and the transport museum.

**Remarks** City centre nursery, convenient for working parents. Cheerful, warm, family atmosphere, with good stimulation from young, qualified nursery nurses. Quality care in a hygienic environment. Lack of natural light is a definite disadvantage, and the uneven floors could lead to even more trips than usual by unsteady toddlers. Although the older age group is in a different building, there are very close links and much shuttling backwards and forwards.

# Tayside

Eighteen nursery schools and 41 nursery classes provide part-time and some full-time nursery education for 35 per cent of Tayside's 3- and 4-year-olds. Tayside has the highest number of full-time places in Scotland. There are no local authority day nurseries, although 12 Child and Family Centres offer some full- and part-time care. Working parents looking for full daycare must try to secure a place with one of the 491 childminders or 35 private day nurseries. Very little provision exists for under-2s, and demand generally exceeds supply throughout the area. 141 thriving playgroups offer part-time facilities only.

**Further information**
For details on day nurseries, childminders and playgroups:
Social Work Department
Tayside House
28 Crichton Street
Dundee DD1 3RA
Tel: (0382) 23281

For details on nursery schools, units and classes:
Education Department
(address and telephone as above)

# FRANCES WRIGHT PRE-SCHOOL CENTRE

Caird Avenue
Dundee DD3 8AR
**Tel:** (0382) 825651

**Owner:** Tayside Regional Council
**Headteacher:** Rhona Armitage, Dip CE, NFFC, Dip Management (Primary School)
**Type:** Nursery school offering full-time places and half-day sessions
**Children:** 3–6yrs. 70 places. 30 places reserved for children with special educational needs. 70 on register
**Hours:** 9am–3.15pm
Morning session 9am–11.30am
Afternoon session 12.45pm–3.15pm
Open 40 weeks a year
**Status:** State pre-school centre
**Number of years open:** 5
**Meals:** Lunch, snacks
**1992 fees:** No fees. 65p per day for lunch
**Waiting list:** Long. 70 names
**Registered by:** Tayside Regional Council

**Premises** A former school for mentally handicapped children, built in 1940 and adapted in 1989 to house this unique nursery school, integrating mainstream and special needs children. Surrounded by a large garden, in a mixed commercial and residential area of Dundee. There is easy access by car and bus. The centre is all on one level, with amazing wall paintings which make an otherwise rather depressing main corridor surprisingly lively. The main nursery is in the middle, adjacent to two rooms designed as bases for children with special educational needs and disabilities. Facilities also include a medical room, physiotherapy and occupational therapy rooms, dining room and a large hall for physical play, with ride-on toys, large construction toys, a slide and a piano. Parents have a well-used family room and a resource base, with separate facilities for the headteacher and staff. There is a crèche for children of students at the College of Further Education which shares the site. The centre is well resourced, with an enormous range of equipment to suit all needs. Outside there is grass and a superb, newly built adventure playground on a special safety surface. Coldside Park is nearby.

**Headteacher & staff** Rhona Armitage has been headteacher since the centre opened five years ago. A qualified primary school teacher, with nursery and infant endorsements, she is responsible for the day-to-day running of the nursery. She reports to the Director of Education. Her large, highly qualified staff team covers a wide range of ages, personalities and experience. Some have special needs qualifications and include a nurse, physiotherapist, occupational therapist and speech therapist. The 23 workers adopt an interdisciplinary approach, where flexibility and the sharing of information are key components. A peripatetic music teacher visits for three or four hours a week and students from many different disciplines, including medical, come for work experience. Nursery staff are encouraged to participate in the many in-service training courses available.

**Children & parents** A complete cross-section of society. Thirty of the children have special educational needs and have been referred by different agencies concerned with their development. They have difficulties ranging from medical disorders such as cerebral palsy, to behavioural problems, social and communication problems and specific language disorders. The centre can cope with all children, except those who require continuous nursing care. Many of the mainstream children come from families living in council flats in the area. Each child has a keyworker, who works alongside the appropriate teacher. Staff/child ratios are 1:10 mainstream; 1:5 special needs. Parents have their own room, with kitchen facilities. Those who have a child with special needs are asked to work in their child's group at least once a week. Communication with parents is seen as vital and there is consultation at every stage. There is no official PTA, but social evenings and fund-raising events are organised regularly. An open-door policy operates for all parents and some help at the weekly swimming sessions. Children go on from here to all types of schools and residential care, some in the private sector.

**Curriculum & activities** All skills are developed by play and the nursery sets out to provide a 'carefully planned play environment, which takes cognizance of different skill areas, but is conducive to integrated development of the whole child'. Two of the teachers are Froebel trained. Because of the wide range of abilities among the children, there is no typical programme, but flexibility to provide a curriculum varied according to each child's needs. All have opportunities to participate in art, craft, sand and water play, music, pretend play, large and small construction play, group games, nature study, looking at books and physical activities. The emphasis is on education as fun. Reading is not formally taught, but children are introduced to pre-literacy skills as appropriate. Integration is considered crucial and up to six special needs children, accompanied by a nursery nurse, attend each mainstream session at any one time. The more vulnerable children stay in their special base and are joined by ten full-time mainstream children each afternoon. Detailed developmental records are kept on each child, which parents see and sign. There are weekly outings to shops, parks, adventure playgrounds and the swimming pool. The centre has the use of a bus and driver. Lunch is provided by a private catering company.

**Remarks** A very special nursery centre, offering parents with children of all levels of ability high-quality, integrated care and pre-school education. Strong team of qualified, highly professional staff. A multi-disciplinary approach, with full parental involvement which benefits all the children equally. A unique and exciting place to be.

## LITTLE ACORN NURSERY

Robert Douglas Memorial Institute
Scone
Perthshire PH2 6RU
**Tel:** (0738) 51311

**Owners/Principals:** Ann Whiteford, Dip CE
Erica Johnstone
**Type:** Nursery school offering morning sessions
**Children:** 2yrs–5yrs 6mths. 36 places. 90 on register
**Hours:** 9am–12 noon
Open 40 weeks a year
**Status:** Private, fee-paying
**Number of years open:** 5
**Meals:** Snacks
**1992 fees:** £4.25 per session
£4.75 per week for one session only
**Waiting list:** Minimal
**Registered by:** Tayside Regional Council

**Premises** A former school building, about 100 years old, now used as a community centre. It stands in a paved area, the old playground, with a fenced-off, grassy garden behind. There is easy access and plenty of room to park in the grounds. Children either walk to school or are brought by car from the surrounding neighbourhood. The nursery uses two of the five rooms in the building, both well lit and decorated. One serves for noisy and messy play and includes a large climbing frame. The room is shared with other community users, so everything has to be cleared away at the end of each session. There are no displays of children's artwork or nursery pictures. The second, smaller room is a quiet area for games, puzzles, pencil and paper work and books. Both rooms have the traditional high windows of old Scottish schools, designed to let in the light but prevent eyes from wandering outside. The building is maintained by a caretaker, who lives in a cottage behind the institute. Everything is neat and tidy, but a little bleak – there are no flowers or plants to be seen. The Robert Douglas Park is just down the road and children are occasionally taken there in the summer.

**Owners/Principals & staff** The school is jointly owned by Ann Whiteford, Dip CE, and Erica Johnstone, who both work in the nursery every day. Ann opened the nursery when she failed to find pre-school education for her own child. Provision in the area is poor. An experienced infant teacher and adult literacy tutor, she has also been Dumfries area chairwoman of the National Childbirth Trust. Erica Johnstone comes from a background in management and administration, which includes time with the library service, specialising in children's books. The owners are also registered playgroup supervisors. There are four other members of staff, all trained teachers, one a gymnast and another a musician. Two are currently following a course run by the region in conjunction with the Scottish Pre-school Playgroups Association. There are four other supply carers in the background who cover for sickness and holidays.

**Children & parents** The children come from similar backgrounds in Scone and rural Perthshire. Virtually all go on to state primary schools. The nursery is able and willing to integrate children with special educational needs. The parents are mainly professional. Most of the mothers do not work outside the home, though many are following college courses. Parents are free to visit the school at any time, but tend not to as the sessions are so short. A termly newsletter keeps them up to date and a complaints and suggestions book is available. Parents join the annual summer outing, organise coffee mornings and help with library visits.

**Curriculum & activities** The nursery aims to prepare children for school, particularly in numeracy and pre-reading skills, but Scottish primary schools do not want structured learning to be provided at this stage. The emphasis is on learning through play following the PPA philosophy. Children learn pencil control, the use of scissors and how to tie laces. Nature study and art and craft form a large part of the curriculum. Apart from a registration form and workbooks used by the children, no written records are kept. Each week usually follows a theme and sessions explore different aspects of the theme. The daily timetable always includes sand, water and painting, large toys on a mat (garage, cars, train set), table-top activities (Lego, Duplo, sticklebricks), a craft table and microwave cookery. Children make or prepare their own mid-morning snacks. These include scones, bread, flapjacks, sandwiches and iced biscuits. The whole group assembles each session for register, news, singing and music and a discussion about the day and weather. Dressing-up clothes are always available. Children have workbooks for pre-reading and pre-writing practice. The session ends with tidy-up time and a story. There is weekly gymnastics for four months of the year. Small group outings take place, and dance and movement weekly.

**Remarks** A good, caring nursery, set up in response to local demand. Shared use of the rather bleak building and lack of stimulating, lively, permanent displays are a disadvantage. Happy and stable staff team, who are there because they love working with children. Clearly it is more a vocation than a job to them. Nursery school provision in the area is poor, and Little Acorn's morning sessions go some way towards satisfying the huge demand.

# Western Isles

No local authority provision in any form – Western Isles stopped providing nursery education in 1984. Working parents in these numerous, sparsely populated islands turn to relatives first, then one of the 30 childminders and finally, if places are available, to just two private day nurseries. 53 playgroups also provide part-time facilities for a few hours/days each week.

**Further information**

For details on day nurseries, childminders and playgroups:
Social Work Department
Registration Office
Sandwick Road
Stornoway PA87 2TD
Tel: (0851) 706072

## RAINBOW NURSERY
42 Newton Street
Stornoway
Isle of Lewis PA87 2RW
**Tel:** (0851) 706252

**Owner/Principal:** Catherine MacPherson, NNEB, City & Guilds Childcare
**Type:** Day nursery offering full- and part-time places
**Children:** 2–5yrs. 16 places. 22 on register

**Hours:** 8am–6pm
Flexible hours
Open 51 weeks a year
**Status:** Private, fee-paying
**Number of years open:** 2
**Meals:** Lunch, snacks
**1992 fees:** £14 per day – under 3
£11.50 per day – over 3
£1.80 per hour – under 3
£1.50 per hour – over 3
**Waiting list:** None kept
**Registered by:** Western Isles Regional Council

# WALES

# Clwyd

Children in Clwyd start full-time education in the September following their 4th birthday. Prior to this, over 80 per cent of 3- and 4-year-olds are offered five 2½-hour sessions per fortnight in a nursery class. Full daycare is left entirely to the private sector, with only 16 registered private nurseries. Playgroups in the area receive no local authority funding. At the time of writing, Clwyd had not published a comprehensive review of all under-5s provision in the county, but it is due to be available by autumn '93.

**Further information**

For details on day nurseries, childminders and playgroups:
Department of Social Services
Shire Hall
Mold CH7 6NN
Tel: (0352) 752121

For details on nursery schools, units and classes:
Education Department
(address and telephone as above)

## LONGFIELDS NURSERY
Sontley Road
Wrexham
Clwyd LL14 6BL
**Tel:** (0978) 350586

**Owner:** Community Studies Centre affiliated to Deeside College. Part of NEWI (North East Wales Institute)
**Manager:** Julia Armstrong
**Officer-in-charge:** Julie Phillips, NNEB
**Type:** Day nursery offering full- and part-time places and half-day sessions
**Children:** 4mths–5yrs. 40 places max. 46 on register

**Hours:** 8.30am–5.30pm
Morning session 8.30am–12 noon
Afternoon session 7pm–5.30pm
Open 51 weeks a year
**Status:** Private, fee-paying, non profit-making
**Number of years open:** 9
**Meals:** Lunch, tea, snacks
**1992 fees:** £53 per week full-time
£6 per session
**Waiting list:** Varies. Early registration advisable
**Registered by:** Clwyd County Council SS
**Under same ownership:** Penardd Nursery, Wrexham; Plas Coch Nursery, Wrexham; Deeside Nursery, Connah's Quay

**Premises** Large, Victorian, detached house, close to the centre of Wrexham, on the once smart, now rather tired, residential side of town. The nursery occupies all the ground floor and an office upstairs. Other offices on the first floor are used by the Community Studies Centre's training department. Toddlers (2½–5 years old) use a large double room for play and table-top activities. The room feels busy and crowded, with large pieces of equipment, tables, chairs and soft cushions on the floor. It has direct access to one of the nursery's two outside play spaces, with lawn, concrete, a huge lockable sandpit and a gate into another, larger area with more grass. Back inside, there is a messy-play room (with lino flooring) for art, craft and water play. Excellent supply of art and craft materials, especially for collage. This room also doubles as a dining room and is next door to the kitchen. Bathroom facilities are awkward – through two fire doors – so children must be accompanied by staff. The baby unit is generally reached via the back entrance. It consists of one large, bright room, with big windows, separated into three by waist-height walls to provide a sleeping area, a playroom and a messy-play/eating space. There is a nappy-changing room, close to the playroom.

**Manager, Officer-in-charge & staff** Julia Armstrong has overall responsibility for Longfields and the three other nurseries belonging to the Community Studies Centre. Julia has 9 years' experience setting up and running day nurseries for NEWI. Most of her time is spent on administration, but she tries to spend some time with children and staff, often covering for holidays or absences. Julie Phillips, NNEB, is the officer-in-charge of day-to-day matters. Bright and cheerful, she was heavily pregnant at the time of our visit. Dot Shaw, SRN, runs the baby room. She has a no-nonsense approach and many years' experience, Babies quickly settle into a routine under her guidance and supervision. Both nursery rooms are well staffed: seven nursery workers – not all qualified – with the 14 babies and six with the 24 toddlers. Qualifications range from NNEB, Cert Ed, B Ed and City & Guilds 324, to PPA certificates. There are no male staff at present. Ancillaries include a cook and a cleaner. Trainees are accepted from time to time. Staff have access to a wide selection of training courses provided by the NEWI.

**Children & parents** Half of the parents using Longfields are students at one of Wrexham's colleges. They are offered assisted places (1992 subsidy of £30 per week), without which most would not be able to afford the fees. Subsidy comes from an access fund given to the college by the Welsh Office. Other subsidised places are provided by Midland Bank for their employees and Social Services for priority cases. The remaining places are available to full-fee paying outside families. There is a varied socal mix, from both urban and rural backgrounds. The children are predominantly English or Welsh (some bilingual), but there is a small Japanese group – Metal Box and Toyota are in the area – whose mothers study English at the college. Children with special educational needs are welcome. Virtually all the children transfer to state primary schools. The nursery has an open-door policy towards parents.

**Curriculum & activities** Learning through play, without pressure. Children are introduced to a variety of stimulating activities in a safe and loving environment. Weekly themes are planned well in advance to ensure that children cover a range of topics and experiences during each term. Babies and older children have access to plenty of art and craft work. Music and singing are done every day. Ample time and space is allotted to developing gross motor skills – climbing apparatus, running and games. Construction sets develop dexterity and hand–eye co-ordination. For the older children, the emphasis is on preparation for school through work with colours, shapes, sorting, grading, early science and number work. This is not primarily a teaching establishment, but the nursery recognises the importance of carefully preparing children well for school. There is no formal teaching of reading or writing. A typical session begins with free play on the large equipment or at tables set out with puzzles, toys and construction sets (annual equipment budget £2000). Circle time follows, with songs, stories and music. After a mid-morning snack, children wade into messy play – sand, water and paint. Staff take turns at organising this session, which is usually related to the current theme. After lunch, there is rest and quiet time. Serious outings are undertaken twice a year, and there are frequent walks and visits to the college gym.

**Remarks** Well-staffed, happy nursery, offering high-quality care. Helped greatly by the blessing and support it receives from the

NEWI. Excellent value for money and generous subsidies for students. Having been a rare and much valued service in the area for some time, Longfields is now having to compete with several private nurseries which have opened recently. This keeps them on their toes, but competition is unlikely to be a serious threat to this well-run nursery.

# Dyfed

The Education Department provides three nursery schools and 130 classes, used predominantly by 3-year-olds. Children are admitted to full-time education as soon as possible after their 4th birthday. Dyfed is a rural area of mainly village schools. Over 40 per cent of 3- and 4-year-olds receive nursery education. There are no local authority day nurseries. The private sector offers eight full-time day nurseries and nearly 200 part-time playgroups. Most parents rely on friends, relatives and registered childminders to meet their childcare needs

## Further information

For details on day nurseries, childminders and playgroups:

Inspection Unit
Social Services Department
9 Quay Street
Carmarthen
Dyfed SA31 3JT
Tel: (0267) 221000

For details on nursery schools, units and classes:
Education Department
1 Penlan Road
Carmarthen
Dyfed SA31 2NH
Tel: (0267) 233333

## ACORN NURSERY & PLAYSCHOOL

Old Login School
Llangunnor Road
Carmarthen
Dyfed SA21 2PG
**Tel:** (0267) 231618

**Joint Owners:** Sheila Morgans
Barbara Russell
**Nursery Nurse:** Mandy Taylor, NNEB
**Type:** Nursery and playschool offering full- and part-time places, plus school holiday care for 5–8yr-olds
**Children:** 0–4yrs. 24 places. 40 on register
**Hours:** 8am–6pm
Flexible hours
Open 51 weeks a year
**Status:** Private, fee-paying
**Number of years open:** 3
**Meals:** Breakfast, lunch, tea
**1992 fees:** £53 per week inc meals

£12 per day inc meals
£1.60 per hour
60p per day for lunch
£15 registration fee
**Waiting list:** Places available
**Registered by:** Dyfed County Council SS

## NANTGAREDIG SCHOOL – NURSERY UNIT

Nantgaredig
Carmarthen
Dyfed SA32 7LG
**Tel:** (0267) 290444

**Owner:** Dyfed County Council LEA
**Headteacher:** Gethin Thomas, Cert Ed
**Teacher-in-charge:** Elspeth James, Cert Ed
**Type:** Nursery class offering part-time places for 1st term and then full-time places thereafter. Mainly Welsh-speaking

**Children:** 3–4½yrs. 30 places. 30 on register
**Hours:** 9am–2.45pm
9am–12 noon (1st term)
9am–12.30pm inc lunch (1st term)
Open 39 weeks a year
**Status:** State nursery class
**Number of years open:** 18
**Meals:** Lunch, milk
**1992 fees:** No fees. 95p per day for lunch
**Waiting list:** Early registration advisable
**Registered by:** Dyfed County Council LEA

# Gwent

Gwent County Council recognises the importance of early years education and offers part-time nursery education to 5,500 of the county's 6,600 3-year-olds. However, in many areas this is little more than two or three sessions a week in a playgroup. Three Social Services nurseries cater for children with special needs. The 17 registered private day nurseries, many of which are concentrated in Newport, mainly offer places to children over 2½ years. Baby places are rare. Working parents use relatives, friends or childminders. Despite sending out a number of questionnaires to the area, response was minimal.

## Further Information

For details on day nurseries, childminders and playgroups:
Department of Social Services
Childminding, Playgroup and Nurseries Section
County Hall
Croesyceiliog
Cwmbran NP44 2XE
Tel: (0633) 838838

For details on nursery schools, units and classes:
Education Department
(address and telephone as above)

# Gwynedd

Gwynedd is trying to expand its early years provision. Three years ago the Education Authority allocated £250,000 to increase the number of playgroups. There are now 144 Welsh-speaking playgroups and 42 run by the PPA. 34 per cent of under-5s are offered part-time nursery education in 19 units attached to primary schools. Full-time daycare is scarce, with relatives and childminders providing the majority of care. 16 private day nurseries are registered by Social Services. At least 60 per cent of the county's under-5s have no access to any form of childcare provision.

**Further information**

For details on day nurseries, childminders and playgroups:
Department of Social Services
Child and Families Office
County Hall
Shirehall Street
Caernarfon LL55 1SH
Tel: (0286) 672255

For details on nursery schools, units and classes:
Education Department
(address and telephone as above)

# Mid Glamorgan

There are no local authority day nurseries for the county's 38,000 under-5s. Private provision is also scarce, with only 11 full-time nurseries. PPA and Welsh-medium playgroups, offering part-time places, are the most popular form of childcare. Some are supported by the local authority, which also funds places in voluntary playgroups for children with special needs. Nursery education is much better, with over 60 per cent of 3- and 4-year-olds offered access to a nursery school or class. The majority of places are full-time. Despite sending out a large number of questionnaires to this area, only one nursery class responded.

**Further information**

For details on private nurseries, childminders and playgroups:
Department of Social Services
Greyfriars Road
Cardiff CF1 3LL
Tel: (0222) 820820

For details on nursery schools, units and classes:
Education Department
County Hall
Cathays Park
Cardiff CF1 3NF
Tel: (0222) 780200

# YSGOL SANTES TUDFUL

Queen's Road
Merthyr Tydfil
Mid Glamorgan CF47 0HE
**Tel:** (0685) 722212

**Owner:** Mid-Glamorgan County Council LEA
**Headteacher:** Wil Morus Jones, qualified teacher
**Teacher-in-charge:** Chris Livesey, Cert Ed
**Type:** Welsh-speaking nursery unit in county primary school offering half-day sessions
**Children:** 3–4yrs. 30 places. 58 on register
**Hours:** Morning session 9.10am–12 noon
Afternoon session 12.50pm–3.30pm
Open 38 weeks a year
**Status:** State nursery unit
**Number of years open:** 20
**Meals:** None
**1992 fees:** No fees. Milk 1p per day. Voluntary contributions for extra-curricular activities
**Waiting list:** Long. Not all can be guaranteed places
**Registered by:** Mid-Glamorgan County Council LEA

**Premises** An integral part of a large primary school, occupying five rooms in the old, stone school building dating from 1913. It is sited above rows of terraced houses and set in beautiful gardens with well-tended lawns and flowerbeds (out of bounds to children). The nursery is in reasonable repair and feels and looks like a proper infant school rather than a nursery. The unit uses former classrooms; two for structured learning with charts, paintings and children's work on the walls; one as a music room with a piano and a good supply of musical instruments; another for messy play such as painting, model making and wet play; and a large well-stocked library also used for table-top work, number games and counting apparatus. Firm wire fencing and lockable gates secure the outside play area, which has a climbing frame, wooden playhouse, bikes, trikes and cars. The nearest park is Thomas Down, visited once a fortnight. It has a newly constructed children's playground and paddling pool.

**Headteacher & staff** Wil Morus Jones has been headteacher for five years and runs the nursery as a fully integrated part of the whole school, staffed by a qualified teacher and a nursery assistant. Many activities correlate with the work of the reception classes. Facilities are shared and children work closely with reception and nursery staff. There is very little staff turnover; staff live close to the school and are part of the local community. All are over 30, have teaching qualifications or degrees and are Welsh-speaking. Training is considered an important, ongoing process, and includes nursery staff (annual budget £1000). Staff meetings are held once a week at least. Students are accepted and visited by their tutors while on placement at the nursery. The school is well known in the county and used as a 'show school' for visitors. It features in training films for heads, deputies and teachers throughout Mid-Glamorgan and has been nominated for the School's Curriculum Award (result pending at the time of writing). The staff/child ratio is 1:15 – not ideal.

**Children & parents** Welsh is the main language of the school. The children, who generally live locally, come from a range of social backgrounds. The majority are not Welsh-speaking when they arrive in the nursery. Parents are asked to encourage their children to watch SC4, to read Welsh books to them and to help them listen to the language as much as possible. English is introduced in the first year of the Junior School. Parents are supportive, interested in the school and play an active role on the PTA. They are not encouraged to drop in unannounced, but are welcome to assist with suitable activities in the classroom. There are open evenings twice a year and children's work and progress is monitored monthly by the nursery teacher. All children are encouraged to wear the school uniform – grey skirt or trousers, white shirt, a green tie with red dragon, and black shoes. There are no children with special educational needs or disabilities at the school and no facilities for integrating them. New parents and children are invited to school for a day, the term before starting. Phasing-in is spread over the first three months of the autumn term.

**Curriculum & activities** A curriculum which aims to develop the whole child intellectually, physically, socially, morally and aesthetically. In reality, the first priority for virtually all nursery children is learning the Welsh language. All activities are geared towards acquiring a basic understanding of Welsh. There is plenty of music -- rousing

Welsh singing, dancing and gym. The classrooms are full of activity and each session is carefully planned in advance. Art and craft is particularly strong. Sand and water play are always available. There is no formal teaching of the 3Rs, but a love of books and picture-reading in the library corner are encouraged. Children learn numbers, colours, fine and gross motor skills and early science in a workshop atmosphere. They are encouraged to work independently, with self-discipline, at their own pace. Equipment and resources are excellent and age-appropriate (annual budget £2000).

There are outings to the garden centre at Ebbw Vale, Penyscynor Wildlife Park and Cardiff Docks. Entertainers visit for a Christmas show. Basic records are kept on each child, and children's progress is monitored once a month by the nursery teacher.

**Remarks** Welsh-speaking nursery unit, run as part of the whole primary school. Children are expected to progress up through the school. One of the county's show schools, used as an example of good practice. Dedicated, qualified staff and a strong, well-defined curriculum.

# Powys

No local authority day nurseries, playgroups, nursery schools or classes. Powys provides no childcare facilities until children enter school full-time, usually at the beginning of the term after their 4th birthday. The 85 PPA and Welsh-medium playgroups offer some part-week play experience to just under 50 per cent of 3- and 4-year-olds. There are 15 small private nurseries, but most parents in this rural area rely on almost 200 childminders or relatives to help with childcare.

**Further information**

For details on private nurseries, childminders and playgroups:

Registration and Inspection Unit
Department of Social Services
County Hall
Llandrindod Wells LD1 5LG
Tel: (0597) 826000

For details on nursery schools, units and classes:

Education Department
(address and telephone as above)

## JOLLY TOTS

Marlow
Middleton Street
Llandrindod Wells
Powys LD1 5DG
**Tel:** (0597) 825553

**Owners/Managers:** Helen Corbett, NAMCW, City & Guilds, Cert of Home Management & Family Care
Carolyn Rees, ICS Child Day Care
Nicky Wenban
**Type:** Day nursery offering full- and part-time places

**Children:** 3mths–5yrs. 12 places. 68 on register
**Hours:** 8.30am–5.15pm
Flexible hours and sessions
Open 50 weeks a year
**Status:** Private, fee-paying
**Number of years open:** 2
**Meals:** Packed lunches. Snacks
**1992 fees:** £2 per hour (less than 6hrs a week)
£1.75 per hour (6–24hrs a week)
£1.60 per hour (25hrs or more a week)
10% sibling discount
**Waiting list:** Book ahead for full-time places.
Part-time places available
**Registered by:** Powys County Council SS

# PARK LANE PEOPLE

Old Stables
Park Lane
Welshpool
Powys SY21
**Tel:** (0938) 552570

**Owner/Principal:** Liz Latham, PPA
**Type:** Day nursery offering full- and part-time and half-day sessions, with after-school and holiday playscheme
**Children:** 4mths–4yrs in nursery. 24 places. 70 on register 4–11yrs after school and holidays. Limited numbers
**Hours:** 8am–6pm
Flexible hours
Open 52 weeks a year (excl bank holidays)
**Status:** Private, fee-paying
**Number of years open:** 3
**Meals:** Breakfast, lunch, snacks
**1992 fees:** £56.75 per week full-time – under 2
£48.50 per week full-time – 2–11yrs
£12.50 per day – under 2
£10.75 per day – 2–11yrs
£6.30–£8.20 for half-day sessions
Minimum charge £3.50
85p per day for lunch
**Waiting list:** Usually about 10. Average wait 4mths
**Registered by:** Powys County Council SS

**Premises**  Tucked away just off busy Welshpool High Street, in a converted stable block behind a large Georgian house. Formerly part of Powys Castle Estate, the nursery is on the ground floor of an attractive stone and slate building – beautiful castle parkland is only 200 yards away. Two play and work rooms lead one into the other, with a cloakroom and toilets in the centre and the baby room at the far end. Clean white walls, pastel fitted carpet throughout and natural wood windows and doors show off an abundance of art, craft and photograph displays and Letterland alphabet friezes. Upstairs, the airy, open-plan roofspace accommodates a newly upgraded kitchen, principal's office, comfortable staff room and small curtained-off sick bay. Maximum use is made of all the available space. Outside, there is a well-fenced, grassy area, but no large fixed play equipment (the high cost of insurance was the reason given). Children play outside each day and in summer are taken on regular picnics, treasure hunts and walks in the castle grounds.

**Principal & staff**  Liz Latham came to the area seven years ago, had difficulty finding an acceptable nursery for her own children, and decided to meet the demand. Apart from attending a PPA Foundation Course, she has no formal childcare qualifications, but a great deal of common sense, energy and leadership skills – and she loves children. Her job is largely administrative. The day-to-day care of the children is ably managed by her NNEB-qualified deputy. She leads a team of three full-time and five part-time carers, many of whom are Welsh-speaking. Unfortunately, the majority are unqualified and young. However, on-the-job training is considered to be very important and all staff, including the principal, were working towards some formal qualification when we visited. There are no local authority nurseries in the area and very few private ones, so most qualified nursery nurses move away to find work or go on to achieve a teaching qualification. The shortage of qualified staff in the area reflects the serious lack of nursery places. Nevertheless, the staff at Park Lane People clearly enjoy working with children and staff turnover is rare.

**Children & parents**  With the exception of Malaysian siblings, all the children are Caucasian, several from homes where Welsh is the first language. Almost all the children have two working parents, many in the medical profession, banking or teaching. Increasing numbers come from farms where for the first time, mothers are taking jobs outside the home. About three-quarters of the children are full-time. They appear secure, happy and well occupied. Virtually all go on to combined nursery/reception classes in local state primary schools at 4. The parents are happy with minimal involvement, but always attend concerts and open evenings. The nursery will take up to two special needs children, and has particular experience of autism and language problems.

**Curriculum & activities**  A structured day, with emphasis on teaching social and practical skills and learning through play. Children are grouped according to age. Under-2s have a more flexible day – more time to settle, longer free play. Older children are taught pre-reading skills, writing patterns and listening skills. Reading and writing are not actively taught, but children leave at 4 years old sufficiently well equipped with the basic skills for these to develop rapidly once they reach primary school. The nursery liaises closely with primary schools in the area and responds to their needs. Children each have their own named basket with their day's work in it to take home. The library is visited once a fortnight, and the local swimming pool used as often as possible, although the staff ratio of 2:5 for swimming is below recommended guidelines. Social education is high on the agenda – the children are encouraged to feed and dress themselves and to be independent as early as possible. Craft activities, storytime, action songs, dance and outside play feature daily. All children leave with complete development records to take to primary school. Meals are a social event. The cook produces imaginative and nutritious menus and caters for special dietary needs.

**Remarks** In an area where nursery provision is extremely scarce, Park Lane People offers an excellent, much-needed and flexible service for working parents. In time, the problem of the lack of qualified staff should be overcome by the policy of on-the-job training and day-release courses. The children are polite, confident and well cared-for. The fees are as high as the area can sustain.

## ST NICHOLAS NURSERY SCHOOL

5 Church Street
Hay-on-Wye
Powys HR3 5DQ
**Tel:** (0497) 821264

**Owner/Headteacher:** Fiona Howard, Cert Ed
**Type:** Nursery school, offering full-time places and half-day sessions
**Children:** 2½–5yrs. Registered for 24 but prefer to take 20 max per session. 55 on register
**Hours:** 9am–4pm
Open 40 weeks a year
**Status:** Private, fee-paying
**Number of years open:** 4
**Meals:** Mid-morning snack, lunch
**1992 fees:** £5.50 per session (inc lunch)
£5.25 per session (excl lunch)
**Waiting list:** 12; all will get places
**Registered by:** Powys County Council SS

**Premises** The owner's large, comfortable, stone-built Georgian house on the main street near the centre of Hay-on-Wye. Nursery school sessions are held in four ground-floor rooms, one of which is kept exclusively for school use and is designated the pre-writing room. Its white walls effectively display several letter friezes and excellent artwork and it includes an attractive, well-equipped play house, dressing-up clothes, and many books in the quiet corner. The large, lived-in, family kitchen doubles as the art, craft and messy-play room, and the walls are covered with superb collages. Two living/sitting rooms are used during school hours for pre-number work and computing, each with a selection of alternative play activities available. To the rear of the house is a large enclosed garden leading to a small orchard overlooking the river Wye to the Welsh hills.

**Principal & staff** Fiona Howard, Cert Ed, mother of two young sons, taught in primary schools in the West Midlands for 15 years before moving to Hay and opening her own nursery school four years ago. Gentle, calm and caring, she and her young, qualified team of staff (one Cert Ed, one NNEB, one City & Guilds Childcare) have created a bright, relaxed but very stimulating environment for the children. The team is warm, welcoming and co-operative – each member with her own responsibilities – ably led by Fiona, who teaches full-time, organises lesson programmes and prepares food before the children arrive. Children are treated tenderly, but firmly, with their individual needs taking priority. The school has visiting music and French teachers and offers piano lessons to those who wish. The staff/child ratio is 1:5.

**Children & parents** Children come from a wide variety of backgrounds, but only a few have two working parents. Most attend because of the pre-school education, rather than their parents' need for daycare. The majority come from within a 12-mile radius. Very few are full-time and most attend for four or five half-day sessions each week. They play happily together, and talk to visitors confidently and politely. They are articulate, interested and busy. Most go on to state primary schools, at 4 if they live in Powys, 5 if they live across the border in Hereford & Worcester. A few transfer to Hereford Cathedral School at a slightly younger age. Although there are no special needs children attending at present, the nursery has had children with learning difficulties, a partially sighted child and a Down's syndrome child in the past and is happy to consider children with disabilities.

**Curriculum & activities** This nursery school aims to provide a stimulating environment for young children to explore, discover and create; to encourage them to think and learn, each at their own pace. Every session begins with a selection of play activities such as jigsaws, Lego, Playmobil or drawing and is a time for everyone to settle in. Songs and rhymes follow, then talking about the current topic. After a break for milk and a slice of apple, comes free playtime (outdoors if fine). Children then divide into four groups, according to age, for four short sessions of art, pre-writing and reading, pre-number work and computing, each held in a different room with a different teacher. Children rotate from one activity to another, often gently taken by the hand and led on by Fiona. There are always play options within the main work activity. Much individual attention. Many learn to read and follow a reading scheme agreed with their feeder school. Weekly swimming lessons at the local school mean that they are all 'water confident'. French and music lessons are offered, and there are Christmas concerts. All children are exposed to a wide range of learning experiences which build confidence and allow them to develop their potential. They transfer happily, very well prepared for school.

**Remarks** A delightful nursery school in a lovely location. Thoughtful and caring principal, supported by lively, qualified staff. High-quality pre-school education at a reasonable price. A 'school in a home' which provides children with confidence, security and a solid learning base.

# South Glamorgan

Approximately 160 playgroups (English- and Welsh-speaking) provide the bulk of the county's provision. Two local authority day nurseries cater for children with special needs, and 40 private nurseries offer some 900 full-time places. Nursery education is available to 55 per cent of under-5s in nursery schools and classes. Over half the places are full-time.

## Further information

For details on day nurseries, childminders and playgroups:
Child and Family Central Support Unit
Maelfa
Llanedeyrn
Cardiff CF3 7PN
Tel: (0222) 732014

For details on nursery schools, units and classes:
Education Department
County Hall
Atlantic Wharf
Cardiff CF1 5UW
Tel: (0222) 872000

# BARNARDO'S FAMILY CENTRE

Grand Avenue
Ely
Cardiff CF5 4LE
**Tel:** (0222) 578918

**Owner:** Barnardo's and South Glamorgan County Council SS
**Project Leader:** Phyllis Watters, NNEB
**Type:** Family centre offering full- and part-time places. Max attendance 2 full days a week
**Children:** 1yr–5yrs. 20 places. 40 on register
**Hours:** 9am–3.30pm
Open 52 weeks a year
**Status:** Charity/state partnership between Barnardo's and Social Services
**Number of years open:** 20 (1½ in current premises)
**Meals:** Lunch, snacks
**1992 fees:** No fees
**Waiting list:** Moderate. Priority to those with the greatest need and Social Services referrals
**Registered by:** South Glamorgan County Council SS

**Premises** Purpose-built, ultra-modern family centre at the end of a row of shops on a large housing estate. There is a spacious main playroom with gym mats, bikes, climbing frame and other large toys surrounded by glass, so that staff can observe without being too conspicuous. Four additional children's rooms are furnished and painted differently, each with library area and loos. The nursery also has a toy library, laundry room for parents' use, a reception room where parents can wait for their children and a 'bring and buy clothes room' where secondhand clothes are sold to raise money for trips. There is a large outside play area with new six-foot-high fencing which has recently been vandalised. Trelai Park is a 20-minute walk from the Centre and is visited once or twice a week, mainly in the summer.

**Project Leader & staff** Phyllis Watters completed her NNEB training with Barnardo's, followed by a post-qualifying course at Bristol University. She has been project leader at the centre for 20 years. Her team of seven staff, three full-time and four part-time, are all qualified and experienced – the majority NNEB. Two nursery nurses are currently learning sign language. Meetings are held once a month with the social worker allocated to the nursery and the administration officer. Staff meetings are held weekly. No member of staff has left the centre in the last two years. Male students have been specifically requested in the past, to provide a good mix, but the unattractive rates of pay mean men tend to move on quickly. Staff are recruited internally through the Barnardo's Journal or sometimes through the local newspaper or Job Centre. Phyllis's role is mainly managerial, but she covers for staff sickness and holidays to keep her in touch with the children. Voluntary helpers and students are welcome. Staff regularly attend courses to update their skills. The staff/child ratio is an excellent 1:3.

**Children & parents** It is a fairly depressed area and many children come from single-parent families or have difficult home lives. There is some cultural mix, but the majority are white, Welsh children. Most go on to local state primary schools. Children are grouped according to age and move from one coloured room to the next, in their groups. They all meet together each day in the large playroom or outside and at mealtimes. The children we observed were obviously happy and relaxed. There is a child with Down's syndrome and others with minor disabilities. Every effort is made to involve parents in the nursery. Each family has a keyworker whom they relate to directly. New children are phased-in gradually, and parents are welcome to stay for as long as their child needs them. Parents usually learn about the nursery through their health visitor or social workers. The nursery operates an open-door policy.

**Curriculum & activities** The nursery aims to work with parents and use their knowledge of each child as a guideline for the teaching of new skills. Each keyworker is responsible for monitoring the children in her care and liaising with parents and other professionals. The children learn through play and are encouraged to take part in a range of different activities, including painting, music, glueing, modelling and reading. Each day starts in family groupings in one of the classrooms for free play and educational work. After this children move into the large playroom, where there are sand and water trays, a home corner, a hospital corner and painting equipment. The playroom is the centre of activity in the afternoon for creative work, but children attending afternoon sessions only do some group work in the classrooms as well. There is plenty of good-quality equipment, child-centred and stimulating. Emphasis is placed on good manners and learning acceptable behaviour. The centre has a detailed document on discipline which applies to both staff and parents visiting the centre. Corporal punishment is not allowed, and persistent bad behaviour is dealt with by removing the child from the room until he/she has regained self-control. Work files are kept on each child, including a developmental chart, photographs and examples of creative work. Parents have open access to all written files and records. The nursery has the use of Barnardo's cottage for two weeks every year and takes eight children at a time, with their parents, for three-day holiday breaks.

**Remarks**  A spotless, modern family centre, with a happy, relaxed nursery. Priority to children in the greatest need. Close partnership with the community. A qualified, experienced care team supports the whole family. Excellent staff/child ratio throughout.

# ROMILLY PARK NURSERY SCHOOL

The Lodge
Romilly Park
Barry
South Glamorgan CF6 8RN
**Tel:** (0446) 749321

**Owner/Principal:** Phyl Lloyd, Cert Ed
**Type:** Day nursery offering full- and part-time places and half-day sessions
**Children:** 18mths–5yrs. 34 places (to be increased to 38). 100 on register
**Hours:** 8.15am–5.30pm
Morning session 8.15am–12.45pm
Afternoon session 1.30pm–5.30pm
Open 51 weeks a year
**Status:** Private, fee-paying
**Number of years open:** 7
**Meals:** Lunch, tea, snacks
**1992 fees:** £12.20 per day inc lunch
£5.50 per session
**Waiting list:** Minimal. Places can usually be guaranteed
**Registered by:** South Glamorgan County Council SS

**Premises**  Chalet-style bungalow, built about 50 years ago on the edge of Romilly Park with a backdrop of beautiful mature trees. The building, owned by the local authority, is ideal for its purpose, as it looks remarkably like a large Wendy house. The nursery is totally enclosed and has a large, attractive, grassy garden. Park by-laws prohibit cars, so parents must park on the road and walk their children the 200 yards to the nursery. There is a large playroom in the centre of the building where children also eat their meals; a messy room; a television room with comfortable chairs in a circle round the television; and a 'make believe' room for imaginative play, with home corner, dressing-up clothes, vacuum-cleaner and pots and pans. A verandah has been enclosed to create a reading corner and reception area. A partitioned-off part of this is used as a rest room, with six beds. Walls are covered in posters and large collages made by the children. The garden is huge and provides a big sandpit, a play house on stilts, with a slide, and a good selection of outdoor equipment.

**Owner/Principal & staff**  Owner/principal Phyl Lloyd, Cert Ed, qualified as a teacher in art and design. She employs a staff of ten female nursery nurses, ranging in age from 17 to 40. There are three full-timers, two of whom are qualified NNEB, the other being a qualified, trained teacher. Other nursery workers have City & Guilds and PPA qualifications. Unqualified staff are required to attend a one-year night-school course on working with under-5s, as well as a first-aid course. The nursery sets out detailed terms and conditions for its staff, and there is a one-month staff induction period, during which new staff are given support, information and advice by their supervisor. Staff meet informally each day and there are after-school staff meetings every two months. Phyl Lloyd regrets that lack of finances prevents her from paying her dedicated staff what she feels they are really worth.

**Children & parents**  The nursery operates a genuine open-door policy and parents are welcome at any time of day, for as long as they like. Children initially attend for short sessions lasting a couple of hours until they are settled. There are no formal groups, except for watching television programmes suitable for a particular age group, or for artwork. Children come from a variety of social backgrounds and there is some cultural mix. Most move to local state primaries and church schools. A high proportion transfer to the Welsh School. Parents are invited to open days and parents' evenings and are encouraged to help out whenever possible. There are fines for late collection – parents pay the member of staff who has stayed behind £2 for every 15 minutes.

**Curriculum & activities** Written timetables are changed weekly and each week children concentrate on a particular subject or theme. The nursery has a good stock of creative and educational toys (annual budget £2000). Every day includes some artwork, sand and water play, free play and, for older children, pre-school work. The learning programme is planned and includes pre-reading, pre-writing and pre-maths work, but does not aim to have children reading or writing by the time they transfer to primary school. Children work in small groups at a table, with a member of staff. Dance and movement, music, singing and percussion take place every day. The school does not pursue any particular philosophy. Phyl Lloyd says, 'Our philosophy is to apply every tactic known to us to enable the children to learn, be happy, secure and ready for school.' Formal record-keeping on developmental progress and individual assessment has just begun. In the summer, children spend a great deal of time outside in the unusually spacious and child-friendly garden or exploring the surrounding parkland. Meals are freshly cooked on the premises and special diets provided. There are twice-yearly outings to Bristol Zoo and Penyscynor Wildlife Park and a Christmas pantomime.

**Remarks** One of very few day nurseries in the area, and definitely one of the greenest urban locations. Children are lively and responsive. After lying empty for 12 years, the building has been transformed into a warm and welcoming nursery. Owner and staff are clearly dedicated to their work.

# West Glamorgan

Top of the Welsh league table for nursery education, with 80 per cent of all 3-year-olds in full- or part-time education, before they start school at rising-5. In total, there are 137 primary schools with nursery classes and two nursery schools. The majority of the 21 private day nurseries offer places for babies from birth. Social Services fund five playgroups for children with special needs, although the policy is to integrate special needs children into ordinary daycare facilities wherever possible. They also sponsor a number of childminders. There are 60 part-time playgroups. There was no response to our questionnaires.

**Further information**

For details on day nurseries, childminders and playgroups:
Development Officer
Department of Social Services
County Hall
Swansea SA1 3SN
Tel: (0792) 471111

For details on nursery schools, units and classes:
Education Department
(address and telephone as above)

# Useful Organisations and Publications

## Organisations

**Childcare Association**
1 Floral Place
Northampton Grove
London N1 2PL
(071) 354 9943

**Daycare Trust**
Wesley House
4 Wild Court
London WC2B 5AU
(071) 405 5617

**Gabbitas Truman & Thring Educational Trust**
6-8 Sackville Street
London W1X 2BR
(071) 734 0161

**Gingerbread**
35 Wellington Street
London WC2E 7BN
(071) 240 0953

**Independent Schools Information Service (ISIS)**
56 Buckingham Gate
London SW1E 6AG
(071) 630 8793/4

**Kids' Club Network**
279-281 Whitechapel Road
London E1 1BY
(071) 247 3009

**London Montessori Centre**
18 Balderton Street
London W1Y 1TG
(071) 493 0165

**MENCAP**
123 Golden Lane
London EC1Y 0RT
(071) 454 0454

**Mudiad Ysgolion Meithrin**
(National Association of Welsh Medium Nursery Schools & Playgroups)
145 Albany Road
Roath
Cardiff CF2 3NT
(0222) 485510

**National Childbirth Trust Headquarters**
Alexandra House
Oldham Terrace
London W3 6NH
(081) 992 8637

**National Childminding Association**
8 Masons Hill
Bromley
Kent BR2 9EY
(081) 460 5427

**National Children's Bureau**
8 Wakeley Street
London EC1V 7QE
(071) 278 9441

**National Consumer Council**
20 Grosvenor Gardens
London SW1W 0DH
(071) 730 3469

**National Private Day Nurseries Association**
24 Bridge End
Rastrick
Brighouse
West Yorkshire HD6 3DH
(0484) 711211

**Pre-school Playgroups Association (PPA)**
61-63 Kings Cross Road
London WC1X 9LL
(071) 833 0991

**NIPPA (Northern Ireland)**
(0232) 662825
**Scottish PPA** (041) 221 4148
**Welsh PPA** (0978) 358195

**Scottish Child and Family Alliance**
Princes House
5 Shandwick Place
Edinburgh EH2 4RG
(031) 228 8484

**Thomas Coram Research Unit**
Institute of Education
University of London
27/28 Woburn Square
London WC1H 0AA
(071) 612 6957

**Voluntary Organisations Liaison Council for Under Fives (VOLCUF)**
77 Holloway Road
London N7 8JZ
(071) 607 9573

**Working for Childcare**
77 Holloway Road
London N7 8JZ
(071) 700 0281

**Working Mothers Association**
77 Holloway Road
London N7 8JZ
(071) 700 5771

## Publications

**(The) Children Act 1989 Guidance and Regulations,** Vol 2, HMSO

**Education Year Book (1994),** Longman Group UK Ltd. (Very expensive; available in public reference libraries)

**Montessori Schools Directory (1992),** Second Edition, available from London Montessori Centre

**Nursery World,** weekly magazine available from newsagents

**Social Services Year Book (1992/3),** Longman Group UK Ltd. (Also expensive; available in public reference libraries)

**'Starting with Quality'** The Report of the Committee of Inquiry into the Quality of the Educational Experience offered to Three and Four Year Olds, HMSO

**Young Children in Group Daycare** (Guidelines for Good Practice), National Children's Bureau

# Index of Nurseries by Name

*italic type = listings*
plain type = full entries

*0-2-5 Nursery, Heaton Mersey, Stockport, Manchester 337*
Abacus Nursery School, Newbury, Berks 31-2
Abbey School Day Nursery, Faversham, Kent 179-80
ABC Day Nursery, Buttershaw, Bradford, W Yorks 452-3
*Abercorn Place School Nursery, Westminster, London 322*
Acorn Day Nursery, Castlethorpe, Milton Keynes, Bucks 46-7
*Acorn Nursery School, Carmarthen, Dyfed, Wales 506*
Acorn Nursery School, Kensington, London 260-1
Acorn Park Nursery, Glasgow, Strathclyde, Scotland 495-6
Acorns Day Nursery, Sevenoaks Primary School, Sevenoaks, Kent 180-2
Acorns Workplace Nursery, Bexley, Kent 182-3
Agnes Hayward Nursery School, Maidenhead, Berks 33-4
Airedale General Hospital Day Nursery, Keighley, Bradford, W Yorks 453-4
Albyn School for Girls Infant Nursery Dept, Aberdeen, Grampian, Scotland 482
Alcester Nursery School, Alcester, Warks 427-8
Alec Hunter Playgroup, Braintree, Essex 124-5
*Ancholme House Nursery, Scunthorpe, Humberside 170*
Annette's Nursery, Bournemouth, Dorset 106
Apple Tree Nursery, Durham 109-10
Appledore Primary School, Bideford, Devon 97-8
*Appollo Day Nursery, Whitworth, Rochdale, Manchester 336*
*Arboretum Nursery School, Nottingham, Notts 372*
Ark Playgroup, Oakham, Rutland, Leics 199-200
Ashfield Nursery School & Parents Centre, Newcastle, Tyne & Wear 414-15

Ashgrove Nursery School, Newry, NI 472-3
Aspley Day Nursery, Kirklees, W Yorks 462-3
Balham Nursery School, Endlesham Road, Wandsworth, London 304-5
Banbury School, Clipper Day Nursery, Banbury, Oxon 374-5
Barnardo's Family Centre, Ely, Cardiff, S Glamorgan, Wales 514-15
Barrachnie Children's Nursery, Glasgow, Strathclyde, Scotland 496-7
Beehive Kindergarten, Onchan, Isle of Man 174-5
*Bembridge School Pre-Prep Department, Bembridge, Isle of Wight 176*
Bilson Family Centre, Cinderford, Glos 134-5
Binswood Nursery School, Leamington Spa, Warks 428-9
*Birch Grove Day Nursery, Rusholme, Manchester 333*
Blundell's Day Nursery, Wandsworth, London 306
Bo Peep Day Nursery, Southend-on-Sea, Essex 125-6
*Body Shop Child Development Centre, Littlehampton, W Sussex 443*
Boundary Oak Nursery Group, Fareham, Hants 142-3
Bram Longstaffe Nursery School, Barrow-in-Furness, Cumbria 86-7
Breakspear Nursery Unit, Ickenham, Hillingdon, London 253-4
*British Red Cross Educare Nursery, Beverley, Humberside 170*
*Broadgate Nursery, Hackney, London EC2 237*
Broadwater Manor Nursery Department, Worthing, W Sussex 443-4
Bubbles Day Nursery/School, Halstead, Essex 126-7
Burnage Children's Centre, Burnage, Manchester 333-4
Burnett Nursery, Warrington, Cheshire 71-2

*Bushey First School Nursery Unit, Merton, London 284*
Busy Bee Day Nursery, Bakewell, Derbyshire 93-4
Busy Bee Nursery School, Hammersmith & Fulham, London 242-3
*Busy Bee Nursery School, Putney, Wandsworth, London 306-7*
Buttons Nursery School, Hanwell, Ealing, London 231
Byron Infant School, Coulsdon, Croydon, London 226-7
Caldecot Primary Nursery Class, Lambeth, London 276-7
*Camden Day Nursery, Camden, London 221*
Cargilfield Nursery, Edinburgh, Lothian, Scotland 488
*Caring Daycare, Haslemere, Surrey 410*
Carlton Road Nursery Unit, Boston, Lincs 206-7
Carol Jane Montessori Nursery School, Enfield, London 233-4
Castle Nursery (The), Edinburgh, Lothian, Scotland 489-90
*Castlereagh Nursery, Belfast, NI 473*
Caterpillars Day Nursery, Bath, Avon 21-2
Cedar Park School Nursery Class, Twyford, Berks 34-5
Celandine Nursery, Yardley Wood, Birmingham, W Midlands 431-2
*Chapel Nursery, Telford, Shropshire 386*
Cheerful Tots Day Nursery, Canterbury, Kent 183-4
Childcare Battle Hill, North Tyneside, Tyne & Wear 420-1
Childcare Wallsend, North Tyneside, Tyne & Wear 421-2
Chiltern Nursery School, Chiltern Nursery Training College, Berks 35-7
Christ the King Primary School – Nursery Class, Reading, Berks 37-8
*City Child, Corporation of London, London 226*
*Clever Clowns Nursery School, Boxley, Maidstone, Kent 185*
Clock Tower Nursery, Lewes, E Sussex 113-14

# 520 INDEX OF NURSERIES BY NAME

Close Nursery School (The), Banbury, Oxon 375-6
Clyde House Day Nursery, Bishopston, Bristol, Avon 23-4
Coigne (The), Minchinhampton, Stroud, Glos 135-6
Community Day Care Group, St Johns, Hereford & Worcester 152-3
Coppice Nursery School, High Wycombe, Bucks 48-9
Cork Street Nursery Centre, Hendon, Sunderland, Tyne & Wear 424-5
*Corner House Day Nursery, Chiswick, Hounslow, London 256*
*Cottam Nursery School, Cottam, Preston, Lancs 190*
Coulsdon Nursery School, Coulsdon, Croydon, London 228-9
*Cozy Corner Playgroup, Crossmaglen, NI 473*
*Cricket Montessori School, Harrow, London 251*
*Croft Family Centre, Nottingham, Notts 372-3*
Croston Nursery School, Croston, Preston, Lancs 190-1
Daisy Chain Montessori School, Lambeth, London 277-8
Daneshill Nursery, Leicester, Leics 200-1
Davison Crèche & Under 5s Club, Worthing, W Sussex 444-5
Defoe Day Care Centre, Hackney, London 237-8
*Dorchester Community Nursery School, Dorchester, Dorset 107*
*Downshire Nursery School, Banbridge, NI 473*
Dulwich College Prep School, Southwark, London 296-7
Dungannon Nursery School, Dungannon, NI 474-5
*Durham University Nursery, Durham 111*
Eager Beavers Nursery, Ashford, Kent 185-6
*Ealing Montessori School, Ealing, London 231-2*
Early Years I, Castle Park Primary, Kendal, Cumbria 87-8
Early Years Day Nursery, Hove, E Sussex 114-15
Eastview Montessori Nursery School, Wavendon, Milton Keynes, Bucks 49-50
Edgbaston Park Nursery, Edgbaston, Birmingham, W Midlands 432-4
Edinburgh Academy Nursery Class, Edinburgh, Lothian, Scotland 490-1
Edinburgh Nursery Crèche (The), Edinburgh, Lothian, Scotland 491-2
Elim Church Day Nursery, Bradford, W Midlands 454-5
Elms Nursery School, Astley Bridge, Bolton, Manchester 327-8
Endcliffe Children's Nursery, Sheffield, S Yorks 399-400
Fair Mile Day Nursery, Fair Mile Hospital, Nr Wallingford, Oxon 376-7
*Fieldhouse Montessori Kindergarten, Credenhill, Hereford & Worcester 153*
First Class Nursery School, Grantham, Linc 207-8
First Steps Day Nursery, Chichester College of Technology, W Sussex 446-7
*Fiveways, Ryde School, Ryde, Isle of Wight 176*
Fleet Street Nursery, Camden, London 221-2
Floral Place Nursery, Islington, London 256-8
Frances Wright Pre-school Centre, Dundee, Tayside, Scotland 501-2
Fulwood Play Centre, Sheffield, S Yorks 400-1
Gamesley Pre-School Centre, Glossop, Derbyshire 94-5
Gardens Nursery School, Southfields, Wandsworth, London 307-8
*Gatehouse Nursery 2, Harmondsworth, Hillingdon, London 254*
*Glenfield Nursery School, Stockton-on-Tees, Cleveland 75-6*
Goldsmiths' College Nursery, Lewisham, London 282-3
Gooseberry Bush Day Nursery, Camborne, Cornwall 78-9
Gosforth Private Day Nursery, Gosforth, Newcastle, Tyne & Wear 415-16
*Grange Hill Nursery School, Goudhurst, Kent 186*
Grays Hall Day Nursery, Sible Hedingham, Essex 128-9
Green Lanes Primary School, Chelmsley Wood, Solihull, W Midlands 439-40
Greenburn Nursery, Aberdeen, Grampian, Scotland 483-4
Greenfields Day Nurseries, Tyldesley, Wigan, Manchester 342-3
Griffin Nursery (Kids Unlimited), Bootle, Sefton, Merseyside 350-1
Grove Nursery School, Headingley, Leeds, W Yorks 464-5
Grove Nursery School, Wimbledon, Merton, London 284-6
Halesfield Day Nursery School, Telford, Shropshire 386-7
*Happy Child Day Nursery, Ealing, London 232*
Happy Days Nursery, Brighton, E Sussex 116-17
Happy Days Nursery, Rudheath, Northwich, Cheshire 72-3
Harvey Road Day Nursery, Cambridge, Cambs 60-1
Hawthorn Cottage Day Nursery & School, St Johns, Hereford & Worcester 153-4
HCAT Nursery, Harrogate College of Arts & Technology, N Yorks 364-6
Headstart Pre-School Centre, Preston, Lancs 191-3
Heaton Nursery School, Heaton, Newcastle-upon-Tyne, Tyne & Wear 416-18
Hendon College Nursery, Colindale, Barnet, London 211-12
Hendon Pre-School, Hendon, Barnet, London 213-14
*Hetton-le-Hole Nursery School, Sunderland, Tyne & Wear 425-6*
Higher Downs Day Nursery, Altrincham, Trafford, Manchester 340-1
Highgate Daycare Nursery, Leverton, Boston, Lincs 208-9
Highview Nursery, Sharples, Bolton, Manchester 328-9
Highweek Nursery, Newton Abbot, Devon 98-100
Hillbury House Nursery School, Hove, E Sussex 117-18
Hirst Wood Nursery School, Shipley, Bradford, W Midlands 455-6
*Histon Nursery School, Histon, Cambs 61*
Holland Park Day Nursery & School House, Kensington, London 262-3
Holly Tree Nursery School, Woolston, Southampton, Hants 141-2
Honeywell Nursery Class, Honeywell Road, Wandsworth, London 308-9
*Hopscotch Nursery School, Chippenham, Wilts 468*

# INDEX OF NURSERIES BY NAME 521

*Hull University Union Day Nursery, Hull, Humberside* 170
*Huntingdon Nursery School, Huntingdon, Cambs* 61
*Independent Day Nursery, Hackney, London* 238
Irwell Vale Private Nursery School, Rossendale, Lancs 193-4
Iverna Gardens Montessori Nursery School, Kensington, London 263-4
Jackanory Nursery, Wallington, Sutton, London 300-1
Jean Jessop Day Nursery, Southport, Sefton, Merseyside 352-3
Joint Colleges Nursery, Cambridge, Cambs 62-3
*Jolly Tots, Llandrindod Wells, Powys, Wales* 510
Joseph's Nursery, Clifton, York, N Yorks 366-7
Kelton Day Nursery, Mossley Hill, Liverpool, Merseyside 345-6
Kids & Co, Donaghmore, Dungannon, NI 475-6
Kindergarten (The), Aberdeen, Grampian, Scotland 484-5
King Richard Nursery, Portsmouth, Hants 143-4
*King St Playgroup, Christ Pieces, Cambridge, Cambs* 63
*Kirklands Day Nursery, Barnard Castle, Co Durham* 111
Knightsbridge Kindergarten, Kensington, London 264-5
*L'Ecole des Petits, Hammersmith & Fulham, London* 243-4
Ladbroke Square Montessori School, Kensington, London 266-7
*Langdale Nursery School, Newcastle, Staffs* 403
Langley Manor Nursery, Langley, Slough, Berks 38-9
Lanherne School Nursery Department, Dawlish, Devon 100-1
Latchmere Infant School Nursery, Kingston-upon-Thames, London 274-5
*Lavenders Day Nursery, Bedford, Beds* 30
Le Monde Petit, Burnley, Lancs 194-5
League of Friends Day Nursery, Canterbury, Kent 186-7
*Park Place Nursery School, Margate, Kent* 188
Leigham Infant School Nursery Unit, Leigham, Plymouth, Devon 101-2
Linda Evans Children's Day Care Centre, Ipswich, Suffolk 406-7
Lingfield Day Nursery, Blackheath, Greenwich, London 235-6
Lion House, Gwendolen Avenue, Putney, Wandsworth, London 309-10
Lisburn Central Nursery Unit, Lisburn, NI 476-7
*Lisvane, Scarborough College Junior School, N Yorks* 367
Little Acorn Nursery School, Scone, Tayside, Scotland 502-3
*Little Acorns Day Nursery, Handforth, Cheshire* 73
Little Acorns Nursery School, Stoneygate, Leicester, Leics 201-2
Little Acorns Nursery, Derby, Derbyshire 95-6
Little Angels Day Care Nursery, Weeford, Staffs 403-4
Little Oaks Nursery School, Sands, High Wycombe, Bucks 51-2
Little Orchard Day Nursery, Chichester, W Sussex 447-8
Little People, Whitehall Park, Islington, London 258-9
Little Red Engine, Grant Road, Wandsworth, London 311-12
*Little School for Little Scholars, Luton, Beds* 30
Little Sparrows Nursery, Ingatestone, Essex 129-30
Littleworld Nursery School, Andover, Hants 144-5
*London Montessori College, Westminster, London* 322
Longfields Nursery, Wrexham, Clwyd, Wales 504-6
Manor House Nursery, Lee-on-Solent, Hants 146
Manor Nursery, Horspath, Oxon 377-8
*Mapperley Plains Primary School Nursery, Nottingham, Notts* 373
Marlin Montessori, Berkhamsted, Herts 161-2
Mary Seacole Day Nursery, Reading, Berks 40-1
Mayfield Junior School Kindergarten, Farnborough, Hants 147-8
MCVS Nursery, Mount Vernon Green, Liverpool, Merseyside 346-7
Meadow Nursery School, Wokingham, Berks 41-2
Meadow View Montessori Nursery School, Rawtenstall, Lancs 196-7
Meadow View Nursery, Newport Pagnell, Bucks 52-3
Meadows Day Nursery, Stocksfield, Northumberland 362
Mews Nursery, Bath, Avon 24-5
*Mill Hill Nursery School, Sunderland, Tyne & Wear* 426
*Millais Day Nursery, Horsham, W Sussex* 448
Millington Road Nursery School, Cambridge, Cambs 63-4
*Minnows, Dents Road, Wandsworth, London* 312
Monkton, Mossley Hill, Liverpool, Merseyside 347-8
Montessori Nursery & Pre-Prep School, Bishops Stortford, Herts 162-3
Montessori Nursery School, Sheffield, S Yorks 401-2
Montessori School Cambridge (The), Chesterton, Cambs 64-6
Moorfield Nursery School, Bingley, Bradford, W Yorks 457-8
Moorlands Children's Nursery, Horwich, Bolton, Manchester 329-31
*Moray Steiner School Kindergarten, Forres, Moray, Grampian, Scotland* 485
Mortlake Day Nursery, Sheen Lane, Richmond, London 289-90
Moss Lea Private Nursery School, Sharples Park, Bolton, Manchester 331-2
Mother Goose Baby Nursery, Peckham, Southwark, London 298-9
Mothercraft Nursery, Hove, E Sussex 118-19
Mount Carmel Kindergarten, St Albans, Herts 163-4
Mount Nursery School (The), Telford, Shropshire 388-9
Mountfields Lodge Nursery, Loughborough, Leics 203-4
Mouse House, Mallinson Road, Wandsworth, London 312-14
Mrs Mynors' Nursery School, Kensington, London 267-8
Mrs Tiggy-Winkle's Day Nursery, Hereford, Hereford & Worcester 154-5
*Nantgaredig School Nursery Unit, Dyfed, Wales* 507
Newburn Manor Nursery School, Newcastle-upon-Tyne, Tyne & Wear 418-19
Newfield Primary School Nursery Unit, Brent, London 217-18
Newfields Childcare Co-operative, Durham 111-12
*Noah's Ark Day Nursery, Richmond, London* 290-1
Noah's Ark, Boutflower Road, Wandsworth, London 314-15

# INDEX OF NURSERIES BY NAME

Noddy's Nursery School, Putney, Wandsworth, London 315
Norland College, Hungerford, Berks 42-4
North Walney Primary School, Barrow-in-Furness, Cumbria 88-90
Norton St Nicholas (C of E) School Nursery Class, Letchworth, Herts 165-6
Nurserytyme, Aylesbury, Bucks 53-5
Oak House Children's Nursery, Aigburth, Liverpool, Merseyside 349-50
Oak House Nursery School, Ross-on-Wye, Hereford, Hereford & Worcester 156-7
Old Buttery Nursery School, Willingham, Cambs 66-7
Old Rectory Day Nursery, Little Billing, Northampton 357-8
*Oops-a-Daisy, Newham, London 288*
Orchard Day Nursery, Caversham, Reading, Berks 44-5
Orchards Day Nursery & Nursery School, Stockport, Manchester 67
*Orchards Day Nursery, Caxton, Cambs 337-9*
Orleans Community Nursery, Twickenham, Richmond, London 291-2
Oval Montessori Nursery School (The), Lambeth, London 278-9
Painter's Cottage, Worcester, Hereford & Worcester 157-9
*Palm Tree Nursery, Douglas, Isle of Man 175*
*Park House Day Nursery, Thetford, Norfolk 355*
Park Lane People, Welshpool, Powys, Wales 511-12
*The Park Nursery School, Wandsworth, London 315*
Park Road Nursery School, Peterborough, Cambs 67-8
Pear Tree Day Nursery, Farnborough, Hants 148-9
Pellon & District Community Day Nursery, Halifax, Calderdale, W Yorks 460-1
Peter Pan Day Nursery, Poole, Dorset 107-8
Pixieland I Day Nursery, Plymouth, Devon 102-3
Playhouse Day Nursery, Long Stratton, Norfolk 356-7
Polly's Day Nursery, Stroud, Glos 136-8
Polwhele House School, Truro, Cornwall 79-80

Pooh Corner Montessori Nursery School, Kensington, London 268-9
*Poppins Day Nursery, Southbourne, W Sussex 449-50*
Priory Day Nursery, Kenilworth, Warks 429-30
Priory Primary Nursery Unit, Dudley, W Midlands 436-7
Prospect House, Putney Hill, Wandsworth, London 316-17
Puffins, Hammersmith & Fulham, London 244-5
Purley Nursery School, Purley, Croydon, London 229-30
Queensmill Nursery Ltd, Hammersmith & Fulham, London 245
Rainbow Corner Day Nursery, Watlington, Oxon 379-80
Rainbow Day Nursery, Bromley, London 219-20
Rainbow Day Nursery, Norton, Cleveland 76-7
Rainbow Nursery 1 & 2, Stoke Newington, Hackney, London 239-40
*Rainbow Nursery, Stornoway, Isle of Lewis 504*
Rawmarsh Nursery School, Rotherham, S Yorks 397-8
Red Balloon, Trinity Road, Wandsworth, London 317-18
Red House Nursery, Westbury Park, Bristol, Avon 25-7
Redford House, Roehampton Institute, Wandsworth, London
Redroofs Nursery, Warmley, Bristol, Avon 318-19
Riverbank Kindergarten & Day Nursery, Ayr, Strathclyde, Scotland 498-9
Rocking Horse Day Nursery School, Redland, Bristol, Avon 28-9
Romilly Park Nursery School, Barry, S Glamorgan, Wales 515-16
Rose Cottage Day Nursery, Shepreth, Royston, Cambs 68-70
Rose Court Preparatory School Nursery Class, Headingley, Leeds, W Yorks 466-7
Rose Montessori School, Hammersmith & Fulham, London 245-6
Rosebrae School Kindergarten, Elgin, Moray, Grampian, Scotland 485-6
*Rouge Bouillon Nursery, St Helier, Jersey 178*
Royal Spa Nursery School, Brighton, E Sussex 119-21
Russell Nursery, Russell School, Petersham, Richmond, London 292-3
St Aidan's School Day Nursery, Carlisle, Cumbria 90-1
St Alphege Infant School Nursery Unit, Solihull, W Midlands 440-1
*St Anne's Nursery, Stirling University, Central, Scotland 480*
St Catherine's Nursery Unit, Barnet, London 214
St Christopher School, Letchworth, Herts 166-7
St Cuthbert's School, Wigton, Cumbria 91-2
St Gabriel's Community Centre Playgroup, Leicester, Leics 204-5
*St Helens College Nursery, St Helens, Merseyside 354*
*St Helen's Montessori School, East Farleigh, Maidstone, Kent 188*
*St John's VC Infants School Nursery Class, Glastonbury, Somerset 390*
St Joseph's (RC) JMI School Nursery Unit, Chelsea, Kensington, London 269-71
St Leonard's Nursery School, Camden, London 223-4
St Mark's Square Nursery School, Camden, London 224-5
St Martin's (C of E) Primary School Nursery Unit, Liskeard, Cornwall 80-1
St Nicholas Garden School, Henley, Oxon 380-1
St Nicholas Nursery School, Hay-on-Wye, Powys, Wales 512-13
St Osburg's Primary School & Nursery, Coundon, Coventry, W Midlands 434-5
St Paul's Nursery School, York, N Yorks 367-9
*St Peter's Nursery School, Kensington, London 271*
*St Peter's Nursery Unit, Stonehouse, Plymouth, Devon 104*
Sandwick Junior High School, Sandwick, Shetland, Scotland 494-5
*Scallywags Private Playgroup, Newtownards, NI 477*
Schoolgate Nursery, Harlow, Essex 130-1
Schoolroom, Putney, Wandsworth, London 320-1
Seaward Day Nursery, Bournemouth, Dorset 108-9
Sevenoaks Day Nursery, Sevenoaks, Kent 188-9

# INDEX OF NURSERIES BY NAME

Severn Lodge Private Nursery, Bolton, Bradford, W Yorks 458-9
*Shepherd's Bush DN, Hammersmith & Fulham, London* 246-7
Simpson Under Fives Resource Centre, Simpson, Milton Keynes, Bucks 55-6
Sinclair Nursery School, Hammersmith & Fulham, London 247-8
Smarties Nursery, Cotton Edmunds, Chester 74-5
Somerset Montessori Nursery School, Taunton, Somerset 390-10
Somerset Nursery 1, Glasgow, Strathclyde, Scotland 449-500
Southbrook Early Education Unit, Daventry, Northants 359-60
*Springwood Nursery School, Roundhay, Leeds, W Yorks* 467
*Square One, Putney, Wandsworth, London* 321
Squirrels Montessori Nursery Centre, Enniskillen, NI 477-8
*Station House Day Nursery, Beeston, Notts* 373
Staunton Park Day Nursery, Havant, Hants 149-50
*Stepping Stones Day Nursery, Bordeaux Vale, Guernsey* 140
*Stepping Stones Nursery, Camden, London* 222
Stepping Stones Nursery School, Nr Marlborough, Wilts 468-9
Studio Day Nursery, Hammersmith & Fulham, London 248-9
Studio Day Nursery, Newport, Isle of Wight 176-7
Studio Montessori School, Kew Gardens Road, Richmond, London 294-5
Summerlane Day Nursery, Barnsley, S Yorks 394-5
Sunfield Day Nursery, St Annes-on-Sea, Lancs 197-8
*Sunflower Montessori School, Richmond, London* 295
*Sunnyside Nursery, Leighton Buzzard, Beds* 30
Sunrise Day Nursery, Basingstoke, Hants 150-1
*Sunshine Day Nursery, Walton, Chesterfield, Derbyshire* 96
Swanpool Children's Nursery, St Johns, Worcester, Hereford & Worcester 159-60
*Swansmere School, Walton-on-Thames, Surrey* 411
Sweet Briar Nursery School, Hoxne, Eye, Suffolk 407-8
Swiftdale Close Day Nursery, Bedlington, Northumberland 363-4
*Tadpoles Nursery School, Chelsea, Kensington, London* 271
Taunton School Kindergarten & Nursery, Taunton, Somerset 391-2
Tavistock Nursery Centre, Tavistock, Devon 104-5
*Teddy's Nursery School, Sandhurst, Surrey* 411
Tenterfield Nursery School, Welwyn, Herts 168-9
*Thomas's Kindergarten, Battersea, London* 321
*Thomas's Kindergarten, Westminster, London* 323-4
Three Bridges First School Nursery Class, Crawley, W Sussex 450-1
Tidworth Clarendon Infant School Nursery Class, Tidworth, Wilts 470-1
*Tiny Tots Day Nursery, Louth, Lincs* 209
Toad Hall Nursery School, Kennington, Lambeth, London 279-80
Tom Thumb Nursery School & Kindergarten, Eastbourne, E Sussex 121-2
Town Mouse Day Nursery, St Peter Port, Guernsey 140
Treliske Pre-Preparatory School Nursery Class, Truro, Cornwall 83-4
*Twickenham Park Day Nursery, Richmond, London* 295
*Unilever Workplace Nursery, Sharnbrook, Beds* 30-1
*Usworth Colliery Nursery School, Sunderland, Tyne & Wear* 426
*Val Mary's Day Nursery, Nottingham, Notts* 373
Valley Road Nursery School, Henley, Oxon 381-2
Victoria House Quality Childcare, Goole, Humberside 170-2
Victoria Private Teaching Nursery, South Tyneside, Tyne & Wear 423-4
Village Day Nursery, Cottingham, Humberside 172-3
Village Montessori School, Lewisham, London 283
Watership Downs Nursery School, Maldon, Essex 132-3
Wellies Day Nursery, North Crawley, Newport Pagnell, Bucks 56-8
Wentworth Nursery School, Hackney, London 240-1
Wessex Gardens Infant & Nursery Schools, Barnet, London 214-15
*West Acton First School, Ealing, London* 232
West Suffolk College Nursery, Bury St Edmunds, Suffolk 408-9
Westfield House Nursery School, Aston, Bampton, Oxon 382-4
Westfields Infants School Nursery Unit, Acomb, N Yorks 369-70
Westfields Private Day Nursery, Cheltenham, Glos 138-9
Westminster Children's Society, Westminster, London 323
Weston Underwood Nursery Class, Weston Underwood, Bucks 58-9
Wheelgate House Nursery & Pre-Prep School, Crantock, Cornwall 81-3
*Willow Cottage, Farmoor, Oxon* 384
Willow Nursery School (The), Lambeth, London 280-1
Willow Tree Nursery, Redhill, Surrey 411-12
Willows County Primary School Nursery Unit, Lichfield, Staffs 404-5
Willows Nursery School, Witney, Oxon 384-5
Wimbledon Park Montessori School, Merton, London 286-7
Winchester House Pre-Prep Nursery Class, Brackley, Northants 360-1
Windmill Nursery School, Camborne, Cornwall 84-5
Wonderland Nursery Ltd, West Drayton, Hillingdon, London 254-5
*Woodland Lodge Kindergarten, Colchester, Essex* 133
*World's End Nursery School, Chelsea, Kensington, London* 272
Wyvern Nursery, Taunton, Somerset 392-3
York College Nursery, Dringhouses, York, N Yorks 370-1
Young England Kindergarten, Westminster, London 324-6
Young Sussex, Hove, E Sussex 122-3
Ysgol Santes Tudful, Merthyr Tydfil, Mid Glamorgan, Wales 509-10
Zebedee Nursery School (The), Kensington, London 272-3

# Index of Nurseries by Region

*italic type* = listings
plain type = full entries

## AVON
Caterpillars Day Nursery, Bath 21-2
Clyde House Day Nursery, Bishopston, Bristol 23-4
Mews Nursery, Bath 24-5
Red House Nursery, Westbury Park, Bristol 25-7
Redroofs Nursery, Warmley, Bristol 27-8
Rocking Horse Day Nursery School, Redland, Bristol 28-9

## BEDFORDSHIRE
*Lavenders Day Nursery, Bedford* 30
*Little School for Little Scholars, Luton* 30
*Sunnyside Nursery, Leighton Buzzard* 30
*Unilever Workplace Nursery, Sharnbrook* 30-1

## BERKSHIRE
Abacus Nursery School, Newbury 31-2
Agnes Hayward Nursery School, Maidenhead 33-4
Cedar Park School Nursery Class, Twyford 34-5
Chiltern Nursery School, Chiltern Nursery Training College, Caversham, Reading 35-7
Christ the King Primary School – Nursery Class, Reading 37-8
Langley Manor Nursery, Langley, Slough 38-9
Mary Seacole Day Nursery, Reading 40-1
Meadow Nursery School, Wokingham 41-2
Norland College, Hungerford 42-4
Orchard Day Nursery, Caversham, Reading 44-5

## BUCKINGHAMSHIRE
Acorn Day Nursery, Castlethorpe, Milton Keynes 46-7
Coppice Nursery School, High Wycombe 48-9
Eastview Montessori Nursery School, Wavendon, Milton Keynes 49-50
Little Oaks Nursery School, Sands, High Wycombe 51-2
Meadow View Nursery, Newport Pagnell 52-3
Nurserytyme, Aylesbury 53-5
Simpson Under Fives Resource Centre, Simpson, Milton Keynes 55-6
Wellies Day Nursery, North Crawley, Newport Pagnell 56-8
Weston Underwood Nursery Class, Weston Underwood 58-9

## CAMBRIDGESHIRE
Harvey Road Day Nursery, Cambridge 60-1
*Histon Nursery School, Histon* 61
*Huntingdon Nursery School, Huntingdon* 61
Joint Colleges Nursery, Cambridge 62-3
*King St Playgroup, Christ Pieces, Cambridge* 63
Millington Road Nursery School, Cambridge 63-4
Montessori School Cambridge (The), Chesterton 64-6
Old Buttery Nursery School, Willingham 66-7
*Orchards Day Nursery, Caxton* 67
Park Road Nursery School, Peterborough 67-8
Rose Cottage Day Nursery, Shepreth, nr Royston 68-70

## CHESHIRE
Burnett Nursery, Warrington 71-2
Happy Days Nursery, Rudheath, Northwich 72-3
*Little Acorns Day Nursery, Handforth* 73
Smarties Nursery, Cotton Edmunds 74-5

## CLEVELAND
*Glenfield Nursery School, Stockton-on-Tees* 75-6
Rainbow Day Nursery, Norton 76-7

## CORNWALL
Gooseberry Bush Day Nursery, Camborne 78-9
Polwhele House School, Truro 79-80
St Martin's (C of E) Primary School Nursery Unit, Liskeard 80-1
Treliske Pre-Preparatory School – Nursery Class, Truro 83-4
Wheelgate House Nursery & Pre-Prep School, Crantock 81-3
Windmill Nursery School, Camborne 84-5

## CUMBRIA
Bram Longstaffe Nursery School, Barrow-in-Furness 86-7
Early Years 1, Castle Park Primary, Kendal 87-8
North Walney Primary School, Barrow-in-Furness 88-90
St Aidan's School Day Nursery, Carlisle 90-1
St Cuthbert's School, Wigton 91-2

## DERBYSHIRE
Busy Bee Day Nursery, Bakewell 93-4
Gamesley Pre-School Centre, Glossop 94-5
Little Acorns Nursery, Derby 95-6
*Sunshine Day Nursery, Walton, Chesterfield* 96

## DEVON
Appledore Primary School, Bideford 97-8
Highweek Nursery, Newton Abbot 98-100
Lanherne School, Nursery Department, Dawlish 100-1
Leigham Infant School Nursery Unit, Leigham, Plymouth 101-2
Pixieland I Day Nursery, Plymouth 102-3
*St Peter's Nursery Unit, Stonehouse, Plymouth* 104
Tavistock Nursery Centre, Tavistock 104-5

## DORSET
Annette's Nursery, Bournemouth 106
*Dorchester Community Nursery School, Dorchester* 107
Peter Pan Day Nursery, Poole 107-8
Seaward Day Nursery, Bournemouth 108-9

## DURHAM
Apple Tree Nursery 109-10
*Durham University Nursery* 111
*Kirklands Day Nursery, Barnard Castle* 111
Newfields Childcare Co-operative 111-12

## EAST SUSSEX
Clock Tower Nursery, Lewes 113-14
Early Years Day Nursery, Hove 114-15
Happy Days Nursery, Brighton 116-17
Hillbury House Nursery School, Hove 117-18
Mothercraft Nursery, Hove 118-19
Royal Spa Nursery School, Brighton 119-21
Tom Thumb Nursery School & Kindergarten, Eastbourne 121-2
Young Sussex, Hove 122-3

## ESSEX
Alec Hunter Playgroup, Braintree 124-5
Bo Peep Day Nursery, Southend-on-Sea 125-6
Bubbles Day Nursery/School, Halstead 126-7
Grays Hall Day Nursery, Sible Hedingham 128-9
Little Sparrows Nursery, Ingatestone 129-30
Schoolgate Nursery, Harlow 130-1
Watership Downs Nursery School, Maldon 132-3
*Woodland Lodge Kindergarten, Colchester* 133

## GLOUCESTERSHIRE
Bilson Family Centre, Cinderford 134-5
Coigne (The), Minchinhampton, Stroud 135-6
Polly's Day Nursery, Stroud 136-8
Westfields Private Day Nursery, Cheltenham 138-9

## GUERNSEY
*Stepping Stones Day Nursery, Bordeaux, Vale* 140
*Town Mouse Day Nursery, St Peter Port* 140

## HAMPSHIRE
Boundary Oak Nursery Group, Fareham 142-3
Holly Tree Nursery School, Woolston, Southampton 141-2
King Richard Nursery, Portsmouth 143-4
Littleworld Nursery School, Andover 144-5
Manor House Nursery, Lee-on-Solent 146

Mayfield Junior School Kindergarten, Farnborough 147-8
Pear Tree Day Nursery, Farnborough 148-9
Staunton Park Day Nursery, Havant 149-50
Sunrise Day Nursery, Basingstoke 150-1

## HEREFORD & WORCESTER
Community Day Care Group, St Johns, Worcester 152-3
*Fieldhouse Montessori Kindergarten, Credenhill, Hereford* 153
Hawthorn Cottage Day Nursery & School, St Johns, Worcester 153-4
Mrs Tiggy-Winkle's Day Nursery, Hereford 154-5
Oak House Nursery School, Ross-on-Wye, Hereford 156-7
Painter's Cottage, Worcester 157-9
Swanpool Children's Nursery, St Johns, Worcester 159-60

## HERTFORDSHIRE
Marlin Montessori, Berkhamsted 161-2
Montessori Nursery & Pre-Prep School, Bishops Stortford 162-3
Mount Carmel Kindergarten, St Albans 163-4
Norton St Nicholas (C of E) School Nursery Class, Letchworth 165-6
St Christopher School Nursery Class, Letchworth 166-7
Tenterfield Nursery School, Welwyn 168-9

## HUMBERSIDE
*Ancholme House Nursery, Scunthorpe* 170
*British Red Cross Educare Nursery, Beverley* 170
*Hull University Union Day Nursery, Hull* 170
Victoria House Quality Childcare, Goole 170-2
Village Day Nursery, Cottingham 172-3

## ISLE OF MAN
Beehive Kindergarten, Onchan 174-5
*Palm Tree Nursery, Douglas* 175

## ISLE OF WIGHT
*Bembridge School Pre-Prep Department, Bembridge* 176
*Fiveways, Ryde School, Ryde* 176
Studio Day Nursery, Newport 176-7

## ISLES OF SCILLY 177

## JERSEY
*Rouge Bouillon Nursery, St Helier* 178

## KENT
Abbey School Day Nursery, Faversham 179-80
Acorns Day Nursery, Sevenoaks Primary School, Sevenoaks 180-2
Acorns Workplace Nursery, Bexley 182-3
Cheerful Tots Day Nursery, Canterbury 183-4
*Clever Clowns Nursery School, Boxley, Maidstone* 185
Eager Beavers Nursery, Ashford 185-6
*Grange Hill Nursery School, Goudhurst* 186
League of Friends Day Nursery, Canterbury 186-7
*Park Place Nursery School, Margate* 188
*St Helen's Montessori School, East Farleigh, Maidstone* 188
Sevenoaks Day Nursery, Sevenoaks 188-89

## LANCASHIRE
*Cottam Nursery School, Cottam, Preston* 190
Croston Nursery School, Croston, Preston 190-1
Headstart Pre-School Centre, Preston 191-3
Irwell Vale Private Nursery School, Rossendale 193-4
Le Monde Petit, Burnley 194-5
Meadow View Montessori Nursery School, Rawtenstall 196-7
Sunfield Day Nursery, St Annes-on-Sea 197-8

## LEICESTERSHIRE
Ark Playgroup, Oakham, Rutland 199-200
Daneshill Nursery, Leicester 200-1
Little Acorns Nursery School, Stoneygate, Leicester 201-2
Mountfields Lodge Nursery, Loughborough 203-4
St Gabriel's Community Centre Playgroup, Leicester 204-5

## LINCOLNSHIRE
Carlton Road Nursery Unit, Boston 206-7
First Class Nursery School, Grantham 207-8
Highgate Daycare Nursery, Leverton, Boston 208-9
*Tiny Tots Day Nursery, Louth* 209

## LONDON
**Barking & Dagenham** 210
**Barnet** 211

# 526 INDEX OF NURSERIES BY REGION

Hendon College Nursery, Colindale 211-12
Hendon Pre-School, Hendon 213-14
*St Catherine's Nursery Unit* 214
Wessex Gardens Infant & Nursery Schools, Golders Green 214-15

**Bexley** 216

**Brent** 216
Newfield Primary School Nursery Unit 217-18

**Bromley** 218
Rainbow Day Nursery 219-20

**Camden** 220
*Camden Day Nursery* 221
Fleet Street Nursery 221-2
*North Bridge House School, Stepping Stones Nursery* 222
St Leonard's Nursery School 223-4
St Mark's Square Nursery School 224-5

**Corporation of London** 225
*City Child* 226

**Croydon** 226
Byron Infant School, Coulsdon 226-7
Coulsdon Nursery School, Coulsdon 228-9
Purley Nursery School, Purley 229-30

**Ealing** 230
Buttons Nursery School, Hanwell 231
*Ealing Montessori School* 231-2
*Happy Child Day Nursery* 232
*West Acton First School* 232

**Enfield** 233
Carol Jane Montessori Nursery School 233-4

**Greenwich** 235
Lingfield Day Nursery, Blackheath 235-6

**Hackney** 237
*Broadgate Nursery, London EC2* 237
Defoe Day Care Centre 237-8
*Independent Day Nursery* 238
Rainbow Nursery 1 & 2, Stoke Newington 239-40
Wentworth Nursery School 240-1

**Hammersmith & Fulham** 242
Busy Bee Nursery School 242-3
*L'Ecole des Petits* 243-4
Puffins 244-5
*Queensmill Nursery Ltd* 245
Rose Montessori School 245-6
*Shepherd's Bush DN* 246-7
Sinclair Nursery School, Sinclair Road 247-8

Studio Day Nursery, Moore Park Road 248-9

**Haringey** 250

**Harrow** 251
*Cricket Montessori School* 251

**Havering** 252

**Hillingdon** 252
Breakspear Nursery Unit, Ickenham 253-4
*Gatehouse Nursery 2, Harmondsworth* 254
Wonderland Nursery Ltd, West Drayton 254-5

**Hounslow** 255
*Corner House Day Nursery, Chiswick* 256

**Islington** 256
Floral Place Nursery 256-8
Little People, Whitehall Park 258-9

**Kensington & Chelsea** 260
Acorn Nursery School 260-1
Holland Park Day Nursery & School House 262-3
Iverna Gardens Montessori Nursery School 263-4
Knightsbridge Kindergarten, Chelsea 264-5
Ladbroke Square Montessori School 266-7
Mrs Mynor's Nursery School 267-8
Pooh Corner Montessori Nursery School 268-9
St Joseph's (RC) JMI School Nursery Unit, Chelsea 269-71
*St Peter's Nursery School* 271
*Tadpoles Nursery School, Chelsea* 271
*World's End Nursery School, Chelsea* 272
Zebedee Nursery School (The) 272-3

**Kingston-upon-Thames** 273
Latchmere Infant School Nursery 274-5

**Lambeth** 275
Caldecot Primary Nursery Class 276-7
Daisy Chain Montessori School 277-8
Oval Montessori Nursery School (The) 278-9
Toad Hall Nursery School, Kennington 279-80
Willow Nursery School (The) 280-1

**Lewisham** 282
Goldsmiths' College Nursery 282-3
*Village Montessori School* 283

**Merton** 284
*Bushey First School Nursery Unit* 284

Grove Nursery School, Wimbledon 284-6
Wimbledon Park Nursery School 286-7

**Newham** 287
*Oops-a-Daisy* 288

**Redbridge** 288

**Richmond-upon-Thames** 289
Mortlake Day Nursery, Sheen Lane 289-90
*Noah's Ark Day Nursery* 290-1
Orleans Community Nursery, Twickenham 291-2
Russell Nursery, Russell School, Petersham 292-3
Studio Montessori School, Kew Gardens Road 294-5
*Sunflower Montessori School* 295
*Twickenham Park Day Nursery* 295

**Southwark** 296
Dulwich College Prep School 296-7
Mother Goose Baby Nursery, Peckham 298-9

**Sutton** 299
Jackanory Nursery, Wallington 300-1

**Tower Hamlets** 302

**Waltham Forest** 303

**Wandsworth** 304
Balham Nursery School, Endlesham Road 304-5
Blundell's Day Nursery, Sheepcote Lane 306
*Busy Bee Nursery School, Putney* 306-7
Gardens Nursery School, Southfields 307-8
Honeywell Nursery Class, Honeywell Road 308-9
Lion House, Gwendolen Avenue, Putney 309-10
Little Red Engine, Grant Road 311-12
*Minnows, Dents Road* 312
Mouse House, Mallinson Road 312-14
Noah's Ark, Boutflower Road 314-15
*Noddy's Nursery School, Putney* 315
*Park Nursery School (The), Wandsworth* 315
Prospect House, Putney Hill 316-17
Red Balloon, Trinity Road 317-18
Redford House, Roehampton Institute 318-19
Schoolroom, Putney 320-1
*Square One, Putney* 321
*Thomas's Kindergarten, Battersea* 321

**Westminster** 322
*Abercorn Place School Nursery* 322

London Montessori College 322
*Thomas's Kindergarten* 323
Westminster Children's Society 323-4
*Young England Kindergarten* 324-6

## MANCHESTER

**Bolton** 326
*Elms Nursery School, Astley Bridge* 327-8
*Highview Nursery, Sharples* 328-9
Moorlands Children's Nursery, Horwich 329-31
Moss Lea Private Nursery School, Sharples Park 331-2

**Bury** 332

**Manchester** 333
*Birch Grove Day Nursery, Rusholme* 333
Burnage Children's Centre, Burnage 333-4

**Oldham** 335

**Rochdale** 335
*Appollo Day Nursery, Whitworth* 336

**Salford** 337

**Stockport** 337
*0-2-5 Nursery, Heaton Mersey* 337
Orchards Day Nursery & Nursery School, Heaton Moor 337-9

**Tameside** 339

**Trafford** 340
Higher Downs Day Nursery, Altrincham 340-1

**Wigan** 342
Greenfields Day Nurseries, Tyldesley 342-3

## MERSEYSIDE

**Knowsley** 344

**Liverpool** 344
Kelton Day Nursery, Mossley Hill 345-6
MCVS Nursery, Mount Vernon Green 346-7
Monkton, Mossley Hill 347-8
Oak House Children's Nursery, Aigburth 349-50

**Sefton** 350
Griffin Nursery (Kids Unlimited), Bootle 350-1
Jean Jessop Day Nursery, Southport 352-3

**St Helens** 353
*St Helens College Nursery* 354

**Wirral** 354

## NORFOLK

*Park House Day Nursery, Thetford* 355

Playhouse Day Nursery, Long Stratton 356-7

## NORTH YORKSHIRE

HCAT Nursery, Harrogate College of Arts & Technology 364-6
Joseph's Nursery, Clifton, York 366-7
*Lisvane, Scarborough College Junior School* 367
St Paul's Nursery School, York 367-9
Westfields Infants School Nursery Unit, Acomb 369-70
York College Nursery, Dringhouses, York 370-1

## NORTHAMPTONSHIRE

Old Rectory Day Nursery, Little Billing, Northampton 357-8
Southbrook Early Education Unit, Daventry 359-60
Winchester House Pre-Prep Nursery Class, Brackley 360-1

## NORTHUMBERLAND

Meadows Day Nursery, Stocksfield 362
Swiftdale Close Day Nursery, Bedlington 363-4

## NOTTINGHAMSHIRE

*Arboretum Nursery School, Nottingham* 372
*Croft Family Centre, Nottingham* 372-3
*Mapperley Plains Primary School Nursery, Nottingham* 373
*Station House Day Nursery, Beeston* 373
*Val Mary's Day Nursery, Nottingham* 373

## OXFORDSHIRE

Banbury School, Clipper Day Nursery, Banbury 374-5
Close Nursery School (The), Banbury 375-6
Fair Mile Day Nursery, Fair Mile Hospital, Nr Wallingford 376-7
Manor Nursery, Horspath 377-8
Rainbow Corner Day Nursery, Watlington 379-80
St Nicholas Garden School, Henley 380-1
Valley Road Nursery School, Henley 381-2
Westfield House Nursery School, Aston, Bampton 382-4
*Willow Cottage, Farmoor* 384
Willows Nursery School, Witney 384-5

## SHROPSHIRE

*Chapel Nursery, Telford* 386
Halesfield Day Nursery School, Telford 386-7

Mount Nursery School (The), Telford 388-9

## SOMERSET

*St John's VC Infants School Nursery Class, Glastonbury* 390
Somerset Montessori Nursery School, Taunton 390-1
Taunton School Kindergarten & Nursery, Taunton 391-2
Wyvern Nursery, Taunton 392-3

## SOUTH YORKSHIRE

**Barnsiey** 394
Summerlane Day Nursery 394-5

**Doncaster** 396

**Rotherham** 396
Rawmarsh Nursery School 397-8

**Sheffield** 398
Endcliffe Children's Nursery 399-400
Fulwood Play Centre 400-1
Montessori Nursery School 401-2

## STAFFORDSHIRE

*Langdale Nursery School, Newcastle* 403
Little Angels Day Care Nursery, Weeford 403-4
Willows County Primary School Nursery Unit, Lichfield 404-5

## SUFFOLK

Linda Evans Children's Day Care Centre, Ipswich 406-7
Sweet Briar Nursery School, Hoxne, Eye 407-8
West Suffolk College Nursery, Bury St Edmunds 408-9

## SURREY

*Caring Daycare, Haslemere* 410
*Swansmere School, Walton-on-Thames* 411
*Teddy's Nursery School, Sandhurst* 411
Willow Tree Nursery, Redhill 411-12

## TYNE & WEAR

**Gateshead** 413

**Newcastle-upon-Tyne** 413
Ashfield Nursery School & Parents Centre 414-15
Gosforth Private Day Nursery, Gosforth 415-16
Heaton Nursery School, Heaton 416-18
Newburn Manor Nursery School 418-19

**North Tyneside** 419
Childcare Battle Hill 420-1
Childcare Wallsend 421-2

# INDEX OF NURSERIES BY REGION

**South Tyneside** 422
Victoria Private Teaching Nursery, Hebburn 423-4

**Sunderland** 424
Cork Street Nursery Centre, Hendon 424-5
*Hetton-le-Hole Nursery School* 425-6
*Mill Hill Nursery School* 426
*Usworth Colliery Nursery School* 426

**WARWICKSHIRE**
Alcester Nursery School, Alcester 427-8
Binswood Nursery School, Leamington Spa 428-9
Priory Day Nursery, Kenilworth 429-30

**WEST MIDLANDS**
**Birmingham** 431
Celandine Nursery, Yardley Wood 431-2
Edgbaston Park Nursery, Edgbaston 432-4

**Coventry** 434
St Osburg's Primary School & Nursery, Coundon 434-5

**Dudley** 436
Priory Primary Nursery Unit 436-7

**Sandwell** 438

**Solihull** 438
Green Lanes Primary School, Chelmsley Wood 439-40
St Alphege Infant School Nursery Unit 440-1

**Walsall** 441

**Wolverhampton** 442

**WEST SUSSEX**
*Body Shop Child Development Centre, Littlehampton* 443
Broadwater Manor Nursery Department, Worthing 443-4
Davison Crèche & Under 5s Club, Worthing 444-5
First Steps Day Nursery, Chichester College of Technology 446-7
Little Orchard Day Nursery, Chichester 447-8
*Millais Day Nursery, Horsham* 448
Poppins Day Nursery, Southbourne 449-50
Three Bridges First School Nursery Class, Crawley 450-1

**WEST YORKSHIRE**
**Bradford** 451
ABC Day Nursery, Buttershaw 452-3
Airedale General Hospital Day Nursery, Keighley 453-4
Elim Church Day Nursery 454-5
Hirst Wood Nursery School, Shipley 455-6
Moorfield Nursery School, Bingley 457-8
Severn Lodge Private Nursery, Bolton 458-9

**Calderdale** 460
Pellon & District Community Day Nursery, Halifax 460-1

**Kirklees** 462
Aspley Day Nursery, Huddersfield 462-3

**Leeds** 464
Grove Nursery School, Headingley 464-5
Rose Court Preparatory School Nursery Class, Headingley 466-7
*Springwood Nursery School, Roundhay* 467

**Wakefield** 467

**WILTSHIRE**
*Hopscotch Nursery School, Chippenham* 468
Stepping Stones Nursery School, Nr Marlborough 468-9
Tidworth Clarendon Infant School Nursery Class, Tidworth 470-1

**NORTHERN IRELAND**
Ashgrove Nursery School, Newry 472-3
*Castlereagh Nursery, Belfast* 473
*Cozy Corner Playgroup, Crossmaglen* 473
*Downshire Nursery School, Banbridge* 473
Dungannon Nursery School, Dungannon 474-5
Kids & Co, Donaghmore, Dungannon 475-6
Lisburn Central Nursery Unit, Lisburn 476-7
*Scallywags Private Playgroup, Newtownards* 477
Squirrels Montessori Nursery Centre, Enniskillen 477-8

**SCOTLAND**
**Borders** 479

**Central** 479
St Anne's Nursery, Stirling University, Bridge of Allan 480

**Dumfries & Galloway** 480

**Fife** 481

**Grampian** 481
Albyn School for Girls Infant Nursery Dept, Aberdeen 482
Greenburn Nursery, Aberdeen 483-4
Kindergarten (The), Aberdeen 484-5
*Moray Steiner School Kindergarten, Forres, Moray* 485
Rosebrae School Kindergarten, Elgin, Moray 485-6

**Highland** 487

**Lothian** 487
Cargilfield Nursery, Edinburgh 488
Castle Nursery (The), Edinburgh 489-90
Edinburgh Academy Nursery Class, Edinburgh 490-1
Edinburgh Nursery Crèche (The), Edinburgh 491-2

**Orkney** 493

**Shetland** 493
Sandwick Junior High School Nursery Class, Sandwick 494-5

**Strathclyde** 495
Acorn Park Nursery, Glasgow 495-6
Barrachnie Children's Nursery, Glasgow 496-7
Riverbank Kindergarten & Day Nursery, Ayr 498-9
Somerset Nursery 1, Glasgow 499-500

**Tayside** 500
Frances Wright Pre-School Centre, Dundee 501-2
Little Acorn Nursery School, Scone 502-3

**Western Isles** 503
*Rainbow Nursery, Stornoway, Isle of Lewis* 504

**WALES**
**Clwyd** 504
Longfields Nursery, Wrexham 504-6

**Dyfed** 506
*Acorn Nursery School, Carmarthen* 506
*Nantgaredig School Nursery Unit* 507

**Gwent** 507

**Gwynedd** 508

**Mid Glamorgan** 508
Ysgol Santes Tudful, Merthyr Tydfil 509-10

**Powys** 510
*Jolly Tots, Llandrindod Wells* 510
Park Lane People, Welshpool 511-12
St Nicholas Nursery School, Hay-on-Wye 512-13

**South Glamorgan** 513
Barnardo's Family Centre, Ely, Cardiff 514-15
Romilly Park Nursery School, Barry 515-16

**West Glamorgan** 516